Frommer's
Ireland 2019

27th Edition

By Jack Jewers

THE TEMPLE BAR

FrommerMedia LLC

Published by
FROMMER MEDIA LLC

Frommer's Ireland 2019, 27th Edition
ISBN 978-1-62887-392-4 (paper), 978-1-62887-393-1 (e-book)

Editorial Director: Pauline Frommer
Editor: Alexis Lipsitz Flippin
Production Editor: Lynn Northrup
Cartographer: Roberta Stockwell
Photo Editor: Meghan Lamb
For information on our other products or services, see www.frommers.com.

Frommer Media LLC also publishes its books in a variety of electronic formats. Some content that appears in print may not be available in electronic formats.

Manufactured in China

5   4   3   2   1

FROMMER'S STAR RATINGS SYSTEM

Every hotel, restaurant and attraction listed in this guide has been ranked for quality and value. Here's what the stars mean:

★ Recommended
★★ Highly Recommended
★★★ A must! Don't miss!

AN IMPORTANT NOTE

The world is a dynamic place. Hotels change ownership, restaurants hike their prices, museums alter their opening hours, and buses and trains change their routings. And all of this can occur in the several months after our authors have visited, inspected, and written about these hotels, restaurants, museums, and transportation services. Though we have made valiant efforts to keep all our information fresh and up-to-date, some few changes can inevitably occur in the periods before a revised edition of this guidebook is published. So please bear with us if a tiny number of the details in this book have changed. Please also note that we have no responsibility or liability for any inaccuracy or errors or omissions, or for inconvenience, loss, damage, or expenses suffered by anyone as a result of assertions in this guide.

CONTENTS

LIST OF MAPS

ABOUT THE AUTHOR

Jack Jewers has written about Ireland for Frommer's since 2006. Born and raised in England, he loved listening to his great aunt's tales about life in Dublin during the civil war. Jack proposed to his Irish-American wife at a spa on the Ring of Kerry. It gets a great review in this book.

ABOUT THE FROMMER TRAVEL GUIDES

For most of the past 50 years, Frommer's has been the leading series of travel guides in North America, accounting for as many as 24% of all guidebooks sold. I think I know why.

Though we hope our books are entertaining, we nevertheless deal with travel in a serious fashion. Our guidebooks have never looked on such journeys as a mere recreation, but as a far more important human function, a time of learning and introspection, an essential part of a civilized life. We stress the culture, lifestyle, history, and beliefs of the destinations we cover, and urge our readers to seek out people and new ideas as the chief rewards of travel.

We have never shied from controversy. We have, from the beginning, encouraged our authors to be intensely judgmental, critical—both pro and con—in their comments, and wholly independent. Our only clients are our readers, and we have triggered the ire of countless prominent sorts, from a tourist newspaper we called "practically worthless" (it unsuccessfully sued us) to the many rip-offs we've condemned.

And because we believe that travel should be available to everyone regardless of their incomes, we have always been cost-conscious at every level of expenditure. Though we have broadened our recommendations beyond the budget category, we insist that every lodging we include be sensibly priced. We use every form of media to assist our readers, and are particularly proud of our feisty daily website, the award-winning Frommers.com.

I have high hopes for the future of Frommer's. May these guidebooks, in all the years ahead, continue to reflect the joy of travel and the freedom that travel represents. May they always pursue a cost-conscious path, so that people of all incomes can enjoy the rewards of travel. And may they create, for both the traveler and the persons among whom we travel, a community of friends, where all human beings live in harmony and peace.

Arthur Frommer

THE
BEST OF
IRELAND

Safety on the
Bridge

Tiny, and with ever-changing scenery, Ireland is an addictive place to explore. Within a few miles you can travel from plunging cliffs and flat pastureland to towering mountains and gloomy peat bogs. You can spend the night in ancient castles or state-of-the-art spa hotels, dine on fine Irish cuisine or snack on crispy fish and chips served in a paper bag. The sheer number of sights, little villages, charming pubs, and adorable restaurants and shops is overwhelming—you always feel that you might be missing something. So it's nice to have somebody to help you focus, and that's why we've put together this list of some of our favorite places and things to do in Ireland. We hope that while you're exploring this magical country, you'll find a few favorites of your own.

THE best PICTURE-POSTCARD TOWNS

o **Adare** (County Limerick): Literally a picture-postcard town—its image has been reproduced alongside a hundred thousand "Wish You Were Heres"—Adare is hardly a secret, but if you manage to visit when the roads aren't clogged with tour buses, you'll leave with a memory card full of photos. See p. 349.

o **Athlone** (County Westmeath): Sitting at the edge of the River Shannon, its streets curving around a fortresslike castle, Athlone is a charmer with a real spirit of fun. Houses are painted in bright hues, and streets are lined with funky boutiques, good restaurants, and lively pubs. See 403.

o **Dalkey** (County Dublin): The cutest of a string of upscale seaside towns unfurling south from Dublin, Dalkey is both a short drive and a million miles away from the busy city. With a castle, lovely beaches, and some fine restaurants, it tempts you into its affluent embrace. See p. 123.

o **Kinsale** (County Cork): Kinsale's narrow streets all lead to the sea, dropping steeply from the hills around the harbor. The walk from Kinsale through Scilly to Charles Fort and Frower Point is breathtaking. Bonus: It's a gourmet hotspot, full of good restaurants. See p. 261.

o **Kenmare** (County Kerry): It's easy to fall in love with Kenmare, with its stone cottages, colorful gardens, and flowers overflowing from

PREVIOUS PAGE: **Carrick-a-Rede bridge.**

Martello fort on Dalkey Island.

window boxes. Home to several elegant hotels, it makes an enchanting base when exploring the Ring of Kerry. See p. 284.

o **Dingle (An Daingean)** (County Kerry): In this charming hilltop medieval town, stone buildings ramble up and down hills, and the small population is relaxed about visitors. You'll find lots of little diners and picturesque pubs, plus a lovely historic church. See p. 319.

o **Ardara** (County Donegal): On the southwest coast of Donegal, tiny Ardara looks as if it were carved out of a solid block of granite. Its hilly streets are lined with boutiques and charming arts shops, many selling clothes made of the famed Donegal wool. See p. 465.

THE best NATURAL WONDERS

o **The Burren** (County Clare): We can guarantee this: The Burren is one of the strangest landscapes you're likely to see anywhere in the world. Its stark limestone grassland is spread with a quilt of wildflowers from as far afield as the Alps, and its inhabitants include nearly every species of butterfly found in Ireland. See p. 334.

o **Mizen Head** (County Cork): While most travelers flock to the better-known Cliffs of Moher (p. 340), you won't find crowds at these majestic sea cliffs at Ireland's southwest tip. Watch the waves crash against the 210m-high (689-ft.) cliffs from the excellent visitor center. See p. 276.

o **Malin Head** (County Donegal): From one extreme to the other—literally! The Malin Head promontory, in the remotest part of Ireland's remotest country, looks out over a seemingly unending sea. Next stop: New York. See p. 474.

Rock climbing at Malin Head.

- **The Twelve Bens** (County Galway): Amid Connemara's central mountains, bogs, and lakes, the rugged Twelve Bens range crowns a spectacular landscape. The loftiest, Benbaun in Connemara National Park, reaches a height of 729m (2,392 ft.). See p. 389.

- **Slieve League** (County Donegal): As the Slieve League peninsula stretches for 48km (30 miles) into the Atlantic, its pigmented bluffs rise to startlingly high sea cliffs. You can also walk along them, if you dare. See p. 460.

- **MacGillycuddy's Reeks** (County Kerry): Cresting grandly over the Iveragh Peninsula, MacGillycuddy's Reeks not only has the best name of any mountain range in Ireland, it also has the highest peak on the island, Carrantuohill (1,041m/3,414 ft.). See p. 291.

- **Giant's Causeway** (County Antrim): At the foot of a cliff by the sea, this mysterious mass of tightly packed, naturally occurring hexagonal basalt columns is nothing short of astonishing. This volcanic wonder, formed 60 million years ago, looks even better when negotiated (cautiously) on foot. See p. 515.

THE best DRIVING TOURS

- **The Ring of Kerry** (County Kerry): It's by far the most well-traveled of Ireland's great routes, but there's no denying the Ring of Kerry's appeal—it's a seductive combination of stunning countryside, charming villages, and inspiring historical sites. The road gets quite busy in summer, but come in the spring or autumn and it's a much more peaceful experience. See p. 306.

o **Slea Head Drive** (County Kerry): This drive, starting from Dingle Town and heading down the Ventry road, follows the sparkling sea past a series of ancient sites such as the Dunbeg Fort and the beehive-shaped Gallarus Oratory. At Dunquin, you can embark on boats to the mysterious abandoned Blasket Islands. See p. 324.

o **Horn Head** (County Donegal): Drive pretty much anywhere in County Donegal, and before long you'll be in beautiful, wild, unspoiled countryside—that's one reason why we never mind getting lost around here. One of the best drives is around Horn Head, near Dunfanaghy, where quartzite sea cliffs glisten as if made of glass when the sun hits them just right. See p. 466.

o **Inishowen Peninsula** (County Donegal): This far-flung promontory in Ireland's northern end stretches out from Lough Foyle to the east and Lough Swilly to the west toward Malin Head, its farthest point. Driving its perimeter, you'll pass ancient sites, pretty villages, and fine sandy beaches in fierce rocky coves. If you are looking to get lost, this is a great place to do it. See p. 471.

o **Antrim Coast** (County Antrim): Sweeping views of midnight-blue sea against gray unforgiving cliffs and deep-green hillsides make this 97km-long (60-mile) coastal route unforgettable. Start in gorgeous Glenarm with its castle walls and barbican gate, then head north along the coast past Bushmills and the Giant's Causeway to Portrush. Best of all, you often have the road quite to yourself. See p. 510.

Children on the Giant's Causeway, a highlight of the Antrim Coast drive.

THE best CASTLES & STATELY HOMES

- **Powerscourt Estate** (County Wicklow): Restored at last to its former glory (at least on the outside) after decades of misfortune and neglect, the magnificent Palladian house at the heart of the Powerscourt estate is surrounded by some of the most exquisite gardens in Ireland. See p. 195.

- **Castletown House** (County Kildare): This grand whitewashed mansion was built in the early 18th century and soon became one of Ireland's most imitated buildings. The grounds house the most delightfully named barn in Ireland. See p. 184.

- **Kilkenny Castle** (County Kilkenny): Although parts of this stout towered castle date from the 13th century, the existing structure looks more like a 19th-century palace. Exquisitely restored, it also has extensive gardens; the old stables now hold art galleries and shops. See p. 230.

- **Bunratty Castle & Folk Park** (County Clare): This grand old castle has been well restored and filled with a curious assortment of medieval furnishings, offering a glimpse into the life of its past inhabitants. This is the first stop for many arrivals from Shannon, so expect crowds. See p. 339.

Kilkenny Castle.

o **Charleville Castle** (County Offaly): Sometimes the castles that leave the biggest impression aren't those in the most impressive states of repair. Not only is Charleville one of the most atmospheric castles in Ireland, it is also reputed to be among its most haunted. See p. 406.

o **Carrickfergus Castle** (County Antrim): This huge Norman fortress on the bank of Belfast Lough is surprisingly intact and well-preserved, complete with an imposing tower house and a high wall punctuated by corner towers. See p. 494.

o **Dunluce Castle** (County Antrim): Set atop a razor-sharp promontory jutting into the sea, these castle ruins are picturesque and evocative. Unlike many other castles, it wasn't demolished by human enemies, but had to be abandoned after a large section collapsed and fell into the breakers below. See p. 513.

THE best PREHISTORIC SITES

o **Hill of Tara** (County Meath): Of ritual significance from the Stone Age to the early Christian period, Tara has seen it all and kept it a secret. This mostly unexcavated site was the traditional center and seat of Ireland's high kings; it's a place to be walked slowly. Although the hill is only 154m (512 ft.) above sea level, on a clear day you can see each of Ireland's four Celtic provinces from here. See p. 176.

o **Newgrange** (County Meath): One of the archaeological wonders of Western Europe, Newgrange is the centerpiece of a megalithic cemetery dating back 5,000 years. Its massive mound and passage tomb are amazing feats of engineering. But the question remains: What was it all for? See p. 178.

o **Knowth** (County Meath): Another great passage tomb, Knowth's awesome presence is matched only by its inscrutability. Hundreds of prehistoric carvings were discovered here when the site was first excavated in the 1960s. And yet nobody seems to quite understand it to this day. See p. 176.

o **Dún Aengus** (County Galway): The eminent archaeologist George Petrie called Dún Aengus "the most magnificent barbaric monument in Europe." No one knows who built this massive stone fort or what year it was constructed. Facing the sea, where its three stone rings meet steep 90m (295-ft.) cliffs, Dún Aengus still stands guard today over the southern coast of Inishmore, the largest of the Aran Islands. See p. 368.

o **Carrowmore and Carrowkeel** (County Sligo): These two megalithic cities of the dead (Europe's largest) may have once contained more than 200 passage tombs. The two together—one in the valley and the other atop a nearby mountain—convey an unequaled sense of the ancient peoples' reverence for the departed. Carrowmore is well

The Hill of Tara, ancient seat of Irish kings, offers amazing views on a clear day.

presented and interpreted, while Carrowkeel quietly awaits those who seek it out. See p. 441.

o **Corlea Trackway** (County Longford): The amazing thing about this simple wooden trackway in a remote bog is just how unbelievably old it is—people were walking its well-preserved planks well over 2,000 years ago. See p. 408.

THE best EARLY CHRISTIAN RUINS

o **Glendalough** (County Wicklow): Nestled in "the glen of the two lakes," this remote monastic settlement was founded by St. Kevin in the 6th century. Today its atmospheric ruins preside over an endlessly scenic setting with lakes and forests surrounding it. It's quite simply one of the loveliest spots in Ireland. See p. 191.

o **Jerpoint Abbey** (County Kilkenny): Jerpoint is the finest of many Cistercian abbeys whose ruins dot the Irish landscape. Somehow, hundreds of years of rain and wind have failed to completely wipe away its medieval carvings, leaving us a rare chance to glimpse how magnificent these abbeys once were. Don't miss the splendid, richly carved cloister. See p. 233.

o **Skellig Michael** (County Kerry): Thirteen kilometers (8 miles) offshore of the Iveragh Peninsula, early Irish monks built this hermitage dedicated to the archangel Michael on a remote, rocky crag rising sharply 214m (702 ft.) out of the Atlantic. Both the journey to Skellig across choppy seas and the arduous climb to its summit are challenging—and equally unforgettable. See p. 310.

o **The Rock of Cashel** (County Tipperary): In name and appearance, "the Rock" suggests a citadel, a place designed more for power than prayer. In fact, Cashel (or *Caiseal*) means "fortress." The rock is a huge outcropping—or an *up*cropping—of limestone topped with beautiful ruins, including what was once Ireland's finest Romanesque chapel. The seat of clerics and kings, it was a power center to rival the Hill of Tara; now the two sites vie for the attention of tourists. See p. 358.

o **Clonmacnoise** (County Offaly): The old Irish high kings came to this place to find spiritual solace, and it's still a profound and thought-provoking place to visit. Don't leave without checking out the monumental ancient slabs, inscribed with personal messages in Celtic script. See p. 407.

o **Inishmurray** (County Sligo): This uninhabited island off the Sligo coast holds another striking monastic ruin, this one surrounded by what appears to be the walls of an even more ancient stone fort. Vikings sought out this remote outpost of peace-seeking monks and destroyed it in A.D. 807. Today its circular walls and the surrounding sea create a stunning view, well worth the effort required to reach it. See p. 444.

Group hike at Glendalough.

THE best MUSEUMS

- **Chester Beatty Library** (Dublin, County Dublin): Not just a library, this is one of Ireland's best museums, with a wealth of books, illuminated texts, and small art objects. Its collection of rare religious manuscripts is among the most unique in the world. See p. 96.

- **National Museum of Ireland: Archaeology** (Dublin, County Dublin): Ireland's National Museum is split into four separate sites, of which this is far and away the best. The collection dates back to the earliest settlers, but it's the relics from the Viking invasion and the early Christian period that dazzle the most. See p. 100.

- **Irish National Famine Museum** (Strokestown Park, County Roscommon): This reflective museum, part of a grand historic estate, does a brilliant job of making the darkest period in Irish history seem immediate and real, including a collection of heartbreaking letters from destitute tenants to their callous landlords. See p. 412.

- **Titanic Belfast** (Belfast, County Antrim): Belfast is incredibly proud of having built the most famous ocean liner in history, despite its ultimate fate—though, as they're fond of saying, "She was alright when she left here." This gleaming, high-tech museum is the best of several *Titanic*-related attractions in Belfast. See p. 488.

- **Ulster Folk & Transport Museum** (Cultra, County Antrim): Ireland has several so-called "living history" museums, where stories of

Titanic Belfast.

people and times past are told through reconstructions of everyday life. This one, just outside Belfast, is one of the liveliest and most engaging. See p. 495.

THE best FOR LOVERS OF LITERATURE

o **Dublin Writers Museum** (Dublin, County Dublin): Filled with letters, manuscripts, personal possessions, and other eclectic ephemera, this great museum in Dublin is a mecca for lovers of Irish literature. Naturally it also has a good bookshop. See p. 97.

o **Davy Byrnes pub** (Dublin, County Dublin): After a stop at the **James Joyce Centre** (see p. 116), make a pilgrimage to this venerable pub, which crops up in Joyce's masterpiece *Ulysses:* The hero, Leopold Bloom, famously orders a lunch of burgundy and a Gorgonzola sandwich here. The pub is acutely aware of its heritage, but knows better than to ruin the appeal by being too touristy. See p. 167.

o **County Sligo:** With its many connections to the beloved poet W. B. Yeats, this county is a pilgrimage destination for poetry fans. The landscape shaped the poet's writing, and many of its landmarks—Lough Gill, Glencar Lake, Ben Bulben Mountain, Maeve's tomb—appear in his verse. Be sure to visit Yeats's dark and somber grave in Drumcliffe. See p. 440.

o **The Aran Islands:** Though playwright John Millington Synge was born in County Dublin, as a leading figure in the Irish literary revival of the late 19th century he became passionately interested in these brooding islands off the Galway coast—the setting for his most famous play, *The Playboy of the Western World.* See p. 368.

o **The Sperrin Mountains:** Nobel prize–winning poet Seamus Heaney (1939–2013) was born in Northern Ireland, between the Sperrin Mountains and Lough Neagh. Even as his literary fame took him around the world, his poetry remained rooted in the boglands, cairns, and farms of his native Ulster. See p. 550.

THE best FAMILY ACTIVITIES

o **Dublin Zoo in Phoenix Park** (Dublin, County Dublin): Kids love this sympathetically designed zoo featuring wild creatures, animal-petting corners, and a train ride. The surrounding park has room to run, picnic, and explore. See p. 121.

o **Irish National Heritage Park** (Ferrycarrig, County Wexford): Millennia of history are made painlessly educational for children and adults at this engaging "living history" museum. It's a fascinating, informative way to while away a couple of hours or more. See p. 218.

A herd of deer browses in Phoenix Park, Dublin.

o **Fota Island & Wildlife Park** (Carrigtwohill, County Cork): In this wildlife park, rare and endangered animals roam freely. You'll see everything from giraffes and zebras to kangaroos, flamingos, penguins, and monkeys wandering the grassland. Add in a tour train, picnic tables, a playground, and a gift shop, and you have the makings of a wonderful family outing. See p. 258.

o **Muckross House & Gardens** (Killarney, County Kerry): Today the gateway to Killarney National Park, this impressive mansion has been preserved in all its Victorian splendor. Nearby, people on the Muckross Historic Farms engage in traditional farm activities while dressed in authentic period clothing. See p. 288.

o **Fungie the Dingle Dolphin Boat Tours** (Dingle, County Kerry): Every day, fishing boats ferry visitors out into the nearby waters to see Fungie, the friendliest dolphin you'll ever meet, swim right up to the boat. You can even arrange an early-morning dolphin swim. The kid-friendly Dingle Oceanworld Aquarium is right by the harbor as well. See p. 320.

o **Bunratty Castle & Folk Park** (Bunratty, County Clare): Kids love Bunratty, which looks every bit as satisfyingly medieval as an old castle should. The grounds have been turned over to a replica 19th-century village, complete with actors playing Victorian residents going about their daily lives. It's great fun to wander through. See p. 339.

o **Galway Atlantaquaria** (Galway, County Galway): Formally known as the National Aquarium of Ireland, this is the place your kids will remember long after they've forgotten the hundredth dolmen you saw by the roadside. Highlights include a tank full of sharks and touch pools where kids can touch curious rays. See p. 384.

THE best HOTELS

- **The Shelbourne** (Dublin, County Dublin): Certainly one of the best hotels in Ireland's capital city, the Shelbourne also holds a unique place in Irish history. See p. 132.

- **The Westbury** (Dublin, County Dublin): What the Shelbourne is to the old Dublin, so this place is to the new: a top-class hotel for fashionistas and sophisticates to rest their well-heeled feet. See p. 132.

- **Powerscourt Hotel** (County Wicklow): Elegant and luxurious, a stay here is like a contemporary reinvention of how grand its namesake, Powerscourt House, must once have been. See p. 200.

- **Monart Spa** (Enniscorthy, County Wexford): A sumptuous countryside retreat, this pampering paradise is consistently rated among the top spas in Ireland. It's a serene, adults-only zone in a lovely setting. See p. 225.

- **Aghadoe Heights** (Killarney, County Kerry): Another of Ireland's top spas, this one overlooks the Lakes of Killarney from a high vantage point just north of the town. See p. 292.

- **Park Hotel Kenmare** (County Kerry): An Irish newspaper recently described this place as "as close as you'll get to Downton Abbey without going on set." The Park Hotel also has one of the very best spas in Ireland. See p. 301.

- **Greenmount House** (Dingle, County Kerry): The views from this charming B&B are as close to your fantasy of an Irish country escape as you'll find anywhere. See p. 322.

- **Gregans Castle Hotel** (Ballyvaughn, County Clare): J. R. R. Tolkien took inspiration for *The Lord of the Rings* while staying at this elegant country house amid the lunar landscape of the Burren. See p. 344.

- **Dolphin Beach House** (Clifden, County Galway): This incredibly special B&B on the Galway coast is a converted early-20th-century homestead with amazing views, gorgeous food, and gregarious hosts. See p. 395.

- **Ashford Castle** (Cong, County Mayo): Live like royalty for a night at this fairy-tale castle in County Mayo. The great and the good have been coming here for decades to see what the fuss is about. The fuss, it turns out, is justified. See p. 432.

- **The Bervie** (Keel, County Mayo): Overlooking the Atlantic Ocean on an island off the Mayo coast, the Bervie is a haven of magnificent views and gourmet food. See p. 433.

- **Temple House** (Ballymote, County Sligo): Proving that not all the best overnight stays are found in luxury hotels, Temple House is a historic countryside B&B that seems in a world of its own. See p. 446.

o **The Merchant** (Belfast, County Antrim): Once a Victorian bank, this stunningly converted hotel is one of the finest places to stay in the trendy capital of Northern Ireland. See p. 496.

o **Castle Leslie** (Glaslough, County Monaghan): This luxurious northern retreat has been a jet-set hideaway for decades. See p. 557.

o **Newforge House** (Magheralin, County Armagh): A supremely relaxing manor house in the middle of the Armagh countryside, Newforge House has sensational food to boot. Come, stay, fall in love. See p. 536.

THE best RESTAURANTS

o **Chapter One** (Dublin, County Dublin): In the vaulted basement of the Dublin Writers Museum, this is one of Dublin's very best restaurants. It's quite a splurge, but come at lunchtime and you can enjoy the same wonderful food at almost half the price. See p. 145.

o **Gallagher's Boxty House** (Dublin, County Dublin): A local man keen on preserving the culinary traditions of his childhood started this captivating—and hugely popular—Temple Bar restaurant. See p. 140.

o **Richmond House** (Cappoquin, County Waterford): One of the real destination restaurants of the southeast, the Richmond House, in a converted 18th-century mansion, serves exquisite seasonal meals, with many ingredients sourced from its own grounds. See p. 216.

o **Café Paradiso** (Cork, County Cork): A vegetarian restaurant that even the most committed meat lover will adore, Café Paradiso is one of the most inventive eateries in Ireland's second city. See p. 251.

o **Fishy Fishy Café** (Kinsale, County Cork): Kinsale is Ireland's unofficial gourmet capital, and the delightful Fishy Fishy is among its best restaurants. The seafood is so local that the menu tells you who caught it—and we're talking dish by dish, name by name. See p. 267.

o **The Oak Room** (Adare, County Limerick): This fine-dining restaurant at the opulent Adare Manor hotel is for special occasions only, but for a real treat, it's simply one of the region's best places to eat. See p. 354.

o **Aniar** (Galway, County Galway): Galway City's most sought-after table has a tiny but perfectly judged menu of innovative modern Irish cuisine—enough to earn a Michelin star, a rarity in Ireland. See p. 374.

o **Inis Meáin** (Inis Meáin, County Galway): Now this is what we call a destination restaurant! Pretty much the main reason for visiting the rather overlooked Aran island after which it is named, this is a place to stay and to savor for days, not just a meal. See p. 373.

o **Wilde's at the Lodge at Ashford** (Cong, County Mayo): On the grounds of Ashford Castle, Wilde's is a joyous restaurant run by a real star of the Irish culinary scene. The dining room has an amazing view of Lough Corrib. See p. 435.

Fishy Fishy Café is just one of several stellar restaurants in Kinsale, County Cork, a magnet destination for food lovers.

o **Ox** (Belfast, County Antrim): Cool and contemporary, this Michelin-starred restaurant is one of Belfast's most sought-after dining hotspots. See p. 501.

o **Mourne Seafood Bar** (Belfast, County Antrim): One of the best restaurants in Northern Ireland, where the fresh Irish seafood is a must-try for Belfast-bound foodies. See p. 502.

o **The Cook & Gardener** (Rathmullan, County Donegal): Ingredients don't get much fresher, picked straight from the garden. And when you've eaten your fill, you can just head upstairs for a restful night's sleep. See p. 470.

IRELAND'S best SHOPPING

o **Avoca** (County Kerry): One of the most Irish of Irish brands, Avoca sells beautiful blankets, clothes, and other woven fabrics made in its traditional workshop in the Wicklow Mountains. The flagship store is in Dublin (p. 153), but our favorite is the little branch clinging to a bend in the road near the Ring of Kerry. See p. 305.

o **Lorge Chocolatier** (County Kerry): French chocolatier Benoit Lorge makes exquisite creations from his workshop just south of Kenmare. The wrapped gift boxes are little works of art in themselves. See p. 305.

o **Brocade and Lime** (County Cork): This wonderful vintage-style clothing boutique sells retro fashions by contemporary Irish designers. It's no surprise that it's got a legion of celebrity fans. See p. 253.

o **Mayfly** (Dublin): Dublin's perpetually cool Temple Bar district is filled with creative, quirky little emporiums, and this is one of the best, selling unique jewelry, vintage fashions, and other irresistible accessories. Look for the cow in the buggy out front! See p. 154.

o **Claddagh Records** (Dublin): One of the best music stores in a country that takes its music very seriously, Claddagh Records is a must for lovers of traditional Irish music. In addition to instruments and sheet music, it sells some great (and tuneful) souvenirs. See p. 153.

o **Steensons** (County Antrim): This elegant, long-established jewelry design firm has recently gained a whole new kind of fame, thanks to its specially commissioned work for *Game of Thrones*. The pieces are as elegant as they are collectible. See p. 504.

o **Belleek China** (County Fermanagh): The world-famous brand of fine china has been furnishing the tables of the upper crust since 1864. The visitor center, near Donegal, has a magnificent collection for sale—and will ship internationally if you're worried about getting your delicate selection home in one piece. See p. 557.

IRELAND'S most OVERRATED

o **Blarney Castle** (County Cork): Though a pretty impressive medieval castle in itself, Blarney has grown to become a veritable font of touristy tat. Before you say "I really must kiss the Blarney stone!" ask yourself this: Do you really want to stand in line for ages so that some strangers can hold you upside-down to twist around and kiss a piece of rock that thousands upon thousands of visitors have already kissed? See p. 243.

o **Cliffs of Moher** (County Clare): The cliffs themselves (pronounced "More") are one of Ireland's great natural wonders. But perhaps, given how they're managed, they'd be better off called the Cliffs of "Gimme More." In practice it's difficult to see them without entering through the gleaming, multimillion-euro visitor center, complete with steep parking charge and—*ka-ching!*—a very well-stocked gift store. See p. 340.

o **The Book of Kells** (County Dublin): No one's saying the book itself isn't beautiful. But to see it (or rather, the tiny portion on display), you'll have to crowd around a small display case with a roomful of people who, like you, have paid handsomely for the privilege. See p. 93. Meanwhile, a short walk away at the **Chester Beatty Library** (p. 96), the stunning collection of illuminated gospels and other ancient religious texts is every bit as magnificent in their artistry—and you can see it for free.

o **The pub crawl:** The idea of the pub crawl, essentially, is to visit as many pubs in a single night as you possibly can, while drinking constantly along the way. At best they're jolly, convivial, well-lubricated affairs. In practice, they're usually loud, rowdy, and fun for no one who isn't several pints down already. You will inevitably encounter groups on pub crawls in big towns and cities, especially on weekends—and especially in places like Dublin's Temple Bar, where they seem to be virtually 24/7. (*Exception:* There are some fantastic pub crawls organized by tour groups, which are really more like walking tours in disguise— such as the Literary and Traditional Irish Music Pub Crawls in Dublin. See p. 107.)

Spectacular as they are, the famous Cliffs of Moher in County Clare suffer from crowds and too many charges.

o **The "Full Irish":** It's amazing how many small B&Bs and hotels assume that everyone's going to like the "full Irish breakfast." Huge plates of sausage links, thick-cut bacon, and black pudding (made from fat, blood, and oatmeal—yum!) are among the meat-heavy delights that await on nearly all breakfast menus. To be fair, they can be delicious. But boy, does it get tedious after a while, and it's surprising how many smaller places still don't offer other choices. We've done our best to point you toward some of the best and most varied breakfast options among the "Where to Stay" listings in this book.

THE best AUTHENTIC EXPERIENCES

o **Seeing a traditional music session at a proper Irish pub:** While there are plenty of shows for the tourist crowd, nothing beats the energy, atmosphere, and authenticity of a genuine small-town traditional music session. The instructions for getting the most out of a session are simple: Buy a pint, grab a seat (preferably one near a smoldering peat fire), and wait for the action to begin. We've listed some of the best places in this book, including pubs such as the **Long Valley** in **Cork** (see p. 254) or **Gus O'Connor's** and **McGann's** in little **Doolin, County Clare** (see p. 342).

o **Getting lost down the back roads of County Kerry:** It's Ireland's most visited county by far, and if you stick to the beaten path, in summer it's thronged with tourists. Instead, veer off onto the winding back roads and allow yourself to get gloriously, hopelessly lost. There are always new discoveries to be made down its breathtaking byways. See p. 302.

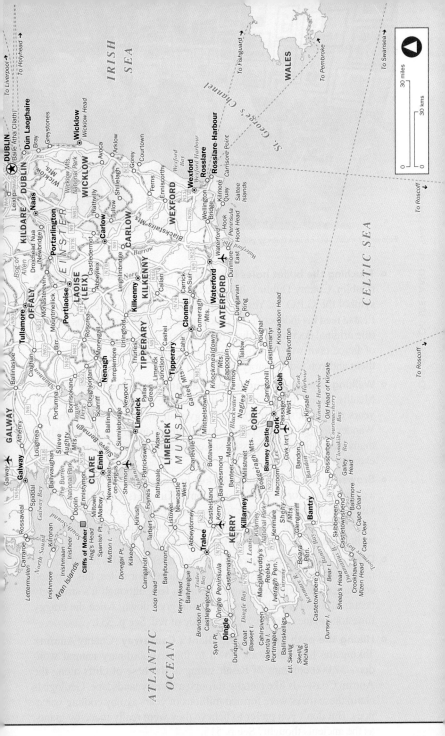

Enjoying a music session in a Galway pub.

o **Touching the bullet holes in the walls of the General Post Office** (Dublin, County Dublin): It's hard to overstate what a potent national symbol the G.P.O. is. Yes, it's still a working post office, but Patrick Pearse read his independence proclamation from its front steps in 1916 (the original document is displayed inside) and in 1922 it was the scene of fierce civil war fighting. Bullet scars still pock the facade. Touch them and you touch history. See p. 111.

o **Walking down the long stone passage at Newgrange** (County Meath): Sacred to the ancients, this passage tomb is more than 5,000 years old—that's older than the Egyptian pyramids or Stonehenge. Wander down the atmospheric central tunnel and try to visualize how many generations have passed since it was built—it's a mind-blowing exercise. See p. 178.

o **Browsing the Old English Market in Cork** (County Cork): Cork is a county made for foodies. In addition to Kinsale (see p. 261), a coastal village that's become a hub for top restaurants, the eponymous main city is home to one of the country's finest (and oldest) food markets. A walk through here is a feast for the senses. See p. 246.

o **Driving through the Burren** (County Clare): Ireland is full of memorable landscapes, but this is the most unique. For miles, this exposed coastal countryside has a haunting, alien feel, although it's strikingly beautiful too. Try to be here as the sun goes down, when the craggy limestone planes turn an evening shade of red. See p. 334.

o **Hiking the path down to the Giant's Causeway** (County Antrim): Taking the half-mile walk down to this extraordinary natural wonder—37,000 columns of basalt sitting at the base of cliffs along the Antrim Coast—is like passing through a fantasy landscape. Geologists claim these rocks were formed millions of years ago by cooling volcanoes. But don't you prefer to believe they were really made by giants, as the ancients thought? See p. 515.

SUGGESTED IRELAND ITINERARIES

2

reland is such a small island that you can cover a lot of ground in a week and feel quite at home within two. But even with the best of intentions and all the energy in the world, you'll never see it all on a short visit.

The suggested itineraries in this chapter will help you get the most out of this extraordinary and varied country—no matter how long you have to see it. If you've only got a week to spend here, the southern regions probably have more to offer. They're generally easier to get around, and the major sights are closer together. If you're traveling with kids, Dublin and County Kerry have particularly rich troves of kid-friendly attractions. However, those in search of the road less traveled will be drawn northward, especially to places such as Mayo, Sligo, and the wilds of Donegal.

All of these tours (except one) assume that you have a week to see the country. Where there's potential for a longer trip, we've given some alternatives for an extended version. Pick and choose the parts that appeal to you, add in your own favorite shopping or scenic drives, and turn it all into a custom-made holiday for yourself.

THE REGIONS IN BRIEF

The island of Ireland is divided into two political units: the **Republic of Ireland,** which makes up the vast majority of the country, and **Northern Ireland,** which along with England, Scotland, and Wales is part of the United Kingdom. Of Ireland's 32 counties, all but 6 are in the Republic.

The ancient Gaelic regions that once divided Ireland are still used in conversation and directions: Ulster is north, Munster is south, Leinster is east, and Connaught is west. Each region is divided into counties:

In Ulster (to the north)   Cavan, Donegal, and Monaghan in the Republic; Antrim, Armagh, Derry, Down, Fermanagh, and Tyrone in Northern Ireland.

In Munster (to the south)   Clare, Cork, Kerry, Limerick, Tipperary, and Waterford.

In Leinster (to the east)   Dublin, Carlow, Kildare, Kilkenny, Laois, Longford, Louth, Meath, Offaly, Westmeath, Wexford, and Wicklow.

In Connaught (to the west)   Sligo, Mayo, Galway, Roscommon, and Leitrim.

DUBLIN & ENVIRONS   With 40% of the Republic's population living within 97km (60 miles) of Dublin, the capital is the center of the profound changes that have transformed Ireland into a prosperous and increasingly

PREVIOUS PAGE: **Downtown Dublin.**

Surfing on Garretstown Beach, near Kinsale, County Cork.

European country. Within an hour's drive of Dublin are Dalkey, Dún Laoghaire, and many more engaging coastal towns, as well as the rural beauty of the Wicklow Mountains and the prehistoric ruins in County Meath.

THE SOUTHEAST   The southeast offers sandy beaches, **Wexford**'s lush and mountainous countryside, **Waterford**'s famous Crystal Factory, Kilkenny's and Cahir's ancient castles, and the Irish National Heritage Park at Ferrycarrig.

CORK & ENVIRONS   **Cork,** Ireland's second largest city, is a buzzy university town and a congenial gateway to the south and west of the island. Within arm's reach are Blarney Castle (and its famous stone), the culinary and scenic delights of Kinsale, the historic emigration port of Cobh, and the dazzling landscape of West Cork.

THE SOUTHWEST   The once-remote splendor of **County Kerry** has long ceased to be a secret, at least during the high season. The Ring of Kerry (less glamorously known as hwys. N70 and N71) encircling the Iveragh Peninsula is Ireland's most visited attraction after the Book of Kells. That's both a recommendation and a warning. While Killarney National Park provides a stunning haven from buses, the town of Killarney is filled with souvenir shops and tour groups. Marginally less visited highlights include the rugged Dingle Peninsula and two sets of islands with rich histories: the Skelligs and the Blaskets.

THE WEST   The west of Ireland offers a first taste of Ireland's wild beauty and striking diversity, especially handy for those who fly into

Shannon Airport. **County Clare**'s natural offerings—particularly the unique landscapes of the Burren—are unforgettable, and the county also has an array of impressive castles: Knappogue, Bunratty, and (just over the county line in Galway) Dunguaire.

GALWAY & ENVIRONS **Galway Town** is busy, colorful, and funky—a youthful port and university town and the self-proclaimed arts capital of Ireland with lots of theater, music, and dance. County Galway is the gateway to **Connemara**'s moody, magical mountains and boglands. Offshore lie the atmospheric, mysterious Aran Islands.

THE MIDLANDS The lush center of Ireland, bisected by the lazy River Shannon, is a land of pastures, rivers, lakes, woods, and gentle mountain slopes. It's a retreat, in high season, from the throngs of tourists who crowd the coasts. The Midlands also hold remarkable sites—Birr Castle and its splendid gardens, for example, and Clonmacnoise, the evocative ruins of a famous Irish monastic center.

THE NORTH SHANNON VALLEY Farther up the coast to the north, past Galway, **County Mayo** offers the sweet town of Westport on Clew Bay and Achill Island (accessible by car), with its beaches and stunning cliff views. **County Sligo** inspired the poetry of W. B. Yeats, and offers a dense collection of stone circles, passage tombs, and cairns at such sites as Carrowmore, Knocknarea, and Carrowkeel.

THE NORTHWEST In Ireland it's easy to become convinced that isolated austerity is beautiful. Nowhere is this more evident than in **County Donegal,** with its jagged, desolate coastline. (If you don't mind the cold, it offers some fine surfing.) Inland, Glenveagh National Park has as much wilderness as you could want.

NORTHERN IRELAND Across the border, Northern Ireland's six counties are a decade and a half into a new era. It's still one of the most underrated parts of Ireland, with such attractions as the stunning **Antrim Coast,** the extraordinary basalt columns of the Giant's Causeway, and the Glens of Antrim. The old city walls of **Derry,** the past glory of Carrickfergus Castle, and **Belfast**'s elaborate political murals make a trip across the border worthwhile.

How to See Ireland

Let's get one thing straight: You don't *have* to rent a car to see Ireland. Millions of people don't. Ireland has a decent public transportation network, and you're spoiled for choice when it comes to tour bus excursions. And that's a fine way to do it. This is *your* trip, after all.

However, if your ideal Ireland involves wandering through the countryside, visiting small villages, climbing castle walls, hailing history from a ruined abbey, or finding yourself alone on a rocky beach—you cannot do those things independently without a car. Out of the main towns, public

IS NORTHERN IRELAND safe to visit?

In short, **yes.** It's been at peace for 20 years. Belfast and Derry are *safer for visitors than almost any comparable American city*, and the Ulster countryside is idyllic and serene. So we really wouldn't worry.

That said, you do need to be aware of a few issues—particularly since many things have been thrown into question after the Brexit vote. Be sensitive to the fact that there are still deep divisions here, and follow these basic rules:

- **Do not** discuss politics with anyone you don't know well.

- **Never** get involved in political or religious arguments relating to Northern Ireland.

- **Avoid** venturing deep into the inner-city areas of Belfast without a guide.

- **Avoid** traditional Catholic or Protestant marches and parades, such as those by the Orange Order. They may look like local color but they can get very unpleasant.

- **Remain** informed. Follow the news to keep abreast of current events and any areas of tension.

transportation exists, but it's slow and limiting. Every major town has car-rental agencies, if you decide to explore by car.

Just remember: They drive on the *left.*

The next step is deciding **where to start.** That decision can be made for you by where your flight terminates. If you're flying into **Shannon Airport** or **Cork Airport,** then it makes geographic sense to start out on the west coast. If you're flying into **Dublin,** you might as well explore that city first, then either head up to the North and the ruggedly beautiful Antrim Coast, or south down to the Wicklow Mountains, Kilkenny, Wexford, and Waterford.

Still, if you fly into Dublin but your heart is in Galway, no worries. You can traverse the width of the country in a few hours, once you get out of Dublin's stultifying sprawl. Just bear in mind that rural roads are not well lit or well signposted, so driving at night should be avoided. Being lost in unfamiliar territory (where it can be many miles between villages) is no fun at all.

THE BEST OF IRELAND IN 1 WEEK

There's something terribly romantic about flying into Dublin. The compact, laidback city awaits a few miles down the road, packed with old-fashioned pubs, modern restaurants, and absorbing sights all laid out for walking. If you've never been here, a couple of days in Dublin make for a quick primer on Ireland. It's just enough time to do some shopping on **Grafton Street,** head up O'Connell Street to the **General Post Office,** and discover the Georgian beauty of **St. Stephen's Green** and **Merrion**

Square. You can give the surface of the city a good brush in a couple of days, and then head south to **Kilkenny** and **Wicklow,** on to **Waterford, Cork,** and **Kerry,** and up to **Clare** for a quick glance before the clock runs out. You'll only be hitting the high points but, as high points go, they're hard to beat.

DAYS 1 & 2: ARRIVE IN DUBLIN

If it happens that you're arriving from North America, you start with an advantage: Most flights arrive early in the morning, which effectively gives you an extra day's sightseeing. Check into your hotel, say yes to any tea and scones offered, take a minute to relax, get a map from your concierge, and then head out on foot.

Stay south of the River Liffey and head down Dame Street to **Dublin Castle** (p. 111), home of the magical **Chester Beatty Library** (p. 96) with its vast collection of gorgeous illuminated manuscripts. Later, take in **St. Patrick's Cathedral** (p. 102) and the vibrant green quadrangles of **Trinity College** (p. 102), before heading down to Merrion Square, with its handsome granite architecture and two of the main sites of Ireland's **National Museum** (a third one is on the west side of the city). The **Archaeology** museum has an extraordinary hoard of ancient gold, while the **Natural History** building contains an array of objects from the ancient past. It's a short stroll from here down to **St. Stephen's Green.** Rest your weary toes and soak up the floral view here, before strolling up **Grafton Street** for some shopping before collapsing in your hotel.

Strolling through Library Square at Trinity College in Dublin.

The Best of Ireland Itineraries

Malin Head

Rathmullan • Bucrana
• Derry

DONEGAL **13**

NORTHERN
IRELAND
(U.K.)

ATLANTIC
OCEAN

Glencolumbkille •

Donegal Bay

Ballyshannon •

Sligo Town •

SLIGO **12**

Achill Island

MAYO **11**

Westport •

Clifden •

GALWAY **9–10**

Galway City •

Galway Bay

REPUBLIC OF IRELAND

*Irish
Sea*

14 **1–2** Dublin

Wicklow •

WICKLOW

3–4

THE BURREN

8
7 Cliffs of Moher ←

CLARE

Bunratty •

Limerick •

Kilkenny •

WATERFORD

Waterford
Town •

*Mouth of the
Shannon*

KERRY

Killarney •
5–6

KILLARNEY
NATIONAL
PARK

CORK

Cork •

4

CELTIC SEA

0 _____ 50 mi
0 _____ 50 km

On **DAY 2,** have a hearty breakfast in your hotel before striking out for the trendy cultural hub of **Temple Bar.** Stroll north to the river, then take a right and walk along the noisy, vibrant waterfront to the landmark **Ha'penny Bridge.** Walk across and head east on **O'Connell Street,** where you can walk past its many statues to the bullet-ridden columns of the **General Post Office** (p. 111), site of the 1916 Easter Rising. After exploring its displays, head farther up O'Connell Street to the **Dublin Writers Museum** (p. 97), which bookish types love for its extensive display of memorabilia. Let someone else do the work in the evening, either on a walking tour—such as the **Irish Music Pub Crawl,** perhaps (p. 107)—or some good-natured scares aboard the **Dublin Ghost Bus** (p. 120). Those in search of less organized fun may prefer the simple, atmospheric pleasure of **An Evening of Food, Folklore & Fairies** (p. 170).

DAY 3: SOUTH TO WICKLOW & KILKENNY

It takes less than 2 hours to drive from the hustle and traffic of Dublin to the peace and quiet of the **Wicklow Mountains** (p. 191). Drive through the town of Enniskerry to the great estate of **Powerscourt** (p. 195) on the south end of the village. After lunching in its Avoca Café, head on to **Glendalough** (p. 191) and feel your soul relax in the pastoral mountain setting of this ancient monastic retreat. From there drive on to the colorful town of **Kilkenny,** where you can spend the rest of the day shopping in its pottery and crafts shops and exploring noble **Kilkenny Castle** (p. 230). This is a good place to spend your first night outside of Dublin.

DAY 4: WEST TO WATERFORD & CORK

Waterford, Ireland's oldest city, is less than an hour south of Kilkenny—you'll get there with plenty of time left for sightseeing. Have a quick look around some or all of the **Waterford Treasures** museums (p. 207) before dropping in for a tour of the **House of Waterford Crystal.** After lunch, you have a choice—either head to **Cork** (p. 240), Ireland's busy second city, or **Kinsale** (p. 261), a quieter harbor town near Cork that has lately become a foodie destination. Each has plenty to keep you busy for the rest of the day and good hotels in which to spend the night.

DAYS 5 & 6: THE RING OF KERRY

If you're not allergic to touristy things, you could stop at **Blarney Castle** (p. 243) on your way out of Cork in the morning; otherwise, on to County Kerry at the southwest tip of the island. Here the most popular place to explore—and one of the busiest tourist spots in Ireland—is the **Ring of Kerry** (p. 284). It is a beautiful drive, filled with historic sites and tiny villages, but you'll have to brave the masses. If you have the stamina, the entire Ring is doable at a reasonable pace over 2 days, although you'd have to skip pretty much everything else around it to make that goal.

Alternatively, you could just explore the short section of the Ring that runs from lovely **Kenmare** (p. 300) to the bucolic peace of **Killarney National Park** (p. 285). Here you can indulge in a buggy ride around the lakes and drink in beautiful landscapes.

DAY 7: COUNTY CLARE

Time is short now, so as you drive through County Clare, promise yourself to come back someday and do it justice. For now, head for the perilously tall **Cliffs of Moher** (p. 340), where the view seems to stretch all the way to America (although the price to park will make you shiver). Then you've another choice: Spend the rest of the day exploring **Bunratty Castle** (p. 339)—where medieval fortress meets historical theme park—or marveling at the otherworldly limestone landscape of the **Burren** (p. 337). Either would be a perfect, quintessentially Irish end to your all-too-short trip.

THE BEST OF IRELAND IN 2 WEEKS

With 2 weeks, your visit to Ireland will be much more relaxed. You can stretch out a bit more in your travels, heading to less crowded counties with more time to meet the locals. In your second week, head up to Galway, Mayo, and Donegal, taking time to smell the heather along the way.

DAYS 1–7

Follow "The Best of Ireland in 1 Week" itinerary, as outlined above.

DAY 8

After spending **DAY 7** exploring County Clare, you'll discover that you need more time to explore this region. If you didn't make it to the **Burren,** spend most of your day here. Otherwise, you could visit another of the county's great medieval buildings such as **Knappogue Castle** (p. 343) or the exquisite ruins of **Corcomroe Abbey** (p. 338). Lovers of live music will want to spend the evening in the pubs of **Doolin** (p. 342), one of the very best places in Ireland for proper traditional music.

DAYS 9 & 10: COUNTY GALWAY

Start the day with a drive up to Galway City (it will take around an hour), your base for **DAY 9.** You could spend a relaxing day walking the delightful streets of this artsy, vibrant town or take a cruise out to the misty **Aran Islands** (see p. 368). If you've got kids to keep amused, take them to the fabulous **Galway Atlantaquaria** (p. 384). On the following day, you can head either east or west. Go west to explore **Connemara National Park** (p. 389), where it's time to get out from behind the wheel, and maybe even see this lovely park by horseback if you're feeling brave. If you head east, you'll be traveling inland for a whistle-stop tour of the Irish Midlands (chapter 11). Either return to your Galway City hotel or pick a B&B in the countryside.

DAY 11: COUNTY MAYO

Drive up from Galway through spectacular scenery, where the rocky shoreline plunges into the cobalt sea in glorious fashion. The south Mayo town of **Westport,** sitting at the edge of a picturesque river, is a delightful place to wander. Probably depending on whether or not you're traveling with youngsters, you could either spend a couple of hours at **Westport House and Pirate Adventure Park** (p. 425) or visit the **National Museum of Ireland: Country Life** (p. 425) near Castlebar. Ancient-history buffs may want to press on to a hotel in County Sligo (see below), but if it's a quiet retreat you're after, drive across the strangely empty flatlands to **Achill Island** (p. 430). The route along the coast and out across the bridge to the island is slow and winding, but the views are fantastic. If you do make it out to Achill, consider an overnight stay at the **Bervie** (p. 433), where the sea is right outside the door.

DAY 12: COUNTY SLIGO

Depending on where you stayed last night, you may be in for a long drive, so start early. **Sligo Town** (p. 438) has a few worthwhile attractions, but mostly it will be useful as a lunch stop. The real reason to come this far lies in the surrounding countryside. There is an astonishing concentration of ancient burial sites here, including **Carrowkeel** and **Carrowmore,** some of the world's oldest pieces of freestanding architecture. Our favorite place to stay the night in these parts is the extraordinary **Temple House** (p. 446).

DAY 13: NORTH TO DONEGAL

You're really entering the wilds of Ireland now. Head up the coast past Donegal Town, then follow the N15 road around the breathtaking coastline to the busy hill town of **Ballyshannon** (p. 458), an excellent spot for crafts shops and glorious hilltop views. The adventurous can explore the **Catsby Cave** (p. 458), a picturesque grotto at the edge of the Abbey River. But here the drive is really the thing, so head on to the darling town of **Glencolumbkille** (p. 458). The excellent folk park here is well worth an hour of your time before you head on to the stone-cut town of **Ardara** at the foot of a steep hill—it's wall-to-wall arts-and-crafts shops and a pleasure to explore. Art lovers won't want to miss the revelatory gallery at **Glebe House** (p. 467). You've spent a lot of time in the car today, but if you can face another

Sunset at the towering sea cliffs of Slieve League, in County Donegal.

40 minutes or so, head for the wonderful **Rathmullan House** (p. 469), an elegant seaside retreat waiting for you on your last night.

DAY 14: HEADING HOME

If your flight leaves late, you could rise early and spend the morning driving up to **Malin Head** (p. 474), the northernmost tip of Ireland. It's a wild and wooly place just a couple of hours' drive from Rathmullan. From there, expect the journey to the airport to take at least 4 hours, but allow plenty of time in case of traffic backups around Dublin—they're virtually constant.

IRELAND FOR FREE OR DIRT CHEAP

Ireland is no longer a cheap country to visit—and hasn't been for some time. The economic crash of the late 2000s and early 2010s drove prices down a bit, but hotels and restaurants are still pricey, and in recent years the euro/dollar exchange rate has not favored travelers from the U.S. But here's the good news: You can visit a lot of great sites for free in Ireland, including some of the biggest tourist attractions in the country. You can also save a lot of money by sticking mainly to places that can be reached by public transport, thus eliminating the need to rent a car (every place we list is easily accessible by train or bus). You'd be surprised by how much of Ireland you can see without blowing the budget. We're starting this tour in Northern Ireland (maybe you got a great deal on a flight to Belfast!), because it's one of the more budget-friendly regions. For more information on train and bus timetables, see **www.irishrail.ie** and **www.buseireann.ie**.

DAY 1: BELFAST

Belfast is rich with free attractions—here are just a few. The excellent **Ulster Museum** (p. 490) displays artifacts from across 9,000 years of Irish history. Right next door is the **Belfast Botanic Gardens & Palm House** (p. 483), only a short walk away from the campus of **Queen's University** (p. 492). **Belfast City Hall** (p. 486) runs free guided tours. Another exceptional Victorian landmark, **Belfast Cathedral** (p. 491), is also free, as is **Cave Hill Country Park** (p. 491), a tranquil place with good walking trails and incredible views of the city. Last but not least, because Belfast is still most famous for the sectarian strife of the mid– to late–20th century, a highlight of your visit may be to view the political murals remaining in what was once the epicenter of the conflict, the **Falls and Shankill roads areas** (p. 487). These neighborhoods are now safe for visitors to explore, and the street art is utterly free to see. To get the most out of them, however, you may want to spend some of that cash you've saved so far on a **Black Taxi Tour** (p. 484).

Catch a train from Belfast to Dublin (Connolly Station). Time: 2 hr. 10 min. Fares start at about €22 for adults.

DAYS 2 & 3: DUBLIN

Ireland's capital is also the number-one destination in the country for free sites. We think the **Chester Beatty Library** (p. 96) is one of the best museums in Europe. The collection of illuminated gospels and early copies of the Bible, Torah, and Koran would justify a steep entrance fee, but it doesn't cost you a cent. Three of the four separate museums constituting the **National Museum of Ireland** are in Dublin—**Archaeology, Natural History,** and **Decorative Arts and History**—and all are free. Each contains incredible treasures, and collectively have enough to keep you occupied for a day or more. All of Dublin's best major art galleries are free, including the **National Gallery of Ireland** (p. 99), the **Irish Museum of Modern Art** (p. 106), the **Temple Bar Gallery** (p. 106), and the excellent **Hugh Lane Gallery** (p. 98). Many of Dublin's most historic public buildings, such as the **Bank of Ireland/Parliament House** (p. 113) and the **Four Courts** (p. 111), don't charge admission. You can walk right into the **General Post Office** on O'Connell Street (p. 111), which is still a working post office, to see a few exhibits devoted to the Easter Rising, including the original Declaration of Independence. There's no charge to visit the **President's House** (Áras an

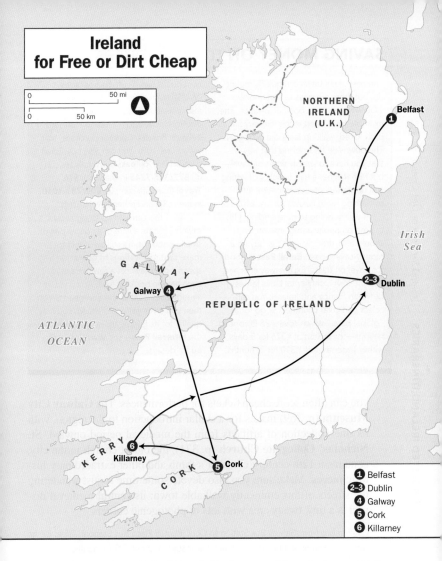

Ireland for Free or Dirt Cheap

0 — 50 mi
0 — 50 km

NORTHERN IRELAND (U.K.)

Belfast ❶

Irish Sea

G A L W A Y

Galway ❹ ← ❷-❸ Dublin

REPUBLIC OF IRELAND

ATLANTIC OCEAN

K E R R Y
Killarney ❻ ← ❺ Cork
C O R K

❶ Belfast
❷-❸ Dublin
❹ Galway
❺ Cork
❻ Killarney

Uachtaráin, p. 113) in Phoenix Park, accessible only by tour (alas, just Sat). Add to this the great public spaces such as **Phoenix Park** (p. 118), **St. Stephen's Green** (p. 119), and **Trinity College** (p. 102), and you'll see it's possible to spend a full 2 days here without spending a penny on sightseeing.

Catch a train from Dublin (Heuston Station) to Galway. Time: 2 hr. 40 min. Fares start at about €33 for adults.

DAY 4: GALWAY

Ireland's artsy, seductive west-coast city offers plenty of free pursuits. The **Galway Arts Centre** (p. 368) usually has good exhibitions, and

33

SAVING MONEY ON trains & buses

The cost of rail travel can quickly mount up, but there are ways to save money. Whenever you can, *book in advance*. The example fares listed in this itinerary are all prebooked; walk-up fares can be higher. The downside for booking that way is that you have to specify times of travel—but Irish Rail has a handy policy of letting you upgrade a prebooked ticket into something more flexible for just €10.

If you're going to be spending a lot of time on public transportation, you should also strongly consider buying a money-saving pass. **Eurail Pass** is good for travel on trains, Expressway coaches, and the Irish Continental Lines ferries between France and Ireland. You can select particular countries, or go for a "global pass," which covers 28 European nations—these start at €376 for 5 days within 1 month, to €1,310 for 3 months'

continuous use. Youth passes (ages 16–25), family, and first-class passes are also available. The passes are valid throughout Ireland (including Northern Ireland). For details or for purchase, visit www.eurail.com. You can also buy Eurail passes from **Railpass** (www.railpass.com; ✆ 877/375-7245 in the U.S.), **STA Travel** (www.sta.com; ✆ 800/781-4040 in the U.S.), and other travel agents.

All of this can add up to significant savings, but be aware of a couple bits of small print. First, it's still advisable to make seat reservations to guarantee a space—this may cost a few extra euro each time in booking fees. And if you're already a resident of the European Union then you can't get one! Instead, you may qualify for its Europeans-only equivalent, the **Interrail Pass**—see **www.interrail. eu** for details.

---

you can often score cheap tickets for performances. The **Galway City Museum** (p. 369) makes for a stellar introduction to the region, with its fine collection of artifacts from the medieval period onward. **St. Nicholas' Collegiate Church** (p. 371), the oldest church in the city, contains a 12th-century crusader's tomb and other extraordinary historic pieces. Make sure you also devote some time to just wandering the streets of this eminently walkable town; its central medieval district is a tiny, twisty area with lots of photogenic corners.

Catch a bus from Galway Bus Station to Cork (Parnell Place Bus Station). Time: 3½ hr. with one change or 4 hr. 20 min. direct. Fares start at about €27 for adults.

DAY 5: GALWAY TO CORK

Busy, youthful Cork City doesn't have a great deal of free historic attractions, but if you're up for a large dose of culture, you'll find plenty to do without paying a cent. Start with a trip to the **Old English Market** (p. 246) for a browse and a cheap lunch. Afterward, head to the **Crawford Art Gallery** (p. 245)—it's one of the very best in Ireland and completely free. More excellent free art is to be found at the **Lewis Glucksman Gallery** (p. 248) on the campus of **University College Cork.** In the evening, check out a few of Cork's exceptional pubs, among the best in the country for traditional music (see "A Tuneful Pint" on p. 256).

Catch a train from Cork to Killarney. Most change at Mallow. Time: 1 hr. 20 min. direct, or 2 hr. with change. Fares start at about €29 for adults.

DAY 6: CORK TO KILLARNEY

It's not exactly difficult to reach **Killarney National Park** (p. 285) from Killarney Town; you just walk toward the cathedral and turn left. This 65sq.-km (25-sq.-mile) expanse of forest, lakes, and mountains is crisscrossed with several well-conceived nature trails, plus more challenging routes for serious hikers. Formerly the grounds of a great mansion, the **Knockreer Estate** (p. 291) still has lovely gardens and beautiful views. Free sites in Killarney Town itself include the rather grand neo-Gothic **St. Mary's Cathedral** (p. 291). For dinner, the frugal traveler will be drawn to the **Laurels** (p. 297)—a lively pub in the center of Killarney town serving steaks, seafood, and stone-baked pizzas, with live music on the side.

Catch a train Killarney to Dublin—again, nearly all change at Mallow. Time: 3½ hr. Fares start at about €44 for adults.

DAY 7: HOMEWARD BOUND...

Assuming your airline will let you fly out of Dublin, an early-ish train back to the capital should allow you some time to pick up any of the

The Long Range, Lakes of Killarney National Park.

SUGGESTED IRELAND ITINERARIES

Ireland for Free or Dirt Cheap

free sites you didn't manage to cover earlier in the tour. Otherwise, you'll have to catch a train straight to Belfast for your flight home (about 7½ hours with up to three changes; fares from Killarney start at about €38 adults). And that's it! You've done a fair bit of Ireland without breaking the bank. Pick your accommodations early and wisely to save the most. Plenty of inexpensive B&Bs are listed in this book for all of these cities. Your other main expense on this itinerary will be rail fares, but you can save money on those too (see "Saving Money on Trains & Buses" on p. 34).

THE BEST OF IRELAND FOR FAMILIES

Traveling with children is always a bit of an adventure, and you'll want all the help you can get. Luckily Ireland—with its vast open countryside, farm hotels, and castles—is like a fairy-tale playground for kids. You may have trouble finding babysitters outside major towns, so just take the kids with you. Most restaurants, sights, and even pubs (during the day) welcome children. The best part of the country for those traveling with kids is arguably Cork and Kerry, where everything seems to be set up for families. Here's a sample itinerary to give you some ideas.

DAYS 1 & 2: DUBLIN

The sprawling greens of **Phoenix Park** (p. 118) are a great place for little ones to let off steam (it's the best place in the city for a picnic, too, if the weather's good). Within the park, **Dublin Zoo** (p. 121) is designed to appeal to the younger ones (you can take a train ride around the zoo, for instance). Inquisitive young minds will be inspired by the cabinets of curiosity at the **National Museum of Ireland: Natural History** (p. 101) and have their interest piqued by Number Twenty-Nine: Georgian House Museum, a house that has been kept exactly as it would have been at the turn of the 19th century. The guides at another museum, the **Little Museum of Dublin** (p. 116), do a great job putting the ordinary lives of Dubliners in the last hundred years into context for younger visitors. But if your youngsters' attention spans demand something a little flashier, try a **Viking Splash Tour** (p. 120), a historical whirl around the city in a World War II amphibious vehicle, complete with headlong splash into the River Liffey. Kids with a high threshold for the ghoulish may get a kick out of the creepy crypts at **St. Michan's Church** (p. 108); if that's too scary, even younger kids are all but guaranteed to love an evening aboard the **Dublin Ghost Bus** (p. 120).

DAY 3: COUNTY CORK

Okay, so it's not exactly untouched by the tourism fairy, but kids find plenty to love about **Blarney Castle** (p. 243), just outside Cork City. They can kiss the famous stone if they don't mind an attendant

REPUBLIC OF IRELAND

Irish Sea

1-2 Dublin

Galway Bay

THE BURREN

Cliffs of Moher

7 C L A R E

Bunratty

6

● Limerick

Mouth of the Shannon

K E R R Y

Killarney

4-5

KILLARNEY NATIONAL PARK

3 ← ● Cork

C O R K

CELTIC SEA

0 — 50 mi
0 — 50 km

1-2 Dublin
3 County Cork
4-5 County Kerry
6 Bunratty Folk Park
7 The Burren

holding them upside-down. A few miles away, the **Fota Island & Wildlife Park** (p. 258) is a well-designed zoo where the docile animals (those that don't bite, kick, or stomp) roam among the visitors.

DAYS 4 & 5: COUNTY KERRY

Kerry is probably Ireland's most kid-friendly county, so there's enough to keep you busy here for at least a couple of days. On the Dingle Peninsula, Fungie, star of the **Dingle Dolphin Boat Tours** (p. 320), has been entertaining kids and grownups alike for the last 30 years. On the Iveragh Peninsula, Kenmare's **Seafari** cruises and seal-watching trips (p. 301) teach kids about conservation issues by putting them in touch with the underwater residents of Kenmare Bay. **Blueberry Hill Farm** (p. 312), in Sneem, is a working, old-fashioned farmstead where kids can help milk cows, make butter, and take part in a treasure hunt. Meanwhile, an underground tour of the atmospheric **Crag Cave** (p. 317) is a surefire winner—as is a stop for high-energy playtime at the **Crazy Cave** (p. 317) adventure playground. And don't overlook what **Killarney National Park** (p. 285) has to offer little ones—what could be better than a ride around the mountains and lakes in an old-fashioned horse-drawn "jarvey"?

37

DAY 6: BUNRATTY FOLK PARK

You could spend most of the day at **Bunratty Castle & Folk Park** (p. 339), an attraction that combines one of Ireland's best medieval castles with a living-history museum. It's a brilliant re-creation of a 19th-century village, complete with costumed actors strolling down the street, chatting to passers-by, and even working in the shops. Bunratty is also the setting for a lively (and hugely popular) **Medieval Banquet.** It's raucous but surprisingly good fun; book an early-evening sitting to suit young bedtimes.

Learning about blacksmithing at the Bunratty Castle & Folk Park.

DAY 7: HEADING HOME

If you have time before the drive back to the airport, head into the otherworldly landscape of the **Burren** (see p. 337), where young imaginations will be fired up by dolmens and other ancient sites. It's also where you'll find the **Burren Birds of Prey Centre** at Aillwee Cave (p. 336), a working aviary full of buzzards, falcons, eagles, and owls in flight.

BEYOND A WEEK...

If your trip extends beyond a week, your family will find plenty of standout attractions for kids farther north.

The **Atlantaquaria** (p. 384), just outside Galway City, is a state-of-the-art aquarium, while pony trekking across **Connemara National Park** (p. 389) is a unique way to see this beautiful, wind-swept landscape.

In Mayo, **Westport House and Pirate Adventure Park** (p. 425) has all the ingredients for high-activity fun; young girls in particular will enjoy learning about the region's real-life pirate hero, **Grace O'Malley** (p. 426).

If you're going as far as Belfast, the attractions around the new Titanic Quarter hold plenty of youthful appeal. Try the hands-on science center, **W5** (p. 493), and the state-of-the-art **Titanic Belfast** museum (p. 488).

Finally, the **Antrim Coast Drive** (see p. 510) has two key high-lights that children will adore: the perilous (but fun) **Carrick-a-Rede Rope Bridge** (p. 512) and the awe-inspiring alien shapes of the **Giant's Causeway** (p. 515).

EXPLORING ANCIENT IRELAND

Ireland has treasured and protected its ancestral past, with mysterious stone circles, cairns, and huge stone tables known as dolmens, standing perfectly preserved in pastures and on hillsides all over the island. Some of the oldest tombs predate the Egyptian pyramids by centuries, and in many cases, while the sites are preserved, their meaning and purpose remain intriguing riddles. To delve into this misty past, you'll need to be intrepid and cover a lot of ground in the car, but it'll be worth it—exploring these rocky symbols can be the most memorable part of any trip to Ireland.

DAY 1: KNOWTH & THE BOYNE VALLEY

After an early breakfast, head north to the rich, rolling Boyne Valley (about an hour's drive north of Dublin off the N2) to the **Brú na Bóinne Visitor Centre** (p. 174) and this extensive Neolithic burial ground. The huge necropolis holds numerous sites, with three open to visitors—**Newgrange** (p. 178), **Knowth** (p. 176), and **Dowth.** Register at the center to tour Newgrange first. A tour here, early in the day before it gets crowded, is spectacular. Next tour is the burial

The megalithic burial site of Newgrange, only an hour north of Dublin.

ground at Knowth, with its extensive collection of passage-grave art. In the afternoon, head down the N3 to the **Hill of Tara** (p. 176). Here mounds and passage graves date from the Bronze Age.

DAY 2: CÉIDE FIELDS

It takes a couple of hours to drive from Dublin to this remote location in north County Mayo, but your efforts will be rewarded. This extraordinary ancient site (p. 427) holds the stony remains of an entire prehistoric farming village on top of a cliff, with a bonus of breathtaking views of the sea and surrounding countryside. Spend the day exploring the 5,000-year-old site, and lunch in the excellent visitor center.

DAY 3: COUNTY SLIGO

In the morning, drive east to County Sligo. On the N4, south of Sligo Town, visit the **Carrowkeel Passage Tomb Cemetery** (p. 441) perched on a hilltop with wide, sweeping views overlooking Lough Arrow. It's often very quiet early in the day—with luck you might have the 14 cairns and dolmens here all to yourself. Then head on to Sligo Town and follow signs to **Carrowmore Megalithic Cemetery** (p. 441). This extraordinary site has 60 stone circles, passage tombs, and dolmens scattered across acres of green pastures. They are believed to predate Newgrange by nearly a millennium. In the afternoon, if you're feeling energetic, climb to the nearby hilltop cairn of **Knocknarea** (p. 445)—thought to be the grave of folklore fairy Queen Maeve.

DAY 4: INISHMURRAY ISLAND

After a relaxing morning, travel by boat to the island of **Inishmurray** (p. 444) off the coast of Sligo. There you can spend the day wandering the impressively complete remains of the early monastic settlement founded in the 6th century. You can still make out its ancient chapels, beehive cells, and altars. If the weather is fine, pack a picnic lunch and eat on the sunny beach. Return to Sligo for the night.

DAY 5: THE BURREN

Today begins with another long drive, but you'll pass through some of the most beautiful parts of Galway and Mayo along the way. **The Burren,** in County Clare, is one of the richest areas of the country for ancient remains from the Neolithic period through medieval times. It has around 120 dolmens and wedge tombs—including the impressive **Poulnabrone Dolmen** (p. 338)—and as many as 500 ring forts. For more on this extraordinary region, see "The Burren" in chapter 9.

DAY 6: SKELLIG MICHAEL

Right after breakfast, head south to County Kerry, where this starkly beautiful island sits 13km (8 miles) off the Iveragh Peninsula, a mute

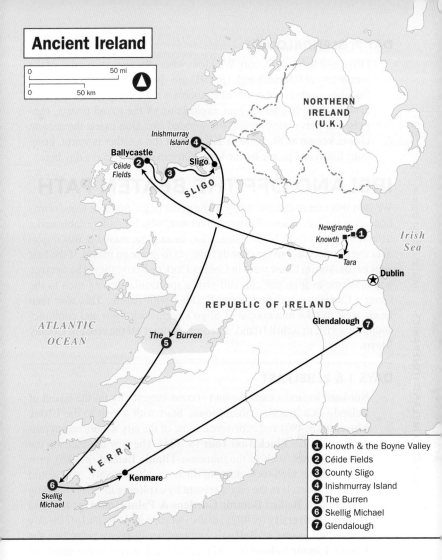

Ancient Ireland

0 ——— 50 mi
0 ——— 50 km

NORTHERN IRELAND (U.K.)

Inishmurray Island **4**

Ballycastle **2**
Céide Fields
Sligo **3**
Sligo

SLIGO

Newgrange **1**
Knowth
Tara

Irish Sea

⊛ Dublin

REPUBLIC OF IRELAND

Glendalough **7**

ATLANTIC OCEAN

The ↙ Burren **5**

KERRY

Skellig Michael **6**
Kenmare

1 Knowth & the Boyne Valley
2 Céide Fields
3 County Sligo
4 Inishmurray Island
5 The Burren
6 Skellig Michael
7 Glendalough

memorial to the hardy souls who once eked out a living amid its formidable cliffs (see p. 310). Deeply observant early Christian monks punished their bodies by living here in miserable conditions, spending their days carving 600 steps into the hard stone, so they could climb up to their beehive huts and icy chapels. Today it is an unforgettable landscape, and the ruins of the monks' homes are profoundly moving. A trip out here by boat and an afternoon's exploration will take up much of the day. Once you return to the mainland, reward yourself with a relaxing evening in Kenmare.

DAY 7: GLENDALOUGH

Drive east today to County Wicklow, where the evocative ruins of the monastery at **Glendalough** (p. 191) are sprawled around two peaceful lakes nestled on the side of a mountain. Get a map from the visitor center before beginning your exploration of the round towers, chapels, and huts dotted around the wooded site. Don't miss the ancient chapel known as **St. Kevin's Kitchen.** If the weather is warm, bring your lunch and picnic by the lake. You can easily spend a day here.

IRELAND OFF THE BEATEN PATH

We start this tour in Belfast, a city in the midst of an immense transformation since the 1998 Good Friday Agreement, which finally established a detente in Northern Ireland. Tourism has steadily increased in this region over the last decade, but the crowds have yet to arrive en masse. If the best sites of the Antrim Coast were in County Cork or Kerry, they'd be overrun with tourists; as it is, you can still visit a spectacular setting such as the Giant's Causeway and find yourself alone with nature. This tour then heads west to take in a couple of Sligo's prehistoric sites and continues south for a visit to Achill Island, a peaceful retreat off the coast of County Mayo.

DAYS 1 & 2: BELFAST

Northern Ireland's capital—and second-largest city on the island of Ireland—is a historic, vibrant town. Start with a visit to the **Ulster Museum** (p. 490) and experience some of the city's more recent past firsthand with a **Black Taxi Tour** (p. 484). The new museums in the Titanic Quarter, such as the immense **Titanic Belfast** (p. 488), provide a more high-tech dose of history; alternatively, you could immerse yourself in the city's present by exploring its busy shopping districts. The **Belfast Botanic Gardens & Palm House** (p. 483) and **Queen's University** (p. 492) are also worth a look. Round off the day with a pint at one of Belfast's extraordinarily pretty pubs, like the **Crown Liquor Saloon** (p. 487), and a meal at one of the small but growing number of world-class restaurants.

DAY 3: COUNTY ANTRIM

One of the North's loveliest counties, Antrim is home to two gorgeous parks: the **Castlewellan Forest Park** (p. 525), with formal gardens and gorgeous woodland walks, and the **Silent Valley Mountain Park** (p. 527), with beautiful walks and even more incredible views. Alternatively, the Antrim Coast road is one of Ireland's great coastal drives—and one of the least spoiled. Few tourists ever venture this far north; those who do will reap spectacular rewards. Start in **Carrickfergus,** with a brief stop to look around its medieval castle

Ireland
Off the Beaten Path

ATLANTIC
OCEAN

DERRY
ANTRIM
Belfast

NORTHERN
IRELAND
(U.K.)

Sligo Town 4-5

Achill
Island 6

SLIGO

Clare
Island

Irish
Sea

REPUBLIC OF IRELAND

Dublin

Shannon River

Shannon
Airport 7

0   25 mi
0   25 km

1-2 Belfast
3 Counties Antrim & Derry
4-5 County Sligo
6 Achill Island
7 Shannon

(p. 494), before heading north along the coast road. For the best
views, take the **Torr Head Scenic Road** (p. 517), located just after
the village of **Cushendun** (p. 512). It's an alternative signposted road
running parallel to the main route, best for those with a good head for
heights. From up here on a clear day, you can see all the way to the
Mull of Kintyre in Scotland. The Antrim Coast's most remarkable
attraction is the **Giant's Causeway** (p. 515), an uncanny natural rock
formation comprised of thousands of tightly packed basalt columns.
You could do the drive in about 2 hours, but you'll want to allow considerably longer than that to give yourself time to stop along the way.
There are places along the coast to spend the night, or you could go
straight on into **Derry** (p. 539). It's about another hour on from the
Giant's Causeway.

DAY 4: DERRY TO SLIGO

Straddling the border between Northern Ireland and the Republic,
this vibrant town for years was synonymous with political strife.
Though it's peaceful these days, it's still a divided place—the residents can't even agree on what to call it. Road signs from the

Republic point to Derry; those in the North point to Londonderry. How can a place like that not be full of character and history? Check out the award-winning **Tower Museum** (p. 544) and the Gothic 17th-century **St. Columb's Cathedral** (p. 544) before recharging for a long drive to County Sligo in the afternoon.

DAY 5: COUNTY SLIGO

Nestled within the gentle, verdant hills of this underrated county are some dramatic archaeological sites. Within a short drive from Sligo Town are two of the most incredible: **Carrowkeel Passage Tomb Cemetery** (p. 441), packed with 14 cairns, dolmens, and stone circles, and the impossibly ancient **Carrowmore Megalithic Cemetery** (p. 441). Here's something to ponder while clambering around the latter: The innocuously named tomb 52A is thought to be 7,400 years old, making it the earliest known piece of freestanding stone architecture in the world.

DAY 6: SLIGO TO ACHILL ISLAND

Just off the coast of County Mayo, this is a wild and beautiful place of unspoiled beaches and spectacular scenery. But you'll also find a handful of excellent little hotels and B&Bs, mostly in the vicinity of **Keel,** the island's most attractive village. This is major outdoor sports territory as well, as the constant wind off the Atlantic Ocean is ideal for windsurfing, hang gliding, and any other sport that depends on a breeze. One of the best (and least-known) discoveries on Achill Island is a deserted village on the slopes of **Mount Slievemore** (p. 430). Not too many people venture up there, making it an even more extraordinary and moving place to visit.

DAY 7: ACHILL ISLAND TO SHANNON

It's a long drive to whichever airport you're flying home from, but a flight out of Shannon will give you the most spectacular route. If you can extend your trip a little, a ferry ride over to Mayo's **Clare Island** (p. 423) is a lovely way to spend a day. Even more peaceful and isolated than its near neighbor, Achill, Clare's permanent population amounts to just 150 people, and you can go a long way without bumping into any of them.

THE BEST OF IRELAND FOR GOLFERS

Golf is the single biggest sporting attraction in Ireland, with nearly a quarter of a million visitors traveling here specifically to play. The Irish landscape and climate, like those of Scotland, seem almost custom-designed for scenic links, fair fairways, green greens, and devilish traps—and there is never a shortage of 19th holes. In short, Ireland is a place of golfing pilgrimage. Every region of the country boasts a few fine 18-hole courses, so no matter where you go, you can easily slip in a rewarding game. Greens fees vary widely, but are often surprisingly modest for non-members, especially on weekdays and at off-peak hours.

If golf is the focus of your vacation, there are a few world-class courses that really shouldn't be missed. The following itinerary is in a way a dream list—you may need to swap out one of these days to do other kinds of sightseeing in these regions. And if you do decide to try to cram in all these elite courses, expect to shell out some hefty greens fees.

Because so many of Ireland's top courses are on the west coast, we begin this itinerary with a flight into Shannon Airport (see p. 563).

DAY 1: COUNTY CLARE

Depending on how early your flight gets in—and how well you can play while jet-lagged—you may even be able to get in a round on Day 1, if you've booked your tee times in advance at **Lahinch Golf Club** (p. 347) on the coast in Lahinch. Stay overnight in County Clare, ready for the scenic drive southwest in the morning.

DAYS 2 & 3: COUNTY KERRY

Heading south to County Kerry (*Tip:* Take the coastal route N67, which incorporates a ferry ride from Killimer to Tarbert), you have a couple of choices just northwest of the town of Tralee: the

The renowned Waterville Golf Links in County Kerry.

Ballybunion Golf Club (p. 319) in Ballybunion, with two esteemed 18-hole clifftop links courses (one of them designed by Robert Trent Jones, Sr.), or the dramatic oceanview Tralee Golf Club (p. 319) in Ardfert, designed by Arnold Palmer. Then continue down to the Ring of Kerry, where you'll stay the night, ready to play on Day 3 at the Waterville Golf Links (p. 299), spectacularly sited overlooking the Atlantic ocean.

DAY 4: COUNTY CORK

It's about a 2½-hour drive east from Kerry to County Cork and the spectacular Old Head Golf Links (p. 269), set on a peninsula just south of the charming town of Kinsale. Named one of *Golf Magazine*'s Top 100 Courses in the World in the 2000s, it charges stiff greens fees—but then, how often do you get to play on a pristine course surrounded by ocean on three sides? Treat yourself to a good dinner that night in Kinsale, one of Ireland's most foodie-friendly towns.

DAYS 5 & 6: DUBLIN

Spend the morning driving cross-country to the Irish capital (if possible stopping along the way to see the stunning medieval ruins of the Rock of Cashel, p. 358, in County Tipperary). One of the world's great golfing cities, Dublin is home to a quarter of Ireland's courses, all within an hour's drive of the city center. Hopefully you've already booked afternoon tee times at either the Portmarnock Golf Club (p. 160), set on a spit of land in Portmarnock, or the Royal Dublin Golf Club (p. 160) on Bull Island in Dublin Bay, near Dollymount. Both are over a century old and have hosted the Irish Open multiple times. Whichever course you play today, you can play the other tomorrow. Both are in the northern suburbs, so do yourself a favor and book a hotel up there, thus avoiding the hassle of getting into and out of the city. Then take public transport into the downtown area for sightseeing, dining, or nightlife.

DAY 7: HEADING HOME

It'll take less than 3 hours to cross the island back to Shannon Airport. So, plenty of time to cram in a few of the sights that you've only heard talked about on the fairway. Book a hotel near the airport so you can get a good night's sleep before flying home.

BEYOND A WEEK...

If you can stretch your vacation by another day or two, you'll be well rewarded if you head up into the less-traveled regions of Northwest Ireland. Fewer golfers make it up here, and the greens fees are therefore much less stratospheric. More important, on the drive up you'll

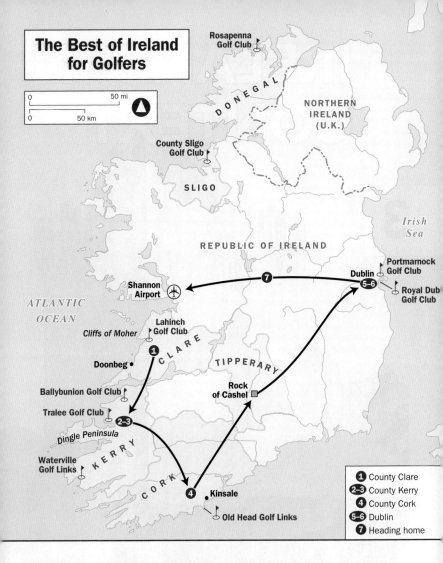

Rosapenna
Golf Club

0   50 mi

0   50 km

DONEGAL

NORTHERN
IRELAND
(U.K.)

County Sligo
Golf Club

SLIGO

*Irish
Sea*

REPUBLIC OF IRELAND

Portmarnock
Golf Club

Dublin

5–6

Royal Dub
Golf Club

Shannon
Airport

7

*ATLANTIC
OCEAN*

Lahinch
Golf Club

Cliffs of Moher

1

CLARE

Doonbeg •

TIPPERARY

Rock
of Cashel

Ballybunion Golf Club

Tralee Golf Club

2–3

Dingle Peninsula

KERRY

Waterville
Golf Links

CORK

4   • Kinsale

Old Head Golf Links

1 County Clare
2–3 County Kerry
4 County Cork
5–6 Dublin
7 Heading home

see some incredibly beautiful countryside that's never mobbed with tourists. **County Sligo Golf Club**, just under 3 hours' drive from Dublin or from Shannon Airport, is a wind-whipped links course edged with wild natural terrain—and it has sweeping views of Sligo Bay and Ben Bulben mountain, immortalized in the poetry of W. B. Yeats. There are two outstanding seaside courses at the **Rosapenna Golf Club** (p. 471) in the Atlantic Highlands of Donegal, a 4-hour drive from Dublin, 5 hours from Shannon. Rosapenna has its own hotel, which may greatly simplify your stay.

IRELAND IN CONTEXT

3

The past decade has been a time of great change for Ireland, as it reels from an ongoing economic crisis and struggles to forge a new political and economic equilibrium. The financial crash of 2008 hit Ireland harder than most other European nations (only Greece and Spain are generally considered to have come off worse), and in many ways the country is still recovering. But while the difficult times are not entirely over, things are getting better. This is certainly a fascinating time to visit and see Ireland in transition. A complex, small country with a tumultuous history, this is a land immensely rich with tradition, beauty, culture, and life.

IRELAND TODAY

The Irish boom economy of the late 1990s changed the country monumentally, resulting in an unprecedented spread of wealth and a huge amount of property development. The excess associated with the boom—business executives flying from Dublin to Galway in their private helicopters for lunch at a particularly good oyster bar, for example, and small apartments in Dublin selling for millions of euro—always seemed unsustainable. And so it was. As suddenly as the boom started, it ended. Over the course of a few weeks in 2008, the economy crashed, sending the country into an economic and political tailspin. Ireland's banks were faced with catastrophic levels of bad debt. As the wave of economic disaster crashed down across Europe, Ireland found itself among the very worst affected.

This all came as a shock to the Irish, who, after more than 15 years of European investment, had begun to believe their newfound affluence would last forever. The chatter of jackhammers formed a constant aural background in nearly every town in the Republic, and the dump truck seemed to be the national symbol of Ireland, as the huge vehicles trundled along by the dozen, carrying tons of gravel and sand to lay new roads and build new neighborhoods. But construction far outpaced demand. Entire subdivisions were built with nobody to live in them—thousands of new homes sat empty. Developers gambling on future growth built shining new ghost towns.

Now, it seems that at last, birdsong is returning to Ireland. The worst years of the crash are behind it, and the economy is turning a corner. But it is a changed country. Experts think this gradual process of recovery

FACING PAGE: **Ross Castle, County Kerry.**

could take years, possibly decades. But Ireland will bounce back. It has been through worse.

THE MAKING OF IRELAND
The First Settlers

With some degree of confidence, we can place the date of the first human habitation of the island somewhere after the end of the last ice age, around the late 8000s B.C. Ireland's first colonizers, Mesolithic *Homo sapiens*, walked, waded, or floated across the narrow strait from what is now Britain in search of flint and, of course, food.

The next momentous prehistoric event was the arrival of Neolithic farmers and herders, sometime around 3500 B.C. Unlike Ireland's Mesolithic hunters, who barely left a trace, this second wave of colonizers began to transform the island at once. They came with stone axes that could fell a good-size elm in less than an hour. Ireland's hardwood forests receded to make room for tilled fields and pastureland. Villages sprang up, and more permanent homes, planked with split oak, appeared at this time.

Far more striking, though, was the appearance of massive megalithic monuments, including court cairns, dolmens (stone tables), round subterranean passage tombs, and wedge tombs. Thousands of these tombs are scattered around Ireland, and to this day only a small percentage of them have been excavated. These megalithic monuments speak volumes about the early Irish. To visit **Newgrange ★★★** (see p. 178) and **Knowth ★★★** (see p. 176) in the Boyne Valley and **Carrowmore ★★★** (see p. 441) in County Sligo is to marvel at the mystical practices of the early Irish. Even today little is known about the meaning or purpose of these mysterious stone relics. Later Celtic inhabitants assumed that the tremendous stones

Mystery surrounds the ancient burial mound of Knowth in County Meath.

monk-y BUSINESS

The Iliad and the Odyssey may have taken place on the turquoise deeps of the Aegean, but it was on the dark waters of the Irish Sea that many classics of Roman and Greek literature survived the sack of Rome and the ensuing Dark Ages. But how did it happen? How did—in the words of bestselling author and historian Thomas Cahill—the Irish save civilization?

The year is 464 A.D. The mighty Roman Empire is on its knees. The Eternal City is under eternal siege, and its great libraries and universities are about to be looted and burned. The world order is quite literally falling apart. Meanwhile, the far-flung backwater of Ireland is undergoing a spiritual revolution. The pagan Gaels are being converted to Christianity by an escaped Roman slave from Wales with a good line in stubbornness. They call him Patricio—known today as St. Patrick.

The Irish wholeheartedly embrace monastic life. Centers of Christian learning pop up across the island, including the remote **Skellig Islands** (p. 310), where monks copy the Bible and other works. Masters of calligraphic arts, they produce beautiful illuminated texts such as the **Book of Kells** (p. 93). Gaeilge becomes the first vernacular language (slang, effectively) in Europe to have been written down. Some of Europe's finest minds flee the continental anarchy for Ireland, bringing books and learning with them. Knowledge-hungry monks duplicate great Latin and Greek works of literature.

After St. Patrick, Irish missionaries such as **Columcille** and **Columbanus** began to look abroad. With the end of the Roman Empire, Europe had become a fragmented patchwork of fiefdoms. The hardy Celtic monks set up new monasteries in France, Germany, Switzerland, and Italy—and they took their skills with them. Beautifully decorated Irish manuscripts from this period have been found as far away as Russia, where the monks continued to advance the art of bookmaking.

and mounds were raised by giants, a race they called the people of the *sí*—a name that eventually became the *Tuatha Dé Danann,* and, finally, *fairies.* Over many generations, oral tradition downsized the mythical people into "little people," who were believed to have led a magical underground life in thousands of *raths* (earthwork structures) coursing the island like giant mole tunnels. All of these sites were believed to be protected by fairies. Tampering with them was thought to bring bad luck, so nobody ever touched them. Thus, they have lasted to this day—ungraffitied, undamaged, unprotected by any visible fences or wires, but utterly safe.

The Celts

Of all the successive waves of outsiders who have, over the years, shaped, cajoled, and pockmarked the timeline of Irish history, none have made quite such an impact as the Celts. They came, originally from Central Europe, in waves, the first perhaps as early as the 6th century B.C. and continuing until the end of the first millennium. They fled from the Roman invasion and clung to the edge of Europe—Ireland being, at the time, about as far as you could go to elude a Roman force. In time, they controlled the island and absorbed into their culture everyone they found there.

Despite their cultural potency, however, the Celts developed little in the way of centralized government, existing instead in a near-perpetual state of conflict with one another. The island was divided among as many as 150 tribes, grouped in alliances under five provincial kings. The provinces of **Munster, Leinster, Ulster,** and **Connaught** date from this period. They fought fiercely among themselves over cattle (their "currency" and standard of wealth), land, and women. No one tribe ever ruled the entire island, though not for lack of trying. One of the most impressive monuments from the era of the warring Celts is the stone fortress of **Dún Aengus,** on the windswept hills of the Aran Islands (see p. 368).

The Coming of Christianity

The Celtic chiefs neither warmly welcomed nor violently resisted the Christians who came ashore beginning in the 5th century A.D. Although threatened, the pagan Celts settled for a bloodless rivalry with this new religion. In retrospect, this may have been a mistake.

Not the first, but eventually the most famous, of these Christian newcomers was a man called Maewyn Succat, a young Roman citizen torn from his Welsh homeland in a Celtic raid and brought to Ireland as a slave, where he was forced to work in a place called the Forest of Foclut (thought to be around modern County Antrim). He escaped on a ship bound for France, where he spent several years as a priest before returning to Ireland as a missionary. He began preaching at sacred Celtic festivals, a tactic that frequently led to confrontations with religious and political leaders, but eventually he became such a popular figure that after his death in 461, a dozen clan chiefs fought over the right to bury him. His lasting legacy was, of course, the establishment in Ireland of one of the strongest Christian orthodoxies in Europe—an achievement for which he was later beatified as **St. Patrick.**

Ireland's conversion to Christianity was a somewhat negotiated process. The church at the time of St. Patrick was, like the man who brought it, Roman. For Ireland, an island still without a single proper town, the Roman system of dioceses and archdioceses simply didn't make sense. So the Irish adapted the church to their own situation. They built isolated monasteries with extended monastic "families," each more or less autonomous.

For several centuries, Ireland flourished in this fashion, becoming a center of monastic learning. Monks and scholars were drawn here in droves, and they were sent out in great numbers as well, to Britain and the Continent, as emissaries for the island's way of thinking and praying.

Like their megalithic ancestors, these monks left traces of their lives behind, enduring monuments to their spirituality. Early monastic sites

Early Christian monks lived in seclusion on Skellig Michael.

such as gorgeous **Glendalough** ★★★ in County Wicklow (p. 191), windswept **Clonmacnoise** ★★★ in County Offaly (p. 407), and isolated **Skellig Michael** off the Kerry coast (p. 310) give you an idea of how they lived, while striking examples of their work can be seen at **Trinity College** ★★ (p. 102), which houses the Book of Kells, and at the **Chester Beatty Library** ★★★ (p. 96) at Dublin Castle.

The Viking Invasions

The monastic city-states of early medieval Ireland might have continued to lead the world's intellectual development—but then the **Vikings** came along and ruined everything.

After centuries of relative peace, the first wave of Viking invaders arrived in Ireland in A.D. 795, making their base in the Southeast, in what is now **Waterford City** (see p. 207). The wealthy Irish monasteries were among their first targets. Unprepared and unprotected, the monasteries, which had amassed collections of gold, jewels, and art from followers around the world, were decimated. The round towers to which the nonviolent monks retreated for safety were neither high enough nor strong enough to protect them and their treasures from the onslaught.

Once word spread of the wealth to be had on the small island, the Scandinavian invaders just kept on coming. Though they were experts in the arts of pillage and plunder, they had no knowledge of or interest in literature. In fact, most didn't know how to read. Therefore, they paid scant attention to the magnificent books they came across, passing them over for more obvious riches. This fortunate quirk of history allowed the monks to preserve their dying culture—and their immeasurably valuable work—for the benefit of future generations.

After the Vikings left, Ireland enjoyed something of a renewal in the 11th and 12th centuries. Its towns grew, its regional kings continued to try (unsuccessfully) to unite the country under a single high kingship, and its church came under increased pressure to conform to the Vatican's rules. All of these factors ripened a prosperous and factionalized Ireland for the next invasion.

It was, tragically, an Irish king who opened the door to the next predator. **Diarmait Mac Murchada,** king of Leinster, whose ambition was to be king of all of Ireland, decided he could do it, with a little help. So he called on **Henry II,** the Norman king of England. Diarmait offered Henry a series of incentives in return for military aid: Not only did he bequeath his eldest daughter to whoever led the army, but he also offered overlordship of the Kingdom of Leinster. To put it bluntly, he made Henry an offer he couldn't refuse. So it was that an English expeditionary force, led by the Earl of Pembroke, Richard de Clare—better known as **Strongbow**—was sent to Diarmait's aid. After a successful invasion, victorious Strongbow remained in Ireland as governor, and thus gave the English their first foothold in Ireland. What Diarmait did not realize, of course, was that they would never leave.

The Norman Invasion

In successive expeditions from 1167 to 1169, the **Normans,** who had already conquered England, crossed the Irish Sea with crushing force. While Dublin Castle was for years the Norman seat of power, over the next century the Norman-English continued to consolidate their power in new towns and cities.

Dublin Castle became the seat of English power in Ireland in the Middle Ages.

Many of these settlers, however, grew attached to the island and began to integrate with the local culture; marriages between the native Irish and the invaders became commonplace. Inevitably, as time passed the Anglo-Normans became more Irish and less English in their loyalties.

Meanwhile, independent Gaelic lords in the North and West maintained their territories. By the late 1400s, English control of the island was effectively limited to **the Pale,** a walled and fortified cordon around what is now greater Dublin. (The phrase "beyond the pale" comes from this—meaning anything that is uncontrollable or unacceptable.)

English Power & the Flight of the Earls

The Tudor dynasty in England, which ruled from 1485 to 1603, changed all that, setting in motion the brutal reconquest of Ireland. In 1542 **Henry VIII** boldly proclaimed himself king of all Ireland—something even his warlike ancestors had stopped short of doing—and later that century his daughter, **Elizabeth I,** declared that all Gaelic lords in Ireland must surrender their lands to her, with the dubious promise that she would immediately grant them all back again.

Unsurprisingly, the proposition was hardly welcomed in Ireland, and a rebel army was raised by Hugh O'Neill and "Red" Hugh O'Donnell, two Irish chieftains. They scored some significant victories early on in their decade-long campaign, most notably over a force led by the Earl of Essex, whom Elizabeth had personally sent to subdue them. Still, by 1603 O'Neill was left with few allies and no option but to surrender, which he did on March 23rd, the day before Elizabeth died. In 1607, after failing to win back much of their power and prestige, around 90 of O'Neill's allies fled to mainland Europe, hoping Spain would try to invade again. This never happened. The **Flight of the Earls,** as it became known, marked a crucial turning point in Irish history—the point at which the old Gaelic aristocracy effectively came to an end.

The Coming of Cromwell

By the 1640s, Ireland was effectively an English plantation. Family estates had been seized and foreign (Scottish) labor brought in to work them. A systematic persecution of Catholics, which began with Henry VIII's split from Rome but did not die with him, barred Catholics from practicing their faith. Resentment against the English and their punitive laws led to fierce uprisings in Ulster and Leinster in 1641, and by early 1642 most of Ireland was again under Irish control. Unfortunately for the rebels, any hope of extending the victories was undermined by internal disunion, and then by a fatal decision to support the Royalist side in the Civil War that had just broken out in England. After King Charles I of England was beheaded in 1648, **Oliver Cromwell,** the commander of the parliamentary forces, was installed as England's ruler. It wasn't long before Cromwell's supporters took on his enemies in Ireland. A year later, the Royalists' stand collapsed in defeat at Rathmines, just south of Dublin.

Defeat for the Royalist cause did not, however, mean the end of war. Cromwell became paranoid that Ireland would be used to launch a French-backed insurgency; he also detested the country's Catholic beliefs. So it was that as the hot, sticky summer of 1649 drew to a close, Cromwell set sail for Dublin with an army of 12,000 men, and a battle plan so ruthless that it remains notorious to this day.

In the town of **Drogheda** (see p. 174), more than 3,552 Irish soldiers were slaughtered in a single night. When a group of men sought sanctuary in the local church, Cromwell ordered the church burned down with them locked inside—an act of such monstrosity that some of his own men risked a charge of mutiny and refused the order. On another day, in **Wexford,** more than 2,000 were murdered, many of them civilians. The trail of destruction rolled on, devastating counties **Galway** and **Waterford.** When asked where the Irish citizens could go to be safe from him, Cromwell famously suggested they could go "to hell or Connaught"—the latter being the most far-flung, rocky, and unfarmable part of Ireland.

After a rampage that lasted 7 months, killing thousands and leaving churches, monasteries, and castles in ruins, Cromwell finally left Ireland in the care of his lieutenants and returned to England. Hundreds of years later, the memory of his infamous violence lingers painfully in Ireland. In certain parts of the country, people still spit at the mention of his name.

The Anti-Catholic Laws

Cromwell died in 1658, and 2 years later the English monarchy was restored. Still, anti-Catholic oppression continued in Ireland. Then in 1685 something remarkable happened: The new Stuart king, **James II,** refused to relinquish his Catholic faith after ascending to the throne. It looked for a while as if Catholic Ireland had found a royal ally at last. However, such hopes were dashed 3 years later, when James was ousted from power, and the Protestant **William of Orange** installed in his place.

James fled to France to raise support for a rebellion and then sailed to Ireland to launch his attack. He struck first at **Derry** (see p. 539), laying siege for 15 weeks, before finally being defeated by William's forces at the **Battle of the Boyne.** The battle effectively ended James's cause, and with it, the hopes of Catholic Ireland for the best part of a century.

After James's defeat, English power was once more consolidated across Ireland. Protestant landowners were granted full political power, while laws were enacted to tamp down the Catholic population. Being a Catholic in late-17th-century Ireland was not exactly illegal per se, but in practice life was all but impossible for those who refused to convert to Protestantism. Catholics could not purchase land, and existing landholdings were split up unless the families who owned them converted to Protestantism. Catholic schools were banned, as were priests and all forms of public Catholic worship. Catholics were barred from holding government office, practicing law, or joining the army. Those who refused to relinquish their faith were forced to pay a tax to the Anglican Church. And, because only landowners were allowed to vote, Catholics whose land had been taken away also lost the right to vote.

The new British landlords settled in, planted crops, made laws, and sowed their own seeds. Inevitably, over time, the "Anglos" became the **Anglo-Irish.** Hyphenated or not, they were Irish, and their loyalties were increasingly unpredictable. After all, an immigrant is only an immigrant for a generation; whatever the birthright of the colonists, their children would be Irish-born and bred. And so an uncomfortable

Canoeing by Trim Castle on the banks of the Boyne River.

sort of stability set in for a generation or three, albeit of a kind that was very much separate and unequal. There were the haves, the wealthy Protestants, and the have-nots, the deprived and disenfranchised Catholics.

This unhappy peace held for some time. But by the end of the 18th century, the appetite for rebellion was whetted again—in the coffee shops and lecture halls of Europe's newest boomtown: **Dublin.**

The United Irishmen & the 1798 Rebellion

By the 1770s, Dublin was thriving as never before. As a center for culture and learning, it was rivaled only by Paris and London; thanks to the work of such architects as Henry Gratton (who designed the **Custom House ★**, p. 110, and the **Four Courts ★**, p. 111), its very streets were being remodeled in a grand, neoclassical style that was more akin to the great cities of southern Italy than of southern Ireland.

While the urban classes reveled in their newfound wealth, the stringent **Penal Laws** that had effectively cut off Catholic workers from their own countryside drove many of them to pour into the city, looking for work. Alongside Dublin's buzzing intellectual scene, political dissent soon brewed. Even after a campaign by Irish politicians succeeded in getting many of the Penal Laws repealed in 1783, Dublin was a breeding ground for radicals and political activists. The results were explosive.

When war broke out between Britain and France in the 1790s, the **United Irishmen**—a nonviolent society formed to lobby for Catholic

The Four Courts, one of Dublin's neoclassical 18th-century landmarks.

Irishmen to be admitted to the Irish Parliament—sent a secret delegation to persuade the French to intervene on Ireland's behalf against the British. Their emissary in this venture was a Dublin lawyer named **Wolfe Tone.** In 1796 Tone sailed with a French force bound for Ireland, determined to defeat forces loyal to the English crown. As luck would have it, though, they were turned back by storms.

In 1798, full-scale insurrection led by the United Irishmen spread across much of Ireland, particularly the southwestern counties of **Kilkenny** and **Wexford,** where a tiny republic was briefly declared in June in Wexford's Bull Ring square (see p. 218). But it was soon crushed by Loyalist forces, which then went on a murderous spree, killing tens of thousands of men, women, and children and burning towns to the ground. The nadir of the rebellion came when Wolfe Tone, having raised another French invasion force, sailed into Lough Swilly in Donegal and was promptly captured by the British. At his trial, Tone wore the uniform of a French soldier; he slit his own throat while in prison waiting to be hung.

The rebellion was over. In the space of 3 weeks, more than 30,000 Irish had been killed. As a final indignity in what became known as **The Year of the French,** the British tricked the Irish Parliament into dissolving itself, and Ireland reverted to strict British rule.

A Conflict of Conflicts

In 1828, a Catholic lawyer named **Daniel O'Connell**—who had earlier formed the Catholic Association to represent the interests of tenant farmers—was elected to the British Parliament as Member of Parliament for Dublin. (His home, in Caherdaniel, County Kerry, can be visited today—see p. 312.) Public opinion was so solidly behind O'Connell, he was able to persuade the British prime minister that the only way to avoid civil war in Ireland was to force a **Catholic Emancipation Act** through Parliament. O'Connell remained an MP until 1841, when he was elected Lord Mayor of Dublin, a platform he used to push for repeal of the direct rule imposed from London after the 1798 rebellion.

O'Connell organized enormous rallies (nicknamed "monster meetings") attended by hundreds of thousands, and provoked the conservative government to such an extent that it eventually arrested him on charges of seditious conspiracy. The charges were dropped, but the incident—coupled with growing impatience toward his nonviolent approach of protest and reform—led to the breakdown of his power base. "The Liberator," as he had been known, faded, his health failed, and he died on a trip to Rome.

The Great Famine

Even after anti-Catholic legislation began to recede, the vast majority of farmland available to Ireland's poor, mostly Catholic rural population was unfertile and hard to cultivate. One of the few crops that could be grown reliably was the potato, which therefore became the staple diet of the rural poor. So when, in 1845, a fungus destroyed much of the potato crop of Ireland, widespread devastation followed. (In Country Kerry's Dingle Peninsula, the **Irish Famine Cottage**—see p. 326—stands as stark evidence of this desolation.)

To label the **Great Irish Famine** of the 1840s and '50s as merely a "tragedy" would be inadequate. It was, of course, tragic—but at the same time, the word implies a randomness to the whole sorry, sickening affair that fails to capture its true awfulness. The fact is that what started out as crop failure was turned into a disaster by the callous response of the British establishment.

As the potato blight worsened, it became apparent to many landlords that their farm tenants would be unable to pay rent. Instead of helping to feed their now-starving tenants, these landlords shipped their grain overseas, determined to recoup what they were losing in rent. The British Parliament, meanwhile, was reluctant to send aid, putting the reports of a crisis down to, in the words of Prime Minister Robert Peel, "the Irish tendency to exaggerate."

People started to die by the thousands.

Eventually it became clear to the government that something had to be done. Emergency relief was sent to Ireland in the form of cheap, imported Indian cornmeal. However, this contained virtually no nutrients. Ultimately, it was malnutrition that spread such diseases as typhus and cholera, which claimed more victims than starvation itself.

To make matters worse, the cornmeal was not simply given to those in need of it. Fearful that handouts would encourage laziness among the

reading LIST

If you want to know about Ireland and the Irish, plenty of talented writers in and out of the country are willing to tell you.

Jonathan Bardon's *A History of Ireland in 250 Episodes* is a good general introduction to Irish history. The book is broken up into 250 short chapters—learned without being too dense, and a very useful primer.

To understand more about the Famine, try the British author **Cecil Woodham-Smith's** *The Great Hunger.* Written in 1962, it's still viewed as the definitive dispassionate examination of this dark period in Irish history.

The author **Tim Pat Coogan,** son of an IRA volunteer, has written two excellent books, *The Irish Civil War* (2001) and *The Troubles: Ireland's Ordeal 1966–1996* (1997), both of which are essential reading for anyone wanting to understand the complexities of 21st-century Ireland.

He also wrote a controversial biography, *Eamon de Valera,* criticizing the former Irish president's actions and legacy.

For a look at Ireland in recent history, try **John Ardagh's** *Ireland and the Irish* (1995) or **F. S. Lyons's** *Ireland Since the Famine* (1973).

The late Dublin-born journalist **Nuala O'Faolain** wrote two top-selling memoirs, *Are You Somebody?* (1996) and *Almost There* (2003), which give the reader an insider's view of living and growing up in modern Ireland.

The late Irish-born American writer **Frank McCourt** earned acclaim and won the Pulitzer Prize for *Angela's Ashes* (1996), his grim memoir of a childhood spent partly in Limerick and partly in Brooklyn. The book is very controversial in Ireland, however—many in Limerick claim it is not an accurate representation of the city during that time.

"shiftless poor," the British government forced people to work for their food. Entirely pointless make-work projects were initiated, just to give the starving men something to do for their cornmeal; roads were built that led nowhere, and elaborate follies constructed that served no discernible purpose. Some of these still litter the countryside today, memorials to cruelty and ignorance.

One of the most difficult things to comprehend, more than a century and a half later, is the sheer futility of it all. For behind the statistics, the memorials, and the endless personal anguish, lies perhaps the most painful truth of all: that the Famine was easily preventable. Enormous cargoes of imported corn sat in Irish ports for months, until the British government felt that releasing them to the people would not adversely affect market rates. Meanwhile, huge quantities of meat and grain were exported from Ireland. (Indeed, in 1847, cattle exports went up 33% from the previous year.)

Given the circumstances, it is easy to understand why so many chose to leave Ireland. More than a million emigrated over the next decade, about three-quarters of them to America, the rest to Britain or Europe. (In County Wexford, the **SS Dunbrody Famine Ship Experience**—see p. 224—movingly depicts this emigration.) They drained the country. In 1841, Ireland's population was 8 million; by 1851 it was 6.5 million.

The Struggle for Home Rule

As the Famine waned and life returned to something like normality, the Irish independence movement gained new momentum. New fronts, both violent and nonviolent, opened up in the struggle for what was now called **Home Rule.** Significantly, the Republicans now drew considerable support from overseas—particularly from America. There, groups such as the **Fenians** fundraised and published newspapers in support of the Irish cause, while more audacious schemes—such as an 1866 "invasion" of Canada with fewer than 100 men—generated awareness, if little else.

Back home in Ireland, partial concessions were won in Parliament. By the 1880s, nationalists such as **Charles Stewart Parnell,** the MP for Meath, were able to unite various factions of Irish nationalists (including the Fenian Brotherhood in America) to fight for Home Rule. In a tumultuous decade of legislation, Parnell came close to winning Home Rule—until revelations about his long affair with Kitty O'Shea, the wife of a supporter, brought about his downfall as a politician.

By 1912, a bill to give Ireland Home Rule was passed through the British House of Commons, but was defeated in the House of Lords. Many felt that the political process was all but unstoppable, that it was only a matter of time before the bill passed fully into law. Then World War I broke out in 1914, forcing the issue onto the back burner once again. Many in the Home Rule movement began to grow tired of pursuing their goal through legal political channels.

The Easter Rising

On Easter Monday 1916, a group of nationalists occupied the **General Post Office ★** (p. 111) in the heart of Dublin, from which they proclaimed the foundation of an Irish Republic. Inside were 1,500 fighters, led by schoolteacher and Gaelic League member **Patrick Pearse** and Socialist leader **James Connolly.**

The British government, panicking over an armed uprising on its doorstep while it fought a massive war in Europe, responded with overwhelming force. Soldiers were sent in, and a battle raged in the streets of Dublin for 6 days before the leaders of the rebellion were captured and imprisoned. (The walls of the post office and other buildings and statues up and down O'Connell Street still have bullet holes in them.) Pearse, Connolly, and 12 other leaders were imprisoned, secretly tried, and speedily executed.

Ultimately, though, the harsh British reaction was counterproductive. The ruthlessness with which the rebellion's ringleaders were pursued and dispatched acted as a lightning rod for many who were still on the fence about how best to gain Home Rule. It's a fact that has become somewhat lost in the ensuing hundred or so years: On that cold Monday morning when Patrick Pearse stood on the post office steps to read a treatise on Irish independence, a great many Irish didn't support the rebellion. Many believed that the best course of action was to lay low until the war had ended, when, they felt, concessions would finally be won. Others felt that the uprising was simply the wrong thing to do, as long as sons of Ireland were sacrificing their lives in the trenches of Europe.

The aftermath of 1916 all but guaranteed, for better or for worse, that Ireland's future would be decided by the gun.

Rebellion & the Anglo-Irish Compromise

A power vacuum was left at the heart of the nationalist movement after the Easter Rising, and it was filled by two men: **Michael Collins** (see p. 274) and **Eamon de Valera.** On the surface, the two men had much in common; Collins was a Cork man who had returned from Britain in order to join the Irish Volunteers (later to become the **Irish Republican Army,** or IRA), while de Valera was an Irish-American math teacher who came back to Ireland to set up a new political party, *Sinn Féin.*

When de Valera's party won a landslide victory in the general election of 1918, its MPs took the provocative step of refusing to take their seats in London. Instead, they proclaimed the first **Dáil,** or independent parliament, in Dublin. De Valera went to rally support for the cause in America, while Collins stayed in Ireland to concentrate on his work as head of the Irish Volunteers. Tensions escalated into violence, and for the next 2 years, Irish nationalists fought a tit-for-tat military campaign against the British in Ireland. The low point of the struggle came in 1920, when Collins ordered 14 British operatives to be murdered in their beds.

Dublin's General Post Office was the scene of fighting in the 1922 Civil War.

In response, British troops opened fire on the audience at a football game at **Croke Park** in Dublin (see p. 114), randomly killing 12 innocent people.

A truce was eventually declared on July 9, 1921. Six months later, the Anglo-Irish treaty was signed in London, granting legislative independence to 26 Irish counties (known together as the **Irish Free State**). The compromise through which that freedom was won, though, was that six counties in the north would remain part of the United Kingdom. Sent to negotiate the treaty, Collins knew that that compromise—which he felt was the best deal he could get at the time—would not be accepted by the more strident members of his rebel group. He also knew they would blame him for agreeing to it in the first place. When he signed the treaty he told the people present, "I am signing my own death warrant."

As he feared, nationalists were split between those who accepted the treaty as a platform on which to build, and those, led by the nationalist de Valera, who saw it as a betrayal. The latter group would accept nothing less than immediate and full independence at any cost. Even the withdrawal of British troops from Dublin for the first time in nearly 800 years did not quell their anger. The result was an inexorable slide into civil war. The flashpoint came in April 1922, when violence erupted around the streets of the capital, raging on for 8 days until de Valera's supporters were forced to surrender.

The government of the fledgling free state ordered that Republicans be shot on sight, leading to the deaths of 77 people. And Collins had been right about his own fate: Four months later he was assassinated while on a visit to his childhood home.

A Republic at Last

The fallout from the Civil War dominated Irish politics for the next decade. De Valera split from the Republicans to form another party, **Fianna Fáil** ("the Warriors of Ireland"), which won the election of 1932 and governed for 17 years. Despite his continuing dedication to the Republican ideal, however, de Valera was not to be the one who finally declared Ireland a republic, in 1948. Ironically, that distinction went to a coalition led by de Valera's opponent, **Douglas Hyde.** Hyde's victory in the 1947 election was attributed to the fact that de Valera had become too obsessed with abstract Republican ideals to govern effectively.

One of the more controversial decisions that Eamon de Valera made while in office was to stay neutral during World War II. His reasons for this decision included Ireland's relatively small size and economic weakness, as well as a protest against the British presence in Northern Ireland. Although that may have made sense to some extent, it left Ireland in the peculiar position of tacitly favoring one side in the war, but refusing to help it. After the death of Adolf Hitler in April 1945, de Valera alienated the Allies further by sending his personal sympathies to the German ambassador. His stance didn't find much favor among the Irish population, either. During the war, as many as 300,000 Irish men still found ways to enlist, in the British or U.S. armies. In the end, more than 50,000 Irish soldiers perished in a war their country had refused to join.

Trouble on the Way

After the war, 2 decades passed without violence in Ireland. Then, in the late 1960s, sectarian conflict erupted in the North. What started out as a civil rights movement, demanding greater equality for Catholics within Northern Ireland, soon escalated into a cycle of violence that lasted for 30 years.

It would be a terrible oversimplification to say that **the Troubles** were a clear-cut struggle between those who wanted complete Irish unification and those who wanted to remain part of the United Kingdom. That was, of course, the crux of the conflict. However, many other factors, such as organized crime and terrorism, together with centuries-old conflicts over religious, land, and social issues, make the conflict even harder for outsiders to understand.

The worst of the Troubles came in the 1970s. In 1972, on a day forever remembered as "Bloody Sunday," British troops inexplicably opened fire on a peaceful demonstration in **Derry** (see p. 539), killing 12 people—many of whom were shot while they tended to the wounds of the first people injured. The IRA took advantage of the mood of public outrage to begin a civilian bombing campaign on the British mainland. The cycle of violence continued for 20 years, inexorably and depressingly. All the while, none of the myriad sides in the conflict would talk to each other. Finally, in the early 1990s, secret talks were opened between the British and the IRA, leading to an IRA cease-fire in 1994 (although the cease-fire held only shakily—an IRA bomb in Omagh 4 years later killed 29, the most to die on any single day of the Troubles).

The peace process continued throughout the 1990s, helped significantly by the mediation efforts of U.S. President Bill Clinton, who became more involved in Irish affairs than any president before him. Eventually, on **Good Friday 1998,** a peace accord was finally signed in Belfast. The agreement committed all sides to a peaceful resolution of the conflict in Northern Ireland, and reinstated self-government for the region in a power-sharing administration. However, it stopped short of resolving the territorial issue once and for all. In other words, Northern Ireland is still part of the U.K., and will be for the foreseeable future.

To some extent, the conflicts rage more bitterly and more divisively than ever before. The difference is that, with notable exceptions, nowadays they are fought through the ballot box, rather than the barrel of a gun. In 2005 the IRA fully decommissioned its weapons, and officially dissolved itself as a paramilitary unit. Since then, there have been wobbles—including the occasional act of violence by splinter groups who don't

A Belfast street mural depicting IRA hunger striker Bobby Sands.

want to accept peace—but these have been very few and far between. Queen Elizabeth's visit to Ireland in 2011, and the 2016 decision by the (Protestant and staunchly pro-British) First Minister of Northern Ireland to attend the centenary celebrations of the Easter Rising in Dublin, have proved hugely symbolic events.

Rebirth

While Northern Ireland struggled to find peace, the Republic of Ireland flourished. The 1990s brought unprecedented wealth and prosperity to the country, thanks in part to European Union subsidies, and partly to a thriving economy, which was nicknamed the **Celtic Tiger** for its new global strength. Ireland became a rich country, widely seen as one of the best places in the world to live and work.

However, that boom came crashing down after the banking crisis of 2008. The Irish government was forced to seek financial aid from the European Union, a package worth more than 50% of the whole economy, to save the country from bankruptcy. The op-ed pages of Irish newspaper expressed real feelings of betrayal and a sense of opportunity lost. Things have improved a lot since then, but the crash changed Ireland for good, as much in terms of its character as mere economics.

The past decade has been one in which Ireland has addressed serious questions about its own identity. Certain things that once seemed indelible to Irish society are now evolving, and the country is becoming more socially liberal. The legalization of abortion, once considered anathema here, is now supported by a majority of people. The influence of the church, while still profound, is less keenly felt than it once was—particularly among the younger generation. One of the most powerful emblems of this change came in 2015, when a referendum to allow **same-sex marriage** passed by a landslide—making this the first country in the world to pass such a law through a popular vote.

IRELAND IN CULTURE

Literature

Ireland holds a place in literature disproportionate to its small size and modest population. Four writers from this tiny country have won the Nobel Prize for literature. Inspired by the country's unique beauty, the inequities of its political system, and its cruel legacy of poverty and struggle, Ireland's authors, poets, and playwrights wrote about the Irish for the Irish, and to raise awareness in the rest of the world. No matter where you live, you've probably been reading about Ireland all your life.

One of the country's best-known early writers was satirist **Jonathan Swift** (see p. 101), who was born in Dublin in 1667. Educated at Trinity College, he left Ireland for England in 1688 to avoid the Glorious Revolution. Though he spent much of his adult life in London, he returned to Ireland when he was over 50 years old, at which point he began to write his most famous works. Greatly moved by the suffering of the poor in Ireland, he translated his anger into dark, vicious humor. His tract *A*

A statue of Irish writer Oscar Wilde in Merrion Square, Dublin.

Modest Proposal is widely credited with inventing satire as we now know it. Swift's best-known works have political undertones—even *Gulliver's Travels* is a political allegory.

Best known for his novel *Dracula,* the novelist and theater promoter **Bram Stoker** was born in Clontarf, a coastal suburb of Dublin, in 1847. As a young man fresh out of Trinity College, he began reviewing theater productions for local newspapers, which is how he met the actor Henry Irving. He spent much of his time promoting and working for Irving, writing novels on the side for extra money. He lived most of his life in England, which largely inspired his work, although it is said that **St. Michan's Church ★★** in Dublin (see p. 108), with its ghostly crypt, and **St. Mary's Cathedral ★** in Killarney (p. 106) contributed to *Dracula*'s creepy feel.

Born in Dublin in 1854, **Oscar Wilde** was a successful student at Trinity College, winning a scholarship to continue his studies in England at Oxford. After a flamboyant time there, he graduated with top honors and returned to Ireland, only to lose his girlfriend to Bram Stoker in 1878, after which he left Ireland forever. His writing—including the novel *The Picture of Dorian Gray,* plays including *The Importance of Being Earnest,* and books of poetry—were often overshadowed by his scandalous personal life. Although a statue of him stands in Dublin in **St. Stephen's Green ★** (p. 119), his works were largely inspired by British and French writers, and he spent the majority of his life abroad.

George Bernard Shaw was born in Dublin in 1856 and attended school in the city, but never went to college. He developed a self-taught literary style. He moved to England as a young man, giving many of his works a distinctly English feel. His plays are known both for their sharp wit and for their sense of outrage over unfairness in society and the absurdity of the British class system. He is the only person ever to have won both the Nobel Prize and an Oscar (for *Pygmalion*).

Born in Sandy Mount outside Dublin in 1865, **William Butler Yeats** attended the Metropolitan School of Art in Dublin, but his poetry and prose were heavily inspired by County Sligo, where he spent much of his time (and where he is buried, in **Drumcliffe** churchyard; p. 442). One of the leading figures of the Irish literary revival in the early 20th century, he won the Nobel Prize in 1923.

James Joyce was born in the Dublin suburb of Rathgar in 1882 and educated at Jesuit boarding schools, and later at Trinity College. He wrote vividly—and sometimes impenetrably—about Dublin, despite spending much of his life as an expat living nomadically in Europe. His controversial and hugely complex novels *Ulysses* and *Finnegans Wake* are his most celebrated (and least understood) works. They and his collection of short stories, *Dubliners,* touch deeply on the character of the people of Dublin. The **James Joyce Centre ★** (p. 116) is a mecca for Joyce fans.

The poet and playwright **Samuel Beckett** was born in 1906 in the Dublin suburb of Foxrock and educated at Trinity College. His work, however, was heavily influenced by German and French postmodernists, and he spent much of his life abroad, even serving with the Resistance in France during World War II. Best known for his complex absurdist play *Waiting for Godot,* he won the Nobel Prize in 1969.

The controversial writer, erstwhile terrorist, and all-round bon vivant **Brendan Behan** was born in Dublin in 1923. Behan came by his revolutionary fervor honestly: His father fought in the Easter Rising and his mother was a close friend of Michael Collins. When he was 14, Behan joined Fianna Éireann, the youth organization of the IRA. An incompetent terrorist, he was arrested on his first solo mission to blow up England's Liverpool Docks when he was 16 years old. His autobiographical book, *Borstal Boy,* describes this period in his life in exquisite detail. His play *The Quare Fellow* made him an international literary star, but he would spend the rest of his life as a jolly, hopeless alcoholic, drinking his way through London, Dublin, and New York, better known for his quick wit and bons mots than for his plays.

Among modern Irish writers, the Nobel Prize–winning poet **Seamus Heaney** may be the best known. Born in 1939 near a small town called Castledawson in Northern Ireland, as a child he won scholarships to boarding school in Derry and later to Queen's University in Belfast. His years studying classic ancient Greek and Latin literature and Anglo-Saxon writing heavily influenced his poetry, but all of his writing is marked by his life in the troubled region where he grew up. His works, including *The Cure at Troy* (based on the works of Sophocles), *The Haw Lantern, The Government of the Tongue,* and a modern translation of *Beowulf* earned him the Nobel Prize in 1995. Heaney's death in the summer of 2013 brought an outpouring of affection from fans across the world.

Other contemporary Irish writers include the award-winning novelist and memoirist **Edna O'Brien** (*The Country Girls, House of Splendid Isolation*); **Marian Keyes** (whose hugely popular novels include *Lucy Sullivan is Getting Married* and *This Charming Man*); **Roddy Doyle** (*The Commitments, Paddy Clarke Ha Ha Ha*); and the late **Maeve Binchy** (*A Week in Winter, Circle of Friends*).

Film & Television

Many controversial, complex, and difficult Irish subjects have been tackled by an international array of directors and actors. Here are some of the better-known ones—and a few obscure gems worth seeking out.

Man of Aran (directed by Robert Flaherty, 1934) is a "docufiction" about life on the Aran Islands. Long respected as a documentary, it's now known that much of it was staged by its American director. Still, it's an interesting view on what the islands looked like in the early 20th century.

Virtually unknown today, ***Maeve*** (directed by John Davis/Pat Murphy, 1982) is a fascinating piece of Irish independent film from the early

1980s, following an Irish expat in England who decides to return to strife-torn Northern Ireland.

The Commitments (directed by Alan Parker, 1991) may be the most famous Irish musical ever made. With its cast of young, largely inexperienced Irish actors playing musicians dedicated to American soul music, it's a delightful piece of filmmaking.

Michael Collins (directed by Neil Jordan, 1996) is a fine biopic about the Irish rebel, filmed largely on location and starring Irish actor Liam Neeson.

Veronica Guerin (directed by Joel Schumacher, 2003) is a dark, fact-based film (with Australian actress Cate Blanchett doing an excellent Irish accent) about a troubled Irish investigative reporter on the trail of a drug boss.

Intermission (directed by Jim Crowley, 2003) is a lively urban romance filmed on location in Dublin, featuring Irish actor Colin Farrell (talking in his real accent for a change). A great look at Dublin right in the middle of its economic boom.

The Wind That Shakes the Barley (directed by Ken Loach, 2006), with a mostly Irish cast and English director, won the Palme d'Or at Cannes for its depiction of Ireland's early-20th-century fight for independence.

Once (directed by John Carney, 2007) is a touching, Oscar-nominated portrait of two struggling young musicians: an Irish singer (played by actor/musician Glen Hansard) and a Czech piano player trying to make it big in Dublin. The film was subsequently turned into a hit stage musical.

The little-seen low-budget *Wake Wood* (directed by David Keating, 2011) is a slice of pure Gothic horror fun. A young Irish couple moves to a new village when their daughter is tragically killed. Turns out the villagers can bring the girl back from the dead—but only for 3 days. When time's up, they refuse to let her go. What could possibly go wrong?

On the other end of the genre scale, *Silence* (directed by Pat Collins, 2012) is a meditative, dreamlike art film about a sound recordist who travels deep into the Irish countryside in search of places completely free of manmade sound (spoiler alert: He has a hard time finding any).

Shadow Dancer (directed by James Marsh, 2012) is an exciting spy thriller set in early 1990s Belfast. A hit at the Sundance Film Festival, the film pulls off the rare trick of being about the Troubles without getting bogged down in politics.

71 (directed by Yann Demange, 2014) has been acclaimed as one of the best films about the Troubles in recent years.

The flipside to Northern Ireland in the '70s is beautifully portrayed in *Good Vibrations* (Glenn Patterson, 2013). The film tells the story of Terri Hooley, who opened a record store in the most bombed street in Belfast—the name reflected his optimistic hope that music could bring warring communities together. The store, which is still open on Winetavern Street in Belfast, went on to spawn a successful record label.

Calvary (directed by John Michael McDonagh, 2014) is a controversial drama about a small-town priest who receives a death threat from one of his parishioners, which leads him to discover dark truths about the community he lives in.

Based on a popular TV sitcom, ***Mrs. Brown's Boys D'Movie*** (directed by Ben Kellett, 2014) is a broad, slapstick comedy about a no-nonsense Dublin matriarch. The film became one of the most successful Irish films of the decade at the box office, despite being almost universally derided as terrible by critics (spoiler alert: They're right).

Brooklyn (directed by John Crowley, 2015) is an incredibly touching drama about a young Irish woman who emigrates to New York in the 1950s. The film, adapted from a novel by Colm Tóibín, was nominated for Best Picture at the Oscars in 2016.

Although it's set in Scandinavia and England, the rip-roaringly good History Channel drama series **Vikings** is almost entirely shot in Ireland. The stunning scenery is a great way to whet your appetite for exploring the Irish countryside.

Music

Music is inescapable in Ireland, and if you hear a band play in a bar and you like them, we strongly advise you to buy a CD from them.

In the days of Internet radio, the best way to discover new sounds is to tune in to Irish radio stations online. An excellent list of stations that stream live (including links) can be found at **www.radiofeeds.co.uk/irish.asp**. Good places to start are the stations run by **RTÉ,** the national broadcaster, particularly the music and entertainment-oriented **2FM** (www.rte.ie/2fm); **Today FM** (www.todayfm.com), a national station that's extremely popular with a young demographic; and **TXFM** (www.txfm.ie), a Dublin-based station that specializes in the latest indie and alternative sounds.

Some cool, quintessentially Irish names to check out, both in and out of the mainstream: **Damien Rice,** who has risen to huge chart success over the past decade; **Lisa Hannigan,** a singer-songwriter with a line in infectiously romantic indie-pop; **Hozier,** a singer-songwriter from County Wicklow who has been making waves globally since 2014; **Burnt Out,** an angsty, artsy pair of indie-punk-influenced artists whose work is deeply rooted in Dublin's working-class culture; rapper **Jafaris,** part of an interesting new wave of Irish hip-hop artists; **Lyra,** a Cork native whose music draws comparisons to Enya and Kate Bush; **Soak,** an absurdly talented young Derry native who's been wowing the music world with her simple but enchantingly beautiful ballads; and **Eden,** an electronic music producer and songwriter who burst onto the international scene in 2016 and has been selling out venues across the world.

Traditional music session in a pub in Donegal.

At the same time, traditional music is alive and well in Ireland, particularly in close association with Irish step dancing. The folk culture is primarily found outside of Dublin, although some pubs in the city do still showcase traditional music. Good places to catch live music are the coastal village of **Doolin,** in County Clare (p. 342), the lively pubs of **Cork City** (p. 240), and the town of **Ballyshannon** in County Donegal (p. 458). Local pubs in small towns almost always can be counted on to host Irish music and sometimes dancing, too.

Social Media

Users of social media, particularly Twitter, can absorb a sense of what modern-day Ireland is really like through the tweets of journalists, thinkers, and just ordinary folk with something to say. Good Irish accounts include **Frank Fitzgibbon** (@FrankSunTimes), editor of the Irish *Sunday Times;* **Hozier** (@Hozier), the delightful Wicklow-born singer-songwriter; the constantly laugh-out-loud funny author **Marian Keyes** (@MarianKeyes); **Colm Tóibín** (@colmtobin), a writer with bone-dry wit who just happens to share the name of a famous author (a frequent cause of misadventure); **Panti Bliss** (@Pantibliss), a Dublin drag queen and activist; radio host **Louise McSharry** (@louisemcsharry), known for discovering some of the hottest talents in Irish music; **Sharon Horgan** (@SharonHorgan), an Irish comedian, mostly based in London, known for her hilarious sketches and hit sitcom *Catastrophe;* and **Amy Huberman** (@amyhuberman), an actress who describes herself as "10% exhausted, 10% feared, and 80% chocolate."

EATING & DRINKING IN IRELAND
Restaurants

Restaurants in Ireland are surprisingly expensive—even after the economic crash, the cost of eating out here is still well above the European average. On the plus side, Ireland's restaurants are varied and interesting—settings range from old-world hotel dining rooms, country mansions, and castles to sky-lit terraces, shopfront bistros, riverside cottages, thatched-roof pubs, and converted houses. Lately, appreciation has grown for creative cooking with an emphasis on locally grown produce and meat.

Before you book a table, here are a few things you should know.

RESERVATIONS   Except for self-service eateries, informal cafes, and some popular seafood spots, most restaurants encourage reservations; most expensive restaurants require them. In the most popular places, Friday and Saturday nights are often booked up a week in advance, so have a few options in mind if you're booking at the last minute.

PRICES   Meal prices at restaurants include national sales taxes (universally referred to as VAT, or Value Added Tax), at the rate of 13.5% in the Republic of Ireland and 20% in Northern Ireland. Many restaurants include the tip as a service charge added automatically to the bill (usually listed at the bottom, just before the bill's total); it generally ranges from 10% to 15%. When no service charge is added, tip around 12% or so, depending on the quality of the service. But do check your bill—some unscrupulous restaurants do not make it clear that you have already tipped, thus causing you to inadvertently tip twice.

The price categories used in this book are based on the price of a complete dinner (or lunch, if dinner is not served) for one person, including tax and tip, but not wine or alcoholic beverages.

TIPS FOR DINING bargains

- If you want to try a top-rated restaurant but can't afford dinner, have your main meal there in the middle of the day by trying the **set-lunch menu.** You'll experience the same great cuisine at half the price.

- Try **pub food.** Pub menus usually include a mix of sandwiches and traditional Irish food, including stews and meat pies. In recent years, many pubs have converted or expanded into restaurants, serving excellent, unpretentious meals at (somewhat) reasonable prices. Check the menu before you sit down at a table (most places post them by their doors).

- Supermarkets and grocery stores in Ireland sell good **premade sandwiches** (much better than supermarket sandwiches in the U.S.) for a few euro. These can make a good, cheap lunch or dinner.

A seafood tower pairs well with a pint of stout in a Dublin pub.

DINING TIPS   Don't be surprised if you are not ushered to your table as soon as you arrive at some upscale restaurants. This is not a delaying tactic—many of the better dining rooms carry on the old custom of seating you in a lounge while you sip an aperitif and peruse the menu. Your waiter then comes to discuss the choices and to take your order. You are not called to the table until the first course is about to be served. You are not under an obligation to have a cocktail, of course. It's perfectly fine to order a soft drink or just a glass of water.

Pubs

The pub is a mainstay of Irish social life—every city, town, and hamlet has a pub. Most people have a "local"—a favorite pub near home—where they go for a drink and conversation with neighbors, family, and friends. Pubs are more about socializing than drinking, and many people you see are just having a soft drink (lime cordial and soda water is a favorite, or orange juice and lemon soda). So even if you don't drink alcohol, feel free to go to the pub. It's a good way to meet locals.

PUB HOURS   Pubs in the Republic set their own hours, although closing times are bound by the type of alcohol license they have. Those with a regular license must shut by 11:30pm from Sunday to Thursday, and 12:30am on Friday and Saturday. Those with late licenses can stay open until 2:30am Monday to Saturday, and 2am Sunday. In Northern Ireland (which is governed by different laws), hours are slightly more restrictive, although this is currently the subject of debate. On Friday and Saturday nights, many pubs stay open until midnight or 1am, and a few even later than that, particularly in large towns and cities. It should also be noted that legal closing times can be hard to police in rural areas.

You'll notice that when the barman calls "closing time," nobody clears out of the pub. "Closing time" is simply the time when the barmen must stop serving alcohol. Expect to hear a shout for "Last orders!" (or the marvelous if antiquated "Time, gentlemen, please!"). Anyone who wants to order his or her last drink does so then. The pubs don't actually close for another 20 to 30 minutes. Eventually, bartenders shout "Time to leave!," lights are turned up brightly, and patrons head to the exit.

TIPS ON ACCOMMODATIONS

Foreign visitors to Ireland should always have at least their first night's room booked, since you will be required to give an address at Immigration when you arrive at the airport. If you need help finding accommodations for subsequent nights once you're in Ireland, contact the local tourism office as soon as possible.

Booking in advance is your best strategy anyway, especially in the summer, when prices can spike up and fall within the course of a week. If you book a month or two in advance, you can often get a better rate at a 4-star hotel than at a 2-star guesthouse—the most expensive hotels often offer in-advance discounts of up to 50%. So before you book that cheap hotel with no services, just have a peek at your dream hotel's prices and see if it's not as cheap, or maybe even cheaper.

Accommodations in Ireland range widely in quality and cost. Often these variations are due to location: A wonderful budget B&B in an isolated area of countryside may be dirt cheap, while a mediocre guesthouse in Dublin or Cork may cost much more. Even in the same lodging, the size and quality of the rooms can vary considerably, especially in older hotels and houses converted to B&Bs. Don't be discouraged by this, but do a little research so you know what you're booking.

Among your various options, **B&Bs** are often hard to beat. These smaller lodgings, usually in residential areas, can be charming and homey—we list several of the best in this book. Breakfast is included in the rate, and it's often hearty. Note that while most B&Bs are regulated and inspected by Ireland's Tourism Quality Services (look for the shamrock seal of approval), many perfectly fine establishments choose not to pay the annual fee that the stamp of approval requires—so don't assume that a place without the shamrock is subpar. **Hidden Ireland** (www.hiddenireland.com; © **098/66650**) is a collection of particularly elegant and unique B&Bs on the higher end of the price spectrum. Another interesting option if you're traveling in the countryside, especially if you're with small children, is a stay in a **farmhouse B&B** on a family-run farm. Contact **B&B Ireland** (www.irishfarmholidays.com; © **071/982-2222**) for an annual guide to farmhouse accommodations.

If you want to stay awhile and establish a base, consider renting a **self-catering** apartment, townhouse, or cottage. Self-catering is a huge business in Ireland. The minimum rental period is usually 1 week, although shorter periods are negotiable in the off-season. Families especially may appreciate the convenience of having more room to spread out and a kitchen for preparing meals. **Rent an Irish Cottage** (www.renta cottage.ie; © **061/411-109**) offers a selection of traditional cottages all over Ireland, fully modernized. The not-for-profit **Irish Landmark Trust** (www.irishlandmark.com; © **01/670-4733**) offers historic properties, refurbished in period style, at prices lower than you might expect. On the more opulent end of the scale, **Elegant Ireland** (www.elegant.ie; © **01/473-2505**) has anything from a chic seaside bungalow to a medieval castle with room for you and 20 of your BFFs.

Nowadays, Ireland's **hostels** are redesigning to attract travelers of all ages, including families. Many have private rooms and may cost a fraction of even a modest bed-and-breakfast. Contact **AnÓige,** the Irish Youth Hostel Association (www.anoige.ie; © **01/830-4555**), or, in the North, **HINI** (Hostelling International Northern Ireland; www.hini.org.uk; © **098/9032-4733**), for listings.

WHEN TO GO

A visit to Ireland in the summer is very different from a trip in the winter. Generally speaking, in summer, airfares, car-rental rates, and hotel prices are highest and crowds are at their most intense. But the days are long (6am sunrises and 10pm sunsets), the weather is warm, and every sightseeing attraction and B&B is open. In winter, you may get rock-bottom prices on airfare and hotels, but it will rain and the wind will blow, and many rural sights and a fair proportion of rural B&Bs and restaurants will be closed.

All things considered, we think the best time to visit is in spring and fall when the weather falls in between seasons, but prices are lower than in high season and the crowds have yet to descend.

Weather

Rain is the one constant in Irish weather, although a bit of sunshine is usually just around the corner. The best of times and the worst of times are often only hours, or even minutes, apart. It can be chilly in Ireland at any time of year, so think *layers* when you pack.

Winters can be brutal, as the wind blows in off the Atlantic with numbing constancy, and strong gales are common. But deep snow is rare and temperatures rarely drop much below freezing. In fact, Ireland is a fairly temperate place: January and February bring frosts but seldom snow, and July and August are very warm but rarely hot. The Irish consider any temperature over 68°F (20°C) to be "roasting" and below 34°F (1°C) bone-chilling.

Average Monthly Temperatures in Dublin

	JAN	FEB	MAR	APR	MAY	JUNE	JULY	AUG	SEPT	OCT	NOV	DEC
TEMP (°F)	36–46	37–48	37–49	38–52	42–57	46–62	51–66	50–65	48–62	44–56	39–49	38–47
TEMP (°C)	2–8	3–9	3–9	3–11	6–14	8–17	11–19	10–18	9–17	7–13	4–9	3–8

HOLIDAYS

The Republic observes the following national holidays, also known as Bank Holidays: New Year's Day (Jan 1); St. Patrick's Day (Mar 17); Easter Monday (variable); May Day (May 1); first Mondays in June and August (summer Bank Holidays); last Monday in October (autumn Bank Holiday); Christmas (Dec 25); and St. Stephen's Day (Dec 26). Good Friday (the Friday before Easter) is mostly observed—all pubs must close on Good Friday, although this archaic law is the subject of hot debate. In the North, the schedule of holidays is the same as in the Republic, with some exceptions: the North's summer Bank Holidays fall on the last Monday of May and August; the Battle of the Boyne is celebrated on Orangeman's Day (July 12); and Boxing Day (Dec 26) follows Christmas.

In both Ireland and Northern Ireland, holidays that fall on weekends are celebrated the following Monday.

Ireland Calendar of Events

For the most up-to-date listings of events, check out **www.discoverireland.ie** and **www.entertainment.ie**.

JANUARY

Funderland. Royal Dublin Society, Ballsbridge, Dublin. An annual indoor fun fair, with white-knuckle rides, carnival stalls, and family entertainment (www.funderland.com; ✆ **01/242-8591**). Smaller events in Cork, Limerick, and Belfast later in the year; check website for details.

FEBRUARY

Audi Dublin International Film Festival. Irish Film Centre, Temple Bar, and various cinemas in Dublin. Ten days of screenings of more than 100 films, from both Ireland and abroad, plus seminars and lectures on filmmaking (www.diff.ie; ✆ **01/662-4620**). Late February and early March.

MARCH

St. Patrick's Dublin Festival. This massive 4-day festival is open, free, and accessible to all. Street theater, carnival acts, sports, music, fireworks, and other festivities culminate in Ireland's grandest parade, with marching bands, drill teams, floats, and delegations from around the world (**www.stpatricksday.ie**). On and around March 17.

St. Patrick's Day Parades. Held all over Ireland and Northern Ireland, celebrating Ireland's patron saint. March 17.

APRIL

Pan Celtic Festival. For 5 days, the wider Celtic family (including Cornwall, Isle of Man, Scotland, Wales, and Brittany) unites for culture, song, dance, sports, and parades with marching bands and pipers. The festival moves to a different part of a Celtic nation or region every year—but Ireland is a frequent host (www.panceltic.ie; ✆ **059/915-8105**). April.

World Irish Dancing Championships. Dublin. The premier international competition in Irish dancing features more than 4,000 contenders from as far away as New Zealand (www.clrg.ie; ✆ **01/814-6298**). April.

Daily Mirror May Day Races. Down Royal Racecourse, Maze, Lisburn, County Antrim. One of the major events on the horse-racing calendar (www.downroyal. com; ✆ **028/9262-1256**).

Deep RiverRock Belfast City Marathon. This 42km (26-mile) race of 17,000 international runners through the city starts at City Hall and finishes at the Maysfield Recreation Centre (www.belfastcity marathon.com; ✆ **028/9060-5933**). Early May.

International Literature Festival Dublin. One of the biggest events in the Irish arts calendar, this 9-day festival draws high-profile authors from around the world. Events take place at venues across the city, including Dublin Castle (http:// ilfdublin.com; ✆ **01/969-5259**). Late May.

Wicklow Arts Festival. Wicklow's big spring event is held over 5 days in Wicklow Town. Many of the music, theater, art, and literary events are free (www. wicklowartsfestival.ie). Late May.

Cat Laughs Comedy Festival. Various venues, Kilkenny Town. Past performers at this international festival of stand-up comedy include American comics Bill Murray, George Wendt, and Emo Phillips, and Ireland's Dara O'Briain (www.the catlaughs.com). Late May or early June.

Taste of Dublin. Iveagh Gardens, Dublin. One of Ireland's biggest and most high-profile food festivals, where for 4 days visitors can sample dishes prepared by some of the country's top chefs and over 100 artisan producers. The event is usually a sellout, so booking is advisable. (https://dublin.tastefestivals.com). Mid-June.

Bloomsday Festival. Various Dublin venues. This unique daylong fest celebrates Leopold Bloom, the central character of James Joyce's *Ulysses,* by replicating the aromas, sights, sounds, and tastes of Dublin on June 16, 1904, the day when *Ulysses* takes place. Ceremonies are held at the James Joyce Tower and Museum;

guided walks visit Joycean sights. Contact the James Joyce Centre, 35 N. Great George's St., Dublin 1 (www.bloomsday festival.ie; ✆ **01/878-8547**). June 11–16.

Cork Midsummer Arts Festival. Emmet Place, Cork City. The program includes musical performances and traditional Irish *céilí* bands, and always has a strong literary content. Bonfire nights are particularly popular (www.corkmidsummer. com; ✆ **021/421-5131**). Mid-June.

Irish Derby. The Curragh, County Kildare. Ireland's version of the Kentucky Derby or Royal Ascot is a fashionable gathering (**Hint:** jackets for men, posh hats for women) of racing fans from all over the world. It's one of the richest middle-distance horse races in Europe. Booking recommended (www.curragh.ie; ✆ **045/441-205**). Late June.

Battle of the Boyne Commemoration. Belfast and other cities. This annual event, often called Orangeman's Day, recalls the historic battle between two 17th-century kings. Protestant parades are held all over Northern Ireland; but don't take the celebratory appearance at face value—they're highly controversial, and inevitably some in urban Belfast and Derry may turn nasty. This may be one better viewed from afar. July 12.

Galway International Arts Festival. Galway City. This 2-week fest features international theater, concerts, literary evenings, street shows, arts, parades, and music (www.giaf.ie; ✆ **091/509700**), followed by the famous **Galway Races** (www.galwayraces.com)—5 days of racing and merriment, music, and song. See www.giaf.ie and p. 381 for details. Mid-to late July.

Fleadh Cheoil na hÉireann. Ireland's premier summer festival of traditional music since 1951 changes its host city every year. Competitions are held to select all-Ireland champions in all categories of instruments and singing. Visit http:// fleadhcheoil.ie to find out this year's location. Early to mid-August.

Lughnasa Fair. Carrickfergus Castle, County Antrim. On the grounds of this 12th-century Norman castle, this event features people in period costumes, medieval games, traditional food, entertainment, and crafts (www.carrickfergus. org; ☏ **028/9335-8000**). Early August.

Dublin Horse Show. RDS Showgrounds, Ballsbridge, Dublin. The most important equestrian event in Ireland. Aside from daily dressage and jumping competitions, highlights include a fashionable ladies' day, nightly formal hunt balls, and the awarding of the Aga Khan Trophy and the Nation's Cup (www.dublinhorse show.com; ☏ **01/668-0866**). Early August.

Kilkenny Arts Festival. Kilkenny Town. Weeklong event has classical and traditional music, plays, readings, films, poetry, and art exhibitions (www. kilkennyarts.ie; ☏ **056/776-3663**).

Puck Fair. Killorglin, County Kerry. In one of Ireland's oldest festivals, the residents of this tiny Ring of Kerry town (see p. 308) capture a wild goat and enthrone it as "king" over 3 days of merrymaking—open-air concerts, horse fairs, parades, and fireworks (www.puckfair.ie; ☏ **066/976-2366**). August 10–12.

Rose of Tralee International Festival. Tralee, County Kerry. A gala atmosphere prevails at this 5-day event (see p. 318), with a full program of concerts, street entertainment, horse races, and a beauty-and-talent pageant leading up to the televised selection of the "Rose of Tralee" (www.roseoftralee.ie; ☏ **066/712-1322**). Mid-August.

National Heritage Week. More than 400 events are held throughout the country—walks, lectures, exhibitions, music recitals, and more (www.heritageweek.ie; ☏ **185/020-0878**). Late August.

SEPTEMBER

Electric Picnic. Stradbally, County Laois. This midsize music festival, held on the grounds of Stradbally Hall, is known for its eclectic lineup. Recent acts have included Sonic Youth, St. Vincent, and Kendrick Lamar. (www.electricpicnic.ie; ☏ **081/871-9300**). Early September.

Irish Antique & Fine Art Fair. Ballsbridge Hotel, Ballsbridge, Dublin. Ireland's premier annual antiques fair, with hundreds of dealers from all over the island (www. iada.ie; ☏ **087/693-3602**).

Lisdoonvarna Matchmaking Festival. Lisdoonvarna, County Clare. Still the biggest and best singles' event, this traditional "bachelor" festival (see p. 345) carries on in the lovely spa town of Lisdoonvarna, with lots of music and dance (www.matchmakerireland.com; ☏ **065/707-4005**). September.

All-Ireland Hurling & Gaelic Football Finals. Croke Park, Dublin. The finals of Ireland's most beloved sports, hurling and Gaelic football, are Ireland's equivalent of the Super Bowl. You can find information at **www.gaa.ie**, or obtain tickets through Ticketmaster (www. ticketmaster.ie; ☏ **081/871-9300**).

Galway International Oyster and Seafood Festival. The highlights of this festival include the World Oyster Opening Championship, a grand opening parade, a yacht race, an art exhibition, a gala banquet, traditional music, and, of course, lots of oyster eating (www. galwayoysterfest.com; ☏ **091/394637**). Late September.

Dublin Theatre Festival. Showcases for new plays by every major Irish company, plus productions from abroad (www. dublintheatrefestival.com; ☏ **01/677-8439**). Late September/mid-October.

OCTOBER

Kinsale Gourmet Festival. Kinsale, County Cork. The foodie capital of Ireland hosts this well-respected annual fest, featuring special menus in all the restaurants and plenty of visiting star chefs (www.kinsalerestaurants.com; ☏ **021/477-3571**). Mid-October.

Baboró International Arts Festival for Children. Galway. A fun-filled, educational festival geared to kids 3 to 12 years of age, with theater, music, dance, museum exhibitions, and literary events (www.baboro.ie; ✆ 091/569-777). Mid-to late October.

Guinness Cork Jazz Festival. Cork City. Ireland's second city stages a first-rate festival of jazz, with an international lineup of live acts playing in hotels, concert halls, and pubs (www.guinness jazzfestival.com; ✆ 021/427-8979). Late October.

SSE Airtricity Dublin City Marathon. More than 20,000 runners from both sides of the Atlantic and the Irish Sea participate in this popular run through the streets of the capital (www.dublin marathon.ie; ✆ 01/623-2250). Last Monday in October.

Wexford Festival Opera. Wexford, County Wexford. Famous as much for its jubilant, informal atmosphere as for acclaimed productions of lesser-known 18th- and 19th-century operatic master-pieces, this festival also has classical-music concerts and more (www.wexford opera.com; ✆ 053/912-2144). Late October/early November.

Cork Film Festival. Cinemas throughout Cork. Ireland's oldest film festival offers a plethora of international features, docu-mentaries, short films, and special pro-grams (http://corkfilmfest.org; ✆ 021/427-1711). Mid-November.

Killarney Christmas Market. Fair Hill, Killarney, County Kerry. Killarney hosts some of the region's best Christmas mar-kets, devoted mainly to quality local crafts and food (www.christmasinkillarney. com; ✆ 064/663-7928). December.

Dublin Docklands Christmas Festival. Part of the traditional run-up to Christmas in Dublin, this huge event all but takes over Docklands. Mostly it's an opportunity to shop (with some 100 different traders), but it also has a fairground and festive food and drink aplenty (www.dublin docklandschristmasfestival.ie; ✆ 01/496-9883). Mid-December until Christmas.

3

IRELAND IN CONTEXT | Ireland Calendar of Events

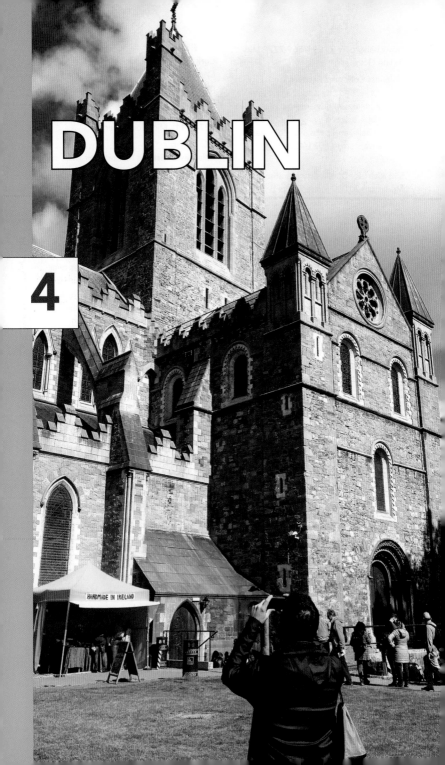

DUBLIN

4

D ublin is an ancient city with a young soul. Its gray stone walls and towers follow the curves of the old River Liffey, as they always have, but the Irish capital is also one of Europe's most youthful cities, with a large population of university students and young workers. In fact, the Dublin of 2019 may not be the Irish city of your imagination. It is by far the island's most cosmopolitan city, and its most diverse. This is a vibrant, modern, European capital, and it wears that status on its sleeve. Busy bars and snazzy restaurants buzz alongside traditional pubs that have stood their ground for centuries. Chic boutiques fill medieval streets beneath historic castle walls. This captivating city is yours to discover—and even if you think you know what to expect, you're almost certain to be surprised by what you find.

ESSENTIALS

Arriving

BY PLANE **Aer Lingus** (www.aerlingus.com; ✆ 081/836-5000), Ireland's national airline, operates regular, direct scheduled flights between Dublin International Airport and numerous cities worldwide. From the United States, direct routes include Boston, Chicago, Hartford, Los Angeles, Miami, New York (JFK and Newark), Philadelphia, Seattle, San Francisco, and Washington D.C. (Not all of these routes operate in winter.) On the return journey, passengers bound for the U.S. may pre-clear customs at Dublin airport (meaning you get to skip passport control on the American side). **American Airlines** (www.aa.com; ✆ 800/433-7300), **Delta** (www.delta.com; ✆ 800/241-4141), and **United** (www.united.com; ✆ 800/864-8331) all fly direct to Dublin from at least one of those same cities. From Canada, direct flights are operated by **Air Canada** (www.aircanada.com; ✆ 888/247-2262). From Australia and New Zealand, **Quantas** (www.qantas.com; ✆ 13-13-13) and **Air New Zealand** (www.airnewzealand.co.nz; ✆ 080/0737-000) both fly to Dublin, with at least one change. Virtually all of the major European airlines have direct flights to Dublin.

   Dublin Airport (www.dublinairport.com; ✆ 01/814-1111) is 11km (6¾ miles) north of the city center. A travel information desk in the arrivals concourse provides information on public bus and rail services

FACING PAGE: **Christ Church Cathedral in Dublin.**

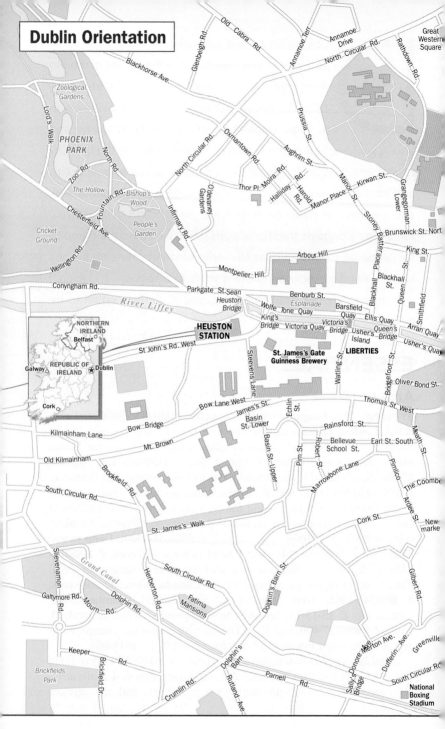

Dublin Orientation

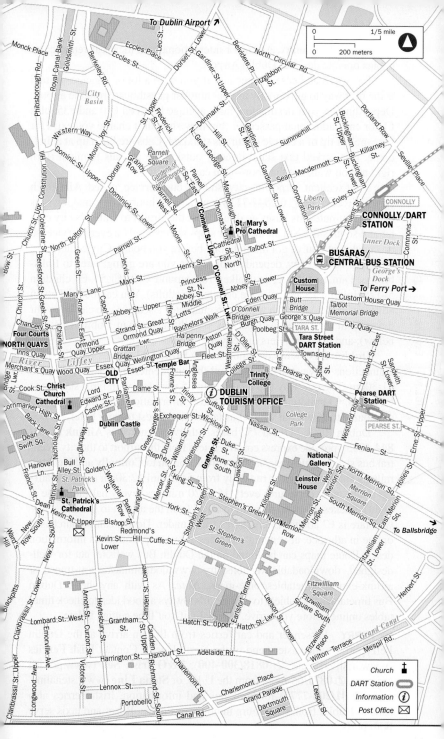

To Dublin Airport ↗

Monck Place

Philipsborough Rd.
Royal Canal Bank
Goldsmith St.
Berkeley Rd.
Eccles Place
Eccles St.
Dorset St. Lower
Gardiner St. Upper
Belvidere Pl.
North Circular Rd.
Fitzgibbon St.

City Basin

Western Way
Mount Joy St.
Frederick St. N.
Denmark St.
Hill St.
Gardiner St. Mid.
Summerhill
Buckingham St. Upper
Buckingham St.
Killarney St.
Portland Row
Seville Place

Dominic St. Upper
Constitution Hill
Granby Row
Parnell Square
Gardens of Remembrance
Parnell Sq. East
Parnell St.
Marlborough St.
Sean Macdermott St. Upper
Sean Macdermott St. Lower
Foley St.
Amiens St.

CONNOLLY

Dorset St. Lower

Dominick St. Lower

Liberty Park

Corporation St.

CONNOLLY/DART STATION

North Bolton St.
Parnell St.
Jervis St.
Moore St.
Cathedral St.
Thomas's St.
St. Mary's Pro Cathedral
Talbot St.
Earl St. North

Inner Dock

George's Dock

Mary's Lane
Mary's St.
Henry St.
Princess St. N.
O'Connell St. Upr.
O'Connell St. Lwr.
Abbey St. Lower
BUSÁRAS/ CENTRAL BUS STATION
To Ferry Port →

Commons

Chancery St.
Green St.
Capel St.
Arran St. East
Abbey St. Upper
Strand St. Great
Abbey St. Middle
Liffey
Lotts
Custom House
Custom House Quay

Four Courts
NORTH QUAYS
Charles St.
Ormond Quay Upper
Ormond Quay Lwr.
Bachelors Walk
O'Connell Bridge
Burgh Quay
Eden Quay
Butt Bridge
George's Quay
Talbot Memorial Bridge
City Quay

Inns Quay
River Liffey
Merchant's Quay
Wood Quay
Grattan Bridge
Essex Quay
Wellington Quay
Ha'penny Bridge
Aston Quay
D'Olier St.
Poolbeg St.
TARA ST.
Tara Street DART Station
Townsend St.
Sandwith St. Lower

Cook St.
Christ Church Cathedral
Lord Edward St.
Parliament St.
Essex St.
Temple Bar
OLD CITY
Fownes St.
Anglesea St.
Fleet St.
Westmoreland St.
College St.
Pearse St.
Shaw St.
Lombard St. East

Cornmarket
High St.
Back Lane
Dame St.
Castle St.
Dublin Castle
Great George's St.
Exchequer St.
Wicklow St.
Trinity St.
Suffolk St.
DUBLIN TOURISM OFFICE
Nassau St.
Trinity College
College Park
Westland Row
Pearse DART Station
PEARSE ST.
Erne St. Upper

Dean Swift Sq.
Nicholas St.
Werburgh St.
Drury St.
King St.
Clarendon St.
Duke St.
Dawson St.
Kildare St.
Fenian St.

Hanover Lane
Bull Alley St.
Golden Ln.
St. Patrick's Park
Whitefriar St.
Peter Row
Aungier St.
Mercer St.
William St. South
Anne St. South
National Gallery
Merrion Sq.
North Merrion Sq.
Holles St.

Francis St.
Dean St.
St. Patrick's Cathedral
Kevin St. Upper
Bishop St.
York St.
Stephen's Green West
St. Stephen's Green North
Leinster House
Merrion St. Upper
South Merrion Sq.
East Merrion Sq.

Ward's Hill
New Row South
Kevin St. Lower
Redmond's Hill
Cuffe St.
St. Stephen's Green
Merrion Row
Merrion St. Lower
To Ballsbridge →

Blackpitts
Clanbrassil St. Lower
New St.
Camden St. Lower
Earlsfort Terrace
Leeson St. Lower
Fitzwilliam Square
Fitzwilliam St. Lower
Herbert St.

Lombard St. West
Heytesbury St.
Grantham St.
Camden St. Upper
Richmond St. South
Hatch St. Upper
Hatch St. Lwr.
Fitzwilliam Square South
Fitzwilliam Place
Wilton Terrace
Grand Canal
Mespil Rd.

Emorville Ave.
Curzon St.
Harrington St.
Harcourt St.
Adelaide Rd.

Clanbrassil St. Upper
Longwood Ave.
Victoria St.
Lennox St.
Portobello
Charlemont St.
Charlemont Place
Grand Parade
Dartmouth Square
Leeson St. Upper

Canal Rd.

Church ✝
DART Station ⬭
Information ⓘ
Post Office ✉

83

throughout the country. All major international and local car-rental companies operate desks at Dublin Airport.

For speed and ease—especially if you have a lot of luggage—a **taxi** is the best way to get directly to your hotel or guesthouse from the airport. Depending on your destination, fares average between €20 and €35, plus €1 for each additional passenger (but they shouldn't charge you extra for luggage). A tip of a couple of euro is standard. Cabs are lined up at a first-come, first-served taxi stand directly outside the arrivals terminal (turn right as you walk out the door—you can't miss it).

An excellent airport-to-city shuttle bus service called **AirCoach** (www.aircoach.ie; ✆ **01/844-7118**) operates 24 hours a day, making runs every 15 minutes. Its buses go direct from the airport to Dublin's city center and south side. Not all the major stops are covered on every service, so do check that you've got the right one before you board. City center fares are €6 to €8 one-way, depending on where you are going; fares to Ballsbridge, Dún Laoghaire, or Dalkey run around €10 (€1.50–€6 children 5–12; children 13 and over are counted as adults). You can buy tickets in advance on the AirCoach website to guarantee a seat, or you can buy your ticket from the driver. AirCoach is slightly faster than Dublin Bus (see below), and takes travelers directly to the hotel districts.

Dublin Bus (www.dublinbus.ie; ✆ **01/873-4222**) has regular daily connections between the airport and the city center from around 6am to 11:30pm. The one-way trip takes about 55 minutes, with fares starting at €4 adults, €3 children. Consult the travel information desk in the arrivals concourse to figure out which bus takes you closest to your hotel.

Dublin Bus's 747 and 757 buses, otherwise known as **Airlink** (✆ **01/ 844-4265**), provide express coach services from the airport to the city's central bus station, **Busáras,** on Store Street, and on to **Connolly** and **Heuston** railway stations. Services run daily from 5am until 12:30am (Sun 7:25am–12:15am), with departures every 15 to 20 minutes (every half-hour late at night); it takes about 40 minutes to travel from the airport to Busáras. One-way fare is €7 adults, €3 children 11 and under. Tickets can be purchased online in advance, at vending machines at bus stops, or at bus information desks. Route maps can be found on the Dublin Bus website, but for well-designed, downloadable versions, try www.dodublin.ie/airport-transfers/airlink-express/timetables/route-maps. *Note:* As with anywhere, Dublin Bus timetables are subject to change. It's always a good idea to check timetables online before you arrive, especially if you'll be getting in late.

BY FERRY Passenger and car ferries from Britain arrive at the Dublin Ferryport, on the eastern end of the North Docks. Contact **Irish Ferries** (www.irishferries.ie; ✆ **0818/300-400**), **P&O Irish Sea** (www.poirish sea.com; ✆ **0871/66-6464** from the U.K), or **Stena Line** (www.stenaline. com; ✆ **01/204-7777**) for bookings and information. Irish Ferries also sails to Dublin from Cherbourg in northern France. Buses and taxis serve both ports.

BY TRAIN Called Iarnród Éireann in Gaelic, **Irish Rail** (www.irish rail.ie; ✆ **1890/77-88-99**) operates daily train service to Dublin from Belfast, Northern Ireland, and all major cities in the Irish Republic, including Cork, Galway, Limerick, Killarney, Sligo, Wexford, and Waterford. Trains from the south, west, and southwest arrive at **Heuston Station,** Kingsbridge, off St. John's Road; from the north and northwest at **Connolly Station,** Amiens Street; and from the southeast at **Pearse Station,** Westland Row, Tara Street. For the lowest fares, buy tickets in advance from the Irish Rail website.

A "living statue" of James Joyce greets tourists.

BY BUS Bus Éireann (www.bus eireann.ie; ✆ **01/836-6111**) operates daily express coach and local bus service from all major cities and towns in Ireland into Dublin's central bus station, **Busáras,** on Store Street. Buy tickets in advance online for the cheapest prices.

BY CAR If you are arriving by car from other parts of Ireland or on a car ferry from Britain, all main roads lead into the heart of Dublin and are well-signposted to **An Lar** (City Centre). The quickest way into Dublin from the airport is to take the Dublin Tunnel. The toll for cars is €3 (€10 Mon–Fri 6–10am). To bypass the city center, follow signs to the East Link toll bridge (€2) or the M50 highway toll (€3.10). The M50 circuits the city on three sides. From Wexford Town, Galway, or Belfast the drive takes around 2 hours; from Cork, 2½ hours. Your car-rental agency should inform you of all anticipated tolls.

Visitor Information

Dublin Tourism operates several walk-in visitor centers in greater Dublin that are open every day except Christmas Day, St. Stephen's Day (December 26), and New Year's Day. The principal center is on Suffolk Street, Dublin 2, open from Monday to Saturday from 9am to 5:30pm, Sunday and public holidays 10:30am to 3pm. (It's easy to spot—just look for the rather racy statue of Molly Malone pushing her cart.) The Suffolk Street office is an excellent resource for travelers, with currency exchange, a car-rental counter, an accommodation reservations service, bus and rail information desks, a gift shop, and a cafe. For accommodation reservations throughout Ireland by credit card (including some good last-minute deals

on Dublin hotels), contact Dublin Tourism via **www.visitdublin.com** or
☎ **1890/324-583.** A tourism center is also in the arrivals concourse of both
terminals at Dublin Airport.

At any of these centers you can pick up the free *Totally Dublin*
(www.totallydublin.ie) monthly entertainment guide. Its website also has
a comprehensive what's-on section. Other go-to entertainment listings
sites include **Visit Dublin** (www.visitdublin.com/whats-on), **TimeOut
Dublin** (www.timeout.com/dublin), and **Dublin.ie** (dublin.ie/whats-on).

City Layout

Dublin is divided by the curves of the River Liffey, which empties into the
sea at the city's eastern edge. To the north and south, canals encircle the
city center: The Royal Canal arcs across the north and the Grand Canal
through the south. Traditionally, the area south of the river has been Dublin's buzzing, prosperous hub. It still holds most of the best hotels, restaurants, shops, and sights, but the Northside is on the upswing, and hip new
bars and hotels give it a trendy edge.

Dublin is compact and easily walked in an hour. In fact, a 45-minute
walk from peaceful St. Stephen's Green, up bustling Grafton Street, and
across the Liffey to the top of O'Connell Street offers a good overview of
the city's prosperous present and storied past.

MAIN STREETS & SQUARES In the town center just south of the river,
the main east-west artery is **Dame Street,** which changes its name to College Green, Westmoreland Street, Lord Edward Street, and High Street at
various points as it connects **Trinity College** with **Dublin Castle** and
Christ Church Cathedral. A short walk north of Dame Street you'll find
the winding medieval lanes of the **Temple Bar** area, Dublin's party central, packed with noisy late-night bars and cheap, cheerful restaurants.

At its eastern end, where Dame Street becomes College Green, the
sturdy gray stone walls of **Trinity College** make an excellent landmark to
get your bearings. At the southwest corner of the campus is the top of

---

Murky Origins

For most visitors, the very word "Dublin" may conjure up a heady, romantic mix of history, but the name actually has a more prosaic origin. It comes from the ancient Celtic words *dubh linn,* meaning "the black pool." Specifically, it refers to a natural inlet where the River Liffey met the River Poddle, and the waters were dark and murky. Long since buried, the inlet is thought to be somewhere around Dublin Castle.

An allusion to these watery origins still survives in the city's Gaelic name, *Baile Átha Cliath,* which means "the town of the hurdled ford"—a ford being a point where a stream or river crosses a road. When fords were "hurdled" in medieval times, it meant that they were covered at low tide with woven sheets of willow, making them easier to cross.

The Liffey Boardwalk follows the river's north bank in Central Dublin.

Grafton Street, a lively pedestrianized lane lined with clothing boutiques and eateries. It leads, eventually, to the bucolic park of **St. Stephen's Green.** From there, head back up Kildare Street past Leinster House (seat of the Irish Parliament) and turn to the right to reach **Merrion Square,** another of Dublin's extraordinarily well-preserved Georgian squares.

To cross the River Liffey and get to the Northside, most visitors choose the photogenic arch of the **Ha'penny Bridge** (see p. 112), while locals take the less attractive **O'Connell Bridge** nearby. You can be different and cross via the Ha'penny's sleekly modern neighbor, the **Millennium Bridge,** which is beautifully illuminated after dark. The O'Connell Bridge leads directly onto broad **O'Connell Street,** the Northside's main thoroughfare. O'Connell Street runs north to **Parnell Square,** which holds a couple of marvelous museums and marks the top edge of central Dublin. The street running along the Liffey's embankment is called the **North Quays** by everyone, though its name changes on virtually every block, reflecting the long-gone docks that once lined it; today a pedestrian boardwalk runs along the riverfront here.

Dublin Neighborhoods in Brief

TRINITY COLLEGE AREA   On the south side of the River Liffey, Trinity College stands at virtually the dead center of the city. Its shady quadrangles and atmospheric stone buildings are surrounded by bookstores, shops, and noisy traffic.

TEMPLE BAR   There are really two Temple Bars, depending on when you visit. During the day, Temple Bar is an artsy, cultured district full of trendy shops and modern art galleries. But such refinement gives way to an altogether more raucous atmosphere at night. With its myriad selection of pubs, bars, and hip clubs, this is definitely where it's at in Dublin after dark.

OLD CITY Dating from Viking and medieval times, the cobblestone enclave of the historic Old City includes Dublin Castle, the remnants of the city's original walls, and Christ Church and St. Patrick's cathedrals.

LIBERTIES Adjacent to Old City, the Liberties district takes its name from the fact that it was once just outside the city walls, and, therefore, exempt from Dublin's jurisdiction. Although it prospered in its early days, Liberties fell on hard times in the 17th and 18th centuries and stayed that way for centuries. For visitors, its main attraction is the Guinness Brewery.

ST. STEPHEN'S GREEN/GRAFTON STREET AREA The main tourist area of the city, this district is home to Dublin's finest hotels, restaurants, and shops. Filled with impressive Georgian architecture, today it is primarily a business and shopping zone.

FITZWILLIAM & MERRION SQUARES Near Trinity College and St. Stephen's Green, these two leafy squares are surrounded by grand Georgian town houses. Some of Dublin's most famous citizens once lived here; today many of the houses are offices for doctors, lawyers, and government agencies.

O'CONNELL STREET (NORTH OF THE LIFFEY) Lined with statues from bottom to top, O'Connell Street was the epicenter of the 1916 Easter Rising and the 1922 Civil War (bullet holes still pock the absurdly ornate statue of its namesake, politician Daniel O'Connell). The surrounding area was fashionable in the 19th century but lost much of its charm as it declined in the 20th century. It has experienced a bit of resurgence in recent years, and now has a few high-profile hotels, shops, and restaurants. With many great pubs and four theaters within walking distance of O'Connell Street, this is also Dublin's theater district.

St. Stephen's Green offers a respite from the Grafton Street shopping crowds.

NORTH QUAYS (THE LIFFEY BOARDWALK)   Once the center of Dublin's shipping industry, the quays are a series of streets filled with office buildings named after the wharves that once stood at water's edge. A modern pedestrian boardwalk now runs from the O'Connell Bridge to Grattan Bridge.

SMITHFIELD   Urban renewal in the 21st century has transformed this formerly seedy market area into a trendy district east of Phoenix Park, with such attractions as the Old Jameson Distillery.

BALLSBRIDGE/EMBASSY ROW   Immediately south of the Grand Canal, this upscale suburb is just barely within walking distance of the city center. Primarily a prestigious residential area, it is also home to hotels, restaurants, and embassies.

GETTING AROUND

If your stay in Dublin is short, geography is on your side. The vast majority of the capital's top sights are concentrated in the city center, which is small and very walkable. This leads to your first, most important (and quite frankly, easiest) decision: If you have a car, leave it behind at your hotel. Dublin's streets are choked with traffic, with baffling one-way streets and inadequate signage. If your feet get tired, there's a good tram and bus system, and taxis are everywhere.

By Bus

After walking, buses are the most convenient and practical way to get around the city center sights. **Dublin Bus** (www.dublinbus.ie; ✆ **01/873-4222**) operates a fleet of double-deckers and single-deckers. Most originate on or near O'Connell Street, Abbey Street, and Eden Quay on the Northside, and at Aston Quay, College Street, and Fleet Street on the south side. Look for bus-stop markers resembling big blue or green lollipops—they're every few blocks on main thoroughfares. To tell where a bus is going, look at the destination street and bus number displayed above its front window; those heading for the city center indicate that with an odd mix of Latin and Gaelic: via an lar.

Bus service runs daily throughout the city, starting at 6am (10am on Sundays), with the last bus at about 11:30pm. On Friday and Saturday nights, **Nitelink** service runs from the city center to the suburbs from midnight to 4am. Buses operate every 30 minutes for most runs; schedules are posted on revolving notice boards at bus stops.

Inner-city fares are based on distances traveled. Daytime journeys that take place entirely within the designated "City Centre Zone" cost €0.50. This zone stretches from Parnell Square in the north to Connolly Station and Merrion Square in the east, St. Stephen's Green in the south, and Ormond Quay in the west. Longer journeys cost anything up to around €5 if you're going as far as the outer suburbs.

You pay on board the bus, using an automatic fare machine located in front of the driver. You can pay in coins or with a smart card known as a **Leap Card** (see below). **No Dublin bus accepts notes or gives change.** If you don't have the exact money in coins, the driver will issue you a "change receipt." You must then take this to the Dublin Bus headquarters on O'Connell Street to collect your change (a process not designed to encourage refunds). The sole exceptions to this rule are routes 747 and 757 (Airlink), which run between the airport and the city center—on those buses, drivers accept notes and give change normally.

By DART

An acronym for Dublin Area Rapid Transit, the electric DART trains travel aboveground, linking the city center stations including **Heuston**, **Connolly Station, Tara Street,** and **Pearse Street** with suburbs and seaside communities. Check a map to see if it serves your area. Service operates roughly every 10 to 20 minutes Monday to Saturday from around 6am to midnight and Sunday 9:30am to 11pm. For further information, check the DART website (www.dart.ie; *℅* **1850/366-222**).

By Tram

The sleek, modern (and wheelchair-accessible) light-rail tram system known as **Luas** runs from around 5:30am to 12:30am Monday to Friday, 6:30am to 12:30am Saturday, and 7am to 11:30pm on Sunday. (The last trams to certain stations are earlier—be sure to check the timetable.) There are two lines, Red and Green: The Green Line runs southeast from St. Stephen's Green to Sandyford and Bride's Glen in the south; the Red Line runs from Connolly Railway Station to the southwestern suburbs of Saggart and Tallaght. For more information, contact Luas (www.luas.ie; *℅* **1850/-300-604**). As this book was being written, the Luas system was being expanded, with a cross-city line connecting the Red and Green lines

---

Leap Cards

If you're likely to use public transport a lot while in Dublin (which we highly recommend), do as the locals do: Get a **Leap Card,** a prepaid smart card for reduced-cost travel on all Dublin buses (including Airlink and Nightlink), DART, Luas, and commuter trains. You can buy Leap Cards at some 400 shops in and around the city—look for the distinctive green logo depicting a somewhat over-excited frog in mid-leap. (In Dublin Airport, you can pick one up at the **Easons, Kiosk,** and **Spa** shops.) Ticket machines in some city center DART and railway stations also dispense Leap Cards. You can also order them online at **www.leapcard.ie**. Unless you're here for more than a week, the best option is to ask for a Visitors' Leap Card, which allows for unlimited travel on the network—including to and from the airport. It costs €10 for 24 hours, €19.50 for 3 days, and €40 for 7 days. They're valid at any time and the clock doesn't start until you first use it.

and a Green Line extension continuing north to Broombridge. Further extensions are planned. Ticket prices depend on the length of your journey and how many city zones it crosses. A single peak-travel journey within the city center (zone 1) costs €1.54, rising to €2.50 for rides to zones 5 to 8. Ticket vending machines are located at every Luas stop. Purchase your ticket in advance using coins, paper money, or a credit card. Leap Cards are also accepted on Luas, and include a small discount.

On Foot

Marvelously compact, Dublin is ideal for walking. Just remember to look right and then left (and in the direction opposite your instincts if you're from North America) before crossing the street. Pedestrians have the right-of-way at specially marked, zebra-striped crossings (these intersections usually have two flashing lights).

By Taxi

Taxis are everywhere in Dublin, and they are a cheap and handy way to get around. You can either hail a cab on the street (if the light on top of the car is lit, it's available) or find one at the many taxi stands (called "ranks") throughout the city—located outside hotels, at bus and train stations, and on prime thoroughfares such as Upper O'Connell Street, College Green, and the north side of St. Stephen's Green. You can also phone for a taxi (see "Fast Facts," p. 92).

By Car

We'll say it again: You do **not** want to drive around Dublin if you can possibly avoid it. However, if Dublin is your first stop on a wider tour of Ireland, you may want to rent a car to leave town and see the rest of the country. If that's the case, try **Hertz** (www.hertz.ie) at Dublin Airport (© **01/844-5466;** or 2 Haddington Rd., Dublin 4 (© **01/668-7566**). **Europcar** (www.europcar. com) also has branches at Dublin Airport (© **01/812-2800**) and Mark Street (off Pearse St.), Dublin 2 (© **01/648-5900**).

[FastFACTS] DUBLIN

ATMs/Banks Nearly all banks are open Monday to Friday 10am to 4pm (to 5pm Thurs). Convenient locations include the **Bank of Ireland,** at 2 College Green, 88 Camden St. Lower, and at Trinity College; and the **Allied Irish Bank (AIB),** at 100 Grafton St. and 37 O'Connell St.

Currency Exchange Currency-exchange services, signposted as **Bureau de Change,** are in most Dublin banks and at many branches of the Irish post office system, known as **An Post.** A bureau de change operates daily during flight arrival and departure times at Dublin Airport. (It's handily situated in the baggage reclaim hall, just opposite carousels 6 to 10—the first ones you come to.) Some hotels and travel agencies offer currency exchange. *Tip:* The best rate of exchange is almost always when you use your bank card at an ATM.

Dentists For dental emergencies, your hotel will usually contact a dentist for you; otherwise, try **Smiles Dental Spa,** 28 O'Connell St. (© **1850/323-323**), or **Molesworth Dental Surgery,** 2 Molesworth Place (© **01/661-5544**).

Doctors & Hospitals For emergencies, dial © **999.** If you need a doctor, have your hotel contact one for you. Otherwise you could try **Dame Street Medical Center,** 16 Dame St. (© **01/679-0754**), or the **Suffolk Street Surgery,** 107 Grafton St. (© **01/679-8181**).

Emergencies For police, fire, or other emergencies, dial © **999.**

Luggage Storage If you arrive at your hotel too early to check in, or if checkout is in the morning and your flight isn't until the evening, many hotels will happily look after your baggage. Alternatively, the **tourism office** (© **01/410-0700**) at 37 College Green, opposite Trinity College, can store bags securely for €5 per 24 hours. There are also luggage facilities in the baggage reclaim hall at Dublin Airport (opposite carousels 6 to 10), and at the Terminal 1 parking lot.

Mail The **General Post Office** on O'Connell St. (© **01/705-7000**) is open Monday through Saturday 8:30am to 6pm. The post office has numerous smaller offices throughout the city.

Pharmacies Dublin does not have 24-hour pharmacies. **City Pharmacy,** 14 Dame St. (© **01/670-4523**), stays open until 9pm weekdays, 7pm Saturday; **Boots the Chemist,** 20 Henry St. (© **01/873-0209**), stays open until 9pm on Thursday, 8pm on Friday, 6pm Sunday, and 7pm all other days. Other branches of Boots are at 12 Grafton St. (© **01/677-3000**) and in the **St. Stephen's Green Centre** (© **01/478-4368**), but not all branches keep the same hours.

Taxis Taxi ranks are outside major hotels, at bus and train stations, and on Upper O'Connell Street, College Green, and St. Stephen's Green. To call a cab, try **NRC Cabs** (© **01/677-2222**), **Trinity** (© **01/708-2222**), or **VIP/ACE Taxis** (© **01/478-3333**).

EXPLORING DUBLIN

Wandering Dublin—just walking down its Georgian streets with a map only in case you get *really* lost—is one of the great pleasures of a visit here. The city center, where the vast majority of the sights are located, is small enough to traverse on foot. One minute you're walking along a quiet, leafy street and suddenly the Irish Parliament appears before you. A few minutes later, it's gorgeous Merrion Square. Then you find yourself facing the granite buildings of Trinity College—and on and on. So pack a sturdy pair of shoes, have your umbrella at the ready, and head out to discover how rewarding this wonderful old town can be.

dublin **PASS**

If you're planning a lot of sightseeing in Dublin, the tourism board would like you to consider purchasing its **Dublin Pass,** which offers free admission to most of the city's major sights, as well as free travel from the airport on the AirCoach shuttle, and discounts at a number of shops, bars, and restaurants.

Unfortunately, the pass is a bit pricey, given that so many of Dublin's sights are free. So our advice is this: If you're going heavy on the sightseeing, buy the pass, but plan carefully how best to use it. For example, consider buying a pass good for 1 or 2 days, and then see all of the city's most expensive sights (the Guinness Storehouse, Kilmainham Gaol, tour

buses and so forth) on those days. On the other days of your trip, you can devote your time to the museums, parks, and galleries that charge no entrance fee. But do add up the admission costs of all your planned sights first, to make sure the pass is right for you.

An adult pass costs €52 for 1 day, €73 for 2 days, €83 for 3 days, and €104 for 5 days. A child's pass costs €31 for 1 day, €41 for 2 days, €52 for 3 days, and €62 for 5 days.

You can purchase a pass at any Dublin Tourism office, or online at **www. dublinpass.ie**. Sometimes discounts are available if you buy one in advance.

Top Attractions

Book of Kells and Old Library ★★ LIBRARY   It's definitely one of Ireland's national treasures, this magnificent hand-drawn manuscript of the four gospels, dating to the year 800, with elaborate calligraphy and colorful illumination drawn by Irish monks. It's an astonishing work of art—but whether it really warrants all the fuss is debatable, especially given the effort involved in seeing it. In high season you may face a lengthy queue, only to find it hard to peer past the hordes of onlookers into the dim glass box where the book is kept—and you're handsomely charged for the privilege. You can secure a more comfortable viewing experience by taking a Trinity College Tour (see p. 102) or by booking fast-track tickets online for an extra €3—these have smaller groups, and more time with the display. Either way, factor in a little extra time to check out the library's handsome **Long Room,** which is included in the price. The grand chained library holds many rare works on Irish history and presents frequently changing displays of classic works. The Book of Kells is located in the Old Library building, on the south side of Library Square, inside Trinity College's main campus.

The Old Library Building, Trinity College, College Green, Dublin 2. www.tcd.ie/visitors/book-of-kells. 🕿 **01/896-2320.** Admission €12 adults; €10 seniors, students, and children; €26 families; admission plus campus tour €14 adults; €13 seniors and students; €28 families. May–Sept Mon–Sat 8:30am–5pm, Sun 9:30am–5pm; Oct–April Mon–Sat 9:30am–5pm, Sun noon–4:30pm. Last admission 30 min. before closing. DART: Pearse St., Tara St., Connolly St. Luas: Lower Abbey St., St. Stephen's Green. Bus: Nassau St. entrance: 25X, 32X, 33X, 41X, 51D, 51X, 58X, 67X, 84X, 92. College Green entrance: 7N, 15N, 15X, 44N, 46N, 48N, 49N, 51D, 51X, 54N, 56A, 70B, 70X, 77A, 77N, 92.

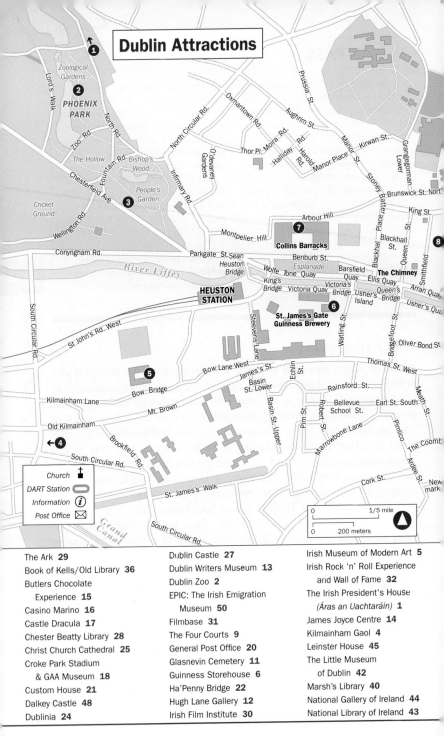

Dublin Attractions

Zoological Gardens

PHOENIX PARK

Lord's Walk

North Rd.

Zoo Rd.

The Hollow

Fountain Rd.

Chesterfield Ave.

Bishop's Wood

People's Garden

Cricket Ground

Wellington Rd.

Conyngham Rd.

Infirmary Rd.

O'Devaney Gardens

North Circular Rd.

Oxmantown Rd.

Thor Pl. Móira Rd.

Halliday Rd.

Harold Rd.

Manor Place

Manor St.

Kirwan St.

Stoney Batter

Aughrim St.

Prussia St.

Grangegorman Lower

Brunswick St. Nort

King St.

Blackhall Pl.

Blackhall St.

Queen St.

Smithfield

Arbour Hill

Montpelier Hill

Collins Barracks

Parkgate St. Sean Heuston Bridge

River Liffey

HEUSTON STATION

South Circular Rd.

St. John's Rd. West

Steevens Lane

Bow Lane West

Bow Bridge

Kilmainham Lane

Mt. Brown

Old Kilmainham

Brookfield Rd.

South Circular Rd.

St. James's Walk

Grand Canal

South Circular Rd.

Benburb St.

Esplanade

Wolfe Tone Quay

King's Bridge

Victoria Quay

Barsfield Quay

Victoria's Bridge

Usher's Island

Ellis Quay

The Chimney

Queen's Bridge

Arran Quay

Usher's Qu

St. James's Gate Guinness Brewery

Watling St.

James's St.

Basin St. Lower

Echlin St.

Basin St. Upper

Pim St.

Robert St.

Rainsford St.

Bellevue School St.

Marrowbone Lane

Earl St. South

Meath St.

Pimlico

The Coomb

Ardee St.

Cork St.

New mark

Thomas St. West

Oliver Bond St.

Bridgefoot St.

Church ✝
DART Station ⬭
Information ⓘ
Post Office ✉

0 _____ 1/5 mile
0 _____ 200 meters

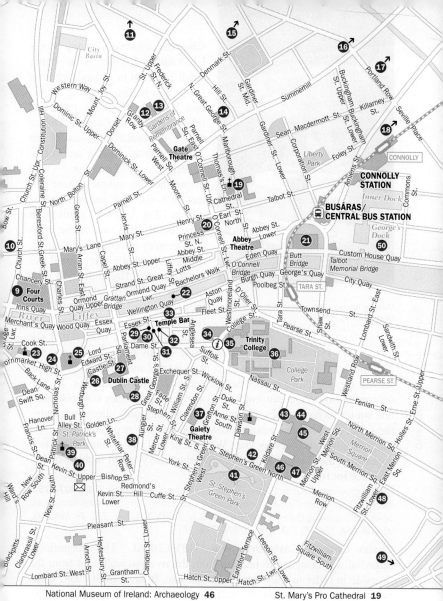

Viewing bibliophile treasures at the Chester Beatty Library.

Chester Beatty Library ★★★

LIBRARY If there's a better small museum in Ireland, we have yet to find it. This dazzling collection of early religious texts and other priceless artifacts in Dublin Castle is named in honor of Sir Alfred Chester Beatty, an Anglo-American industrialist who bequeathed his unique private collection to the Irish nation when he died in 1968. And what a collection it is! Beatty was one of the great 20th-century adventurer-collectors, of the kind that simply could not exist today. Highlights of the bequest include breathtaking illuminated gospels and early Bibles (including the oldest known fragment in existence, from A.D. 150); impeccable 15th-century Qurans; Quranic scrolls from the 8th and 9th centuries; and sacred Buddhist texts from Burma and Tibet. Look for the ancient Egyptian love letter, near the entrance to the upper floor. There's no translation—a museum employee once told us that they commissioned one but it was far too racy to display! Though the core collection remains the same, exhibits are constantly changing, and you're unlikely to see the same manuscripts on every visit. Why queue and pay a tenner to see two pages from the Book of Kells when you can lose yourself in this wonderful place for free?

On the grounds of Dublin Castle, Dame St., Dublin 2. www.cbl.ie. ✆ **01/407-0750.** Mon–Fri 10am–5pm (Nov–Feb closed Mon), Sat 11am–5pm, Sun 1pm–5pm. Luas: Jervis, St. Stephen's Green. DART: Tara St. Bus: 37, 39, 39A, 39B, 39C, 49, 49A, 49X, 50, 50X, 56A, 65X, 70, 70A, 70X, 77, 77A, 77X, 123.

Christ Church Cathedral ★★

CATHEDRAL This magnificent cathedral was designed to be seen from the river, so walk to it from the riverside in order to truly appreciate the size. It dates from 1038, when Sitric, Danish king of Dublin, built the first wooden Christ Church here. In 1171, the original foundation was extended into a cruciform layout and rebuilt in stone under the leadership of the Norman warrior Strongbow. The present structure dates mainly from 1871 to 1878, when a huge restoration took place—work that remains controversial to this day, as much of the building's old detail was destroyed in the process. Still, magnificent stonework and graceful pointed arches survive. (There's also a statue of Strongbow inside, and some believe his tomb is here as well, although historians are not convinced.) The best way to get a glimpse of what the

Christ Church Cathedral.

original building must have been like is to visit the 12th-century crypt, which has been kept untouched. *An intriguing side note:* Christ Church once displayed what was believed to be the preserved heart of St. Laurence O'Toole (1128–80). However, in 2012, the holy relic was stolen in an audacious nighttime raid. Nothing else was taken, including items of much higher value, leading police to surmise that the heart was stolen to order for a macabre collector. But stunner of stunners: In April 2018, the heart was found by the local police (Gardaí) undamaged, in Phoenix Park, and quickly handed over to the Archbishop of Dublin for ultra-safekeeping.

Christchurch Place, Dublin 8. www.christchurchdublin.ie. ✆ **01/677-8099.** Admission €6.50 adults; €5 seniors and students; €2.50 children (aged 5 to 15); €16 families. Free entry for prayer or services. Guided tours available (€10.50, €28 families). Apr–Sept Mon–Sat 9:30am–7pm; Sun 12:30–2:30pm, 4:30–7pm; Mar and Oct Mon–Sat 9:30am–6pm; Sun 12:30–2:30pm, 4:30–6pm; Nov–Feb Mon–Sat 9:30am–5pm, Sun 12:30–2:30pm. Last entry 45 min. before closing (Mon–Sat). Bus: 37, 39, 39A, 39B, 39C, 39X, 49, 49A, 49X, 50X, 54A, 56A, 70, 70A, 70X, 78A.

Dublin Writers Museum ★★ MUSEUM   Manuscripts, early editions, personal possessions, and other pieces of ephemera relating to Ireland's most famous writers are on display at this fascinating museum in Parnell Square. The exhibits are laid out across two rooms, tracing the development of Irish literature up to the present day. Lovers of Behan, Joyce, Shaw, Stoker, Wilde, Yeats, and other greats of the canon will find plenty to savor here—from the trivial (Brendan Behan's postcard from Los Angeles extolling its virtues as a place to get drunk) to the profound (a first edition of Patrick Kavanagh's *The Great Hunger,* complete with a handwritten extra section that his publisher refused to publish, fearing it too controversial). You can take a self-guided audio tour, and there's an excellent bookshop—of course. Talks, readings, and other special events are occasionally held here; call or check the website for details. 18 Parnell Sq., Dublin 1. www.writers museum.com. ℂ **01/872-2077.** Admission €8 adults; €7.50 seniors and students; €4.70 children; €20 families. Mon–Sat 10am–5pm, Sun 11am–5pm. Last admission 45 min. before closing. Bus: 1, 2, 8, 14, 14A, 16, 16A, 19, 19A, 33X, 39X, 40, 40A, 40B, 40C, 41X, 48A, 58X, 70B, 70X, 116, 120, 123, 145.

Hugh Lane Gallery ★★ ART MUSEUM   This small art gallery, housed in the glorious classical Charlemont House, punches well

Letters and mementoes of Ireland's greatest writers are displayed at the Dublin Writers Museum.

above its weight. The strong collection of Impressionist works includes Degas's *Sur la Plage,* Manet's *La Musique aux Tuileries,* and Daumier's *In the Omnibus* (stolen from the gallery in 1992 but recovered in 2014). There are also sculptures by Rodin; a stunning collection of Arts and Crafts stained glass by Dublin-born artist Harry Clarke (don't miss his masterpiece, *The Eve of St. Agnes*); and numerous works by modern Irish artists. One room holds the maddeningly cluttered studio of the Irish painter Francis Bacon, moved here from London and reconstructed behind glass. They

local hero: **SIR ALFRED CHESTER BEATTY**

Few people embody the term "citizen of the world" as much as Sir Alfred Chester Beatty. Born in New York in 1875, Beatty launched an American mining business that earned him the nickname "the King of Copper"—and a multimillion-dollar fortune to boot. This fabulous wealth gave him the means to pursue his passion for ancient manuscripts and works of art, and by the time he was an old man, his collection rivaled that of some of the world's greatest museums.

Beatty became a British citizen in the 1930s and was knighted by Queen Elizabeth in 1954, after he made a generous bequest to the British Museum. However,

he left the vast majority of his collection to Ireland—his ancestral home and a place dear to his heart. In return Beatty was made an honorary Irish citizen in 1957. He died 11 years later in Monaco, but was brought back to Dublin for a state funeral—still to date the only civilian to be given this honor.

Despite all this, Beatty is a surprisingly little-known figure in his adoptive home today. Many Dublin guides don't list the Chester Beatty Museum among the city's top attractions, and in our experience a good many Dubliners have never even heard of the collection, or the man himself. What an injustice!

moved everything—right down to the dust. This is an excellent, compact art museum, and a great place to spend an afternoon.

Parnell Sq. North, Dublin 1. www.hughlane.ie. © **01/222-5550.** Free admission. Tues–Thurs 9:45am–6pm, Fri 9:45am–5pm, Sat 10am–5pm, Sun 11am–5pm. Closed Mon. Bus: 1, 2, 8, 10A, 14, 14A, 16, 16A, 19, 19A, 33X, 39X, 40, 41X, 46A, 46B, 46X, 48A, 58C, 58X, 70B, 70X, 116, 145.

Kilmainham Gaol ★★★ HISTORIC SITE   Anyone interested in Ireland's struggle for independence from British rule should not miss visiting this former prison. Within these walls, political prisoners were incarcerated, tortured, and killed from 1796 until 1924. The leaders of the 1916 Easter Uprising were executed here, along with many others. Future president Eamon de Valera was its final prisoner. An exhibition illuminates the brutal history of the Irish penal system; there's also a well-presented historical film. An art gallery on the top floor houses thought-provoking exhibitions. To walk along these corridors through the grim exercise yard, or to venture into the walled compound, is a moving (at times even overwhelming) experience that will linger in your memory. Only a limited number of tickets are sold each day, and visits are by guided tour only. Prebooking online is the best way to guarantee you'll get in on the day of your choice, especially in summer.

Inchicore Rd., Kilmainham, Dublin 8. http://kilmainhamgaolmuseum.ie. © **01/453-5984.** Admission €9 adults; €7 seniors; €5 students and children; €23 families. Jan–May daily 9:30am–5:30pm; June–Sept daily 9am–6:45pm; Oct–Dec daily 9:30am–5:30pm. Last admission 1 hr. before closing. Luas: Suir Rd. Bus: 13, 40, 51B, 51C, 63, 69, 78A, 79, 123, 206.

National Gallery of Ireland ★★ ART MUSEUM   George Bernard Shaw loved this place so much that he left it one-third of his royalties in perpetuity after he died. He saw it as paying a debt, so important was the gallery to his education. It is still a place to wander, wonder, and just be in thrall to so much beautiful art. Highlights of the permanent collection include paintings by Caravaggio, Gainsborough, Rubens, Goya, Rembrandt, Monet, and Picasso. The Irish national portrait collection is housed in one wing, while another area is devoted to the career of Jack B. Yeats (brother of W. B. Yeats), an Irish painter of some note. A 6-year, €30-million renovation finished in 2017 reopened two wings and added a glass-covered courtyard. (Check out the gravity-defying, 7m/22-ft. freeform sculpture by Cork artist Joseph Walsh, which stands sentinel over the new, light-filled space.) Major exhibitions change regularly, and the subjects are often more imaginative than just the usual run of retrospectives and national landscapes. In keeping with the "art for all" ethos that so enamored Bernard Shaw, entry to the permanent collection and many of the temporary shows is free.

Merrion Sq. West, Dublin 2. www.nationalgallery.ie. © **01/661-5133.** Free admission. Mon–Wed and Fri–Sat 9:15am–5:30pm, Thurs 9:15am–8:30pm, Sun 11am–5:30pm, public holidays 10am–5:30pm. DART: Pearse. Luas: St. Stephen's Green, Grafton St. Bus: 4, 7, 8, 39a, 46a.

National Museum of Ireland: Archaeology ★★★ MUSEUM
The most impressive of the four sites that collectively make up the
National Museum of Ireland, this excellent museum is devoted to
the ancient history of Ireland and beyond—from the Stone Age up to the
Early Modern period. Highlights include a stunning collection of Viking
artifacts from the archaeological digs that took place in Dublin from the
1960s to the early 1980s—a haul so important that in one fell swoop
the history of Viking settlement in Ireland was rewritten. There is also an
enormous range of Bronze Age gold and metalwork, as well as iconic
Christian treasures from the Dark Ages, including the Ardagh Chalice, the
Moylough Belt Shrine, and the Tara Brooch. It's not just the relics of
ancient Irish people that can be seen here—there are also four "bog bodies," human beings whose remains were naturally preserved in bogs,
sometime between 400 and 200 B.C. Other notable artifacts include
Ralaghan Man, a carved wooden Bronze Age statue from County Cavan;
a collection of 2nd-century Roman figurines and homewares; and an
extraordinary granite table made in Egypt circa 1870 B.C.

Kildare St., Dublin 2. www.museum.ie. ℂ **01/677-7444.** Free admission. Tues–Sat
10am–5pm, Sun 2–5pm. Luas: St Stephen's Green. Bus: 25, 33, 41, 51, 66, 67, 84.

**National Museum of Ireland: Decorative Arts & History, Col-
lins Barracks** ★★ MUSEUM   As the name of this branch of the
National Museum of Ireland suggests, the collection tells the story of Irish
(and world) history through fashion, jewelry, furniture, and other decorative
arts, with the bulk of the collection spanning the 1760s to the 1960s. One
gallery is devoted to the work of Eileen Gray (1878–1976), an Irish architect and furniture designer who became one of the most important figures of
the Modernist movement; another showcases the extraordinary collection
of Asian art bequeathed to the Irish nation in the 1930s by Irish-American
philanthropist Albert Bender. Set in a converted 18th-century army building, this branch of the National Museum isn't entirely devoted to the arts;

Monumental Wit

Few cities have such a love-hate relationship with their statues as Dublin. Locals
have an acerbic rhyming nickname for
each one, many of them unprintable.
The very buxom statue of Molly Malone
(heroine of the Irish folk song, who
sold "cockles and mussels, alive alive,
oh...") in front of the tourism office on
Suffolk Street is variously known as "the
Tart with the Cart," "the Trollop with
the Scallop," or "the Flirt in the Skirt."
In the same vein, the James Joyce
statue on O'Connell Street is "the Prick
with a Stick"; the statue of Anna Livia
(a character in Joyce's *Finnegans Wake*
who symbolized the Liffey), rising from
an ornamental pond in Croppies Park,
is "the Floozie in the Jacuzzi"; and,
depending on whom you talk to, the
Spire of Dublin on O'Connell Street is
either "the Stiletto in the Ghetto,"
"the Skewer in the Sewer," "the Stiffy
by the Liffey," or "the Nail in the
Pale."

hard to love: **JONATHAN SWIFT**

The acerbic 18th-century wit Jonathan Swift, author of *Gulliver's Travels*, was born in Dublin, and except for a decade or so in England lived in Ireland most of his life. After trying (and failing) to win a position at the English court, he became a Church of Ireland clergyman. Yet he continued to write and publish essays and poetry—in fact, he wrote his most controversial works while acting as dean of St Patrick's Cathedral.

Many nations might have banned Swift for his scandalous writing. He certainly could not live in England—his works were considered too shocking. But the Irish always forgave him, and the church protected him, even after he published his most infamous essay, "A Modest Proposal," in 1729. In that essay, still read in English classes around the world, he advocated (ironically) that the Irish sell their children to be eaten as food in order to solve the problem of Irish poverty. He assured the reader that Irish babies would be delicious "whether stewed, roasted, baked or boiled..."

Satire was relatively unknown at the time, and many readers at first believed he was seriously recommending cannibalism. The essay caused public outrage and calls for him to be punished. But the church stood by him, as did the town, allowing him to continue to push the limits of 18th-century patience.

Swift believed passionately in humane treatment for the mentally ill, which in his time was unheard of. When he died, he bequeathed much of his estate to found St. Patrick's Hospital for the mentally ill. Typically, though, he couldn't just leave it at that. He wrote one last caustic verse about himself, and the country he loved:

"He left the little wealth he had
To build a house for fools and mad;
Showing in one satiric touch
No nation needed it so much."

eight galleries cover Irish military history from the 16th century to the present day, including a fascinating section about the Easter Rising of 1916.
Collins Barracks, Benburb St., Dublin 7. www.museum.ie. ✆ **01/677-7444.** Free admission. Tues–Sat 10am–5pm, Sun 2–5pm. Luas: Museum. Rail: Heuston. Bus: 39B, 70N.

National Museum of Ireland: Natural History ★★ MUSEUM
The core collection at this museum has changed little since the museum was founded in the mid–19th century, and that's part of the attraction. Its display cases are filled with native Irish animals, from stuffed birds and mice to the skeletons of enormous sea creatures. While there are recent additions—including the Discovery Zone, in which visitors can open a series of drawers to discover unusual specimens within—it feels quaintly old-fashioned. Upstairs you'll find the most unique parts of the collection, such as the avian galleries and the "crystal jellies" collection—beautiful oversize glass models of microscopic sea creatures, made in the 19th century by the eccentric and brilliant Blaschka brothers of Dresden. There's no doubt that this is a strange place—the locals call it "the dead zoo." Still, kids find it fascinating, and it is, in many ways, a trip into the past.
Merrion St., Dublin 2. www.museum.ie. ✆ **01/677-7444.** Free admission. Tues–Sat 10am–5pm, Sun 2–5pm. Luas: St Stephen's Green. Bus: 4, 7, 8, 39a, 46a.

Richmond Barracks ★★ HISTORIC SITE   Like Kilmainham Gaol (p. 99), these austere, forbidding buildings will forever be associated with the Easter Rising of 1916. As many as 3,000 prisoners were held here immediately after the failed rebellion, with many going to the executioner shortly afterward—including a good number of its leaders, who were taken to be shot at Kilmainham. To commemorate the centenary of the Rising in 2016, Richmond Barracks was reopened as an informative and powerful museum. A guided tour also takes in adjacent **Goldenbridge Cemetery.** Founded by Daniel O'Connell in 1829, it was the first (official) Catholic burial ground in Ireland to be built since the Reformation—until then, the law only allowed Catholics to be buried in Protestant grounds, using Protestant rites. Exhibitions here are thoughtfully done and clearly presented, with the role of women in the Easter Rising often given particular prominence. And about time, too.

Signposted off Bulfin Rd., Dublin 8. www.richmondbarracks.ie. ✆ **01/222-8400.** Admission €6 adults; €3 seniors, students, and children; €19 families. Guided tours €2 extra on all prices. Mon–Fri 10am–12:45pm, 1:45–4pm; Sat–Sun 10:45am–1pm. Closed Bank Holidays. Bus: 13, 13a, 40, 68.

St. Patrick's Cathedral ★★ CATHEDRAL   The largest—and most famous—church in Ireland, St. Patrick's is one of the most beloved places of worship in the world. The original church was built between 1220 and 1260 in honor of Ireland's patron saint, on a site where Patrick was said to have baptized converts; most of what you see now dates from the 14th century, along with some 19th-century renovations. The building is mainly Early English in style, with a square medieval tower that houses the largest ringing peal bells in Ireland; its spire, nearly 150 feet tall, soars above the city's low skyline. This is the national cathedral for the whole of Ireland, and it feels like the church of the nation, with its grand nave, glorious high ceiling, and historic displays. Tucked away at the back of the cavernous nave is a moving collection of war memorials, including a very low-key tribute to the Irish dead of World War II. (Ireland was neutral in that war, but still around 300,000 men volunteered to fight with the Allies.) You can also see the tomb of the satirical 18th-century writer Jonathan Swift (see p. 101), once a dean at this cathedral. Admission includes an irregular program of lunchtime classical-music recitals—call or check the website for details.

St. Patrick's Close, Dublin 8. www.stpatrickscathedral.ie. ✆ **01/453-9472.** Admission €6.50 adults; €5.50 seniors and students; €3.50 children; €16 families. Mar–Oct Mon–Fri 9:30am–5pm; Sat 9am–6pm; Sun 9–10:30am, 12:30–2:30pm, and 4:30–6pm. Nov–Feb Mon–Fri 9:30am–5pm; Sat 9am–5pm; Sun 9am–10:30am and 12:30–2:30pm. Guided tours Mon–Sat 10:30am and 2:30pm. Last admission 30 min. before closing. Bus: 49, 54a, 56a, 77a, 151.

Trinity College ★★ UNIVERSITY   The oldest extant university in Ireland, Trinity was founded in 1592 by Queen Elizabeth I to offer an education to the children of the upper classes and protect them from the "malign" Catholic influences elsewhere in Europe. Now it is simply the

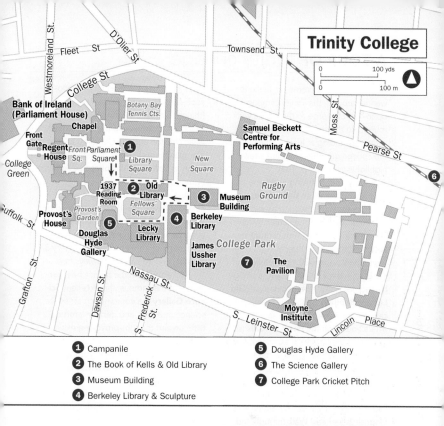

Trinity College

0   100 yds
0   100 m

Westmoreland St.
Fleet St
D'Olier St
College St
Townsend St.
Moss St.
Pearse St.

Bank of Ireland
(Parliament House)
Botany Bay
Tennis Cts.
Chapel
Front
Gate
Regent
House
Front
Sq.
Parliament
Square
Samuel Beckett
Centre for
Performing Arts
College
Green
1
Library
Square
New
Square
Rugby
Ground
6
1937
Reading
Room
2 Old
Library
Fellows'
Square
3 Museum
Building
Suffolk St.
Provost's
House
Provost's
Garden
5
Douglas
Hyde
Gallery
Lecky
Library
4
Berkeley
Library
James
Ussher
Library
College Park
7
The
Pavilion
Grafton St.
Dawson St.
S. Frederick St.
Nassau St.
Moyne
Institute
S. Leinster St.
Lincoln Place

1 Campanile
2 The Book of Kells & Old Library
3 Museum Building
4 Berkeley Library & Sculpture
5 Douglas Hyde Gallery
6 The Science Gallery
7 College Park Cricket Pitch

most respected university in Ireland. Among its alumni are Bram Stoker, Jonathan Swift, Oscar Wilde, and Samuel Beckett, as well as an array of rebels and revolutionaries who helped create the Republic of Ireland. Step through the portico off College Green, into the historic gray stone courtyard, and it wouldn't take much more than a lick of fog and a top hat or two to make you think you'd stepped back in time a century or more. The campus spreads across central Dublin just south of the River Liffey like a low-slung castle, with charming cobbled squares, lush gardens, and picturesque quadrangles. Most of the architecture dates from the 17th

Trinity College is the oldest university in Ireland.

103

A TOUR OF trinity college

A beautiful, grand, romantic place to wander around, the Trinity campus is open free of charge to the public year-round. No trip to Dublin is complete without spending at least a little while on the college grounds. Here are a few highlights (see map p. 103).

Trinity's most striking and famous monument, the white **Campanile,** or bell tower, grabs your attention as soon as you enter through the main archway. Dating from the mid–19th century, it stands on the site of the college's original foundations, from 300 years earlier.

Built in the 18th century to a design by Thomas Burgh, the neoclassical **Old Library Building** is the only building on campus you have to pay to see. It's where you'll find the **Book of Kells** (see p. 93) and the library's magnificent **Long Room**—both of which are unmissable.

Home to the geography and geology departments, the **Museum Building** is one of Trinity's hidden gems. Built in the mid–19th century, it has Byzantine and Moorish influences. Walk through and look up to the glorious domed ceiling and the green marbled banisters.

Set between these two architectural masterpieces, the stark 1967 **Berkeley Library Building** sharply divides opinion with its austere modernism. Designer Paul Koralek's library honors Bishop

George Berkeley, famed for his philosophical theory of "immaterialism" (things that can't be proven cannot exist), which went against the theories of both Isaac Newton and the Catholic Church. The gleaming sculpture outside the library is *Sphere with Sphere* by Arnaldo Pomodoro (1983).

Also facing the Old Library across Fellows Square, the 1970s **Arts Building** includes the **Douglas Hyde Gallery,** with a regularly changing program of modern art. Exhibitions switch out about every 3 months, and admission is always free.

Tucked away in the far northeastern corner of the campus, the excellent **Science Gallery** is a combination art space, science museum, and debating forum, with fun and thought-provoking exhibitions, workshops, public lectures, and even shows. Entry is free, except to certain special events. See **www.science gallery.com** for more details.

One of the more benign remnants of English rule, the **College Park Cricket Pitch** is a small park where you'll often find a cricket match in progress on summer weekends. The sport is notoriously arcane for the uninitiated—but everyone can enjoy the picturesque sight of the players in their white uniforms.

to the 19th century. You can wander the campus for free (see above); alternatively, between May and September, the university's official tourism partner, **Authenticity Tours,** offer an excellent tour of all the main sights, including a ticket for the Old Library and the Book of Kells (see p. 93).

College Green, Dublin 2. www.tcd.ie. ℂ **01/896-1000.** Campus tours €6; tours including Old Library €13 adults, €12 seniors and students, €26 families. Library and Book of Kells only €12 adults, €10 seniors and students. Call or go online for times. DART: Pearse St., Tara St., Connolly St. Luas: Lower Abbey St., St. Stephen's Green. Bus: College Green entrance: 7N, 15N, 15X, 44N, 46N, 48N, 49N, 51D, 51X, 54N, 56A, 70B, 70X, 77A, 77N, 92. Nassau St. entrance: 25X, 32X, 33X, 41X, 51D, 51X, 58X, 67X, 84X, 92.

More Attractions

ART MUSEUMS

Filmbase ★ ARTS CENTER   The stripped-down, artsy cousin to the Irish Film Institute (see below), Filmbase has a free exhibition space on its ground floor, usually featuring a free show from local contemporary artists. Filmbase also runs special cinema-related events all year, including talks and screenings. On Saturdays the **Temple Bar Food Market** (p. 158) takes place directly outside.

2 Curved St., off Temple Bar, Dublin 2. www.filmbase.ie ✆ **01/679-6716.** Free admission. Event prices vary. Bus: 27, 40, 49, 54A, 56A, 65, 65B, 68, 68A, 69, 69X, 77A, 77X, 79, 79A.

Irish Film Institute ★ ARTS CENTER   This arthouse film institute is a hip Temple Bar hangout for Dublin cinephiles. It houses three cinemas, the Irish Film Archive, a library, a small but comprehensive bookshop, a busy bar, and a cafe that's a good place for a cup of coffee on a cold afternoon. Although the emphasis is on Irish cinema, groundbreaking films from all over the world are shown here, with a good mixture of new and older titles. *Wild Strawberries* is a bimonthly film club for the over-55s; see a classic movie with free tea or coffee. Many of the special film-related events are free.

6 Eustace St., Dublin 2. www.ifi.ie. ✆ **01/679-3477.** Free admission. Cinema tickets €8–€10. Mon–Sun 12:30pm–10pm. Bus: 27, 40, 49, 54A, 56A, 65, 65B, 68, 68A, 69, 69X, 77A, 77X, 79, 79A.

The Dublin Web Fest is one of many cinema-related events hosted at Filmbase.

Irish Museum of Modern Art ★ ART MUSEUM   Set in a beautiful 17th-century former hospital building, this small but handsome museum has a strong collection of modern art dating from the 1940s to the present day. Highlights include a striking series of mid-1970s photographs by Serbian conceptual artist Marina Abramovic; etchings and lithographs by Alice Maher, Louis le Brocquy, and Marcel Duchamp; and the Madden Arnholz Collection, made up of around 2,000 old master prints, including works by Rembrandt. The beautifully restored grounds are also used as an exhibition space, with a number of changing pieces displayed among the formal lawns and clipped box hedges.

Royal Hospital, Military Rd., Kilmainham, Dublin 8. www.imma.ie. © **01/612-9900.** Free admission. Tues–Fri 11:30am–5:30pm, Sat 10am–5:30pm, Sun and public holidays noon–5:30pm. Last admission 45 min. before closing. Closed Mon. Luas: Heuston. Bus: 13, 40, 79, 79A, 123, 145.

Temple Bar Gallery + Studios ★★ ART GALLERY/STUDIOS   This big, rambling art gallery sums up all that is good about Temple Bar. Founded in 1983 in the heart of Dublin's "Left Bank," it's one of the largest studio and gallery complexes of its kind in Europe. It's filled with innovative work by contemporary Irish artists—more than 30 of them, in a variety of disciplines, including sculpture, painting, printing, and photography. The colors and creativity are dazzling, and it's run by helpful, friendly people. Only the gallery section is open to the public, but you can make an appointment in advance to view individual artists at work. The Studios host free talks and discussion panels, featuring the great and the good of the Irish arts scene. Call or go online for details.

5–9 Temple Bar, Dublin 2. www.templebargallery.com. © **01/671-0073.** Free admission. Tues–Sat 11am–6pm. Bus: 26, 37, 39, 39A, 39B, 39C, 49X, 50X, 65X, 66, 66A, 66B, 66D, 67, 67A, 69X, 70, 70A, 77X.

CHURCHES & CATHEDRALS

St. Audeon's Church ★ CHURCH   Near the only remaining gate of the Old City walls (dating from 1214), this is said to be the one surviving medieval parish church in Dublin. Although it is partially in ruins, significant parts have survived, including the west doorway, which dates from 1190, and the 13th-century nave. (*Note:* While this St. Audeon's is Church of Ireland, nearby is another St. Audeon's Church, dating only to 1846 and Catholic. There, Father "Flash" Kavanagh used to say the world's fastest Mass so that his congregation could be out in time for the football matches.) Entrance to the ancient St. Audeon's is through a visitor center, which offers a self-guided exhibit on the church's history; visits to the church itself are by guided tour (Apr–Oct only).

14 High St., Dublin 8. www.heritageireland.ie. © **01/677-0088.** Free admission. Apr–Oct daily 9:30am–5:30pm. Bus: 49X, 50X, 51B, 51C, 51N, 54A, 78A, 206.

St. Mary's Pro Cathedral ★ CATHEDRAL   No, there isn't a pro and amateur league for cathedrals in Ireland—"pro" simply means

DUBLIN walking tours

Small and compact, Dublin was made for walking, and some of the best experiences the city has to offer involve taking it at your own pace, map in hand. If you'd like more guidance, however, consider one of the following tour services.

You could hardly be in better or more learned hands than with the **Historical Walking Tours of Dublin** (www.historical tours.ie; ✆ **087/688-9412**), whose guides are all post-grad students at Trinity College, Dublin. Established for nearly 30 years, these engaging tours offer peerless historical insight. Tours leave from the front gates of Trinity College on College Green daily at 11am and 3pm May to September; daily at 11am April and October; and Friday to Sunday at 11am November to March. Tickets cost €12 adults, €10 students and seniors (accompanied kids are free), and you can just pay the guide on the day. An intriguing variety of private tours are also available—subjects include Medieval Dublin; Revolutionary Dublin; and even the Story of Irish Food. These need to be booked in advance and cost €160.

If you prefer to take in the sights at a more leisurely pace, with a bit of liquid refreshment to keep things lively, try the **Literary Pub Crawl** (www.dublinpub crawl.com; ✆ **01/670-5602**). Walking in the footsteps of Joyce, Behan, Beckett, Shaw, and other Irish literary greats, this tour visits Dublin's most famous pubs and explores their deep literary connections. Actors provide humorous performances and commentary between stops. Tours start upstairs at the **Duke Pub,** 8 Duke Street (✆ **01/679-9553**), daily at 7:30pm April to October; and Thursday to Sunday at 7:30pm November to March. Tickets are €14 adults, €12 students. A limited number of tickets are sold at the Duke on the night (cash only), but it's best to book online. No children are allowed, for obvious reasons, but the tour organizers are keen to stress that the

tour is both safe and enjoyable for women traveling alone.

More excellent sightseeing for the thirsty can be enjoyed on the **Traditional Irish Music Pub Crawl** (www.musical pubcrawl.com; ✆ **01/475-3313**). Tours are led by two professional musicians, who sing as you make your way from one famous musical pub to another in Temple Bar. The evening is touristy, but the music is good. Tours meet upstairs at **Oliver St. John Gogarty's** pub, Fleet Street and Anglesea Street (✆ **01/671-1822**). Tours run daily at 7:30pm April to October; and Thursday to Saturday at 7:30pm November to March. The cost is €14 adults, €12 students. Another higher-priced option also includes a show and a meal at Flanagan's on O'Connell Street. You can book in advance or buy on the night; again, no children are allowed. The same company has recently started doing an early-evening version that ends with dinner and a live show—and children are allowed. It starts at 6pm, also at the Oliver Street John Gogarty's, and dinner is served at 7:15pm in **Flanagan's Restaurant** on O'Connell Street (✆ **01/873-1388**). The all-inclusive price is €43 adults, €41 students, €25 students, and €130 families.

If you're looking for less booze and more history, the **1916 Rebellion Walking Tour** (www.1916rising.com; ✆ **086/ 858-3847**) takes you into the heat of the action at the General Post Office, explaining how the anger rose until the rebellion exploded on Easter Sunday in 1916. The 2-hour tour is well-thought-out and run by local historians who authored a book on the events of that year. Tours are at 11:30am Monday to Saturday and 1pm Sunday from March to October; and at 11:30am on Friday and Saturday and 1pm Sunday in November and February. Tickets cost €13 per person. Booking is advisable. Meet at the International Bar, 23 Wicklow St. (✆ **086/ 858-3847**).

"temporary." And therein lies a fascinating piece of historical trivia. Contrary to popular belief, Dublin has no Roman Catholic cathedral (St. Patrick's and Christ Church have been part of the Anglican Church of Ireland since the 16th century). But the Vatican views Christ Church as Dublin's "true" Catholic cathedral. Therefore, St. Mary's has been designated the "temporary" official Catholic cathedral in Dublin...since 1820. Tucked away on a rather unimpressive back street, it's nonetheless the heart of the city's Northside. It was built between 1815 and 1825 in Greek Revival Doric style, with an exterior portico modeled on the Temple of Theseus in Athens, with six Doric columns. The Renaissance-style interior is patterned after the Church of Saint-Philippe du Roule of Paris. The church is noted for its awe-inspiring Palestrina Choir, which sings a Latin Mass Sundays at 11am during school terms.

83 Marlborough St., Dublin 1. www.procathedral.ie. © **01/874-5441.** Free admission. Mon–Fri 8am–5pm; Sat 8am–7pm; Sun 9am–1:45pm and 5–7:30pm; public holidays 10am–1:30pm. DART: Connolly, Tara St. Luas: Abbey St. Bus: 2, 3, 4, 5, 7, 7A, 7B, 7D, 8, 10, 10A, 11, 11A, 11B, 13, 20B, 27, 32X, 33X, 39X, 40A, 40C, 41, 41A, 41B, 41C, 41X, 42, 42A, 42B, 43, 51A, 116, 123, 130, 142, 747.

St. Michan's Church ★★ CHURCH

Built on the site of an early Danish chapel (1095), this 17th-century edifice has fine interior woodwork and an organ (dated 1724) on which Handel is said to have played his *Messiah.* The humble whitewashed interior is almost puritan in its simplicity, but it's in the underground vaults where the church's real claim to fame lies—and, be warned, it's about as macabre as it gets. Something about the atmospheric conditions down here drastically slows decomposition, and the mummified remains of several people have lain for centuries in an extraordinary state of preservation. A few still have their hair and fingernails; on others you can see desiccated internal organs under the skin. The tallest mummy is known as "the Crusader"; his legs were broken in order to fit him into the coffin. Others in residence include "the Nun" and "the Thief"; their true identities were lost when the church records were destroyed during the Civil War in 1922. It's creepy as all get-out, but fascinating. It is said that Bram Stoker was inspired to write *Dracula* in part by having visited as a child. And we can believe it! *Note:* The church is wheelchair-accessible, but the vaults are not.

Church St., Dublin 7. © **01/872-4154.** Admission €5 adults; €4 seniors and students; €4 children; €15 families. Crypt: Mid–Mar to Oct Mon–Fri 10am–12:45pm and 2–4:30pm; Sat 10am–12:45pm. Nov to mid–Mar Mon–Fri 12:30–3:30pm; Sat 10am–12:45pm. No crypt tours Sun. Luas: Four Courts, Smithfield. Bus: 51D, 51X.

St. Teresa's Church ★ CHURCH

After years of anti-Catholic legislation, this was the first Catholic church to be legally and openly erected in Dublin, following the Catholic Relief Act of 1793. While the foundation stone was laid in 1793, many enlargements followed, until it reached its present neo-Gothic form in 1876. Among the artistic highlights are

John Hogan's *Dead Christ,* a sculpture displayed beneath the altar, and Phyllis Burke's seven beautiful stained-glass windows.

Clarendon St., Dublin 2. www.clarendonstreet.com. ℂ **01/671-8466.** Free admission; donations welcome. Daily 8am–8pm or longer. Bus: 15A, 15B, 44, 61, 100X, 101X, 109, 111, 133, 140.

St. Werburgh's Church ★ CHURCH Although the neoclassical 18th-century exterior is hardly insignificant, you'd be forgiven for missing St. Werburgh's, as it doesn't look particularly churchlike. There's a reason for this—the spire was demolished in 1803, ostensibly because it was in bad repair, although the true reason was that the British were worried that it could be used by snipers to target nearby Dublin Castle. The building itself dates from the late–12th century, although it was rebuilt several times—the present interior was modeled in 1877. Jonathan Swift (see p. 101) was baptized here in 1677. The ornately carved wooden pulpit dates from the 1700s. Note the enormous cast-iron bell in the middle of the nave (you can hardly miss it). It doesn't, in fact, come from the old tower; it was placed here in honor of Napper Tandy, a leader of the 1798 rebellion, whose name is carved into the metal. To see inside the church you usually have to call first, or you could drop by no. 8 Castle Street (just around the corner) to ask the caretaker to let you in.

Werburgh St., Dublin 2. ℂ **01/478-3710.** Free admission. Open by appointment May–Sept. Bus: 49X, 50X, 54A, 56A, 77, 77A, 77X, 78A, 150, 151.

Whitefriar Street Carmelite Church ★ CHURCH This 19th-century Byzantine-style church is unexpectedly (perhaps dubiously) one of the city's most romantic spots, as it holds the relics of St. Valentine. The pieces of bone are believed to be authentic; they were given to the church by Pope Gregory XVI in 1836. They're kept in a casket on an altar to the right of the main altar, but once a year (on St. Valentine's Day, of course), they are carried out in procession for a special Mass. The church also holds an icon known as **Our Lady of Dublin,** a 15th-century woodcarving that, in 1824, was rescued from a nearby farm where it had been used as a pig trough.

56 Aungier St., Dublin 2. www.whitefriarstreetchurch.ie. ℂ **01/475-8821.** Free admission. Mon, Wed, Fri 7:30am–6pm; Tues 7:30am–9pm; Sat 7:30am–7pm; Sun 7:30am–8pm. Bus: 16, 16A, 19, 19A, 83, 122, 155.

DISTILLERIES

Guinness Storehouse ★ MUSEUM Opened in 1759, the Guinness Storehouse is one of the world's most famous breweries, producing the distinctive dark stout that is known and loved the world over. You can explore the Guinness Hopstore, tour a converted 19th-century building housing the World of Guinness Exhibition, and view a film showing how the stout is made; then move on to the Gilroy Gallery, dedicated to the graphic design work of John Gilroy (whose work you will have seen if you've ever been in an Irish pub); and last but not least, stop in at the

Sample the famous stout along with 360-degree city views at the Guinness Storehouse's Gravity Bar.

breathtaking **Gravity Bar.** Here you can sample a glass of the famous brew in the glass-enclosed bar 61m (200 ft.) above the ground, complete with 360-degree views of the city. Ticket prices vary based on the time of day—early-morning tickets are as low as £17.50. Check online for discounts.

St. James's Gate, off Robert St., Dublin 8. www.guinness-storehouse.com. ℂ **01/408-4800.** Admission €25 adults; €20 seniors and students over 18; €16 children 13–17 (children 13 and under free); €47 families. Sept–June daily 9:30am–7pm (last admission 5pm); July–Aug daily 9am–8pm (last admission 6pm). Luas: St. James's Hospital. Bus: 123.

The Old Jameson Distillery ★ FACTORY TOUR   Easy to spot from nearly a mile away by its chimney-shaped glass viewing tower, this working distillery is the place to come if you want to learn about one of Ireland's most famous whiskeys. After right-in-front-of-your-eyes demonstrations, you get to sip a little of the old firewater yourself. A couple of lucky people on each tour are selected to be "tasters" and sample different Irish, Scotch, and American whiskeys. Tours run throughout the day, about every 30 minutes, and last an hour. You can get a 10% discount by booking online.

Bow St., Smithfield Village, Dublin 7. www.jamesonwhiskey.com. ℂ **01/807-2355.** Admission €20 adults; €16 seniors and students; €10 children under 18. Mon–Thurs 10am–6pm (last tour 5:30pm); Fri–Sat 10am–7:30pm (last tour 7pm); Sun 10am–6pm (last tour 5:30pm). Luas: Smithfield. Bus: 67, 67A, 68, 69, 79, 90.

HISTORIC ARCHITECTURE & BUILDINGS

Custom House ★ ARCHITECTURAL SITE   Completed in 1791, this beautifully proportioned Georgian building has a long classical facade of graceful pavilions, arcades, and a central dome topped by a statue of Commerce. The 14 keystones over the doors and windows are known as the

Riverine Heads, because they represent the Atlantic Ocean and the 13 principal rivers of Ireland. Although it burned to a shell in 1921, the building has been masterfully restored. The exterior is the main attraction here, and most of the interior is closed to the public; those with a real interest in finding out more about the building can drop by the small visitor center, which has exhibits and an audiovisual presentation telling the story of its reconstruction.

Custom House Quay, Dublin 1. ℰ **01/888-2000.** Admission €1 adults; €3 families; students free. Visitor center: Mid-Mar to Nov Mon–Fri 10am–12:30pm and 2–5pm; Sat–Sun and public holidays 2–5pm. Dec to mid-Mar Wed–Fri 10am–12:30pm and 2–5pm; Sun 2–5pm. Luas: Busáras. Bus: 27C, 41X, 53A, 90, 90A, 92, 151, 747, 748.

Dublin Castle ★ CASTLE   The center of British power in Ireland for more than 700 years, this 13th-century castle was finally taken over by the new Irish government in 1922. You can wander the grounds for free, but they're somewhat plain—the police and government agencies use a significant section of the castle as office space. You'll need to take a guided tour to see the impressive State Apartments, the early-18th-century Treasury, and the Gothic-style Chapel Royal, with its fine plaster decoration and carved-oak gallery. The castle's only extant tower—a 13th-century structure once used to imprison suspected traitors—now holds a small museum dedicated to the Garda. In 1583 the castle's Upper Yard was the scene of Ireland's last trial by mortal combat; today it is dominated by an impressive Georgian structure called the Bedford Tower. The Irish crown jewels were kept in the tower until they were stolen in 1907 (they have never been recovered). If it's open, check out the Medieval Undercroft, an excavated site on the grounds where an early Viking fortress once stood. *Note:* This is a government building, so some areas may be closed for state events.

Dame St., Dublin 2. www.heritageireland.ie. ℰ **01/645-8813.** Guided tour €10 adults; €8 seniors; €8 students; €4 children 12–17; €24 families. Mon–Sun and public holidays 9:45am–5:45pm (last admission 30 min. before closing). Luas: Jervis, St. Stephen's Green. Bus: 9, 13, 14, 15, 15A, 15B, 16, 27, 40, 49, 54A, 56A, 65, 68, 77A, 83, 122, 123, 140, 150, 151, 747.

The Four Courts ★ ARCHITECTURAL SITE   Home to the Irish legal courts since 1796, this fine 18th-century building was designed by James Gandon (who also designed the Custom House; see p. 110). It is distinguished by its graceful Corinthian columns, massive dome, and exterior statues of Justice, Mercy, Wisdom, and Moses. Badly damaged by the fighting during the Civil War of 1922, this building was later artfully restored, although some details, such as the statues of famous Irish lawyers that once adorned the niches of the Round Hall, were lost. No public tours are offered, sadly, but if you want to see the interior, slip in to watch a trial in progress.

Inns Quay, Dublin 8. www.courts.ie. ℰ **01/888-6000.** Luas: Four Courts. Bus: 25, 25A, 51D, 51X, 68, 69, 78, 79, 79A, 83, 151, 172.

General Post Office ★ HISTORIC SITE   Don't be fooled by the nondescript name: With a facade of Ionic columns and Greco-Roman pilasters 60m long (197 ft.) and 17m high (56 ft.), this is more than a post office—it is the symbol of Irish freedom. Built between 1815 and 1818, it was the main stronghold of the Irish Volunteers during the Easter Rising. On Easter Sunday, 1916, Patrick Pearse stood on its steps and read a proclamation declaring a free Irish Republic. It began, "In every generation the Irish people have asserted their right to national freedom and sovereignty." Then he and an army of supporters barricaded themselves inside. A siege ensued that ultimately involved much of the north of the city. Before it was over, the building was all but destroyed. It had barely been restored before civil war broke out in 1922, and it was heavily damaged again. It's still a working post office today, although the small **Letters, Lives, and Liberty Museum** does house a few diverting exhibits, including the original Declaration of Independence. That's all very much a secondary attraction, though; touching the bullet holes in the walls out front is a far more powerful way to experience a sense of this building's history.

O'Connell St., Dublin 1. www.anpost.ie. ✆ **01/705-8833.** Free admission (museum €2). Post Office building: Mon–Sat 8:30am–5pm. Closed public holidays. Museum: Mon–Sat 10am–5pm. Luas: Abbey St. Bus: 10, 10A, 32X, 33X, 39X, 40A, 40C, 41X, 46A, 46B, 46C, 46D, 46E, 116, 123, 145, 747.

Ha'penny Bridge ★ LOCAL LANDMARK   Built in 1816, and one of the earliest cast-iron bridges in Europe, the graceful pedestrian-only Ha'penny Bridge (pronounced *Hay*-penny) is the still the most attractive of Dublin's bridges. Officially named the Liffey Bridge, it's universally known by the toll once charged to cross it: half a penny. The turnstiles were removed in 1919 when passage was made free. The bridge is at its prettiest after sundown, when the old lamps atop its three filigreed arches are lit, and the underside at each end is illuminated in green. In recent years it became traditional for couples to leave padlocks latched onto the bridge, with their names inscribed, before throwing the keys into the water. Dublin's city government now forbids the practice, seeing them more as an eyesore (and a hazard to the bridge) than a symbol of eternal love.

Connects Wellington Quay and Lower Ormond Quay, Dublin 2. Luas: Jervis. Bus: 39B, 51, 51B, 51C, 51D, 51X, 68, 69, 69X, 78, 78A, 79, 79A, 90, 92, 206.

Leinster House ★ ARCHITECTURAL SITE   The home of the Dáil (Irish House of Representatives) and Seanad (Irish Senate), this is the modern center of Irish government. Dating from 1745, it was originally known as Kildare House and was the seat of the Dukes of Leinster. Like the Parliament House building (see p. 113), it is said to have been a major influence on the architects of Washington, D.C.; the resemblance to Irish-born James Hoban's design for the White House, built 78 years later, is certainly clear enough. When the Dáil is not in session, tickets are available for guided tours, three times a day, on Mondays and Fridays. You don't have to book in advance, but tour numbers are strictly limited. To reserve tickets, the events desk prefers an e-mail (event.desk@oireachtas. ie; include your full name, address, and telephone number), or you can call (© **01/618-3271** or **3781**). *Note:* You need to bring photo I.D. (such as a driver's license or passport) to gain admission, and leave large or bulky bags at home. Because this is a government building, you should arrive a few minutes early to allow for security checks before your tour.

Kildare St. and Merrion Sq., Dublin 2. www.oireachtas.ie. © **01/618-3186** or 01/618-3781. Free admission. Entry by guided tour only, Mon and Fri 10:30am, 2:30, 3:30pm. (Additional tours when Dáil and Seanad in session: Tues and Wed 7pm and 8pm.) DART: Pearse St. Luas: St. Stephen's Green. Bus: 4, 7, 11, 14, 15, 15A, 15B, 25A, 25B, 38, 38A, 39, 39A, 46A, 66, 66A, 66B, 67, 120, 128, 145.

Parliament House ★ ARCHITECTURAL SITE The grand colonnaded facade of this building was allegedly the model for the Capitol building in Washington, D.C., with one key difference: It's completely devoid of windows. When Parliament House was built in the 1730s, it had windows, but they were bricked up in the early 1800s for security reasons. The Irish Parliament met here until 1801, when, by an extraordinary quirk of history, it was tricked into voting for its own abolition. (William Pitt the Younger, then Prime Minister of Britain, had promised sweeping reform of the anti-Catholic laws if Ireland agreed to a formal union with Britain. They did so, but then Pitt was deposed by King George III, the reforms never happened, and the Irish lost what little self-government they had.) Today the building is a branch of the **Bank of Ireland,** but you can see parts of the magnificent interior featuring oak woodwork, 18th-century tapestries, and a sparkling crystal chandelier. Friendly porters are on hand to fill you in on the history. In our experience, they may also give informal tours of rooms you can't normally see, if you ask nicely.

2 College Green, Dublin 2. © **01/671-1488.** Free admission. Mon–Wed and Fri 10am–4pm, Thurs 10am–5pm. DART: Tara St. Luas: St. Stephen's Green, Jervis St. Bus: 9, 13, 16, 27, 40, 54a, 65, 65b, 68, 77a, 83, 150.

The President's House (Áras an Uachtaráin) ★★ HISTORIC HOUSE Set in Phoenix Park, Áras an Uachtaráin was once the Viceregal Lodge, the summer retreat of the British viceroy, whose main digs were in Dublin Castle. From what were never humble beginnings, the original 1751 country house was expanded several times, gradually becoming the splendid neoclassical white mansion you see today, which now serves as the official residence of Ireland's president. Guided tours leave from the Phoenix Park Visitor Centre every Saturday. After an introductory historical film, a bus brings visitors to and from the house for a 1-hour tour of the state reception rooms (tours run a little longer in summer, when the gardens are included on the itinerary, weather permitting). Since the building is still the official home of the Irish president, a strictly limited number of tickets are given out, on a first-come, first-served basis. The house may occasionally be closed for state events, so call ahead.

Note: For security reasons, no backpacks, travel bags, strollers, cameras, or mobile phones are allowed on the tour.

Tour departs from Phoenix Park Visitor Centre, Dublin 8. www.president.ie. ℭ **01/677-0095** (Phoenix Park visitor center). Free admission. Sat tours hourly 10:30am–3:30pm. Bus: 37.

MUSEUMS & LIBRARIES

Croke Park Stadium & GAA Museum ★ SPORTS MUSEUM

Croke Park is the headquarters, and main sports ground, of the Gaelic Athletic Association (GAA), which oversees most of the traditional Irish sports—including hurling, rounders (similar to baseball), and Gaelic football. Their museum does a good job of setting out the history of these games and putting them into the wider historical context of the importance of sport to the Irish way of life. The interactive exhibits include a large video archive, and you can take a tour of the stadium, too. But the most excitement, of course, happens on match days—check the website if you want to come and hear the roar of the crowd for real.

Jones Rd., Dublin 3. www.crokepark.ie. ℭ **01/819-2323.** Tour and museum: €14 adults; €11 seniors and students; €9 children under 12; €34–€38 families. Museum only: €7 adults; €6 seniors and students; €5 children under 12; €18–€20 families. Museum open Mon–Sat 9:30am–5pm, Sun 10:30am–5pm (June–Aug open until 6pm Mon–Sat); on match days, call to confirm hours. Tour times: July–Aug hourly 10am–4pm (10am–3pm Sun); Sept–June Mon–Fri 11am, 1, 3pm (also 4pm in June); Sat 10am, 11am, noon, 1, 2, 3pm; Sun 11am, noon, 1, 2, 3pm (also 10am in June). On match days, call to confirm hours. Bus: 3, 11, 11a, 16, 16a, 41.

EPIC: The Irish Emigration Museum ★★ MUSEUM

This modern, well-designed museum tells the story of how and why millions of people emigrated to these shores in search of a better life—and the impact they made on other countries when they got there. The exhibits have a heavily interactive element, with plenty of high-tech storytelling. While not aimed specifically at children, it certainly does enough to keep younger visitors entertained as well as informed—for example, you've given a "passport" with your ticket, which you can get stamped in each of the 20 galleries. There's also a Genealogy Centre on-site if you want help in exploring any of your own connections to the far-reaching Irish diaspora.

The CHQ Bldg., Custom House Quay, Dublin 1. www.epicchq.com. ℭ **01/906-0861.** Admission €14 adults; €12 seniors; €12 students; €7 children 6–15; children 5 and under free; €35 families. Genealogy Centre only: €9.50. Daily 10am–6:45pm (last admission 5pm; open until 8pm Thurs). Luas: George's Dock. DART: Connolly, Tara St.

Glasnevin Cemetery & Museum ★ CEMETERY

North of the city center, the Irish national cemetery was founded in 1832 and covers more than 50 hectares (124 acres). Most people buried here were ordinary citizens, but there are also many famous names on the headstones, ranging from revolutionary commander Taoiseach (prime minister), and president Eamon de Valera, to other political heroes and rebels including Michael Collins (see p. 274), Daniel O'Connell, Countess Constance Markievicz (see p. 443), and Charles Stewart Parnell. Literary figures also have their place here—including writers Christy Brown (immortalized in the film *My Left Foot*) and Brendan Behan. A small museum is devoted to the cemetery and its famous occupants. Guided tours run daily, or you can download a self-guided-tour app for your smartphone for €10 via the cemetery website. Maps showing who's buried where are sold in the flower shop at the entrance.

Finglas Rd., Glasnevin, Dublin 11. www.glasnevintrust.ie. ℰ **01/882-6550.** Museum and tour €13 adults; €10 seniors, students, and children; €35 families. Museum only €6.50 adults; €4.50 seniors, students, and children; €20 families. Museum: Daily 10am–5pm (including Bank Holidays). Tours daily 11:30am and 2:30pm. Bus: 4, 9, 40, 83, 140, 58X, 66X, 67X, 70X, 84X, 92.

Irish Rock 'n' Roll Museum Experience and Wall of Fame ★

MUSEUM   Not so much a museum as a tour of a demo studio with a few exhibits thrown in, the Rock 'n' Roll Museum opened to some fanfare in 2015. The tour culminates with the chance to form a "band" with your fellow visitors and lay down a track in the studio. Exhibits on display include vintage instruments and assorted memorabilia, such as a blank check signed by Bono for an autograph hunter. Outside, on Curved Street, is the **Irish Music Wall of Fame,** where giant photographic portraits of Ireland's top music stars, including Van Morrison, U2, and the Cranberries, adorn one side of the building.

Curved St., off Temple Bar, Dublin 2. http://irishrocknrollmuseum.com. ℰ **01/635-1993.** Tours (must be prebooked) €14.40 adults; €12.60 seniors, students, and children 12–17; €7.20 children 11 and under; €11.25 families. Daily 11am–5:30pm. DART: Tara St. Luas: Jervis St., St. Stephen's Green. Bus: 9, 13, 16, 27, 40, 54a, 65, 65b, 68, 77a, 83, 150.

The Irish Music Wall of Fame adorns a sidewall of the Irish Rock 'n' Roll Museum Experience.

James Joyce Centre ★ MUSEUM   This idiosyncratic museum is set in a handsome Georgian house that once belonged to the Earl of Kenmare. Joyce himself never lived here; however, he was rather taken with a former owner of the house named Denis Maginni—an eccentric Irishman, who added an "i" to his name to give himself an air of Italian sophistication. (Maginni appears as a character in Joyce's masterpiece *Ulysses*.) Today the center functions as both a small museum and a cultural center devoted to Joyce and his work. Actual exhibits are a little thin on the ground, but they hold interesting (at least for Joyce fans) lectures and special events, and also organize a Joyce-themed walking tour of Dublin. Unsurprisingly, this place becomes an explosion of activity around Bloomsday (June 16th), the date upon which *Ulysses'* fictional events take place. Unlike the rest of Dublin, which makes do with a single day of celebrating its most famous 20th-century literary hero, the James Joyce Centre turns it into a week-long festival.

35 North Great George's St., Dublin 1. www.jamesjoyce.ie. ✆ **01/878-8547.** Admission €5 adults; €4 seniors, students, and children. Apr–Sept Mon–Sat 10am–5pm, Sun noon–5pm; Oct–Mar Tues–Sat 10am–5pm, Sun noon–5pm. Last admission 30 min. before closing. Bus: 1, 4, 7, 7b, 7d, 8, 9, 11, 13, 16, 38, 38a, 38b, 40, 44, 122, 123, 140, 747.

The Little Museum of Dublin ★★★ MUSEUM   Stuffed full of ephemera relating to the lives of ordinary Dubliners—art, toys, photographs, newspapers, prints, and other artifacts of the everyday—this delightful little museum chronicles what it was like to live in the city throughout the 20th century. Thoughtfully laid out inside a beautifully preserved Georgian town house, the vast majority of the items on display were donated by the people of Dublin, and the collection is being added to all the time. Among the curios are genuine documents of social history, including items relating to the First World War, the struggle for independence, and the suffrage movement. Several objects have charming anecdotes connected—such as the music stand that, in June 1963, was hurriedly borrowed from the home of a local antiques dealer by visiting U.S. President John F. Kennedy, when he realized he had nowhere to put his papers during a speech. While it probably packs more of an emotional punch for native Dubliners, the exhibits tell a captivating story for outsiders as well. Entry is by guided tour (on the hour, every hour); tours are lively and informative, and guides are great with children. Do book tickets online in advance during the high season, as tours quickly fill up. *Note:* **DoDublin** bus tour tickets (see p. 120) include free entry to the museum—but it's first come, first served, so be sure to reserve your place on a tour.

15 St. Stephen's Green, Dublin 2. www.littlemuseum.ie. ✆ **01/661-1000.** Admission €10 adults; €8 seniors and students; €5 children; €20 families. Deluxe ticket (includes private guided tour) €12. Daily 9:30am–5pm (open until 8pm Thurs). Luas: St. Stephen's Green. Bus: 15X, 32X, 39X, 41X, 46X, 51X.

Marsh's Library ★★ LIBRARY   Founded by the wonderfully named Narcissus Marsh, the Archbishop of Dublin, in 1701, this library is still much today as it was in the archbishop's time. Tall, long rows of books sit between paneled walls, and rolling ladders slant upward so readers can reach the high shelves. It is a magnificent example of a 17th-century scholar's library, its shelves filled with scholarly volumes, chiefly focused on theology, medicine, ancient history, and maps, along with Hebrew, Greek, Latin, and French literature. Remaining are the wire cages in which readers would be locked in with the more valuable tomes. It's still a working library, but readers are no longer imprisoned with their books. The library has a particularly excellent collection of books by and about Jonathan Swift (see box p. 101), including volumes

Founded in the 17th century, Marsh's Library is full of rare scholarly tomes.

DUBLIN | Exploring Dublin

with his editing comments in the margins. Ironically, Swift himself said of Archbishop Marsh, "He is the first of human race, that with great advantages of learning, piety, and station ever escaped being a great man."

St Patrick's Close, Dublin 8. www.marshlibrary.ie. ℂ **01/454-3511.** Admission €3 adults; €2 seniors and students; children under 16 free. Mon and Wed–Fri 9:30am–5pm; Sat 10am–5pm. Closed public holidays and last week in Dec. Bus: 49, 49A, 50X, 54A, 56A, 77A, 77X, 150, 151.

National Library of Ireland ★ LIBRARY   If you're coming to Ireland to research your roots, one of your first stops should be this library, where thousands of volumes and records yield ancestral information. Open at this location since 1890, it's also the principal library of Irish studies, particularly noted for its collection of first editions and the papers of Irish writers and political figures, such as W. B. Yeats, Daniel O'Connell, and Patrick Pearse. Parts of the collection are always on display to the general public (the exhibition devoted to Yeats is particularly good). The library also has an unrivaled collection of maps of Ireland. A specialist **Genealogy Advisory Service** is open Monday to Friday 9:30am to 4:45pm, and Saturdays in June to September from 9:30am to 12:45pm. It's free of charge and you don't have to make an appointment.

Kildare St., Dublin 2. www.nli.ie. ℂ **01/603-0200.** Free admission. Mon–Wed 9:30am–7:45pm, Thurs–Sat 9:30am–4:45pm (reading rooms close 12:45pm on Sat), Sun 1–4:45pm (exhibits only, reading rooms closed). DART: Pearse. Bus: 7B, 7D, 10, 10A, 11, 11A, 11B, 14, 14A, 15, 15A, 15B, 15C, 20B, 25X, 32X.

PARKS & GARDENS

Phoenix Park ★ PARK   The vast green expanses of Phoenix Park are Dublin's playground, and it's easy to see why. This well-designed, user-friendly park is crisscrossed by a network of roads and quiet pedestrian walkways that make its 704 hectares (1,739 acres) easily accessible. Avenues of oaks, beech trees, pines, and chestnut trees are shady hideaways, or you can sun yourself in broad expanses of grassland; livestock graze peacefully on pasturelands, deer roam the forested areas, and horses romp on polo fields. It's a relaxing place to spend a restful afternoon, but there's also plenty to do here should you feel active. The home of the Irish president (see p. 113) is in the park, as is the Dublin Zoo (see p. 121). The visitor center is partly located inside **Ashtown Castle,** a tower house built in the 1430s that—hard to believe, but true—was only discovered in 1978, when a later building that had completely enveloped it was being demolished. Free parking is adjacent to the center. Also next to the center, the quaint **Phoenix Park Tea Rooms** (✆ **01/677-0900**) serves snacks and light lunches; it also has toilets. The park is 3km (2 miles) west of the city center on the north bank of the River Liffey.

Phoenix Park, Dublin 8. www.phoenixpark.ie. ✆ **01/677-0095.** Free admission. Park open 24 hr.; visitor center 9:30am–5:30pm. Tea Rooms: Mar–Oct Mon–Fri 9:30am–5pm, Sat–Sun 9:30am–5:30pm; Nov–Feb Mon–Fri 9:30am–4pm, Sat–Sun 9:30am–5pm. Last admission 45 min. before closing. Bus: Castleknock Rd. entrance: 37. Navan Rd. entrance: 37, 38, 39, 70. North Circular Rd. entrance: 46A.

Horse and carriage ride through Phoenix Park.

HORSE-DRAWN carriage tours

Touristy it may be, but there's something hard to resist about the idea of clattering over Dublin's cobblestoned streets in a horse-drawn carriage, with a driver who will comment on the sights as you clop past. Drivers and their carriages congregate at the Grafton Street side of St. Stephen's Green. Simply walk up to one and arrange your tour—anything from a short swing around the green to a half-hour Georgian tour or an hour-long Old City tour.

Rides are available on a first-come, first-served basis from April to October (weather permitting) and cost about €30 to €60 for one to four passengers.

Alternatively, to book a tour in advance, **Bernard Fagan Horse Drawn Carriages** (www.horsedrawncarriages dublin.com; ✆ **086/874-8691**) is one recommended company. Tours are customized to what you're interested in seeing; prices vary, but expect to pay upwards of €25 per person for an hour-long tour.

St. Stephen's Green ★ PARK   This lovely city center park is filled with public art, and there always seems to be something new and imaginative hidden amid its leafy walkways. Among them is a beautiful statue commemorating the Irish rebel Wolfe Tone (beside an affecting monument to the Great Famine) and a garden of scented plants for blind visitors. This is a great place for a summer picnic. If the weather's fine, you can take a buggy ride through the park (see above).

Dublin 2. Luas: St. Stephen's Green. Bus: 20B, 32X, 33X, 39X, 40A, 40C, 41X, 46B, 46N, 46X, 51X, 58X, 70B, 70X, 84X, 92.

Especially for Kids

Sure, Dublin is rich in history and culture, but if you've got restless kids in tow, museums and historic buildings can get old fast. Luckily, the Irish capital also has a good complement of attractions that are tailor-made for families. Besides the attractions listed below, consider taking the **Viking Splash Tour** or the **Dublin Ghost Bus** (see p. 120), or, if you've got jaded teenagers, **Castle Dracula** (p. 123) or the **Irish Rock 'n' Roll Museum Experience** (p. 115). A seaside excursion to the heritage village of **Dalkey** (p. 123) or the oceanfront resort town of **Bray** (p. 159) can also be a welcome antidote to city touring. And don't overlook **Butlers Chocolate Experience** (p. 121), a treat for any kid with a sweet tooth.

The Ark: A Cultural Centre for Children ★ ARTS CENTER   This is a great option for children who are makers, thinkers, doers, listeners, and watchers. Age-specific programs are geared to small groups of kids from 2 to 12 years old. Mini courses (1 to 2 hours long) are designed around themes in music, visual arts, and theater; there are also workshops in photography, instrument making, and the art of architecture. The custom-designed arts center has three modern floors that house a theater, a gallery, and a workshop for hands-on learning sessions. Tickets include

Convenient, comfortable, and—remember this when the heavens open in June—relatively immune to inclement weather, bus tours are a great way to pack a lot of sightseeing into a little time. And while Dublin has more than its fair share of standard tourist buses, some are more original.

For a lively tour of Dublin's Viking history, the **Viking Splash Tour** (www.vikingsplash.ie; ☏ **01/707-6000**) in a reconditioned World War II amphibious "duck" vehicle starts on land and eventually splashes into the Grand Canal. Viking helmets, though supplied, are optional. Tickets are €27 adults, €24 seniors and students, €18 children 13 to 17, €13 children 2 to 12, and €75 to €85 families. Children under 2 aren't allowed for safety reasons.

Of the many "hop on, hop off" bus tours of the city, one of the best is the **DoDublin** tour (www. dodublin.ie; ☏ **01/844-4265**). The 24-stop tour runs all around the city center, taking in sights such as **Trinity College** (see p. 102), **Dublin Castle** (p. 111) and the **Guinness Storehouse** (p. 109). You can leave and rejoin the tour at any point, and as many times as you like within a 24- or 48-hour period, depending on which ticket you buy. The cost includes free entry into the **Little Museum of Dublin** (see p. 116); but you'll still need to book yourself on a tour) and the option of a free walking tour with a local guide. Buses run all day, every 15 minutes from 9am daily; the last tour starts its loop at 5pm. Every other bus is multilingual. Tickets cost €22 adults, €20 seniors and students, €10 children. Two kids ages 13 and under travel free with every adult. Check for online discounts. DoDublin also runs full-day excursions to attractions such as **Glendalough** (see p. 191) and **Powerscourt** (p. 195). See website for details.

A spooky evening tour in a bus decked out in, um...spooky wallpaper, **Dublin Ghost Bus** (www.dodublin.ie/city-sightseeing-tours/ghostbus; ☏ **01/844-4265**) addresses Dublin's history of felons, fiends, and phantoms. You'll see haunted houses, learn of Dracula's Dublin origins, and even get a crash course in body snatching. It's all ghoulish fun but actually quite scary in places, so it's not recommended for kids who don't have "teen" in their age. Tickets cost €28.

Likewise, the entertaining **Gravediggers Tour** (www.thegravedigger.ie; ☏ **085/102-3646**) takes you in pursuit of a few ghoulish and well-intentioned scares. Just when it all seems like too much for the faint-hearted, the bus stops at the Gravediggers Pub by Glasnevin Cemetery (see p. 114) for a fortifying drink—included in the ticket price of €25. Live actors and 4D technology help bring the whole experience to life. Or should that be...

one child and one adult; prices vary, but expect to pay around €6 to €12 for most events. Check the current themes and schedule on the Ark's very helpful website, and book well ahead.

11a Eustace St., Dublin 2. www.ark.ie. ☏ **01/670-7788.** Ticket prices vary. Event times vary; call ahead. DART: Tara St. Luas: Jervis, St. Stephen's Green. Bus: 15E, 15F, 16, 16A, 16C, 19, 19A, 19C, 49, 49A, 50, 51, 51B, 51C, 54A, 56A, 65, 65B, 68, 69, 69X, 77, 77A, 77X, 78, 78A, 79, 79A, 83, 121, 122, 123, 150, 151.

Dublinia ★ HERITAGE SITE   Covering the history of Dublin from the Viking age through medieval times, this child-friendly history experience is presented as a series of interactive tableaux—complete with sound effects, smells, and audio "reconstructions" of *olde worlde* Dublin. (They're such effective earworms, in fact, that adults may find themselves thinking about them months later.) Kids can try on clothes like the ones their ancestors may have worn, or even find themselves placed in the Dublin stocks. Check the website for details of special tours, with costumed guides, and other family-friendly activities. Climb the 96 steps to the top of their new viewing tower, which was once part of the (now otherwise vanished) medieval **Church of St. Michael the Archangel.** Dublinia is right across from Christ Church Cathedral (see p. 96), making this an excellent payoff for any little ones who patiently trudged around that historic but austere building. You'll save money when you buy combined tickets for the two.

St. Michael's Hill, Christ Church, Dublin 8. www.dublinia.ie. 🕐 **01/679-4611.** Admission €9.50 adults; €8.50 seniors and students; €6 children; €25 families. Mar–Sept daily 10am–6:30pm; Oct–Feb daily 10am–5:30pm. Last admission 1 hr. before closing. Luas: Four Courts. Bus: 49, 49A, 54A, 123.

Dublin Zoo ★★   A perennial kid-pleaser, this modern, humane zoo in Phoenix Park provides a home for more than 235 species of wild animals and tropical birds. The animals live inside a series of realistically created habitats such as the African Savanna, home to giraffes, rhinos, and ostriches; the Gorilla Rainforest, a 12,000sqm (7½-sq.-mile) enclosure that houses five lowland gorillas; Asian Forest, home to Sumatran tigers and lions; the South American House, with an eclectic range of almost unbearably cute species, including tiny pygmy marmosets and two-toed sloths; and the new Pacific Coast, where you can watch sea lions swim underwater and view a flamingo aviary that's big enough for the gracious birds to take flight. Playgrounds and gift shops are scattered throughout. Feeding times and scheduled talks are posted on the zoo website (several times daily March–Sept; weekends only Oct–Feb). A restaurant is on-site, as well as plenty of smaller cafes and picnic areas for those who prefer to bring their own meals.

Phoenix Park, Dublin 8. www.dublinzoo.ie. 🕐 **01/474-8900.** Admission €17.50 adults; €13.50 seniors and students; €13 children 3–15; €6.50 special-needs child; €10 special-needs adult; €49–€57 families. Mar–Sept daily 9:30am–6pm; Oct 9:30am–5:30pm; Nov–Dec 9:30am–4pm; Jan 9:30am–4:30pm; Feb 9:30am–5pm. Last admission to zoo 1 hr. before closing; last admission to African Savanna 30 min. before closing. Luas: Heuston (15-min. walk). Bus: 25, 26, 46A, 66, 66A, 66B, 67, 69.

Outlying Attractions

Butlers Chocolate Experience ★ FACTORY TOUR   Ireland is awash with brewery tours, but rare is the chance to look around a real-life chocolate factory. The world-famous chocolatiers, whose cafes are scattered throughout Dublin, have been based in the city since the 1930s. The delectable confections are now produced at a less-than-lovely industrial park on the road to Malahide, but like all the best soft-centered

Painting chocolate bears at Butlers Chocolate Experience.

chocolates, the sweet part is on the inside. The tour takes you around the factory to see the luxury chocolate makers in action, with tastings aplenty. At the end you get to decorate your own chocolate figure. The factory is completely accessible to wheelchair users. Space is quite limited; you'll have to book tours in advance. No chocolates are made on Saturday, so the weekday tours are definitely the most fun.

Clonshagh Business and Technology Park, Oscar Traynor Rd., Dublin 17. www.butlers chocolates.com/chocolateexperience. ✆ **01/851-2151.** Admission €13 adults and children; €47.50 families. Mon–Sat 10am, 12:30, 3:30pm. Booking essential. Bus: 130. From Dublin, take R105 to R107 toward Malahide; after about 3.5km (2½ mi.), turn left onto Oscar Traynor Rd., take 5th right turn and look for sign on the left.

Casino Marino ★★ ARCHITECTURAL SITE   Stand down, gamblers—this "casino" simply means "little house." Built around 1770, this unique and unexpected little architectural gem sits in the middle of a suburban park. The tiny neoclassical exterior is exquisitely proportioned, with Corinthian columns and elaborate detail around the white stone cornices. Inside, unlikely though it seems from the compact exterior, 16 rooms are decorated with rich 18th-century architectural details, such as beautiful plasterwork ceilings and subtly curved windows. Entry is by tour only, but the cheerful guides help put it all into context.

Casino Park (signposted from R107, Malahide Rd.), Dublin. www.heritageireland.ie. ✆ **01/833-1618.** Admission €7 adults; €5 seniors; €3 children and students; €12 families. June–Sept 10am–6pm; mid-Mar to May and Oct daily 10am–5pm; closed Nov to mid-Mar except for prebooked groups. Last admission 45 min. before closing. Bus: 14, 27, 27A, 27B, 42, 43, 128.

Castle Dracula ★ INTERACTIVE ENTERTAINMENT   Well, this is a novel way to spend Saturday night. Part live theater, part museum, this homage to Dublin-born author Bram Stoker is set up as a tour of "Castle Dracula," through a series of elaborately constructed sets and tunnels. Costumed actors try to scare you and make you laugh in almost equal measure, while you learn more about Bram Stoker and the Dracula phenomenon along the way. (They even have a real lock of Stoker's hair, allegedly taken from his corpse by his wife). The tour ends in an underground auditorium made to look like a spooky graveyard, where you watch a live show that includes comedy and two magicians. The emphasis overall is on laughs rather than scares (although there are a few of the latter, so no kids under 14 are allowed—nor are pregnant women, supposedly, although who are they kidding?). You meet at the reception lobby of the Westwood Club, a modern gym, which somehow adds to the bizarreness of the whole experience. Tickets must be booked in advance. Clontarf DART station is right next door, or it's about a 15-minute cab ride from the center of Dublin.

Meet at Westwood Gym, Clontarf Rd. (next to Clontarf DART), Dublin. www.castle dracula.ie. ✆ **01/851-2151.** Admission €25 adults; €20 seniors, students, and children 15–18. Late Feb to Aug Sat only 7pm (arrive 6:45pm). May not run every week—check website for schedule. DART: Clontarf. Bus: 130.

Dalkey Castle & Heritage Centre ★ HERITAGE SITE   Housed in a 15th-century tower house, this center tells the history of venerable Dalkey town in a few sweet, if unsophisticated, displays. Tours run by costumed guides tell the tale of the building (complete with live performance), or you can duck out of the (lengthy) tour and take in the view from the battlements instead. Adjoining the center is a medieval graveyard and the **Church of St. Begnet** (Dalkey's patron saint), whose foundations date back to Ireland's early Christian period. Dalkey itself is worth a wander; a heritage town with plenty of historic buildings, it also has lots of charming pubs, restaurants, and charming boutiques. If you enjoy country walks, climb **Dalkey Hill** in Dalkey Hill Park, just south of town, for great views of Killiney Bay, Bray Head, and Sugarloaf Mountain. From Coliemore Harbour, a 10-minute walk from the train station, you can take a 5-minute ferry ride to clamber around rocky, abandoned **Dalkey Island,** with its ruined church and guard tower, wild goats, and seal colony.

Castle St., Dalkey (16km/10 mi. southeast of Dublin on R119). www.dalkeycastle.com. ✆ **01/285-8366.** Admission €9 adults; €8 seniors and students; €7 children 5–12; €25 families. Mon and Wed–Fri 10am–5pm; Sat–Sun 11am–5pm. DART: Dalkey. Bus: 7D, 59.

WHERE TO STAY IN DUBLIN

With a healthy mix of plush hotels and grand old guesthouses, Dublin excels in providing a place to rest your head at the end of a day. Unfortunately, finding a really great, *affordable* place to stay is a tougher prospect

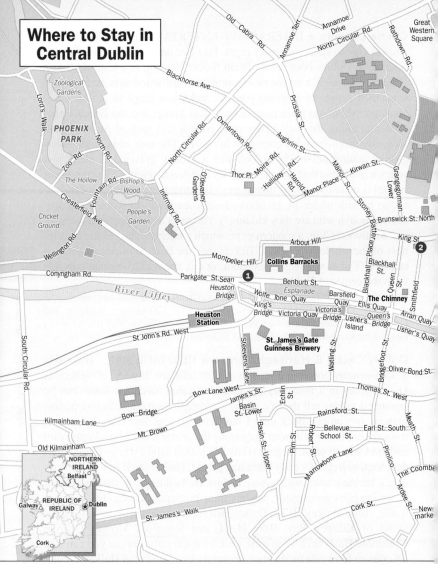

Where to Stay in Central Dublin

Academy Plaza **4**
Ashling Hotel **1**
Buswells **17**
Camden Court Hotel **20**
The Clarence **8**
The Conrad **19**
Dublin Citi Hotel **12**
Eliza Lodge **9**
Harding Hotel **7**
Hotel Riu Plaza The Gresham **5**

Maldron Hotel Smithfield **2**
The Merchant House **11**
The Morrison **6**
Radisson Blu Royal **14**
The Shelbourne **18**
Temple Bar Hotel **10**
Trinity Lodge **16**
The Westbury **15**
The Westin **13**
The White Cottages **3**

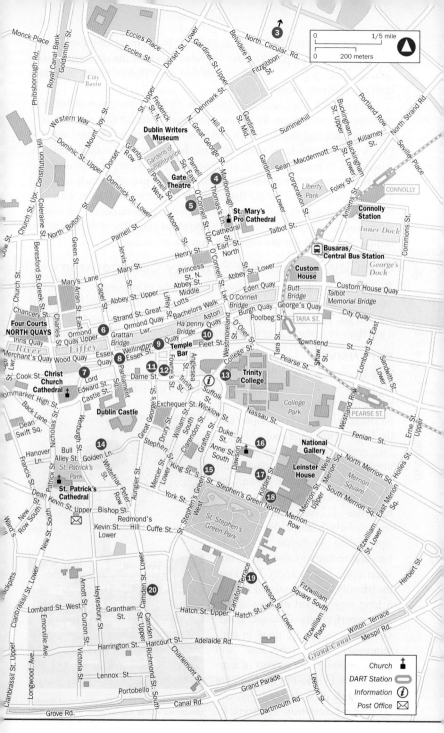

in the summer. In this book we have tried to list as many of these finds as we can. If you're prepared to stay slightly outside of the city center, your options open up quite a bit (remember that most Dublin travel, including taxis, is relatively cheap).

Try to book your accommodations as far in advance as possible. The most sought-after places fill up fast. And don't write off four-star hotels—frequent sales and discounts can make them cheaper than budget options. Check your dream hotel's website first, before making a final decision. Always try to book online—many hotels offer web-only special deals.

Irish immigration authorities require visitors to have already arranged a place to stay at least for the first night. If you arrive in Dublin without a reservation, however, don't despair. One of the best sources of last-minute rooms (often at a discount) is **www.visitdublin.com**. The website lets you browse hotels and guesthouses with immediate availability.

Old City, Temple Bar & Trinity College Area

Temple Bar is the youngest, most vibrant niche in a young, vibrant town. Stay here and you'll be on the doorstep of practically anywhere you'd want to go. That said, it can get *very* noisy at night, so request a room on a top floor or at the rear of the establishment if you want some shut-eye.

EXPENSIVE

The Clarence ★★ Back in the 1990s, when the Celtic Tiger was starting to roar, the Clarence became something of a symbol of the "new" Dublin. Chic, fashionable, and with megastar owners to boot (Bono and the Edge from U2), it spoke of Dublin's revival as a modern and cultured capital city. These days, with the economy slowing down, the Clarence has lost some of its original luster—U2 have sold their share, and a refurbishment is overdue. The surrounding profusion of trendy bars and restaurants also means that street noise is a problem. However, the friendly and professional staff go a long way toward making up for any imperfections. Pleasant, good-size guest rooms are done in contemporary tones (chocolate and cream or white with accents of scarlet and black). Most of the furniture is the work of Irish designers, and beds are luxuriously comfortable.

The Octagon Bar in the Clarence hotel draws celebrities, not to the exclusion of regular folk.

Prices are high, but check the website for package deals and special offers, particularly in the off-season. The trendy **Cleaver East** restaurant serves ultra-contemporary Irish fare, and stopping by the lovely **Octagon Bar** for a pint of Guinness is a must, even if you're not staying here. The basement **Liquor Rooms** nightclub, which has a nice retro speakeasy vibe, is one of the coolest places in Temple Bar for late-night cocktails (see p. 166).

6-8 Wellington Quay, Dublin 2. www.theclarence.ie. ℂ **01/407-0800.** 50 units. €200–€230 double, €350–€390 suite. Breakfast €15–€19. Dinner, bed-and-breakfast packages available. Valet parking €5 per hr. **Amenities:** Restaurant; bar; gym; room service; spa; Wi-Fi (free). Bus: 26, 66, 66A, 66B, 66D, 67, 67A.

Eliza Lodge ★   Located in the middle of Temple Bar, above a popular Italian restaurant and overlooking the Liffey, this smart guesthouse could hardly feel more in the thick of the action. Guest rooms are simple and compact, with large windows letting in plenty of natural light, although the modern bathrooms are shoebox size. It's also pricey, given the no-frills amenities—they don't service your room during your stay, for instance—but what you're really paying for here is the convenience of the location. And that, like so many other hotels in this 'hood, is both its biggest asset and greatest liability. Temple Bar rarely sleeps, and Eliza Lodge sits on a busy traffic intersection. So if you're a finger-on-the-pulse type, step right in! But if you're a very light sleeper, you might want to look elsewhere—or at least pay extra for an upper-floor room (which also gets you a nice view of the river).

23–24 Wellington Quay (corner of Eustace St.), Dublin 2. www.elizalodge.com. ℂ **01/671-8044.** 18 units. €179–€329 double. Discount parking at nearby lot (€7 overnight, €14 for 24 hr.). Breakfast included. Dinner, bed-and-breakfast packages available. **Amenities:** Restaurant; Wi-Fi (free). Bus: 26, 39B, 51, 51B, 51C, 51D, 51X, 66, 66A, 66B, 66D, 67, 67A, 68, 69, 69X, 78, 78A, 79, 79A, 90, 92, 206, 748.

Radisson Blu Royal ★★   The exterior of this hotel is nothing to write home about—it's a nondescript 1980s building a few blocks from St Patrick's Cathedral, surrounded by bland office buildings. But don't let appearances fool you. Inside, it's all about convenience and comfort. There's a sophisticated restaurant, **V'nV,** and three bars—ranging from a glitzy cocktail bar (the **O Bar**) to a quiet lounge (the **Vintage Room**), perfect for after-dinner conversation. Bedrooms are spacious and modern, with new, comfortable beds and large bathrooms equipped with baths and separate walk-in showers. Soundproofing is excellent throughout. Service is friendly and helpful across the board. All the technology is modern, and the Wi-Fi is fast. Here, you're an 8-minute walk from Dublin Castle and the Old City, and 12 minutes' stroll from Temple Bar. Guests have free access to the nearby Iveagh Club gym and swimming pool. All in all, if you're looking for a central, reliable option, this is the place. It's nothing flashy, but absolutely everything you need.

Golden Lane, Dublin 8. www.radissonblu.com. ℂ **01/898-2900.** 150 units. €190–€280 double. Parking €15. Breakfast included. **Amenities:** Restaurant; bar; room service; Wi-Fi (free). Bus: 27, 49, 54a, 56a, 77a, 150, 151.

The Radisson Blu Royal's bar showcases elite whiskies and cognacs.

The Westin ★★   With its grand, imposing facade (thanks to its former incarnation as a bank), this hotel boasts an interior with handsome original 19th-century features. Even those parts that feel more modern have an impeccably well-maintained elegance to them. The large guest rooms have a refined decor, with wide leather headboards and outrageously comfortable beds. The **Mint Bar** remains a fashionable hangout for the Dublin glitterati, and the **Exchange** restaurant serves excellent modern European food. The only thing missing is a spa, but you can book pampering treatments in your room.

Westmoreland St., Dublin 2. www.thewestindublin.com. ✆ **01/645-1000.** 163 units. €450–€600 double, €650–€800 suite. Breakfast included. Dinner, bed-and-breakfast packages available. Valet parking €25 per day. **Amenities:** Restaurant; bar; gym; room service; Wi-Fi (€15/day; free for Starwood Preferred members). Bus: 1, 7B, 7D, 9, 11, 13, 16, 16C, 25N, 26, 33N, 39N, 40, 41N, 44, 100, 133.

MODERATE

Buswells ★★   An old-school air pervades this rather traditional mid-priced hotel, a 5-minute walk from Grafton Street. The Georgian building's original features have been carefully maintained, from the intricate cornices of 19th-century plasterwork to the marble fireplaces, which warm the lobby on cold days. It can come as a surprise, therefore, to find that the small but decently furnished guest rooms are modern in style (rather bland, even, compared to the grand lobby). Similarly, the bar and restaurant are more cheaply furnished than the lovely building deserves. Guests with mobility problems should ask for a room on a lower floor, as the old building (actually three town houses merged together) has many staircases. But even with its faults, this is a charming place on a peaceful street, with friendly staff and quiet rooms. Plus, you're in the very heart of the action here—just a few minutes' walk to Trinity College in one direction and St. Stephen's Green in the other.

23–25 Molesworth St., Dublin 2. www.buswells.ie. © **01/614-6500.** 69 units. €180–€240 double. Hotel covers cost of parking at nearby lot (overnight only). Cheaper rates do not include breakfast. **Amenities:** Restaurant; bar; room service; Wi-Fi (free). DART: Pearse. Bus: 7B, 7D, 10, 10A, 11, 11A, 11B, 13, 14, 14A, 15, 15A, 15B, 15C, 15X, 20B, 25X, 32X, 27C, 33X, 39B, 40A, 40C, 41X, 46A, 46B, 46C, 51D, 51X, 58X, 67X, 84X, 92.

Dublin Citi ★ This small, friendly hotel almost qualifies as budget for the location. It's in the thick of the action, sure enough—the shortest of strolls takes you to Trinity College and Grafton Street in one direction, and Temple Bar in the other. Full marks for convenience! Light sleepers beware, however: Dame Street is one of the busiest thoroughfares in the city, and it only seems to get noisier every year. (What's more, there's a busy bus stop by the little plaza next door.) The friendly staff does its best to ameliorate all this—providing free earplugs to guests, for instance—but an upper-floor room is a must. Bedrooms are compact but cozy, with street views and a neutral, modern decor. A few have decorative stone balconies, or quirky little references to the historical nature of the building, such as a (functioning) faux 1940s-style telephone. The hotel has a lively bar downstairs, but you're hardly short of options in these parts. An arrangement with a local gym allows you to use its facilities for free, including a pool, sauna, and steam room. *Note:* Prices plummet by up to two-thirds in the off-season.

48–49 Dame St., Dublin 2. www.dublincitihotel.com. © **01/679-4455.** 27 units. €134–€235 double. No children under 3. Discount parking at nearby lot (€12 per day). Breakfast not included in lower rates. **Amenities:** Bar; room service; use of nearby gym; Wi-Fi (free). Bus: 27, 40, 49, 54A, 56A, 65, 65B, 68, 68X, 69, 69X, 77A, 77X, 79, 79A, 150.

Temple Bar Hotel ★ This cheerful, well-run hotel certainly wins in the location stakes, sitting right in the middle of trendy Temple Bar. Guest rooms are pleasant, decorated in a clean, modern style, with big, comfortable beds. Executive rooms offer extra space for a small premium. Teeny-tiny "Pod" rooms provide the best value but absolutely no space. **Toast,** the in-house restaurant, has a good, reasonably priced menu. The downstairs bar has live music nightly, which can make sleeping a bit of a challenge, but this is Temple Bar, and if you're up for a party, a dozen other lively pubs are within a stone's throw. Check the website for off-season discounts.

10 Fleet St., Dublin 2. www.templebarhotel.com. © **01/612-9200.** 129 units. €230–€290 double. Breakfast included. **Amenities:** Bar; room service; Wi-Fi (free). DART: Pearse. Bus: 100X, 133.

INEXPENSIVE

Harding Hotel ★ Just central enough not to require a long trek to the main tourist sites, but far enough to escape the inevitable nighttime crowds of nearby Temple Bar, this is a reasonable option on the western edge of the city center. The polished wood and bright, floor-to-ceiling windows of the cheerful lobby give off a pleasantly old-fashioned vibe. The comfortable, if plain, guest rooms are good value. Even in high season, you can occasionally find a double room for less than €125, and triple rooms typically cost just a little bit more than standard doubles. This makes the Harding a standout option for families. It's not fancy, but it's pleasant and clean and has everything you need.

Copper Alley, Fishamble St., Dublin 2. www.hardinghotel.ie. ☏ **01/679-6500.** 52 units. €124–€186 double. No parking. Breakfast not included in lower rates. **Amenities:** Restaurant; bar; accessible rooms; Wi-Fi (free). Bus: 37, 39, 39A, 39B, 39C, 39X, 49, 49A, 49X, 50, 50X, 56A, 70, 70A, 70X.

The Merchant House ★   Mainly geared toward business travelers and couples, the accommodations here are different from that in a conventional hotel. The Merchant House is a series of spacious guest suites, with various services attached but no dedicated reception area. The upside to this is more room—which is great for groups, although no children are allowed. The downside is that, while the entrance is secure and private, the building isn't staffed all the time. Also, travelers who prefer their local color less, well, colorful, should be warned that it's next door to a fetish store—albeit a fairly discreet one. The suites themselves are extremely well designed, with lovely architectural touches as well as flatscreen TVs and elegant contemporary furnishings. The bed-and-breakfast rate includes daily housekeeping service and breakfast at a nearby cafe.

8 Eustace St., Dublin 2. www.themerchanthouse.eu. ☏ **01/633-4447.** 4 units. €180–€205 double. No children. No parking. Breakfast not included in lower rates. **Amenities:** Wi-Fi (free). Bus: 39B, 49X, 50X, 65X, 77X.

O'Connell Street Area/North of the Liffey

The Northside has some good offerings in the way of hotels. Though in some respects a less sought-after area, it's still very central and within walking distance of all the major sights and shops. Hotel rates tend to be lower than they are a 5-minute walk away, across the river.

EXPENSIVE

The Morrison ★★   Rooms at this chic hotel owned by Doubletree Hilton verge on futuristic, with ultra-modern furniture, moody uplighting, and a host of flashy extras, such as 40-inch HDTVs. Bathrooms are surprisingly utilitarian, given how fancy everything else. But it's all ruthlessly clean. Every inch is painted in a million shades of white, with endless crisp, straight lines and plenty of fancy gizmos (the hotel has in-house tech support should the Wi-Fi let you down).The art can be a bit of an acquired taste, but song lyrics painted onto the walls here and there add an edge of Irish literary romance. There's a good restaurant, the **Morrison Grill,** and a funky cocktail lounge, **Quay 14.** The staff is excellent, and regulars swear the amazing service never falters.

Lower Ormond Quay, Dublin 1. www.morrisonhotel.ie. ☏ **01/887-2400.** 138 units. €315–€345 double. No children under 3. Discount parking at nearby lot (€12/day). Breakfast included. **Amenities:** Restaurant; bar; room service; gym; Wi-Fi (free). Bus: 25, 25A, 25B, 25N, 25X, 26, 66, 66A, 66B, 66N, 66X, 67, 67N, 67X, 69N.

MODERATE

Hotel Riu Plaza The Gresham ★★   One of Dublin's most historic hotels, the Gresham first opened in 1817, though it was almost destroyed during the Easter Rising of 1916. Most of the current building dates from the 1920s. The public areas retain a glamorous Art Deco feel, preserved during a big modernization of the hotel in the mid-aughts. Although the suites and deluxe rooms are opulent, the cheaper guest rooms are quite basic—but they're comfortable, quiet, and, most important, surprisingly affordable for a hotel with this kind of pedigree. The **Writer's Lounge,** a beautiful remnant of its Jazz Age heyday, is a popular spot for afternoon tea. Overlooking both the hotel lobby and busy O'Connell Street, it's a good perch for people-watching. The main O'Connell Street taxi rank is directly outside, and it's about a 15-minute walk to Temple Bar.

23 Upper O'Connell St., Dublin 1. www.gresham-hotels.com. ✆ **01/874-6881.** 298 units. €198–€270 double. No children under 3. Discount parking at nearby lot (€15 overnight). Breakfast not included in lower rates. Dinner, bed-and-breakfast packages available. **Amenities:** 2 restaurants; 2 bars; room service; discounted use of nearby gym and pool (€10); Wi-Fi (free). Luas: Abbey St. Bus: 2, 3, 4, 5, 7, 7A, 7B, 7D, 8, 10, 10A, 11, 11A, 11B, 13.

INEXPENSIVE

Academy Plaza Hotel ★★   Owned by the Best Western chain, this large, modern, low-frills option is popular with business travelers and well located for travelers exploring central Dublin. The lobby is small but pleasant, with wood paneling and leather furniture; rooms are compact and simple, with cream walls, rust-and-brown-hued carpet, and windows well-insulated from street noise. Some rooms are bigger than others, so if size matters, request a deluxe room. Bathrooms are decent and modern, with showers above the baths. The buffet breakfasts are sizeable, if not terribly varied, and can be delivered to your room (for a charge). The staff is pleasant, and the location, for the money, is very good.

10-14 Findlater Place, off O'Connell St., Dublin 1. www.academyplazahotel.ie. ✆ **01/878-0666.** 304 units. €160–€190 double. Parking €12 per day. Breakfast included. **Amenities:** Wi-Fi (free). Luas: Abbey St. Bus: 2, 3, 4, 5, 7, 7A, 7B, 7D, 8, 10, 10A, 11, 11A, 11B, 13.

St. Stephen's Green/Grafton Street Area

St. Stephen's Green may be only a 10-minute walk from the hustle and bustle of Temple Bar and Trinity College, but it's infinitely calmer and less harried. This is a good area if you're looking for a little peace and quiet.

EXPENSIVE

Conrad Dublin ★★   The Dublin outpost of Hilton's high-end brand is all about the luxury. Beds in the spacious, modern guest rooms are sumptuously comfortable (and refreshingly large for a European hotel, even in the cheapest rooms). Color schemes of chocolate and cream, or oatmeal and royal blue, help convey an air of elegance without feeling too fussy.

Thoughtful touches, such as Nespresso machines in every room, are welcome. In general, this place feels somewhat like an American-style business hotel, geared more toward professional travelers on expense accounts than tourists. But that's not always a bad thing. Some rooms were being refurbished as this book was being written, and the lobby has been redesigned with a stylish bar and bistro, which offers an excellent afternoon tea and is popular with locals.

Earlsfort Terrace, Dublin 2. http://conradhotels3.hilton.com. ℗ **01/602-8900.** 191 units. €330–€600 double, €490–€790 suite. Valet parking €19 per day. Breakfast included. **Amenities:** Bar; restaurant; room service; gym; Wi-Fi (€5/day). Bus: 126.

The Shelbourne ★★★   Dublin hotels simply don't come with a better historic pedigree than this—the Irish constitution was written in this very building (room 112, to be precise). A feeling of *fin de siècle* elegance pervades throughout the grand lobby rooms, with high plaster ceilings, crystal chandeliers, and a winding iron staircase. Guest rooms have a much more discreet, contemporary elegance, with extremely luxurious beds and a host of modern extras tucked in among the glitz. The spa is excellent, and a gorgeous old bar is popular with local writers and politicians. Afternoon tea at the Shelbourne is a true Dublin institution; consider splurging on tea or a drink in the lobby, even if you can't spring for a night here.

27 St. Stephen's Green, Dublin 2. www.marriott.co.uk. ℗ **01/663-4500.** 190 units. €410–€510 double, €1,485–€1,600 suite. Valet parking €25 per day. Breakfast €21–€29. Dinner, bed-and-breakfast packages available. **Amenities:** 3 restaurants; 3 bars; gym; spa; accessible rooms; Wi-Fi (free). Luas: St. Stephen's Green. Bus: 7B, 7D, 10, 10A, 11, 11A, 11B, 14, 14A, 15, 15A, 15B, 15C, 15X, 20B, 25X, 32X, 39X, 40A, 40C, 41X, 51X, 70B, 84X.

The Westbury ★★★   Basically conceived with well-heeled shopaholics in mind, this top-end hotel on busy Grafton Street is a luxurious and stylish retreat. The lobby is vast and grand, with sofas designed to keep your posture perfect as you gossip. Bedrooms are huge and modern, with subtle floral wallpaper, handmade furniture, and soothing beige and cream tones. Beds are comfortable (although with so much space to spare, they could be bigger), and a few are modern-style fourposters. **Wilde,** the excellent Modern Irish restaurant, is a beautiful space overlooking Grafton Street; it also serves an excellent afternoon tea. Check the website for some enticing package deals, including dinner, bed-and-breakfast, and theater options.

Grafton St., Dublin 2. www.doylecollection.com/hotels/the-westbury-hotel. ℗ **01/602-8900.** 205 units. €420–€520 double, €490–€630 suite. Parking €20 per day. Breakfast included. **Amenities:** 2 restaurants; bar; room service; gym; Wi-Fi (free). Bus: 11, 11a, 11b, 14, 14a, 15a, 15c, 15x, 20b, 27c, 33x, 39b, 41x, 46b, 46c.

MODERATE

Camden Court Hotel ★★   Although not exactly budget, this large hotel just south of St. Stephen's Green is great value for what you get. A "practical base" kind of hotel, rather than one overflowing with character and charm, the Camden Court is nonetheless well equipped, with good-size, modern guest rooms (especially the family rooms) and even a pool.

You'd pay significantly more if this place were just a few blocks farther north; the only real drawback is that you're a 10- to 20-minute walk away from the center, but a bus stop is just steps away. The traditional pub next door, the **Bleeding Horse,** is a good spot for a pint of Guinness with locals.

Camden St. Lower (near junction with Charlotte Way), Dublin 2. www.camdencourt hotel.com. ✆ **01/475-9666.** 246 units. €190–€210 double. Free parking. Breakfast not included in lower rates. **Amenities:** Restaurant; bar; accessible rooms; beauty salon; gym; pool; room service; Wi-Fi (free). Luas: Harcourt St. Bus: 15X, 16, 16A, 19, 19A, 65, 65B, 65X, 83, 122.

Smithfield

MODERATE

Ashling Hotel ★★   Close to Heuston Station and Phoenix Park on the western end of the city center, the Ashling is a modern six-story hotel. Basic double rooms have generic corporate-style decor, but deluxe rooms are more distinctive and spacious, with comfortable beds and large windows overlooking the city. **Chesterfield's** restaurant serves classic Irish fare, including a daily lunchtime "carvery" (roast meat, potatoes, and vegetables, served buffet-style). Central Dublin is a 10-minute tram ride or a 25-minute walk, but, handily, this is the last stop before the airport on the Airlink bus (see p. 84). *Tip:* Stroll through Coppies Memorial Park, opposite the hotel, to see the semi-nude bronze statue of Anna Livia, a character in James Joyce's *Finnegans Wake.* She appears to float above a pool of water—thus earning her the nickname "the Floozie in the Jacuzzi." For more on the acerbic wit of Dublin statues' nicknames, see p. 100.

Parkgate St., Dublin 8. www.ashlinghotel.ie. ✆ **01/677-2324.** 225 units. €215–€260 double, €290–€315 suite. Parking (€10/24 hr.). Breakfast included. Dinner, bed-and-breakfast packages available. **Amenities:** Restaurant; bar; Wi-Fi (free). Luas: Museum. Bus: 25, 26, 66, 66A, 66B, 67, 69.

Maldron Hotel Smithfield ★   Part of a small Irish hotel chain, the Maldron Smithfield is a good midpriced option, a stone's throw from the Old Jameson Distillery and a 10-minute walk from St. Michan's Church. The guest rooms are modern and comfortable, with good soundproofing. Go for an upper-floor room with a balcony if you can; the view across the low-slung skyline of Dublin's Northside is lovely, particularly at sunrise and sunset. The onsite restaurant and bar have fairly limited offerings, but right outside, around Smithfield Square, are several bars and restaurants. Alternatively, the front desk can order you a pizza from a local delivery company (there's a menu in your room; pay in cash). While you're here, you should definitely visit the **Cobblestone** (see p. 167), probably the best pub in Dublin for live traditional music, and less than 30 seconds from the hotel's front door (turn left and you're facing it, right next to the colorful mural).

Smithfield Terrace, Dublin 7. www.maldronhotelsmithfield.com. ✆ **01/485-0900.** 92 units. €160–€190 double, €200–€235 suite. Parking (€10/24 hr.). Breakfast included. **Amenities:** Restaurant; bar; Wi-Fi (free). Luas: Smithfield. Bus: 37, 39, 39A, 70, 83, 83A, 747.

Trinity Lodge ★   This small hotel is full of quirks—not all of them convenient (there's no elevator and plenty of stairs, for instance), but the bedrooms are comfortable, contemporary, and surprisingly large for a place in this price range. A converted town house, the hotel was built in 1785, and some of the bedrooms retain a historic feel, while others are more modern. Quadruple rooms offer outstanding value for families. From South Frederick Street it's a short walk to Trinity College and all the action; it's also—a comparative rarity in the city center—generally quite peaceful at night. Breakfast is good, with cold and hot options, but it's served in a separate building, which—depending on where your room is—might mean walking outside briefly.

12 South Frederick St., Dublin 2. www.trinitylodge.com. ✆ **01/617-0900.** 16 units. €140–€180 double. 2-night minimum on some summer weekends. Discounted parking at nearby lot (€17.50/24 hr.). Continental breakfast included. **Amenities:** Wi-Fi (free). Rail: Connolly. Luas: St. Stephen's Green. DART: Pearse. Bus: 7B, 7D, 10, 10A, 11, 11A, 11B, 14, 14A, 15, 15A, 15B, 15C, 15X, 20B, 25X, 27C, 32X, 33X, 39B, 41X, 46B, 46C, 51D, 51X, 58X, 67X, 84X, 92.

Ballsbridge & the Southern Suburbs

South of the canal, this prestigious Dublin residential neighborhood is coveted for its leafy streets and historic buildings. Half the foreign embassies in Dublin are located in this district. It's also growing as a hotel quarter—the distance from the city center means that you'll get much more for your money by staying here.

EXPENSIVE

InterContinental Dublin ★★   This purpose-built modern hotel has been outfitted in a traditional style, more redolent of a country house than you'd think from the imposing brick-and-glass exterior. From the elegantly simple guest rooms, with their sumptuously comfortable beds, to the outstanding full-service spa, the hotel offers a host of thoughtful touches. All rooms are spacious, and bathrooms are marble luxury. Downstairs, the **Seasons** restaurant is gorgeous, with peaceful green views. The **Reading Room** and **Lobby Lounge** are perfect places to linger over tea or a drink. In fact, the only downside is the location. Views over the rooftops of Ballsbridge are never going to equal the kind of city vista you get downtown—but you make up the difference in tranquility and beauty. (And it's only a short train or taxi ride into the city center.)

Simmonscourt Rd., Ballsbridge, Dublin 4. www.intercontinental.com/dublin. ✆ **01/665-4000.** 195 units. €265–€380 double, €385–€490 suite. Valet parking (free). Breakfast not included in lower rates. **Amenities:** Restaurant; bar; spa; pool; Wi-Fi (€15). DART: Sandymount. Bus: 4, 7, 7N, 8, 27X.

MODERATE

Aberdeen Lodge ★★   Drive up to this elegant Regency building in the springtime, and its front is so covered in ivy, it looks like a vertical lawn with spaces cut for the windows. Inside, the decor is rather endearingly

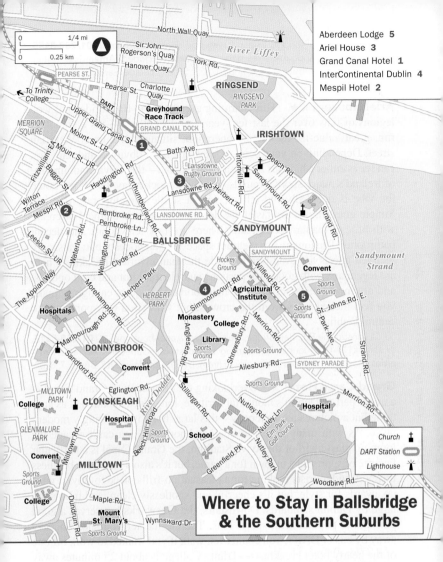

Where to Stay in Ballsbridge & the Southern Suburbs

old-fashioned; neat-as-a-pin public spaces have heavy, antique-style furnishings and embroidered pillows scattered hither and thither. Guest rooms are comfortable and quiet, if a little plain, but modern bathrooms are a big plus. Some have views of the large garden, where guests can take tea—often in the company of the hotel's friendly cat. Aberdeen Lodge is a short walk to the nearest DART station, and from here it's a hop to the city center. Alternatively, a 5-minute stroll takes you to a pleasant walking path through a park beside the coast. If you do come this way, look for the gray stone tower stuck rather ignominiously between a public toilet and a payphone—it's an example of a Martello Tower, a small defensive fortification built by the British to ward off a feared invasion from France in the early 19th century.

53–55 Park Ave., Ballsbridge, Dublin 4. www.aberdeen-lodge.com. ℂ **01/283-8155.**
11 units. €210–€240 double. Free parking. Breakfast included. **Amenities:** Restaurant; bar; use of nearby spa; Wi-Fi (free). DART: Sydney Parade, Sandymount. Bus: 2, 3, 18, 84N.

Ariel House ★★★

This charming guesthouse in Ballsbridge has won legions of fans over the last few years. And rightly so—it's a smoothly run, great value-for-the-money operation, situated on a quiet Victorian street. Depending on your point of view, the most obvious landmark you can see is either a hideous blot or a great day out—the Aviva Stadium, one of Ireland's major sports grounds, literally a block away. Inside the hotel, the vibe is decidedly old-school, with a subtle contemporary flourish. Simple guest rooms are tastefully decorated in earthy oatmeal or cream with brocade-pattern bedspreads. There are tiny televisions and decent bathrooms. The lounge is a pleasant space with an honesty bar; musically inclined guests are even free to tickle the piano ivories. Breakfasts here are legendary, with good-size portions and plentiful hot and cold options, and afternoon tea is served. The neighborhood is quiet enough to make you feel tucked away from the crowds, but with good transport links to central Dublin.

50–54 Lansdowne Rd., Ballsbridge, Dublin 4. www.ariel-house.net. ℂ **01/668-5512.**
37 units. €115–€135 double. Free parking. Breakfast not included in lower rates. **Amenities:** Honesty bar; room service; Wi-Fi (free). DART: Lansdowne Rd. Bus: 4, 7, 8, 84.

Grand Canal Hotel ★

Overlooking the 18th-century Grand Canal—a major part of Dublin's industrial heritage, long since abandoned as anything but a picturesque waterway—this large hotel is a strikingly modern place. As with many hotels in this neighborhood, you can't escape the looming glass swirl of the Aviva Stadium; the Grand Canal is a particular favorite of sports fans in town for a game, but it's also a haven for business travelers and tourists looking for a pleasant no-frills place to stay. It wins no awards for style, but it's cheerful and spotlessly clean, and rooms are large by Dublin standards. Downstairs, the **Gasworks** bar serves a good pint and is popular with sports fans. The city center is a short journey away by bus or DART. You could even walk if you wanted to work off one of the hearty hotel breakfasts—Trinity College is about 25 minutes away on foot.

Grand Canal St. Upper, Ballsbridge, Dublin 4. www.grandcanalhotel.ie. ℂ **01/646-1000.** 142 units. €180–€195 double. Theater and O2 Arena packages available. Free parking. Breakfast not included in lower rates. **Amenities:** Restaurant; bar; accessible rooms; Wi-Fi (free). DART: Grand Canal Dock. Bus: 4, 5, 7, 7A, 8, 45, 63, 84.

Mespil Hotel ★

Another reasonable option in Ballsbridge, the Mespil is about a 15-minute walk from St. Stephen's Green. Accommodations here are certainly of a higher standard than what you're likely to find uptown for the same price. (Stays of more than 1 night usually qualify for discounts when you book online.) The guest rooms are spacious and feature modern decor and comfortable beds. Bathrooms are large, and many have walk-in rainfall showers. The street below can be quite noisy—ask for a top-floor room. In common with most hotels of this type, breakfast is served buffet-style—tasty and excellent fuel for a day wandering the city. One other nice little bonus: An excellent gourmet food market is held just outside by the canal every Thursday from 11am to 2pm (see **www.irishvillagemarkets.com** for details).

50–60 Mespil Rd., Dublin 4. www.mespilhotel.com. ℭ **01/448-4600.** 255 units. €255–€295 double. Parking (limited). Breakfast €12. **Amenities:** Restaurant; bar; gym; room service; accessible rooms; Wi-Fi (free). Bus: 10, 10A, 15X, 49X, 50X, 66D, 92.

North of Dublin

The seaside suburb of Skerries is most definitely outside of the city—about 30km (18½ miles) from Temple Bar—but transport links are reasonably good. Of course, those seeking peace and quiet at the end of the day will see this as a selling point.

INEXPENSIVE

The White Cottages ★★★   The sea is an ever-present feature at this pleasant, whitewashed little B&B in Skerries, a pretty commuter town just north of Dublin. The coastline is literally feet away from the wooden terrace at the back, and the sound of the waves can help soothe you to a restful sleep at night. Guest rooms are decorated in summery white and blue colors, with jaunty, candy-striped accents. The owners are welcoming and extremely helpful—Joe, the co-owner, is a mine of information about the local area, and his wife, Jackie, displays some of her art around the house. Breakfasts are good, and in summer you can get afternoon tea (€20) or a "romantic picnic" lunch (€25), although you'll have to fend for yourself at dinnertime. (Joe can provide an exhaustive list of places to eat nearby.) The only major snag is that Skerries is far outside of the city; the train journey to the center takes about 40 minutes, and the bus takes over an hour. Still, it's nothing more than local commuters do every day, and you'll be hard-pressed to find a more tranquil and welcoming retreat after a long day of sightseeing.

Balbriggan Rd., Skerries, Co. Dublin. www.thewhitecottages.com. ℭ **01/849-2231.** 4 units. €100 double. Free parking. Breakfast included. **Amenities:** Picnic lunches; Wi-Fi (free). Rail: Skerries. Bus: 33.

WHERE TO EAT IN DUBLIN

The economic boom years of the early 2000s in Dublin brought with it a new generation of international, sophisticated restaurants. Ireland embraced foodie culture in a way it never really had before. When the economy crashed, however, so too came a minor resurgence in the popularity of traditional Irish fare, even in expensive restaurants. That's not to say that the food in Dublin is on the downswing—far from it—it's just become easier to find traditional Irish food in the city than it was a decade ago, as Ireland re-embraces and reinvents its food heritage.

Where to Eat in Dublin

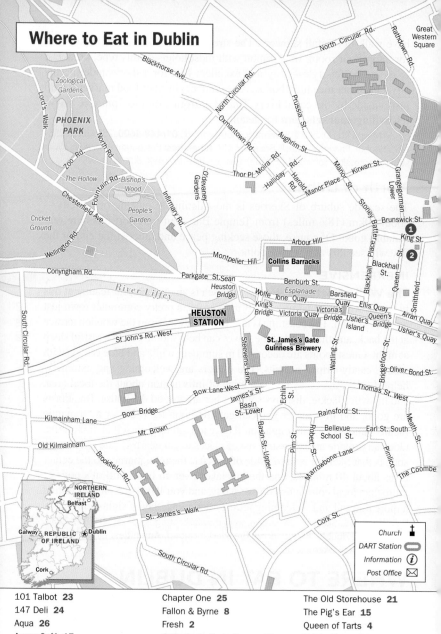

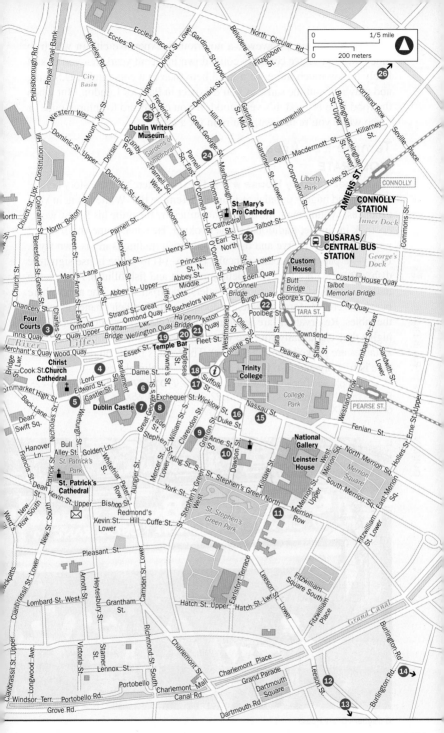

Dublin remains, however, a notoriously expensive city in which to dine out. Prices have certainly come down in recent years, but you're still likely to pay much more for a meal here than in a comparable U.S. city, and maybe about the same as you'd expect in Paris or London. But when the food here is good, it's very good. If you can afford to splurge once or twice while you're in town, you're in for a treat.

Temple Bar Area

MODERATE

Gallagher's Boxty House ★★★ IRISH   There's a great story behind this tiny and hugely popular restaurant in Temple Bar. While living in Venezuela as a young man, the owner was struck by the pride his fellow workers took in simple, traditional home cooking. He came home and founded a restaurant to preserve and update some Irish traditions in his own style. Boxty—a paper-thin potato pancake (see p. 141)—is the house signature dish, served with a variety of delicious meat and fish fillings. Also on the menu are thick steaks, seafood chowders, and Irish stews. The atmosphere buzzes as crowds form outside the door, waiting for their chance at one of the tables. Reservations are recommended on weekends, but even on busy nights they can usually squeeze you in (*squeeze* being the operative word, as tables are packed tightly together). The food is fresh and delicious; service is friendly and fast. One of our favorite Dublin places.

20–21 Temple Bar, Dublin 2. www.boxtyhouse.ie. ✆ **01/677-2762.** Entrees €15–€25. Daily 11am–10:30pm. Luas: Jervis. Bus: 22, 39B, 49X, 50X, 65X, 66, 66A, 66B, 66D, 67, 67A, 69X, 77X.

Gallagher's Boxty House.

boxty

"Boxty on the griddle, boxty on the pan. If you can't bake boxty, sure you'll never get a man."

—Traditional Irish rhyme

Boxty—which comes from an old Gaelic term meaning "poor bread"—is a traditional Irish food, with recipes handed down in families from parent to child through generations. It's basically a thin potato pancake, made with buttermilk and sometimes eggs, that's cooked, crepe-like, on a griddle pan, and then stuffed with meat or vegetable filling and wrapped up like a tortilla.

Each region has its own distinctive spin on the boxty. Although boxty is usually fried, it can also be baked or served as a dumpling (similar to the Polish pierogi). More often than not, modern chefs will accompany their boxty with meat or fish, in various creative (and delicious) ways.

The Old Storehouse ★★ IRISH/PUB   There isn't much in the way of innovation on the menu of hearty Irish classics at this popular pub in Temple Bar—and that's precisely why it's so popular. What you get is delicious traditional pub food mixed with just a hint of bistro style around the edges: dishes like Irish stew; West of Ireland seafood chowder; bangers and mash (sausages and mashed potato) with ale gravy; and cottage pie (ground beef and vegetable pie, topped with mashed potato). There's a small wine list, but the beer selection is better. As much of a draw as the food is the nightly live music, all traditional and all free, with up to 20 acts a week in the summer. The Old Storehouse doesn't accept reservations, so be prepared to wait for a table when it's busy.

Crown Alley, off Cope St., Dublin 2. www.theoldstorehouse.ie. ✆ **01/607-4003.** Entrees €14–€22. Daily noon–11:30pm (to 12:30am Fri and Sat). Bus: 39B, 49X, 50X, 65X, 77X.

INEXPENSIVE

Gourmet Burger Kitchen ★★ BURGERS   This upscale British-New Zealand chain has recently started springing up in Ireland, and a welcome import it is, too—they make some of the most reliably good burgers in town. Portions aren't huge, but there's something for everyone—get yours classic and simple, or opt for one of the more imaginative creations (such as the chicken, Camembert, and cranberry burger; or the spicy Habanero, with a fruity chile-tomato salsa). There are even some good veggie choices, such as a delicious homemade falafel burger, served with tahini and Sriracha sauce. Dessert options are a little limited, but the enormous malted shakes more than make up for that. Other Dublin branches are at 5 South Anne St. (✆ **01/672-8559**) and 14 South William St. (✆ **01/679-0537**).

Temple Bar Sq., Dublin 1. www.gbk.ie. ✆ **01/670-8343.** Entrees €8–€13. Mon–Wed 11am–10pm, Thurs 11am–11pm, Fri–Sat 9:30am–11pm, Sun 9:30am–10pm. Luas: Jervis. Bus: 22, 39B, 49X, 50X, 65X, 66, 66A, 66B, 66D, 67, 67A, 69X, 77X.

Queen of Tarts ★★ CAFE   This cheerful little tearoom in the heart of Temple Bar is a delightful pit stop for a pot of tea and some form of sweet, diet-busting snack. Cakes and tarts are the specialty; it's all good, but try the lemon meringue pie or the old-fashioned Victoria sponge (yellow cake with a jam and cream filling and a dusting of sugar on top). They also serve delicious, generously proportioned breakfasts until 11:30am during the week, 1pm on Saturday, and a decadent 2pm on Sunday. At lunchtime you can order soups or sandwiches, but it's the cakes that keep us coming back. A second branch is just around the corner on Lord Edward Street, directly opposite the junction with Cork Hill (with City Hall on the corner).

Cow's Lane, Dame St., Dublin 2. www.queenoftarts.ie. Ⓒ **01/633-4681.** Breakfast €5–€12, lunch €6–€12. Mon–Fri 8am–7pm, Sat–Sun 9am–7pm. Bus: 37, 39, 39A, 39C, 70, 70A.

Trinity College Area

EXPENSIVE

The Pig's Ear ★★★ MODERN IRISH   A deliciously inventive approach to traditional Irish tastes pervades at this super-cool restaurant overlooking Trinity College. But this isn't one of those trendy eateries where the menu is too concerned with being clever to be satisfying. Here, classic ingredients are offered with modern flair: cod with smoked black lard and mint, beef short rib with garlic and bone marrow, or fried salmon served with hay-smoked mussels and brown shrimp. Dishes on the constantly changing menu are light and beautifully presented in an atmosphere of modern elegance. This is one of the city's top restaurants, and one of its trendiest, so make reservations as early as you can.

4 Nassau St., Dublin 2. www.thepigsear.ie. Ⓒ **01/670-3865.** Entrees €18–€28. Mon–Sat noon–2:45pm and 5:30–10pm. DART: Pearse St. Bus: 25X, 32X, 33X, 41X, 51D, 51X, 58X, 67X, 84X, 92.

The Vintage Kitchen ★★★ IRISH   An antidote to over-fussy fine dining, the Vintage Kitchen is a stripped-down, funky little restaurant. Vintage artworks line the dining room—everything's for sale, but there are no fixed prices, so just make an offer if you like something. It's a small place with a limited number of tables, and they don't even have an alcohol license—you're encouraged to BYOW for a small corkage fee of €3. But you can see why people crowd in: The classic cooking is truly excellent, artfully presented in a contemporary style and generously proportioned. Start with the Cajun-style seafood chowder before tackling slow-roasted lamb shank with roasted carrots and treacle gravy, or hake with samphire (a sea vegetable), leeks, and red pepper puree. If dinner prices are a bit steep for you, come for lunch—main courses are just €13, and small plates half that. Make reservations for dinner.

7 Poolbeg St., Dublin 2. www.thevintagekitchen.ie. Ⓒ **01/679-8705.** Fixed-price menus: lunch €21–€28, dinner €30 two courses, €36 three courses. Daily noon–2:30pm; 5:30–10pm. DART: Tara St. Bus: 65, 65B.

MODERATE

Avoca Café ★★ CAFE   So much better than just another department store cafe, this eatery on the top floor of the famous Avoca shop is a great place for breakfast, lunch, or a mid-shopping snack. The morning menu is more varied and interesting than at most hotels: free-range scrambled eggs with arugula salad, several types of pancakes, French toast, and even the ubiquitous "full Irish." Lunches are healthy and delicious—think superfood salad with roasted butternut squash, quinoa, and blueberries, or rotisserie chicken with Caesar salad. The delicious soups are famous among locals. Or just drop in for an afternoon slice of cake and a restorative cup of tea.

11–13 Suffolk St., Dublin 2. www.avoca.ie. ✆ **01/677-4215.** Breakfast €3–€12, lunch €6–€17. Mon–Fri 9:30am–5:30pm (serving coffee and scones only 4:30–5:30pm), Sat 9:30am–5pm (coffee and scones until 5–5:30pm), Sun 11am–5pm (coffee and cakes until 5:30pm). Bus: 15X, 32X, 33X, 39X, 41X, 51D, 51X, 58X, 70X, 84X.

The Bank on College Green ★★ PUB   With undoubtedly one of Dublin's most jaw-droppingly handsome interiors, this place would be worth visiting even if it didn't serve great pub food. Built as a bank in 1895, at the height of Victorian opulence, it preserved several remnants of the original when it was converted into a pub (including the wonderful old-style safes that you can still see downstairs). In the hour after local offices close, you'd be lucky to walk in and snag a table right away, but waiting for a table at least gives you an opportunity to admire the beautiful architecture. Tucked away behind the bar are bronze busts of the seven signatories of the 1916 Proclamation of Independence. A small and fairly traditional lunch menu of burgers, fish and chips, sandwiches, and salads gives way to a more extensive selection in the evening, including steaks, pasta, and sharing plates. Come for the leisurely Sunday brunch and sample a traditional roast.

20 College Green, Dublin 2. www.bankoncollegegreen.com. ✆ **01/677-0677.** Entrees €10–€25. Mon–Wed 11am–12:30am, Thurs–Sat 11am–1:30am, Sun 11am–midnight. Bus: 15X, 32X, 33X, 39B, 39X, 41X, 49X, 50X, 51X, 58X, 65X, 70X, 77X, 84X.

Near Dublin Castle

MODERATE

Brasserie Sixty6 ★★ IRISH/INTERNATIONAL   This cheerful, well-run bistro near Trinity College is a popular choice with locals for special occasions. Prices are not cheap, but the food is reliably excellent. Roast meats cooked rotisserie-style are a house specialty. Try the beef filet with fondant potatoes, or dig into a plate of juicy prawns flavored with sea salt and jalapeño peppers, served with crab claws, lemongrass, and thick-cut French fries. Vegetarians are catered to as well, with choices such as vegetable tagine or spinach and ricotta tortellini, and pretty much all of the food here is celiac-friendly. Service is topnotch and the portions generous. The pre-theater menu is a good value (€30 for three courses, served all night Sun–Wed and until 6:30pm Thurs–Sat). A popular Sunday brunch served until 3:30pm is accompanied by a jazz band.

66 South Great Georges St., Dublin 2. www.brasseriesixty6.com. ℰ **01/400-5878.** Entrees €12–€33. Mon–Fri noon–10pm, Sat–Sun 10am–10pm. Bus: 15E, 15F, 16, 16A, 19, 19A, 65, 65B, 65X, 83, 122.

Fallon & Byrne ★★ MODERN EUROPEAN   A top-floor adjunct to the wonderful food and wine store **Fallon & Byrne Food Hall** (p. 157), this restaurant serves delicious seasonal Irish fare sourced from artisan producers. Nothing seems to have come very far: crab from the tiny port of Castletownbere, County Cork; lamb from Lough Erne; oysters from Carlingford. The menu keeps a nice balance between ambitious dishes and more down-to-earth options, so while you may find, say, filet of turbot served with pink grapefruit and crushed new potatoes, you could just as easily opt for a simple burger topped with Cashel bleu cheese and smoked bacon. They also have vegetarian and vegan menus. And if you prefer to fend for yourself, an enormous selection of deli items is downstairs, available to go.

11–17 Exchequer St., Dublin 2. www.fallonandbyrne.com. ℰ **01/472-1010.** Entrees €12–€33. Wed–Thurs noon–3pm, 6–10pm; Fri–Sat noon–3pm, 6–11pm; Sun noon–4pm, 6–9pm; Mon–Tues noon–3pm, 6–9pm. Bus: 15E, 15F, 16, 16A, 19, 19A, 65, 65B, 65X, 83, 122.

San Lorenzo's ★★ BREAKFAST/ITALIAN   This upscale Italian restaurant serves creative, Italian-influenced meals daily for lunch and dinner, when it tends to fill with the local business crowd. But that's not what it's famous for in Dublin. San Lorenzo's is one of the most popular spots in town for brunch on weekends. Abandon your hotel buffet, and come here for the heavenly French toast topped with caramelized bananas, Coco Pops (a chocolatey breakfast cereal), whipped cream, and thick chocolate sauce; or opt for the Belgian waffles with salted caramel ice cream. Many of the savory options have a Latin edge: huevos rancheros, brunch tacos, and even a pulled-pork hash. Just be prepared to wait for a table—the locals love this place.

South Great Georges St., Dublin 2. www. sanlorenzos.ie. ℰ **01/478-9383.** Brunch €22–€27, lunch entrees €7–€16, dinner entrees €9–€36. Mon–Fri 11am–3:30pm, 5–10pm; Sat 10am–3:30pm, 5–10pm; Sun 10am–4pm, 5:30–9pm. Bus: 15E, 15F, 16, 16A, 19, 19A, 65, 65B, 65X, 83, 122.

San Lorenzo's popular French toast, topped with a Coco Pops square.

INEXPENSIVE

Leo Burdock's ★ FISH & CHIPS   Proof that not all good food experiences come with a hefty price tag, Leo Burdock's is probably the most famous fish and chip shop in Ireland. In fact, it's virtually *de rigueur* for passing celebrities to pop in; the photographic "wall of fame" includes Sandra Bullock, Russell Crowe, and Tom Cruise. But don't come expecting cutting-edge cuisine, because Leo Burdock's still trades on the same simple, winning formula it has used since 1913: battered fresh fish (cod, sole, ray, or scampi) and thick chips (like very fat steak fries), all cooked the old-fashioned way, in beef drippings. There are other options on the menu, including hamburgers, but frankly, what's the point of coming to a place like this if you don't order the one thing for which it's world-famous?

2 Werburgh St., Dublin 8. www.leoburdock.com. © **01/454-0306.** Entrees €3–€8. Daily noon–midnight. Bus: 49X, 50X, 54A, 50X, 56A, 77, 77A, 77X, 78A, 150, 151.

O'Connell Street Area/North of the Liffey
EXPENSIVE

Chapter One ★★★ MODERN IRISH   The atmospheric vaulted basement of the excellent Dublin Writers Museum (see p. 97) houses one of the city's most feted restaurants, with a fixed-price menu that uses innovative techniques and organic ingredients. Feast on gourmet dishes that fuse diverse ingredients, such as smoked eel with kohlrabi and yogurt, or salt-marsh duck with Madeira and salted grapes. The separate vegetarian menu is small but suitably inventive. Book the chef's table, located in the kitchen, if you want the full experience. The wine list is excellent; consider splurging on a Meerlust Rubicon 2013, an outstanding and little-seen South African vintage with a sublime, smoky flavor.

19 Parnell Sq. North, Dublin 1. www.chapteronerestaurant.com. © **01/873-2266.** Four-course fixed-price dinner menu €80. Tues–Sat 12:30–2pm, 7:30–10pm. Luas: Abbey St. DART: Connolly St. Bus: 1, 2, 14, 14A, 16, 16A, 19, 19A, 33X, 39X, 41X, 48A, 58X, 70B, 70X.

MODERATE

101 Talbot ★★ IRISH/INTERNATIONAL   This cheery and informal spot, a 3-minute walk from the General Post Office on O'Connell Street, is strong on delicious Irish cuisine with global influences and a healthy twist. The bright, airy dining room is lined with modern art. Specials may include seabass with pesto and Parmesan mashed potato, or pheasant with a stuffing of chestnuts and squash. The early-bird menu (two courses €21; 5–7:15pm) is a particularly good deal and popular with pre-theater diners attending the Abbey Theatre just around the corner.

101–102 Talbot St., Dublin 1. www.101talbot.ie. © **01/874-5011.** Entrees €16–€24. Tues–Sat noon–3pm, 5–11pm. Luas: Abbey St. Bus: 20B, 32X, 33X, 41, 41A, 41B, 41C, 42, 42A, 42B, 43, 51A, 130, 142.

Winding Stair ★★ MODERN IRISH   A sweet old bookstore downstairs and a chic restaurant upstairs, Winding Stair is just a stone's throw from the Ha'penny Bridge. The views of the Liffey are romantic, but it's the inventive modern Irish cooking that pulls in the crowds for lunch and dinner. After a starter of Irish chowder with chorizo and treacle bread, you could opt for slow-braised beef with parsnip mash, or sea trout with trout caviar and pickled cucumber. The enormous wine list, which is help-

The Winding Stair, a chic and inventive restaurant above a vintage bookstore.

fully arranged by character rather than region, features several decently priced options. The fixed-price lunch (€22–€27) and the pre-theater menus (€27–€31) are great value for money.

40 Lower Ormond Quay, Dublin 1. www.winding-stair.com. ✆ **01/872-7320.** Entrees €23–€28. Mon–Thurs noon–5pm, 5:30–10:30pm; Fri noon–4pm, 5–10:30pm; Sat–Sun 5:30–10:30pm. Luas: Jervis. Bus: 39B, 51, 51B, 51C, 51D, 51X, 68, 69, 69X, 78, 78A, 79, 79A, 90, 92, 206.

INEXPENSIVE

147 Deli ★★ DELI   Widely viewed as among the best sandwich makers in the city, the team at 147 pride themselves on piling it high and making it fresh. This small place just off O'Connell Street might not look like much from the outside, but sandwich magic is happening behind that counter. It has a few tables at the back where you can sit down with your pulled pork and slaw on sourdough bread, or New York–style Reuben, among many others. If you're feeling ambitious, try your luck with whatever this week's special might be. There are also plentiful vegetarian options and outstanding coffee. Whatever way you go, you're likely to be happy. In the morning you can also get poached eggs, fresh cinnamon buns, and breakfast sandwiches. If you're feeling run-down, try the minidoughnuts—the sugar will save you.

147 Parnell St. Rotunda, Dublin 1. ✆ **01/872-8481.** Sandwiches €10. Mon–Fri 8am–5pm, Sat 10am–5pm. Luas: Abbey St. DART: Connolly St. Bus: 1, 2, 14, 14A, 16, 16A, 19, 19A, 33X, 39X, 41X, 48A, 58X, 70B, 70X.

Smithfield Area

INEXPENSIVE

Fresh ★ INTERNATIONAL   No, you haven't come to the wrong place—this is a supermarket. But step inside and you'll be met with a row of fresh cooking stations serving up delicious street food from around the world. The Mexican stand is popular, but for us the real standout is the incredible pan-Asian station, where a delicious pad Thai or crispy chili chicken can be whipped up in minutes, completely from scratch. Delicious, quality fast food doesn't come much fresher than this. Portion sizes are generous, and you can get a full meal, with nibbles on the side, for well under €20. There are a few tables, or you can get it all to go. It's a great option for lunch or an early, no-fuss dinner—but be aware that the food stations usually wind down by around 7pm.

Smithfield Sq., Dublin 7. © **01/485-0272.** Hot food €4–€13. Mon–Fri 7am–10pm, Sat–Sun 8am–10pm. Luas: Smithfield. Bus: 37, 39, 39A, 70, 83, 83A, 747.

Namaste India ★★ INDIAN   This exceptional takeout has served many a hungry late-night, post-pub customer in this part of Dublin over the years. And while it may look rough-and-ready, the cooking is some of the best Indian food in the city. Everything is prepared in an open kitchen right in front of you—as tantalizing as it is hypnotic—and everything is to-go only. If, alas, your hotel doesn't allow takeout food in the guest rooms, our advice is this: Smuggle! Cheat! Every mouthful will be worth it. Try a classic jalfrezi or Madras, with your choice of meat, prawns, or vegetables, or perhaps a juicy, barbecued chicken tikka, with pilau rice (spiced with cumin and cardamom). Be sure to order a few poppadoms (large pieces of very thin, fried crispbread made from chickpeas) and a naan bread to mop up the thick, perfectly balanced sauces. No frills, no fuss, just deliciously authentic cooking.

88 North King St., Dublin 7. www.namasteindia.ie. © **01/485-0272.** Entrees €7–€12. Mon–Thurs 4pm–1am, Fri 3:30pm–3:30am, Sat 4pm–3:30am, Sun 4pm–1am. Luas: Smithfield. Bus: 37, 39, 39A, 70, 83, 83A, 747.

St. Stephen's Green/Grafton Street Area

EXPENSIVE

Bang ★ MODERN IRISH   The presence of so many Irish place names on the menu indicates how much this place has embraced the Slow Food ethos. Many ingredients are regionally sourced from specialist Irish producers, with local flavors prevailing throughout: You may find Thornhill duck breast served with black garlic; chicken with black pudding and buckwheat; or a tasty filet of roast hake in a brown butter emulsion. The wine list is expertly chosen, and there's a delightful seasonal cocktail menu—if it's on the menu when you're there, try the beehive julep, with spiced whiskey, Manuka honey, and black-walnut bitters.

11 Merrion Row, Dublin 2. www.bangrestaurant.com. © **01/400-4229.** Entrees €22–€33. Lunch Tues–Sat noon–3pm; dinner Mon–Fri 5:30–10pm, Sat 5–11pm, Sun 5–9:30pm. Luas: St. Stephen's Green. Bus: 25X, 51D, 51X, 65X, 66X, 67X, 77X.

INEXPENSIVE

Bewley's ★ CAFE   A Dublin landmark since 1927, Bewley's has a literary pedigree as well as a historic one: James Joyce was a regular (it makes an appearance in his book *Dubliners*), and a host of subsequent literary greats made this their regular stop-off for a cup of joe and a slice of cake. It's still hugely popular, but not just for coffee; you can get a pretty good pizza, salad, or burger here, in addition to a more modest menu of light snacks. ***Fun fact:*** The ornate faux-Egyptian facade (incongruously framing its never-really-used full name, "Bewley's Oriental Café") is a relic of a European craze for all things Ancient Egyptian, following the discovery of Tutankhamen's tomb just 5 years before the cafe opened.

78–79 Grafton St., Dublin 2. www.bewleys.com. © **01/672-7720.** Breakfast €3–€13.50, lunch and dinner entrees €7.50–€11. Mon–Wed and Fri–Sat 8am–8pm, Thurs 8am–9pm, Sun 9am–8pm. Bus: 11, 11A, 11B, 14, 14A, 15A, 15C, 15X, 20B, 27C, 33X, 39B, 41X, 46B, 46C.

Lemon Crepe & Coffee Co. ★★ CAFE   This simple, straightforward eatery on busy Dawson Street serves fresh hot crepes, pancakes, eggs, and sandwiches, all made to order. Walk straight to the bar to order your California omelette, with guacamole and bacon, or Power Crepe, filled with spinach, cheddar, and ham. The cafe serves both sweet crepes (with fillings like fruit, chocolate, and Nutella) and savory crepes (choose from cheese, meats, fish, or veggies), as well as a variety of sandwiches, waffles, and pancakes. Find a seat at one of the long shared tables inside, or, if the weather's fine, sit out front and watch the city go by. It might not be the healthiest meal you have all day, but it will be delicious. The coffee is also excellent here, and the staff are friendly. A second location is on William St. South.

60 Dawson St., Dublin 2. www.lemonco.com. © **01/672-8898.** Entrees €3–€10. Mon–Wed and Fri 7:30am–7:30pm, Thurs 7:30am–8:30pm, Sat 8:30am–7:30pm, Sun 9:30am–6:30pm. Bus: 11, 11A, 11B, 14, 14A, 15A, 15C, 15X, 20B, 27C, 33X, 39B, 41X, 46B, 46C.

Sweet and savory crepes headline the menu at Lemon Crepe & Coffee Co.

Fitzwilliam Square Area

EXPENSIVE

The Sussex ★★ IRISH   One of the best proponents of gastropub cuisine—the reinvention of traditional Irish cooking into something chic and fashionable—is this refined pub (above another popular bar) 10 minutes' walk south of St. Stephen's Green. The menu takes classic pub fare and prepares it beautifully, in dishes like beer-battered fish and chips with pea and mint puree; linguine served with tiger prawns, clams, garlic, and chile; and a delicious house burger topped with cheddar cheese from County Cork. For dessert, try the *posset* (a syllabub-like concoction containing cream and lemon) served with spiced shortbread. As you'd expect, all the ingredients are sourced as locally as possible, with plenty of attention to what's in season. The wine and ale lists are well curated, with lots of reasonably priced options. *Tip:* The lunch menu is an edited version of what's for dinner—but cheaper.

9 Sussex Terrace (at junction of Sussex Rd., above M. O'Briens Pub), Dublin 4. www.thesussex.ie. ℭ **01/676-2851.** Entrees €15–€32. Lunch Mon–Fri from noon, dinner Mon–Sun from 5pm. Bus: 7B, 7D, 11, 11A, 11B, 27C, 39B, 39X, 46B, 46C, 46D, 46E, 58C, 58X, 70B, 70X, 116.

Ballsbridge & the Southern Suburbs

MODERATE

Roly's Bistro ★ BISTRO   This lovely, easygoing bistro, just down the street from the United States Embassy, is one of the best places to eat south of the city center. Local meats and fish predominate; start with some chestnut, mushroom, and rosemary soup with hazelnut cream, or perhaps a Dublin Bay prawn cocktail. For the main event, try the roast Clare Island salmon with wilted greens, or, for a dose of traditional comfort food, a Kerry lamb and vegetable pie. There's also an adjacent cafe. Reservations are recommended for the restaurant.

7 Ballsbridge Terrace, Dublin 4. www.rolysbistro.ie. ℭ **01/668-2611.** Entrees €14–€27. Mon–Fri 7:30am–10:30pm, Sat–Sun 9am–10:30pm. Bus: 4, 7, 8, 18.

North of Dublin

EXPENSIVE

Aqua ★★★ SEAFOOD   With a jaw-dropping view over Dublin Bay, this has to be one of the most romantic dining spots in the region. Service is excellent—attentive without being overbearing—and the seafood is delicious and fresh as can be. You might start with a half-dozen oysters from Connemara in County Galway, before moving on to Bere Island scallops with carrot puttee, or a dish of pasta with salmon, smoked coley, and mussels in a saffron cream sauce. It's not cheap, but it's reliably good. Howth is a small commuter suburb of Dublin, about 16km (10 miles) northeast of the city center. The restaurant is a 10-minute walk from the

Waterside dining at Aqua Restaurant.

Howth DART station, while a cab here from the city should run you about
€30. Definitely worth the splurge.

1 West Pier, Howth, Co. Dublin. www.aqua.ie. ✆ **01/832-0690.** Entrees €26–€45.
Lunch Tues–Sat 12:30–5:30pm, Sun noon–5pm; dinner Tues–Sat 5:30–9:30pm, Sun
6–8:30pm. DART: Howth. Bus: 31.

South of Dublin

MODERATE

The Merry Ploughboy ★ IRISH/PUB   An exuberant live show of
traditional music and dancing accompanies dinner at this hugely popular
pub in Rathfarnham, one of Dublin's farther-flung southern suburbs. Admit-
tedly it's all very touristy, but you certainly get your money's worth—the
show runs for 2 hours, and the menu, while limited, is actually pretty good.
Expect plates of beef braised in Guinness and served with roasted root vegetables, or scampi cooked in tempura batter, served with chips (thick fries).
The only real drawback is the time it takes to get here (Rathfarnham is about
6km/3¾ miles from the city center), although a dedicated minibus will
deliver you there and back to the city for a bargain round-trip price of €9.

Edmondstown Rd., Rockbrook, Rathfarnham, Dublin 16. www.mpbpub.com. ✆ **01/
493-1495.** Dinner and show €50. Bar menu €5–€22. Daily dinner arrive 6:30–7pm,
show 8–10pm. Bar food: Mon–Sat 12:30–9:30pm, Sun 12:30–8pm. Special bus serves
six locations in central Dublin (€9 per person; must be prebooked).

SHOPPING

There's no question, Dublin is a fantastic city for shopping. Independent
shops and boutiques line up alongside their chain-store rivals, and you can
often find excellent craftsmanship in the form of hand-woven wool

blankets and clothes, high-quality crafts and antiques, and chic fashions from the seemingly limitless line of Dublin designers.

The hub of mainstream shopping south of the Liffey is indisputably **Grafton Street,** with its mix of big chains, chi-chi department stores, and little shops. It's also a popular site for street performers, where you're almost guaranteed an impromptu show, rain or shine. Grafton Street is crowned by the city's most fashionable department store, Brown Thomas (known as BT; see p. 155), and the jeweler Weir & Sons (p. 158), but much better shopping is on the smaller streets radiating out from Grafton, such as **Duke, Dawson, Nassau,** and **Wicklow** streets, where you'll find shops that specialize in books, handicrafts, jewelry, gifts, and clothing. For clothes, look out for tiny **Cow's Lane,** off Lord Edward Street—it's popular with those in the know for its excellent boutiques selling the works of local designers. Also in Grafton's penumbra are **William Street South, Castle Market,** and **Drury Street,** all of which have smart boutiques and irresistible tiny shops. On William Street South, check out the **Powerscourt Townhouse Centre,** a small, elegant shopping center in a grand Georgian town house (see p. 154). Not far away, the **George's Street Arcade** is a marvelous clutter of bohemian jewelry, used books, vintage clothes, and other things appealing to the alternative crowd (they even have a resident fortune-teller).

HOURS   Generally, Dublin shops are open from 9am to 6pm Monday to Saturday and until 9pm on Thursday. Most shops have Sunday hours, although these vary; some open at 9am, but most are open 11am to 6 or 7pm.

SHOPPING MALLS   Dublin has several clusters of shops in **multistory malls** or ground-level **arcades,** ideal for indoor shopping on rainy days. On the Northside, these include the **ILAC Centre,** off Henry Street (www. ilac.ie; ✆ **01/828-8900**), and the **Jervis Shopping Centre** (www.jervis.ie; ✆ **01/878-1323**), at 125 Abbey Street. On the south side, there's the small **Royal Hibernian Way,** 49–50 Dawson Street (✆ **01/679-5919**); the gleaming wrought-iron-and-glass **St. Stephen's Green Centre** at the top of Grafton Street (www.stephensgreen.com; ✆ **01/478-0888**); and the **Powerscourt Townhouse Centre,** 59 William Street South (www.powerscourt centre.com; ✆ **01/679-4144**). In the southern suburbs, about 8km (5 miles) south of the city center, the large **Dundrum Town Centre** on Sandyford Road (www.dundrum.ie; ✆ **01/229-1700**) has several major fashion outlets.

Grafton Street bustles with shoppers and passersby.

Art & Antiques

Caxton ★★   Antique prints from the 16th, 17th, and 18th centuries are a specialty of this wonderful art store. (In 2012, someone even identified a lost Renaissance masterpiece among the stock.) The prices can be astronomical, but even if you're not buying, for lovers of the antiquarian browsing here is like being a kid in a candy store. 63 Patrick St., Dublin 8. ✆ **01/453-0060.** Bus: 49, 54A.

Christy Bird ★   Variety is our specialty proclaims a sign at this appealing antique store, which has been in business since the 1940s. And it certainly lives up to the promise, stocked with a happy jumble of knick-knacks, collectibles, tat, and genuine antiques. The joy is that you never quite know what you're going to find. 32 South Richmond St., Dublin 2. www.christybird.com. ✆ **01/475-4049.** Luas: Charlemount, Harcourt St. Bus: 14, 14A, 14B, 15, 15B, 65B, 74, 83, 128.

Danker Antiques ★★   This friendly, approachable dealer, in an arcade just off Dawson Street, has a fine collection of antique silver tableware and jewelry. It specializes in designs from the Celtic Revival period of the early 20th century, and usually has some beautiful Art Deco pieces as well. 10 Duke St., 1st Floor, Dublin 2. www.dankerantiques.com. ✆ **01/677/4009.** Luas: Dawson St. Bus: 7b, 7d, 11, 37, 38, 38a, 38b, 38d, 39, 39a, 39x, 44, 46a, 46e, 61, 70, 84x, 116, 118, 145, 722.

The Doorway Gallery ★★★   Both new and established Irish artists display their work at this cheerful art gallery. There's always something wonderful to discover, and many prices are affordable, too. 24 S. Frederick St., Dublin 2. www.thedoorwaygallery.com. ✆ **01/764-5895.** Bus: 4, 7, 8, 7B, 7D, 25, 25A, 25B, 25X, 26, 27X, 46A, 66, 66A, 66A, 66B, 66X, 67, 67X, 120, 145.

Green on Red ★★   Outstanding contemporary art can be found at this little gallery in the docklands, about a mile northwest of the city center. It holds a dozen or so exhibitions per year. Park Lane, Spencer Dock, Dublin 1. www.greenonredgallery.com. ✆ **087/245-4282.** Rail: Docklands. Luas: Spencer Dock. Bus: 151.

Books & Stationery

Eason ★   There are outlets of this popular book chain all over Ireland, but this multi-story shop on O'Connell Street is one of Ireland's oldest, having been in business since 1819. Pretty much everything you could want is here, from history and local-interest titles to the latest bestsellers. Dublin has 15 other Eason branches, including ones at Nassau Street and Heuston Station. 40 Lower O'Connell St. www.easons.com. ✆ **01/858-3800.** Luas: Abbey St. Bus: 1, 11, 38, 38A, 38B, 39N, 88N, 120, 122, 123, 747.

Hodges Figgis ★   Another enormous *grande dame* Dublin bookshop, this one's even older than Eason—they've been dealing in the printed page here since 1768. Now owned by the Waterstones chain, Hodges Figgis one of the go-to places in the city for books of all kinds. 56–58 Dawson St., Dublin 2. www.waterstones.com/bookshops/hodges-figgis. ✆ **01/677-4754.** Bus: 15A, 15B, 44, 61, 140.

The Pen Corner ★★★   Keeping the flame alive for the dying art of letter writing, this place is an utter delight. The Pen Corner sells exquisite fountain pens, paper, and other writing implements, and also stocks beautiful notebooks and cards. 12 College Green, Dublin 2. ℂ **01/679-3641.** Luas: Abbey St. Bus: 9, 13, 16, 16C, 19, 49N, 54A, 83, 83A, 122, 123, 150, 747, 869.

Ulysses Rare Books ★★   When lovers of Irish literature and antiquarian books die, if they've been good, they get to spend eternity in this shop. Formerly called Cattach Books, this is where to come for rare copies of Joyce, Yeats, Wilde, Behan, Stoker, and just about every luminary of the Irish canon you can think of. Prices range from the barely affordable (€375 for a rare 1927 *Dracula*) to the stratospheric (€35,000 for a first-edition *Ulysses*), but it's simply heaven to browse. 10 Duke St. (off Grafton St.), Dublin 2. www.rarebooks.ie. ℂ **01/671-8676.** DART: Pearse. Bus: 10, 11A, 11B, 13, 20B.

CDs & Music

Claddagh Records ★★★   Renowned among insiders in traditional Irish music circles, this is where to find "the genuine article" in traditional music and perhaps discover a new favorite. Not only is the staff knowledgeable and enthusiastic about new artists, but they're also able to tell you which venues and pubs are hosting the best music sessions that week. 2 Cecilia St., Dublin 2. www.claddaghrecords.com. ℂ **01/677-0262.** Luas: Jervis. Bus: All An Lar (cross-city) buses.

Waltons ★★   A longtime favorite among Dublin's musically inclined (of which you may have noticed there are many), Waltons has been in business since the 1920s. Its excellent stock of Irish folk instruments includes pennywhistles, flutes, accordions, and pipes. It also has a huge range of traditional Irish music CDs, books, and T-shirts. 69 South Great George's St., Dublin 2. www.waltons.ie. ℂ **01/475-0661.** Bus: 15E, 15F, 16, 16A, 19, 19A, 65, 65B, 65X, 83, 122.

Crafts, Design & Housewares

Avoca Handweavers ★★★   A Dublin institution, Avoca is a wonderland of vivid colors, intricately woven fabrics, soft blankets, light woolen sweaters, children's clothes, and toys, all in a delightful shopping environment spread over three floors near Trinity College. All the fabrics are woven in the Vale of Avoca in the Wicklow Mountains (see p. 198). The store also sells pottery, jewelry, vintage and antique clothing, food, and adorable little things you really don't need, but can't live without. Hands down, this is one of the best stores in Dublin. The top-floor **cafe** is a great place for lunch (see p. 143). 11–13 Suffolk St., Dublin 2. www.avoca.ie. ℂ **01/677-4215.** Bus: All An Lar (cross-city) buses.

The Design Tower ★★   A cutting-edge convocation of hot designers and craftspeople work at this former sugar refinery at the Grand Canal Quay on the eastern side of the city. Occupants include Seamus Gill, who makes extraordinary, almost organic-seeming silverware; conceptual artist and fashion designer Roisin Gartland; and jewelry designer Brenda Haugh, whose

work includes interesting modern interpretations of Celtic motifs. Some designers here have walk-in shops, but most prefer appointments, so call ahead if you want to see someone specific. The Design Tower is near the Grand Canal Dock DART station, or about a 20-minute walk from Grafton Street. Trinity Centre, Pearse St. and Grand Canal Quay, Dublin 2. www.thedesigntower.com. ℃ **01/677-5655.** DART: Grand Canal Dock. Bus: 1, 2, 3, 50, 56A, 77A.

Powerscourt Townhouse Centre.

House of Ireland ★ An excellent "one-stop shop" for quality Irish souvenirs, this is the place to come for Waterford and Galway crystal, Belleek china, soft wool knits, linens, and clothing by big-name Irish designers such as Eugene and Anke McKernan, John Rocha, and Louise Kennedy. It's touristy, yes, but filled with wonderful, Irish-made items. If you've left your souvenir shopping until the last minute, two smaller outlet branches are at Dublin Airport. 37–38 Nassau St., Dublin 2. www.houseofireland.com. ℃ **01/671-1111.** Bus: 15X, 25X, 32X, 33X, 39X, 41X, 51D, 51X, 58X, 67X, 70X, 84X, 92.

Mayfly ★★★ This Temple Bar charmer (look for the cow in the buggy out front) is a treasure trove for deliciously creative, artsy gifts, jewelry, clothing, and other doodads that are impossible to resist. Artists whose work is for sale include Courtney Tyler, who turns old watch faces into interesting jewelry, and James Carroll, a designer of furniture and home-wares known for his unusual and playful creations. 11 Fownes St. Upper, Dublin 2. www.mayfly.ie. ℃ **086/376-4189.** Bus: 39B, 49X, 50X, 65X, 77X.

Moss Cottage ★★★ A real one-of-a-kind craft store, Moss Cottage is the kind of place where you go in for a browse and leave with bags full of souvenirs and a mental note to e-mail the lovely owner photos of all your finds *in situ* back home. It specializes in "upcycling"—converting old junk into beautiful things—and stocks everything from scented candles to vintage homewares. The shop is in the suburb of Dundrum, about 7km (4½ miles) south of the city center. 4 Pembroke Cottages, Main St., Dundrum, Dublin 14. www.mosscottage.ie. ℃ **01/215-7696.** Luas: Dundrum. Bus: 14, 14C, 44, 44B.

Powerscourt Townhouse Centre ★★ In a restored 1774 town house, this four-story complex consists of a central sky-lit courtyard and more than 60 boutiques, craft shops, art galleries, snack bars, wine bars, and restaurants. The wares include all kinds of crafts, antiques, paintings, prints, ceramics, leatherwork, jewelry, clothing, chocolates, and farmhouse cheeses. You can also book a behind-the-scenes tour to learn more about the house's history, where you'll poke around the old kitchen and cellars, the former Lord and Lady's bedrooms and dressing rooms, the music room, ballroom, and dining room. For details and booking, contact Shireen Gail at © **086/806-5505** or e-mail shireengail@gmail.com. 59 S. William St., Dublin 2. www.powerscourtcentre.com. © **01/679-4144.** DART: Pearse. Luas: St. Stephen's Green. Bus: 11, 11A, 11B, 14, 14A, 15A, 15C, 15X, 20B, 27C, 32X, 33X, 39B, 39X, 41X, 46B, 46C, 46N, 46X, 51X, 58X, 65X, 70X, 84X.

Department Stores

Arnotts ★★ Ireland's original department store, Arnotts first opened its illustrious doors in 1843. Its selection of womenswear, menswear, gifts, and beauty products is enormous. Weary shoppers will also be delighted to find a branch of that most famous of Dublin coffeehouses, Bewley's, next to the Abbey Street entrance on the lower ground floor. Arnotts stays open for late shopping until 9pm on Thursdays and 8pm on Fridays. Henry St., Dublin 1. www.arnotts.ie. © **01/805-0400.** Luas: Abbey St. Bus: 1, 7, 7B, 7D, 8, 11, 38, 38A, 38B, 39N, 40, 88N, 120, 122, 123, 747.

Brown Thomas ★★★ The top-hatted doorman out front sets the tone for this great old Dublin institution filled with designer clothes and accessories. We've always found this a relaxed and friendly place, even if the credit card takes a bit of a beating. Stop by for most of the major fashion labels before getting your nails done, having a one-to-one at the cosmetics counters, or indulging at the bar and cafe or the elegant restaurant. 88–95 Grafton St., Dublin 2. www.brownthomas.com. © **01/605-6666.** Luas: St. Stephen's Green. Bus: 11, 11A, 11B, 14, 14A, 15A, 15C, 15X, 20B, 27C, 32X, 33X, 39B, 39X, 41X, 46B, 46C, 51X, 58X, 70X, 84X.

Harvey Nichols ★ The only Irish outpost of the famous British department-store chain, "Harvey Nicks" is as renowned for its outstanding food court as it is for its high-end fashion and beauty. There's also a good steakhouse and trendy cocktail bar. Harvey Nichols is in the Dundrum Town Centre mall, 8km (5 miles) south of Dublin city center. It has late-night shopping until 9pm Wednesday to Friday. Dundrum Town Centre, Sandyford Rd., Dundrum, Dublin 16. www.harveynichols.com. © **01/291-0488.** Luas: Dundrum. Bus: 14, 14a, 17, 44, 48, 48N, 75.

Fashion & Clothing

Alias Tom ★★ This has long been one of Dublin's top boutique clothing stores. Alias Tom made its name in menswear, but now sells designer fashions (mostly Italian) for women, too. Prices tend to be high, but so does the quality. Duke Lane, Grafton St., Dublin 2. www.aliastom.com. © **01/671-5443** (menswear); © **01/677-8842** (womenswear). Bus: 15A, 15B, 44, 61, 100X, 101X, 111, 133, 140.

BT2 ★ A cutting-edge spin-off from the department store Brown Thomas (see p. 151), BT2 sells youthful designer fashions for men and women. It also has the biggest denim bar in Ireland, full of hip brand names such as Supertrash and Seven For All Mankind. BT2 has another branch in the Dundrum Town Centre mall (see p. 151). 28–29 Grafton St., Dublin 2. www.bt2.ie. © **01/605-6747.** DART: Pearse. Bus: 10, 11A, 11B, 13, 20B.

China Blue ★ Shelves upon shelves of women's and men's footwear can be found at this trendy shoe store—including an enticing range of designer Doc Martens. It also carries a good selection of kids' shoes. Merchants Arch, Temple Bar, Dublin 2. www.chinablueshoes.com. ✆ **01/671-8785.** Bus: 25, 25A, 25B, 25N, 37, 39A, 51D, 67N, 69, 69X, 70, 70N, 79, 79A.

Costelloe & Costelloe ★ This sweet clothing and accessories store sells a great range of handbags, pashminas, shrugs, and—delightfully—colorful fascinators and headpieces. Best of all, prices are thoroughly reasonable. 14A Chatham St., Temple Bar, Dublin 2. https://costelloeandcostelloe. com. ✆ **01/671-4209.** DART: Tara St. Bus: 15A, 15B, 44, 61, 140.

Design Centre ★★★ Located in the Powerscourt Townhouse Centre (see p. 154), this is a great showcase for Irish fashion designers, both new and established. A lot of what's on offer is unsurprisingly expensive, but you can sometimes walk away with a bargain. Powerscourt Townhouse Centre, Dublin 2. www.designcentre.ie. ✆ **01/679-5863** or 679-5718. DART: Pearse. Luas: St. Stephen's Green. Bus: 11, 11A, 11B, 14, 14A, 15A, 15C, 15X, 20B, 27C, 32X, 33X, 39B, 39X, 41X, 46B, 46C, 46N, 46X, 51X, 58X, 65X, 70X, 84X.

Kevin & Howlin ★ There's nothing cutting-edge whatsoever about this place—and that's just why people like it. Dublin's go-to store for Donegal tweed, it's been selling hand-woven jackets, coats, hats, and other traditional Irish countrywear since 1936. 31 Nassau St., Dublin 2. www. kevinandhowlin.com. ✆ **01/633-4576.** DART: Pearse. Bus: 7B, 7D, 25, 25A, 25B, 25X, 26, 46A, 66, 66A, 66B, 66X, 67, 67X, 145.

Louise Kennedy ★★★ Undoubtedly one of the biggest names in contemporary Irish fashion—so respected that she was put on a postage stamp a few years ago—Louise Kennedy has dressed everyone from heads of state to Hollywood superstars. Her boutique in Merrion Square showcases the best of her current collection. Among the items she's famous for is the gorgeous "Kennedy bag," a limited-edition handbag that is a must-have among the Irish *glitterati*—yours for a mere €1,500. 56 Merrion Sq., Dublin 2. www.louise kennedy.com. ✆ **01/662-0056.** DART: Pearse. Bus: 25, 25A, 25B, 26, 66, 66A, 66B, 67.

Om Diva ★★★ Proof that not every designer emporium has to be the kind of place where they check your credit rating at the door, Om Diva is a delightful, cheery shop, with a great selection of designer women's fashion, handmade jewelry, vintage clothes, and accessories. One of Dublin's real finds. 27 Drury St., Dublin 2. www.omdivaboutique.com. ✆ **01/679-1211.** Bus: 9, 16, 16A, 83.

Gourmet Food

Butlers Chocolate Café ★★ These chocolatiers now sell their delicious wares all over the world, but the business is still owned and run by the same Dublin family who founded it in 1932. Their Chocolate Cafés are all over Dublin, including Grafton Street, Henry Street, and the airport, but the one on Wicklow Street is the flagship. In addition to an enormous selection of gourmet chocolates, it sells cakes, cookies,

STEP away FROM THE LEPRECHAUN: THREE ALTERNATIVE DUBLIN SOUVENIRS

Sure, you can stop by any of the multitude of souvenir stores in Dublin for a keychain shaped like a shamrock, or a T-shirt with an "amusing" slogan ("Irish I were drunk!" "Fifty Shades of Green!"). But unless your friends really *do* want a hat shaped like a pint of Guinness, you'll score better points back home with one of these more authentic mementos.

○ **A pennywhistle.** At Waltons (see p. 153), which has been in the music business since the 1920s, you'll find instruments both traditional and modern, ranging from an authentic bodhrán (drum) for about €50, to an "absolute beginners" Dublin tin whistle set, complete with DVD tutorial and songbook, for €17.

○ **Flapjacks.** If you ask for a flapjack in Ireland, you won't get a pancake, but a sweet biscuit (cookie to North Americans) made from rolled oats, butter, brown sugar, and honey, often with fruit, nuts, or yogurt added. These traditional treats can be bought in boxes at food stores, or grab one in a coffee shop for a euro or two. They stay fresh for a few days, and are sturdy enough to survive the trip home.

○ **Hedgerow jam.** Known for its soft-as-silk hand-woven wool items, Avoca Handweavers (see p. 153) offers more than just lovely clothing. You can also pick up a jar of their traditional Irish breakfast marmalade or the delightfully named hedgerow jam—each an Avoca specialty costing €5. (Meanwhile, buy yourself a luxurious Avoca blanket, dyed with traditional methods in vibrant shades of blue, green, or pink—a relative bargain, given their quality, starting at around €50.)

flapjacks—and a mean cup of joe. The hot chocolate is spectacular; try the white chocolate version for the purest hit of sweet choccy joy. True addicts can take a tour of the Butlers factory, just north of Dublin (see p. 156). 24 Wicklow St., Dublin 2. www.butlerschocolates.com. ✆ **01/671-0591.** Bus: 9, 16, 49N, 54A, 65, 65B, 68, 68A, 83, 83A, 100X, 101X, 109, 111, 122, 133, 150.

Fallon & Byrne Food Hall ★★★   This exceptional artisan food and wine store is like a high-end deli crossed with an old-fashioned grocer's—albeit a posh modern version. Produce is laid out in open crates, and shelves are stocked with epicurean treats of all kinds, including cheese, charcuterie, and a great selection of wine. There's also an outstanding restaurant on the top floor (see p. 144). 11–17 Exchequer St., Dublin 2. www.fallonandbyrne.com. ✆ **01/472-1010.** Bus: 9, 16, 16C, 49N, 65, 65B, 68, 68A, 83, 83A, 122, 150.

Sheridans Cheesemongers ★★★   Serious cheese lovers need look no further than this wonderful cheesemonger on South Anne Street. They stock around 100 different varieties of cheese—French, English, Italian, you name it—but traditional Irish varieties are their particular specialty. They also sell other deli items, such as wine and cold meats, and do sandwiches to go. 11 South Anne St., Dublin 2. www.sheridanscheesemongers.com. ✆ **01/679-3143.** Bus: 15A, 15B, 44, 61, 140.

TEMPLE BAR street markets

On weekends, chic Temple Bar shopping isn't only indoors—it spills outside into three of Dublin's finest street markets.

The most glamorous of the three is the **Designer Mart,** a showcase for fashion designers and craftspeople from all over Ireland, which takes place in uber-trendy Cow's Lane every Saturday from 10am until 5pm. The more low-key **Book Market** takes up residence in Temple Bar Square all weekend, from 11am to 6pm; there's always some piece of printed treasure or other to be unearthed among its secondhand book stalls.

A must for foodies, the **Food Market** makes its presence felt most of all, as tempting aromas waft around Meeting House Square (outside Filmbase; see p. 105) from 10am to 5pm on Saturday. Should the weather take a turn for the worse, a fancy retractable roof will keep you dry while you deliberate over which Irish farmhouse cheese to take away, before waiting in line for a freshly cooked snack.

For details on the Temple Bar street markets, check out **www.templebar.ie**.

Jewelry

DESIGNyard ★★★   Some of Ireland's leading designers of contemporary jewelry have creations for sale here. Prices tend to be quite high—the cheapest items are around €100 and rise to thousands—but you'll be walking away with something beautiful and unique. They carry an especially beautiful range of engagement rings. 25 S. Frederick St., Dublin 2. www. designyard.ie. *©* **01/474-1011.** DART: Pearse. Bus: 7B, 7D, 25, 25A, 25B, 25X, 26, 46A, 66, 66A, 66B, 66X, 67, 67X, 145.

Gollum's Precious ★   Come here for classic vintage and designer jewelry—especially French—with a particularly good collection of contemporary pearl earrings, bracelets, and necklaces. Ground floor, Powerscourt Centre, Dublin 2. www.gollumspreciouspowerscourt.yolasite.com. *©* **01/670-5400.** DART: Pearse. Luas: St. Stephen's Green. Bus: 11, 11A, 11B, 14, 14A, 15A, 15C, 15X, 20B, 27C, 32X, 33X, 39B, 39X, 41X, 46B, 46C, 46N, 46X, 51X, 58X, 65X, 70X, 84X.

Rhinestones ★   This small but delightful jewelry store specializes in costume jewelry, contemporary and vintage. The antique pieces go back to the early Victorian age, but the mid-20th-century collection has a particular air of glamour. 18 St. Andrews St., Dublin 2. *©* **01/679-0759.** Bus: 9, 13, 16, 16C, 49N, 54A, 83, 83A, 100X, 101X, 109, 111, 122, 123, 133, 150, 747, 869.

Weir & Sons ★★   Established in 1869, this is the granddaddy of Dublin's fine-jewelry shops. It sells new and antique jewelry, as well as silver, china, and crystal. The ground floor of the main branch on Grafton Street also has a section devoted to 17th-, 18th-, and 19th-century antique silver from Ireland and Britain. A second branch can be found in Dundrum, about 7km (4⅓ miles) south of the city center. 96–99 Grafton St. and 1–3 Wicklow St., Dublin 2. www.weirandsons.ie. *©* **01/677-9678.** Bus: 15X, 32X, 33X, 39X, 41X, 51X, 58X, 70X, 84X.

Specialist

Forbidden Planet ★ Geeks, assemble! This treasure trove of comics, books, DVDs, and other assorted memorabilia celebrates everything cult. The range of comics and graphic novels is enormous. 5–6 Crampton Quay, Dublin 2. www.forbiddenplanet.co.uk. ℭ **01/671-0688.** Luas: Jervis. Bus: 25, 25A, 25B, 25N, 37, 39, 39A, 51D, 67N, 69, 69X, 70, 70N, 79, 79A.

The R.A.G.E. ★★ Imagine the kind of shop where 1980s teenagers hung out in John Hughes movies, and you've got this place about right. It stands for Record Art Game Emporium, and everything here is vintage—plenty of classic vinyl (all of which can be sampled first). You can even play some of the old video games on an original arcade machine. 16B Fade St., Dublin 2. www.therage.ie. ℭ **01/677-9594.** Bus: 9, 16, 49N, 65, 65B, 68, 68A, 83, 83A, 122.

SPORTS & OUTDOOR PURSUITS

BEACHES Plenty of fine beaches are accessible by city bus or DART, which follows the coast from Howth, north of the city, to Bray, south of the city in County Wicklow. Some popular beaches include **Dollymount,** 5km (3 miles) away; **Sutton,** 11km (6¾ miles) away; **Howth,** 15km (9⅓ miles) away; and **Portmarnock** and **Malahide,** each 11km (6¾ miles) away. The southern commuter town of **Dún Laoghaire** (pronounced Dun *Lear*-y), 11km (6¾ miles) away, makes a particularly good day trip. Not only does it offer a beach (at Sandycove) and water sports, but it also has a long bayfront promenade, plenty of interesting shops, and a bucolic park to wander around in. For more details, inquire at the Dublin Tourism office.

GOLF Dublin is one of the world's great golfing capitals, with a quarter of Ireland's courses—including 5 of the top 10—within an hour's drive of the city. Visitors are welcome, but phone ahead and make a reservation. The following four courses—two parkland and two links—are among the best 18-hole courses in the Dublin area.

Elm Park Golf & Sports Club ★, Nutley Lane, Donnybrook, Dublin 4 (www.elmparkgolfclub.ie; ℭ **01/269-3438**), is a beautifully manicured par-69 course in the residential, privileged south side of Dublin, only 6km (3¾ miles) from

Sailing at Dún Laoghaire.

the birds of BULL

With a wealth of estuaries, salt marshes, sandflats, and islands, Dublin Bay provides a varied habitat for a number of bird species, making it surprisingly rewarding for bird-watching expeditions. Your all-around best bet lies just north of Dublin city harbor, in the suburb of Clontarf: a bird sanctuary called **Bull Island,** also known as the North Bull.

Bull Island isn't an island at all, but a 3km (2-mile) spit of marshland connected to the mainland by a bridge. It was inadvertently created early in the 19th century by Captain William Bligh, of *Mutiny on the Bounty* fame. As head of the Port and Docks Board, Bligh ordered the construction of a harbor wall at the

mouth of the River Liffey, in an effort to stop the bay from silting up. In fairly short order the shifting sands created this small landmass, a unique beachscape of dunes, salt marsh, and extensive intertidal flats that attracts thousands of seabirds.

Hundreds of species have been recorded on Bull Island, and some 40,000 birds regularly shelter and nest. In winter, they are joined by tens of thousands of migrants from the Arctic Circle, along with North American spoonbills, little egrets, and sandpipers. Together, they all make a deafening racket. A visitor center is open daily 10am to 4:30pm; admission is free.

the city center. Greens fees are €80. Nonmembers are not allowed after midday on weekends.

The respected links course at **Portmarnock Golf Club ★**, in Portmarnock (www.portmarnockgolfclub.ie; ℂ **01/846-2968**), lies about 16km (10 miles) from the city center on Dublin's Northside, on a spit of land between the Irish Sea and a tidal inlet. Opened in 1894, this par-72 championship course has over the years hosted many leading tournaments, including the Dunlop Masters (1959, 1965), Canada Cup (1960), Alcan (1970), St. Andrews Trophy (1968), and many an Irish Open. You won't be surprised, then, to discover that fees are a bit pricey. Greens fees are around €225 weekdays (€145 Nov–Mar), €250 weekends. The price includes lunch.

Often compared to Scotland's St. Andrews, the century-old **Royal Dublin Golf Club ★**, Bull Island, Dollymount, Dublin 3 (www.theroyal dublingolfclub.com; ℂ **01/833-6346**), is a par-73 championship seaside links on an island in Dublin Bay, 4.8km (3 miles) northeast of the city center. Like Portmarnock, it has been rated among the world's top courses and has played host to several Irish Opens. The home base of Ireland's legendary champion Christy O'Connor, Sr., the Royal Dublin is well known for its fine bunkers, close lies, and subtle trappings. Greens fees are €150 Monday to Thursday and €175 Friday to Saturday (€80–€90 Nov–March); a second round may be played at half-price if space is available. Before 8:30am and after 4:30pm green fees are €95 Monday to Thursday and €105 Friday to Saturday.

St. Margaret's Golf & Country Club ★ in Skephubble, St. Margaret's (www.stmargaretsgolf.com; ℂ **01/864-0400**), is a stunning, par-72 parkland course 4.8km (3 miles) west of Dublin Airport. Greens fees are around €25 Monday to Thursday; €30 Friday; €45 Saturday to Sunday, or slightly less in winter.

HORSEBACK RIDING For trail riding through Phoenix Park, **Ashtown Riding Stables** (www.ashtownstables.com; ✆ **01/838-3807**) is ideal. It's in the village of Ashtown, adjoining the park and only 10 minutes by car or bus (no. 37, 38, 39, 70, or 120) from the city center. You can also get there by train from Dublin Connolly station in less than 15 minutes; Ashtown station is directly opposite the stables.

WATERSPORTS Certified level 1 and level 2 instruction and equipment rental for three watersports—kayaking, sailing, and windsurfing—are available at the **Surfdock Centre,** Grand Canal Dock Yard, Ringsend, Dublin 4 (www.surfdock.ie; ✆ **01/668-3945**). The center has 17 hectares (42 acres) of enclosed fresh water for its courses.

SPECTATOR SPORTS

GAELIC SPORTS If your schedule permits, try to get to a **Gaelic football** or **hurling** match—the only indigenously Irish games and two of the fastest-moving sports around. Gaelic football is vaguely a cross between soccer and American football; you can move the ball with either your hands or feet. **Hurling** is a lightning-speed game in which 30 men use heavy sticks to fling a hard leather ball called a *sliotar*—think field hockey meets lacrosse. Both amateur sports are played every weekend throughout the summer at local fields, culminating in September with the **All-Ireland Finals,** the Irish version of the Super Bowl. For schedules and admission fees, phone the **Gaelic Athletic Association,** Croke Park, Jones Road (www.gaa.ie; ✆ **01/836-3222**).

RUGBY & SOCCER The **Aviva Stadium,** 62 Lansdowne Road (www.avivastadium.ie; ✆ **01/238-2300**), is, depending on your perspective, either a gleaming modern monument to Irish sports or one of Dublin's biggest eyesores. Either way, you really can't miss it. This is the official home of both the national rugby and football (soccer) teams.

GREYHOUND RACING Races are held throughout the year at **Shelbourne Park Greyhound Stadium,** South Lotts Road, and **Harold's Cross Stadium,** 151 Harold's Cross Road. Both can be contacted via the **Irish Greyhound Board** (www.igb.ie) or call ✆ **1890/269-269.**

HORSE RACING The closest racecourse to the city center is the **Leopardstown Race Course,** off the Stillorgan road (N11), Foxrock (www.leopardstown.com; ✆ **01/289-0500**). This modern facility with all-weather, glass-enclosed spectator stands is 9.7km (6 miles) south of the city center. Racing meets—mainly steeplechases, but also a few flats—are scheduled throughout the year, two or three times a month.

DUBLIN AFTER DARK

Nightlife in Dublin is a mixed bag of traditional old pubs, where the likes of Joyce and Behan once imbibed and where Irish music is often reeling away, and cool modern bars, where the hottest new international sounds fill the air and the crowd knows more about Prada than the Pogues. There's little in the way of crossover, although there are a couple of quieter bars and a few with an alternative angle.

WHAT'S ON   Aside from the eternal elderly pubs, things change rapidly in the world of Dublin nightlife, so pick up a copy of local listings magazines, such as *Totally Dublin* (p. 86) if you're looking for the very latest in the club scene. The tourism website **www.ireland.com** offers a "what's on" daily guide to cinema, theater, music, and whatever else you're up for—click "Destinations" and "Dublin City" from the front page, then follow the "Things to Do" link. You can search by type of experience or view complete events listings by date. The **Dublin Events Guide,** at **www.dublinevents.com**, also provides a comprehensive listing of the week's entertainment possibilities.

TICKETS   As with any big city, ticket prices for shows vary considerably, from around €5 to over €100. Advance bookings for most large concerts, major plays, and so forth can be made through **Ticketmaster Ireland** (www.ticketmaster.ie; ℰ **81/871-9300** or 353/818-719-300 internationally, including Northern Ireland). The best way to arrange tickets is online or by phone, but if you prefer to speak to a human being in person, you can also drop by one of the small Ticket Centres—central Dublin locations are at **Ticketron,** Jervis Shopping Centre, Jervis Street, and St. Stephen's Green Shopping Centre, St. Stephen's Green; **FAI Umbro Store,** the Football Association of Ireland, 15 Westmoreland St.; and the Pavillion at **The Hub,** Dublin City University, Glasnevin.

Arenas & Concert Venues

3Arena ★   This enormous indoor arena (previously known as **the O2**) is the biggest venue in Dublin, and the fifth-best attended in the world at this writing. It's the go-to place for major international acts, standup comedy, and other big-ticket entertainment events—all top-of-the-bill stuff. North Wall Quay, Dublin 1. www.3arena.ie. Box office: ℰ **081/871-9300;** Inquiries: ℰ **01/819-8888.** Luas: The Point. Bus: 151.

National Concert Hall ★★   If classical music is more your thing, this is the place to come. The program also covers opera, world music, jazz, show tunes, and musicals. Something is on virtually every night; check the website for full listings. Earlsfort Terrace, Dublin 2. www.nch.ie. ℰ **01/417-0000.** Luas: Harcourt. Bus: 100X, 101, 101X, 109, 111, 126, 133.

Vicar Street ★★   This much-loved venue is definitely not Dublin's largest—its capacity is roughly ¹⁄₁₄th that of the 3Arena (see above)—but it attracts consistently big names in music and standup comedy. 58–59 Thomas St., Dublin 8. www.vicarstreet.ie. ℰ **01/775-5800.** Bus: 13, 25N, 40, 69N, 123.

Bars

Dublin bars generally open at noon and may stay open as late as 2:30am, depending on the day of the week.

37 Dawson Street ★★ This sumptuous cocktail bar is crammed with antiques and curios—everything from a stuffed bull's head on a polished wood wall to old anatomical drawings and ornate vases. Its cocktail list is as extensive and imaginative as the quirky surroundings would suggest, and at the back of the building is a proper, old-style whiskey bar. There's also a good restaurant. 37 Dawson St., Dublin 2. www.37dawsonstreet.ie. ✆ **01/902-2908.** Luas: St. Stephen's Green. Bus: 15A, 15B, 44, 61, 140.

Café en Seine.

Café en Seine ★★ At this elegant, 1920s-style cafe/bar, the interior is all terribly Gatsby, with hanging lamps, glass ceilings, faux-baroque furniture, and polished brass statuettes. The cocktail list is straight-up fun, the whiskey menu a page long, and the atmosphere appropriately decadent. They also serve a bistro menu until 9pm, and on Sundays there's a popular jazz brunch from noon to 5pm. 40 Dawson St., Dublin 2. www.cafeenseine.ie. ✆ **01/677-4567** for bookings after 6pm and other inquiries. ✆ **01/699-3328** for bookings. Mon–Fri 10am–6pm. Luas: St. Stephen's Green. Bus: 15A, 15B, 44, 61, 140.

Dakota ★★ Small but perfectly curated, this stylish bar on South William Street has a hip clientele and an outstanding selection of bottled beers and cocktails. The crowd is young and the atmosphere raucously sophisticated. 9 S. William St., Dublin 2. www.dakotabar.ie. ✆ **01/672-7969.** Bus: 9, 16, 49N, 54A, 65, 65B, 68, 68A, 83, 83A, 122, 150.

The Woolshed Baa and Grill ★ Looking for somewhere to watch a big game? This is the place. Enormous TV screens flank the bar, showing whatever's hot in the sporting world—football (the European kind), rugby, U.S. sports (including football, the American kind), and whatever else is on the schedule. They also serve crowd-pleasing bar food. Parnell St., Dublin 1. www.woolshedbaa.com. ✆ **01/872-4325.** Luas: Jervis. Bus: 13, 40, 40B, 40D, 140.

Comedy Clubs

The International Bar & Comedy Cellar ★★ Hosted by the International Bar, the Comedy Cellar is one of the country's top comedy clubs, showcasing the best young pretenders in the world of Irish standup every Wednesday night. Keep an eye on the website and the club's Facebook

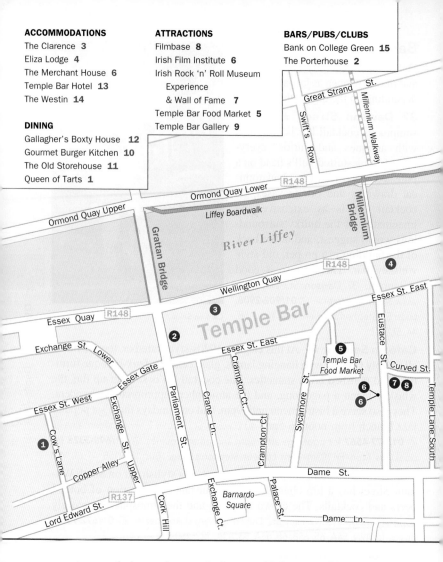

page to see who's on when you're in town. Tickets cost €10. The Internatio-nal, 23 Wicklow St., Dublin 2. www.international-bar.com. ℭ **01/677-9250.** Wed 9:30pm (doors open 9pm). Bus: 16, 49N, 54A, 83, 83A, 100X, 101X, 109, 111, 133, 150.

Laughter Lines ★★   What is it about Dublin on a Wednesday that everybody needs cheering up? Another midweek pub takeover, this one happens at the Duke on Duke Street, every Wednesday night at 8:30pm (show starts 9pm). The talented company improvises sketches according to whatever the audience suggests. It's chaotic and great fun. Tickets are €5. The Duke, Duke St., Dublin 2. www.laughterlinesdublin-com.webs.com. ℭ **01/679-9553.** Wed 8:30pm. €5. Bus: 11, 11A, 11B, 14, 14A, 15A, 15C, 15X, 20B, 27C, 33X, 39B, 41X, 46B, 46C.

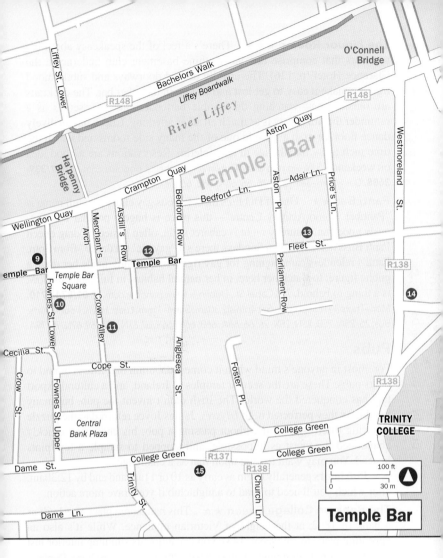

Nightclubs

Admission to nightclubs varies, from free if you arrive early-ish, to around €20 for the very fanciest places. Prices are usually higher on Friday and Saturday nights. Check club websites before going so you won't be surprised.

Lillie's Bordello ★   One of Dublin's real "VIP" clubs, this long-time celebrity magnet has a notoriously snooty door policy and plenty of roped-off areas to make you feel either special or excluded, depending which side you're on. So, if glamour is your thing, put on your glitziest gear and act like you just *belong* inside. 2 Adam Court, Grafton St., Dublin 2. www.lilliesbordello. ie. ✆ **01/679-9204.** Daily 11pm–3am. Bus: 15A, 15B, 44, 61, 100X, 101, 101X, 111, 140.

The Liquor Rooms ★★★   There's a feel of the speakeasy about the two bars that comprise this labyrinthine basement club underneath the Clarence Hotel (p. 126). The artfully draped doorways and subtle mood lighting make it easy to get lost and end up in the other bar. The cocktails are outstanding—watching the nimble bartenders at work serves as a reminder that mixology is as much an art as anything. Check out the lively dance floor, or grab a table in one of the many side rooms and watch the time melt away like the ice in an appletini. Reservations are a good idea on weekends. 5 Wellington Quay, Dublin 2. www.theliquorrooms.com. 𝒞 **087/339-3688.** Daily 5pm–3am. Bus: 26, 66, 66A, 66B, 66D, 67, 67A.

Panti Bar ★★   One of Dublin's most famous gay clubs—its full name is "Pantibar Homo Activity Centre"—this place is hugely popular and riotously good fun. Saturday night is cabaret night, often hosted by drag queen Panti Bliss herself, and on Sundays there's a "gay ole' tea dance" from 3pm. Panti's relentless campaigning for gay rights has recently made her quite a public figure; to watch her here, in her natural habitat, in full fabulous flow, is a thing to behold. 7–8 Capel St., Dublin 1. www.pantibar.com. 𝒞 **01/874-0710.** Mon–Thurs 4–11:30pm, Fri–Sat 4pm–12:30am, Sun 4–11pm. Luas: Jervis, Four Courts. Bus: 25, 25A, 25B, 25N, 25X, 26, 66, 66A, 66B, 66N, 66X, 67, 67N, 67X, 69, 69N, 79, 79A.

Pubs

Foremost in anyone's mind when it comes to Dublin nightlife is bound to be its pubs. These are the secular temples of Ireland, and a cultural export that has conquered the world. The Irish didn't invent the pub, but many would say they perfected it. In *Ulysses,* James Joyce referred to the puzzle of trying to cross Dublin without passing a pub; his characters quickly abandoned the quest as impossible, and stopped to sample a few pints instead. You may want to look upon that as a challenge.

   Pub hours generally begin as early as 10 or 11am and end by 12:30am, after which you'll need to head to a nightclub if you crave more action.

The Bank on College Green ★★   This handsome place was built as a bank in 1892, at the height of Victorian opulence. While it's also an appealing place to eat (see p. 143), you can enjoy its stunning interior just as well by simply grabbing a pint or a wee dram. 20 College Green, Dublin 2. www.bankoncollegegreen.com. 𝒞 **01/677-0677.** Opens daily at 11am, closes after midnight. Bus: 15X, 32X, 33X, 39B, 39X, 41X, 49X, 50X, 51X, 58X, 65X, 70X, 77X, 84X.

The Brazen Head ★★★   This is a serious contender for the coveted title of "oldest pub in Ireland," having served the locals continually since at least 1661 (although an alehouse was reputedly on the same spot for hundreds of years before that—they claim 1198 as the foundation date, and who's to argue?). It was once a hangout for Irish revolutionaries, and Joyce mentioned the place in *Ulysses,* although today it's more famous for lively traditional music sessions. Every night features a different act; worthies who've played here include Van Morrison, Tom Jones, and Garth Brooks.

Dublin's oldest pub, the Brazen Head.

20 Lower Bridge St., Dublin 8. www.brazenhead.com. ℂ **01/677-9549.** Luas: Smithfield. Bus: 25, 25A, 25B, 25X, 26, 37, 39, 39A, 51D, 51X, 66, 66A, 66B, 66X, 67.

The Cobblestone ★★★ We recently asked a Dublin taxi driver to recommend the best place for live music in Temple Bar. Answer: "Now why would you bother, when the Cobblestone is so close?" This is an authentic musician's place, as much a traditional music venue as a pub, such is the standard of the music. Free sessions are in the front bar nightly, with ticketed acts in the **Backroom,** a dedicated performance space. The pub is on the Northside, 5 minutes' walk from the Old Jameson Distillery (p. 110). 77 North King St., Smithfield, Dublin 7. www.cobblestonepub.ie. ℂ **01/872-1799.** Opens at 4pm Mon–Sat, 1:30pm Sat–Sun; closes at 11:30pm Sun–Thurs, 12:30am Fri–Sat. Bus: 37, 39, 39A, 70, 70N.

Davy Byrnes ★★ "He entered Davy Byrnes," wrote Joyce of Leopold Bloom, the hero of *Ulysses.* "Moral pub. He doesn't chat. Stands a drink now and then. But in a leap year once in four. Cashed a cheque for me once." Given its impeccable literary connections, it's no surprise that so many writers make this pub a pilgrimage spot when they're in town. Joyce himself was a regular, although the food has improved since his day—the menu of pub classics and sandwiches is actually pretty good, and reasonably priced. *Ulysses* fans will be delighted to hear that you can still order a gorgonzola sandwich, Bloom's snack of choice. 21 Duke St., off Grafton St., Dublin 2. www.davybyrnes.com. ℂ **01/677-5217.** Bus: 11, 11A, 11B, 14, 14A, 15A, 15C, 15X, 20B, 27C, 33X, 39B, 41X, 46B, 46C.

Listen to the Music

When you're out for a night of traditional Irish folk music, you should know that some pubs charge and some do not; if the band is playing informally in the main bar, as often happens, there's no charge, although they will probably pass a hat at some point, and everybody should toss in a few euro. If there is a charge, the music often happens in a separate room from the main pub, and the charge will be noted on the door; cover is usually about €5 to €10, and you pay as you go in, cash only.

And don't worry. If they're selling CDs they'll make sure you know about it. (They'll probably autograph them too, after the set.)

Doheny and Nesbitt ★★★ From the outside, this pub brings to mind a Victorian medicine cabinet, all polished wood with a rich blue-and-gold sign. Its proximity to the political heart of the capital makes it a perennial hangout for politicos, lawyers, economists, and those who write about them—which can make for some spectacularly good eavesdropping. (Its name inspired a catchphrase, "the Doheny and Nesbitt School of Economics," to describe the movers and shakers who used to shoot the breeze here during Ireland's boom years of the 1990s and 2000s.) To admire its cozy interior, a midweek daytime visit is best—this place gets packed in the evenings (especially summer weekends), even more so when a big sports match is on. 5 Baggot St. Lower, Dublin 2. www.dohenyandnesbitts. ie. ☏ **01/676-2945.** Bus: 10, 10A, 25X, 51D, 51X, 65X, 66D, 66X, 67X, 77X.

Grogan's Castle Lounge ★★★ There's a friendly, chatty vibe at this satisfyingly old-fashioned place, considered one of Dublin's "quintessential" pubs. You'll find little modern about the dimly lit, atmospheric interior, save for the incongruous art collection on the walls (if you like a piece, ask—most of it is for sale). Grogan's reputation rests mostly on its eclectic clientele, ranging from grizzled old folks who've been coming here for years to hipsterish artsy types in search of a low-fi hangout. 15 S. William St., Dublin 2. ☏ **01/677-9320.** Bus: 15, 32X, 33X, 39X, 41X, 51X, 58X, 70X, 84X.

Kehoe's ★★ This lovely old pub is virtually sepia-toned, with its burnt-orange walls and acres of polished walnut. That's an appropriate analogy for the atmosphere, too—easy-going and frequently packed in the evenings. Kehoe's is best enjoyed in daylight hours, when you can observe the local characters and soak up the old-school Irish pub atmosphere. A particularly appealing feature is the original "snugs"—tiny private rooms, almost like booths. 9 South Anne St., Dublin 2. www.louisfitzgerald. com/kehoes. ☏ **01/677-8312.** Bus: 15A, 15B, 44, 61, 140.

The Long Hall ★★★ The gorgeous, polished walnut-and-brass interior of this Victorian pub is liable to elicit purrs of delight from thirsty patrons as soon as they walk in the door. Undoubtedly one of Dublin's most...well, *Irish* of pubs, the Long Hall is named for the bar that runs the entire length of the interior. Regulars have to fight for space alongside the tourist crowd, but it's more than worth squeezing in for a look at the interior. Not that staying here for a few pints is anything like a chore. 51 S. Great George's St., Dublin 2. ℂ **01/475-1590.** Open from 4pm Mon–Wed, 1pm Thurs–Sat, 3pm Sun. Bus: 11E, 15F, 16, 16A, 19, 19A, 39X, 65, 65B, 65X, 83, 122.

The Merry Ploughboy ★   In many ways this is the antithesis to the Cobblestone (see p. 167), in that its live music show is very much for tourists—cheesy, but good fun and hugely popular. They will even ferry you here from the city center and take you back again for just €9 round-trip (see p. 150 for full review). Edmondstown Rd., Rockbrook, Rathfarnham, Dublin 16. www.mpbpub.com. ℂ **01/493-1495.** Daily dinner arrive 6:30–7pm, show 8–10pm. Bar food: Mon–Sat 12:30–9:30pm, Sun 12:30–8pm. Special bus from six central Dublin locations (€9 per person; must be prebooked).

Neary's ★   A favorite hangout of Dublin's theatergoers—and actors, stage crews, and just about everyone else from the Gaiety Theatre (below) next door—it's full of Victorian features, such as the wonderful globe lanterns out front, held aloft by a brass arm emerging from the brickwork. The upstairs bar is a quiet retreat during the day. 1 Chatham St., Dublin 2. ℂ **01/677-8596.** Luas: St. Stephen's Green. Bus: 15A, 15B, 61, 140.

The Porterhouse ★★   This lovely pub in Temple Bar was the first in Dublin to sell only microbrewery beers. Most are produced by the Porterhouse's own mini-chain, and the range is constantly updated, so you never know what you'll get from one visit to the next. A relaxed, jovial vibe and hearty pub lunches make it a perfect pit stop on a long day's sightseeing. There's also live music every night. 16–18 Parliament St., Dublin 2. www. porterhousebrewco.ie. ℂ **01/679-8847.** Bus: 13, 27, 37, 39, 39A, 40, 49, 51D, 54A, 56A, 65, 65B, 68, 68A, 69, 69X, 70, 77A, 77X, 79, 79A, 83, 123, 145, 747.

Theater

Abbey Theatre ★   Since 1903, the Abbey has been the national theater of Ireland, and it remains one of the most respected and prestigious theaters in the country. The original theater, destroyed by fire in 1951, was replaced in 1966 by the current functional, although uninspired, 492-seat house. In addition to its main stage, the theater has a 127-seat basement studio, the **Peacock,** where it presents newer, more experimental work. 26 Lower Abbey St., Dublin 1. www.abbeytheatre.ie. ℂ **01/878-7222.** Ticket prices generally €13–€40. Event times vary; call ahead. Rail: Tara St., Connolly. Luas: Abbey St. Bus: 2, 3, 4, 5, 7, 7A, 7B, 7D, 8, 10, 10A, 15, 15A, 15B, 15C, 15E, 15F, 20B, 27B, 27C, 29A, 31, 31B, 32, 32A, 32B, 32X, 33, 33X, 38, 38A, 38C, 41, 41A, 41B, 41C, 41X, 42, 42A, 42B, 43, 45, 46A, 46B, 46C, 46E, 51A, 70B, 70X, 121, 122, 130, 142, 145.

Gaiety Theatre ★   The elegant little Gaiety, opened in 1871, hosts a varied array of performances, everything from opera to classical Irish plays and Broadway-style musicals. (The Gaiety's annual pantomime, or Christmas show, is a big event on the city's theatrical calendar.) And when

SPINNING AN IRISH yarn OR TWO

The concept of the wonderful **An Evening of Food, Folklore & Fairies ★★★** is timeless, yet brilliant in its simplicity. No high-tech smoke and mirrors, just compelling tales from Irish folklore, passionately told by masters of the storytelling craft. To be clear, this is storytelling for all ages, not just children, and it's a brilliant revival of an ancient art. The whole thing takes place in an atmospherically lit room inside the **Brazen Head** pub (see p. 166), one of Dublin's oldest. During dinner, the storytellers spin their absorbing yarns. The meal, included in the price, is suitably traditional as well: beef-and-Guinness stew or bacon and cabbage with mashed potatoes. If you haven't had your fill of Irish tradition by the end of it all, you can go downstairs and listen to live music in the bar.

The storytelling evenings are held nightly at 7pm, every night of the week (except Jan and Feb, when it's only Thurs and Sat nights). Tickets are €46 adults, €42 seniors and students, €29 children (minimum age 6). Contact www.irishfolktours.com (✆ **01/218-8555**).

the thespians leave, the partygoers arrive: On Friday and Saturday from midnight on, the place turns into a nightclub, with four bars hosting live bands and DJs, spinning R&B, indie, blues, or hip hop. There are even occasional cult movie showings. Don't forget to check out the ornate decor before you get too tipsy. The Gaiety Theatre, South King St., Dublin 2. www.gaietytheatre.ie. ✆ **081/871-9388.** Ticket prices generally €15–€50. Event times vary; call ahead. Luas: St. Stephen's Green. Bus: 11, 11A, 11B, 14, 14A, 15A, 15C, 15X, 20B, 27C, 33X, 39B, 40A, 40C, 41X, 46B, 46C, 46N, 46X, 51X, 58X, 67X, 70X, 84X.

The Gate Theatre ★   Just north of O'Connell Street off Parnell Square, this 370-seat theater was founded in 1928 by Irish actors Hilton Edwards and Micheál Mac Liammóir to provide a venue for a broad range of plays; its program today still includes a blend of modern works and the classics. Although less known by visitors, the Gate is easily as distinguished as the Abbey. Cavendish Row, Parnell Sq., Dublin 1. www.gatetheatre.ie. ✆ **01/874-4045.** Ticket prices generally €20–€30. Event times vary; call ahead. Bus: 1, 2, 14, 14A, 16, 16A, 19, 19A, 33X, 39X, 40, 40A, 40B, 40C, 41X, 48A, 58X, 70B, 70X, 120. 123.

DAY TRIPS FROM DUBLIN

5

D riving in or out of Dublin along the big, bland motorway, it's easy to dismiss the region immediately surrounding the city's urban sprawl. However, you'll find plenty to do within an hour's drive north, south, or west of Dublin. Rural landscapes, ancient ruins, stately homes—some of Ireland's most iconic sights are surprisingly close to the city. And although it's possible to see any of them on a quick day trip, some fine hotels and restaurants reward visitors who opt to stay overnight instead.

North of Dublin, you'll find the remnants of ancient civilizations at prehistoric sites Newgrange and Knowth. A short distance away, the green hills around the Boyne Valley hold the long-lost home of early Irish kings, who once reigned with a mixture of mysticism and force.

West of Dublin is Kildare, Ireland's horse country. Even if you're not into horseracing, some handsome historic homes and other sites make this area worth checking out.

South of Dublin, the Wicklow Mountains rise from the low, green countryside, dark and brooding. It's a beautiful region, dotted with early Christian ruins and peaceful river valleys. The hills are perfect for a day trip from Dublin, and make a good starting point for a driving tour of the south of Ireland.

ESSENTIALS
Arriving

BY CAR   Most of the attractions listed in this chapter are easily accessible by car in about an hour from Dublin. The roads are good in the regions around the city, although traffic can be a problem—particularly during rush hour, when all roads around Dublin slow to a crawl. In reasonable traffic, Newgrange and Knowth are about an hour north of the city; Kildare Town and its nearby attractions are just under an hour to the southwest; and Glendalough is about an hour's drive south. You can get excellent maps from any one of the **Dublin Tourism** visitor centers (www.visit dublin.com; ✆ **1890/324-583**).

BY BUS   **Bus Éireann** (www.buseireann.ie; ✆ **01/836-6111**) operates services from the central bus station (Busáras) out to each of the regions listed in this chapter, although there aren't always practical links to the more remote sites. If you're looking to visit attractions by bus, the best bet is probably to take a tour—see the box on p. 175.

PREVIOUS PAGE: Browne's Hill Dolmen in County Carlow, south of Dublin.

Day Trips from Dublin

Counties Louth & Meath

Drogheda **6**
Hill of Tara **11**
Knowth **8**
Loughcrew **2**
Monasterboice **4**
Newgrange **7**
Newgrange Farm **9**
Old Mellifont Abbey **5**
Proleek Dolmen **1**
St. Colmcille's House **3**
Trim Castle **10**

County Kildare

Castletown **12**
The Curragh Racetrack **15**
Irish National Stud **13**
Irish Pewtermill **20**
Japanese Gardens **14**
Moone High Cross **19**
St. Brigid's Cathedral **16**

Counties Wicklow & Carlow

Browne's Hill Dolmen **26**
Glendalough **22**
Glenmacnass Waterfall **23**
Huntington Castle **27**
Mount Usher Gardens **24**
The Powerscourt Estate **18**
Russborough House **17**
St. Mullin's Monastery **28**
Vale of Avoca **25**
Wicklow Mountains National Park **21**

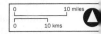

Irish Rail (www.irishrail.ie; ✆ **1850/366-222**) trains leave Dublin's Heuston station for Kildare at least once an hour. The journey takes between 25 and 45 minutes. Several direct trains depart daily from Dublin's Connolly station to Wicklow; the journey takes an hour.

NORTH OF DUBLIN: COUNTIES MEATH & LOUTH

North of Dublin's conurbation, the River Boyne rolls through the rich, fertile countryside of counties Meath and Louth. The Boyne is more than a river—it's an essential part of Irish lore, linking Ireland's ancient past (the prehistoric passage tombs of Newgrange, the storied Hill of Tara) with more modern history (the infamous 1690 Battle of the Boyne, when the Protestant King William III defeated the exiled Catholic King James II for the crown of England). Today the Boyne Valley is a much more peaceful place, but it offers visitors a wealth of historic treasures tucked away among miles of farmland and smooth, rolling hills.

Visitor Information

The **Dundalk Tourist Office** is on Market Square, Dundalk, Co. Louth (✆ **042/935-2111**). It's open Monday to Saturday from 9:30am to 1pm and 2pm to 5pm. The **Drogheda Tourist Office** (West St., Drogheda, Co. Louth; ✆ **041/987-2843**) is open Monday to Saturday from 9:30am to 5:30pm (closed Sun Dec–Apr). The **Bru na Boinne Visitor Center,** the center for Newgrange (see p. 178) and Knowth (p. 176), is at Newgrange, Donore, Co. Meath (✆ **041/988-0300**), and keeps the same hours as those ancient sites.

Exploring North of Dublin

On the surface, County Meath looks like placid farm country—little but rolling hills covered in emerald green grass. But don't be fooled. Its most breathtaking historical sights lie underground. Meath's fertile soil and rich riverland has attracted settlers for more than 8,000 years, and much of what they left behind has yet to be found. Archaeologists believe that they have uncovered only a fraction of the archaeological wealth of this region; new discoveries are made constantly.

Drogheda ★ TOWN A modest industrial commuter town of 30,000 people, 56km (35 miles) north of Dublin, Drogheda (pronounced *Draada* in the local accent) has two historic churches—both, confusingly, with the same name. The bigger of the two, **St. Peter's Roman Catholic Church,** in the town center, is remarkably impressive, with its French Gothic rose window and imposing 68m (222-ft.) spire. But its main claim to fame is more grisly; St. Peter's contains the shrine of St. Oliver Plunkett (1625–81), the Archbishop of Armagh, who was beheaded in London for his part in an alleged plot to assassinate King Charles II—becoming the last

Although you'll need a car to fully explore what the regions around Dublin have to offer, it's possible to see virtually all of the big attractions by taking guided bus tours. Most leave from central Dublin, quite early in the day, and deposit you back around 5 or 6pm. Book tours directly with the operator; the Dublin tourist offices can also help. Here are a few of the most popular ones.

Newgrange Tours by Mary Gibbons (www.newgrangetours.com; ✆ **086/355-1355**) are among the most respected of the guided tours that visit the ancient burial site. Mary is an excellent guide, and her tours have an allocated entry slot at Newgrange, meaning you don't have to wait. Tours run daily from several pickup points in Dublin, between 9:30am and 10:10am Monday to Friday (returning about 4:30pm); and 7:40am and 8:15am Saturday and Sunday (returning about 3:15pm). The cost is €40, or €35 for students.

Glendalough Bus (www.glendaloughbus.com; ✆ **01/281-8119**) runs day trips from the north side of St. Stephen's Green (opposite the Starbucks at St. Stephen's Court) to Glendalough every day at 11:30am. Tickets cost €20, and you buy them from the driver.

The **Wild Wicklow Tour** (www.wildwicklow.ie; ✆ **01/280-1899**) takes in Dún Laoghaire Harbour and Dalkey, before heading to Glendalough and the Sally Gap. They even take you to a pub for lunch (not included in the price). The tours—which are perhaps skewed toward youthful travelers—leave from several points in Dublin, "early but not too early" (8:50am–9:40am). Tickets cost €28 adults, and €25 seniors, students, and children.

Paddy Wagon Tours (www.paddywagontours.com; ✆ **01/823-0822**) run a number of rather touristy trips from Dublin to places all over Ireland, from near (**Kilkenny** and **Glendalough**) to about the farthest you can get from Dublin and still be in Ireland (the **Dingle Peninsula, Cliffs of Moher,** and **Giant's Causeway**). Tickets start at €25 and rise to around €85. The longest day tours take about 12 hours, door to door. Paddy Wagon also runs multi-day tours that include accommodations; see the website for details.

Catholic martyr to die in England. His severed head can still be seen, shriveled and wizened inside a glass case, as the gruesome centerpiece to his shrine. The other St. Peter's, **St. Peter's Church of Ireland,** a simple graystone church at the northern end of the town, has its own notorious backstory, dating to 1649, during Oliver Cromwell's bloody conquest of Ireland. On September 11, after an 8-day siege, around 2,000 Irish soldiers loyal to the deposed monarch, Charles I, were massacred. Fleeing the carnage, 140 took refuge in St. Peter's steeple. Refusing to heed their surrender, Cromwell ordered them burned alive using wood from the pews—an act so heinous that some of his own men refused, risking a charge of mutiny. St. Peter's has been rebuilt twice since the terrible event. (Check out the spooky carved skeletons on one tomb in the nave.) The small **Drogheda Museum** is located in the 17th-century **Millmount Fort,** overlooking the town, where the walls were finally breached at the end of the siege. Tours cost €3, but they're a little long, so stick with the self-guided version.

St. Peter's R.C. Church: West St. www.saintoliverplunkett.com. © **041/983-8536.** Daily 10am–5pm. **St. Peter's Church of Ireland:** Peter St. and William St. www.stpetersdrogheda.ie. No phone. Daily 10am–3pm. **Millmount Fort:** Off John St. www.millmount.net. © **041/983-3097.** Admission €5.50 adults; €4 students and seniors; €3 children; €8 families. Mon–Sat 10am–5:30pm, Sun/holidays 2–5pm.

Hill of Tara ★★ ANCIENT SITE   Legends and folklore place this hill at the center of early Irish history. Ancient tombs have been discovered that date back to the Stone Age; pagans believed that the goddess Queen Maeve reigned from here. By the 3rd century, a ceremonial residence had been built here for the most powerful men in Ireland—the high kings, who ruled as much by myth as by military strength. Every 3 years they would hold a weeklong *feis* (a kind of giant party-cum-government-session), at which more than 1,000 princes, poets, athletes, priests, druids, musicians, and jesters celebrated. Laws were passed, disputes settled, and matters of defense decided. After the last *feis* was held in A.D. 560, Tara went into a decline as the power shifted. Today, little is left of the hill's great heritage, save for grassy mounds and some ancient pillar stones. All that survives of the Iron Age forts are depressions in the soil. That said, it's still a great spot with views that extend for miles. You can learn the hill's history at a visitor center in the old church beside the entrance. Guided tours are available for those who want to know what lies beneath the smooth, green surface.

Signposted on N3, about 12km (7.4 miles) south of Navan, Co. Meath. www.hillof tara.org. © **046/902-5903** (visitor center); 041/988-0300 (out of season). Admission €5 adults; €4 seniors; €3 students and children; €13 families. Hill open year-round. Visitor Centre: Mid-May to mid-Sept daily 10am–6pm.

Knowth ★★★ ANCIENT SITE   This extraordinary prehistoric burial site was only discovered in 1968, and much of it is yet to be excavated. It is mainly composed of two massively long underground burial chambers, the longer of which stretches for 40m (131 ft.). In the mound, scientists found the largest collection of passage tomb art uncovered thus far in Europe, as well as a number of underground chambers and 300 carved slabs. Surrounding the mound, 17 satellite graves are laid out in a mysterious, complex pattern. And still, nobody can give a definitive answer to the biggest riddle of all: What was it all for? Even now, many of Knowth's secrets have not been uncovered—excavation work is constant here, and you may get a chance to see the archaeologists digging. All tickets for Knowth and **Newgrange** ★★★ (see p. 178) are issued at the Brú na Bóinne Visitor Centre near Donore. There is no direct access to the monument; a shuttle bus takes visitors over. And as with Newgrange, it's advisable to book tickets comfortably in advance of your visit—the site can get extremely busy in summer, and space is limited.

Brú na Bóinne Visitor Centre, on N51, 2km (1¼ miles) west of Donore, Co. Meath. www.knowth.com. © **041/988-0300.** Visitor center and Knowth: €6 adults; €4

A Stone Age burial ground, Knowth contains Europe's largest collection of passage tomb art.

seniors, students and children; €14 families. Combined ticket with Newgrange: €13 adults; €10 seniors; €8 students and children; €30 families. Open daily June to mid-Sept 9am–7pm; May and late Sept 9am–6:30pm; Feb–Apr, Oct 9:30am–5:30pm; Nov–Jan 9am–5pm.

Loughcrew Cairns and Gardens ★★ ANCIENT SITE   Loughcrew is a two-for-one deal: beautiful 19th-century pleasure gardens dotted with lakes, perfect for picnicking, and, just a short distance away, one of the biggest megalithic burial grounds in Ireland. The 30 passage tombs of Loughcrew are known locally as *Slieve na Calliaghe,* which translates as "The Hill of the Witch." With such an atmospheric name you'd expect something good to look at, and sure enough, the three hills topped like crowns with symmetrical tombs can be seen from miles away. The site is aligned with both the equinox and the pagan day of Samhain (Halloween), so that twice a year the dawn sun lights a heavily carved stone within one cairn. Crowds gather each year to see the phenomenon. Access to the cairns is free, but you need to pick up the key from the **Limetree Coffee Shop,** the wooden chalet-like building near the garden gatehouse; in summer it's open daily from 11am to 5pm, in winter 10am to 4pm on weekdays, 11am to 4pm on weekends. From N3, take R195 through Oldcastle toward Mullingar; 2.4km (1½ miles) out of Oldcastle, look for the signposted left turn and follow signs.

Outside Oldcastle, Co. Meath. www.loughcrew.com. © **049/854-1356.** Free admission to cairns. Gardens: €6 adults; €5 seniors; €3 children; €20 families. Tours €20 per group. Mid-Mar to Oct Mon–Fri 9:30am–5:30pm, Sat–Sun 11am–5:30pm; Nov to mid-Mar Sat–Sun 11am–4pm.

Monasterboice ★ RELIGIOUS SITE   This atmospheric monastic site holds a peaceful cemetery, one of the tallest round towers in Ireland, ancient church ruins, and two excellent high crosses, all surrounded by trees and green fields. The site is said to have been founded in the 4th century by a follower of St. Patrick named St. Buithe. The name "Buithe" was corrupted to Boyne over time, and thus the whole region is named after him. A small monastic community thrived here for centuries, until it was seized and occupied by Vikings in the 10th century. The Vikings were, in turn, defeated by Donal, the high king of Tara, who is said to have single-handedly killed 300 of them. Today only a little is left, but the **Muiredeach's High Cross** is worth the trip all on its own. Dating from 922, the near-perfect cross is carved with elaborate scenes from the Old and New Testaments (see box p. 179). Two other high crosses are more faded, and one was smashed by Cromwell's forces. The site is now accessible to wheelchair users.

Off the main Dublin road (N1), 9.7km (6 miles) NW of Drogheda, near Collon, Co. Louth. Free admission. Daily dawn–dusk.

Newgrange ★★★ ANCIENT SITE   Ireland's best-known prehistoric monument is one of the archaeological wonders of Europe. Built as a burial mound more than 5,000 years ago—long before the Egyptian pyramids or Stonehenge—it sits atop a hill near the Boyne, massive and mysterious. Newgrange is so old, in fact, that when it was being built there were still woolly mammoths living in parts of Europe. The mound is 11m (36 ft.) tall and approximately 78m (256 ft.) in diameter. It consists of 200,000 tons of stone, a 6-ton capstone, and other stones weighing up to 16 tons each, many of which were hauled from as far away as County Wicklow and the Mountains of Mourne. Each stone fits perfectly in the overall pattern, and the result is a watertight structure, an amazing feat of engineering. The question remains, though: Why? Even as archaeologists found more elaborate carvings in the stones, they deduced no clues as to whether it was built for gods, kings, or long-forgotten rituals. Inside, a passage 18m (59 ft.) long leads to a central burial chamber that sits in pitch-darkness all year, except for 5 days in December. During the winter solstice (December 19–23), a shaft of sunlight travels down the arrow-straight passageway for 17 minutes, where it hits the back wall of the burial chamber. You can register for a lottery to be in the tomb for this extraordinary event, although competition is fierce—and these days it's livestreamed on the Internet too. As part of the daily tour, you can walk down the passage, past elaborately carved stones and into the chamber, which has three sections, each with a basin stone that once held cremated human remains. *Tip:* The site has no direct access; you have to come via the Brú na Bóinne Visitor Centre near Donore, where you park and take a shuttle bus the rest of the way. As with Knowth (p. 176) you should book as soon as you know the day you'll be coming—space is limited and it's one of the most popular historic sites in the country.

Brú na Bóinne Visitor Centre: on N51, 2km (1¼ miles) west of Donore, Co. Meath. www.newgrange.com. ☏ **041/988-0300.** Visitor center and Newgrange: €7 adults; €6 seniors; €4 students and children; €16 families. Combined ticket with Knowth: €13 adults; €10 seniors; €8 students and children; €30 families. Open daily June to mid-Sept 9am–7pm; May and late Sept 9am–6:30pm; Feb–Apr, Oct 9:30am–5:30pm; Nov–Jan 9am–5pm.

HIGH CROSSES: icons OF IRELAND

You see them all over Ireland, often in the most picturesque rural surroundings, standing alone like sentries: high Celtic crosses with faded stories carved into every inch of space. Haunting and ancient as they seem to us today, when they were created, these carved stones served a practical purpose: They were books, of sorts, in the days when books were rare and precious. Think of the carvings, which illustrate biblical stories, as cartoons explaining the Bible to an illiterate population. Originally, the crosses were probably brightly painted, but the paint has long been lost to the wind and rain.

The **Muiredeach's High Cross** (see p. 177) at Monasterboice has carvings telling, from the bottom up, the stories of Adam and Eve, Cain and Abel, David and Goliath, and Moses, as well as the wise men bringing gifts to the baby Jesus. At the center of the old cross, the carving is thought to be of Revelations, while at the top St. Paul stands alone in the desert. The western side of the cross tells the stories of the New Testament, with, from the top down, a figure praying, the Crucifixion, St. Peter, Doubting Thomas, and, below that, Jesus's arrest. On the base of the cross is an inscription of the sort found often carved on stones in ancient Irish monasteries. It reads in Gaelic, "A prayer for Muiredach for whom the cross was made." Muiredach was the abbot at Monasterboice until 922, so the cross was probably made as a memorial after his death.

Another excellent example of a carved high cross is the **Moone High Cross ★**, which is not too far away (see p.186). Really intrigued by high crosses? Then head southwest to the **Ahenny High Crosses** in County Tipperary (see p. 356).

5

Newgrange Farm ★ FARM   After all that history, the kids will thank you for bringing them to this busy farm, where farmer Willie Redhouse and his family offer a 1½-hour tour. You can feed the ducks, groom a calf, and bottle-feed the lambs and kid goats. Children can hold a newborn chick, pet a pony, play with the pigs, and look at pheasants and rare birds in the aviaries. Tractor rides cost an extra €2.50. The high point of the week occurs every Sunday afternoon (and on Irish national holidays), when the sheep take to the track with teddy bear jockeys for the weekly derby. (Call to check race times.) Demonstrations show farm skills such as threshing and horseshoeing, and sheepdogs show off their herding skills. The farm has kids' play areas, a coffee shop and plenty of picnic space. The price is a little steep, but family discounts kick in at just one adult and one child.

Off N51, 3.2km (2 miles) east of Slane (signposted off N51 and directly west of Newgrange monument), Co. Meath. www.newgrangefarm.com. ✆ **041/982-4119.** Admission €5 adults; €4 seniors; €3 students and children; €13 families. Visitor center open June–Aug daily 10am–6pm; last admission 45 min. before closing.

Old Mellifont Abbey ★ RELIGIOUS SITE/RUINS   Founded in the 12th century, this was the first Cistercian monastery on the island, and it grew to be the most important. Much of it is gone now, but enough is left to give you an idea of what Mellifont was like in its day, when it was the center of Cistercian faith in Ireland, with more than 400 monks living and working within its walls. You can see the outline of the cross-shaped nave, as well as the remains of the cloister, refectory, and the warming room (the only part of the monastery with heating—after all, monks were supposed to live lives of suffering). Mellifont was closed in the 16th century during Henry VIII's dissolution of the monasteries, and a manor house was soon built on the site for an English landlord, using the abbey stones. A century later, that house would be the last place where Hugh O'Neill, the final Irish chief, stayed before surrendering to the English and

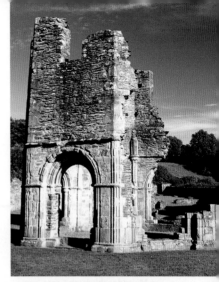

The ruins of Old Mellifont Abbey in County Louth, the first Cistercian monastery in Ireland.

then fleeing to Europe in 1607 (see "English Power & the Flight of the Earls," p. 55). At the informative visitor center next door, you can find out more about the monastery and its long, complex history.

Tullyallen, signposted off R168, 9.7km (6 miles) west of Drogheda, Co. Louth. www. heritageireland.ie. © **041/982-6459** or 041/982-3071 (out of season). Admission €4 adults; €3 seniors; €2 students and children; €10 families (free admission mid-Sept to mid-May). Visitor center open late May to early Sept, daily 10am–6pm; last admission 45 min. before closing.

Proleek Dolmen ★ ANCIENT SITE   This huge dolmen is said to resemble a giant's finger when viewed from a distance. That is subjective, to say the least. But fingerlike or not, it's an impressive sight. A massive 35-ton capstone looks alarmingly precarious, balanced on top of three smaller stones like a crude, misshapen tripod. The top of the capstone is invariably covered with pebbles, thanks to a local legend that says if you can throw a stone and it stays there, your wish will come true. You can reach the dolmen down a paved footpath from the parking lot of the **Ballymascanlon House Hotel** (www.ballymascanlon.com; © **042/935-8200**) near Dundalk; the dolmen is a 5-minute walk away. To find the hotel from Dublin, take exit 18 for Dundalk North off the M1, then take the N52 off the first roundabout, and the road to Ballymascanlon from the second. The hotel is about 3km (1¾ miles) down this road.

On the grounds of the Ballymascanlon House Hotel, Dundalk, Co. Louth. No phone. Free admission.

St. Colmcille's House ★ RELIGIOUS SITE   Sitting incongruously near more modern houses in Kells, like a memory of Ireland's distant past, this narrow gray stone house is all that's left of a long-lost monastic settlement that once stood where the town now sprawls. Most of the nearly windowless building dates to the 10th century, although some sections predate that by another hundred years. Some experts believe it was once a scriptorium, where monks wrote and illuminated books—and quite possibly where the Book of Kells (see p. 93) was produced. The first-floor room still contains traces of an ancient fireplace and entryway; a narrow staircase ascends to a dark vault just under the roof.

About 180m (590 ft.) NW of St. Columba's Church, Church Lane, Kells, Co. Meath. No phone. Free admission. June–Sept 10am–5pm. Ask for key from caretaker, Mrs. Carpenter, who lives next door to the oratory on Church Lane, opposite the churchyard.

Trim Castle ★ CASTLE A skeletal reminder of the clout once wielded by Anglo-Normans in Ireland, this ruined edifice is an inspiring sight. The Norman lord Hugh de Lacy occupied the site in 1172 and built the enclosed cruciform keep. In the 13th century, his son Walter enlarged the keep, circled it with a many-towered curtain wall, and added a great hall as an upgraded venue for courts, parliaments, and feasts. After the

> ### A Gruesome Find at Trim Castle
>
> In 1971, when excavation work was underway at Trim Castle, workers made a macabre discovery: While digging to the south of the central keep, they uncovered the remains of 10 headless men. Historians believe that the bodies date from the 15th century. During a time of high crime in 1465, King Edward IV ordered that all robbers be beheaded, and their heads displayed on spikes to intimidate those who might be considering a career in crime. Presumably, these men had all suffered that fate.

17th century, though, it was abandoned and lay in ruins for hundreds of years. Few paid much attention to it, until Mel Gibson chose to use it as a setting for the 1995 film *Braveheart*. The Irish Heritage Service restored it as a "preserved ruin." Entry to the main part of the castle is by guided tour only, but arrive early if you're visiting in summer—space is limited and the tour can't be booked in advance, so it often sells out. *Note:* The hour-long tour is unsuitable for small or unruly children, and for anyone unable to maneuver steep climbs or afraid of formidable heights.

Castle St., Trim, Co. Meath. www.heritageireland.ie. 📞 **046/943-8619.** Admission €5 adults; €4 seniors; €3 students and children; €13 families. Mid-Mar to Sept daily 10am–5pm; Nov to Jan weekends 9am–4pm; Feb to mid-Mar daily 9:30–4:30pm; last admission 1 hr. before closing.

Where to Stay North of Dublin

Bellinter House ★★ On the banks of the River Boyne outside Navan, this imposing graystone Palladian country house was designed by the same man who built Russborough House (p. 196) and Powerscourt (p. 195). The hotel has been restored to resemble a 19th-century country getaway, with an atmosphere of relaxed elegance. The lounges are gorgeous, with oak-paneled walls, fires crackling at the hearth, and deep leather chairs to sink into with a good book. Most guest rooms are less glamorous than the public areas, however; the more expensive rooms are, inevitably, the most beautiful. But all have large, modern bathrooms and comfortable beds. The restaurant is highly rated for its butter-rich, French-influenced Irish cuisine and locally sourced meat and produce. Breakfasts are huge—even the tea selection is enormous. The tiny spa has a hot tub and steam room, and guests are free to explore the sprawling grounds and fish on the river. Excursions to nearby sites can be arranged. Get directions from the hotel before setting out—on a tiny farm road, this place can be hard to find.

Bellinter, Navan, Co. Meath. www.bellinterhouse.com. ⓒ **046/903-0900.** 34 units. €120–€260 double. Free parking. Breakfast included. **Amenities:** Restaurant; bar; spa; Wi-Fi (free).

Ghan House ★★   Overlooking Carlingford Lough, Ghan House is a sweet, old-fashioned hotel. The good-size guest rooms are traditionally furnished, with antiques and sofas. Most are in the main 17th-century building, though there is also a modern extension, and many have views of the lake or mountains. "Superior" rooms have half-tester beds and deep Victorian bathtubs. The award-winning restaurant serves excellent modern-Irish menus—think roasted boar or fresh local beef—and the owners hold cooking and wine-tasting classes on-site. Check the website for special offers, including great dinner-bed-and-breakfast packages, starting at about €120 per person.

2 Ghan Rd., Carlingford, Co. Louth. www.ghanhouse.com. ⓒ **042/937-3682.** 12 units. €80–€160 double. Free parking. Breakfast included. **Amenities:** Restaurant; bar; Wi-Fi (free).

Headfort Arms Hotel ★   This pleasant, cheery hotel is a 5-minute walk from St. Colmcille's House (see p. 180) in the center of Kells. The picture-postcard facade—all hanging baskets and neat little shutters—gives way to a more modern interior, and bedrooms are simple but large and tidy. Executive rooms have two copper-sprung beds, and family rooms offer plenty of space for kids. The hotel restaurant, the **Vanilla Pod ★★** (ⓒ **046/924-0084;** see p. 183), is one of the best in the area. The small spa offers massage and beauty treatments at extremely reasonable prices—several cost just €25 on Wednesdays only.

Headfort Pl., Kells, Co. Meath. www.headfortarms.ie. ⓒ **046/924-0063.** 45 units. €95–€125 double. Free parking. Breakfast included. **Amenities:** Restaurant (dinner only except Sun lunch); bar; room service; spa; Wi-Fi (free).

Trim Castle Hotel ★   This modern hotel is a stone's throw from the castle (you really could hit it with a rock quite easily, not that we're encouraging you). The hotel lounges and restaurants are bright and cheerful. Guest rooms are not huge but are well-appointed, with modern bathrooms. Some rooms have direct views of the evocative ruins. The good, bistro-style restaurant offers reasonably priced classic Irish fare (€25 for three courses), and a lovely rooftop patio overlooking the castle is a fine place to take a coffee and soak up the view. Book early for the best rates. There are lots of half-priced deals, in the spring in particular.

Castle St., Trim, Co. Meath. www.trimcastlehotel.com. ℂ **046/948-3000.** 68 units. €110–€175 double. Free parking. Breakfast included. **Amenities:** Restaurant; bar; room service; Wi-Fi (free).

Where to Eat North of Dublin

The Bay Tree ★★★ IRISH   This restaurant isn't much to look at from the outside, but inside it's a cozy, romantic option. The cooking is top-notch, allowing the freshest, local ingredients—some of which come from their own gardens—plenty of space to shine without overloading the palate. Start with a fig and Roquefort tart garnished with 25-year-old balsamic, then try the salmon with red onion marmalade, or the slow-cooked beef short rib with thyme jus. Follow it up with a rich sticky toffee pudding with hot toffee sauce, or a super-fresh baked Alaska. The Bay Tree has an attached B&B, the **Belvedere House,** where pleasant, modern bedrooms cost around €90 to €100 per night.

Newry St., Carlingford, Co. Louth. www.belvederehouse.ie. ℂ **042/938-3848.** Entrees €20–€26. Mon–Sat 6–9pm; Sun 1–7pm.

Burke's Restaurant ★ INTERNATIONAL   The Burke family have run this friendly, unpretentious little diner for over 25 years, making it a local institution. The enormous, overflowing full Irish breakfasts are a staple (and pretty reasonable at €8, given that it provides carbs enough to keep you going for a week). The lunch menu focuses on unpretentious comfort food: fried chicken, burgers, and fresh local fish. Drop by in the afternoon for tea and sample the delicious house-recipe pancakes. The restaurant is just around the corner from St. Peter's Church on West Street.

6 Peter St., Drogheda, Co. Louth. ℂ **041/984-3498.** Entrees €7–€15. Mon–Sat 9:30am–6pm.

Vanilla Pod ★★ MODERN EUROPEAN   Imaginative Irish cooking with international influences is the focus of this great little restaurant in Kells. The menu is seasonal and showcases regional flavors in dishes like rack of local lamb with mint and coriander (cilantro) salsa; scallops with a black pudding crumb; or duck potstickers with a homemade summer berry jam. Vanilla Pod is in the popular **Headfort Arms Hotel** (see p. 182).

The Headfort Arms Hotel, John St., Kells, Co. Meath. www.headfortarms.ie. ℂ **046/924-0084.** Entrees €16–€26. Mon–Thurs 5–10pm, Fri–Sat 5–11pm, Sun 12:30–9:30pm.

WEST OF DUBLIN: COUNTY KILDARE

The flatlands of Kildare are rich in more ways than one. The fertile soil produces miles of lush pastures perfect for raising horses, and the population is one of the most affluent in the country, with plenty of cash for buying horses. Driving through the smooth rolling hills, home to sleek thoroughbreds, you might notice a similarity to the green grass of Kentucky—in fact, the county is twinned with Lexington, Kentucky. This is the home of the Curragh, the racetrack where the Irish Derby is held, and of smaller tracks at Naas and Punchestown.

Once the stronghold of the Fitzgerald Clan, Kildare is named after the Irish *cill dara,* or "Church of the Oak Tree," a reference to St. Brigid's monastery, which once sat in the county, surrounded by oak trees. Brigid (see box p. 187) was a bit ahead of her time as an early exponent for women's equality—she founded her co-ed monastery in the 5th century.

Visitor Information

The **Kildare Heritage Centre** is in Market Square, Kildare Town (www.www.kildareheritage.com; © **045/530672**). It's open Monday to Saturday from 9:30 to 1pm and 2 to 5pm (1:30–4pm the rest of the year).

Exploring West of Dublin

Castletown ★★ HISTORIC HOUSE   The fine, symmetrical architecture of this spectacular Palladian-style mansion has been imitated many times across Ireland over the centuries. Made of clean, white stone, with elegant rows of tall windows, Castletown was built between 1722 and 1729, designed by Italian architect Alessandro Galilei for then-speaker of the Irish House of Commons, William Connolly. Today, it's beautifully maintained, and the fully restored interior is worth the price of admission. Visitors are free to wander around the surrounding parkland, and a cafe offers tea and cakes should you need a break. Two interesting follies on the estate were built as make-work for the starving population during the Famine: One is a graceful obelisk, the other an extraordinarily playful barn, created as a higgledy-piggledy inverted funnel, around which winds a stone staircase. It is aptly named the "Wonderful Barn."

Signposted from R403, off main Dublin-Galway Rd. (N4), Celbridge, Co. Kildare. www.castletownhouse.ie. © **01/628-8252.** House: €10 adults; €8 seniors; €5 students and children; €25 families. Grounds: €3 adults; €2 seniors; students and children; €10 families. Tours mid-Mar to early Nov Mon–Sun 10am–6pm. Last admission 1 hr. before closing. Tours at 11am and 3pm. Grounds 10am–5pm year-round. Call ahead to confirm times, as they change frequently.

The Curragh ★ RACECOURSE   The country's best-known racetrack, the Curragh has hosted races for hundreds of years. The first recorded race took place here in 1727, but historians believe races were held here long before then. Today it's a modern flat track—there's nothing left of whatever may have stood here centuries ago. But its place in history is assured, and it is home to the **Irish Derby,** the premier horse race of Ireland, held every June and July. Races take place at least one Saturday a month from March to October. The Curragh website has full

A mare and foal at the Irish National Stud, home of many of Ireland's finest thoroughbred racehorses.

details on all races and tickets, including premium packages. Derby day tickets are inevitably more expensive than for other races; expect to pay upwards of €30 or €50 with transport to and from Dublin (prebooking is essential). The nearest train station is Kildare Town (a free shuttle runs from there to the track on race days); trains run direct from Waterford, Cork, Limerick, Galway, and Dublin's Heuston station, with fares starting at around €15. **Dublin Coach** (www.dublincoach.ie; ℭ **01/465-9972**) runs a "Race Bus" from Westmoreland Street in central Dublin; fares start at around €10.

Dublin-Limerick Rd. (N7), Curragh, Co. Kildare. www.curragh.ie. ℭ **045/441205.** Standard race days €15 adults; €8 seniors and under 25; children under 16 (with adult) free. Classic race days €20 adults; €10 seniors and under 25; children under 16 (with adult) free. Hours vary; 1st race usually 2pm, but check newspaper sports pages.

Irish National Stud with Japanese Gardens & St. Fiachra's Garden ★ FARM/GARDENS Many of Ireland's fastest horses have been bred on the grounds of this famous stud farm. Horse lovers and racing fans will be in heaven, walking around the expansive grounds and watching the well-groomed horses being trained. There are exhibits on racing, steeplechase, hunting, and show jumping, plus a rather macabre display featuring the skeleton of Arkle, one of Ireland's most famous horses. The tranquil **Japanese Garden,** dating from 1906, has pagodas, ponds, and trickling streams, and the beautifully designed visitor center has a restaurant and shop. A garden dedicated to St. Fiachra—the patron saint of gardeners—lies in a beautiful natural setting of woods and wetlands, and a reconstructed hermitage features a Waterford crystal garden of rocks and delicate glass orchids.

Off the Dublin-Limerick Rd. (N7), Tully, Kildare, Co. Kildare. www.irishnationalstud.ie. ⓒ **045/522963.** Admission €13 adults; €10 seniors and students; €7 children 5–15; €30 families. Daily 9am–6pm; last admission 1 hr. before closing. Tours daily 10:30am, noon, 2pm, and 4pm (fewer tours likely outside of summer season).

Irish Pewtermill Centre ★ CRAFT FACTORY   In an 11th-century mill originally constructed for the nunnery of St. Moling, Ireland's oldest pewter mill makes a nice diversion. It has a little museum devoted to the craft, but the skilled artisans who work here are the main attraction, still casting pewter in antique molds, some of which are 300 years old. Casting takes place most days, usually in the morning—make an appointment in advance if you want to watch the craftsmen or visit the museum (both are free). The showroom has a wide selection of high-quality, hand-cast pewter gifts for sale, from bowls to brooches, at reasonable prices.

Timolin-Moone Rd. (signposted off N9 in Moone), Co. Kildare. ⓒ **087/909-0044.** Free admission. Mon–Fri 10am–4:30pm, Sat–Sun 11am–4pm. Museum and workshop open by appointment only.

Moone High Cross ★ RELIGIOUS SITE   Amid the picturesque ruins of Moone Abbey, this magnificent high cross (see box p. 179) is nearly 1,200 years old. The abbey, established by St. Columba in the 6th century, lies in evocative ruins around it. The cross features finely crafted Celtic designs as well as biblical scenes: the temptation of Adam and Eve, the sacrifice of Isaac, and Daniel in the lions' den. Among the carvings are several surprises, such as a carving of a Near Eastern fish that reproduces when the male feeds the female her own eggs, which eventually hatch from her mouth.

Signposted off N9 on southern edge of Moone, Co. Kildare. No phone. Free admission. Daily dawn–dusk.

St. Brigid's Cathedral ★ CHURCH   Built on the site of St. Brigid's monastery, which was founded in the 5th century, this beautiful 13th-century church dominates central Kildare. Its exquisite stained-glass windows portray Ireland's three great saints: Patrick, Colmcille, and Brigid. The round tower on the grounds is the second tallest in the country (33m/108 ft.); it dates to the 10th century, although its original pointed roof was later replaced by a Norman turret. If the groundskeeper is in, you can climb the stairs to the top for €7. Near the tower, a strange-looking stone with a hole at its top is known as the "wishing stone"—according to lore, if you put your arm through the hole and touch your shoulder when you make a wish, then your wish will come true. The cathedral is closed to visitors from October to April, but you can usually visit the grounds

Modern-day feminists have embraced this 5th-century Irish saint, and for good reason. Brigid was a headstrong girl who fought against the oppressive, patriarchal rules of her time. When her father picked a husband for her, she refused to marry him. Legend holds that when her father insisted that the wedding should go forward, she pulled out her own eye to prove she was strong enough to resist his plans. He backed down, and the mutilated girl joined a convent. When she took her vows, however, the bishop accidentally ordained her as a bishop rather than a nun. It is said that as soon as that happened, she was miraculously made beautiful again.

As she grew older, Brigid remained a rebel. She founded a monastery in Kildare, but insisted that it be open to both nuns and monks—something

unheard of at that time. Word of the monastery, and of its unusual abbess, soon spread throughout Europe, and she became a powerful figure in European Christianity. Her followers marked their homes with a plain cross woven from river reeds. In some Irish homes, you'll still find crosses made in precisely that way.

One of Brigid's strangest rules for her monastery was that a fire should always be kept burning, day and night, tended by 20 virgins. Long after she died, the fire at St. Brigid's burned constantly, tended as she said it should be. This continued as late as 1220, when the bishop of Dublin insisted that the tradition, which he viewed as pagan, be stopped. But there is still a fire pit at **St. Brigid's Cathedral ★** (see above), and a fire is lit in it every February 1, on St. Brigid's feast day.

year-round, free, by inquiring at the Heritage Centre on Market Square (p. 184).

Market Sq., Kildare Town, Co. Kildare. ✆ **045/521229.** Free admission to Cathedral; round tower €7. Cathedral: May–Sept Mon–Sat 10am–1pm, 2–5pm; Sun 2–5pm; last admission 15 min. before closing. Closed Oct–Apr. Grounds: daily, dawn–dusk.

Where to Stay West of Dublin

Barberstown Castle ★★   Although parts of this hotel were built as recently as the early 2000s, enough genuine old castle is still on view as you approach for it to look and feel satisfyingly, well, *castle*-like. The oldest section dates from the 12th century, and even the modern guest rooms manage to feel pleasantly antique; some have four-poster beds. Family rooms are available, too. The formal **Barton Rooms** restaurant serves classic (and quite pricey) Irish bistro fare. There's also a tearoom called **Clapton's Lounge**—a reference to the fact that Barberstown Castle was the home of rock star Eric Clapton in the 1980s.

On R403, Straffan, Co. Kildare. www.barberstowncastle.ie. ✆ **01/628-8157.** 55 units. €160–€200 double, €215–€245 suite. Free parking. Breakfast included. **Amenities:** Restaurant; room service; Wi-Fi (free).

Dollardstown House ★★   This large, salmon-pink manor house, about 10 minutes' drive from the Moone High Cross (see p. 186), would be

Dining in the castle's keep at Barberstown Castle.

a charming place to stay even without such warm and friendly owners—but as it is, you're made to feel like a houseguest at a grand country pad. Owners Antoinette and Andrew know just how to put guests at ease (the delicious, home-baked scones on arrival help), and they've done a beautiful job restoring Andrew's ancestral home. The building dates mostly to the 1690s, though parts are older. The pleasant (and very spacious) bedrooms are decorated in a tasteful Georgian style and have recently been renovated—though be aware that not all rooms have a private bath. One room is a family room (about €30 extra). Breakfasts are, of course, delicious (try the homemade soda bread and fall in love), and while there's no restaurant, you can prebook evening meals, prepared by a local chef.

Athy, Co. Kildare. www.dollardstown.com. © **059/862-2012.** 4 units. €90–€120. Free parking. Breakfast included. **Amenities:** Wi-Fi (free).

Martinstown House ★★ An elegant country house getaway near the famous Curragh racecourse (see p. 184), Martinstown dates mostly from the 1830s. Bedrooms are decorated with more than a few nods to its early Victorian origins, with heritage color schemes and antique-style furniture. Excellent four-course dinners (€50) are served around a single, long, candlelit table, which gives the appealing sense of an upper-class house party from a bygone age. Expect seasonal fare such as roast duck with spiced red cabbage, or grilled sole with lemon and caper butter. *Note:* Although the Curragh is just 8km (5 miles) away, a frustrating road layout means driving between the Martinstown and the racecourse takes up to a half-hour each way.

Off L6078 (follow signs for Martinstown), Ballysaxhills, Curragh, Co. Kildare. www.martinstownhouse.com. © **045/441269.** 6 units. €175–€295 double. Free parking. Breakfast included. **Amenities:** Restaurant; Wi-Fi (free).

Where to Eat West of Dublin

Cunningham's ★ THAI/PUB FOOD   Inside and out, Cunningham's is a fairly traditional, run-of-the-mill Irish pub—which makes it all the more unlikely that it also serves some of the best Thai food in the area. Delicious authentic-style meals are prepared by the Thai chef, Chock, and served in the bar nightly. You could go for a spicy red, green, or panang curry, made with coconut and chili, or a classic pad Thai served with crispy wontons. The menu also has a selection of traditional pub options, such as burgers and steaks, but it's the Thai food that packs in the crowds. Some nights include live music.

Main St., Kildare, Co. Kildare. www.cunninghamskildare.com. ℂ **045/521780.** Entrees €11–€21. Mon–Thurs 5–11:30pm; Fri 5pm–12:30am; Sat 1pm–12:30am; Sun 1–11pm.

Silken Thomas ★ INTERNATIONAL   Named for a real-life knight and dashing rebel (see box p. 190), this atmospheric pub offers simple, tasty, unfussy meals in a jovial atmosphere. The menu is something of a global tour, with Mexican fajitas, Chinese stir-fries, and Indian curries happily served alongside burgers, salads, fish and chips, and other familiar Irish fare. There's also a carvery (station serving roast meat and vegetables) from noon daily. A second dining room houses **Chapter 16 ★**, a more formal dining space with a slightly pricier, bistro-style menu (steaks, pasta, fresh fish, and the like).

The Square, Kildare, Co. Kildare. www.silkenthomas.com. ℂ **045/522232.** Entrees €13–€26. Silken Thomas: Mon–Sat 8am–around 10pm (pub open later). Chapter 16: Mon–Fri 6–10pm; Sat noon–2pm, 5:30–10pm; Sun noon–2pm, 5:30–9:30pm.

Trax Brasserie ★★ IRISH   This laid-back but elegant brasserie in tiny Naas, about 22km (13½ miles) northeast of Kildare, is a real find. The 1880s building was originally a railway shed, hence the subtle hints of the industrial in the dining room, such as exposed stone walls and "slabs of slate" serving plates. The fixed-price two- and three-course menus focus on classic Irish and European flavors. You might start with some hot fish cakes, before tucking into a plate of chicken supreme with prosciutto ham, mozzarella, and sundried tomatoes, or hake with a chive and lemon butter sauce. Early-bird menus (€22 for two courses, €26 for three) are served until 6:30pm nightly.

Friary Rd., Naas, Co. Kildare. www.traxbrasserie.ie. ℂ **045/889333.** Fixed-price menus €27–€30. Wed–Sat 5–10pm; Sun 1–7:45pm.

Sports & Outdoor Pursuits in Kildare

CYCLING   Kildare's flat-to-rolling landscape is perfect for gentle cycling. Bike rental shops are surprisingly few in County Kildare, but **Cahill Cycles,** Fishery Lane, Naas, Co. Kildare (www.cahill.ie; ℂ **045/881-585**), comes highly recommended.

local hero: **SILKEN THOMAS**

Nobleman and rebel rolled into one, Silken Thomas was an unlikely revolutionary.

More properly known as Thomas FitzGerald, the 10th Earl of Kildare, he was born in 1513 to illustrious parents—his father was governor of Ireland—and spent much of his childhood at the court of King Henry VIII in England.

Thomas returned to Ireland as a young man, all set to follow in his father's footsteps and rule on behalf of the king. However, when word reached him that his father had fallen out with Henry and been executed, Thomas raised a rebellion.

It began with a blistering attack on Dublin Castle. Even though that failed, the English were rattled. Thomas and his men retreated to the relative safety of County Kildare, expecting a counter-attack at any moment. And indeed it came...but by stealth. While Thomas was temporarily absent from his garrison, a guard was bribed to let in a small group of English soldiers, who massacred everybody inside.

Despite that huge blow to the rebellion, Thomas and his remaining men fought valiantly on for a while longer. The struggle was futile, however, and Thomas eventually agreed to surrender in return for a promise that he and his closest compatriots would be spared. But King Henry wasn't one for keeping his word. Thomas and his men were sentenced to death by hanging, drawing, and quartering.

What happened next is enough to make the blood run cold. On a bleak February morning in 1537, the men were dragged through the streets of London to a site of public execution. Thomas and the others were hanged by the neck, but cut down before they died. Then they were cut open, their bowels and genitals removed and then burned in front of their eyes. They were finally killed by beheading, after which their corpses were cut into quarters and placed on spikes. Such was the wrath of kings.

Despite this most chilling end, Thomas remains a folk hero in Ireland. But why the unusual nickname? The sobriquet "Silken Thomas" comes from a wonderful footnote to history. It is recorded that Thomas was a dashing and handsome man, always dressed in the height of fashion. And when his army of 200 men rode into battle, they wore strands of silk streaming from their helmets.

GOLF The flat plains here create excellent parkland layouts, including the Arnold Palmer–designed, par-72 **Kildare Hotel & Country Club** (also known as the **K Club**) in Straffan, Co. Kildare (www.kclub.com; ℡ **01/601-7200**). The club has two courses, with greens fees ranging from around €90 to €250.

HORSEBACK RIDING While you're in horse country, why not arrange a saddle trek in the Kildare countryside? Contact the **Kill International Equestrian Centre,** Kill, Co. Kildare (www.killinternational.ie; ℡ **045/877-333**). Private lessons cost around €50 per person, with discounts if you book as a group.

WALKING The way-marked **Grand Canal Way,** a long-distance walking path that cuts through part of Kildare, passes through such scenic towns as Sallins, Robertstown, and Edenderry, where you can find a room and stock up on provisions. For more information, go to **www.irishtrails. ie/Trail/Grand-Canal-Way/18**, or contact the Kildare tourist office.

SOUTH OF DUBLIN: COUNTIES WICKLOW & CARLOW

Wicklow's northernmost border is just a dozen or so miles south of Dublin, making it one of the easiest day trips from the city. The centerpiece of the region is the beautiful **Wicklow Mountains,** traversed by the well-marked **Wicklow Way** walking path, which wanders for miles past mountain tarns and secluded glens. Tucked into the mountains are the isolated monastery of **Glendalough** and picturesque villages such as **Roundwood, Laragh,** and **Aughrim.** Along the coast, the bright and busy upscale town of **Bray** is 12.6km (7¾ miles) south of Dún Laoghaire. Farther south are the sweet little harbor town of **Greystones** and, just inland, the charming riverside village of **Avoca.** A handful of historic homes dot the countryside.

Just over the border of County Wicklow lies **County Carlow,** one of Ireland's smallest counties, bordered to the east by the Blackstairs Mountains and to the west by the fertile limestone land of the Barrow Valley and the Killeshin Hills. Its most prominent feature is the 5,000-year-old granite formation known as **Browne's Hill Dolmen.**

Visitor Information

The **Wicklow Tourist Office,** Fitzwilliam Square, Wicklow Town (www.visitwicklow.ie; ✆ **040/469117**), is open Monday to Friday year-round between the slightly odd hours of 9:20am and 5:15pm (closed weekends). The **Carlow Tourist Office,** Library Building, College Street, Carlow Town (www.carlowtourism.com; ✆ **059/913-0411**), is open year-round Monday to Friday 9:30am to 5pm and Saturday 10am to 4pm. Both are usually open all weekend in summer; call before you visit.

Exploring South of Dublin

Browne's Hill Dolmen ★ ANCIENT SITE   Resembling an elephant about to topple slowly to one side, this megalithic stone table has crouched in this green field for millennia. No one knows its purpose, though archaeologists suspect the dolmen was built to mark the burial place of a long-dead king. The gigantic stack of stones is estimated to be 5,000 years old, and for many centuries, people believed it had been built by giants. Today, archaeologists say the vast capstone—believed to weigh a colossal 100 tons—was likely rolled into place up an earthen ramp that was then destroyed. Faced with the sheer massiveness of these stones, you may prefer to stick with the tale about the giants.

Off Rathvilly Rd., Carlow, Co. Carlow. No phone. Free admission. Daily dawn–dusk. Access via parking lot and enclosed pedestrian pathway.

Glendalough ★★★ RELIGIOUS SITE   Tucked away amid deep forests and surrounded by rolling hills, this evocative, misty glen is a truly magical place. First established by a monk known as St. Kevin in the 6th century, Glendalough was originally devoted to Christian worship and scholarly learning. Sacked first by the Vikings and later by the English, it was eventually abandoned by the monks who sought refuge here. Those beautiful round towers were actually hideouts with retractable ladders that the monks would pull up after them when the raiders arrived. Most of the buildings were destroyed in repeated attacks, but enough survives to ensure the ruins are a striking and atmospheric spectacle. The site sprawls, so stop by the visitor center at the entrance to pick up a map. Each of the many walking trails traversing the area takes in different hidden ruins among the lakes and hills. Highlights include the oldest ruins, the **Teampall na Skellig,** across the lake at the foot of towering cliffs (unfortunately, there's no boat service and they cannot be visited), and the cave known as **Kevin's Bed,** believed to be where St. Kevin lived when he first arrived at Glendalough. Follow the path from the upper lake to the lower lake to walk through the remains of the monastery complex. There's a nearly perfect round tower, 31m (102 ft.) high and 16m (52 ft.) around the base, as well as hundreds of timeworn Celtic crosses and several chapels. One of these is St. Kevin's Chapel, often called **St. Kevin's Kitchen,** a fine specimen of an early Irish barrel-vaulted oratory with a miniature round belfry rising from a stone roof. Climb the hills to take in the beauty of this extraordinary site from above.

Signposted from R756, 2km (1.3 miles) west of Laragh, Co. Wicklow. www.heritage ireland.ie. ℂ **040/445-352.** Admission €5 adults; €4 seniors; €3 students and children; €13 families. Mid-Mar to mid-Oct daily 9:30am–6pm; mid-Oct to mid-Mar daily 9:30am–5pm; last admission 45 min. before closing.

A reflective moment above the lakes of Glendalough.

DARKNESS & light: THE RISE & FALL OF GLENDALOUGH

The ruins of Glendalough date from the 6th century, when a monk named Coemgen chose this secluded setting to build a great church. He is generally thought to be have been born in 498, to parents named Coemlog and Coemell, at a place called "the Fort of the White Fountain" in Leinster. However, given that many sources cite the date of his death as 618—which adds up to a highly improbable lifespan of 120 years—none of this is certain. "Coemgen" was later anglicized to Kevin, the name by which he was eventually canonized in 1903.

It is thought that Kevin chose this site because of its isolation, although there's also a Bronze Age tomb here, suggesting that the place already had some religious significance when Kevin arrived.

Over the next 4 centuries, Kevin's church became a center of religious learning, attracting thousands of students from all over Europe. Unfortunately, Glendalough's success was also its downfall. The monastery soon came to the attention of the Vikings, who pillaged it repeatedly between A.D. 775 and 1071. On one such raid they stole timbers that they used to construct the biggest Viking ship ever known to have been built.

Despite suffering centuries of attack, the monastery at Glendalough always somehow managed to rebuild and bounce back. The crushing blow, however, came in 1398, when it was virtually destroyed by invading English troops. Even then, attempts were made to resuscitate it once more, and the monastery limped along—just a shadow of all it had been—until the 17th century, when it was finally abandoned forever.

Glenmacnass Waterfall ★ NATURE SITE   A wide strip of silver running down a rugged hill, the Glenmacnass Waterfall is more pretty than spectacular. It doesn't plummet so much as slip through the rugged countryside and down the side of Mt. Mullagheleevaun. From the parking lot near the top of the hill there's a well-signposted path to the falls, but take care on the rocks, which can be slippery.

Laragh, Co. Wicklow. Follow Military Rd. through the Sally Gap and Laragh to the top of Glenmacnass Valley, and then watch for signs to the waterfall. Free admission.

Huntington Castle ★★ CASTLE   This place has all the makings of a spectacular haunting. It's built on the site of a 14th-century abbey, which was itself built on top of a Druid temple (a modern shrine to the Egyptian Goddess Isis lies in the basement). And it certainly looks the part—the rambling, 17th-century crenelated manor house is overgrown with vines that turn blood-red in the fall. It should come as no surprise then that the castle claims to be the most haunted building in Ireland. The owners say it is plagued by ghosts of druids who cause mists in the fields and showers of blood. Other than that, it's very nice. The interior can only be seen by guided tour, which includes areas that were closed until recently, such as the old kitchens and drawing room. The gardens are beautiful—many of the plants date back to the 18th century—and the unusual 17th-century water features have been restored to working condition. Don't miss the walking path guarded on either side by ancient yew trees. An adventure playground keeps little ones busy. If you're not afraid of ghosts, the castle offers bed-and-breakfast and self-catering accommodations in the elegant Georgian gatehouse; e-mail info@huntingtoncastle.com for prices and information.

Clonegal, Co. Carlow (off N80, 6.5km/4 miles from Bunclody). www.huntington castle.com. ℂ **053/937-7160.** Guided tours: €9 adults; €5 children. May–Sept daily tours hourly 2–5pm. Gardens and playground only: €5 adults, €2,50 children. May–Sept daily 10am–5pm. May, Sept weekends only (same hours). Gardens and playground only: €5 adults, €3 children. May–Sept daily 10am–5pm; last admission 1 hr. before closing.

Armor and hunting trophies line a hallway in rambling Huntington Castle.

Mount Usher Gardens ★★ GARDENS   Spreading out on 8 hectares (20 acres) at the edge of the River Vartry, this peaceful and romantic site was once an ancient lake. Since 1868 it's been a riverside garden, designed in a distinctively informal style, with fiery rhododendrons, fragrant eucalyptus trees, giant Tibetan lilies, and snowy camellias competing for your attention. Attuned to their natural setting, these gardens have an almost untended feel—a sort of floral woodland. A spacious cafe, run by the fantastic Avoca chain, overlooks the river and gardens. The courtyard at the garden entrance

---

A DAY IN bray

At the southern terminus of the DART line from Dublin, the oceanfront resort town of **Bray** is a great option for an afternoon excursion from the city. Its chief attraction is the **National Sea Life Centre** aquarium (Strand Rd.; www.visitsealife.com/bray; ℂ **01/286-6939**), at the center of a charming boardwalk that also features arcades, games, and other family amusements. But locals know that Bray's greatest pleasure is the stunning coastal view of Killiney Bay, Dalkey Island, and Bray from the rocky promontory of **Bray Head.**

Follow the beachside promenade south through Bray; at the outskirts of town, the promenade turns left and up, beginning the ascent of Bray Head. Shortly after the ascent begins, a trail branches to the left—this is the cliffside walk, which continues another 5km (3 miles) along the coast to Greystones. From the center of Greystones, a train will take you back to Bray. This is an easy walk, about 2 hours each way, but don't attempt it in bad weather or strong winds, when the cliffside path becomes treacherous.

contains an interesting assortment of shops selling seeds, gardening supplies, and books.

Ashford, Co. Wicklow (off the N11). www.mountushergardens.ie. © **040/440205.** Admission €7.50 adults; €6.50 seniors and students; €3.50 children 4–16; free for children under 4. Daily 10am–5pm; last admission 1 hr. before closing. Avoca Garden Café: Mon–Fri 9:30am–5pm, Sat–Sun 10am–5pm.

The Powerscourt Estate ★★★ GARDENS/HISTORIC HOUSE

The 20th century was not kind to this magnificent estate. It took more than 30 years to restore the Palladian house to its former glory (see box p. 196) after being abandoned and then gutted by fire. The gardens, however, remained gorgeous, with classical statuary, a shady grotto made of petrified moss, a peaceful Japanese garden, and a massive, over-the-top fountain from which statues of winged horses rise. Landscaper Daniel Robertson designed the gardens between 1745 and 1767. Legend has it that thanks to crippling gout, he oversaw the work while being carted around in a wheelbarrow, sipping port as he went. When the bottle was dry, work was done for the day. The whole thing is impressive enough that in 2014 *National Geographic* magazine named Powerscourt's the third-greatest gardens in the world. At the estate's garden center you can learn everything there is to know about the plants that thrive here, and even pick up seeds to take home (although beware of Customs rules for such things). A few rooms of the house are open to the public 1 or 2 days a week, but a unique new addition is open daily, year-round: **Tara's Palace,** an

The magnificent Palladian manor of Powerscourt House.

elaborate and detailed 18th-century palace built in miniature. Displayed in a small museum devoted to historic dollhouses, it took a team of crafts-people 2 decades to complete. And 2018 saw the addition of the **Cool Planet Experience,** a high-tech visitor center aimed at teaching children about human-made climate change and how the world might combat it. The estate also has a playground and gift shops. If you feel energetic, fol-low the well-marked path over 7km (4 miles) to the picturesque **Powers-court Waterfall**—the highest in Ireland at 121m (397 ft.); you can also drive here, following signs from the estate. Powerscourt is only about 20km (12½ miles) south of Dublin, and can be reached by city buses 44 or 185 to Enniskerry village, approximately a 25-minute walk from the estate.

On R760, Enniskerry, Co. Wicklow. www.powerscourt.ie. ✆ **01/204-6000.** Gardens: €10 adults (€7.50 Nov–Feb); €8.50 seniors and students (€7 Nov–Feb); €5 children 5–12 (€3.50 Nov–Feb); children under 5 free; €25 families (€18 Nov–Feb). Tara's Palace: €5 adults; €4 seniors and students; €3 children; €12 families. Cool Planet: €10 adults; €5 children; €20 families. Waterfall: €6 adults; €5 seniors and students; €3.50 children 2–12; €16 families. Gardens: Daily 9:30am–5:30pm (or at dusk if earlier). Gar-den Pavilion: Mon–Sat 9:30am–5:30pm, Sun 10am–5:30pm. Ballroom and Garden Rooms: May–Sept Sun–Mon 9:30am–1:30pm; Oct–Apr Sun 9:30am–1:30pm. Tara's Palace: Mon–Sat 10am–5pm, Sun noon–5pm. Cool Planet: Daily 10am–5pm. Powerscourt Waterfall: May–Aug 9:30am–7pm (last admission 6pm); Mar–Apr and Sept–Oct 10:30am–5:30pm (last admission 5pm); Nov–Feb 10:30am–4:30pm (last admission 3:30pm). Last admission to gardens ½ hr. before closing.

Russborough House ★★ HISTORIC HOUSE   Sprawling low across the green landscape, this somber graystone villa was built between 1741 and 1751. The designer was Richard Cassels, the same man who designed the much more fanciful Powerscourt House (see above). Today, however, Russborough is known not for its architecture but for housing a small but mighty art gallery. In the 1950s, the house was bought by Sir Alfred Beit, a member of the De Beers diamond family, specifically to hold his massive personal art collection, and it displays one of the most exquisite small rural art collections you're likely to find anywhere. Although many of the most valuable paintings have been moved to other museums after a series of rob-beries, you can still view works by Vermeer, Gainsborough, and Rubens. The house can be explored only by guided tour, and there is certainly a lot to see: ornate plaster ceilings by the Lafranchini brothers, huge marble mantelpieces, and fine displays of silver, porcelain, and furniture. Kids will be amused by a fiendish maze, a "fairy trail" on the grounds that tells the story of Russborough's resident fairy, and sheepdog demonstrations daily at 2pm (in good weather). The grounds also contain traditional craft work-shops where you can see artisans in action, including a blacksmith and a candlemaker. The estate's other main attraction is the **National Bird of Prey Centre** (www.nationalbirdofpreycentre.ie; ✆ **045/857-755**), home to hawks, owls, falcons, and eagles from different parts of the globe. Check the website for details on how to book a private "hawk walk" through the grounds with a trainer and one of the resident big birds. The center is open

THE curse OF POWERSCOURT HOUSE

This grand house in Enniskerry has a history of misfortune. It was designed in the 18th century by Richard Cassels, whose other work includes Russborough House (see above) and Dublin's Parliament building (p. 113). The same family lived in the building for 350 years until the 1950s, but their fortunes gradually declined. By the time they moved out and donated the once-magnificent house to the state, it was in terrible condition, and the country had little money to restore it. Plagued with financial problems, the renovation limped along, eventually taking two decades to complete.

Finally, in 1974, the work was done, and a grand reopening was planned. But just one day before the event was due to take place, a fire broke out, completely gutting the building. (The beauty of the original interiors can be seen in Stanley Kubrick's *Barry Lyndon,* which finished filming here just months before the devastating conflagration.) So the slow process of reconstruction began again—and this time the renovation lasted more than 30 years.

At last, though, the house has a new lease on life as one of the region's biggest tourist attractions. Even though only a small part of the restored interior may currently be seen (and only for a few hours a week), the estate is still worth a visit for its gorgeous exterior architecture and exquisite gardens.

daily July to September, Wednesdays to Sundays April to June, and weekends only October to March.

Signposted from N81, 3.2km (2 miles) south of Blessington, Co. Wicklow. www.russboroughhouse.ie. © **045/865-239.** House: €12 adults; €9 seniors and students; €6 children 6–15; free children 5 and under; €30 families (includes maze entry). Maze: €3, or €10 families. Sheepdog demonstration €5. Fairy trail €3. National Bird of Prey Centre: €9 adults; €7 seniors; €6 students and children 6–15; €25 families. May–Sept daily 10am–5pm (tours hourly); Mar, Oct, and Dec daily tours 1 and 2pm; April and Oct Mon–Fri noon–3pm, Sat–Sun and holiday Mon tours noon, 10am–5pm. Parklands daily 9am–6pm. National Bird of Prey Centre: Sat–Sun 11am–5pm. All-day parking €2.

St. Mullin's Monastery ★ RELIGIOUS SITE   This monastery's idyllic setting—in a sleepy hamlet beside the River Barrow, surrounded by low hills—is reason enough for a visit. These are the ruins of a monastery founded by St. Moling (Mullin) in roughly A.D. 614. Plundered again and again by the Vikings in the 9th and 10th centuries, it was annexed in the 12th century by a nearby Augustinian abbey. Here, too, are a steep grassy motte (the mound on which a castle was built) and the outline of a bailey (the outer wall or court of a castle) constructed by the Normans in the 12th century. In the Middle Ages the monastery ruins were a popular destination, especially at the height of the Black Death in 1348. By tradition, pilgrims would cross the river barefoot, circle the burial spot of St. Mullin nine times, and drink from the healing waters of the saint's well. These ruins and waters are still the subject of an annual pilgrimage on or near July 25. Adjoining the monastery buildings is an ancient cemetery still in use, where, contrary to common practice, Protestants and Catholics have long lain side by side. A number of rebels from the 1798 Rising are buried here.

On the Barrow Dr., 12km (7½ miles) north of New Ross, St. Mullins, Co. Carlow. Free admission. Daily dawn–dusk.

Vale of Avoca ★ NATURE SITE   Basically a peaceful, green river valley, the Vale of Avoca is the "Meeting of the Waters" where the Avonmore and Avonbeg rivers join to form the Avoca River. Pleasant as it is, we'd probably never have heard of it were it not for the 19th-century poet Thomas Moore, who wrote, "There is not in the wide world a valley so sweet / As the vale in whose bosom the bright waters meet…" Three kilometers (2 miles) away, the charming riverside village of **Avoca** makes a good stop. Here you can tour the traditional mills where **Avoca Handweavers** still make their coveted blankets, sweaters, and other beautiful homewares, nearly 300 years after they spun their first looms. You can watch the weavers at work on a free tour of the woolen mill, which also has a wonderful gift shop (of course). The mill is signposted on the R754 road heading north out of the village.

Rte. 755, Avoca, Co. Wicklow. Shop: Daily 9am–6pm summer, 9:30am–5:30pm winter.

Wicklow Mountains National Park ★★★ NATURE SITE Sprawling around Glendalough, this hilly national park is popular with hikers walking the Wicklow Way, a trail that cuts across the park (see p. 201). In the high season, you'll find an information station at the Upper Lake at Glendalough where you can get maps and route guides. Behind the center is a sweet little "sensory garden" (free admission), containing a variety of plants chosen for their scent, texture, and even the sounds of the wildlife they attract. The closest parking is at Upper Lake, where you'll pay a couple of euro per car; or just walk up from the visitor center at Glendalough (p. 191), where the parking is free. *Note:* The Irish National Parks and Wildlife Service warns that ticks carrying Lyme disease are known to live in the hills. Although the risk of contracting the disease is small, you should dress in long sleeves, wear a hat, avoid hiking in shorts, and check for ticks afterward. Don't panic too readily if you find one, though; ticks need to be attached for at least 24 hours for infection to take place, and fewer than 100 cases are reported annually in the whole of Ireland. In the parks service's reassuring words, "remember, be aware, but don't worry."

Glendalough, Co. Wicklow. www.wicklowmountainsnationalpark.ie. © **040/445325.** Free admission. Glendalough Visitor Centre: €5 adults; €4 seniors; €4 students and children; €13 families. Park open 24 hours. Visitor Centre open May–Sept daily 10am–5:30pm; Oct weekends 10am–5:30pm; Nov–Jan weekends 9:30am–4:30pm; Feb–April weekends 10am–5:30pm. Last admission to center 45 min. before closing.

Where to Stay South of Dublin

BrookLodge & Macreddin Village ★★   A winning combination of top-end hotel, spa, and holiday village, BrookLodge is a luxurious hideaway. Guest rooms are understated and contemporary in design, while

Heathlands mantle the panoramic Wicklow Mountains.

suites—which come with a stylish mezzanine level—offer plenty of extra room for not much greater cost. The hotel is surrounded by an entire village of activities, from golf, hiking, and horseback riding to an artisan baker, deli, and crafts store. The award-winning spa, **Wells,** is worth trying out—most 1-hour treatments cost around €75. The main restaurant, the excellent **Strawberry Tree** ★★★ (see p. 201), was the first in Ireland to gain full organic certification—many of the ingredients are so local that there's a good chance your dinner was at least partly foraged by the kitchen staff.

Macreddin Village (btw. Aughrim and Aghavannagh), Co. Wicklow. www. brooklodge.com. ✆ **040/236444.** 86 units. €170–€295 double, €170–€320 suite. Free parking. Breakfast included. **Amenities:** 2 restaurants; 2 pubs; golf course; gym; pool; room service; spa; Wi-Fi (free).

The Lord Bagenal ★   This cheerful, modern hotel on the banks of the River Barrow loses points for character, but the air-conditioned bedrooms are spacious and comfortable. Ask for a room with a view of the river. This is a good choice for families; in addition to family rooms that cost very little more than doubles, the staff here will help organize activities, such as kayaking or fishing on the Barrow, and the bar even has a designated family area. The in-house restaurant serves rich, French-influenced cuisine in a formal setting, while the bar, with its cozy open fires and relaxed atmosphere, offers a simple, crowd-pleasing menu (steaks, burgers, local fish, and the like).

Main St., Leighlinbridge, Co. Carlow. www.lordbagenal.com. ✆ **059/977-4000.** 39 units. €105 double, €145 suite. 2-night minimum on summer weekends. Breakfast included. **Amenities:** Restaurant; bar; room service; Wi-Fi (free).

Powerscourt Hotel ★★★ The grand, sweeping Palladian-style frontage of this gorgeous hotel, part of the Marriott chain, is almost as impressive as its namesake, Powerscourt House (see p. 195). Guest rooms are large and elegantly furnished; some have balconies with views of the Wicklow Mountains. Everything here is way above par. The lounges are gorgeous, with soaring ceilings, beautiful furniture, and exquisite views. The in-house spa, **Espa,** is positively sci-fi in its sleek, high-tech design—the pool is lit by illuminated Swarovski crystals—and the list of treatments includes everything from hot stone and aromatherapy treatments to an 80-minute "shillelagh massage" in which you are, we kid you not, rubbed with a lucky stick. The hotel has three eateries of varying levels of formality: The **Sika** restaurant, overlooking nearby Sugar Loaf Mountain, serves outstanding modern European cuisine (plaice [flatfish] with kohlrabi and samphire, for instance, or beef with Madeira sauce). The **Sugar Loaf** lounge is marginally less formal and offers a gorgeous afternoon tea (€39 per person). If you're looking for something casual, **McGill's Pub** is the place to go. Needless to say, service throughout is impeccable.

Powerscourt Estate, Enniskerry, Co. Wicklow. www.powerscourthotel.com. ✆ **01/274-8888.** 200 units. €220–€355 double, €275–€395 suite. Free parking. Breakfast €28. **Amenities:** 2 restaurants; bar; gym; pool; pub; room service; spa; Wi-Fi (free).

Wicklow Way Lodge ★★ Though the outside of the building looks plain, it's hard to fault this modern B&B, just 6km (4 miles) from Glendalough (see p. 191). Guest rooms are simple but tastefully furnished, with lots of polished wood and toasty underfloor heating. Rooms also have—how could they not?—enormous windows to take advantage of the picture-perfect surroundings. There's one family room (children are charged at a 50% reduction on the adult rate), but because of the split-level design of the house, very young kids aren't allowed. Hosts Marilyn and Seamus are a joy, genuinely kind and helpful and full of tips for the best walking paths. There's homemade bread at breakfast, with fresh local eggs—and try the porridge, too! A haven of tranquility and charm.

Oldbridge, Roundwood, Co. Wicklow. www.wicklowwaylodge.com. ✆ **01/281-8489.** 5 units. €100–€110 double. Free parking. Breakfast included. **Amenities:** Wi-Fi (free in lounge only).

Where to Eat South of Dublin

Brunel ★★ MODERN IRISH Winner of plenty of accolades over the years, Brunel continues to uphold its reputation for excellent modern Irish cooking. All meats and produce are sourced regionally. The menu changes regularly, but expect to find such dishes as sage gnocchi with feta cheese, or beef filet with asparagus and mashed potato. Vegetarians are well-served, with a full menu of nonmeat choices.

At the Tinakilly Country House Hotel, Rathnew, Co. Wicklow (on R750, off the N11). www.tinakilly.ie. ✆ **040/469274.** Reservations recommended. Entrees €18–€32. Daily noon–4pm, 6–10pm.

WALK THIS WAY: hiking IN COUNTY WICKLOW

Loved by hikers and ramblers for its peace, isolation, and sheer beauty, the **Wicklow Way** is a 132km (82-mile) signposted walking path that follows forest trails, sheep paths, and country roads from the suburbs south of Dublin up into the Wicklow Mountains and down through country farmland to Clonegal.

It takes about 5 to 7 days to walk its entirety, with overnight stops at B&Bs and hostels along the route. Most people, however, choose to walk sections as day trips. (**Tip:** The southern section, through Tinahely, Shillelagh, and Clonegal, is much gentler and less hilly.) You can pick up information and maps at the Wicklow National Park center at Glendalough, or get more information on the Wicklow Way at **www.irishways.com**.

St. Kevin's Way, an ancient pilgrims' route more than 1,000 years old, has recently been restored. The path runs for 30km (19 miles) through scenic countryside from Hollywood to Glendalough, following the route taken by pilgrims who visited the ancient monastic site. As it winds among roads, forest paths, and open mountainside, the route visits many of the historical sites associated with St. Kevin, as well as areas of geological interest and scenic beauty.

Leaflets containing maps and route descriptions for other walks can be found at tourist offices. Folks who prefer less-strenuous walking may enjoy the paths around the lakes at **Glendalough.**

5

Chakra by Jaipur ★★ INDIAN   If you need a break from Irish food, or just fancy something a little more adventurous, this outstanding Indian restaurant is a great choice. It's not the most idyllic location, in a concrete-and-glass shopping mall down a rather nondescript street in Greystones, but inside the decor is bright and cheerful. And the food is truly excellent, inflecting classic Indian flavors with local accents. You might start with a plate of duck flavored with star plum gel and tangerine peel, before following on to a traditional butter chicken made with honey and fenugreek, or the succulent *neelgiri jhinga*—griddled shrimp spiced with carom and cilantro.

1st floor, Meridian Point, Church Rd., Greystones, Co. Wicklow. www.jaipur.ie. ℂ **01/201-7222.** Entrees €15–€36. Mon–Sat 5–11pm, Sun 1–10pm.

Poppies ★ DELI/IRISH   This is a great pit stop for a cheap and cheerful lunch in Enniskerry, a few minutes' drive from Powerscourt House (see p. 195). Don't expect anything fancy, but it's all freshly made—panini, sandwiches, salads, quiches, and meat pies. The shepherd's pie is a local favorite. Treat yourself to one of the delicious cakes for dessert. You can also get anything on the menu to go.

The Square, Enniskerry, Co. Wicklow. www.poppies.ie. ℂ **01/282-8869.** Entrees €7–€10. Daily 8am–6pm.

The Strawberry Tree ★★★ MODERN IRISH   The main restaurant of the excellent **BrookLodge** complex (see p. 198) is rightly regarded as

201

one of the best places to dine in the region. The beautiful, blue-tinged dining room makes a wonderful setting for any gathering. This was the first restaurant in Ireland to receive full organic certification, and that ethos guides the outstanding modern Irish menu, which takes localism seriously. Depending on the season, you might find wild monkfish with courgette (zucchini) and fill cream, or beef filet with lemon yogurt or ramson (a wild-growing herb native to northern Europe) and bone gravy. If you're feeling gregarious, book a place at the "big table"—a communal table that seats up to 40, at which you're served a set menu in the style of a feast.

At the BrookLodge, Macreddin Village (btw. Aughrim and Aghavannagh), Co. Wicklow. www.brooklodge.com. ⓒ **040/236444.** Fixed-price menus €65–€85. Tues–Sun 7–9pm (also Mon in Aug only).

Sports & Outdoor Pursuits in Wicklow

CYCLING   To hire a mountain bike, go to **Wicklow Adventures,** Hidden Valley Holiday Park, in Rathdrum (www.wicklowadventures.ie; ⓒ **086/727-2872**). Rentals are €15 per day, including helmet, hi-vis jacket, bike lock, and map. **Cycling Safaris** (www.cyclingsafaris.com; ⓒ **01/260-0749**) offers a weeklong tour of Dublin and Wicklow starting at €840 per person, including bed, breakfast, and 1 night's dinner; it also offers 3- and 4-night tours.

HORSEBACK RIDING   The hillside paths of Wicklow are perfect for horseback riding. More than a dozen stables and equestrian centers in the area offer horses for hire and riding lessons. Rates average around €30 to €50 per hour. **Brennanstown Riding School,** Hollybrook, Kilmacanogue, Co. Wicklow (www.brennanstownrs.ie; ⓒ **01/286-3778**), offers beginner's treks up the picturesque Little Sugar Loaf Mountain, which has views across Dublin Bay.

WATERSPORTS & ADVENTURE SPORTS   Deep in the Wicklow Mountains, the Blessington Lakes are a 2,000-hectare (4,940-acre) playground of tranquil, clean, speed-boat-free water. At the Hidden Valley Holiday Park in Rathdrum, **Wicklow Adventures** (www.wicklowadventures.ie; ⓒ **086/727-2872**) offers a variety of high-octane outdoor activities, including kayaking and laser tag. They also provide cycle tours and bike hire (see above).

Scenic Sally Gap in the Wicklow Mountains National Park tempts hikers and cyclists.

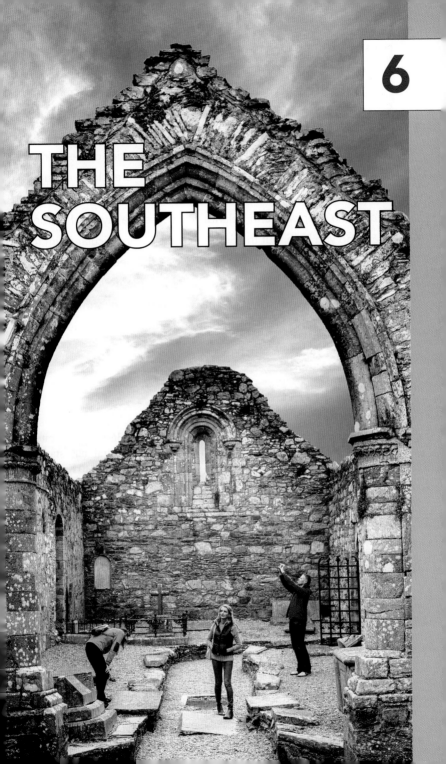

THE SOUTHEAST

t doesn't take long to feel like you're deep into the Irish countryside as you travel to the counties south of Dublin. For a start, the accent changes—subtly but unmistakably, a mellifluous dialect creeps in, peppered with unique words and phrases (remnants, so it is said, of the ancient Yola language once spoken in the region). The three main counties of the Southeast—**Waterford, Wexford,** and **Kilkenny**—are close enough together that you could use any as a base for exploring the region by car. Like everywhere in Ireland, you sense the layers of history all around you here, but the Southeast has one particular claim to fame—it's Viking country! Waterford was the seat of the Norse invasion of Ireland, and Waterford City has plenty left to see of that unique heritage. "City," by the way, is a relative term out here: Despite being the largest population center of the region, it is home to just 53,000 residents.

ESSENTIALS
Arriving

BY BUS **Bus Éireann** (www.buseireann.ie; © **01/836-6111**) operates direct service several times a day from Dublin's central bus station (**Busáras**) into Kilkenny, Wexford, and Waterford. The journey to Kilkenny takes upwards of 2 hours; to Wexford and Waterford, closer to 3.

BY TRAIN **Irish Rail** (www.irishrail.ie; © **1850/366-222**) operates several trains daily between Dublin and Kilkenny, Wexford, and Waterford. The journey to Kilkenny takes about 90 minutes; to Waterford, a little over 2 hours; and to Wexford, 2½ hours.

BY FERRY Ferries from Britain sail to Rosslare Harbour, 19km (12 miles) south of Wexford Town. See **Irish Ferries** (www.irishferries.ie; © **0818/300-400**) or **Stena Line** (www.stenaline.com; © **01/907-5555**) for bookings and information.

BY CAR The journey from Dublin to Kilkenny, Waterford, or Wexford is nearly all via motorway. From Dublin to Wexford, take N11 south. For Kilkenny, take E20, then M7 southwest out of Dublin, then split off onto M9. If you're heading to Waterford, stay on M9 for another 50km (31 miles) after the turnoff for Kilkenny. The drive to Kilkenny is about 1½ hours, and

PREVIOUS PAGE: **The haunting ruins of Ardmore Cathedral, southwest of Waterford City.**

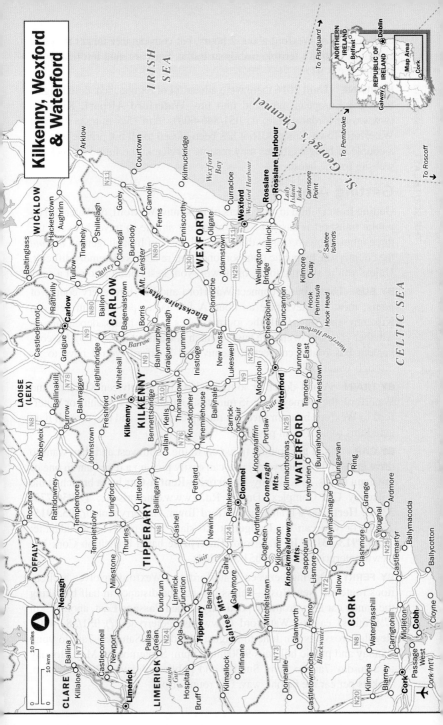

Kilkenny, Wexford & Waterford

IRISH SEA

NORTHERN IRELAND
Belfast

REPUBLIC OF IRELAND

Galway

Dublin

Map Area

Cork

To Fishguard →
To Pembroke →
To Roscoff →

St. George's Channel

CELTIC SEA

WICKLOW

Arklow
Courtown
Kilmuckridge
Baltinglass
Hacketstown
Aughrim
Shillelagh
Gorey
Camolin
Tinahely
N11
Ferns
Enniscorthy
Oilgate
Wexford Bay
Curracloe
Wexford
Wexford Harbour
Rosslare
Rosslare Harbour
Lady Island Lake
Camsore Point

CARLOW

Rathvilly
Tullow
Clonegal
Bunclody
N80
Ballon
N30
Adamstown
N25
Wellington Bridge
Kilmore Quay
Castledermot
Carlow
N9
Mt. Leinster
N90
Saltee Islands
Slaney
Graigue
Leighlinbridge
Blackstairs Mts.
Clonroche
Hook Peninsula
Hook Head

LAOISE (LEIX)

Ballinakill
N78
Ballyragget
Borris
Ballymurphy
Graiguenamanagh
Drummin
New Ross
Lukeswell
Cheekpoint
Duncannon
Waterford Harbour
Abbeyleix
Durrow
Whitehall
Freshford
Barrow
N9
Ballyhale
Mooncoin
Suir

KILKENNY

Bennettsbridge
N10
Thomastown
Inistioge
N25
Dunmore East
Johnstown
Nore
Kilkenny
Kells
Knocktopher
Waterford
Tramore
Annestown

WATERFORD

Callan
Knockmoylan
Carrick-on-Suir
Portlaw
N25
Bunmahon
Dungarvan
Ring
Roscrea
N76
Ninemilehouse
Knockanaffrin
Kilmacthomas
Rathdowney
Fethard
Comeragh Mts.
Lemybrien
Ballymacmague
Templemore
Littleton
Ballingarry
Clonmel
Kilcommon
Grange
Ardmore
Ballymacoda

TIPPERARY

Templetuohy
Thurles
Cashel
Ardfinnan
Clogheen
Cappoquin
N72
Clashmore
Youghal
Milestone
Newinn
N24
Knockmealdown Mts.
Lismore
N25
Castlemartyr
OFFALY
Cahir
Mitchelstown
Tallow
Ballycotton
Nenagh
N7
Dundrum
Bansha
Galtee Mts.
Glanworth
Fermoy
N8
Cloyne
Galtymore

CLARE

Ballina
Killaloe
Castleconnell
Newport
Pallas Grean
Oola
Limerick Junction
Tipperary
N73
Blackwater
Doneraile
Castletownroche
Watergrasshill
Midleton
Cobh

LIMERICK

Limerick
N24
Hospital
Lough Gur
Kilfinane
Kilmallock
Kilmona
Blarney
Carrigtohill
Passage West
Cork
Cork Int'l
Bruff
N20
CORK

10 miles
10 kms

to Waterford or Wexford about 2 hours, but considerably longer if you're caught in Dublin's terrible rush-hour traffic. For car-rental information in Dublin, see p. 91.

BY PLANE   Until 2016 there were a handful of regular, scheduled flights from the European mainland into tiny **Waterford Airport,** Killowen (www.waterfordairport.ie; ℭ **051/846-600**), 9km (5⅔ miles), south of Waterford Town. Since 2016 it has been closed to all but private jets, but a couple of budget airlines may resume service in the future—check the website for the latest.

Getting Around

Getting from Dublin to the centers of Kilkenny, Wexford, or Waterford by public transport is easy. It's also relatively simple to travel between the three cities. However, as with most rural areas in Ireland, getting *around* the countryside by public transport once you're here is extremely difficult. Unless you're sticking to the big towns, your best option is to rent a car.

BY BUS   Direct buses connect Waterford and Wexford every couple of hours; most journeys take an hour. A few buses per day run between Kilkenny and Waterford; the journey takes 1 to 2 hours, depending on whether you have to change buses (which you almost always do). No convenient bus routes connect Kilkenny and Wexford; you'll have to go through Waterford.

BY TRAIN   A half-dozen or so trains daily travel between Kilkenny and Waterford; the journey takes 35 minutes. Getting from Kilkenny or Waterford to Wexford by train involves multiple changes and can take all day; avoid this route if at all possible.

BY CAR   If you take public transport to the Southwest and then want to drive around the countryside, you can easily pick up a rental car in one of the main towns. In Kilkenny, **Enterprise-Rent-a-Car** has a branch at the Kilkenny Car Complex, Dublin Rd. (www.enterprise.ie; ℭ **056/775-3318**). **Hertz** has a branch in Wexford Town, on Ferrybank (ℭ **053/915-2500**), or you can try **Budget** at Rosslare Ferryport (www.budget.ie; ℭ **053/913-3318**). In Waterford, **Enterprise** has a branch on Cork Rd. (www.enterprise.co.uk; ℭ **051/304-804**).

BY FERRY   Driving between Waterford and Wexford involves a circuitous route via New Ross—unless you cut the distance in half by taking the handy car ferry from the poetically named **Passage East,** about 12km (7½ miles) east of Waterford (www.passageferry.ie; ℭ **051/382-480**). Regular crossings run June to August Monday to Saturday 7am to 9pm, Sunday and public holidays 9:30am to 9pm; September to May Monday to Saturday 7am to 8pm, Sunday and public holidays 9:30am to 8pm. Tickets per car are €8 one-way, €12 round-trip.

COUNTY WATERFORD

Waterford City's unprotected location at the edge of the ferocious Atlantic Ocean makes it Ireland's Windy City, where a sea breeze is always blowing. Not only is it the main seaport of southeast Ireland, its oceanside location has a lot to do with its status as the oldest city in the country, founded by Viking invaders in the 9th century.

Visitor Information

The **Waterford Discover Ireland Centre** is at 120 Parade Quay, Waterford (www.discoverireland.ie; © **051/875-823**). It's open Monday to Friday 9am to 5pm (sometimes later in summer) and on summer weekends only.

Exploring Waterford City

Bishop's Palace ★★ MUSEUM   One of three separate museums that are known collectively as **Waterford Treasures,** the Bishop's Palace focuses on life in the city from 1700 until the mid–20th century. The collection covering the 18th century is by far the most impressive, including furniture, art, fashion, and some exquisite glass and silverwork. The Georgian drawing room is dominated by Willem Van der Hagen's fascinating 1736 landscape painting of Waterford City—the oldest landscape of an Irish city in

The Georgian Drawing Room at the Bishop's Palace.

local hero: THOMAS FRANCIS MEAGHER

The **Granville Hotel** ★★ on Waterford Quay (see p. 214) has another claim to fame—as the birthplace of the colorful 19th-century politico Thomas Francis Meagher. Twice elected mayor of Waterford (the city's first Catholic mayor since the 16th century), Meagher was arrested for treason in 1848 after joining an anti-British rebellion. His death sentence, however, was commuted to exile in Australia—from where he eventually escaped. Fleeing to America, the wily Meagher resurfaced in the Civil War as a senior Union officer. By 1867, he had become governor of the Montana Territory, only to die suddenly, falling from a steamboat into the Missouri River. Or was he pushed? Rumor had it that he was assassinated in retaliation for his military campaigns against Native American tribes.

existence—depicting long-vanished Waterford landmarks such as the medieval Christ Church Cathedral, demolished in 1773. Appropriately enough, given its close proximity to the famous factory (see p. 210), the museum also holds the earliest surviving pieces of Waterford Crystal, including a decanter dating from 1789. The Bishop's Palace, itself an elegant example of Georgian architecture, was built by Richard Cassels (1690–1751), who was also the architect of **Leinster House** ★ in Dublin (see p. 112).

The Mall. www.waterfordtreasures.com/bishops-palace. ✆ **076/102501.** Admission €7 adults; €6 seniors and students; free for children under 14. Combined ticket with Medieval Museum €10 adults; €9 seniors and students; free for children under 14. Mon–Fri 9:15am–6pm; Sat 9:30am–6pm; Sun and public holidays 11am–6pm (closes 5pm daily Sept–May).

Christ Church Cathedral ★ CATHEDRAL Waterford's most important church building is a beautiful example of late-18th-century architecture. The Italianate style that so enthralled the Georgians is on full display here—so much so that the interior looks almost like a stately home rather than a place of worship. Corinthian columns top grand marble plinths, rising up to meet the stucco, with its delicate filigreed detail. The current building, designed by John Roberts, was finished in 1773, replacing one built by the Vikings in the 11th century. (One solitary pillar remains from the original building.) This was where Strongbow, the first English lord to invade Ireland, married an Irish princess—thus gaining a permanent foothold into Irish nobility. Christ Church's Catholic counterpart, the Holy Trinity Cathedral (also designed by John Roberts), is on Barronstrand Street (p. 210).

Cathedral Square. www.christchurchwaterford.com. ✆ **051/858958.** Free admission. Easter–Oct Mon–Sat 10am–5pm; Oct–Easter Mon–Sat noon–3pm.

City Hall ★ MUSEUM Headquarters of the local city government, this late-18th-century building houses a few pieces of interesting local memorabilia, including an exhibit on the extraordinary life of the Zelig-like 19th-century politician Thomas Francis Meagher (see box above).

The Mall. ✆ **051/860856.** Free admission. Mon–Fri 9am–5pm.

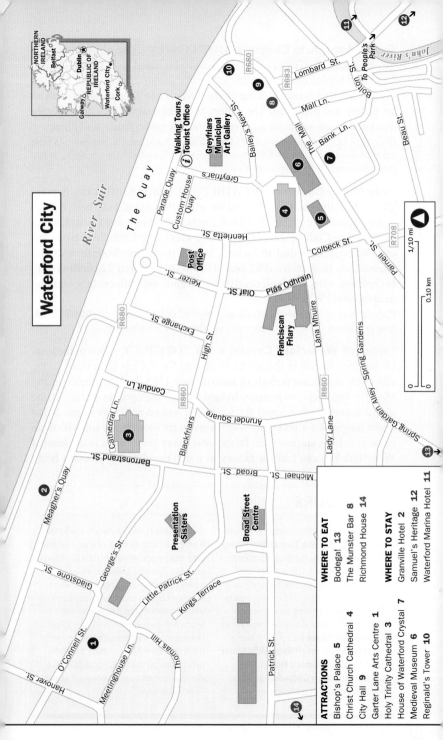

Waterford City

ATTRACTIONS

Bishop's Palace **5**
Christ Church Cathedral **4**
City Hall **9**
Garter Lane Arts Centre **1**
Holy Trinity Cathedral **3**
House of Waterford Crystal **7**
Medieval Museum **6**
Reginald's Tower **10**

WHERE TO EAT

Bodega! **13**
The Munster Bar **8**
Richmond House **14**

WHERE TO STAY

Granville Hotel **2**
Samuel's Heritage **12**
Waterford Marina Hotel **11**

Garter Lane Arts Centre ★ ARTS CENTER   One of Ireland's larg-est arts centers, the Garter Lane occupies two buildings on O'Connell Street. Number 5 holds exhibition rooms and artists' studios, and no. 22a, a former Friends meeting house, is home of the Garter Lane Theatre, along with an art gallery and courtyard. The gallery showcases works by contemporary and local artists, and hosts a varied program of music, dance, and films.
O'Connell St. www.garterlane.ie. ℂ **051/855038.** Many events and exhibits free; ticketed events around €9–€20. General opening: Tues–Sat 11am–5:30pm; indi-vidual performance and event times vary.

Holy Trinity Cathedral ★ CATHEDRAL   Waterford has two impres-sive cathedrals, one Catholic and the other Protestant, both built by one equal-opportunity architect, John Roberts (the other being Christ Church Cathedral in Cathedral Square, p. 208). This is the Catholic version, the only baroque cathedral in Ireland. It has 10 unique Waterford crystal chandeliers. Roberts lived 82 years (1714–96), fathered 22 children with his beloved wife, and built nearly every significant 18th-century building in and around Waterford.
Barronstrand and Henrietta sts. www.waterford-cathedral.com. ℂ **051/875166.** Free admission. Open daily; hours vary but generally 7:30am–7pm.

House of Waterford Crystal ★ FACTORY TOUR   One of the best-known Irish brands in the world, Waterford Crystal has been made in the city (with significant periods of hiatus) since 1783. In 2009, the company filed for bankruptcy—perhaps Ireland's most high-profile victim of the global financial crisis—and for a while it looked as if this iconic brand might disappear for good. But new owners were soon found, and with them came this shiny, purpose-built factory and visitor center, right in the heart of Waterford. You can tour the factory to watch the glittering products being

---

EPIC TOURS to go

For those who like their history entertain-ing and fast, the **Epic Tour of the Viking Triangle** offered by the Waterford tour-ism office takes in 1,100 years of local history in 45 minutes. Enthusiastic cos-tumed guides take you to several points of interest within the so-called "Viking Triangle" of central Waterford, starting at the **Bishop's Palace** (see p. 207) and moving swiftly through **Reginald's Tower** (p. 212), the **Chorister's Hall** (p. 211), and **Christ Church Cathedral** (p. 208). You don't get to linger inside any of

these places (some you won't see further than the lobby), so think of it as a whistle-stop history primer, rather than anything in depth. The tour's raucous style is heavy on audience participation, which may not be to everybody's taste, but kids will get a kick out of the dressing-up antics and wacky vibe. Tours cost €7 and operate daily May through September at noon and 2pm. Meet outside the Bish-op's Palace on the Mall. For details, see www.waterfordtreasures.com and select "The Experience."

Watch fine crystal being blown in the Waterford Crystal factory.

molded, blown, cut, and finished, mostly using traditional methods that have changed little in 200 years. Or, if you'd rather just drop in for sparkly souvenirs, you can hit the enormous gift shop without taking the tour.

The Mall. www.waterfordvisitorcentre.com. ✆ **051/317000.** Admission €12.60 adults; €12 seniors; €11 students; €6 children 6–17; free for children 5 and under; €35 families. Tour: Apr–Oct Mon–Sat 9am–4:15pm, Sun 9:30am–4:15pm; Nov–Feb Mon–Fri 9:30am–3:15pm; Mar Mon–Sat 9am–3:15pm, Sun 9:30am–3:15pm. Store: Apr–Oct Mon–Sat 9am–6pm, Sun 9:30am–6pm; Mar Mon–Sat 9am–5pm, Sun 9:30am–5pm; Nov–Dec Mon–Sat 9:30am–5pm, Sun noon–5pm; Jan–Feb Mon–Sat 9:30am–5pm.

Medieval Museum ★★ MUSEUM   The latest addition to the multi-site Waterford Treasures, the Medieval Museum has some beautiful artifacts from the city's medieval period, including richly embroidered cloth-of-gold vestments, intricate metal badges worn by pilgrims to the Holy Land, and the lavishly illustrated Charter Roll of Waterford dating from 1373. The building itself is as much of a treasure as the items on display. Though a modern design, the museum incorporates two medieval structures that were inaccessible for years: the 15th-century **Wine Vault** and the impressive 13th-century **Chorister's Hall,** with its vaulted stone ceiling, which now forms one of the main areas of the museum.

Cathedral Square. www.waterfordtreasures.com/medieval-museum. ✆ **051/849501.** Admission €7 adults; €6 seniors and students; free for children under 14; combined ticket with Bishop's Palace €10 adults; €9 seniors and students. Mon–Fri 9:15am–6pm, Sat 9:30am–6pm, Sun 11am–6pm (closes at 5pm daily Sept–May). Last admission 40 min. before closing.

Reginald's Tower ★★ MUSEUM
Claimed to be Ireland's oldest building that's still in day-to-day use, Reginald's Tower was built around the
year 1000 by the Viking invaders
who founded the city. Today it houses
a museum devoted to that period in
Waterford's history. While much of it
is interpretive in nature, with plaques
that tell the story in absorbing detail,
a surprising number of actual items
are on display too: fragments of
Viking pottery, coins, and jewelry,
including the stunning Waterford
Kite Brooch, an ornamental clasp
dating from the late 11th century,
intricately patterned with fine threads
of gold and silver. Be careful when

The modern Medieval Museum incorporates
within it some impressive chambers from the
Middle Ages.

climbing the old stone staircase—in order to confound attackers, these
"stumble steps" were designed to be deliberately uneven, hence easy to trip
over (also oriented in such a way to make wielding a sword impossible if
you're right-handed—so better leave yours behind). The Quay. www.waterfordtreasures.com/reginalds-tower. ✆ **051/304220.** Admission €5 adults; €4 seniors; €3 students and children; €13 families. Late Mar to mid-
Dec daily 9:30am–5:30pm; Jan to early Mar Wed–Sun 9:30am–5pm. Last admission
30 min. before closing.

Waterford City Walking Tours ★★ TOURS Local guide Jack
Burtchaell is well versed in the history, folklore, and witty anecdotes of
his home city. From mid-March to October he conducts this engaging
hour-long tour of the old city twice daily, leaving from the tourist office at
11:45am and 1:45pm, and the reception area of the Granville Hotel on the
Quay at noon and 2pm. You don't have to book in advance—just show up
a little before departure time. The Quay. www.jackswalkingtours.com. ✆ **051/873711.** Tour €7. Mid-Mar to Oct
daily 11:45am, 1:45pm.

Farther Afield in County Waterford

Ardmore High Cross ★ RELIGIOUS SITE Ardmore (Irish for "the
great height") is a very ancient Christian site—St. Declan, its founder, is
said to have been a bishop in Munster as early as the mid-4th century, well
before St. Patrick came to Ireland. Tradition has it that the small stone oratory in a cemetery high above Ardmore marks his burial site. St. Declan's
Oratory is one of several stone structures composing the ancient monastic
settlement. The most striking is the perfectly intact 30m-high (98-ft.)
round tower. On-site are also ruins of a medieval cathedral and, nearby, St.

Declan's well and church. Ardmore is near the border with County Cork, about 70km (43 miles) southwest of Waterford City.

On R673, Ardmore, Co. Waterford. Free admission. Daily dawn–dusk. From the main N25 road, turn onto R673 and follow signs to Ardmore.

Lismore Castle Gardens and Arts ★★ GARDENS/GALLERY High above the River Blackwater, this turreted medieval fortress dates from 1185, when Prince John of England (later the infamously bad King John who signed the Magna Carta) established a castle on this site. The grounds, surrounded by thick defensive walls dating from 1626, are spread across nearly 3 hectares (7 acres). They're peaceful and quite lovely to walk around, dotted with sculptures and offering views of the massive castle (which is, sadly, not open to the public). Also on the grounds is **Lismore Castle Arts** (www.lismorecastlearts.ie; ✆ **058/54061**), a gallery devoted to contemporary visual arts, with a good program of exhibitions. Big-name artists featured here have included Ai Weiwei and Dorothy Cross. Entry is included in the price for the gardens. The gallery recently opened a second space at **St. Carthage Hall,** located on Chapel Street in Lismore (✆ **058/54061**), open Friday to Sunday noon to 5pm, during exhibition periods only (call or go online to check the schedule). Admission is free.

Lismore, Co. Waterford (6.5km/4 miles west of Cappoquin via N72). www.lismore castlegardens.com. ✆ **058/54061.** Gardens and gallery: €8 adults; €6.50 seniors, students, and children; €20 families. Mid-Mar to mid-Oct daily 10:30am–5:30pm; last admission 1 hr. before closing.

Waterford City Walking Tours are led by the knowledgeable Jack Burtchaell.

Walk the grounds around turreted Lismore Castle, which dates to the 12th century.

A WALK TO mahon falls

The point where the narrow Mahon River reaches the top of the Comeragh Mountains makes for a beautiful, rugged view, as it tumbles hundreds of feet down the rocky slopes in a spray of silvery white. The walk to the falls is popular with hikers, both for the sheer stony loveliness of it (you can see all the way from the falls to the sea) and because it's a fairly short distance—about a 15-minute walk in each direction. The 80m (262½ ft.) waterfalls are on the R676 between Carrick-on-Suir and Dungarvan. At the tiny village of Mahon Bridge, 26km (16 miles) south of Carrick-on-Suir, turn west on the road marked for Mahon Falls, then follow signs for the falls and the Comeragh Drive. In about 5km (3 miles), you reach a parking lot along the Mahon River (in fact, just a tiny stream). The trail begins across the road. Follow the stream along the floor of the valley to the base of the falls. From here you can see the fields of Waterford spread out below you, and the sea a glittering mirror beyond. Walking time is about 30 minutes round-trip.

Mahon Falls in the Comeragh Mountains.

Where to Stay in County Waterford

Granville Hotel ★★   With its elegant, sienna-colored frontage, this welcoming hotel was built in the late 1700s and has been in business continuously since 1865. The interior retains something of a manor house feel, with rich color schemes, deep red carpeting, and antique furniture. Guest rooms are comfortable and reasonably spacious—although not all have air-conditioning, so make sure you request this when you book if it's important to you. Some rooms overlook Waterford Quay, with its field of gently bobbing yacht masts. The hotel bar is popular with locals, and the **Bianconi Restaurant** offers excellent Irish and European cooking. Staff could hardly be friendlier or more helpful. Book one of the relaxing (and reasonably priced) massage treatments in the **Therapy Room.**

Meagher's Quay. www.granville-hotel.ie. ℱ **051/305555.** 98 units. €120–€140 double. Breakfast not included in lower rates. Dinner-bed-and-breakfast packages available. Parking at Clock Tower lot (opposite the hotel) €2 per hour/€16 per day. **Amenities:** Restaurant; bar; room service; Wi-Fi (free).

Samuel's Heritage ★★ This charming B&B on the outskirts of Waterford (just a little too far to be considered walking distance from the center) overlooks open fields on one side and the River Suir on the other. Sally, Des, and family have converted their home into a modern, well-equipped lodging, with surprisingly good amenities for a countryside B&B, such as a mini-gym and infrared sauna. The bright and cheery guest rooms have ample space and a few extras such as flatscreen TVs and free Wi-Fi. Family rooms sleep up to four. The delicious breakfast options include smoked salmon with eggs from their own hens.

Halfway House, Dunmore Rd. www.samuelsheritage.com. © **051/875094.** 6 units. €80–€90 double. Rates include breakfast. Free parking. **Amenities:** Gym; sauna; Wi-Fi (free).

Waterford Marina Hotel ★ This modern, well-run hotel overlooking the River Suir isn't particularly characterful, but it's in a great location, a short walk from the center of Waterford. Rooms are clean and have everything you need, including comfortable beds. Family rooms are an exceptionally good value and sleep up to four, usually for just €10 or €20 more than the standard double rates. Some bedrooms have lovely views over the water. Special offers are often listed on the website, including packages that cover dinner in the excellent restaurant. *Tip:* Ask for an upper-floor room—the views are better, and, since there can be street noise at night, particularly on weekends, you're just a bit above the ruckus.

Canada St. www.waterfordmarinahotel.com. © **051/856-600.** 81 units. €106–€131 double. Free parking. Breakfast not included in lower rates. **Amenities:** Restaurant; bar; room service; accessible rooms; Wi-Fi (free).

Where to Eat in County Waterford

Waterford's restaurant scene is pretty impressive for such a small city. Luxury restaurants such as **Richmond House** (see p. 216) really raise the bar, but cheaper options also abound, and it's perfectly possible to dine well without stretching the wallet.

Bodega! ★★ MODERN IRISH/EUROPEAN A restaurant with an exclamation point in the name isn't really the sort of place you'd expect to sit up straight, and Bodega! certainly does its best to cultivate a funky vibe. Order a cocktail and nibble on a tasting platter, or go all out on a full meal: smoked and local market fish cooked in ginger beer batter, for instance, or Kilmore Quay haddock with peas and cockles. The word "local" appears reassuringly often on the menu. The long cocktail list should help maintain the buzz.

54 John's St. www.bodegawaterford.com. © **051/844177.** Fixed-price menu €23–€33. Entrees €16–€29. Mon–Sat noon–10pm.

The Munster ★ BISTRO This cozy bar, across the street from the House of Waterford Crystal visitor center (see p. 210), serves a smallish menu of unpretentious, traditional pub grub—steaks, Irish stew, seafood pie, and an enormous house burger. The early-evening menu has a few more ambitious choices, such as chicken breast with chorizo and Parmesan cream, or salmon fishcake served with chili jam. It may lack frills, but it's good food.

Bailey's New Street. www.themunsterbar.com. ℂ **051/874656.** Entrees €10–€14. Mon 12:30–2:30pm; Tues–Fri 12:30–2:30pm, 5–9pm; Sat 5–9pm; Sun 4–8pm.

Richmond House ★★★ MODERN IRISH   The grounds of this 18th-century mansion hide away a bountiful produce patch, where the chef gets most of the fruit and vegetables for the restaurant's kitchen. This is something of a dining destination for people in this part of Ireland, and it's easy to see why—the food is a hugely successful combination of Irish and Continental flavors. Menus change daily, according to what's fresh and in season, but you're likely to find locally sourced lamb, beef, and seafood served with sides like champ (mashed potato and spring onion) or something freshly picked from the garden. The wine list includes a better-than-average selection of wines by the glass—a relief, given the price of dinner. Those wanting to sample some of this sumptuous home cooking on a budget may want to check out the early-bird menus (€28–€35) served until 7:30pm daily. Richmond House also has a few guest rooms (around €120–€170 per night; family rooms available) if you like it so much you don't want to leave.

Signposted from N72, Cappoquin. www.richmondhouse.net. ℂ **058/54278.** Fixed-price menus €25–€55. Daily 6–9:30pm (closes 9pm Sun). Closed Dec 22–Jan 10.

Sports & Outdoor Pursuits in Waterford

CYCLING   From Waterford City, you can ride 13km (8 miles) to Passage East and take the ferry (fare with bicycle €2 one-way, €3 round-trip) to Wexford and the beautiful Hook Peninsula (see p. 222). Or continue on from Passage East to Dunmore East, a picturesque seaside village with a small beach hemmed in by cliffs. The road from there to Tramore and Dungarvan is quite scenic. To rent wheels, try **Greenway Bike Hire** at 2 Grattan Quay, Waterford City (www.greenwaywaterfordbikehire.ie; ℂ **086/129-2724**). It charges €15 per day for adults, €10 for children.

FISHING   **Knockaderry Reservoir** is an enormous 28-hectare (70-acre) fishery 12km (7½ miles) southwest of Waterford City, great for catching rainbow trout. You can purchase permits (€25) from the Centra supermarket on the main R680 road in Kilmeaden; boats can be hired for €15 from Pat Smith, treasurer of the local angling association (ℂ **051/384428**). The **Fort William Fishery,** Glencairn, Lismore (www.fortwilliamfishing.ie; ℂ **087/855-7218**), is renowned for its wild salmon; permits cost between €30 and €100 per day, depending on the month. They also rent cottages, sleeping up to 8, for €600 to €900 per week; see the website for details.

GOLF   County Waterford has rich pickings for golf fans. Clubs and resorts include three 18-hole championship courses. **Waterford Castle**

Vast flotillas of colorful sails and wet-suited windsurfers spring up all along Ireland's coasts these days as the sport of windsurfing continues to boom in popularity. Windsurfing schools with boards for rent can be found in most regions of the country, with the greatest concentration on the southeast and southwest coasts.

In the southeast, the top spots are **Cahore** and **Rosslare** in County Wexford, and **Dunmore East** and **Dungarvan** in County Waterford. Beyond the southeast, check out **Cobh** in County Cork (see p. 259), **Brandon Bay** on the Dingle Peninsula (see p. 330), **Roundstone** in Galway (see p. 389), **Achill Island** in Mayo (see p. 430), and in Donegal, **Magheroarty** (see p. 471) and **Rossnowlagh** (see p. 463).

Hotel & Golf Resort, The Island, Ballinakill, Waterford (www.waterford castleresort.com/golf-home.html; ⓒ **051/878203**), is a par-72 parkland course; greens fees are around €25 to €50. **Faithlegg Golf Club,** Faithlegg House, Waterford (www.faithlegg.com; ⓒ **051/382000**), a par-72 parkland course beside the River Suir, charges greens fees of €25 to €50. **Dungarvan Golf Club,** Knocknagranagh, Dungarvan (www.dungarvan golfclub.com; ⓒ **058/43310**), a par-72 parkland course, has greens fees of €30 to €40, with a few discounts to be had if you book online.

SAILING, WINDSURFING & SEA KAYAKING   From May to September, the **Dunmore East Adventure Centre,** Dunmore East (www.dunmore adventure.com; ⓒ **051/383783**), offers courses of 1 to 5 days that cost around €90 to €275, including equipment rental. Summer programs for children are also available.

COUNTY WEXFORD

The countryside in this area feels so peaceful and bucolic, Dublin might as well be hundreds of miles away. Wexford is known for its long stretches of pristine beaches and for the evocative historic monuments in Wexford Town and on the Hook Peninsula. The modern English name of Wexford evolved from *Waesfjord,* which is what the Vikings called it when they invaded in the 9th century. The Normans captured the town at the end of the 12th century; you can still see remnants of their fort at the Irish National Heritage Park.

Visitor Information

The **Wexford Tourist Office** is on Crescent Quay, Wexford (www.visit wexford.ie; ⓒ **053/912-3111**). It's open Monday to Saturday from 9am to 5:30pm. From late July to mid-August it's also open on Sundays from 10:30am to 5pm.

Exploring Wexford Town

The Bull Ring ★ SQUARE/STATUE   In the 17th century, this town square was a venue for bull baiting, a sport introduced by the butcher's guild. (Tradition maintained that after a match, the hide of the ill-fated bull was presented to the mayor and the meat was used to feed the poor.) But it played a greater part in history in 1798, when the first declaration of an Irish republic was made here. A memorial statue honors the Irish pikemen who fought for the cause. Today, activity at the ring is much tamer: An excellent outdoor market is held every Friday from 9:30am to 2pm and Saturday from 9:30am to 1pm.

Off N. Main St.

Cornmarket ★ SQUARE   Until a century ago, this central marketplace buzzed with the activity of cobblers, publicans, and more than 20 other businesses. Today it's just a wide street dominated by the Wexford Arts Centre, a structure dating from 1775.

Off Upper George's St.

Irish National Heritage Park ★★ HERITAGE SITE   On the banks of the River Slaney, just outside of Wexford Town, this 14-hectare (35-acre) living-history park is great fun. It provides an ideal introduction for visitors of all ages to life in ancient Ireland, from the Stone Age to the Norman invasion. Each reconstructed glimpse into Irish history is well crafted and has its own natural setting and wildlife. There's also a nature trail and interpretive center, complete with gift shop and cafe. Kids can easily be kept amused for half a day here.

Ferrycarrig (about 4.8km/3 miles west of Wexford, signposted from N11). www.inhp. com. ✆ **053/912-0733.** Admission €10 adults; €8 seniors and students; free for children 4 and under; €23–€25 families. May–Aug daily 9:30am–6:30pm (last admission 5pm); Sept–Apr daily 9:30am–5:30pm (last admission 3pm).

John Barry Monument ★ STATUE   This bronze statue, a gift from the American people in 1956, faces out to the sea as a tribute to the titular Mr. Barry, a Wexford native who became the father of the American Navy. Born at Ballysampson, Tacumshane, 16km (10 miles) southeast of Wexford Town, Barry immigrated to the colonies while in his teens and volunteered to fight in the American Revolution. One of the U.S. Navy's first commissioned officers, he became captain of the *Lexington.* In 1797, George Washington appointed him commander-in-chief of the U.S. Navy.

Crescent Quay.

St. Iberius Church ★ CHURCH   Erected in 1660, St. Iberius was built on hallowed ground—the land has been used for houses of worship since Norse times. The church has a lovely Georgian facade and an interior known for its superb acoustics. Concerts are sometimes held here; see local listings for details.

N. Main St. No phone. Free admission. Mon–Sat 9:30am–4pm.

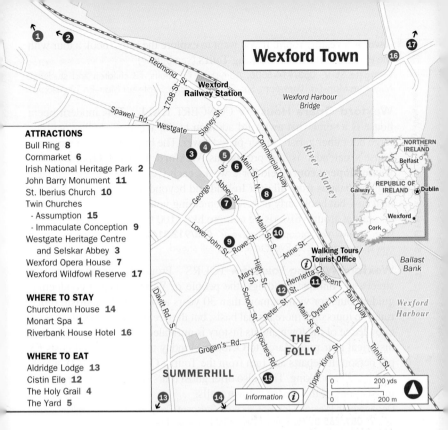

Wexford Town

ATTRACTIONS
Bull Ring **8**
Cornmarket **6**
Irish National Heritage Park **2**
John Barry Monument **11**
St. Iberius Church **10**
Twin Churches
  - Assumption **15**
  - Immaculate Conception **9**
Westgate Heritage Centre
  and Selskar Abbey **3**
Wexford Opera House **7**
Wexford Wildfowl Reserve **17**

WHERE TO STAY
Churchtown House **14**
Monart Spa **1**
Riverbank House Hotel **16**

WHERE TO EAT
Aldridge Lodge **13**
Cistin Eile **12**
The Holy Grail **4**
The Yard **5**

The Twin Churches: Church of the Assumption and Church of the Immaculate Conception ★ CHURCHES

Dominating Wexford's skyline, a pair of 69m (226-ft.) spires top these twin Gothic Revival structures (1851–58), designed by architect Robert Pierce, a pupil of Augustus Pugin (designer of the Houses of Parliament in London). Mosaics on the main doors of both churches give a good bit of local history.

Bride and Rowe sts. © **053/912-2055.** Free admission; donations welcome. Daily 8am–6pm.

Westgate Heritage Centre and Selskar Abbey ★ RELIGIOUS SITE/MUSEUM

The **Westgate Heritage Centre** is housed in what was once a tollgate on the western approach to the city, part of the town's 12th-century defensive walls. The center has some diverting exhibits relating to Wexford's town history, plus an informative film. Opening times are somewhat variable, so it's a good idea to call ahead. Adjacent to the center is the picturesque **Selskar Abbey,** where the first Anglo-Irish treaty was signed in 1169; it's said that Henry II spent Lent 1172 at the abbey doing penance for (unintentionally, so the story goes) having Thomas à Becket murdered. Although the abbey is mostly in ruins, its choir is part of a Church of Ireland edifice, and a portion of the original tower is a vesting room. If you want to explore the ruins, book a tour with the excellent **Wexford Walking Tours** (see below).

Westgate St. ✆ **053/914-6506.** Admission €7 adults; €3 children and students. May–Aug Mon–Fri 10am–6pm, Sat–Sun noon–6pm; Sept–Apr Mon–Fri 10am–5pm.

Wexford Opera House ★ CONCERT HALL   This modern opera house is a somewhat awkward addition to the Wexford skyline, with its large but rather garish copper-plated tower. The biggest event in the opera house's calendar is the prestigious **Wexford Festival Opera** (**www. wexfordopera.com**), held for 2 weeks each October/November, attracting aficionados from all over Ireland and beyond. Opera lovers will be in heaven—but book early if there's something you really want to see. Tickets start at around €10, rising to more like €100 for the best seats.

High St. www.wexfordoperahouse.ie. ✆ **053/912-2144.** Ticket prices vary; generally between €15–€35. Event times vary; call ahead.

Wexford Walking Tours ★★ TOURS   Proud of their town's ancient streets and antique buildings, the people of Wexford began conducting guided tours for visitors more than 30 years ago. Now the tourism office runs the tours on a more formal basis, but they're still led by locals, whose knowledge of the town and its history is unrivaled. The regular 90-minute historical tour runs March to October Monday to Saturday, and costs €5 per person. It departs at 11am from the Tourist Office (see p. 217), which also handles booking. They also offer ghost tours and a walk of the surviving sections of the medieval town walls.

Departs from Wexford Tourist Office on Crescent Quay. www.wexfordwalkingtours. net. ✆ **087/265-8276.** Tour €7. Mar–Oct Mon–Sat 11am.

Wexford Wildfowl Reserve ★ NATURE RESERVE   This national nature reserve is part of the unfortunately named North Slob, adjacent to Wexford Harbour, 5km (3 miles) east of Wexford Town. About 10,000 Greenland white-fronted geese—more than one-third of the world's population—winter here, as do brent geese, Bewick's swans, and wigeons. The reserve has a visitor center, an informational film, an exhibition hall, and an observation tower and blinds.

North Slob. www.wexfordwildfowlreserve.ie. ✆ **076/100-2660.** Free admission. Daily 9am–5pm. (Gates locked at 5pm.)

Farther Afield in County Wexford

Hook Lighthouse & Heritage Centre ★★ LIGHTHOUSE   The Hook Peninsula (see p. 222) is one of southern Ireland's loveliest drives, full of captivating vistas and hidden byways to discover. Nestled at the end of it all is this picturesque old lighthouse, the oldest part of which dates from the 13th century, making it the world's oldest lighthouse still in continuous use. Guided tours do an excellent job of telling the history of the lighthouse and of the surrounding peninsula, which has been

occupied since at least the 5th century A.D. There is an active program of special events too, from art courses to ghost tours. *Tip:* The drive from Waterford is drastically shorter if you take the Passage East car ferry (see p. 206).

Hook Head. www.hookheritage.ie. ℂ **051/397-055.** Admission €9 adults; €8 seniors and students; free for children 4 and under; €12–€24 families. Visitor center: Jan–Aug daily 9:30am–6pm; Sept–Dec 9:30am–5pm. Lighthouse tours: June–Aug half-hourly 10am–5:30pm (later during peak periods); Sept–May half-hourly 10am–5pm. 30km (18⅔ miles) SE of Waterford, 47km (29 miles) SW of Wexford.

Hook Lighthouse.

Irish Agricultural Museum and Famine Exhibition ★★

MUSEUM Absorbing and at times deeply affecting, this excellent museum on the grounds of Johnstown Castle illuminates how important agriculture has been to the history of this region. Exhibits are devoted to, among other things, traditional crafts, dairy farming, country furniture, and historic machinery. Of course, no farming museum in Ireland would

Johnstown Castle, home of the Irish Agricultural Museum.

A TRIP THROUGH history: EXPLORING THE RING OF HOOK

A wild and rugged place of rocky headlands and secluded beaches, the **Hook Peninsula** juts out between Bannow Bay and Waterford Harbour in southwest County Wexford. In medieval times, these inlets were significant landing spots for travelers from Britain to Ireland, as archaeological remains attest. Today, the peninsula is a popular driving or cycling route (see map p. 223), as well as a magnet for hikers on the Wexford Coastal Pathway (see p. 228) and for birders watching the spring and fall passerine migration.

Start your exploration at the town of **Wellington Bridge** 22km (14 miles) southwest of Wexford Town via R7333. Just west of Wellington Bridge on R733 is a roadside stop on the left by a cemetery; from here you can look across Bannow Bay to the ruins of **Clonmines,** a Norman village established in the 13th century. It's a fine example of a walled medieval settlement, with remains of two churches, three tower houses, and an Augustinian priory. You can drive to the ruins—just follow R733 another mile west to a left turn posted for the Wicklow Coastal Pathway, and continue straight on this road where the pathway turns right. The ruins are on private land, so ask permission at the farmhouse at the end of the road.

Continuing west on R733, turn left on R734 at the sign for the Ring of Hook, and turn right at the sign for **Tintern Abbey ★** (see p. 224). Founded by Welsh monks in the 13th century, its beautiful grounds contain a restored stone bridge that spans a narrow sea inlet.

As R734 continues south, you come to **Baginbun Head,** where the Norman presence in Ireland was first established with a victory over the Irish at the Battle of Baginbun. Today it's a peaceful scene, with a fine beach nestling against the cliffs, but from the beach you can still see the outline of the Norman earthwork fortifications on the head.

The **tip of the peninsula,** with its line of low cliffs eroded in places for blowholes, has been famous for shipwrecks since Norman times. Its historic **lighthouse** (see p. 220) has been on this site since the early 13th century.

The Ring of Hook road returns along the western side of the peninsula, passing the beaches at **Booley Bay** and **Dollar Bay.** On a promontory overlooking the town of **Duncannon** is a **fort** built in 1588 to protect Waterford Harbour from the Spanish Armada. Just north of Duncannon, along the coast at the village of **Ballyhack,** a ferry runs to County Waterford (see p. 206), and there's a Knights Hospitallers castle on a hill.

A visit to the Hook Peninsula wouldn't be complete without a stop at **Dunbrody Abbey,** in a field beside the road about 6.5km (4 miles) north of Duncannon. The abbey, founded in 1170, is a magnificent ruin and one of the largest Cistercian abbeys in Ireland. Despite its grand size, it bears remarkably little ornamentation. Tours are sometimes available; inquire at the visitor center across the road.

be complete without mention of its greatest catastrophe: the Great Famine, which killed about a million people in the mid–19th century (and was responsible for the emigration of a million more). A special section puts it all into perspective in a thought-provoking way. Johnstown Castle was

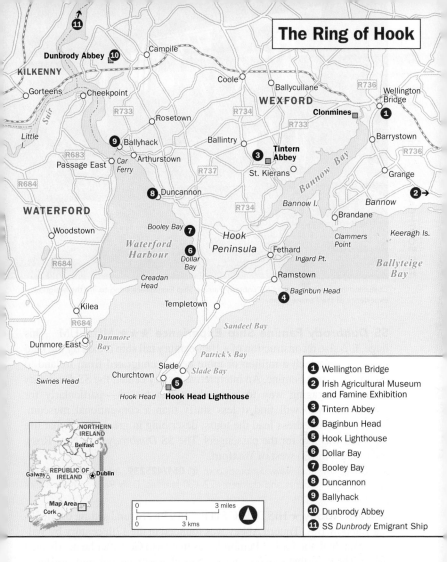

The Ring of Hook

1. Wellington Bridge
2. Irish Agricultural Museum and Famine Exhibition
3. Tintern Abbey
4. Baginbun Head
5. Hook Lighthouse
6. Dollar Bay
7. Booley Bay
8. Duncannon
9. Ballyhack
10. Dunbrody Abbey
11. SS *Dunbrody* Emigrant Ship

built in the 1400s; today it's used as a government building, but you can wander the beautiful grounds.

Johnstown Castle Estate, Bridgetown Rd., off Wexford-Rosslare Rd. (N25). www.irishagrimuseum.ie. ✆ **053/918-4671.** Gardens and museum: €8 adults; €6 seniors; €4 students and children; €24 families. Museum only: €6 adults; €5 seniors; €4 students and children; €20 families. Gardens only: Mar–Oct €3 adults; €2 seniors; €1 students and children; €8 families; Nov–Feb free. Museum: Mar–Oct Mon–Fri 9am–5pm (July–Aug 9am–6pm), Sat–Sun and public holidays 11am–5pm (July–Aug 11am–6pm); Nov–Feb Mon–Fri 9am–4pm, Sat–Sun and public holidays 11am–4pm. Gardens: Mar–Oct daily 9am–5:30pm (July–Aug 9am–6:30pm); Nov–Feb daily 9am–4:30pm.

Costumed interpreters at the SS *Dunbrody* Famine Ship Experience bring to life the emigrant experience of the Famine years.

SS *Dunbrody* Famine Ship Experience ★★★ MUSEUM   This huge, life-size reconstruction of a 19th-century tall ship is exactly the kind of vessel on which a million or more people emigrated from Ireland to escape the Great Famine. An interpretive history center, the SS *Dunbrody* offers an engaging way to learn about that history—particularly for youngsters, who will find it less stuffy than a conventional museum. Actors in period dress lead the tours, describing in great detail what life on board was like for the passengers. The SS *Dunbrody* is in New Ross, 36km (22⅓ miles) west of Wexford.

The Quay, New Ross. www.dunbrody.com. ✆ **051/425239.** Admission €10 adults; €8 seniors; €6 students and children; €22–€30 families. Daily 9am–6pm. First tour 9:45am; last tour 5pm.

Tintern Abbey ★ HISTORIC SITE   In a lovely rural setting overlooking Bannow Bay, Tintern Abbey was founded in the 12th century by William Marshall, the Earl of Pembroke, as thanks to God after he nearly died at sea. The parts that remain—nave, chancel, tower, chapel, and cloister—date from the early 13th century, though they have been much altered since. The grounds are extraordinarily beautiful and include a stone bridge spanning a narrow sea inlet. A visitor center has exhibitions on the history of the abbey, as well as a small cafe.

Note: This is not the Tintern Abbey that William Wordsworth wrote about in his famous poem of the same name; however, the monks who named this abbey were Cistercians from the other Tintern, located in Wales; they simply gave this one the same name.

Saltmills, New Ross. ✆ **051/562650.** Admission €5 adults; €4 seniors; €3 students and children; €13 families. Apr to early Nov daily 10am–5pm. Signposted 19km (12 miles) S of New Ross off of R733.

Where to Stay in County Wexford

In Wexford, choice within the town is limited; you'll do much better opting for a place in the countryside, where there's a satisfying mixture of bucolic farmhouses and luxurious getaways.

Churchtown House ★★   This sweet country-house B&B is only a 10-minute drive from the ferry port at Rosslare, yet it's a peaceful, relaxing location. Guest rooms are spacious with decent-size beds, with views over 3.2 hectares (8 acres) of park and woodland. The handsome white house was built in 1703, and has been a guesthouse since the 1990s. The hosts are especially accommodating to guests who must leave early to catch a ferry (breakfast can be served super-early, with notice). There's no restaurant, but they'll happily point you to their favorite local eateries.

Tagoat, Rosslare, Co. Wexford. www.churchtownhouse.com. ℂ **053/913-2555.** 11 units. €105–€125 double. Breakfast included. **Amenities:** Wi-Fi (free).

Monart Spa ★★★   A luxurious, restorative, grownup retreat, Monart is consistently named among the top spas in Ireland (Condé Nast even declared it the third best in the world a few years ago)—and for good reason. It's a sumptuous, impeccably designed place, nestled beside a lake and a verdant forest. Guest rooms are surrounded by woodland, and some have little balconies overlooking the grounds. The restaurant is excellent, though expensive (€45 for three courses, and many dishes have an extra cost). The heavenly spa has a thermal suite (free to use for guests) equipped with two pools, a salt grotto, indoor and outdoor saunas, and an aroma steam room. Check the website for package deals, particularly midweek specials. To maintain the air of serenity, no children are allowed at Monart.

On L6124, The Still (about 5.2km [3⅓ miles] W of Enniscorthy). www.monart.ie. ℂ **053/923-8999.** 70 units. €113–€146 double, €300–€546 suite. Free parking. Rates include breakfast. Dinner-bed-and-breakfast and spa packages available. **Amenities:** 2 restaurants; bar; afternoon tea; cafe; pool; room service; spa; Wi-Fi (free).

Riverbank House Hotel ★★   This cozy midsize hotel just outside the town center in Wexford has lovely views of the River Slaney. Rooms overlooking the river have suitably huge picture windows. Beds are comfortable and very large; some are four-posters. Family rooms cost just €30 more than doubles (though they aren't that much bigger, with one double and one single bed). The bar and restaurant are pleasant spaces, filled with natural light. The casual pub-style food is good, too—unfussy, international dishes of the something-for-everyone variety—and in good weather you can dine on the terrace overlooking the river. The genuinely cheerful staff helps things run smoothly. All in all, this is a thoroughly decent, near-budget option about a 10-minute walk from central Wexford.

The Bridge. www.riverbankhousehotel.com. ℂ **053/912-3611.** 23 units. €130–€160 double. Free parking. Breakfast not included in lower rates. **Amenities:** Restaurant; bar; room service; Wi-Fi (free).

Creative cuisine at Aldridge Lodge in Duncannon, County Wexford.

Where to Eat in County Wexford

Aldridge Lodge ★★★ IRISH   This wonderful restaurant near the village of Duncannon has been wowing diners for over a decade. The menu very much depends on what's in season, but specialties of the talented chef, Billy Whitty, include Bluebell Falls goat-cheese mousse, beef filet with cauliflower puree, and wild venison with hazelnuts. The tasting menu is a delight, bucking the trend for an endless procession of bite-size plates in favor of four balanced and well-designed courses (thoroughly reasonable, too, at just €40 per head). Aldridge Lodge also has three elegant bedrooms for €90 per night; dinner-bed-and-breakfast packages are good value for the money.

Duncannon, Co. Wexford. www.aldridgelodge.com ℰ **051/389116.** Set menus €35–€40. Reservations essential. Wed–Sat 6–9:30pm; Sun 1–2pm, dinner seatings 5:30 and 8:30pm.

Cistin Eile ★★ MODERN IRISH   Gaelic words painted on the dining room wall translate to "hunger makes a great sauce"—a wry nod to tradition that nicely sums up this place. Wexford native and rising star chef Warren Gillen deeply embraces the flavors of his home region yet gives them a contemporary edge. Haddock with wild garlic pesto, 10-hour-cooked local beef, crispy polenta with pumpkin and mushroom—all are elegantly presented without a hint of pretension. One of the nicest things about Cistin Eile is how relaxed it feels; Warren often greets guests at the

local hero: **JFK, GREAT-GRANDSON OF NEW ROSS**

U.S. President John F. Kennedy was born in America, but Patrick Kennedy (1823–58), his great-grandfather, was a son of Ireland, raised in the small waterfront city of New Ross in County Wexford. That connection to the Kennedy family history draws thousands of visitors a year.

New Ross is a modest-size working city, with rows of stone buildings leading down to a busy port that's usually dotted with fishing boats. It was from this port that Patrick Kennedy sailed to England in 1848. After working for a time in Britain, in 1849 he boarded a packet ship in Liverpool, the *Washington Irving,* and traveled to the U.S. to begin a new life.

The house near New Ross where he lived until 1848 has been converted into a museum dedicated to the Kennedy family's Irish history. The **Kennedy Homestead** (www.kennedyhomestead. ie; (✆ **051/388264**) in the tiny village of Dunganstown, 8km (5 miles) south of New Ross, is a humble, one-story traditional stone building. John F. Kennedy himself visited the homestead in June 1963, meeting his cousins during what he reportedly called "the happiest four days of my life." The story of that visit is

one of the exhibits at the modern visitors' center on the grounds, where you can see also rare memorabilia (some acquired through the Kennedy Library archival collection in Boston), and learn what the family's life was like in the dangerous world of 19th-century Ireland, as well as the circumstances that led to Patrick Kennedy's decision to emigrate. It's open daily 9:30am to 5:30pm (last admission 5pm); entry costs €8 adults, €7 seniors, €6 students, and €22 families.

Another nearby JFK site of interest is the **JFK Memorial Park & Arboretum** (www.heritageireland.ie; (✆ **051/388171**), a beautiful lakeside garden and wildlife haven dedicated to the late president. It's just a memorial—there's no strong connection between the family and the park—but it's a popular stop for those visiting the area. It's signposted from R733, about 12km (7½ miles) south of New Ross. Opening times are: May to August daily 10am to 8pm; April and September daily 10am to 6:30pm; and October to March daily 10am to 5pm. Last admission is 45 minutes before closing. Entry costs €5 adults, €4 seniors, €3 students and children, and €13 families.

door personally and chats with them at their tables. *Tip:* Lunch here is surprisingly affordable.

80 South Main St., Wexford, Co. Wexford. (✆ **053/912-1616.** Lunch entrees €4–€13. Dinner set menu €35. Reservations recommended. Mon–Tues noon–3pm; Wed–Sat noon–3pm, 6–9pm. Closed Sun.

The Holy Grail ★ PAN-ASIAN The eclectic mix at this cheerful restaurant in New Ross includes Indian, Chinese, and Thai flavors alongside more traditional European dishes (though not at the same time). The approach can feel somewhat unfocused, but the food is good. Try the tasty mango curry, made with tiger prawns and succulent raw mangoes, or, if you're feeling more local in your tastes, go for a filet of salmon with white

walk this way: **THE WEXFORD COASTAL PATHWAY**

Along the entire coastline you'll see brown signs with a picture of a hiker on them, marking the **Wexford Coastal Pathway,** which meanders along the coast via pristine beaches and country lanes—and, unfortunately, some stretches of busy roads. At the north end, however, there's a peaceful beach walk from **Clogga Head** (County Wicklow) to **Tara Hill,** 14km (8 miles) south, ending with panoramic views from atop Tara Hill. South of Wexford town, another good section runs from **Rosslare Harbour** around Carnsore Point to **Kilmore Quay.**

Yet another fine coastal walk is near Wexford town in the **Raven Nature Reserve,** an area of forested dunes and uncrowded beaches. To get there, take R741 north out of Wexford, turn right on R742 to Curracloe village, and at Curracloe turn right to drive just over a mile to the beach parking lot. The nature reserve is to your right. By car it's a half-mile south, but you can also walk there along the beach. It's 5km (3 miles) to Raven Point, where at low tide you can see the remains of a shipwreck, half-buried in the sand.

wine sauce. A good early-bird deal is offered on weekdays: a two-course meal for two, with a bottle of house wine, for €49.50.

8 Irishtown, New Ross, Co. Wexford. www.theholygrailwexford.com. ℂ **053/914-4100.** Entrees €13–€23. Reservations recommended. Mon–Thurs noon–2:30pm, 4:30–10pm; Fri–Sun noon–10:30pm.

The Yard ★★ BRASSERIE   There are two sides to this place; drop in at lunchtime for a restorative, hearty, but informal meal (beer-battered cod and chips, perhaps, or a tasty burger), or come in the evening for a more elaborate brasserie-style menu, combining traditional Irish flavors with wider influences. Start with a tasty chicken salad, then go for an herby roast chicken with carrot and tarragon, or barbecued monkfish tale with saffron custard and peperonata. Come on Thursday or Friday night for the great-value set menu: four courses for just €30, plus free entry to the **Centenary Stores** (www.thestores.ie; ℂ **053/912-4424**), a popular nightclub on Charlotte Street. Open Thursday to Saturday evenings, the **Little Yard** is an alternative dining space, part bar, part tapas restaurant. It's also open Sunday nights on holiday weekends.

3 Lower Georges St., Wexford, Co. Wexford. www.theyard.ie. ℂ **053/914-4083.** Entrees €17–€28. Mon–Sat noon–10pm.

Sports & Outdoor Pursuits in Wexford

BEACHES   County Wexford's beaches at **Courtown, Curracloe, Duncannon,** and **Rosslare** are good for walking, jogging, and swimming.

BIRD & WILDLIFE WATCHING   Besides the **Wexford Wildfowl Reserve ★** (see p. 220), bird-watchers head for **Hook Head** (see p. 220), a good spot in spring and autumn for seeing the passerine migration. In addition to swallows, swifts, and warblers, look out for the less common cuckoos, turtle-doves, redstarts, and blackcaps.

Kilmore Quay Angling (www.kilmoreangling.com; ✆ **087/213-5308**) offers an "eco-cruise" around the Saltee Islands, to see seals and birds (without landing); expect to pay around €20 adults, €10 children.

In May, June, and July, **Great Saltee Island** is excellent for watching seabirds, when the island's southern cliffs become mobbed with nesting birds and their young. Plentiful species include puffins, which nest in underground burrows, as well as graceful guillemots, cormorants, kitti-wakes, gannets, and Manx shearwaters. The island is privately owned, but visitors are welcome so long as they do not disturb the bird habitat and the island's natural beauty. You can usually charter a boat to the Saltees from the Kilmore Quay; alternatively, try **Sailing Ireland** (www.sailingireland.ie; ✆ **053/913-9163** or 086/171-3800). Landings generally take place only in summer, and not in rough weather.

CYCLING From Wexford, the road north up the coast through Curracloe to Blackwater is a scenic day trip. You can rent mountain bikes in Wexford Town at **Hayes Cycle Shop,** 108 South Main St. (www.hayescycles.com; ✆ **053/912-2462**).

DIVING The Kilmore Quay area, south of Wexford Town, offers some of the most spectacular diving in Ireland, especially around the Saltee Islands and Conningbeg rocks. Wrecks off the coast lie at depths of around 60m (200 ft.). For all your diving needs, consult the **Pier House Diving Centre,** Kilmore Quay (✆ **053/29703;** e-mail scubabreaks@eircom.net).

COUNTY KILKENNY

Like so many Irish towns, Kilkenny City stands on the site of an old monastery from which it takes its name. A priory was founded here in the 6th century by St. Canice; in Gaelic, *Cill Choinnigh* means "Canice's Church." In medieval times, it was a prosperous walled city. Much of its medieval architecture has been skillfully preserved, including long sections of the medieval wall. Farther afield from the county seat, the gentle countryside is full of captivating old ruins, from the majestic **Kells Priory** to the haunting remains of **Jerpoint Abbey.**

Visitor Information

The **Kilkenny Tourist Office** is at Shee Alms House, Rose Inn Street, Kilkenny (www.kilkennytourism.ie; ✆ **056/775-1500**). It's open May to September Monday to Saturday 9am to 5:30pm, Sunday 10:30am to 4pm; October to April Tuesday to Saturday 9am to 5pm. It sometimes closes for lunch on quieter days.

Exploring Kilkenny City

Black Abbey ★ CHURCH
Nobody is quite sure why this Dominican church, founded in 1225, is named Black Abbey. It may be because the Dominicans wore black capes over their white habits, or perhaps because the Black Plague claimed the lives of eight priests in 1348. The abbey's blackest days came in 1650, when Oliver Cromwell used it as a court from which to dispense summary justice, before destroying it completely; by the time he left, all that remained were the walls. The abbey was rebuilt and opened in 1816 as a church; a new nave was completed in 1866, and the entire building was fully restored in 1979. Among the elements remaining from the origi-

Founded by Dominican friars in the 13th century, Black Abbey today makes a dramatic setting for a music concert.

nal abbey are an alabaster sculpture of the Holy Trinity that dates from 1400, and a pre-Reformation statue of St. Dominic carved in Irish oak, which is believed to be the oldest such piece in the world. The huge Rosary Window, a stained-glass work of nearly 45sq.m (484 sq. ft.) representing the 15 mysteries of the rosary, was created in 1892 by Mayer of Munich.

Abbey St. (off Parliament St.). ✆ **056/772-1279.** Free admission; donations welcome. Apr–Sept Mon–Sat 7:30am–7pm, Sun 9am–7pm; Oct–Mar Mon–Sat 7:30am–5:30pm. No visits during worship.

Kilkenny Castle ★★★ CASTLE Standing majestically beside the River Nore on the south side of Kilkenny City, this landmark medieval castle was built in the 12th century and remodeled in Victorian times. From its sturdy corner towers to its battlements, Kilkenny Castle retains the imposing lines of an authentic fortress. The exquisitely restored interior includes a library, drawing room, and bedrooms, all decorated in 1830s style. The former servants' quarters are now an art gallery. The 20-hectare (49-acre) grounds include a riverside walk, extensive gardens, and a well-equipped children's playground. This is a very busy site, so arrive early (or toward the end of the day) to avoid waiting.

The Parade. www.kilkennycastle.ie. ✆ **056/770-4100.** Admission €8 adults; €6 seniors; €4 students and children; children 5 and under free; €20 families. June–Aug daily 9am–5:30pm; Apr–May and Sept 9:30am–5:30pm; Oct–Feb 9:30am–4:30pm; Mar 9:30am–5pm. Guided tours only Nov–Jan. Last admission 30 min. before closing (45 min. Nov–Jan).

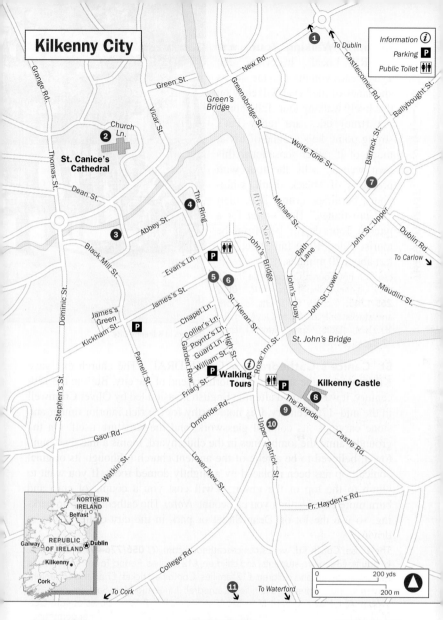

Kilkenny City

Information ⓘ
Parking P
Public Toilet 🚻

NORTHERN IRELAND
Belfast

REPUBLIC OF IRELAND
Galway • Dublin ✈
Kilkenny •
Cork •

0   200 yds
0   200 m

ATTRACTIONS
Black Abbey **3**
Kilkenny Castle **8**
St. Canice's Cathedral **2**
Smithwick's Experience Kilkenny **4**

WHERE TO STAY
Lawcus Farm Guesthouse **11**
Pembroke Hotel **10**
Rosquil House **1**

WHERE TO EAT
Campagne **7**
Gourmet Store **5**
Kyteler's Inn **6**
Ristorante Rinuccini **9**

Kilkenny Walking Tours ★★

TOURS Local historian Pat Tynan leads you through the streets and lanes of medieval Kilkenny on this lively walking tour. Tall-sounding (true) tales are really Pat's strong point; he's a mine of trivia, much of it rather sensational (his own website sells the tour with promises of "black death, whippings, burnings, crime, jails, theft and prostitutes." How's *that* for a pitch?). Tours depart daily from the tourist office, Rose Inn Street, and last about 70 minutes.

c/o Kilkenny Tourist Office, Rose Inn St. www.kilkennywalkingtours.ie. ☎ **087/ 265-1745.** Tickets €7 adults, seniors, and students. Mid-Mar to Oct Mon–Sat 10:30am, 12:15, 3pm; Sun 11:15am, 12:30pm.

Buskers in Kilkenny City.

St. Canice's Cathedral ★★ CATHEDRAL

The church that gave Kilkenny its name stands at the northern end of the city. Built in the 12th century, it was restored after the English invasion led by Oliver Cromwell in the mid–17th century. It is noteworthy for the rich interior timber and stone carvings, its colorful glasswork, and the structure itself. On the grounds, amid the tombstones in the churchyard, looms a massive round tower, believed to be a relic of the ancient church (although its original conical top has been replaced by a slightly domed roof). If you want to climb to the top of the tower, it will cost you a couple of euro and burn more calories than you can count. *Note:* The cathedral has no parking, so use the lot on Dean Street or park in the city center if you're driving.

The Close, Coach Rd. www.stcanicescathedral.com. ☎ **056/776-4971.** Cathedral: €4 adults; €3 seniors, students, and children; €12 families. Round Tower: €4 adults; €4 seniors, students, and children; €12 families. Combined ticket: €7 adults; €6 seniors, students, and children; €15 families. Cathedral: June–Aug Mon–Sat 9am–6pm, Sun 1–6pm; Apr–May and Sept Mon–Sat 10am–5pm, Sun 2–5pm (closes at 4pm Oct–Mar); Oct–Mar Mon–Sat 10am–1pm and 2–4pm. Round Tower (weather permitting): June–Aug Mon–Fri 9am–6pm, Sun 1–6pm. Last climb 30 min. before closing. No children under 12 allowed to climb the round tower.

Smithwick's Experience Kilkenny ★ FACTORY TOUR

Established in 1710 by John Smithwick, the St. Francis Abbey Brewery occupies a site that once belonged to the 12th-century abbey of the same name. A popular local beer called Smithwick's is produced here, as are

Budweiser and Land Kilkenny Irish beer. In 2014, the old Victorian brewery building was repurposed as a shiny new visitor center, which acts as the starting-off point for an informative tour of the grounds. The tour is as much about the history of brewing as an appreciation (with tastings!) of the famous product itself. A highlight—if you can call it that—is a stop by the ruined 12th-century abbey, still located on the brewery grounds. It would qualify as picturesque if it wasn't thoughtlessly hemmed in by industrial warehouses and a large parking lot.

Parliament St. www.smithwicksexperience.com. © **056/778-6377.** Admission €15 adults; €13 seniors and students 18 and older; €9 students under 18; €38 families. No high heels or open-toe sandals. Mar–Oct daily 10am–6pm; Nov–Feb 11am–5pm. Last tour 1 hr. before closing.

Farther Afield in County Kilkenny

Duiske Abbey ★ CHURCH   A fine example of an early Cistercian abbey, Duiske Abbey was founded in 1204. Although it was officially suppressed in 1536, monks continued to occupy the site for many years. In 1774, the tower of the abbey church collapsed. In 1813, the roof was replaced and religious services returned to the church, but the abbey didn't approach its former glory until the 1970s, when a group of locals mounted a reconstruction effort. Now, with its fine lancet windows and a large effigy of a Norman knight, the abbey is the pride of Graiguenamanagh. The adjacent visitor center has an exhibit of Christian art and artifacts.

Upper Main St., Graiguenamanagh. © **059/972-4238.** Free admission; donations welcome. Daily 8am–6pm.

Dunmore Cave ★ UNDERGROUND CAVERNS   This gloomy series of chambers, formed over millions of years, contains some fine calcite formations. The caves have been known to humans for at least a millennium; they are first recorded in written records from the 9th and 10th centuries. These records, known as the *Triads of Ireland,* indicate that a bloody Viking massacre took place here in the year A.D. 928. No conclusive proof has ever been found, but evidence unearthed by archaeologists in more recent years confirms that Vikings used the caves. Exhibits at the visitor center tell the story. Access to the cave is by guided tour only. Dunmore is about 11km (7 miles) from Kilkenny City.

Off Castlecomer Rd. (N78), Ballyfoyle. © **056/776-7726.** Admission €5 adults; €4 seniors; €3 students and children; €13 families. Mid-June to early Sept daily 9:30am–6:30pm (last tour 5pm); Mar to mid-June and early Sept to Oct daily 9:30am–5pm (last tour 4pm); Nov to Feb Wed–Sun 9:30am–5pm (last tour 3pm). Tours may end early in winter depending on sunset.

Jerpoint Abbey ★★ CHURCH   About 18km (11 miles) southeast of Kilkenny, this atmospheric Cistercian monastery dates from the 12th century. Highlights of the ethereal ruins, which are preserved in a peaceful country setting, include a sculptured cloister arcade, Romanesque architecture in the north nave, and unique stone carvings on the medieval tombs (some of which supposedly have traces of original paint on them, but we've never been able to find it). The staff is quite friendly and knowledgeable about the local area. Ask for details of where to find the mysterious, ghostly ruins of the **Church of the Long Man,** about 16km (10 miles) away. If you're lucky, they'll be able to direct you—it's very hard to find otherwise, and a local secret you may find yourself sworn to keep. *Tip:* If you're here in spring or autumn, plan your visit toward the end of the day. Wandering around these ancient places as the setting sun blushes the walls in peach and gold is an unforgettable experience.

On N8, 2.5km (1½ miles) SW of Thomastown. www.heritageireland.ie. ✆ **056/772-4623.** Admission €5 adults; €4 seniors; €3 students and children; €13 families. Early Mar–Sept daily 9am–5:30pm; Oct daily 9am–5pm; Nov to mid-Dec daily 9:30am–4pm. Closed early Dec to early Mar (except for prebooked tours).

Jerpoint Glass Studio ★ CRAFT STUDIO   Here you can witness the creation of Jerpoint glass, which you've probably been admiring in shops all across Ireland. The lines of the glasses, goblets, and pitchers are simple and fluid, highlighted by swirls of color. Watch the glass being blown and then blow your budget next door at the shop.

Stoneyford. www.jerpointglass.com. ✆ **056/772-4350.** Shop and gallery: Mar–Oct Mon–Sat 10am–6pm; Sun and public holidays noon–5pm. Nov–Feb Mon–Fri 10am–5pm, Sat noon–5pm (closed Sun). Glassblowing demonstrations Mon–Thurs 10am–4pm, Fri 10am–1pm. No demonstrations on public holidays.

Kells Priory ★★ RELIGIOUS RUINS   With its encompassing fortification walls and towers, Kells is a glorious ruined monastery enfolded into the sloping south bank of the King's River. In 1193, Baron Geoffrey FitzRobert founded the priory and established a Norman-style town beside it. The current ruins date from the 13th to 15th centuries. The priory's wall has been carefully restored, and it connects seven towers, the remains of an abbey, and foundations of chapels and houses. You can tell by the thick walls that this monastery was well fortified, and those walls were built for a reason—it was frequently attacked. In the 13th century, it was the subject of two major battles and burned to the ground. (Despite the similar name, this is not the same monastery where the famous Book of Kells, see p. 93, was stored for years before being moved to Dublin in the 1650s. That monastery is in County Meath, just off M3, about 65km/40 miles north of Dublin.) The priory is less than a half-mile from the village of Kells, so if you have some time to spare, cross the footbridge behind it, which takes you on a beautiful stroll across the river and intersects a riverside walk leading to a picturesque old mill.

Kells. ✆ **056/775-1500.** Free admission. Take N76 S from Kilkenny, follow signs for R699/Callan and stay on R699 until you see signs for Kells.

Where to Stay in County Kilkenny

Lawcus Farm Guesthouse ★★★ Perfect peace and tranquility await you at this gorgeous farmyard B&B, deep in the Kilkenny countryside. Make no mistake: This is the real deal ("Helping us on the farm at feeding time is greatly appreciated," says the website), but hosts Mark and Anne Marie go out of their way to welcome guests. The early-19th-century farmhouse has been beautifully renovated. Guest rooms are cozy and decent-sized, with plenty of natural light. Some have original fireplaces; one has exposed graystone walls and an antique-style brass bed. It's a pastoral setting to die for—you're right next to a river, where you can go wild-water swimming or even try your hand at fishing for trout. Home-cooked breakfasts are delicious, but you'll have to fend for yourself at dinner. (Luckily, your hosts can recommend a string of nearby places.) They've opened a self-contained lodge for couples, the Tree House, which sits on a rocky outcrop down by the river—what romantic bliss!—and costs €250 for 2 nights, including breakfast in the main house. The only snag in this rural idyll? Lawcus Farm doesn't accept credit cards or checks, so make sure you're able to pay in cash.

Stoneyford. www.lawcusfarmguesthouse.com. © **086/603-1667.** 6 units. €100–€120 double. Free parking. Breakfast included. Discounts for stays of 3 or more nights. Children under 5 free (1 per party). **Amenities:** Wi-Fi (free). From the R713, pass Stoneyford sign and turn to the right of the small bridge; follow signs to B&B.

Pembroke Hotel ★★ Just a few streets away from Kilkenny Castle (from the upper floors you can see the castle's turrets poking up over rooftops), this is a cosmopolitan hotel in the center of Kilkenny City. Bedrooms are modern and comfortable, with plenty of room, if not a great deal of character. The in-house **Statham's Restaurant** serves good modern Irish cooking, and certain nights in summer features barbecue. The sophisticated bar is a lively spot for a cocktail or glass of wine. Guests get free use of a local gym and pool, a 10-minute walk away.

Patrick St. www.kilkennypembrokehotel.com. © **056/778-3500.** 74 units. €150–€217 double. Free parking. Rates include breakfast. **Amenities:** Restaurant; bar; gym and pool (10-min. walk); room service; Wi-Fi (free).

Rosquil House ★★ Comfortable and friendly, this modest little B&B is great value for the money. Your hosts, Rhoda and Phil, greet guests with genuine warmth and enthusiasm, making them feel immediately at home. The house was purposely built as a B&B, so the bedrooms are spacious and well-proportioned. One room is fully accessible for those with mobility problems. Family rooms cost about €10 to €20 extra. Public areas, including a large guest lounge, are tastefully decorated in color schemes of chocolate and cream, with polished wood floors. The breakfasts cooked by Phil are delicious. The only downside is that you're a little far from the action, with central Kilkenny about a 15-minute walk away.

Castlecomer Rd. www.rosquilhouse.com. ℂ **056/772-1419.** 7 units. €80–€95 double. Parking at nearby lots €4–€5 overnight; €5–€16 24 hr. Rates include breakfast. **Amenities:** Wi-Fi (free).

Where to Eat in County Kilkenny

Campagne ★★★ BISTRO   The chef at this outstanding French-Irish restaurant, about a 10-minute walk from Kilkenny Castle, once ran the kitchen at Dublin's superlative **Chapter One** ★★★ (see p. 145). The sleek and atmospherically lit dining room has colorful modern art on the walls; the menu is short but subtly inventive: monkfish with *coco de paimpol* beans, pheasant in pastry with parsnip puree, or perhaps beef filet in a buttery bearnaise sauce with a Parmesan cheese croquette. A full vegetarian menu is always available. For dessert, try the warm caramelized pear with cinnamon ice cream. The extensive wine list is well chosen, with particularly strong French options. Locals make this their top choice for special occasions—but if you find the prices too high, come for the early-bird menu, very decently priced at €35 for three courses.

5 The Arches, Gashouse Lane. www.campagne.ie. ℂ **056/777-2858.** Entrees €29–€33. Dinner Wed–Sat 6–10pm; lunch Fri–Sun 12:30–2:30pm. Open Sun nights on Bank Holiday weekends. Closed Mon and Tues.

Gourmet Store ★ DELI/CAFE   Very good for a quick lunch on the go, this cafe in the center of Kilkenny is popular with local workers who come for tasty sandwiches and bagels. There's a great stock of deli goods, so you can put together your own picnic hamper, or the folks behind the counter will do it for you—perfect for when you need a quick bite on the road. A lot of the off-the-shelf products are local and small-brand, including jams and chutneys that make great gifts and edible souvenirs.

56 High St. ℂ **056/777-1727.** All items €4–€10. Mon–Sat 8am–5:30pm.

Kyteler's Inn ★ PUB   In business for over 6 centuries, this vintage inn serves decent pub

Historic Kyteler's Inn in Kilkenny City.

food—sandwiches, Irish stew, burgers, fish and chips—but it's the atmosphere you really come for. With all the exposed flagstones and cozy nooks, it's hard to think of a more satisfyingly Irish-looking pub. The place is named after noted hellraiser Alice Kyteler, who died in 1324. She poisoned at least three of her husbands, ran the inn as a den of debauchery, and was sentenced to be burned as a witch. But she escaped, and nobody saw or heard from her again. Unless, that is, you believe some of the more colorful tales about this place after dark…

Kieran St. www.kytelersinn.com. © **056/772-1064.** Lunch entrees €8–€14. Dinner entrees €8–€24. Mon–Fri 11am–11:30pm, Sat 11am–2am, Sun 12:15pm–midnight (food served until about 10pm).

Ristorante Rinuccini ★★★ ITALIAN   This extremely popular restaurant opposite Kilkenny Castle packs in diners for delicious Italian food with an Irish accent. The basement-level dining room gets very busy, but the food more than makes up for it. The homemade pasta is as good as you'd expect, and on the specials board, local produce really comes into its own—catch of the day fresh from Kilmore Quay; Silver Hill duck baked with sweet aurum (an Italian orange liqueur); or supreme of Irish chicken with white wine sauce. Desserts are equally good—try the homemade chocolate tart served with honey ice cream. The tasty cheese plate is filled with selections imported from Italy. Make reservations if you're coming on a weekend.

1 The Parade. www.rinuccini.com. © **056/776-1575.** Entrees €17–€29. Reservations recommended. Mon–Fri noon–2:30pm, 5–10pm; Sat noon–3pm, 5–10pm; Sun noon–9pm.

Sports & Outdoor Pursuits in Kilkenny

GOLF   **Mount Juliet Golf and Country Club** in Thomastown (www.mountjuliet.ie; © **056/777-3000**) is an excellent course 16km (10 miles) south of Kilkenny City. The 18-hole, par-72 championship course, designed by Jack Nicklaus, charges greens fees of €100. Even closer to the city is the 18-hole championship course at the **Kilkenny Golf Club** in Glendine (www.kilkennygolfclub.com; © **056/776-5400**), an inland par-71 layout with greens fees around €35 to €60.

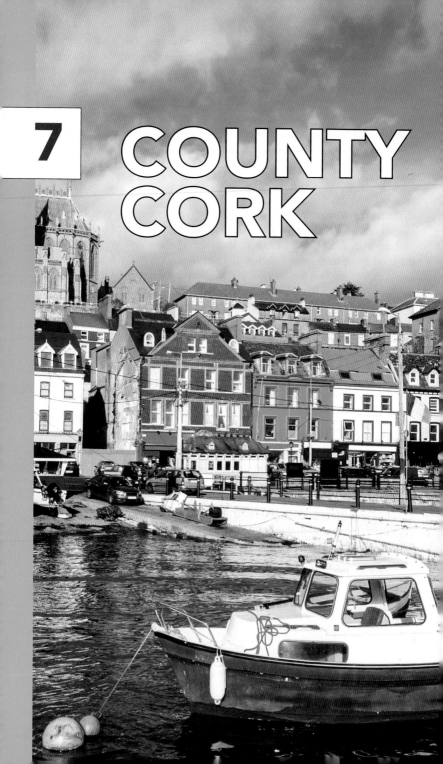

7 COUNTY
CORK

T he largest of Ireland's counties, Cork is also one of its most diverse. It encompasses a lively capital city, quiet country villages, rocky hills, picturesque beaches, and long stretches of flat, green farmland. Here, workaday Irish life meets modern tourism (this is where you find Blarney Castle, after all), and somehow manage to coexist gracefully. St. Fin Barre founded Cork in the 6th century, when he built a monastery on a swampy estuary of the River Lee, giving the place the rather generic Gaelic name of *Corcaigh*— which, unromantically, means "marsh." Range beyond Cork City to visit the pretty harbor town of Kinsale, famous for spearheading Ireland's gourmet food scene in the 1990s and 2000s; the storied seaport of Cobh in East Cork; or the barren beauty of Cape Clear Island in craggy West Cork.

ESSENTIALS
Arriving

BY BUS **AirCoach** (www.aircoach.ie; ✆ **01/844-7118**) runs a regular direct service from Dublin to Cork City. You can catch the bus either at Dublin Airport or Westmoreland Street, in the center of Dublin; from there, the journey to Patrick's Quay in the center of Cork takes 3 hours, traffic permitting. Buses leave at 25 minutes past the hour from Terminal 2 (starting at 6:25am), 5 minutes later from Terminal 1, and then on the hour from Aston Quay, with the final bus of the day leaving Terminal 2 at 25 minutes past midnight (from Aston Quay at 1am). One-way tickets are €17 adults, €10 children under 13; round-trip tickets are €27 adults, €20 children. You can sometimes (but not always) get a discount for booking online. In Cork City, **Bus Éireann** (www.buseireann.ie; ✆ 021/450-8188) runs from the Parnell Place Bus Station to all parts of the Republic. Bus 226 connects Cork with Kinsale. Buses also arrive on Pier Road.

BY TRAIN **Iarnród Éireann/Irish Rail** (www.irishrail.ie; ✆ 185/036-6222) travels to Cork City from Dublin and other parts of Ireland. Trains arrive at Kent Station, Lower Glanmire Road, in eastern Cork City (✆ 021/455-7277). Kinsale does not have a train station.

BY FERRY There are no longer any direct ferry routes into Cork from Britain. However, **Brittany Ferries** (www.brittany-ferries.com;

FACING PAGE: **The harbor at Cobh, County Cork.**

(✆ **021/427-7801**) sail a few times per week between Roscoff, in France, and Cork's Ringaskiddy Ferryport.

BY CAR Cork is easily reachable on the N8 from Dublin, N25 from Waterford, and N22 from Killarney. To rent a car in Dublin, see p. 91; to rent a car at Shannon Airport, see p. 334. To hire a car in Cork, try **Enterprise Rent-A-Car,** Kinsale Road (✆ **021/497-5133**), or **Hertz** at Cork Airport (✆ **021/496-5849**).

BY PLANE **Cork Airport,** Kinsale Road (www.corkairport.com; ✆ **021/413131**), is served by several airlines, including **Aer Lingus, British Airways, Flybe,** and **Ryanair.** Cork recently overtook Shannon as the Republic of Ireland's second busiest airport (and the fourth in Ireland overall, after Dublin and the two airports in Belfast). It has direct flights to and from several European countries, including the U.K. and in France. However, it has stopped running any scheduled flights to other airports in Ireland.

Visitor Information

The **Cork Tourist Office** is at the appropriately named Tourist House at 42 Grand Parade, Cork (www.corkcity.ie; ✆ **021/425-5100**). It's generally open Monday to Saturday 9am to 5pm (closed Sun). The **Kinsale Tourist Office** on Pier Road, Kinsale (www.kinsale.ie; ✆ **021/477-2234**), is open Monday to Saturday 9am to 5pm (closed Sun). The **Cobh Tourist Office,** in the Sirius Arts Centre, the Old Yacht Club Building, Lower Road, Cobh (✆ **021/481-3301**), is open Monday to Friday 9am to 5:30pm and Saturday to Sunday 10:30am to 4:30pm. **Seasonal tourist offices** operate at the Jameson Centre, Midleton (✆ **021/461-3702**), and Market Square, Youghal (✆ **024/92447**).

CORK CITY

Cork City might as well be called Dublin South. It's far smaller than the capital, with 125,000 residents, but it's a busy, attractive, cultured place. Cork City is home to a major university, which keeps the population young, the creative class dynamic, the pubs interesting, and the number of affordable restaurants plentiful. It also, statistically, has one of the mildest climates in Ireland—temperatures in the city rarely get below freezing or above 25° C (77° F), whatever the time of year. Cork isn't as instantly crowd-pleasing a city as, say, Dublin—it has severe traffic congestion and can feel gritty and overcrowded. For its fans, however, these flaws merely underscore the sense that it's a real, working town, with wonderfully varied offerings. Because of the limited parking, Cork is best seen on foot; it's compact enough for that to be feasible. A signposted Tourist Trail can guide you to the major sights.

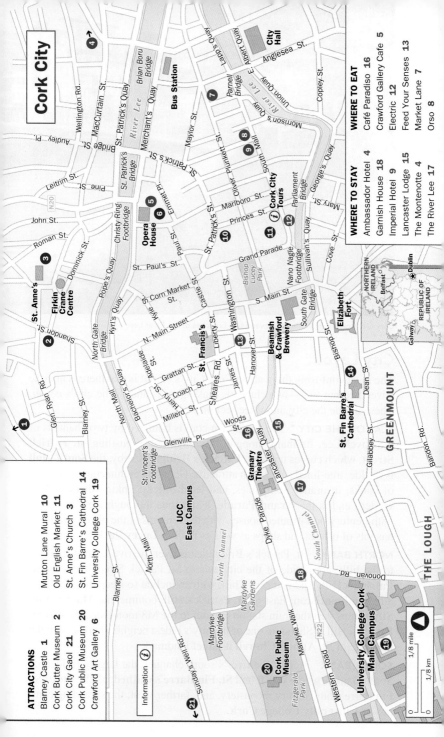

Cork City

ATTRACTIONS

Blarney Castle **1**
Cork Butter Museum **2**
Cork City Gaol **21**
Cork Public Museum **20**
Crawford Art Gallery **6**
Mutton Lane Mural **10**
Old English Market **11**
St. Anne's Church **3**
St. Fin Barre's Cathedral **14**
University College Cork **19**

Information ⓘ

WHERE TO STAY

Ambassador Hotel **4**
Garnish House **18**
Imperial Hotel **9**
Lancaster Lodge **15**
The Montenotte **4**
The River Lee **17**

WHERE TO EAT

Café Paradiso **16**
Crawford Gallery Cafe **5**
Electric **12**
Feed Your Senses **13**
Market Lane **7**
Orso **8**

NORTHERN
IRELAND
Belfast ○
REPUBLIC OF
IRELAND
Galway ○   ✪ Dublin

Cork City's center is an island between two branches of the River Lee.

City Layout

The most confusing thing about Cork City's layout is that there is not one River Lee but two—two channels making an island of the city's center. These divide the city into three sections:

FLAT OF THE CITY   The downtown core is bounded by two channels of the River Lee. Its main shopping thoroughfare is bustling **St. Patrick Street,** which curves up to **St. Patrick's Bridge.** Nearby, the **South Mall** is a wide, tree-lined street with attractive Georgian architecture and a row of banks, insurance companies, and legal offices; linking them at their western end is the **Grand Parade,** a spacious thoroughfare that blends 18th-century bow-fronted houses with the remains of the old city walls. It has lots of offices and shops as well as **Bishop Lucey Park.**

NORTH BANK   St. Patrick's Bridge leads over the river's north channel to the hilly north side of the city, where St. Patrick Street becomes **St. Patrick's Hill.** And is it ever a hill, with an incline so steep that it's virtually San Franciscan. East of St. Patrick's Hill, commercial **MacCurtain Street** runs past the train station and out to the M8 motorway. West of St. Patrick's Hill is Shandon, one of the city's oldest neighborhoods, with the tall spire of **St. Anne's Church** its chief landmark.

SOUTH BANK   Across the river's south channel, the largely residential South Bank is where you'll find **St. Fin Barre's Cathedral,** the site of St. Fin Barre's 6th-century monastery, and, farther west, the sprawling campus of **University College Cork.**

Exploring Cork City

Blarney Castle ★ CASTLE   Though the runaway favorite for the hotly contested title of "cheesiest tourist attraction in Ireland," Blarney Castle is undeniably an imposing structure. Constructed in the late 15th century, it was once much bigger; the massive square tower is all that remains of the original medieval building. But, be honest, that's not why you've heard of this place, right? Its most famous attraction, and probably the most disappointing magical rock you'll ever kiss in your life, is the eponymous "Blarney Stone." Whoever first decided that this particular slab had mystical powers certainly didn't have the convenience of visitors in mind; after trudging up a series of poorly lit narrow staircases, you'll find it wedged underneath the battlements, far enough to make it uncomfortable to reach, but not so far that countless tourists cannot lie down, stick their heads outside, and kiss it in hopes of achieving lifelong loquaciousness. There's no extra charge for kissing the Blarney Stone, though it's customary to tip the attendant who holds your legs (you might want to do it *before* you're slung over the edge). Have we sold you on the experience yet? Snark aside, there is definitely more to see here. Take time to explore the atmospheric dungeons penetrating the rock at the base of the castle, and if you need a break from the masses, the gardens are not only very pretty, but much less crowded. On the grounds is the later **Blarney House,** built in 1874 in the then-fashionable Scottish Baronial style with imposing graystone and filigreed turrets that resemble a mini-Hogwarts. It's still a private residence, but you can tour the interior from June to August only, Monday to Saturday from 10am to 2pm. Blarney Castle is 8km (5 miles) outside the city on R617. You can easily get here by bus; the number 215 stops about twice an hour (once per hour on Sun). Ask the driver to let you off at the stop nearest the castle. *Tip:* Save a few euro on the ticket price by booking online.

Blarney, Co. Cork. www.blarneycastle.ie. © **021/438-5252.** Admission €16 adults; €13 seniors and students; €7 children 8–16; €40 families. June–Aug Mon–Sat 9am–7pm, Sun 9am–6pm; May and Sept Mon–Sat 9am–6:30pm, Sun 9am–6pm; Mar–Apr and Oct daily 9am–6pm; Nov–Feb daily 9am–5pm. Public holiday hours same as Sun. Last admission generally 30 min. before closing; closes at dusk if earlier.

The Gift of Gab (Or Is It Just Blarney?)

Can being held upside down and backward from the top of a tall castle to kiss a rock really bring you the ability to talk up a storm? Well, Blarney Castle's association with the gift of gab does go back a long way. The popular version has it that Queen Elizabeth I (1533–1603) invented the notion in a fit of exasperation at then–Lord Blarney's tendency to prattle on at great length without ever agreeing to anything she wanted. The custom of actually kissing the stone, though, is less than a century old. Nobody knows quite when, how, or why it started, but around here they've got a thousand possible tales, some involving witches and others the crusaders. But don't believe them— it's all a bunch of...

An attendant hoists tourists down to kiss the Blarney Stone at Blarney Castle.

Cork Butter Museum ★ MUSEUM   With a name like that, it's no surprise that this place has turned up on several "world's quirkiest museums" lists, but the fun little Cork Butter Museum is more than just a celebration of tasty Irish dairy produce. From 1770 until the 1920s, Cork was the largest exporter of butter in the world, peaking at half a million casks annually by the turn of the 20th century. The museum chronicles that industrial past, using butter as a springboard to explore wider stories about Irish farming, society, and industry, from the Middle Ages onward. It's surprisingly enlightening.

John Redmond St. www.corkbutter.museum. ✆ 021/430-0600. Admission €4 adults; €3 seniors and students; €2 children under 18; children 11 and under free. Mar–Oct daily 10am–5pm; Nov–Feb Sat–Sun 11am–3pm. Closed Mon–Fri Nov–Feb.

Cork City Gaol ★ HERITAGE SITE   Like something out of a Victorian novel, this early-19th-century jail is an austere and highly atmospheric building. It opened in 1824 as a women's prison. Famous inmates included the extraordinary Countess Constance Markievicz (1868–1927). The first woman elected to the British parliament, she was sentenced to death for her part in the 1916 Easter Rising (her sentence was commuted because of her sex, to which she responded "I do wish you had the decency to shoot me"). Earlier in its history, the jail was the last place in Ireland many convicts were held before being shipped off to Australia. This colorful past is well-presented, with the aid of costumed mannequins in key positions. Somewhat incongruously, in 1927, after the building ceased to be used as a prison, it became the site of Ireland's first radio station. A small museum tells this story, complete with a restored studio from the period. Special evening tours (€10 per person) take place a couple of times per month, though you must have a group of at least eight and book at least a week ahead—check the website for upcoming dates.

Convent Ave., Sunday's Well. www.corkcitygaol.com. © **021/430-5022.** Free admission. Tues–Fri 10am–4pm; Sat 11am–4pm; Sun 2–4pm. Closed Sun Oct–Mar.

The atmospheric Cork City Gaol.

Cork Public Museum ★ MUSEUM   This simple, rather endearing civic museum is a good place to get an overview of the city's history. Displays include a few objects from Cork's ancient past—including an Iron Age helmet and some of the oldest tools ever discovered in Ireland. But it's strongest when it comes to the traditional crafts made in the city during the 19th and 20th centuries, including silverware and intricate lace from the Victorian period. There are also very good collections relating to the lives of local revolutionaries, including Michael Collins (see p. 274). The museum is located on the west side of Cork, in the middle of Fitzgerald Park—near the Western Road, where many of the city's B&Bs are located (see "Where to Stay" on p. 248). It's about a 10-minute walk from the city center.

Fitzgerald Park. www.corkcity.ie. © **021/427-0679.** Free admission. Mon–Fri 11am–1pm, 2:15–5pm; Sat 11am–1pm, 2:15–4pm; Sun 3–5pm. Closed Sun Oct–Mar.

Crawford Art Gallery ★★★ ART MUSEUM   One of the best art galleries in Ireland, the Crawford has impressive collections of sculpture and painting. The Irish School is particularly well-represented with works from John Butts (1728–65), including his fine 1755 panorama of Cork City, and Dublin-born Harry Clarke (1889–1931), one of the most celebrated illustrators of the early 20th century, who also produced some extraordinary, early Deco–influenced stained glass. The gallery has a strong collection of works by female Irish artists from the mid–19th century onward; check out the extraordinary abstract work of Mainie Jellett (1897–1944) and the Cubist painter Norah McGuinness (1901–80). The gallery also has a program of temporary exhibitions. The **Crawford Gallery Café** ★★ (see p. 251) is a good spot for a light lunch.

Emmet Place. www.crawfordartgallery.ie. © **021/480-5042.** Free admission. Mon–Wed and Fri–Sat 10am–5pm, Thurs 10am–8pm. 2nd floor closes 4:45pm daily. Closed Sun and public holidays.

CORK: THE rebel CITY

Travel in County Cork today, and all that appears in front of you are rolling green hills and bucolic farmscapes. But this county was once at the heart of the battle for Ireland's soul.

For centuries, the county had a reputation for defiance and revolt. Once the seat of power in South Munster, it changed hands many times as the English and Irish battled for control. Devastated by the Great Famine, Cork became a center of the 19th-century Fenian movement, when the label "Rebel Cork" was first widely used. It certainly lived up to the name during Ireland's 20th-century battle for independence. It was a battle of wills, and Cork refused to give in.

The British troops occupying Cork—a paramilitary force nicknamed the "Black and Tans" for the color of their uniforms—were among the most repressive in the country. The struggle came to a head in 1920 when Thomas MacCurtain, mayor of Cork City, was killed by the Black and Tans. His successor, Terence MacSwiney, was arrested, and later died in a London prison after a hunger strike lasting 75 days.

On December 11 of that year, after an attack by the IRA, the British forces set fire to Cork city center, apparently as payback. The library, the City Hall, and almost all the buildings on St. Patrick Street were burned to the ground. More than 300 buildings were destroyed in the ensuing conflagration—virtually the entire city was smoldering rubble. As the fires blazed, two men suspected to be members of the IRA were shot as they slept, also allegedly by the occupying military troops.

The atrocity left a bitter legacy, ensuring that the battle would wage on in Cork, even as peace talks took hold elsewhere in Ireland. It ensured that Cork would resist any peace agreements to the end, even a treaty negotiated by Cork native son Michael Collins (see p. 274). And it ensured that Cork natives would embrace their identity as Rebel Cork forevermore.

Mutton Lane Mural ★ PUBLIC ART   This riotously colorful mural along the walls of Mutton Lane, down one side of the Mutton Lane Inn, is intended to represent the essence of Cork. It depicts musicians performing the traditional "Pana Shuffle," and all of the characters featured are real local people. It is a vivid evocation of peace and community spirit, beloved locally—so much so, claim the owners of the pub, that it has never been vandalized by graffiti (impossible to prove, of course). The mural was painted by local artist Anthony Ruby in 2004. Its historical provenance can be dated by the following message, which is hidden within the colorful scene: "dedicated to everyone except George Bush."
Mutton Lane, off St. Patrick St.

Old English Market ★★ MARKET HALL   The name of this bustling food market harks back to the days of English rule—it was first granted a charter in 1610 during the reign of King James I. The current market building dates from 1788, although it was redesigned after being gutted by fire in the 1980s. Inside is a cornucopia of fresh produce, including super-traditional Cork delicacies—some of them tempting, others less palatable to outsiders. (Mmm, tripe! Pig's trotters? Anyone?) Happily, more modern refreshments and takeaway snacks are also there to sate your hunger.

Grand Parade; enter from Patrick St., Grand Parade, Oliver Plunkett St., or Princes St. www.englishmarket.ie. *©* **021/492-4258.** Free admission. Mon–Sat 8am–6pm.

St. Anne's Church ★ CHURCH   Cork's most recognizable landmark, also known as Shandon Church, is famous for its giant pepper-pot steeple and eight melodious bells. Pretty much wherever you stand in the downtown area, you can see the stone tower crowned with a gilt ball and distinctive fish weathervane. The clock, added in 1847, made it the first four-faced clock tower in the world (beating London's Big Ben by just a few years). Until fairly recently, due to a quirk of clockworks, it was known as "the four-faced liar" because each side showed a different time—except on the hour when they all somehow managed to synchronize. Disappointingly, perhaps, that charming oddity has now been repaired. Climb the 1722 belfry tower for a chance to ring the famous Shandon Bells. (Be warned, though: It's 132 steps up to the belfry, and the gap narrows to a claustrophobic half-meter—that's just over 1½ feet—near the entrance to the belfry.) If you continue on the somewhat precarious climb past the bells, you'll be rewarded with spectacular views over the surrounding countryside.

Church St., Shandon. www.shandonbells.ie. *©* **021/450-5906.** Free admission. Clock tower €5 adults; €4 seniors and students; €3 children; €12 families. June–Sept Mon–Sat 10am–5pm, Sun 11:30am–4:30pm; Mar–May and Oct Mon–Sat 10am–4pm, Sun 11:30am–4pm; Nov–Feb Mon–Sat 11am–3pm, Sun 11:30am–3pm. Public holiday hours same as Sun. Last entry to tower 20 min. before closing.

St. Fin Barre's Cathedral ★ CATHEDRAL   With its three soaring spires dominating the Cork skyline, this Church of Ireland cathedral sits on the very spot St. Fin Barre chose in A.D.. 600 for his church and school. A much smaller medieval tower was demolished to make way for the current building, which dates from the early 1860s—there's nothing left of the original, although a few pieces of decorative stonework were salvaged and can be viewed inside. The architect, William Burges (1827–81), won a competition staged to create a new Anglican cathedral in the city; his design embraced the French Gothic style popular at the time. The interior is highly ornamented with

The elegant Gothic Revival St. Fin Barre's Cathedral stands atop Cork City's monastic foundations.

some stunning mosaic work. The bells were inherited from a 1735 church that also previously stood on this site. The cathedral hosts occasional exhibitions; check the website for listings of what's on.

Bishop St. www.corkcathedral.webs.com. ☏ **021/496-3387.** Admission €6 adults; €5 seniors and students; €3 children 15 and under. Apr–Oct Mon–Sat 9:30am–5:30pm; Sun 12:30–2:30pm and 4:30–5pm; Nov–Mar Mon–Sat 9:30am–5:30pm. Closed certain public holidays; call to check.

University College Cork and Glucksman Gallery ★★ UNIVERSITY

Part of Ireland's national university, with about 7,000 students, this center of learning is housed in a pretty quadrangle of Gothic Revival–style buildings. Colorful gardens and wooded grounds grace the campus. An audio tour of the campus takes in the **Crawford Observatory,** the Harry Clarke stained-glass windows in **Honan Chapel,** the landscaped **President's Garden,** and the **Stone Corridor,** a collection of stones inscribed with the ancient Irish *ogham* written language. You can also join an hour-long guided tour, given by students, leaving from the visitor center at 3pm from Monday to Friday, or noon on Saturdays. Also on the campus, the innovative **Lewis Glucksman Gallery** (www.glucksman. org; ☏ **021/490-1844**) has an excellent program of exhibitions. Expect to see cutting-edge photography, painting, sculpture, and a few items from the university's ever-expanding permanent collection. A good cafe and shop are also on-site. Admission to the Glucksman is free, though a donation of €5 per person is requested.

Visitor Centre: North Wing, Main Quad, Western Rd. www.ucc.ie/en/discover/visit/centre. ☏ **021/490-1876.** Free admission. Visitor Centre: Mon–Fri 9am–5pm, Sat noon–5pm. Glucksman Gallery: Tues–Sat 10am–5pm, Sun 2–5pm.

ORGANIZED TOURS

Cork City Tours ★ Riding on open-top buses, you can hop on and off to explore the sights of Ireland's second city. The buses run all day in a loop from March through October (as frequently as every half-hour in July and Aug). Tour highlights include the Cork City Gaol, St. Anne's Church, and U.C.C. (University College, Cork). While the tour begins at the tourist office (42 Grand Parade), you can buy a ticket on the bus at several stops; check out the route on the Cork City Tours website.

www.corkcitytour.com. ☏ **021/430-9090.** Tickets €15 adults, €13 seniors and students; €5 children 5–18; children under 5 free; €35 families. Number of tours according to seasonal demand. June–Aug daily tours every half-hour 9:30am–7:05pm; Apr–May and Sept–Oct daily tours every 45 min. 9:30am–4:15pm; Mar and Nov daily tours every 90 min. 9:30am–4:45pm. Times refer to start of tours at Grand Parade or St. Patrick St.; complete circuit takes about 75 min.

Where to Stay in Cork City

Cork City is filled with B&Bs and small hotels, particularly along Western Road. They vary in quality, but among them are some interesting, decently priced options.

EXPENSIVE

The River Lee ★★   A 5-minute walk from the city center, this shiny, modern hotel overlooks the River Lee (as you may have guessed). Guest rooms are quietly chic, with an understated modern style and huge windows that make the most of city views. Executive rooms have fancy extras such as Nespresso coffee machines and access to a private lounge with panoramic views of the city. The attached health club includes a (nearly) Olympic-size indoor swimming pool. The substantial breakfast buffet (€14) offers much more than the usual options.

Western Rd. www.doylecollection.com/hotels/the-river-lee-hotel. *©* **021/425-2700.** 182 units. €160–€240 double. Free parking (underground lot). Breakfast not included in lower rates. Dinner, bed-and-breakfast packages available. **Amenities:** Restaurant; room service; spa; swimming pool; Wi-Fi (free).

MODERATE

Imperial Hotel ★★   This city center hotel is surprisingly affordable for the amenities it offers, with elegantly restored public areas that are redolent of a much more expensive kind of hotel altogether. The guest rooms are perhaps a little plain by comparison, and the most basic rooms are small, but upgrading just a little gets you ample space and a bit more style. The hotel has four restaurants; the **Pembroke** specializes in local meats and seafood. And you can unwind in the **Escape Spa,** which offers a long list of indulgent, revitalizing treatments, starting at about €85 for a 50-minute facial, or back, neck, and shoulder massage. Check the website for dinner-bed-and-breakfast packages, as well as inclusive spa deals.

76 South Mall. www.flynnhotels.com. *©* **021/427-4040.** 130 units. €200–€245 double, €511–€851 suite. Parking at nearby lot (€10 per 24 hr.). Breakfast included. **Amenities:** Restaurants; bar; room service; spa; Wi-Fi (free).

Lancaster Lodge ★   One of many small hotels on Western Road, Lancaster Lodge is modern and well-run and offers good value for your money. The purple color scheme in some of the public areas might be a bit garish for some, but guest rooms are big, with contemporary furnishings. Suites, which don't cost a great deal more than the standard doubles, come with Jacuzzi baths. Breakfast is better than you might expect from a budget hotel, and although it doesn't serve dinner, central Cork is only a short walk away.

Lancaster Quay, Western Rd. www.lancasterlodge.com. *©* **021/425-1125.** 48 units. €140–€165 double, €170–€190 suite. 2-night minimum on some summer weekends. Free parking. Breakfast not included in lower rates. **Amenities:** Room service; Wi-Fi (free).

The Montenotte ★★   Those who like to stay perched above the action, rather than right in the thick of it, will doubly appreciate one of the chief selling points of the stylish Montenotte: fantastic views across Cork City and the River Lee. Converted and renovated top-to-bottom from what used to be a rather sorry Best Western, the hotel is a sophisticated, fun place to stay. The cool, modern color schemes in the good-size guest rooms are offset with traditional patterns. The **Panorama Bistro** offers topnotch bistro cooking—with a superb view from the dining room, of course. There's even an in-house cinema, where dinner-and-movie specials are offered a few nights each month.

Middle Glanmire Rd. www.themonottehotel.com. ✆ **021/453-0050.** 108 units. €134–€231 double. Free parking. Breakfast not included in lower rates. Dinner, bed-and-breakfast packages available. **Amenities:** Restaurant; bar; cinema; gym; room service; swimming pool; Wi-Fi (free).

INEXPENSIVE

Ambassador Hotel ★   The impressive redbrick exterior of this hilltop 1870s mansion on the northeast outskirts of Cork gives way to a glossy lobby, with black-and-white checkered floors and twinkly chandeliers. The guest rooms are modestly decorated, with traditional-style furnishings. Pay the extra for an upper-floor room with a city view. A pleasant bar is filled with floor-to-ceiling bookcases, and the on-site restaurant is handy for a hotel that's a mile or so from the center of town, although it's hardly a trek by taxi. Be aware that the Ambassador can get booked up by wedding parties in the summer.

Military Hill. www.ambassadorhotel.ie. ✆ **021/453-9000.** 70 units. €127–€155 double. Free parking. Breakfast included. **Amenities:** Restaurant; bar; gym; room service; Wi-Fi (free).

Garnish House ★★   Another standout among the plethora of B&Bs and hotels in the Western Road neighborhood, Garnish House is a sweet and friendly place to stay. You're hardly through the door before you're offered an afternoon tea, complete with delicious homemade scones. Guest rooms are pleasant with good-size beds, and some rooms have Jacuzzi baths. Breakfasts are outstanding; in addition to the usual hearty "full Irish" options, you could have French toast, pancakes, lentil ragout, stuffed tomatoes, salmon and dill tarts, or scrambled eggs with avocado—more choices than some restaurants around here offer at dinner. For those who want a little extra freedom, self-catering options include a one-bedroom apartment and a full town house directly across the street.

1 St. Mary's Villas, Western Rd. www.garnish.ie. ✆ **021/427-5111.** 14 units. €92–€125 double. Free parking. Breakfast not included in lower rates. **Amenities:** Wi-Fi (free).

Where to Eat in Cork City

Cork's reputation as a kind of cultural "Dublin South" is burnished by its restaurant scene, smattered with trendy eateries. (Nearby Kinsale, however, is where the county really goes to let its collective belt out—see p. 261.)

Cafe Paradiso ★★★ VEGETARIAN   An inventive, classy vegetarian restaurant on the Western Road strip, Cafe Paradiso does such magnificent things without meat that even passionate carnivores will find plenty to love. Start with a bowl of hot parsnip and lemongrass soup, then tuck into some chile-glazed tofu with pak choi, or a delicious risotto made with sage and roasted sunchoke tomato. Desserts are heavenly; if it's on the menu, try the dark chocolate mousse served with popcorn and whiskey salted caramel. For those who prefer to roll (or should we say bounce) straight from table to bed, the cafe also has guest rooms for €220 per couple, per night.

16 Lancaster Quay. www.cafeparadiso.ie. © **021/427-7939.** Fixed-price menus: two- course €33, three-course €40. Mon–Sat 5:30–10pm. No children after 7pm. Closed Sun.

Crawford Gallery Café ★★ CAFE   A big step up from the average cafe tacked onto an art gallery, the Crawford is as much a great little bistro as it is a convenient spot for a coffee or light nibble. It's open for breakfast, which certainly provides some excellent options if you can't face another hotel morning meal. Expect to find tempting treats such as spiced scones, American-style pancakes, and delicious eggs Florentine with organic spinach on the menu. Lunchtime is when this place gets busiest, though, and the lineup changes regularly with plenty of daily specials like chorizo bean cassoulet or smoked salmon salad with horseradish dressing.

At the Crawford Gallery, Emmet Place. www.crawfordgallerycafe.com. © **021/427-4415.** Breakfast €4.50–€10.50, lunch €10.50–€15. Mon–Sat 8:30am–4pm; closed Sun.

Electric ★★ MODERN IRISH/SEAFOOD   You could easily get swept up in the romance of this trendy but unpretentious restaurant, with a dining room overlooking the river and the city skyline beyond. The smallish menu focuses on casual but upscale comfort food: roast chicken with red wine jus, short ribs with duck-fat roast potatoes, or perhaps a juicy burger served with chips and pink peppercorn coleslaw. You can also order from a slightly more casual selection in the bar. In addition, there is the **Fish Bar** (evenings only), where you can eat super-fresh seafood while perched on bar stools overlooking the river. Despite its popularity, you can usually get a table at Electric if you arrive early—a full fifth are held back every night.

41 South Mall. www.electriccork.ie/restaurant.   © **021/422-2990.** Entrees €8.50–€46. Daily 10am–10pm. Fish Bar open evenings only; no children in the Fish Bar.

> ### Brewing Up Loyalty
>
> There is a definite sense of civic loyalty when it comes to drinking stout in this town. Yes, Ireland is known for its love of Guinness, but in Cork you're more likely to find locals drinking the two locally brewed stouts—Murphy's or Beamish. In fact, walk into any pub and order a "home and away" and you'll be presented with a pint of Murphy's and one of Guinness.

Feed Your Senses ★★ SPANISH   This small and intimate restaurant just west of the city center has a warm, upbeat vibe. The cozy dining room is decorated in a rustic taverna style. The food is billed as tapas, but plates are really quite generously proportioned. Try a fluffy tortilla with a serving of *albondigas* (Spanish meatballs, here made with Irish beef and pork) or maybe some *chorizos con vino* (fried chorizo sausage cooked in red wine). There's a good wine list, although the lusty, full-bodied house red is delicious enough accompaniment by itself.

27 Washington St. ℗ **021/427-4633.** Entrees €5–€21.50. Tues–Wed and Sun 5–9pm, Thurs 5–9:30pm, Fri–Sat 5–10pm. Closed Mon.

Market Lane ★★ IRISH   This friendly, informal downtown restaurant serves Irish-inflected bistro food. It's a let-down-your-hair kind of place, with the menu consisting mostly of traditional, unpretentious cooking, done very well. Think sophisticated comfort food: apricot-stuffed chicken with roast potatoes, or baked cod with carrot and swede (rutabaga) boxty—a traditional kind of potato pancake (see box p. 141). Try the delicious marmalade and vanilla bread and butter pudding for dessert. The early-bird menu is a deal at €25 for three courses (Mon–Thurs 5–7pm, Sun 1–7pm). Gourmet sandwiches are served at lunchtime.

5–6 Oliver Plunkett St. www.marketlane.ie. ℗ **021/427-4710.** Entrees €15–€27. Mon–Wed noon–9:30pm, Thurs noon–10pm, Fri–Sat noon–10:30pm, Sun 1–9:30pm.

Orso ★★★ IRISH/MEDITERRANEAN   This place is like a ray of warm Mediterranean sunshine in downtown Cork City. Traditional flavors of southern Europe and North Africa meet Irish influences, and the result is nothing short of delightful. It's open all day, so you can pop in for a breakfast of Syrian *manoushi* bread with poached egg and caramelized onion, or smoked salmon and scrambled eggs. The lunch menu is long and varied, but it's really at dinnertime when the excellent cooking comes into its own. Plates could include scallops with samphire and sumac, or *sfeehas*—small Lebanese pies made with spiced lamb and fennel. Nearly everything on the wine list is available by the glass, and the small cocktail menu is intriguing—try the delicious house Bellini.

8 Pembroke St. www.orso.ie. ℗ **021/243-8000.** Entrees €8–€21.50. Mon 8:30am–6pm, Tues–Thurs 8:30am–10pm, Fri–Sat 8:30am–10:30pm, Sun (Dec only) 1–10pm.

Cork City Shopping

St. Patrick Street is the main shopping thoroughfare, though many stores are scattered throughout the city on side streets and in lanes. In general, shops are open Monday to Saturday 9:30am to 6pm, unless indicated otherwise. In the summer, many shops remain open until 9:30pm on Thursday and Friday, and some are open on Sunday.

Winthrop Arcade, off Winthrop Street, is the best of a handful of covered shopping arcades in the city. The main full-size shopping mall is **Merchant's Quay Shopping Centre,** Merchant's Quay and St. Patrick Street (www.merchantsquaycork.com; ℗ **021/427-5466**).

Cork's best department store is **Brown Thomas,** 18-21 St. Patrick Street (www.brownthomas.ie; ℂ **021/480-5555**), its three floors filled with the same kind of upscale items found in the main branch in Dublin (see p. 155). Just next door is the Cork outpost of another popular department store, **Debenhams,** 12-17 St. Patrick St. (www.debenhams.ie; ℂ **021/464-8400**), a particularly good bet for clothes and housewares.

BOOKS

Easons ★ The large and nicely designed Cork branch of this major Irish bookstore chain has titles on just about everything under the sun, from bestsellers to travel guides (you know, just in case you lose this one). It's directly across from Debenhams department store. 113–115 St. Patrick's St. www.easons.com. ℂ **021/427-0477.**

Vibes and Scribes ★ This cheery secondhand bookstore stocks titles in a huge array of genres, as well as gifts and crafty knick-knacks. A second branch, also selling stationery and art and craft supplies, is at 3 Bridge St. (ℂ **021/450-5370**). 21 Lavitt's Quay. www.vibesandscribes.ie. ℂ **021/427-9535.**

FASHION & CLOTHING

Blarney Woollen Mills ★ On the grounds of **Blarney Castle** ★ (see p. 243), this is the flagship outlet of an Irish chain that specializes in traditional Irish gear: Aran sweaters, cashmere and other knitwear, tweeds, country clothing, capes, and accessories. It also stocks a large range of Irish crafts, such as Waterford crystal and Celtic-style jewelry. It's open until 6pm daily. On the grounds of Blarney Castle, Blarney. www.blarney.ie. ℂ **021/451-6111.**

Brocade and Lime ★★★ This wonderful vintage-style clothing store sells retro-inspired (but brand-new) fashions, all the work of a talented coterie of Irish designers. They include Orla Kiely, who specializes in swinging '60s prints; Alicia Estrada, whose Stop Staring label features clothes that hark back to 1940s film noir; and What Katie Did, a supercool brand of 1950s-influenced lingerie, favored by celebrities including Kate Moss, Penelope Cruz, and Christina Hendricks. 4 Cornmarket St. www.brocadeandlime.ie. ℂ **021/427-8882.**

Monreal ★★ Designer handbags, belts, and other accessories are for sale at this boutique in the Winthrop Arcade. The gorgeous stock of shoes includes some rather cool lace-up Wellington boots—a handy way of staying stylish, whatever the Irish weather throws at you. Winthrop Arcade, off Winthrop St. www.monreal.ie. ℂ **021/480-6746.**

Cork City After Dark
PUBS

An Spailpin Fánac ★★ One of Cork's oldest pubs (it opened in 1779), this is a wonderful spot to hang out with a pint and while away an hour or two. It's also one of the best pubs in the city for live music (see box p. 256). 28–29 S. Main St. ℂ **021/427-7949.**

Enjoying a drink in one of Cork's historic pubs.

The Idle Hour ★ This is the sort of place you go if you want some good lively craic (fun), loud music, and a young crowd. It's an extremely popular pub, especially during sports matches, shown here on huge TVs. Albert Quay. ℰ **021/496-5704.**

John Henchy & Sons ★★ Full of appealing Victorian features, this fantastic pub looks as if it has hardly changed since it first opened in 1884. It's got a private area ("snug") that was originally built to allow ladies to visit the pub without fear of impropriety. 40 St. Luke's. ℰ **021/450-7833.**

The Long Valley ★★ A cheerful, gregarious air pervades at this long-standing favorite of the Cork pub scene. The crowd is a good mix of stalwart locals and hip young things. It also has a good program of live music and spoken word. 10 Winthrop St. ℰ **021/427-2144.**

CLUBS: COMEDY, DANCE & MUSIC

Bowery ★ One of the most popular nightspots in Cork, the Bowery offers several options. Downstairs are two sophisticated bars, the **Bowery** and the **Berwick Room,** which cultivate a decadent vibe with just a hint of the bordello. Upstairs, DJs spin the latest cuts and eclectic sets in the **Stage Room,** as well as in the **Rooftop Bar,** overlooking the nearby park. It's open Friday and Saturday from 11pm until 2am. 21 Tuckey St. www. bowery.ie. ℰ **087/688-4868.** Cover €10 and up.

Havana Browns ★ This busy nightclub attracts the kind of young party crowd that is drawn to a bit of glamour like moths to a flame. After negotiating your way past the notoriously surly bouncers, relax in one of the three bars or work your moves on the dance floor, with its high tech LED illuminations. The club is open every night from 11pm until 2am. Hanover St. www.havanabrowns.ie. ✆ **021/465-8100.** Cover €10 and up.

THE PERFORMING ARTS

Cork Opera House ★ Near the river on Emmet Place, the Cork Opera House is the region's preeminent venue when it comes to opera and other live concerts (classical, trad, folk, rock, country), plus dance, standup, and more. Emmet Place. www.corkoperahouse.ie. ✆ **021/427-0022.** Tickets around €18–€50.

The Firkin Crane Cultural Centre ★★ Named after two Danish words for measurements of butter, the Firkin Crane is set in a quirky Victorian-era rotunda on the North Bank, just downhill from St. Anne's Church. It's one of Ireland's major centers for contemporary dance, hosting touring companies in addition to showcasing new talent. Many performances are free. The only downside is that performances are infrequent—usually just a handful per month—and the most headline-grabbing tend to be during the Guinness Jazz Festival (see box below). John Redmond St., Shandon. www.firkincrane.ie. ✆ **021/450-7487.** Ticket prices and performance times vary by event.

Sports & Outdoor Pursuits in Cork City

GAELIC GAMES Hurling and Gaelic football are both played on summer Sunday afternoons at Cork's **Pairc Ui Chaoimh Stadium,** Marina Walk (✆ **021/201-9200**). The stadium recently underwent a €30-million redevelopment. Check the local newspapers for match listings or visit the **Gaelic Athletics Association** website at www.gaa.ie.

WHALE-WATCHING Whale-watching is a popular activity in summer, and one of the best companies is the aptly-named **Whale of a Time** (www.whaleofatime.ie; ✆ **086/328-3250**), which uses rigid inflatable boats to cause less disruption to the creatures of the deep. Departing from Cork Harbour, the searches take in the waters around Ram Head and Kinsale. Prices per person are around €35 for a 90-minute "family trip," or €70 for a 4-hour "enthusiasts trip." **Kinsale Angling** (see "Fishing," p. 269) also offers dolphin, whale, and seal-watching trips.

The Guinness Cork Jazz Festival

Held every year since 1978, this is Ireland's biggest and most prestigious jazz festival. Big names such as Ella Fitzgerald, Oscar Peterson, and Stephane Grappelli have played here over the years, with more than 1,000 performers from all over the world taking part annually. It's held at various citywide venues in late October. Visit **www.guinnessjazz festival.com** for details. Tickets go on sale in early September; prices vary and some events are free.

Cork has a deserved reputation as home to some of Ireland's best pubs for live, traditional music. It's virtually a rite of passage to catch a session while enjoying a pint or two (and it's stout in these parts, by the way—Murphy's or Beamish, not Guinness—if you really want to fit in).

You can just follow your ears to find the best places, but to get you started, here are a few of the most respected spots. **An Bodhran** (the name refers to a type of drum made from goatskin), 42 Oliver Plunkett St. (℃ 021/427-4544), has live sessions nightly, as does the cozy **An Spailpín Fánach** (which means "the Wandering Migrant Worker"), 27 South Main St. (℃ 021/427-7949). The succinctly named **Sin é** (literally, "That's It"), 8 Coburg St. (℃ 021/450-2266), has been one of Cork's top live-music pubs for decades. It has sessions most nights at 7pm, but those on Tuesday, Friday, and Sunday are particularly good. There's traditional Irish music every Thursday night at the atmospheric **Long Valley Bar**, 10 Winthrop St. (www.thelongvalley bar.com; ℃ 021/427-2144)—but if you've had your fill of the pennywhistle by this point, come on Monday nights at 9:30 to catch the lively program of spoken-word events; see www.obheal.ie for more details.

DAY TRIPS TO EAST CORK

Along the coast just east of Cork City are a number of attractions worth venturing away from the city for, most within an easy hour's drive. While families will probably make a beeline for **Fota Wildlife Park** on the shore of Lough Mahon, the small inland town of Midleton attracts foodies thanks to **Ballymaloe House** and its famous cooking school. A vital piece of Ireland's history is told at the harbor town of **Cobh,** which under its former name Queenstown was once Ireland's chief port of emigration. If you have more time to spend, farther east are some pleasant beach resorts such as **Ballycotton** and, near the Waterford border, **Youghal** (pronounced *Yawl*).

Arriving

If you're driving from Cork City, take the main Waterford road (N25) east. Exit at R624 for Fota and Cobh; Midleton and Youghal have their own signposted exits. **Irish Rail** (www.irishrail.ie; ℃ 021/455-7277) operates daily train service between Cork City and Cobh via Fota Island. The journey takes about half an hour. **Bus Éireann** (www.buseireann.ie; ℃ 021/450-8188) also provides daily service from Cork City to Cobh and other points in East Cork.

Exploring East Cork

Ballymaloe Cookery School ★★ SCHOOL Professional and amateur cooks flock here from all over the world to sit near the whisk of Darina Allen. It all started with Darina's mother-in-law, Myrtle, whose

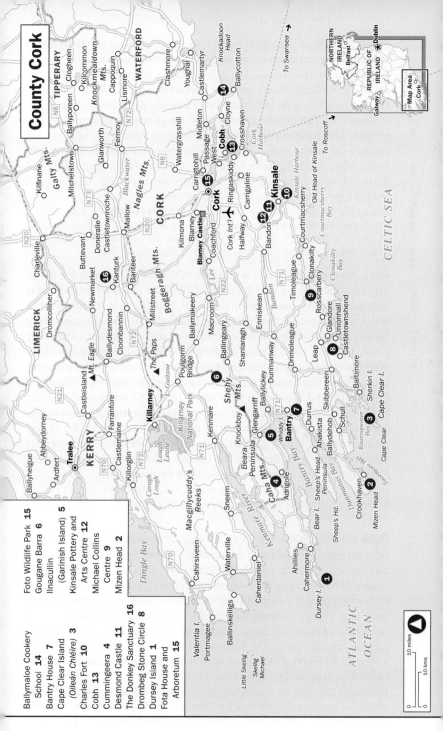

County Cork

TIPPERARY
WATERFORD
LIMERICK
KERRY
CORK

ATLANTIC OCEAN

CELTIC SEA

To Swansea
To Roscoff

Map Area
Cork

NORTHERN IRELAND
Belfast
REPUBLIC OF IRELAND
Galway
Dublin

evangelization of Ireland's bounty of fresh produce at **Ballymaloe House ★★★** restaurant (see p. 260) elevated Irish "country house" cooking to gourmet status. The Allen family's success led to the founding of this cooking school, the most famous in Ireland, which offers dozens of courses ranging in length from a half-day to 12 weeks. Prices start at about €50. The extensive **gardens** on the grounds are open to visitors all year. The **Ballymaloe Shop,** open 10am to 5pm daily, sells kitchen produce (including Ballymaloe's own delicious brand of relish) and craft items, while the **Ballymaloe Café** offers light lunches, afternoon tea, and lip-smackingly good cakes. Weather permitting, you can usually get a guided tour of the gardens for €5 per person.

Shanagarry, Midleton. www.cookingisfun.ie. ✆ **021/464-6785.** Half-day courses from €60–€195. Open year-round; schedule varies. Admission to gardens €6 adults; €4 seniors and students, €3 children; €15 families. Gardens and farm: June–Sept daily 11am–5:30pm; Oct–May Mon–Sat 11am–5:30pm (closed Sun).

Fota House & Gardens ★★ HISTORIC HOUSE   This is one of two popular attractions on Fota Island, a small island in Cork Harbour that is fully accessible by road. Built in the 1820s, Fota House is considered to be one of the finest example of a Regency mansion in Ireland. You can wander the elegant, classically-influenced interior by yourself, or take a tour (daily 11am, 12:30, 2, and 3:30pm—booking is advised). The house also maintains a working Victorian kitchen garden, which you can tour along with the house. House tours cost €8 adults, €6 seniors and students, €3 children, and €19 families; kitchen garden tours are €5 adults, €4 seniors and students, €14 families. Meanwhile the free-to-visit **Fota Arboretum** is a must-see for horticulturalists. Laid out at around the time the house was built, the 27-acre grounds include walled gardens, with several exotic plants that defy the odds and thrive here, thanks to the island's unusually mild microclimate. *Note:* The gardens are open year-round, but the house is not.

Fota Island, Carrigtwohill. http://fotahouse.com. ✆ **021/481-5543.** House: €8 adults; €6 seniors and students; €3 children; €19 families. Arboretum: Free. House: Apr–Sept daily 10am–5pm.

Fota Wildlife Park ★★ ZOO   If only all zoos were like this thoughtfully designed park. Many of the animals—including kangaroos, macaws, and lemurs—have the run of 16 hectares (40 acres) of grassland, free to roam without any apparent barriers and mingling with human visitors and each other. Only the more dangerous animals, such as cheetahs and gibbons, are behind conventional fencing. Besides close contact with a menagerie of exotic creatures, kids can be entertained by a tour train, picnic area, and gift shop. The **Savannah Café** (one of two in the park) has a view of the meerkat exhibition, so you may find yourself being watched by curious eyes while you eat your lunch.

Fota Island, Carrigtwohill. www.fotawildlife.ie. ✆ **021/481-2678.** Admission €16.50 adults; €12 seniors and students; €11 children 3–15, children 2 and under free; €48–€64 families. Daily 10am–4:30pm. Last entry 1½ hr. before closing.

If you're a foreigner with an Irish surname, this bustling seaside town could be more important to you than you realize. Cobh (pronounced *cove*, meaning "haven") used to be called Queenstown, and it was once Ireland's chief port of emigration. For thousands of Irish emigrants, particularly during the Famine years and in the early 20th century, Cobh was the last bit of Ireland they ever saw. It was also the last port of call for the RMS *Titanic* before it sank in April 1912. That story is expertly told at **Cobh: The Queenstown Story** (Deepwater Quay; www.cobhheritage.com; ℂ 021/481-3591). Part of the Cobh Heritage Centre, the exhibition is open from May to October daily 9:30am to 6pm; and November to April Monday to Saturday 9:30am to 5pm and Sunday and public holidays 11am to 5pm. Last admission is 1 hour before closing. Tickets cost €10 adults, €8 seniors and students, €5 children, and €25 families.

A short walk from the Cobh Heritage Center, the **Lusitania Memorial** (Casement Sq.) commemorates the British luxury liner sunk just off the Cork coast by a German U-boat on May 7, 1915, killing 1,198 passengers. Queenstown was the base for the heroic Irish rescue efforts that saved 764 lives. Across Casement Square from the memorial, the **Titanic Experience** (www.titanicexperiencecobh.ie; ℂ 021/481-4412) is more of a themed attraction than a museum—it's just a few re-created rooms from the ship and a series of exhibits about the ill-fated voyage, emptying into a very busy gift shop. From April to September it's open daily from 9am to 6pm, with tours every 15 minutes; from October to March the opening times are 10am to 5:30pm, tours every 30 minutes. The last tour starts 45 minutes before closing. Entry costs €10 adults, €8 seniors and students, €7 children 4 to 16, and €20 to €31 families.

Frankly, your time would be better spent climbing the hill to the handsome neo-Gothic **St. Colman's Cathedral** (www.cobhcathedralparish.ie; ℂ 021/481-3222). Started in 1868, the cathedral was the country's most expensive religious building of its time. The largest of its 47 bells weighs 3½ tons, and the organ has nearly 2,500 pipes. The interior is vast and ornate, including a beautiful nave and precipitously high chancel arch. It is also a popular venue for concerts and recitals.

If you want to discover more about Cobh's role in the *Titanic* story, an hour-long **walking tour** visits several related sites, putting it all into the context of the town's maritime history. In truth, this is a general historical tour of the town with just a couple of *Titanic* connections, but it's informative nonetheless. The tour departs from the Commodore Hotel, 4 Westbourne Place, at 11am and 2pm daily. (From Oct–Mar, the tour only runs if there are prebookings.) It costs €12.50 adults, €5 children age 11 and under (plus a €1.50 booking fee). For bookings, call ℂ 021/481-5211 or visit **www.titanic.ie**.

Harbor view of historic Cobh.

Where to Stay in East Cork

Ballymaloe House Hotel ★★   Most famous for being Ireland's best-known cookery school—you can take wonderful day and half-day courses here (see p. 256)—Ballymaloe is also an inviting country hotel. Comfortable guest rooms are furnished in traditional country-house decor, with floral-print wallpaper, antique-style furniture, and original art on the walls. If you want a bit more privacy, you can choose from several self-catering options, including cottages, a faux castle tower (complete with balcony on the battlements), and cabin-style chalets. The kitchen is the real draw here—the restaurant produces fantastic gourmet dinners nightly, lavish five-course affairs with seasonal menus (€75 per person); Sunday features a slightly simpler buffet spread—just as well if you've already had the €45 Sunday lunch. The (largely French) wine list is extensive and unusually high-tech—ask to be given the iPad version to check out video information pages.

Shanagarry, Midleton. www.ballymaloe.ie. © **800/323-5463** in the U.S., or 021/465-2531. 33 units. €255–€315 double. Breakfast included. Dinner, bed-and-breakfast packages available. Closed early Jan to early Feb. **Amenities:** Restaurant; room service; Wi-Fi (free).

Students cooking up a storm at Ballymaloe Cookery School.

Bayview Hotel ★ If ever there was a view that qualified as "wow factor," this would be it: miles of coastline dotted with islands, and boats bobbing gently in the harbor. Guest rooms are basic but pleasant, with modern furnishings (superior rooms, with a little more space, can be had for €20 extra). Each room has a view of the sea. The **Capricho** restaurant serves good modern Irish cuisine, using plenty of local produce, including fish direct from the pier and meat from local and regional farms; prices are high (€25–€28 for a main course) but there aren't a lot of alternatives around here. Hotel guests have free use of a swanky new spa and health club at sister property **Garryvoe Hotel** (www.thebayviewhotel.com; ⓒ 021/464-6746), about 5 minutes' drive down the coast. Check the website for deals and special offers, including dinner, bed-and-breakfast packages and senior discounts.

Ballycotton. www.thebayviewhotel.com. ⓒ **021/464-6746.** 35 units. €117–€157 double, €177–€217 suite. Breakfast included. 2-night minimum on summer weekends. **Amenities:** Restaurant; bar; use of nearby health club; room service; Wi-Fi (free). Closed Nov–Easter.

Where to Eat in East Cork

Don't miss the nightly five-course gourmet dinners at the **restaurant at Ballymaloe House ★★★** (see p. 260), its food sourced from local producers and Ballymaloe's own farm. It also serves a Sunday buffet.

Gilbert's ★ IRISH A lively and laid-back little bistro, Gilbert's serves a fine menu of bistro classics, complemented by a few distinctly regional flavors. Appetizers are kept fairly light and simple—a plate of calamari rings, a simple bruschetta—and the bistro classic main courses are all crowd pleasers, from beef and Guinness stew to tempura-battered fish and chips. A pared-down version of the same menu is available at lunch, plus hearty sandwiches (steak, smoked salmon, honey-roast ham).

11 Pearse Sq., Cobh. www.gilbertsincobh.com. ⓒ **021/481-1300.** Entrees €17–€25. Mon–Fri 5–9pm, Sat noon–9pm, Sun 1–8pm. Closed Mon–Wed in winter.

Trade Winds ★ INTERNATIONAL This popular spot overlooks the harbor in Cobh, just a 5-minute walk from **Cobh: The Queenstown Story** (see p. 259). The seafood is particularly good here—monkfish in garlic sauce, scallops flavored with honey and mustard—or you can opt for one of the extremely generous steaks, served with a rich pepper sauce. At any time you can choose from the full bistro-style main menu, or opt for a lighter (and cheaper) bar snack. Some evenings include live music.

16 Casement Sq., Cobh. ⓒ **021/481-3754.** Entrees €10–€28. Tues–Fri noon–3pm, 6–10:30pm, Sat 6–10:30pm, Sun noon–7pm. Closed Mon.

KINSALE

A half-hour's drive south of Cork City (take N27 to the R600, a.k.a. Kinsale Road, or N71 to the R607), **Kinsale** is a charming fishing village sitting on a picturesque harbor, surrounded by green hills. Considered the

Kinsale's historic harbor is a welcome haven for sailboats.

gateway to the western Cork seacoast, this artsy town of 3,000 residents enchants with its narrow winding streets, well-kept 18th-century houses, imaginatively painted shopfronts, window boxes overflowing with colorful flowers, and a harbor full of sailboats. Picturesque as it is, however, Kinsale has a more eventful history than you might think. In 1601, it was the scene of a major sea battle between Protestant England and Catholic Spain—one in which Irish rebels played a covert part. You can learn all about this fascinating conflict on one of local man Don Herlihy's absorbing Kinsale Historic Strolls (see p. 263).

Exploring Kinsale

Charles Fort ★ HISTORIC SITE   Southeast of Kinsale, at the head of the harbor, this coastal landmark dating from the late 17th century was named after Charles II, who was king of England and Ireland at the time it was built. A classic star-shaped fort, it was constructed after the Battle of Kinsale (1601) to replace medieval Ringcurran Castle, which had been reduced to rubble by the English army. The building was strengthened throughout the 18th and 19th centuries, and the fort remained in use as a military garrison right up until the British left in 1921. It suffered extensive damage during the civil war, and has only recently been restored. Across the river, the smaller **James Fort** dates to the reign of King James I (1603–25) and was later captured in 1690 by the forces of (Protestant) King William I during his war with the deposed (Catholic) James II—part of the same conflict that is still commemorated by Protestant "Orange marches" in Northern Ireland.

Summercove. www.heritageireland.ie. ℭ **021/477-2263.** Admission €5 adults; €4 seniors; €3 students and children; €13 families. Mid-Mar to Oct daily 10am–6pm; Nov to mid-Mar daily 10am–5pm. Last admission 1 hr. before closing.

Desmond Castle ★ MUSEUM   This small, squat stone fortress doesn't really look like a castle, in part because it sits incongruously halfway up a residential street. Built around 1500 as the Customs house for Kinsale Harbour, in the late 17th century it was turned into a prison—at which time its history took several dark detours, including a fire that gutted the building in 1747, roasting alive the 54 French soldiers imprisoned within. Later, during the potato famine, it was used as a workhouse. Inside is an unusual little museum, which tells the extraordinary tale of the Irish exiles who helped transform the global wine trade from the 17th century onward.

Cork St. www.heritageireland.ie. ℭ **021/477-4855.** Admission €5 adults; €4 seniors; €4 students and children; €13 families. Mid-Apr to early Oct daily 10am–6pm. Closed early Oct to mid-Apr.

Kinsale Historic Stroll ★★★ TOURS   One of the most pleasant ways to spend an hour in these parts is to take local resident Don Herlihy's excellent walking tour—or "historic stroll," as he prefers to call it—of Kinsale town. Don and his fellow guide, Barry Moloney, have been leading visitors around the main sights since the mid-1990s, and their local knowledge is second to none. Highlights include the 12th-century St. Multose Church; a walk past Desmond Castle (see above); and the harbor, where the 17th-century Battle of Kinsale is recounted with an enthusiasm only found in people who really love their subject. Don asserts that the battle was perhaps the most significant turning point in Irish history, and when you hear his argument firsthand, you're inclined to agree. The tour starts outside the tourist office at 11:15am every day. From May to September, there's also an earlier tour at 9:15am (except Sun). You pay at the end or, in their words, "drop out for free if you're

Biking down the hilly streets of Kinsale.

not delighted." That probably doesn't happen very often. If you prebook, you're given a free historic chart designed by Don.

Departs from Kinsale Tourist Office, Pier Rd. www.historicstrollkinsale.com. ℂ 021/477-2873 or 087/250-0731. Tours €7 adults; €1 children. May–Sept Mon–Sat 9:15 and 11:15am, Sun 11:15am; Mar–Oct daily 11:15am. Nov to mid-Mar prebooking only.

Kinsale Pottery and Arts Centre ★ ART STUDIO   This excellent ceramics workshop outside of Kinsale sells beautiful, original items of pottery from delicate tea sets and tableware to ornamental masks. The shop is full of surprises, and prices aren't too steep for the quality of what's on offer. A two-floor gallery always has some interesting pieces on display. If you're looking for an alternative way to spend a day or more, the workshop also runs pottery courses where you can learn the basics of the craft and go home with your own creations. Prices start at around €40 for a half-day adult course (plus the cost of shipping what you make after it's fired, finished, and glazed, if you're unable to pick it up in person a week later). All materials are included in the price, as is lunch for the adult courses. From Pearse Street in Kinsale, turn left at the junction with the Blue Haven hotel on your right, then follow signs to Bandon and Innishannon. Take this road up the big hill, past the Kinsale sports ground, and look for signs to Kinsale Pottery on the left.

Ballinacurra. www.kinsaleceramics.com. ℂ **021/477-7758.** Free admission. Daily 10am–5pm.

Where to Stay in Kinsale

Actons Hotel ★   Built in the mid–19th century, this pleasant, well-run property overlooking Kinsale Harbour has been a hotel since the 1940s, though a recent renovation has smoothed out a few wrinkles. Guest rooms aren't huge, but they're nicely designed, with very large beds and lovely harbor views. In a town where it's easy to find accommodations with character but lacking modern conveniences, you'll welcome the few extras such as an elevator (rare around here) and a swimming pool. The hotel's two restaurants are good, but you've also got Kinsale and all its wonderful restaurants on your doorstep.

Pier Rd. www.actonshotelkinsale.com. ℂ **021/477-9900.** 74 units. €195–€205 double. Free parking. Breakfast included. Dinner, bed-and-breakfast packages available. **Amenities:** 2 restaurants; bar; room service; gym; pool; Wi-Fi (free).

Blue Haven Hotel ★★   There's something wonderfully old-school about this chic town house hotel in the middle of Kinsale. The rooms are traditionally decorated with antique-style furniture and heritage print wallpaper. Appropriately enough for a hotel in such a foodie town, the hotel has three restaurants, all of them good: a bar and bistro, a seafood café, and a tapas bar. The only snag is street noise, so ask for an upper-floor room if you're a light sleeper.

3–4 Pearse St. www.bluehavenkinsale.com. ℂ **021/477-2209.** 17 units. €180–€230 double. Parking at nearby lots around €1 per hr. Breakfast included. Midweek and weekend deals available. **Amenities:** 2 restaurants; bar; room service; Wi-Fi (free).

THE scilly WALK

Effectively a miniscule suburb across the harbor from Kinsale, the village of Scilly—yes, pronounced "silly"—clings to a strong sense of its own identity. Its unusual name is thought to hark back to fishermen from the Scilly Isles (off the coast of Cornwall, England) who settled here during the 17th century.

To explore the area, follow the signposted pedestrian path that runs along the sea from Scilly to Charles Fort. (You can pick up maps of the full route at the Kinsale tourism office.) Take the righthand road around the village, skirting along the coast, and join the marked pedestrian trail by the waterside. Along here are lovely views across the harbor to Kinsale and the stout remains of **James Fort** (see p. 262).

You'll pass another tiny hamlet on the outskirts of Kinsale, **Summer Cove,** which is as sweet a place as its halcyon name suggests. Black-and-white toy-town houses, with splashes of green and red, face the harbor as gulls circle overhead and the waves froth and bubble along the harbor walls.

A short walk uphill from Summer Cove lies **Charles Fort** (see p. 262), built to defend the port from foreign invaders. Local lore has it that until the 19th century, access to this stretch of water was controlled by a massive chain floating on timber kegs between the two shores that could be drawn tight at a moment's notice.

The Scilly Walk ends here, but if you continue south along the sea, you'll find another path that follows the headland to the tip of **Frower Point,** which affords great views across the harbor to the Old Head of Kinsale. The total distance from Kinsale to Frower Point is 8km (5 miles) each way, and every part of it is rewarding.

Desmond House ★★ This lovely, historic B&B is one of the best places to stay in Kinsale. Desmond House was built in the mid–18th century and, according to host Michael McLaughlin, is one of the oldest and best-preserved Georgian buildings in town. Michael is a genuine and charming man. Guest rooms are generously sized, with big, comfortable beds, and the modern bathrooms are furnished with whirlpool tubs. Many of the ingredients for the delicious breakfasts come straight from the **Old English Market** ★★ in Cork (see p. 246).

42 Cork St. www.desmondhousekinsale.com. ℂ **021/477-3575.** 4 units. €150 suite. Parking at nearby lots around €1 per hr. Breakfast included. 2-night minimum on summer weekends. **Amenities:** Wi-Fi (free).

Pier House ★★ There's something wonderfully bright and cheerful about this sweet place. Hosts Pat and Anne have done a beautiful job converting the 19th-century town house into a B&B, with chic color schemes and subtle splashes of modern art. A few of the rooms have little balconies, and guests are welcome to bring wine back with them if they want to spend a leisurely hour admiring the views of the harbor or garden. Breakfasts are delicious and plentiful. You'll have to fend for yourself at dinner, but this is hardly a chore in foodie-friendly Kinsale.

Pier Rd. www.pierhousekinsale.com. ℂ **021/477-4169.** 10 units. €100–€140 double. Parking for bikes and motorbikes only; car parking at nearby lots around €2 per hr. Breakfast included. **Amenities:** Wi-Fi (free).

Where to Eat in Kinsale

Bastion ★★★ IRISH This funky, creative restaurant opened in 2014 and fast became a hit with local diners. The menu is divided between a full a la carte selection and small plates, served tapas style (try the amazing homemade hummus if it's on the menu). Irish flavors are brought to the fore and updated, usually with deliberately no-nonsense names—"beef and onions" is actually a tender filet served with smoked potato cream and onion crumble, while the tasting menu rather delightfully offers servings of "leg in the egg" (confit duck in egg yolks) or "rest of the duck" with baked salted carrots. The exquisitely presented desserts

Milk Market square in Kinsale.

are a treat—try the poached pear with mascarpone, perhaps washed down with a sweet glass of orange muscat.

Corner of Main and Market sts. www.bastionkinsale.com. ✆ **021/470-9696.** Entrees €24–€34. Fixed-price menus €45–€65. Wed–Sun 5–11pm. Closed Mon–Tues.

Black Pig Winebar ★★★ BISTRO/TAPAS "In the company of best friends, there is never enough wine" says the inscription in the sunny courtyard of this seductive cafe-bar. It has won hearts as much for the atmosphere as for the excellent food and wine. Gently flickering candlelight and bookcases filled with well-thumbed tomes set the laidback tone. The menu has plenty of local specialties: smoked duck breast served with a salad of orange and rocket (arugula); rich and creamy Dingle crab ravioli; or perhaps a delicious plate of scallops from Kilmore Quay. The wine list is outstanding, with over 170 vintages on offer. The Black Pig is a popular spot, especially on weekends, so booking is advisable—although in our experience they'll try to squeeze you in even if it's late.

66 Lower O'Connell St. ✆ **021/477-4101.** Entrees €8–€18. Wed–Sun 5:30pm–midnight.

Finns' Table ★★★ MODERN IRISH The menu here is ambitious without being overly complicated, and with plenty of space to let the ingredients breathe. As you'd expect from Kinsale, the seafood on the menu comes directly from the harbor, so you never know exactly what will end up in the kitchen. However, on a typical night you could find a filet of John Dory with fennel croquettes, or turbot with baby leeks and lime. While the standout dishes tend to be seafood, there's plenty more to choose from, and the meats are all sourced from the owner's parents, who run a butcher shop in nearby Mitchelstown.

6 Main St. www.finnstable.com. ℭ **021/470-9636.** Entrees €23–€38. Wed–Mon 6–10pm (till 9:30pm in winter).

Fishy Fishy ★★★ SEAFOOD   Widely respected, hugely popular, and yet brilliantly simple, the Fishy Fishy is one of the best restaurants in Kinsale. The owners also have a gourmet store and fish-and-chips shop on Guardwell Street, but this is their flagship. The skillfully prepared fresh seafood comes from a small number of trusted local suppliers. And we do mean local: Shane catches the cod and turbot, Maurice provides the crab, Christy, David, and Jimmy catch the prawns—you get the idea. Exactly what's cooking depends on the day's catch, but you can expect to find the signature Fishy Fishy pie of salmon and shellfish in a creamy sauce with a breadcrumb topping, and a plate of classic fish in tempura batter with home-made chips (remember, that means thick-cut fries around here). Reservations are only taken for dinner, so this place gets packed during lunchtime.

Crowleys Quay. www.fishyfishy.ie. ℭ **021/470-0415.** Entrees €19–€28. Mar–Oct daily noon–9pm; Nov–Feb Sun–Wed noon–4pm, Thurs–Sat noon–9pm. Closed Jan.

Man Friday ★★★ MODERN IRISH/SEAFOOD   The dining room at Man Friday overlooks the bay in Scilly, a perfect setting for the reliably excellent food served here. We can't resist the seafood—smoked salmon rolls stuffed with shrimp, plaice with crab and lemon butter, and a delightfully retro-style sole Colbert—although the beef and lamb options are excellent, too. For dessert, try the sticky toffee pudding with butterscotch sauce. Sunday lunch (€29.50 for three courses) is quite an event, and always very popular—be sure to book ahead, and best not plan to do much with the rest of the day afterward except relax and digest. Ask to sit in the conservatory for the most heavenly views.

Scilly. www.manfridaykinsale.ie. ℭ **021/477-2260.** Entrees €20–€31. Mon–Sat 5–9:30pm, Sun 4–9:30pm.

Max's ★★★ MODERN IRISH   A husband-and-wife team has run Max's since the '90s, and they're still effortlessly adept at making diners feel welcome. The menu changes seasonally, but the main flavors are all

---

Kinsale Food Festival

Food lovers from all over Ireland—and even farther afield—descend on Kinsale for a weekend each October when the **Kinsale Gourmet Festival** takes over town.

The event's calendar changes every year, but always includes plenty of cooking demonstrations and other lively activities.

Restaurants join in the fun by hosting parties, special tastings, "meet the chef" events, and other culinary happenings. Many of these are free, although some of the bigger events and banquets charge €20 to €100 per ticket. It's magnificent, Bacchanalian fun. Learn more and book tickets at www.kinsalerestaurants.com.

local—meat from Kilbrittain, a little village down the coast, and shellfish caught close enough that they could have been carried to the door. (The catch of the day is posted on the website if you want to know what to expect.) Max's also has a full vegetarian menu and plenty of kids' options. The early-bird menu (a thoroughly reasonable €26 for two courses) is served until 7:15pm (7pm on Sat).

48 Main St. www.maxs.ie. ℃ **021/477-2443.** Entrees €23–€29. Daily 6–10pm. Closed Jan to early Mar.

Poet's Corner ★ CAFE   Drop in to this charming little cafe for a freshly baked scone, a cup of herbal tea (the choice is huge), or coffee and a toasted sandwich. As the name suggests, this place styles itself as a "reading cafe"; not only can you buy books here, but bring them two books in good condition and they'll let you swap it for another one from their secondhand collection. The "Irish Corner" is filled with interesting books and other information about the area.

44 Main St. www.poetscornerkinsale.com. ℃ **086/227-7276.** Lunch items €5–€10. Daily 9:30am–6pm.

The Spaniard ★★ BISTRO   The portrait on the sign of this atmospheric old inn shows Don Juan de Aguila, the Spanish commander who led a force of 4,000 men, assisted by local Irish revolutionaries, against the English at the Battle of Kinsale in 1601. The English won, but Don Juan became a hero in local folklore. The present inn dates from around 50 years after the battle—so some of its first patrons were probably veterans—and it's still a satisfying place with an old-world look. The restaurant serves excellent, homey pub food; the menu in the bar is just as good, and cheaper, too. Try the house special chowder, followed by a plate of fresh brill with leek and fennel, or a hearty beef rib in red wine gravy. An eclectic program of live music features everything from straight-up Irish folk to Russian Gypsy bands.

Junction of Scilly and Lower Rd. www.thespaniard.ie. ℃ **021/477-2436.** Entrees €14–€25. Mon–Thurs 10:30am–11:30pm, Fri–Sat 10:30am–12:30am, Sun 12:30–11:30pm. (Food served until about 9pm daily.)

The Steakhouse ★★ GRILL   In a town full of wonderful restaurants noted mostly for their seafood, this superb grill will delight devoted carnivores. The restaurant sources its beef from the southwest region—particularly the Cork native Dexter breed, which lends itself particularly well to rib-eye—and serves it up with delicious comfort-food sides. It also serves a range of gourmet burgers. It's not all about the beef, either, with daily seafood, chicken, and duck specials. Leave room for the house-special chocolate pudding with whipped cream.

18–19 Lower O'Connell St. www.thesteakhouse.ie. ℃ **021/470-9850.** Entrees €16–€35. Mon–Fri 5:30–9pm, Sat 5:30–10pm, Sun 1–3pm and 5:30–10pm. Closes 9pm and Mon–Tues in winter.

The historic inn the Spaniard celebrates Irish resistance at the Battle of Kinsale.

Sports & Outdoor Pursuits in Kinsale

FISHING Kinsale is one of the southern Irish coast's sea-angling centers. The area has numerous shipwrecks for wreck fishing (not the least of them the *Lusitania,* near the Old Head of Kinsale). Try **Kinsale Angling** (1 Rampart Lane, The Ramparts; www.kinsale-angling.com; ✆ **021/477-4946**) for charter boats. They also run whale- and dolphin-watching trips. Prices vary widely, so call or e-mail for more information.

GOLF Embraced by the sea on three sides, the nothing-short-of-spectacular **Old Head Golf Links** (www.oldhead.com; ✆ **021/477-8444**) is Tiger Woods's favorite Irish course. Named one of *Golf Magazine*'s "Top 100 Courses in the World" in the 2000s, it is hauntingly beautiful, rain or shine. The course retains a resident environmentalist to ensure that crucial wildlife habitats are not disturbed. But golfing here costs big money: Greens fees in summer are a whopping €275 weekdays/€300 weekends for one 18-hole round, and €450 for 36 holes. In the winter, prices drop by around €180 for one 18-hole round, and €300 for 36 holes.

SAILING There's excellent sailing out from Kinsale Head. **Sovereign Sailing** (www.sovereignsailing.com; ✆ **087/617-2555** or ✆ 086/858-6212) offers a full range of yacht-sailing options for all ages and levels of experience. Between March and November, full- or half-day sails from Kinsale leave every day. Rates vary widely based on the kind of sailing you try, but a half-day trip on a 27-foot day yacht costs €150 for up to three people, €200 for up to five. They can also provide lunch.

WATERSPORTS The **Oysterhaven Activity Centre** (www.oysterhaven. com; ✆ **021/477-0738**), 8km (5 miles) from Kinsale, rents windsurf gear, dinghies, and kayaks. The cost ranges from around €20 to €40 for wind-surfing equipment, €15 to €25 for kayaks, and €12 per hour (€18 for 2 hr.) for SUPs (stand-up paddleboards). Windsurfing lessons cost €50 for a 2½-hour taster session, up to €95 for a full day. Things get pretty busy during summer, so try to book ahead as much as possible.

WEST CORK

You might say that West Cork is like County Kerry without the crowds. Like Kerry, it's got a photo-friendly craggy topography and jagged Atlantic coastline; and also as in Kerry, it's impossible to make good time on the narrow, sinuous roads here, as they twist along rivers, through valleys, around mountains, and through lovely small towns. Those willing to slow down and go with the flow are amply rewarded. You'll probably come across a few rural intersections that are completely lacking in signage, and end up slowing down for at least one herd of sheep ambling down a country lane. In places, the public route that hugs the coast narrows to just one lane and delivers heart-stopping views. Over time, you may come to think of the roads here as one of West Cork's great pleasures.

Some of the most beautiful coastal scenery (and severe weather) is on West Cork's islands. **Cape Clear,** home to a bird-watching observatory, is also a well-known Gaeltacht: Schoolchildren and adults alike come here to work on their Gaelic skills each summer. **Dursey Island,** off the tip of the Beara Peninsula, is accessible by cable car. **Garinish Island** in Glengarriff is the site of Ilnacullin, an elaborate Italianate garden.

Arriving

N71 is the main road into West Cork from north and south, looping around its coast; the east-west N22, on its way from Cork City to Killarney, also passes through West Cork. **Bus Éireann** (www.buseireann.ie; ✆ **021/450-8188**) provides daily bus service to and from the principal towns in West Cork.

Exploring West Cork

Bantry House ★★ HISTORIC HOUSE   Built around 1750 for the earls of Bantry, this Georgian house holds furniture and *objets d'art* from all over Europe, including Aubusson and Gobelin tapestries said to have been made for Marie Antoinette. The gardens, with original statuary, are beautifully kept—climb the steps behind the building for a panoramic view of the house, gardens, and Bantry Bay. Check out the informative exhibition on the ill-fated Spanish Armada, which, led by the Irish rebel Wolfe Tone, attempted to invade the country near Bantry House in 1769. Fully guided tours (included in the ticket price) take place daily at 2pm;

walk this way: **THE SHEEP'S HEAD LOOP**

A jagged strip of land reaching out into the Atlantic on the western side of County Cork, the Sheep's Head Peninsula is well worth a visit. It's a place of wild, rocky scenery, ice-blue lakes, and spectacular coastal views. It is also an isolated place; you'll likely find yourself alone for large stretches of time, with the expansive sea views all to yourself. Which, in bustling modern Ireland, is enough to make it worth the trip.

To see it the easy way, drive the **Sheep's Head Loop,** which begins just outside Bantry along the tiny road to Kilcrohane. It takes you through the coastal village of **Ahakista,** where you can stop to explore a Bronze Age stone circle, and on to tiny **Durrus,** home to the rocky ruins of the Cool na Long Castle. The main draw here, though, is the natural beauty. The north side of the peninsula is all sheer cliffs and stark, rocky scenery, unmarred by modern development (the sunsets on this side are unbelievable), while the more lush south-side road runs right along the wondrous Dunmanus Bay.

To explore the peninsula in more depth, however, you could walk the **Sheep's Head Way,** voted "Best Walk in Ireland" by *Country Walking* magazine a few years ago. The windy coastal walk is certainly ambitious, making an 89km (55-mile) loop around the peninsula. Most walkers choose to explore only the tip, from the point where the road ends down to the stumpy 1960s-era lighthouse, which keeps oil tankers from running aground. If you try the longer walk, be aware that the route is rough in places, particularly on the north side. The south side of the peninsula is greener and the path well-travelled.

The *Guide to the Sheep's Head Way* by Stephen Bosch (2003), available in local shops and tourist offices, combines history, poetry, and topography in a fantastic introduction to the region. The lavishly illustrated guide *Walking the Sheep's Head Way* by Amanda Clarke (2014) helpfully breaks the walk into all its various stages.

otherwise, you're free to wander around by yourself. And if you really love it here, you can spend the night (doubles €180–€230).

Bantry. www.bantryhouse.com. ✆ **027/50047.** Admission €11 adults; €8 seniors and students; €3 children 6–16; children under 6 free; €26 families. Gardens only €5. June–Aug daily 10am–5pm; Apr–May and Sept–Oct Tues–Sun and public holiday Mon 10am–5pm. Closed Nov–Mar.

Cape Clear Island (*Oileán Chléire*) ★★ HERITAGE/NATURE SITE

The southernmost inhabited point in Ireland, 13km (8 miles) off the mainland, Cape Clear Island has a permanent population of just a hundred residents. It is a bleak place with a rock-bound coastline and no trees to break the rush of sea wind, but it's also starkly beautiful. In early summer, wildflowers brighten the landscape, and in October, passerine migrants, some on their way from North America and Siberia, fill the air. Seabirds are abundant during the nesting season, especially from July to September. A bird observatory is at the **North Harbour,** with a warden in residence from March to November. **Ciarán and Mary O'Driscoll,** who operate a B&B on the island (www.capeclearisland.eu; ℂ 028/39153 or 086/366-5078), also run boat trips for bird-watchers and have a keen eye for vagrants (the avian kind). You can get to the island by ferry with **Cape Clear Ferries** (www.capeclearferries.com; ℂ **028/39159** or 41923; €17 adults, €7 children, €40 families) and explore it all at your own pace; alternatively, you can take **Fastnet Tours'** Fastnet Rock Lighthouse Tour (www.fastnettour.com; ℂ **087/389-9711**), a ferry trip that runs a couple of times a week from June to August, weather permitting (call for current sailing times). After visiting the island's tiny heritage center, you're taken out for a boat ride around **Fastnet Rock,** a craggy outcrop in the Atlantic. Home to nothing but a weather-beaten lighthouse, Fastnet was traditionally known as "Teardrop Island," not for its shape, but because it was the last piece of Ireland emigrants saw on their way to America. Note that Fastnet Tours must be booked at least 3 days in advance. The cost is around €35 per person (€80 families); book online for a 10% discount.

Cape Clear Island. www.oilean-chleire.ie.

The Donkey Sanctuary ★ ANIMAL SANCTUARY   A real tear-jerker, this one: a charity that rescues abandoned and abused donkeys and nurses them back to health. A few here have been voluntarily relinquished by owners who are no longer able to care for them, but the majority have sadder histories. The donkeys live out their days at this quiet, bucolic place, where they receive medical aid and plenty of TLC. Visitors can meet the gentle patients and learn their stories. The emphasis is on happy endings. Seeing these animals given a new lease on life can be a touching and even profound experience for kids.

Liscarroll, near Mallow. www.thedonkeysanctuary.ie. ℂ **022/48398.** Free admission. Mon–Fri 9am–4:30pm; Sat, Sun, and public holidays 10am–5pm.

Drombeg Stone Circle ★★ ANCIENT SITE   This ring of 13 standing stones is the finest example of a megalithic stone circle in County Cork. The circle dates from 153 B.C., and little is known about its ritual purpose. However, the remains of two huts and a cooking area, just to the west of the circle, give some clue; it is thought that heated stones were placed in a water trough (which can be seen adjacent to the huts), and the hot water was used for cooking. This section has been dated to sometime between A.D.. 368 and 608.

Signposted off R597 between Rosscarbery and Glandore, just east of Drombeg village. No phone. Free admission (open site).

Dursey Island ★★ HERITAGE/NATURE SITE   This is a real adventure—a barren promontory extending into the sea at the tip of the Beara Peninsula. The island offers no amenities for tourists, but the adventurous will be rewarded with beautiful seaside walks, a 200-year-old signal tower, and a memorable passage from the mainland via cable car. To get

Walk to Abandoned Cummingeera

Stark and eerie, **Cummingeera** ★ is an abandoned village in a wild, remote valley near Lauragh, on the Kerry side of the Beara Peninsula. The walk to the village gives you a taste for the rough beauty of this mountainous area, and a sense of the extent to which people in pre-Famine Ireland would go to find a patch of arable land. To get to the start of the walk, take R571 from Castletown up along the coast toward the town of Lauragh. Just west of Lauragh, turn onto the road for Glanmore Lake, signposted on the right. After approximately 1km (⅔ mile), turn right at a road posted for "stone circle." Continue 2km (1¼ miles) to the point at which the road becomes dirt, and park on the roadside. From here, there is no trail—just walk up the valley to its terminus, about 2km (1¼ miles) away, where the ruins of a village hug the cliff's base. Where the valley is blocked by a headland, take the route around to the left, which is less steep. Return the way you came. The whole walk—4km (2½ miles)—is of moderate difficulty.

there, take R572 past Cahermore to its terminus. As you sway wildly in the wooden cable car, you'll wonder whether or not to be reassured that someone saw fit to place the text of Psalm 91 inside. ("If you say 'the Lord is my refuge,' and you make the most high your dwelling, no harm will overtake you.") You may even be sharing your car with sheep or cows—it's also used to transport livestock to and from the island. At this point you might be wondering whether a ferry would have been a wiser option. It wouldn't: Apparently the channel between the island and mainland is just too treacherous to permit regular crossing by boat. Cable cars run all year, 7 days a week, from about 9:30am to 8pm, with long breaks at lunch and supper times (June–Sept they may run continuously, however). Crossings can't be prebooked—it's always first come, first served—but be sure to check return times with the operator before you go. The island has no shops, pubs, restaurants, or lodging of any kind (save for a few cottages for rent, by prebooking only; see website for details). Bring food, water, and warm clothing. The crossing is very popular in summer, and numbers are sometimes restricted on the island on particularly busy days. For up-to-date schedule information, call the **Skibbereen Tourist Office** at ℂ **028/21766.**

Dursey Island. www.durseyisland.ie. No phone. Cable-car round-trip €10 adults, €5 children. Daily 9:30am–1pm, 1:30–5pm. Last cable car journey 30 min. before closing. About 21km (14 miles) west of Castletown-Bearhaven (follow R572).

Gougane Barra ★★ HERITAGE/NATURE SITE   One of Western Ireland's most beautiful spots, Gougane Barra (which means "St. Fin Barre's Cleft") is the name of both a tiny old settlement and a forest park a little northeast of the Pass of Keimaneigh, 24km (15 miles) northeast of Bantry, and well signposted off R584. If you're coming from the east, it's about 30km (18.6 miles) southwest of Macroom. Its loveliest feature is a

local hero: **MICHAEL COLLINS**

Among the heroes of Ireland's struggle for independence, Michael Collins seems to be Cork's favorite native son. Affectionately referred to as "the Big Fella," Collins was the commander-in-chief of the army of the Irish Free State, which finally won the Republic's independence from Britain in 1921.

Collins was born in 1890, and, along with seven brothers and sisters, he was raised on a farm in Sam's Cross, just outside the little town of **Clonakilty.** He immigrated to England at 15, like many other young Irish men seeking work in London. In his 20s, he joined the Irish revolutionary group, the Irish Republican Brotherhood (I.R.B.) and first came to fame in 1916 as one of the planners and leaders of the Easter Rising (see p. 61). Although it aroused passions among the population, the Rising was in fact a military disaster, and Collins—young but clever—railed against its amateurism. He was furious about the seizure of prominent buildings—such as Dublin's General Post Office (see p. 111)—that were impossible to defend, impossible

to escape from, and difficult to get supplies into.

After the battle, Collins was arrested and sent to an internment camp in Britain, along with hundreds of other rebels. There his stature within the I.R.B. grew, and by the time he was released, he had become one of the leaders of the Republican movement. In 1918, he was elected a member of the British Parliament, but like many other Irish members, he refused to go to London, instead announcing that he would sit only in an Irish parliament in Dublin. Most of the rebel Irish MPs (including Eamon de Valera) were arrested by British troops for their actions, but Collins avoided arrest, and he later helped de Valera escape from prison. Over the subsequent years, de Valera and Collins worked together to create an Irish state.

After lengthy political wrangling and much bloodshed (Collins orchestrated an assassination that essentially wiped out the British secret service in Ireland), Collins was sent by de Valera in 1921 to negotiate a treaty with the British government. In the meeting, British Prime

still, dark, romantic lake, which is the source of the River Lee. This is where St. Fin Barre founded a monastery, supposedly on the small island connected by a causeway to the mainland. Though nothing remains of the saint's 6th-century community, the setting is idyllic, with rhododendrons spilling into the still waters where swans glide by. The island now holds an elfin chapel and eight small circular cells dating from the early 1700s, as well as a modern chapel. Signposted walks and drives lead through the wooded hills.

7km (4½ miles) west of Ballingeary (signposted off R584). Park admission €5 per car (in coins).

Ilnacullin (Garinish Island) ★★ GARDEN Officially known as Ilnacullin, but usually referred to as Garnish (or "Garinish"), this little island is a beautiful and tranquil place. It used to be little more than a barren outcrop, whose only distinguishing feature was a Martello tower left over from the Napoleonic Wars of the early 19th century. Then, in 1919,

Minister David Lloyd George agreed to allow Ireland to become a free republic, as long as that republic did not include the largely Protestant counties of Ulster, which would stay part of the United Kingdom. Knowing he could not get more at the time and determined to end the violence, Collins reluctantly agreed to sign the treaty, hoping to renegotiate later. After signing the document Collins said, "I have just signed my death warrant."

As he'd expected, the plan tore the new Republic apart, dividing the group now known as the IRA into two factions: those who wanted to continue fighting for all of Ireland, and those who favored the treaty. Fighting soon broke out in Dublin, and the civil war was underway.

Collins had learned many lessons from the Easter debacle, and now his strategy was completely different. His soldiers operated as "flying columns," waging a guerrilla war against the enemy—suddenly attacking, and then just as suddenly withdrawing, thus minimizing their losses and leaving the opposition baffled.

The battles stretched on for 10 months. In August 1922, Collins, weary of the war, was on a peace mission in his home county. Stopping at a pub near his mother's birthplace, he and his escort were on the road near Béal na Bláth when Collins was shot and killed. Precisely who killed him—his own men or the opposition—was never known. On his rapid rise to the top, he'd made too many enemies. He was 31 years old.

The **Michael Collins Centre** (www. michaelcollinscentre.com; © **023/884-6107**), located on the farm where he grew up, is a good place to learn more about the man. In addition to an hour-long tour, featuring a film and a visit to the actual ambush site, the center runs in-depth guided trips around the local area. (These last 3½ hours are probably for Collins devotees only.) The center is signposted off N71, 5.6km (3½ miles) west of Clonakilty. It's open mid-June to mid-September, Monday to Friday 10:30am to 5pm and Saturday 11am to 2pm. Admission is free.

the English landscaper Harold Peto was commissioned to create an elaborately planned Italianate garden, with classical pavilions and myriad unusual plants and flowers. The island's unusually mild microclimate allows a number of subtropical plant species to thrive here; George Bernard Shaw is said to have written *St. Joan* under the shade of its palm trees. The island can be reached for €10 per person round-trip (€5 children 6–15) on a covered ferry operated out of Glengarriff by **Blue Pool Ferry** (www.bluepoolferry.com; © **027/63333**) or **Harbour Queen Ferries** (www.harbourqueenferry.com; © **027/63116**). Boats run back and forth about every 20 to 30 minutes. *Note:* The Harbour Queen doesn't take credit cards. The nearest ATMs are in Bantry.

Glengarriff. www.garnishisland.com. © **027/63040.** Admission (gardens) €5 adults; €4 seniors; €3 students and children; €13 families. July–Aug Mon–Fri and Sun 9:30am–5:30pm, Sat 9:30am–6pm. June Mon–Fri and Sun 10am–5:30pm, Sat 10am–6pm. Apr–May and Sept–Oct daily 10am–5:30pm. Last landing 1 hr. before closing. No landings Nov–Mar.

Mizen Head ★★ VIEWS At Mizen Head, the very extreme southwest tip of Ireland, the land falls precipitously into the Atlantic breakers in a procession of spectacular 210m (689-ft.) sea cliffs. You can cross a suspension bridge to an old signal station, now a visitor center, and stand on a rock promontory at the southernmost point of the mainland. The sea view is spectacular, and it's worth a trip regardless of the weather. On wild days, tremendous Atlantic waves assault the cliffs, while on clear days, dolphins leap from the waves and seals bask on the rocks. A huge renovation in the early 2010s added new bridges, viewing platforms, and a simulated ship's bridge. On the way out to Mizen Head, you'll pass Barleycove Beach, a gorgeous stretch of sand and rock.

The suspension bridge to Mizen Head.

From Ballydehob, take R592 and then R591 to Goleen and follow signs to Mizen Head. www.mizenhead.ie. ✆ **028/35115** or 35000. Admission €7.50 adults; €6 seniors and students; €4.50 children 5–13; children 4 and under free; €25 families. June daily 10am–6pm; July–Aug daily 10am–7pm; mid-Mar to May and Sept–Oct daily 10:30am–5pm; Nov to mid-Mar Sat–Sun 11am–4pm. Also daily during Feb school holiday week 11am–4pm.

Where to Stay in West Cork

Glebe Country House ★ About halfway between Cork and Kinsale, this place was built as a rectory in the late 17th century. Bedrooms are comfortable and traditionally furnished, with views of the idyllic gardens. The owners are real foodies: The breakfast menu is longer and more imaginative than most places this size (try the cheesy French toast), and the five-course dinners, made with plenty of local produce, are delicious. Dinners are also thoroughly reasonable, at €35 per head, although you must book by noon. If you're after a bit more seclusion, two self-catering cottages are on the grounds.

Balinadee (off Balinadee center), Bandon. www.glebecountryhouse.ie. ✆ **021/477-8294.** 9 units. €110–€150 double. Free parking. Breakfast included. €400–€570 per week self-catering apts. **Amenities:** Restaurant; Wi-Fi (free). Closed in winter.

Inchydoney Lodge & Spa ★★★ So close to the beach you could almost dive into the Atlantic from your balcony, this famously luxurious spa hotel is one of the best in the region. The spa specializes in thalassotherapy treatments, using seawater, although the full list of what's offered may relax you just by reading it. Guest rooms are sophisticated and modern, with huge windows that open out onto amazing views of the sea (of course). The **Gulfstream Restaurant** serves French- and Mediterranean-influenced cooking, with fresh seafood a particular specialty. The hotel also has a pub and bistro if you're after something simpler. Unlike some high-end spas, Inchydoney is a great option for families, with its dedicated Children's Lounge daycare; the hotel can also arrange family-friendly activities such as kayaking, whale-watching, and cycling.

Clonakilty. www.inchydoneyisland.com. ⓒ **023/883-3143.** 67 units. €190–€290 double. Free parking. Breakfast included. Dinner, bed-and-breakfast packages available. **Amenities:** 2 restaurants; bar; pool; room service; spa; Wi-Fi (free).

Longueville House Hotel ★★ The bright pink frontage of this grand but delightfully relaxed country house, built in 1720, is your first indication that this isn't a place to stand on ceremony. Sure enough, your hosts, the O'Callaghans, soon make you feel right at home. William O'Callaghan trained with the renowned French chef Raymond Blanc, and he puts the skills he learned to wonderful use here (see the **President's Restaurant ★★★,** p. 278). The hotel also does a proper afternoon tea and Sunday lunch. Spacious bedrooms reflect the heritage of the building, with appealingly traditional style and antique furniture. The hotel and restaurant are closed Monday and Tuesday; from November to March they're only open Friday through Sunday afternoon.

Mallow. www.longuevillehouse.ie. ⓒ **022/47156.** 22 units. €150–€195 double, €185–€215 suite. Free parking. Breakfast included. Dinner, bed-and-breakfast packages available. **Amenities:** Restaurant; room service; Wi-Fi (free).

Where to Eat in West Cork

Blairscove ★★ IRISH This has to be one of the most picturesque dining rooms in Ireland—a former barn, which may have originated as an 18th-century watchtower. The menu isn't cutting-edge, but that's kind of the point. Instead what you get (after a charmingly retro buffet of appetizers) are traditional Irish flavors elegantly updated, such as rack of lamb with braised chicory and sorrel pesto, or hake served in a mustard, dill, and white-wine sauce. Desserts are rich and delicious. If you want to make even more of a night of it, Blairscove offers B&B lodging for €190 to €260 a night and self-catering cottages from upwards of €644 a week.

Barley Cove Rd., Durrus. www.blairscove.ie. ⓒ **027/61127.** Three-course fixed-price menus €60. Mid-Mar to Oct Tues–Sun 6:30–10pm. Closed Nov to mid-Mar.

Good Things ★ MODERN IRISH The "good things" that this sophisticated cafe promises are simple, tasty, healthful meals, using plenty of local produce. You might start with a salad of seasonal vegetables, then try the roasted brined chicken (brining gives the meat a juicy tenderness) with pumpkin and herb stuffing, or the Growers' Plate—a vegetarian cornucopia made with aubergine (eggplant), spiced chickpeas, and cumin. There's also a cookery school here, where you can learn about everything from vegetarian cooking to fermenting seaweed; 1-day courses start at about €160.

Dillon's Corner, 68 Bridge St., Skibbereen. www.thegoodthingscafe.com. ☏ **028/51948.** Entrees €18–€28. Mon and Thurs–Sat noon–3pm, 6–9pm; Tues–Wed noon–3pm. Closed Sun. Closed Nov to mid-Mar.

The Heron's Cove ★★ SEAFOOD

It's all about the bounty of the sea at this laid-back restaurant about 15km (9 miles) from **Mizen Head** (see p. 276). All the seafood is caught on the West Cork coastline; expect Bantry Bay organic salmon, tempura monkfish, or perhaps some lemon sole filet prepared in a creamy white-wine sauce. You can sit outside on a terrace overlooking the harbor if the weather's good. It also offers B&B lodging in pleasant guest rooms with views of the harbor for €80 to €100 per night (€115–€120 per night for family room).

Harbour Rd., Goleen. www.heronscove.com. ☏ **028/35225.** Entrees €17–€27. Daily 7–9:45pm. Essential to call ahead in winter: Restaurant closes in quiet periods and hours may vary at other times.

Mary Anne's ★ SEAFOOD/PUB FOOD

The handsome exterior of this friendly pub in Castletownshend, near Skibbereen—in fact, the *only* pub in the village—is a photo op waiting to happen. The ochre paint and neat black windows look so satisfyingly publike that it may as well be on the front of a postcard (for all we know, it might well be). Fortunately, the food is just as good. This being the West Cork coast, the seafood is often what stands out—fresh, local crab salad, local scallops, fish pie with plenty of, guess what, local ingredients—but there are meatier choices as well, such as roast duck in a sauce of blood orange and star anise, or lamb chops. You can eat in a little courtyard terrace if you're blessed with sunshine.

Castletownshend, Skibbereen. ☏ **028/36146.** Entrees €15–€27. Daily 11am–11pm (food served until about 9pm).

The President's Restaurant ★★★ FRENCH/IRISH

The restaurant of the excellent **Longueville House Hotel** (see p. 277) is one of the finest in the region. Chef William O'Callaghan—who, along with his wife, Aisling, also runs the hotel—trained under famed French chef Raymond Blanc at Le Manoir aux Quat'Saisons, one of the most famous restaurants in England. Local ingredients (many from the restaurant's own farm and kitchen garden) feature heavily in the Irish-French menus, including Castletownbere cod, local beef, and honey from the house hive. The evening menu can be taken as a seven-course tasting menu, or a three-course version with more regular portion sizes. A lavish lunch is served on Sundays (€40 per person, €20 children). The hotel website suggests that guests at the hotel might like to take a quick nap in front of the fire afterwards—excellent advice after a meal like that.

Mallow. www.longuevillehouse.ie. © **022/47156.** Set menu €55; tasting menu €65. Reservations essential, at least 24 hr. in advance. Wed–Thurs 6:30–8pm; Fri–Sat 6:30–9pm; Sun 12:30–2:15pm, 6:30–8pm. Closed Mon–Tues year-round.

Sports & Outdoor Pursuits in West Cork

BEACHES **Barleycove Beach** is a vast expanse of pristine sand with a fine view out toward the Mizen Head cliffs; despite the trailer park and holiday homes on the far side of the dunes, large parts of the beach never seem to get crowded. Take R591 to Goleen, and follow signs for Mizen Head. **Inchydoney Beach,** on Clonakilty Bay, is famous for both its gorgeous beach and the luxe **Inchydoney Lodge & Spa** (see p. 276).

CYCLING The **Mizen Head, Sheep's Head,** and **Beara peninsulas** offer fine roads for cycling, with great scenery and few cars. The loop around Mizen Head, starting in Skibbereen, is a good 2- to 3-day trip; a loop around the Beara Peninsula from Bantry, Glengarriff, or Kenmare takes at least 3 days at a casual pace. In Skibbereen, 18- and 21-speed bicycles can be rented from **Roycroft Cycles,** Heron Court, Town Car Park (www.westcorkcycles.ie; © **028/21235**); expect to pay around €15 to €20 per day, €70 to €80 per week.

DIVING The **Baltimore Diving Centre** in Baltimore (www.baltimore diving.com; © **028/20300**) provides equipment and boats to certified divers to explore the many shipwrecks, reefs, and caves off Cork's western coast. Cost is €30 to €65 per dive. Various 2-hour to 15-day certified PADI courses are available for all levels of experience.

FISHING The West Cork coast is known for its many shipwrecks, making this one of the best places in Ireland for wreck fishing. **Courtmacsherry Sea Angling Centre,** Woodpoint House, Courtmacsherry (www. courtmacsherryangling.ie; © **023/884-6427**), offers packages that include bed-and-breakfast in an idyllic 18th-century stone farmhouse, plus a day's sea angling aboard an Aquastar fishing boat that can reach the wreck of the *Lusitania* in about 40 minutes. A day's fishing costs around €70 per person (€80 to go out to a wreck). Rod hire is €10 per day. They also run 2-hour dolphin- and whale-watching excursions for €35 per person. B&B rates starts at €40 per person, €70 with dinner—and fish is likely to be on the menu.

KAYAKING With hundreds of islands, inviting inlets, and sea caves, the coast of West Cork is a sea kayaker's paradise. **Lough Ine,** one of the largest saltwater lakes in Europe, offers warm, still waters for beginners, a tidal rapid for the intrepid, and access to a nearby headland riddled with caves. In Skibbereen, **Atlantic Sea Kayaking** (www.atlanticseakayaking.com;

© **028/21058**) specializes in guided trips around Galley Head in Clonakilty and Mizen Head.

WALKING   A spectacular coastal walk begins along the banks of **Lough Ine,** cupped in a lush valley of exceptional beauty. To get there, follow signs for Lough Ine along R595 between Skibbereen and Baltimore; a parking lot is at the northwest corner of the lake. The wide trail proceeds gradually upward from the parking lot through the woods on the west slope of the valley; once you reach the hilltop, you'll see a sweeping view of the coast from Mizen Head to Galley Head. Walking time to the top and back is about 1½ hours.

An easy 2-hour seaside walk on the **Beara Peninsula** begins at Dunboy Castle, a ruined 19th-century manor house about 1 mile west of Castletownbere on R572. Just down the road are the ruins of a medieval fortress; beyond, the trail (a section of the O'Sullivan Beara trail) continues to the tip of Fair Head through rhododendrons, with fine views across to Bere Island.

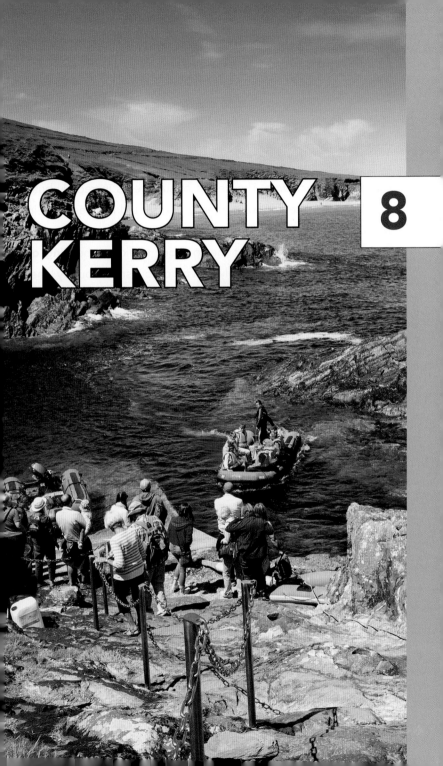

COUNTY KERRY

8

Known for rolling green fields, vibrant little towns, and craggy ocean vistas, County Kerry is one of those places visitors to Ireland keep at the top of their lists. Charming villages like colorful Kenmare and bustling historic towns like Killarney make perfect stops on any Irish tour. Its peaceful green valleys are just what you hope for when you come to Ireland. That said, with massive popularity come massive crowds. The height of summer is incredibly busy here—if it's peace you want, ideally, you should hit these hills in the late spring or fall. But there's an antidote for even the busiest times: Should you find that the tour bus traffic on the **Ring of Kerry** is getting to you, simply turn off onto a small country lane, and within seconds you'll find yourself virtually alone in the peaceful Irish countryside.

ESSENTIALS
Arriving

BY BUS   Bus Éireann (www.buseireann.ie; ✆ 064/663-0011) operates regularly scheduled service into Killarney and Dingle from all parts of Ireland.

BY TRAIN   Trains from Dublin, Cork, and Galway arrive daily at the **Killarney Railway Station** (www.irishrail.ie; ✆ 064/663-1067), Railway Road, off East Avenue Road. Kenmare and Dingle do not have train stations.

BY CAR   Getting to Killarney from Cork is easy—just head northeast out of Cork City on N22; the distance is about 85km (53 miles). To get to Killarney from Dublin, take M7 southwest to Limerick, then N21 (which also leads to Tralee, gateway to the Dingle Peninsula), and N22 to Killarney. The total journey is about 310km (193 miles). Kenmare and Killarney are connected by the main N71 Ring of Kerry Road; they're only 33km (20½ miles) apart, but allow plenty of time because of the winding nature of the road (and, in summer, tour-bus traffic). To hire a car in Killarney, try **Budget** at the International Hotel on Kenmare Place (www.budget.ie; ✆ 064/663-4341) or **Enterprise** at the Gleneagles Hotel, Muckross Road (www.enterprise.ie; ✆ 064/663-1393). For details

PREVIOUS PAGE: Small inflatable boats carry visitors to the remote Blasket Islands.

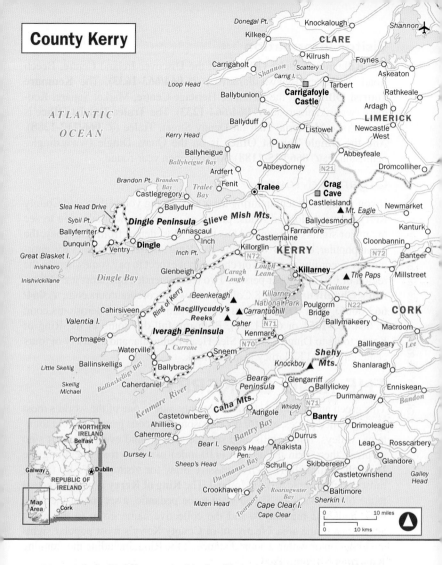

County Kerry

on car rentals in Dublin, see p. 91; for Shannon Airport car rentals, see p. 334.

BY PLANE   Aer Lingus (www.aerlingus.com; ℂ 081/836-5000) has two flights per day from Dublin into the miniscule **Kerry County Airport** in Farranfore (www.kerryairport.ie; ℂ **066/976-4644**), about 16km (10 miles) north of Killarney. A handful of flights fly every week from London's Lupton and Stanstead airports, and Frankfurt's Hahn airport, operated by **Ryanair** (www.ryanair.com; ℂ **0871/246-0000** in the U.K. or 1520/444-004), with fewer flights scheduled in winter.

Visitor Information

The **Killarney Tourist Office** is at the Discover Ireland Centre, Beech Road, Killarney (www.killarney.ie; ✆ **064/663-1633**). The **Kenmare Tourist Office** is at the Kenmare Heritage Centre, Market Square, Kenmare (www.kenmare.ie; ✆ **064/664-1233**). The **Tralee Tourist Office** is at the Ashe Memorial Hall on Denny Street, Tralee (✆ **066/712-1288**). And the **Dingle Tourist Office** is on the Quay, Dingle (www.dingle-peninsula.ie; ✆ **066/915-1188**). All stay open year-round.

Organized Tours

8

If you're not confident in hiring a car and driving yourself around County Kerry's tourist-clogged roads, plenty of companies will take you to see the major sights on organized bus tours. Most depart from **Killarney,** the most popular base for exploring the Ring of Kerry. Prices vary enormously according to what you choose, but expect to pay somewhere in the region of €20 to €50 per person. Two recommended operators are **Corcoran's Chauffeur Tours,** 8 College St. (www.corcorantours.com; ✆ **064/663-6666**), and **Dero's Tours,** 22 Main St. (www.derostours.com; ✆ **064/663-1251** or 663-1567). Both run full-day tours of the Ring of Kerry, tours to Dingle and the Slea Head Peninsula, and a variety of tours centered around Killarney National Park.

THE RING OF KERRY

This green and beautiful stretch of countryside is one of the world's most photographed places, and for good reason: Gorgeous panoramas of mountains, valleys, rolling hills, and seaside wait around every curve. It's no surprise, then, than the 178km (110-mile) two-lane road encircling the **Iveragh Peninsula** is such a massive draw for visitors—it's by far the most popular scenic drive in Ireland. The **Ring of Kerry** is both the actual name of the road—or, if you want to be pedantic, a section of the N70, N71, and N72 highways—and the collective name given to the many attractions in the area. Nearly all of County Kerry's most popular sights are either on or within a short distance of the Ring, including the stunning **Killarney National Park.**

What you won't find, at least in the summertime, is much in the way of peace. Bicyclists avoid the route because of the scores of tour buses thundering down it from early morning until late in the day. You can drive either way along the Ring of Kerry, but a counterclockwise route gives you the best views. Very large vehicles are always meant to travel this way to avoid accidents and nasty traffic jams around the Ring's perilously narrow bends.

Of course, if you yearn for peace and quiet, you can simply skedaddle off that busy highway and onto the many narrower country roads. There's so much beauty here, it doesn't really matter how you choose to

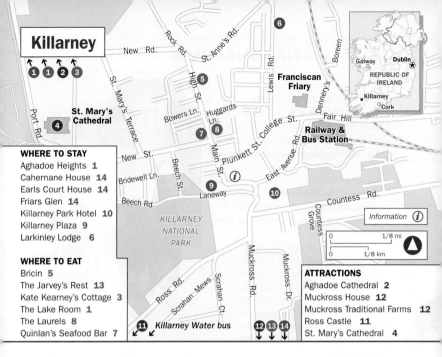

Killarney

↑ ① ↑ ① ② ↑ ③

New Rd.   Rock Rd.   St. Anne's Rd.   ⑥

St. Mary's Terrace   St. Mary's Cathedral   ④   Port Rd.

⑤   High St.   Bowers Ln.   Huggards Ln.

⑦   ⑧

Franciscan Friary   Lewis Rd.   Dennery's   Boreen

Fair Hill   Railway & Bus Station

New St.   Bridewell Ln.   Beech St.   Beech Rd.

Main St.   Plunkett St.   College St.

⑨   Laneway   ⓘ   ⑩   East Avenue Rd.   Countess Rd.

KILLARNEY NATIONAL PARK

Countess Grove

Information ⓘ

0 — 1/8 mi
0 — 1/8 km

Ross Rd.   Scrahan Mews   Scrahan Ct.   Muckross Rd.   Muckross Dr.

⑪ ← ← Killarney Water bus

⑫ ⑬ ⑭ ↓ ↓ ↓

Ireland map: Galway, Dublin ★, REPUBLIC OF IRELAND, Killarney, Cork

WHERE TO STAY
Aghadoe Heights 1
Cahernane House 14
Earls Court House 14
Friars Glen 14
Killarney Park Hotel 10
Killarney Plaza 9
Larkinley Lodge 6

WHERE TO EAT
Bricin 5
The Jarvey's Rest 13
Kate Kearney's Cottage 3
The Lake Room 1
The Laurels 8
Quinlan's Seafood Bar 7

ATTRACTIONS
Aghadoe Cathedral 2
Muckross House 12
Muckross Traditional Farms 12
Ross Castle 11
St. Mary's Cathedral 4

see it. Often the greatest pleasures can be found during a scenic drive along a side road or on a quiet byway just begging to be explored.

The small but busy town of **Killarney** is the area's main hub. It's conveniently sited on the edge of spectacular **Killarney National Park,** which includes the breathtaking **Killarney Lakes** and the scenic **Gap of Dunloe.** Most people traveling the route start and finish at Killarney, but smaller, quieter **Kenmare** makes for a good alternative base.

Killarney & Killarney National Park

Killarney's ample stock of restaurants, pubs, and hotels keeps it buzzing with visitors throughout the year. Given this, tourism is a bit more in-your-face here than anywhere else in Kerry—in the summer its narrow streets are prone to tour-bus traffic jams. That aside, Killarney has much to offer, and plenty of beauty to go with the bustle.

The main attraction is the valley in which Killarney nestles—a verdant landscape of mist-wreathed lakes and rugged hills so spectacular that author and playwright Brendan Behan once said, "Even an ad man would be ashamed to eulogize it." Escaping the crowded streets to explore the quiet rural splendor of the 65-sq.-km (25-sq.-mile) **Killarney National Park** could hardly be easier. The main visitor center is just 7km (4½ miles) south of the city, or you could merely walk to the cathedral and cross the road at the back—this is the boundary of the **Knockreer Estate ★** (see p. 291), which is itself a section of the park.

killarney **NATIONAL PARK**

A huge, rambling wilderness with breathtaking scenery, **Killarney National Park ★★★** is an essential stop along the Ring of Kerry. Within the park's limits are lakes, mountains, and two estates—**Muckross** and **Knockreer** (see p. 288 and 291). The main visitor center for the park, located in **Muckross House** (☏ 064/663-1440), is clearly signposted. Stop by here to pick up maps before you get started. The visitor center is open daily from 9am to 5:30pm; hours may vary in winter.

Cars are banned from most of the trails that traverse the park, so you'll have to explore it on foot—or else hire a **"jarvey,"** or "jaunting car," an old-fashioned horse-and-buggy. Jarveys can be booked at the National Park Visitor Centre at **Muckross House** or from **Killarney Jaunting Cars,** Muckross Close (www.killarneyjauntingcars.ie; ☏ **064/663-3358**). Drivers also often congregate in one of the small parking lots on the main N72 Ring of Kerry Road, between the edge of Killarney Town and the entrance to Muckross House.

Jaunting cars, or "jarveys," bustle around Killarney National Park.

Three lakes dot the park. The largest, the **Lower Lake,** is sometimes called Lough Leane or Lough Lein, translated as "the lake of learning." It's more

TOWN LAYOUT

Killarney may be the most important town in the region, but this is Ireland, so this "metropolis" is much smaller than you'd expect, with a full-time population of only about 14,000. Of course this number can swell considerably at the height of tourist season—and it feels like it. The town is laid out around one central thoroughfare, **Main Street,** which confusingly changes its name to **High Street** at the northern end. The principal cross streets are **New Street** and **Plunkett Street** (which becomes **College Street**). The Deenagh River edges the western side of town, and **East Avenue Road** edges the eastern side. The busiest section of town is at the southern tip of Main Street, where it curves to meet East Avenue Road, then curves again to head south to the Muckross road and the entrance to Killarney National Park.

There is limited local bus service, but the best and fastest way to get around is almost always on foot. (Those with mobility problems might find it easier to call a taxi than look for a bus—nowhere is all that far from than 6km (3¾ miles) long and holds 30 small islands that seem to rise from the mist. The most celebrated of Killarney's islands, the lovely **Innisfallen** ★★ (see p. 288), can be found on Lower Lake. Nearby are the **Middle Lake** or Muckross Lake, and the smallest of the three, the **Upper Lake.**

Here are several marked trails for exploring the beauty of Killarney Park:

Blue Pool Nature Trail: Starting behind the Muckross Park Hotel, this trail winds for a relaxing 2.3km (1.5 miles) through coniferous woodland beside a small lake. The trail is named for the lake's unusually deep blue-green color, a result of copper deposits in the soil.

Cloghereen Nature Trail: Incorporated into a small section of the Blue Pool trail (see above), this walk is fully accessible to blind visitors. A guide rope leads you along the route, lined by plants identifiable by scent and touch. An audio guide is available from the Muckross House visitor center for a small deposit.

Mossy Woods Nature Trail: One of the park's gentler trails, this route starts from Muckross Lake and runs just under 2km (1.2 miles). The moss-covered trees and rocks it passes are a major habitat for bird life. You'll also see several strawberry trees (*Arbutus*), something of a botanical mystery—they're common in these parts but found almost nowhere else in Northern Europe. The route offers incredible mountain views.

Old Boat House Nature Trail: This short lakeside walk begins at the 19th-century boathouse below Muckross Gardens and goes .8km (½ mile) around a small peninsula by Muckross Lake.

Arthur Young's Walk: Starting on the road to Dinis Island, this longer (4.8km/3 miles) hike traverses natural yew woods, then follows a 200-year-old road on the Muckross Peninsula.

Audioguides for all trails can be obtained at the Muckross House visitor center.

anywhere else in this town, so fares are low.) A signposted **Tourist Trail** visits all the highlights; it takes less than 2 hours to complete. Pick up a booklet outlining the trail's sights at the tourist office.

TOP ATTRACTIONS IN KILLARNEY & KILLARNEY NATIONAL PARK

Gap of Dunloe ★★★ VIEWS A narrow pass between the Purple Mountains and the dark, rocky hills known as MacGillycuddy's Reeks, the winding Gap of Dunloe rises through mountains and wetlands just west of Killarney National Park. The route through the gap (called Gap of Dunloe Road, naturally) passes craggy hills, meandering streams, and deep gullies, and it ends in the park at the Upper Lake. Some of the roads can be difficult around here, so many people choose to explore by bicycle (see p. 299) or by "jarvey" (see box p. 286). While cars are not strictly banned from this road (which is not technically part of Killarney National Park), it's not advisable to drive all the way through the Gap. Drive into

Biking is the best way to explore the Gap of Dunloe, just outside Killarney National Park.

the scenic countryside—perhaps as far as **Kate Kearney's Cottage** (see p. 296)—park your car, and then proceed on foot or by bike.

Signposted from N72 (Ring of Kerry Rd.), Killarney.

Innisfallen ★★ HERITAGE/NATURE SITE   Shrouded in forest, this small island appears to float peacefully on the Lower Lake in Killarney National Park. Behind the trees is what's left of a 7th-century monastery that flourished for 1,000 years. It's thought that Brian Boru, the great Irish chieftain, and St. Brendan the Navigator received their education here. From 950 to 1320, the "Annals of Innisfallen," a chronicle of early Irish history, was written at the monastery. You can reach Innisfallen by row-boat in the summer season only, available for rental at **Ross Castle ★** (p. 290).

Lower Lake, opposite Ross Castle, Ross Rd. (signposted from N71, Ring of Kerry Rd.), Killarney.

Muckross House & Gardens ★★ HISTORIC HOUSE   This elegant, neo-Gothic Victorian house at the entrance to Killarney National Park was built in 1843. Guided tours offer an enlightening glimpse at how both masters and servants of the house once lived—the grand, *Downton Abbey*–like formal dining room contrasts starkly with the Victorian kitchens and servants' quarters below stairs. The landscaped gardens are beautiful and a riot of color in high summer. The pleasant cafe, overlooking some manicured flowerbeds, is a lovely spot to linger over a cup of tea. A traditional weavers' and craft shop is also on the grounds, along with the evocative ruin of the 15th-century **Muckross Abbey,** founded about 1448 and burned by Cromwell's troops in 1652. The abbey's central feature is a vaulted cloister around a courtyard that contains a huge yew tree, thought to be as old as the abbey itself. William

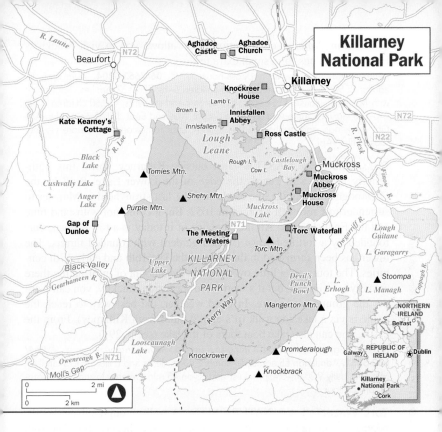

**Killarney
National Park**

Makepeace Thackeray once called it "the prettiest little bijou of a ruined abbey ever seen."

On N71 (Ring of Kerry Rd.), 6km (3¾ miles) south of Killarney. www.muckross-house.ie. ☏ **064/667-0144.** Admission €9 adults; €7.50 seniors and students; €6 children 6–18; €28–€32 families. Joint ticket with Muckross Traditional Farms: €15 adults; €13 seniors and students; €10.50 children 6–18; €40–€45 families. July–Aug daily 9am–7pm; Sept–June daily 9am–5:30pm. Last admission 1 hr. before closing.

Muckross Traditional Farms ★★ HERITAGE SITE   Not far from the Muckross House estate, these farms demonstrate traditional life as it was in previous centuries in County Kerry. It's cleverly done—the farmhouses and barns are so authentically detailed that you feel as if you've dropped in on the real deal. In a way, you have. Work really happens here: Farmhands work the fields, while the blacksmith, carpenter, and wheelwright ply their trades. Women draw water from the wells and cook meals in historically accurate kitchens. There's also a petting zoo, where kids can handle some of the animals. A coach constantly circles the grounds, ferrying those with mobility problems between different areas of the farm. *Note:* A combination ticket allows you to visit Muckross House & Gardens for a small extra fee.

Kenmare Rd. (N71). www.muckross-house.ie. ✆ **064/663-0804.** Admission €9 adults; €7.50 seniors and students; €6 children 6–18; €28–€32 families. Joint ticket with Muckross House: €15 adults; €13 seniors and students; €10.50 children 6–18; €40–€45 families. June–Aug daily 10am–6pm; May and Sept daily 1–6pm; Mar–Apr, Oct weekends, and public holidays 1–6pm. Last admission 1 hr. before closing. Closed Nov–Apr.

Ross Castle ★ CASTLE Just outside Killarney Town, this 15th-century fortress still guards the edge of the Lower Lake. Built by the O'Donoghue chieftains, the castle was the last stronghold in Munster to surrender to Cromwell's forces in 1652. But it could not withstand time and the English army: All that remains of it today is a tower house surrounded by a fortified *bawn* (walled garden) with rounded turrets. The tower has been furnished in the style of the late 16th and early 17th centuries. The tours are a little overlong for the amount of information there actually is to impart, but it's worth it to see inside. Luckily, you can wander the grounds at leisure. In good weather, the best way to reach the castle is via a lakeside walk (it's 3km/2 miles from Killarney). From the castle, you can also take boat tours of the lake (see p. 291).

Ross Rd., signposted from N71 (Ring of Kerry Rd.). www.heritageireland.ie. ✆ **064/663-5851.** Admission €5 adults; €4 seniors; €3 students and children; €13 families. Mar–Oct daily 9:30am–5:45pm. Last admission 45 min. before closing. No photography on tour.

Torc Waterfall ★★ NATURE SITE A walk through sylvan woods, populated with red deer, brings you to this popular beauty spot. The 18m (60 ft.) falls are impressive, and well worth the 5-minute walk from the dedicated parking lot on the Ring of Kerry Road. More strenuous but even more rewarding is the climb up the 100 or so steps next to the Falls, which take you up to **Friar's Glen**—so-called because it was a hideout for priests during Cromwell's invasion—with its sweeping views across the Killarney Lakes. The river that feeds the Falls rises on a mountainside a few miles away; the source is evocatively known as the Devil's Punchbowl.

Off N71, about 1.5km (¾ mile) S of Muckross House (in the direction of Kenmare), Killarney.

OTHER ATTRACTIONS IN THE KILLARNEY AREA

Aghadoe Cathedral ★ RUINS/RELIGIOUS SITE These evocative ruins look more like a crumbling parish church than a cathedral, but that's exactly what stood here until the hamlet of Aghadoe was sacked by the forces of Oliver Cromwell in 1652. Ivy grows along a roofless nave, and decaying stone walls give way to a hillside graveyard. The tiny round tower, a few yards away, is the sole remnant of a monastery dating from 1027. Adjacent to the ruins is a viewpoint with breathtaking views over the Lower Lake, 1.6km (1 mile) away. Squint and you can also see Ross Castle on the far shore. There's a small (free) parking lot next to Aghadoe

Heights Hotel (p. 292) just across the street. It's worth booking afternoon tea at the hotel—the dining room has extraordinary views of the lake. And the scones and cakes are to die for.

About 5km (3 miles) NW of Killarney off N22/L2019; Ard Na Be Rd., Aghadoe. Follow signs for Aghadoe Heights. Free admission. Daily dawn–dusk.

Killarney Water Bus ★ BOAT TOURS From the harbor at **Ross Castle** ★ (see p. 290), the **MV Pride of the Lake** takes you on an hour-long waterborne cruise. The covered boat ride is a little on the touristy side, but the views of the park from the lake are gorgeous. You can also take a tour that combines a lake cruise with a "jaunting car" ride around the park. **Tip:** You can get to the pier by Ross Castle on a free shuttle bus from Killarney town center. It leaves Scotts Street (by the junction with East Avenue Road) a quarter of an hour before each sailing. Lake cruises are strictly limited to 80 people, so you may want to book ahead at busy times—but be sure to bring a printout of the confirmation or they won't let you board.

The Pier, Ross Castle, Ross Rd., off N71 (Ring of Kerry Rd.), Killarney. www.killarney laketours.ie. ✆ **064/663 2638.** €10 adults; €5 children under 16; free for children 3 and under. Mar–Oct daily 11am, 12:30, 2:30, and 4pm. Times may change according to weather.

Knockreer Estate ★ GARDENS The grand old house that once stood here burned down in the early 20th century; what you see today is a modern building of the same name on the same site, which serves as the park's education center. Still, the estate's lovely old gardens remain, with 200-year-old trees setting off sweet wildflowers and azaleas to fragrant effect. A signposted walk takes you past beautiful views of the Lower Lake and the valley; a pathway leads down to the River Deenagh. Main access to Knockreer is through Deenagh Lodge Gate, opposite St. Mary's Cathedral in Killarney town.

Main entrance on Cathedral Place, off New St., Killarney. Free admission.

St. Mary's Cathedral ★ CATHEDRAL If you think this limestone cathedral looks more Castle Dracula than local church, it may be because New Street was once the home of Bram Stoker, who spent summers in Killarney while he was a student at Trinity College Dublin. Officially known as the Catholic Church of St. Mary of the Assumption, it's designed in the Gothic Revival style and laid out in the shape of a cross. Construction began in 1842, was interrupted by the Famine, and concluded in 1855 (although the towering spire wasn't added until 1912).

Cathedral Place, off New St. ✆ **064/663-1014.** Free admission. Daily 9am–6pm.

The Meeting of the Waters ★ NATURE SITE One of the most tranquil spots in Killarney National Park (not to be confused with the more famous place with the same name in County Wicklow—see p. 198), this is where the Upper, Middle, and Lower Lakes converge. You can hike from Muckross House (about 5km/3 miles), or park at the unmarked lot about 1.6km (1 mile) south of the Torc Waterfall (p. 290) parking area on the main Ring of Kerry Road. From here, the walk down a signposted path takes about 15 minutes, although "unofficial" side paths also lead you to the shore at different points. These can give you just as lovely views, and be free of people, but take care—the ground can be uneven. Good, sturdy walking shoes are recommended.

Off N71, about 2.4km (1½ miles) S of Muckross House, Killarney.

WHERE TO STAY IN KILLARNEY
Expensive
Aghadoe Heights ★★★ Luxurious, welcoming, and with one of the best views in Ireland, this is among the country's top spa hotels. Perched on a hill to the north of Killarney Town, this modernist building boasts floor-to-ceiling windows that take in the full, glorious panorama of Lough Lein in Killarney National Park. (In winter an atmospheric fluke can mean that you're literally above the clouds here, an effect that's nothing short of fairy-tale.) Guest rooms have all been renovated in the past couple of years—it's worth paying a little extra for a lakeview room—and suites are positively apartment-sized. The **Lake Room** (p. 296) serves French-influenced seasonal Irish cuisine with an emphasis on fresh seafood in an elegant atmosphere. Alternatively, you can graze on lighter fare in the adjacent lounge and piano bar. Service is excellent throughout, but it's in the restaurants that the staff really shines. When you're not sightseeing you can relax in the opulent **Voya** spa and thermal suite, or if that feels like work, you can even call the "bath butler" to prepare a relaxing soak in your guest room. If all this isn't enough to charm you into a state of hotel bliss, the delightful staff surely will. Take time to explore the ethereal ruins of **Aghadoe Cathedral,** directly across the road from the hotel (p. 290).

About 5km (3 miles) NW of Killarney, signposted off N22; Ard Na Be Rd., Aghadoe. www.aghadoeheights.com. ✆ **064/663-1766.** 74 units. €259–€319 double, €409–€600 suite. Free parking. Breakfast included. Spa- and dinner-bed-and-breakfast packages available. **Amenities:** 2 restaurants; bar; pool; room service; spa; tennis court; Wi-Fi (free).

Cahernane House ★★ A neo-Gothic mansion on the outskirts of Killarney National Park, Cahernane is a luxurious retreat. The decor is authentically grandiose: Public areas have the feel of a traditional

ENExJOYING spa life, IRISH STYLE

It's fair to say Ireland is blessed with more than a few top-rated spas—and some of the top spas cluster around Kenmare and Killarney. The best spas use the beautiful natural settings to spectacular effect, and borrow their treatments from the Irish countryside. Everything from Irish spring water to peat mud and local river stones are used to coax forth beauty from tired, work-dulled skin and hair. None of these spas are cheap, but they're a wonderful way to treat yourself on the road.

All guests at the **Aghadoe Heights Hotel & Spa ★★★** (see p. 292) outside Killarney are welcome to spend an hour in its exquisite thermal suite for the relatively small fee of €25. With a wide array of steam rooms, saunas, tropical showers, cooling rooms, and hot tubs, that's a luxuriant 60 minutes. Once you're fully relaxed, you might sample one of the spa's numerous massages or facials, using Aveda products. Treatments range from about €65 to €225.

The **Easanna Spa** at the **Sheen Falls Lodge,** off N71, Kenmare (www.sheen fallslodge.ie; © **064/664-1600**) features a pool shaped like a flower, each petal forming a kind of relaxation space. You can have a hot stone massage or facial and then float off in total relaxation.

Room rates here start at around €330 in high season. Treatments range from about €45 to €110.

The spa at the **Killarney Park Hotel,** off East Avenue in the center of Killarney (www.killarneyparkhotel.ie; © **064/663-5555**) is a modern, peaceful oasis, with a soothing pool and such exotic treatments as the coconut rub and milk ritual wrap, in which you are soaked in milk and wrapped in foil; or the lime and ginger salt glow, designed to revitalize tired skin. Rooms here start at around €250 (not including breakfast). Treatments range from about €65 to €125.

The **Sámas spa** in the elegant **Park Hotel Kenmare,** Shelbourne Street, Kenmare (www.parkkenmare.com; © **064/664-1200**) has won awards for its unique design. You can soak in the warm spa pool while gazing out over the mountains nearby. Spend an hour relaxing in the thermal suite (rock sauna, ice fountain, tropical mist shower), before moving on to your facial, wrap, or massage. Unlike the other spas listed, this one is strictly for guests only, although sometimes exceptions are made when it's not too busy. Rooms start at about €330; treatments range from around €140 to €245.

gentlemen's club, filled with antique furniture, stag heads on the wall, and the scent of a peat fire hanging heavy in the air. Guest rooms are more modern, though no less elegant, and some bathrooms have deep claw-foot tubs. Many of the rooms have private patios. The house has two restaurants: the excellent, formal **Herbert Room,** and the more relaxed **Cellar Bar,** where you can take lighter meals among the beautifully lit arches of an old wine cellar. Fields and farmland surround the hotel, and the misty mountains of the park linger in the distance. Check the website for special offers, including dinner-bed-and-breakfast deals.

Muckross Rd. www.cahernane.com. © **064/663-1895.** 38 units. €215–€275 double, €350–€385 suite. Free parking. Breakfast included. **Amenities:** Restaurant; bar; room service; Wi-Fi (free).

Killarney Park ★★   This popular hotel and spa won Trip Advisor's top Ireland hotel award in 2018, and it's easy to see why. Conveniently located in the center of town, the lemon-yellow, five-story building has appealing arched attic windows. Rooms are not huge, but they're comfortable and were recently redone. Premium rooms are larger and have king beds and separate seating areas. The attention to detail is what most regulars rave about—staff are friendly, service attentive and cheerful. Afternoon tea is popular with visitors and locals alike. The **Park Restaurant** offers upscale, French-influenced Irish cuisine in an elegant atmosphere. On cool nights, open fires bring warmth to the dining room. The **Elemis spa** is an oasis with an indoor pool and outdoor hot tubs overlooking the hills outside the town. Indulge in a treatment if you can.

East Ave. www.killarneyparkhotel.ie. ✆ **064/663-5555.** 67 units. €190–€215 double, €215–€290 premium. Free parking. Breakfast included. **Amenities:** Restaurant; bar; room service; Wi-Fi (free).

Moderate

Earls Court House ★★   Just outside the center of Killarney, on a quiet street with views of the mountains, Earls Court House is a pleasingly old-fashioned kind of B&B. Guest rooms are simple but elegant, featuring polished wood furniture and buttermilk-colored walls. A few have four-poster beds (at an extra cost of €20 per night). Flatscreen TVs mounted to the walls add a modern touch. You can take afternoon tea in one of the two guest lounges (included in the price of your room), and optional light suppers are served until early evening. The excellent, varied breakfasts include fresh, home-baked bread and pastries. Check the website for special seasonal offers.

Woodlawn Rd. www.killarney-earlscourt.ie. ✆ **064/663-4009.** 24 units. €140–€160 double. Free parking. Breakfast included. 2-night minimum summer weekends. **Amenities:** Library; Wi-Fi (free).

Friars Glen ★★★   Nestled in the cleft of a lush and verdant glen inside Killarney National Park, this delightful B&B could hardly be friendlier or better run. Hosts John and Mary (and their two dogs) welcome guests like old friends; they really take pride in their region, and love to help visitors plan explorations of the park and the Ring of Kerry. They will organize tours on your behalf and can even provide babysitting in the evenings with a bit of notice. The building itself looks like an old farmhouse, but is actually contemporary and very well-designed, with plenty of authentic materials and exposed stone. Guest rooms are cozy and simple, with wood furniture and decent-size bathrooms. Ask for a room with a view; the vistas across the surrounding glen are inspiring. Breakfast is served until a very civilized 10am. Dinner isn't offered, but the place is only a short drive south of Killarney. From the N71, turn east just south of the Muckross Park Hotel.

Mangerton Rd., Muckross. www.friarsglen.ie. ✆ **064/663-7500.** 10 units. From €120 double. Free parking. Breakfast included. **Amenities:** Wi-Fi (free).

Killarney Plaza ★ This large, modern hotel couldn't have a better location if you like to be in the thick of the action—it's right in the middle of Killarney town center. The accommodations are functional, contemporary, and comfortable rather than luxurious—think U.S. chain hotel and you're close enough. (Indeed, this place is big with tour groups, from the U.S. and elsewhere.) The buffet breakfast offers a vast selection, and there are two in-house restaurants—although being this centrally located in Killarney, you're hardly short of choice at your doorstep. The spa offers reasonably priced treatments (an hour-long aromatherapy massage costs €89, for example). Those arriving by car will be happy to know the hotel has its own underground lot (parking can be a nightmare in the center of town), although the spaces are so tight you may wonder if you'll ever get out again.

Town Centre, Killarney. www.killarneyplaza.com. © **064/662-1111.** 198 units. €158–€178 double. Free parking. Breakfast included. **Amenities:** 2 restaurants; 3 bars; pool; spa; Wi-Fi (free).

Inexpensive

Larkinley Lodge ★★ A great option just a few blocks from the center of Killarney, Larkinley Lodge is a stylish, modern B&B in a beautifully converted town house. Toni and Danny Sheehan are gregarious hosts, with an eye for detail. Guest rooms are small, but just the right mix of traditional and modern, with minimal clutter and muted color schemes. Triple rooms only cost a little more than doubles. Don't miss the home-baked scones at breakfast. The location is only about a 10-minute walk into central Killarney, not far from great pubs and restaurants, yet in a quiet neighborhood where you can escape the evening street noise—sometimes a problem in this lively town. *Note:* Larkinley Lodge has a 2-night minimum stay, year-round.

Lewis Rd. www.larkinley.ie. © **064/622-2447.** 6 units. €129. Minimum 2 nights. Free parking. Breakfast included. **Amenities:** Wi-Fi (free).

WHERE TO EAT IN KILLARNEY

Expensive

Bricin ★★ IRISH Located above a craft store on Killarney's main street, this is a long-standing favorite on the local dining scene. *Bricin* means "little trout" in Gaelic, and seafood is one of the strong points of the traditional Irish menu. Locally reared meat is also often on the menu, served with interesting sauces—lamb with Madeira and rosemary, say, or steak with brandy, bourbon, and pepper. It is the house specialty for which this place is renowned, however: boxty, a savory pancake stuffed with several different types of filling (see box p. 141). The dining room is an old-fashioned kind of place, complete with stained-glass windows and an open fireplace. Bricin serves a great-value early-bird menu (€22 for two courses) until 6:45pm.

26 High St. www.bricin.com. © **064/663-4902.** Fixed-price menus €23–€37. Two courses €23–€26. Tues–Sat 6–9pm. Closed early Jan–early Mar; closed Tues–Wed in winter.

The Jarvey's Rest ★ IRISH   This popular pub is not nearly as old as it tries to appear, with a roomful of exposed beams and rows of tankards on the ceiling, as if any moment now a crowd of jolly drinkers might swipe them down and roar a drunken toast. But it has charm. The menu is crowd-pleasing stuff—a good local seafood chowder, fish and chips, or a juicy burger served in a brioche bun. If it's on the menu when you're there, try the lemon meringue pie, served with fresh berries. A lively show of traditional Irish music and dancing kicks in at 8pm on Saturday nights in April and May, which expands to Tuesday, Wednesday, Thursday, and Saturday nights from June to October.

At the Muckross Park Hotel, Muckross Rd. www.jarveys.ie. ℂ **064/662-3400.** Entrees €11–€25. May Mon–Thurs 5pm–midnight, Fri–Sun noon–midnight; June–Oct daily noon–midnight (food served until 9:30pm). Also open St. Patrick's Day weekend and on school holiday weeks in late Feb and Easter. Closed rest of year.

Kate Kearney's Cottage ★ INTERNATIONAL   Unofficially considered the gateway to the Gap of Dunloe, this cheerful pub is hugely popular. It's a little touristy (a dead giveaway is the in-house souvenir shop), but the atmosphere is upbeat and traditional, and the stick-to-your-ribs pub food is pretty tasty. The menu offers steaks, burgers, and bistro-style classics, best washed down with a restorative pint. Semi-regular "Irish Nights" offer a package of dinner and a show of traditional music; call or check the website for upcoming dates. The pub is named after a feisty local woman who carved out a reputation as a maker of illegal *potcheen* (moonshine) that she called Mountain Dew.

Gap of Dunloe, Beaufort, signposted from N72 (Ring of Kerry Rd.). www.katekearneyscottage.com. ℂ **064/664-4146.** Entrees €14–€20. Daily noon–11pm (food 6:30–9:30pm).

The Lake Room ★★★ MODERN IRISH   The main restaurant at the **Aghadoe Heights** hotel (p. 292) overlooks the Lower Lake, a special-occasion view if ever there was one—with sumptuous cooking to match. Local seafood is, of course, a specialty, with a constantly changing menu that might include Atlantic cod with orange poached chicory, or halibut in a delightfully sweet vanilla butter. Meatier choices include Kerry beef, cooked to perfection, perhaps finished with black currant jus. The wine list is excellent—if you're

At the aptly named Lake Room, gourmet dining comes with a side of Killarney lake views.

having fish, try a glass of the fragrant Picpoul, a steal at €8. While this undoubtedly qualifies as fine dining, the staff cultivates a relaxed air. On our last visit, the waiter even ended the meal by showing us photos of his new puppy—it's that kind of place.

At Aghadoe Heights Hotel, about 5km (3 miles) NW of Killarney, signposted off N22. www.aghadoeheights.com/dining/the-lake-room. © **064/663-1766.** Fixed-price four-course menu €55. Entrees €25–€36. Daily 6:30–9:30pm.

The Laurels ★ INTERNATIONAL   The menu at this busy pub in the center of Killarney is populist fare. Starters include deep-fried brie with red currant sauce and chicken wings, while entrees range from a generous steak served with peppercorn sauce and French fries to traditional Irish dishes such as Irish stew or potato cakes with gravy. It also serves a massive seafood platter that must be seen to be believed. The lunch menu is much simpler, offering "doorstep" (very thick cut) sandwiches, burgers, salads, and the like. In summer, the pub features lively music sessions several times a week.

Main St. www.thelaurelspub.com. © **064/663-1149.** Entrees €17–€29. Mon–Thurs 10:30am–11:30pm, Fri–Sat 10:30am–12:30am, Sun 12:30–11pm. (Food served until about 9:30pm.)

Quinlan's Seafood Bar ★ SEAFOOD   This casual eatery is where the locals go when they're craving fish. With a seafood counter up front, selling straight from the boat, the fare here is simple and straightforward—fish and chips, with a light batter and a giant portion of chunky fries, come hot from the fryer. Have it with mushy peas, and you're deep into a true Irish dinner. If you fancy more sophisticated dishes, the menu obliges, with scallops in butter, boiled Irish lobster, lemon sole in a buttery sauce, or prawns so fresh they all but swim off the plate. The white, clean dining room is nothing fancy, but it does the job.

77 High St. www.kerryfish.com/seafoodbar-killarney. © **064/662-0666.** Entrees €7–€14. Daily noon–9pm.

KILLARNEY SHOPPING

Shopping hours in Killarney are usually Monday to Saturday 9am to 6pm, but from May through September many stores are open every day until 9 or 10pm. Although Killarney has more souvenir and craft shops than you can shake a shillelagh at, here are a few of the best.

Aran Sweater Market ★   Rows of soft wool sweaters, skirts, hats, and scarves in colors ranging from traditional cream to bright blues, reds, and ochre await in this town center store. All are Irish made, most from pure wool. College Square. www.aransweatermarket.com. © **064/662-3102.**

Bricin ★   This little craft store sells traditional ceramics, jewelry, and clothes. Many of the wares on sale here were made locally. Upstairs is one of the town's best restaurants (p. 295). 26 High St. © **064/663-4902.**

The Dungeon Bookshop ★   One of Killarney's most popular independent bookstores, the Dungeon stocks a good range of secondhand books. 99 College St. www.dungeonbookshop.goldenpages.ie. ℭ **064/663-6536.**

Killarney Art Gallery ★★   This gallery showcases work from respected Irish artists as well as new and local talent. A second branch is in Aghadoe, just northwest of central Killarney. 32 Main St. www.killarney artgallery.com. ℭ **087/276-7999.**

Mr. McGuire's Olde Sweet Shop ★★   This charming traditional candy store is a delight for kids of all ages. Candy is measured out from tall jars into little bags, or you can pick out some very giftable packages straight from the shelf. Closed weekdays in winter. College Square. ℭ **064/667-1764.**

Mucros Craft Centre ★★   Part of the Walled Garden, a small shopping complex on the grounds of **Muckross House** ★★ (see p. 288), this place has a good stock of Irish crafts, pottery, clothing, cards, and quality gifts—and many items are made locally. Muckross House, Muckross Rd. www. muckross-house.ie. ℭ **064/667-0147.**

KILLARNEY AFTER DARK

The mainstay of nightlife in Killarney is the lively pub scene. The town has more than its fair share of good places to enjoy a pint and some live traditional music. All of these places can get pretty packed on a busy summer's night—so come early to stand a chance of getting a seat.

Killarney Grand ★★   This hugely popular pub is one of the best places in the region to hear traditional Irish music—and for free. Nightly live sessions start at 9pm; after 11pm it turns into a nightclub. The atmosphere gets pretty raucous, and the crowds can really pack in here (definitely standing-room-only), but the music is always good. Some of the biggest names in Irish music have played here over the years; you never know when you might catch the next big thing. A "neat" dress code is enforced at the door—you don't have to wear your best duds, but don't be too scruffy, either. Main St. www.killarneygrand.com. ℭ **064/663-1159.**

The Laurels ★   Another very popular pub for live music, here the traditional music sessions take place several times a week, usually starting at around 9pm. The pub also serves good food, including stone-baked pizzas (see p. 297). Main St. www.thelaurelspub.com. ℭ **064/663-1149.**

O'Connors ★★   At this traditional-feeling pub, the program of live music is extensive, with bands playing every night—scheduled and, occasionally, spontaneous. It doesn't stop there, either; you might catch a play, some standup comedy, or even a spoken-word event. Check the website for what's coming up. 7 High St. www.oconnorstraditionalpub.com. ℭ **064/663-9424.**

Tatler Jack ★ For Gaelic sports fans, this is the place to go. Football and hurling matches are shown on big-screen TVs, and traditional music is played on many nights in summer. Expect to find a raucous atmosphere. Plunkett St. © **064/663-2361.**

SPECTATOR SPORTS IN KILLARNEY

GAELIC GAMES The people of Killarney are passionately devoted to the national sports of hurling and Gaelic football, and games are played almost every Sunday afternoon in summer at **Fitzgerald Stadium,** Lewis Road (www.gaa.ie; © **064/836-3222**). For complete details, consult the local *Kerryman* newspaper or the Killarney Tourist Office.

HORSE RACING Killarney has two annual horse-racing meets, in early May and mid-July. Each event lasts for 3 or 4 days and draws large crowds. For more information, contact the **Killarney Racecourse,** Fossa (www.killarneyraces.ie; © **064/663-1125**), or the tourist office.

OUTDOOR PURSUITS IN THE RING OF KERRY

CYCLING **Killarney National Park,** with its lakeside and forest path-ways, trails, and roads, is a paradise for bikers. Bike rental charges aver-age around €20 to €25 per day, €80 to €90 per week. Bicycles can be rented from **Killarney Rent-a-Bike,** Lower New Street or 49 High St. (www.killarneyrentabike.com; © **064/663-1282**).

FISHING Fishing for salmon and brown trout in Killarney's unpolluted lakes and rivers is a popular pastime. Brown trout fishing is free on the lakes, but a permit is necessary for the rivers Flesk and Laune. Salmon fishing anywhere requires a permit. Permits, tackle, bait, rod rental, and other fishing gear can be obtained from **O'Neill's,** 6 Plunkett St. (© **064/663-1970**). The shop also arranges boat rentals and *ghillies* (fishing guides) for around €50 to €100 per day on the Killarney Lakes, leaving from Ross Castle.

GOLF Overlooking the Atlantic Ocean, on the southwestern part of the Ring of Kerry, the par-72 **Waterville Golf Links,** Waterville (www.watervillegolflinks.ie; © **066/9476-4102**), is considered one of the best courses in Ireland. The 6,200-yard course also has the distinction of con-taining a "Mass Hole," a relic of the days when Catholic Mass had to be celebrated in secrecy. Greens fees are €210 weekdays, €230 weekends. Daily second rounds are €100 to €110; early or late €150 and November to March €75. Visitors are always welcome at the twin 18-hole champion-ship courses of the **Killarney Golf & Fishing Club,** Killorglin Road (N72), Fossa (www.killarney-golf.com; © **064/663-1034**), 5km (3 miles) west of the town center. Widely praised as one of the most scenic golf set-tings in the world, it has two 18-hole courses—Killeen and Mahony's Point—with gorgeous lake and mountain layouts. (A third course,

At Kenmare's annual Fair Day, every August 15, local livestock, horses, and sheepdogs for sale throng the town streets.

Lackabane, is currently being redeveloped.) Greens fees are €45 to €110, depending on the course and the time of day.

HORSEBACK RIDING   Many trails in the Killarney area are suitable for horseback riding. Hiring a horse costs from €40 per hour at **Killarney Riding Stables,** N72, Ballydowney (www.killarneyridingstables.com; ℂ **064/663-1686**). Lessons and weeklong trail rides can also be arranged.

Kenmare

Kenmare is a sweet little town with flower boxes at every window, lots of restaurants, and plenty of places to stay. Originally called Neidin (pronounced Nay-*deen,* meaning "little nest" in Irish), Kenmare is indeed a little nest of verdant foliage and colorful buildings nestled between the River Roughty and Kenmare Bay. And while it certainly gets more than its fair share of visitors in the summer, Kenmare isn't as frenetic as Killarney. If you crave a quieter life, this can make it a more pleasant place to stay—especially if you have the freedom of a car.

EXPLORING KENMARE

Kenmare Druid Circle ★ PREHISTORIC SITE   On a small hill near the market square (see p. 301), this large Bronze Age druid stone circle is magnificently intact, featuring 15 standing stones arranged around a central boulder that still bears signs (circular holes, a shallow dent at the center) of having been used in ceremonies. To find it, walk down to the market square and follow signs on the left side of the road. There's no visitor center and no admission fee; it's just sitting in a small paddock, passed by the traffic of everyday life.

Off the Square, Kenmare.

Kenmare Farmer's Market ★ MARKET If you're visiting midweek, be sure to check out this small but lively open-air market held every Wednesday in Kenmare's main square. The emphasis is on food produce from small, artisan producers from across the region and beyond. You'll also find rustic crafts. Traders may come here from quite far afield to sell their wares, although the bulk of what's for sale is locally sourced. It's a fun market to browse your way through.

The Square. Kenmare. Wed 10am–4pm. Some stalls may close in bad weather.

Seafari ★★ BOAT TOUR A good option for families, this 2-hour cruise aboard a 15m (49-ft.) covered boat makes for an engaging introduction to Kenmare Bay and its wildlife—specifically the dolphins, sea otters, and gray seals you'll most likely see frolicking nearby. Boats depart from the pier next to the Kenmare suspension bridge. The family ticket includes coffee, tea, cookies, a lollipop for kids, and a drink of rum for the grownups. They'll also lend you a pair of binoculars if you need one. Live entertainment sometimes follows you on board, from kid-friendly puppet shows to traditional Irish music. Reservations are recommended.

3 The Pier, Kenmare. www.seafariireland.com. ℰ **064/664-2059.** €25 adults; €20 students; €15 teenagers; €12.50 children 11 and under then €7.50 per extra child; €60 families. Apr–Oct, two sailings daily; call or check website for departure times.

WHERE TO STAY IN KENMARE

Expensive
Park Hotel Kenmare ★★★

The noble graystone house holding the elegant Park Hotel was described by the Irish *Independent* newspaper as "as close as you'll get to Downton Abbey without going on set." And that's about right. The circa-1897 building rambles through large, perfectly decorated rooms, each more glorious than the last, with open fireplaces, grand oil paintings, and imposing staircases galore. All around are spectacular

Captain Raymond welcomes passengers on the 2-hour Seafari cruise of Kenmare Bay.

301

The Best Drive in Ireland?

It takes about 45 minutes to drive between Killarney and Kenmare, but it's one of the most picturesque routes in the country. It's easy enough to find—just follow signs for N71 through Killarney National Park, taking care not to get onto the quicker but infinitely less romantic back roads instead (your GPS may try and take you this way by default). If you're setting out from Kenmare, the drive begins along gentle foothills; from Killarney, it's sun-dappled, sylvan woods. Either way, before long you hit wide, sweeping vistas of lakes and mountains, guaranteed to catch your breath and steal your heart. Fortunately there are plenty of places to pull over and gawp at the scenery, including **Ladies' View**—so-called because it was, apparently, a favorite of the ladies-in-waiting to Queen Victoria. The viewpoint has a handy cafe (closed at press time but scheduled to reopen by summer 2018). All of the best viewpoints have small, free parking areas, so don't be tempted to pull over illegally on the narrow road. Just make sure you've got enough space in your camera for all those dreamy pictures.

views of mirrorlike lake and green, rolling hills. This is a formal place—staff are polite but not snobbish and will help arrange anything you need, including sightseeing excursions and horse-riding expeditions. But the extraordinary **Sámas spa** (see p. 293) might prove so distracting that you forget to go sightseeing at all. Bedrooms are quiet and unusually spacious for Ireland; all are impeccably decorated, some with four-poster beds. The in-house restaurant is known for its Irish-European cuisine and formal atmosphere; four-course set menus cost around €70.

Kenmare High St., Kenmare. www.parkkenmare.com. ✆ **064/664-1200.** 46 units. €190–€225 double. €320–€390 suite. Free parking. Breakfast included. **Amenities:** Restaurant; bar; room service; spa; Wi-Fi (free).

Moderate

Sallyport House ★★   An extremely good value for the money, this peaceful 1930s mansion-turned-B&B in Kenmare is filled with interesting antiques, lending a touch of old-school luxury to its already traditional charms. (Thanks to a wealthy industrialist ancestor, there's a story behind most of them.) Guest rooms are comfortable and spacious. A few rooms have intricately carved antique four-poster beds. The house is surrounded by beautiful countryside, and some rooms look out over an idyllic lake. Breakfasts are delicious, and the service is warm and accommodating without ever being intrusive.

Shelbourne St., Kenmare (just S of junction with Pier Rd.). www.sallyporthouse.com. ✆ **064/664-2066.** 5 units. From €135 double. Free parking. Breakfast included. **Amenities:** Wi-Fi (free).

Shelburne Lodge ★★   This cozy 18th-century house was originally the country home of William Petty, the Lord Shelburne (1737–1805), a Dublin-born landowner who was responsible for building much of the modern town of Kenmare. He later became Prime Minister of Great Britain and Ireland, and in 1783 he signed the Treaty of Paris, which formally ended the

American War of Independence, bringing peace between Britain and the U.S. His home is in good hands nowadays, thanks to wonderful hosts Tom and Maura Foley. Rooms have an old-fashioned air with antique furniture, huge beds, and color schemes of yellow and peach. Public areas have a similar feel—the guest sitting room is so packed with handsome furniture that it's like walking through an antique shop. A lovely, manicured lawn is out back, and the center of Kenmare is only a short walk away.

Cork Rd., Kenmare. www.shelburnelodge.com. ⓒ **064/664-1013.** 9 units. €100–€160 double. Free parking. Breakfast included. **Amenities:** Wi-Fi (free). Closed Dec–Feb.

Inexpensive

Sea Shore Farm ★★ A modern house overlooking Kenmare Bay and the mountains beyond, this is a special place to stay. Floor-to-ceiling windows take full advantage of the magnificent surroundings. The guest rooms are large (very large in some cases) and tastefully furnished. The guest lounge has a library of travel books, though you may find yourself too distracted by the views to concentrate. Kenmare is a short drive away or a captivating 15-minute walk through the countryside—the better to work off those indulgent breakfasts. Hosts Mary and Owen make everything run smoothly and are always full of helpful suggestions for things to do. They have an encyclopedic knowledge of the local area.

Sea Shore, Tubrid. www.seashorekenmare.com. ⓒ **064/664-1270.** 5 units. €90–€110 double. Free parking. Breakfast included. **Amenities:** Wi-Fi (free).

WHERE TO EAT IN KENMARE

Expensive

The Lime Tree ★★ MODERN IRISH This internationally praised restaurant in a charming historic building offers an elegant twist on Irish comfort food. The menu is smart and varied without being overly complicated, with plenty of locally sourced ingredients—black pudding from Sneem, salmon from Kenmare, County Kerry lamb. You might start with a "deconstructed prawn cocktail" with cognac-infused sauce, then go on to a baked filet of salmon with lemon crumb crust, or breast of free-range duck with a spicy ginger and rhubarb chutney. Try the crepes for dessert, served with pralines and a deliciously rich butterscotch sauce. The wine list is excellent, with lots of choices by the glass as well as the bottle.

Shelbourne St., Kenmare. www.limetreerestaurant.com. ⓒ **064/664-1225.** Entrees €18–€29. Apr–Oct daily 6:30–9:30pm.

The Mews ★★ MODERN IRISH/INTERNATIONAL A relative newcomer to Kenmare, the Mews has fast become one of the town's destination restaurants. Local seafood and meats are specialties, presented in a subtly modern style—never overly fussy, but with welcome touches of invention. A bowl of traditional chowder is prepared with vermouth; a simple salmon filet is accompanied by curried pomegranate. Vegetarians are catered to with more than just a token option—if it's on the menu, try the delicious Indian dahl turnover, served with a flavorful garlic raita. A dessert of chocolate terrine with blueberry ice cream is enough to send chocoholics back to their hotel with a smile that will last until morning. Children are only allowed at the early dinner seating.

Henry Court, off Henry St., Kenmare. www.themewskenmare.com. ⓒ **064/664-2829.** Entrees €18–€30. Wed–Thurs 6–9pm; Fri–Sun 5:30–9pm. Closed in winter. No children after 7pm.

Packie's ★★ IRISH   Packie's has been a local favorite in Kenmare for years. The candlelit dining room is atmospheric, and the crowd is as much residents as visitors. And it's easy to understand why—the food is unpretentious but delicious, using a bounty of local ingredients. Choose from steak, lamb, or perhaps super-fresh seafood, all simply prepared but melt-in-your-mouth tasty. Desserts are worth leaving room for. The reasonably priced wine list offers plenty of choices available by the glass.

Henry St., Kenmare. www.kenmare.com/packies. ⓒ **064/664-1508.** Entrees €17–€34. Mon–Sat 5:30–10pm. Closed Sun. Closed Feb.

Moderate

The Boathouse Bistro ★ BISTRO/SEAFOOD   This casual seafood bistro at Dromquinna Manor has an outside seating area overlooking Kenmare Bay, making it perfect for a warm summer night. The menu serves dishes like pan-seared salmon or the house-special fishcakes with mango salsa. Or you could just have a burger and sea-salted French fries while you take in the wonderful view. This is a good stop for lunch on a sunny day, especially when the weather's fine and you can sit outside. It closes for much of the off-season.

On N70, 5km (3 miles) W of Kenmare. www.dromquinnamanor.com. ⓒ **064/664-2889.** Entrees €15–€32. July–Aug daily 12:30–9pm; May–June and Sept Tues–Sun 12:30–9pm; Oct Thurs–Sun 12:30–9pm; Mar–Apr weekends 12:30–9pm. Closed Nov–Feb.

Number 35 ★★ IRISH/INTERNATIONAL   "Local produce" is a term that you'll see a lot in the best restaurants, but this place really takes it a step further—all the meat it serves was reared on its own farm. The menu is short and simple; you might start with some pork sausages (free-range, though you knew that anyway), followed by a Moroccan lamb tagine, or roast chicken served with butternut squash. There's a good wine list, and an equally good selection of Irish craft beers—perfect to wash down a hearty plate of comfort food. The dining room is small and this place can get packed, so make reservations.

35 Main St., Kenmare. www.no35kenmare.com. ⓒ **064/664-1559.** Entrees €18–€27; three-course fixed-price menu €30. Sun–Tues and Thurs 12:30–4pm, 5:30–9:30pm; Fri–Sat 12:30–4pm, 5:30–10pm. Closed Wed.

Inexpensive

Maison Gourmet ★ BAKERY   A little touch of *La Vie parisienne* on the very un-French streets of Kenmare, this artisan bakery serves freshly made sandwiches, salads, soups—and excellent coffee. The patisserie is so tempting it's hard even to walk past this place without dreaming of a delicious slice of cake or tart. Eat in or take out.

26 Henry St., Kenmare. ☎ **064/664-1857.** All items €4–€10. Daily 8am–6pm. Closed Mon. Opening times may vary in winter.

Pyro ★ PIZZA   Run by the unusual team of an artist and an Olympic skier, this funky little pizza place is tucked away down a small alleyway, right next door to the Mews (p. 303). And we do mean little—it has just a handful of tables, so this might be a better takeout option. The pizzas have quirky names like the "Pizza of Knowledge" (salmon, zucchini, and cream sauce—the name is an obscure pun on ancient Celtic folklore) or the "We Will Flog It" (smoked chicken, spinach, and barbecue sauce). Expect loads of veggie options, too. Diners with smaller appetites can order a mini-version of any pizza for half-price. *Note:* Pyro appears to be closed in winter; call beforehand to check.

Henry Court, off Henry St., Kenmare. http://pyro.ie. ☎ **064/664-8441.** Entrees €8–€14. Daily 4–10pm.

Wharton's Traditional Fish & Chips ★★ FISH & CHIPS   Not actually a restaurant at all, but a food truck that you'll usually find parked in the main square, Wharton's is proof that not all the best dining experiences come with a hefty price tag, This is an outstanding "chipper," with a traditional menu—who would have it any other way with fish and chips?—although asking if you'd prefer your fish battered or fried in breadcrumbs is a nice twist. It's nothing fancy, but that's half the point—this is real Irish fast food.

The Square, Kenmare. ☎ **083/348-7505.** Entrees €6–€10. Daily around noon–10pm; hours vary in winter.

KENMARE SHOPPING

The Ring of Kerry has many good craft and souvenir shops, but those in and around Kenmare offer some of the best choices in terms of quality. Kenmare shops are open year-round, usually Monday to Saturday 9am to 6pm. From May to September, many shops remain open until 9 or 10pm, and some open on Sunday from noon to 5 or 6pm.

Avoca at Moll's Gap ★★   Creative, colorful, and with what must be one of the world's best appointed parking lots, this branch of Avoca is on a mountain pass just off the main Ring of Kerry Road, north of Kenmare. Though quite small, it sells a good selection of the crafts, knitwear, and upscale knick-knacks for which the Wicklow-based company is famous. The cafe upstairs is also a great pit stop for a light lunch or cup of tea.

Moll's Gap (on R568, signposted from main N71 Ring of Kerry Rd.). www.avoca.ie. ☎ **064/663-4720.** Mon–Fri 10am–5pm; Sat–Sun 10am–5:30pm. Closed Jan to mid-Mar.

Lorge Chocolatier ★★   Benoit Lorge makes his exquisite artisanal chocolates at this workshop, 10km (6 miles) south of Kenmare on the N71 road. They're wonderful creations, elegantly presented—the gift boxes are little works of art in themselves. Too bad their precious, tasty cargo must be eaten. All of it. Right now. N71, Bonane, near Kenmare. www.lorge.ie. ℂ **064/667-9994.**

Quills Woollen Market ★   Housed in a delightfully multicolored row of shops in the center of Kenmare, this long-standing business specializes in traditional Irish knitwear—particularly heavy-knit Aran sweaters, coats, and cardigans. It also sells Irish tweeds, shawls, linens, and various home-decor pieces like plush sheepskin rugs. It's a great place to stock up on authentic souvenirs. Other branches of Quills are in Killarney, Glengarriff, Ballingeary, and Sneem. Main St. www.irishgiftsandsweaters. com. ℂ **064/663-2277.**

SPORTS & OUTDOOR PURSUITS IN KENMARE

ADVENTURE SPORTS   **Eclipse Ireland,** Blackwater Bridge, Kenmare (www.eclipseireland.com; ℂ **064/668-2965**), offers a host of high-thrills activities and outdoor fun, including kayaking, archery, raft building, mud surfing, and trekking. It's not just high-energy activities, either—you can even opt for a session of laughter yoga. See the website for the full list.

CYCLING   You could conceivably cycle directly from Kenmare to Killarney National Park (about 13.2km/8½ miles), although the main Ring of Kerry Road is narrow, with sharp bends, and can get clogged with tour-bus traffic in summer. Ask for alternative cycling routes when you rent bikes, either from **Finnegan's Corner** at 37 Henry St., Kenmare (ℂ **064/664-1083**), or **Eclipse Ireland,** Blackwater Bridge, Kenmare (www.eclipseireland.com; ℂ **064/668-2965**). Rates are around €20 per day.

Driving the Ring of Kerry Road

Whether you're setting out from Kenmare or Killarney, it's best to follow the Ring of Kerry tourist route in a counterclockwise direction. This means that you'll begin by heading west out of Killarney on the N72 road. (The road number will change to N70 for most of the loop as it circumnavigates the Iveragh Peninsula; it becomes N71 when you swing back through Kenmare.) About 22km (16½ miles) northwest from Killarney is

---

SOS: GPS

You can drive either way along the Ring of Kerry, but we recommend a **counterclockwise** route for the most spectacular views. Drivers of very large vehicles also stick to this direction in order to avoid bottlenecks on the perilously narrow bends. This all worked fine for years—until modern technology intervened with the spread of GPS technology. Now some drivers unfamiliar with the route are being sent by their devices in a clockwise direction, thus causing all sorts of chaos, including some of the worst traffic jams ever seen on the Ring. These problems are rare, but expect high traffic in the summer.

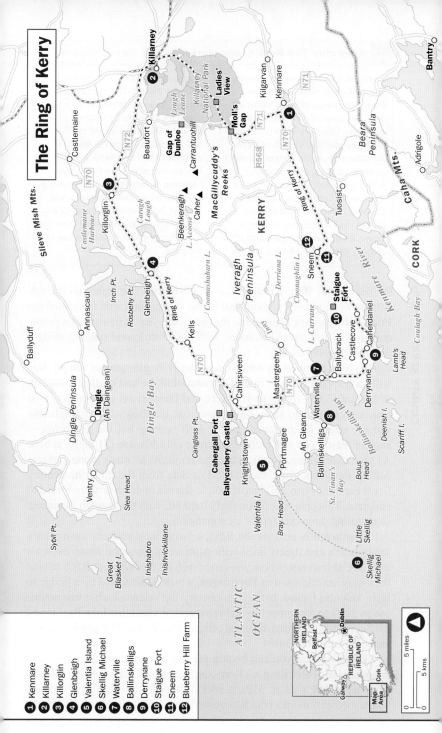

The Ring of Kerry

slieve Mish Mts.

Dingle Peninsula

Dingle (An Daingean)

Killarney

Ladies' View

Moll's Gap

Kilgarvan

Kenmare

Bantry

Beara Peninsula

Adrigole

Caha Mts.

CORK

KERRY

Iveragh Peninsula

Beaufort

Gap of Dunloe

Carrantuohill

MacGillycuddy's Reeks

Beenkeragh

Caher

L. Acoose

Killarney National Park

Lough Leane

Killorglin

Castlemaine

Castlemaine Harbour

Rosbehy Pt.

Inch Pt.

Annascaul

Ballyduff

Ventry

Sybil Pt.

Sea Head

Great Blasket I.

Inishabro

Inishvickillane

Dingle Bay

Glenbeigh

Kells

Cahirsiveen

Mastergeehy

Waterville

Canglass Pt.

Cahergall Fort

Ballycarbery Castle

Knightstown

Valentia I.

Bray Head

Portmagee

An Gleann

Ballinskelligs

St. Finan's Bay

Bolus Head

Little Skellig

Skellig Michael

ATLANTIC OCEAN

Ballinskelligs Bay

Deenish I.

Scariff I.

Lamb's Head

Derrynane

Caherdaniel

Castlecove

Ballybrack

Staigue Fort

Sneem

Kenmare River

Tuosist

Coulagh Bay

Carragh L.

Caragh Lough

Commashaharn L.

Inny

L. Currane

Derriana L.

Cloonaghlin L.

Moll's Gap

N71

N72

N70

R568

Ring of Kerry

Locations

1. Kenmare
2. Killarney
3. Killorglin
4. Glenbeigh
5. Valentia Island
6. Skellig Michael
7. Waterville
8. Ballinskelligs
9. Derrynane
10. Staigue Fort
11. Sneem
12. Blueberry Hill Farm

NORTHERN IRELAND

Belfast

REPUBLIC OF IRELAND

Galway

Dublin

Map Area

Cork

5 miles

5 kms

307

Killorglin: The Puck Stops Here

Sleepy little **Killorglin** wakes up every year on August 10, when the annual **Puck Fair** (www.puckfair.ie) incites a 3-day explosion of merrymaking and pageantry. One of Ireland's last remaining traditional fairs, it's technically an agricultural show; the apex of the event involves capturing a mountain goat (which symbolizes the *puka* or *puki*, a mischievous Celtic sprite), which is then declared "King Puck" and paraded around town on a throne, wearing a crown. It's bonkers, but quite a lot of fun. Nobody knows how it began, but one story dates to Cromwell's invasion of Ireland in the mid–17th century. English soldiers, foraging for food in the hills above the town, tried to capture a herd of goats. One goat escaped to Killorglin and alerted the villagers to mount a defence. Others say the fair is pre-Christian, connected with the Pagan feast of Lughnasa on August 1. As you cross the old stone bridge over the River Laune, look out for the whimsical statue of the goat on the eastern side—and know that it stands in honor of this town's love for the *puka*.

the next major stop: **Killorglin,** a smallish town that lights up in mid-August when it hosts a traditional horse, sheep, and cattle fair called the **Puck Fair** (see box above). For the rest of the year, Killorglin is a pretty, quiet town, well worth a wander, with the River Laune running straight through the town center.

As you continue on what is now the N70, glimpses of Dingle Bay will soon appear on your right. **Carrantuohill,** Ireland's tallest mountain at 1,041m (3,414 ft.), is to your left, and bleak vistas of open bog land constantly come into view. Along this coast, the Ring winds around cliffs and the edges of mountains, often with nothing but the sea below—another reason you will probably average only 50kmph (31 mph), at best. As you travel along, you'll notice the remnants of many stone cottages dotting the fields along the way. Most date from the mid-19th-century Great Famine, when millions of people starved to death or were forced to emigrate. This area was particularly hard hit, with the Iveragh Peninsula alone losing three-quarters of its population.

Glenbeigh is next on the Ring, a sweet little seafront town with a sandy beach and streets lined with palm trees. Continue along the sea's edge to **Cahirsiveen,** where you can branch off the N70 onto R565 to visit the lovely seaside town of **Portmagee,** which is connected by a bridge to leafy **Valentia Island.** In the 18th century, the Valentia harbor was notorious as a refuge for smugglers and privateers; it's said that John Paul Jones, the Scottish-born American naval officer in the War of Independence, also anchored here quite often.

From Valentia you can book a seat on a ferry to arguably the most magical site of the Ring of Kerry, an island just off its shore: **Skellig Michael ★★★** (see p. 310), a rocky pinnacle towering over the sea, where medieval monks built a monastery in exquisite isolation. Today, the ruins of their church, reached by way of rambling stone staircases up the sides of cliffs at the edge of the cobalt sea, still convey a sense of deep spirituality. Seabirds nest here in abundance, and more than 20,000 pairs of gannets inhabit neighboring **Little Skellig** during the summer nesting season. The crossing to the island can be rough and will even be canceled in stormy weather, so you'll want to visit on as clear and calm a day as possible. The Skelligs have become more famous recently—key parts of *Star Wars* were filmed here (it's the spectacularly rugged island where Luke Skywalker exiles himself in *The Force Awakens* and *The Last Jedi*— and where Rey finds him), so ferry seats must be booked well in advance.

Head next for **Waterville,** an idyllic beach resort located between Lough Currane and Ballinskelligs Bay. For years it was a favorite retreat of Charlie Chaplin; there's even a statue of him near the beach. Here's another rewarding detour: Follow the sea road north of Waterville (R567) to the Irish-speaking village of **Ballinskelligs ★★** (see p. 311), with its medieval monastery slowly rotting away. The scenic **Skellig Ring** coastal drive leads from here; a sandy Blue Flag beach is just past the post office by Ballinskelligs Bay, and at the end of the beach are the remnants of a 16th-century castle.

Continuing on the N70, the next point of interest is **Derrynane ★★** (see p. 312), at **Caherdaniel.** Derrynane is the former seat of the O'Connell clan and erstwhile home to Daniel O'Connell, "the Liberator"

Monks once lived in these stone beehive huts atop Skellig Michael.

a great, mysterious wonder:
A TRIP TO THE SKELLIG ISLANDS

"Whoever has not stood in the graveyard on the summit of that cliff, among the beehive dwellings and beehive oratory, does not know Ireland through and through…

—George Bernard Shaw

The craggy, inhospitable Skellig Islands rise precipitously from the sea. Here gray skies meet stormy horizons about 14km (8 miles) off the coast of the Iveragh Peninsula. From the mainland, Skellig Michael and Little Skellig appear impossibly sharp-angled and daunting even today—just imagine how perilous the mere act of getting there would have been in the 6th and 7th centuries. Back then, a group of monks built a community on the steepest, most wind-battered peaks. Over time, they carved 600 steps into the cliffs and built monastic buildings hundreds of feet above the ocean. The complex is now a UNESCO World Heritage Site.

There is something tragic and beautiful about the remains of the ancient oratories and beehive cells there. Historians know very little about these monks and how they lived, although they obviously sought intense isolation. Records relating to the Skelligs indicate that even here, all but completely hidden, the monastery was discovered by Vikings, who attacked it as they did all the Irish monastic settlements. Monks were kidnapped and killed in attacks in the 8th century, but the settlement always recovered. To this day, nobody knows why the monks finally abandoned the rock in the 12th century.

Landing is only possible on **Skellig Michael ★★★,** the largest of the islands on clear, sunny days. Due to its protected status, there's an annual quota for the number of visitors allowed. Although the island has always been a popular attraction, this was rarely a problem in the past—until *Star Wars* came along. Filming *The Force Awakens* and *The Last Jedi* in 2014 and 2016 changed everything. Demand to visit Skellig Michael skyrocketed. What was once a small, rural sight is now massive business…but one that's still run like a small, rural sight. So, if you want to have the unique experience of making

who freed Irish Catholics from the last of the English Penal Laws in the 19th century. From there, watch for signs to the prehistoric ruins of **Staigue Fort ★★** (see p. 312), about 3km (2 miles) off the main road in a farmer's field.

Sneem, the next village on the circuit (see **Blueberry Hill Farm ★★,** p. 312), is a colorful little hamlet where houses are painted in vibrant shades, creating a beautiful tableau. The colorss—blue, pink, yellow, and orange—burst out on a rainy day, like a little touch of the Mediterranean. There's not much to do in Sneem, but it's worth a stop just to see it. From here, you're no distance at all from Kenmare, and you've made your way around the Ring.

landfall on Skellig Michael in the summer, it's a bit tricky. Boat tours to the island are run by individual locals rather than a central ferry company. About a dozen companies offer this service, most contactable only via their cellphones or at their stalls on the beach near Portmagee. Bookings need to be made early these days—especially if you're travelling in the summer. **The Skellig Michael Cruises Company** is one of a few boat services currently offering online booking, and it has a good word-of-mouth reputation (www.skelligmichaelcruises.com; ✆ **087/6178114**). Another recommended option with online booking is **Casey's Skellig Island Tours,** which also offers an eco-tour of the puffins and other rare birds that inhabit the islands (http://skelligislands.com; ✆ **66/9472437**). You'll find a list of other boat operators on the Portmagee town website (www.portmagee.ie/). The Cork and Kerry tourism offices can also assist, as can your hotel.

Most, though not all, tours leave from Portmagee harbor; be sure to check when you book.

Whether or not you're making the trip out there, the **Skellig Experience** (www.skelligexperience.com; ✆ **066/947-6306**) is an excellent visitor center devoted to the islands and their history. It tells you all about the extraordinary history of these ancient edifices and also offers boat trips out to see the islands. The center, which is on Valentia Island (reached via a road bridge from Portmagee), is open daily 10am to 6pm in May, June, and September; 10am to 7pm in July and August; and weekdays only 10am to 4:30pm in March, April, October, and November. Last entry is 1 hour before closing. Admission costs €5 adults, €4 seniors and students, €3 children, and €14 families.

The visitor center also offers boat trips around the Skelligs; the cost of admission plus a cruise is €30 adults, €28 seniors and students, €18 children, and €85 families. Note that these trips only cruise *around* the Skelligs, however, and **do not make landfall.** If you want to see the ruins on Skellig Michael up close, you'll have to go with one of the independent boat operators listed above.

TOP ATTRACTIONS ON THE RING OF KERRY DRIVE

Ballinskelligs & the Skellig Ring ★★ RUINS/RELIGIOUS SITE West of Waterville, across a small bay, the coastal village of Ballinskelligs contains the absurdly picturesque ruins of **St. Michael Ballinskelligs,** a medieval priory overlooking the sea. A beautiful sandy beach also features the remnants of a 16th-century castle. Ballinskelligs is a starting point for the so-called **Skellig Ring,** a stunning coastal drive that takes in some of the best viewpoints of the mysterious Skellig Islands (see box p. 310). It also passes through some of the most dramatic scenery in the county, and with the merest fraction of the traffic that can clog the Ring of Kerry. Be warned, however: Its very remoteness means that this route can be tough going, and the roads are very mountainous in places. This is also the edge of Gaeltacht territory, where Irish is the primary language on road signs. To find the Ring, head south through Ballinskelligs. About 0.5km (⅓ mile) after the pink An Post building, you'll come to a cross-roads. The Skellig Ring (*Morchuaird na Sceilge* in Gaelic) is signposted to the right. The signs continue throughout the route.

Visitor Information Point: Cafe Cois Trá, Ballinskelligs Beach, Ballinskelligs. ℂ **066/947-9323.** Cafe open daily 9am–6pm (hours may be reduced in winter).

Blueberry Hill Farm ★★ HERITAGE SITE   Looking for a way to amuse younger children for half a day? Try this working farm, which still follows traditional farming methods. As part of the half-day tours, you can help milk cows, make butter, and take part in a treasure hunt. Children get to interact with the animals and can help out at feeding time. A cafe sells fresh, homemade scones and other treats. The whole experience is very friendly, authentic, and can be delightful for the little ones. Book ahead in the high season, as tours are limited to small groups. Full-day courses in such skills as basket weaving, blacksmithing, food preserving, and beekeeping are available for adults.

Signposted from R568 (Sneem-Killarney Rd.), Sneem. www.blueberryhillfarm.ie. ℂ **087/364-7371.** Admission €20 adults and children; family groups (4 or more) €15 per person. Tours daily 10am and 3pm. Tours may not run in winter or bad weather; call ahead.

Derrynane House National Historic Park ★★ HISTORIC HOUSE   Irish political leader and Parliament member Daniel O'Connell (1775–1847) became known as "the Great Liberator" for his successful campaign to repeal the laws that barred Catholics from holding office. He became particularly famous in his lifetime for his so-called "monster meetings," vast public rallies held across the country (one, on the Hill of Tara, was reckoned to have been attended by nearly a million supporters). His house at Caherdaniel contains a museum devoted to his life, featuring various artifacts and items from his personal archives. Not everything will be of interest to those who aren't already familiar with his story, but a few pieces—such as the gilded carriage from which he triumphantly greeted crowds after a brief spell as a political prisoner—are definitely worth seeing. Take time to wander the vast, scenic grounds.

Signposted from N70 (Ring of Kerry Rd.), approx. 2.5km (1½ miles) from Caherdaniel. www.heritageireland.ie. ℂ **066/947-5113.** Admission €5 adults; €4 seniors; €3 students and children; €13 families. Mid-Mar to Sept daily 10:30am–5:15pm; Oct Wed–Sun and public holidays 10am–5pm; Nov to mid-Dec weekends 10am–4pm. Last admission 45 min. before closing.

Staigue Fort ★★ ANCIENT SITE   This well-preserved, surprisingly large prehistoric fort is built of rough stones without mortar of any kind. The walls are 4m (13 ft.) thick at the base. Historians are not certain what purpose it served—it may have been a hilltop fortress or just a kind of prehistoric community center—but experts think it dates from around 1000 B.C. It's an open site with no visitor center. Look for signs, and hike up the path through the field. It's quite something to see.

Off N70 just outside Castlecove, on a small farm road (follow signs 4 km/2½ miles to site). Daily 9am–7pm.

WHERE TO STAY ALONG THE RING OF KERRY

Although the Ring of Kerry is easily driven as a day excursion from Killarney or Kenmare, don't overlook the option of staying overnight in the countryside or in one of the small towns along the Ring—and it just may save you a few euros, too.

Moderate

Iskeroon ★★★ In a spectacularly beautiful setting on the Ring of Kerry, looking out across the Derrynane coast and out to the Skellig Islands, this extraordinary bed-and-breakfast is a serene and special place to stay. Built in the 1930s, the house isn't large, but this merely adds to the feeling of special care and attention you experience from the moment you walk through the door. The suite, with heated stone floors, king-size beds, handmade furniture, and beautiful pieces of art, has been elegantly renovated. Fresh ingredients are provided for breakfast, but you prepare it yourself in the suite's kitchenette—and there's no better location to enjoy a leisurely breakfast than your balcony overlooking the sea. The former coach house on the grounds is rented out on a weekly basis as a full self-catering accommodation. Each is big enough for just two people, making this ideal for a peaceful, romantic getaway. The only downside is the minimum stay—3 nights in the suite, a week in the cottage—but that might not feel like a chore once you're here. Needless to say, it can get booked up far in advance. From the Scariff Inn, follow signs for Bunavalla Pier, then signs to Iskeroon.

Bunavalla (halfway between Waterville and Caherdaniel). www.iskeroon.com. ✆ **066/947-5119.** 2 units. Suite €100 per night. Apartment €400–€450 per week. Free parking. Breakfast included. 3-night minimum stay. 5% discount for 4 nights or more; 2.5% charge for credit cards. **Amenities:** DVD player/library; kitchenette; Wi-Fi (free).

Picín ★★ Romantic and secluded, Picín is a place to live out your Irish country cottage fantasy. It's just one double room, but guests have a private entrance, with a garden-facing terrace and their own sitting room with a wood-burning stove. The bathroom is enormous, with a deep clawfoot tub and even an old wooden loveseat. Upstairs, the bedroom is an oasis of peace and calm. Hosts Amelia and Nick Etherton are a delight and so considerate—prepare to be welcomed with cake and smiles. Breakfasts are delicious, too. Pet the ponies, take a countryside walk, and just relish living this life for a few days. The only snag is that you have to fend for yourself at dinner, but Caherdaniel is a short drive away—or you can borrow a barbecue grill. Picín is just off the Ring of Kerry Road, between Caherdaniel and Castlecove (on the left if you're coming from Caherdaniel). There is a sign, but it's small and low to the ground.

Off N70, about 3.8km (2⅓ miles) E of Caherdaniel. www.picincottage.com. ℭ **066/ 947-5894.** 1 unit. Suite €110–€120. Free parking. Breakfast included. **Amenities:** Wi-Fi (free).

QC's ★★   More of a restaurant-with-rooms than a small hotel, QC's is nonetheless a stylish and unique place to stay on the Ring of Kerry. Bedrooms are open-plan contemporary spaces with a minimalist vibe: polished wood floors, huge skylights, and claw-foot tubs next to the bed, plus a few high-tech extras such as Bose stereos. The guest lounge looks as if it's tumbled from the pages of a decor magazine, featuring deep velvet sofas and a cozy wood-burning stove. The superb downstairs restaurant specializes in fresh seafood, taking pride in local flavors cooked to perfection, such as Valentia scallop Mornay, or local steak filet with scallion mashed potatoes.

Main St., Cahersiveen. www.qcbar.com. ℭ **066/947-2244.** 5 units. €170–€180 double. Free parking. Breakfast included. **Amenities:** Wi-Fi (free).

Inexpensive

Coffey River's Edge ★   A bright, cheery building overlooking the River Laune in the center of Killorglin, Coffey's is an exceptional value for the money. Most rooms are decently sized (one upstairs is quite small, though), with double beds and contemporary wood furniture. Breakfasts are served in a dining room overlooking the river and picturesque stone bridge, or in fair weather, on a large guest balcony and deck. No evening meal is served, but pretty Killorglin is right at your doorstep. Owners Finbarr and Anne are both keen golfers and will happily arrange a game for you at a local course.

The Bridge, Killorglin. www.coffeysriversedge.com. ℭ **066/976-1750.** 11 units. €80–€90 double. Free parking. Breakfast included. **Amenities:** Wi-Fi (free).

WHERE TO EAT ON THE RING OF KERRY DRIVE

Expensive

Jack's Coastguard Restaurant ★★★ SEAFOOD/MODERN IRISH This cheery restaurant lists "Water's Edge" as its address. That's not so much a street name as a description; it's right on the harbor in Cromane, a tiny village near Killorglin. The dining room is a bright, modern space boasting beautiful views of the bay, while a pianist plays away in the corner. The menus hit elegant notes with choices like crispy salmon with leek, tomato, and chive, or supreme of chicken with fennel. For dessert, try the delicious marscapone cheesecake. The restaurant is attached to a popular local pub, which hosts live music every Monday night in summer.

Water's Edge, Cromane Lower, Killorglin. www.jackscromane.com. ℭ **066/976-9102.** Entrees €18–€35. Thurs–Sun 6–9pm. Sun lunch 1–3pm. Closed Tues. Reservations encouraged.

Nick's Restaurant & Gastro Bar ★★ SEAFOOD/IRISH   The Rat Pack feel to this restaurant's name says everything about its old-school credentials. Nick's is quite famous in this part of Ireland—it's been here since 1978—and although you won't find cutting-edge modern cuisine here, it still deserves its reputation as one of the better places to eat along the Ring of Kerry. Choose from two dining areas: the formal restaurant or the "Gastro Bar," where a simpler (and less expensive) selection is served in more relaxed surroundings. In the main restaurant, dine on catches of the day (naturally), grilled sole, a monkfish and prawn thermidor, or a classic seafood platter. You can also order grilled steaks and lamb. The bar menu offers simpler but nonetheless classy options: Thai beef and asparagus salad; beef, lamb, or pulled-pork burgers; or perhaps a steaming bowl of creamy seafood Mornay. Everything is served to the gentle melodies of live piano accompaniment. The same as it ever was.

Lower Bridge St., Killorglin. www.nicks.ie. ✆ **066/976-1219.** Entrees €14–€36. Tues–Sun 4:30–10pm.

Moderate

The Blind Piper ★ IRISH   This friendly, lively pub is one of the top places to eat in Caherdaniel. The menu strikes a nice balance between straightforward "pub grub" and something a little more sophisticated—cheeseburger made with brie on a focaccia bun, for example, or tempura-battered fish and chips. Live traditional music sessions liven the place up on Thursday nights from 9:30pm. The Blind Piper is a bit hard to find, partly because it doesn't have a proper street address. Take the main N70 road through Caherdaniel, and then take the turn next to the big red building in the center of the village. (There's usually a handmade sign here pointing you in the right direction.) The pub is painted bright yellow.

Off main Ring of Kerry Rd. (N70), Caherdaniel. ✆ **066/947-5126.** Entrees €11–€20. Mon–Thurs 11am–11:30pm, Fri–Sat 11am–12:30am, Sun 12:30–9pm.

The Blue Bull ★ IRISH   This great little pub in tiny, picturesque Sneem serves traditional fare in a couple of cozy dining spaces. The menu doesn't deviate too far from Irish pub classics, but it does it all very well—Irish stew, fish and chips, mussels in garlic sauce, steaks, sandwiches, and salads. The crowd, a good mix of hungry tourists and easygoing locals settling down at the bar, makes for a congenial atmosphere. This is a straight-up traditional pub with a bar area in the front separate from the dining rooms. It's a great spot for eavesdropping on a few conversations, and possibly being asked your opinion about the topic of the day.

South Square, Sneem. ✆ **064/664-5382.** Entrees €8–€18. Mon–Sat 11am–around midnight, Sun noon–11pm (food until about 9pm).

Inexpensive

Bake My Day ★★ BAKERY   Perfect for a simple, tasty lunch on the go, this charming bakery serves delicious sandwiches and cakes. It's all homemade and available to go if you prefer. Try the open crab

walk this way: **THE KERRY WAY**

Serious hikers test their chops on the **Kerry Way,** a long-distance trail that traverses extraordinary scenery while roughly following the Ring of Kerry. Ireland's longest marked hiking trail, the 202km (126-mile) route includes several "green roads" (old, unused roads built as Famine relief projects and now converted into walking paths).

The first stage, from Killarney National Park to Glenbeigh, travels inland over rolling hills and past pastoral scenes. The second stage circles the Iveragh Peninsula and takes in spectacular ocean views, passing through picturesque towns including Cahersiveen, Waterville, colorful Sneem, and lovely

Kenmare. The final inland walk brings you via the old Kenmare Road back to Killarney.

The walk is steep in places—the highest point is 385m (1,200 ft.) in a section known as Windy Gap. There are long stretches of wilderness between civilization—walkers attempting the entire path, or even substantial portions of it, need to prepare carefully. But some short stretches can be easily accessed and make for gentle afternoon walks, suitable for amateurs.

Maps outlining the route, and the best short walks, are available from the Killarney and Kenmare tourist offices. For details, see **www.kerryway.com**.

sandwich—something of a specialty—or you can order soup, quiche, or the all-day breakfast if you're after something hot and savory. Right down to the homemade brown bread, all is fresh and tasty as it should be. Even the most enthusiastic dieter will be tempted by the delectable cakes and pies. The coffee's good, too. What more could you want to pep you up for an afternoon of exploring the Ring of Kerry?

On N70, Castlecove, Caherdaniel ⓒ **086/088-9253.** €5–€10. Daily 10am–6pm. Hours may be reduced in winter.

TRALEE

Sandwiched between the Ring of Kerry and the Dingle Peninsula, Tralee doesn't quite live up to its singsong pretty name. Mostly it's a place you go *through,* rather than to. With a population of 24,000, the town is nearly twice the size of Killarney, but this is a workaday place, rather than a tourist center, and there's not much here for visitors. In fact, it can feel a bit rough at times—especially on weekend nights, when the town's many bars are packed. However, it has some attractive Georgian architecture and a few sights worth seeing, with a couple more offerings in the countryside nearby.

Exploring In & Around Tralee

Blennerville Windmill ★★ LANDMARK Reaching 20m (66 ft.) into the sky, this snow-white windmill must surely be the most photographed object in Tralee. Perched at the edge of the river, the windmill has blades that still turn, which makes it rare in this part of the world. Built in 1800, it flourished until 1850, when it was largely abandoned. After decades of neglect, it was restored and is now fully operational. You can climb to the top and see some of its complex inner workings in detail. The visitor complex has an exhibition on the Famine years (when Blennerville was a major point of emigration), plus an audiovisual theater, craft workshops, a model railway exhibition, and a cafe. The windmill is about a mile outside of central Tralee on the N86.

Windmill St., Blennerville. © **066/712-1064.** Admission €5 adults; €4 seniors and students; €3 children; free for children under 6; €15 families. No credit cards. June–Aug daily 9am–6pm; Apr–May, Sept–Oct daily 9:30am–5:30pm. Closed Nov–Mar.

Crag Cave ★★ UNDERGROUND CAVERNS Although they are believed to be more than a million years old, these limestone caves were not discovered until 1983. The guides accompany you 3,753m (12,310 ft.) into the well-lit cave passage on a 35-minute tour revealing massive stalactites and fascinating caverns. It's very touristy, but interesting nonetheless. There is a children's play area (endearingly called **Crazy Cave**), although it costs extra. The **Garden Restaurant** is a useful stop for lunch if you need a quick bite. On the same site is **Kingdom Falconry,** where you can watch birds of prey.

College Rd., Castleisland (turn left off N21 onto Main St., then left onto College Rd.) www.cragcave.com. © **066/714-1244.** Caves: €12 adults; €9 seniors and students; €5 children; €30–€35 families. Kingdom Falconry: €8 adults, seniors, and students; €5 children 5–16; free for children 4 and under; €20–€27 families. Crazy Cave: €8 per child for 2 hr. play (accompanying adults free), or €11 including cave tour; €5 children 2 and under. July–Aug daily 10am–6:30pm; mid-Mar to June and Sept–Dec daily 10am–6pm; Jan to mid-Mar Fri–Sun, 10am–6pm. Tour times: May–Aug, every half-hr.; off-season no set times.

Kerry County Museum ★ MUSEUM Spanning several thousand years of history, up to the present day, this museum's galleries cover Kerry's ancient past; the coming of the Normans and the medieval period; the Famine years; and the struggle for independence. The high-tech audiovisual presentation includes a tour of the county using archival footage to show how it looked half a century ago. In the Knight's Hall and Medieval Experience, you can wander around a re-created medieval town, with requisite sound effects, dressed-up mannequins, and the like. The museum is in the same building as the Tralee tourism office.

Ashe Memorial Hall, Denny St., Tralee. www.kerrymuseum.ie. © **066/712-7777.** Admission €5 adults; free for accompanying children; €10 families. June–Aug daily 9:30am–5:30pm; Sept–May Tues–Sat 9:30am–5pm.

The Seanchaí: Kerry Writers' Museum ★ MUSEUM This imaginative museum's innovative displays often feel more like art installations devoted to the life and work of various Kerry writers from the past and present. Life-size statues sit hunched over books and even propping up a bar, with the text of their best-known works covering them from head to toe. Herein also lies the drawback—Kerry simply hasn't produced many "big beasts" of Irish literature, so the writers celebrated here probably

COULD YOU BE THE rose OF TRALEE?

Beauty pageants may have gone out of fashion in much of the world, but at the annual **Rose of Tralee,** they're still going strong.

A 19th-century song about a pretty local girl named Mary O'Connor is at the root of this world-famous beauty contest. William Mulchinock's tear-jerker tune about the girl he was stopped by fate from marrying so caught the public's imagination that more than 100 years later, it is still performed in Irish pubs worldwide. Thus, in 1959 the idea was born for a contest to find the loveliest lass in Tralee and crown her.

Every August, the town fills with striking young women, those who make them beautiful, and people who want to look at them. The contest rules are fairly generous in terms of who is Irish, not to mention Traleean—the rules require contestants to be of Irish birth *or ancestry,* so past winners have been from places as far-flung as the U.S. and Australia. The festival lasts 5 days, during which time the entire town becomes somewhat obsessed with it—restaurants, pubs, and theaters all get involved in hosting events related to the Rose of Tralee. In recent years they've also added a men's section, the "Escort of the Year."

If you want to join in the fun, or if you know a pretty girl with an Irish last name, contact the **Rose of Tralee Festival Office** (www.roseoftralee.ie; ✆ **066/712-1322**).

won't ring many bells for the casually interested. But part of the pleasure is discovering new names and hitherto unfamiliar works. A busy schedule of events fills the summer months; check the website for details. Listowel is 26km (16 miles) northeast of Tralee on N69.

24 The Square, Listowel. www.kerrywritersmuseum.com. ✆ **068/22212.** Free admission. Guided tours €5 adults; €4 seniors and students; €3 children; €12 families. June–Aug Mon–Sun 9:30am–5:30pm; Sept–Nov, Mar–May Mon–Fri 10am–4pm. Last tour 1 hr. before closing. Closed Dec–Feb.

Where to Stay & Eat in Tralee

Ballygarry House ★★   On the outer edge of Tralee, this pleasant country inn is ensconced amid lush gardens. Built as a manor house in the 18th century, it has retained plenty of its original features. Elegant guest rooms maintain the country-mansion air, and superior rooms are surprisingly spacious, with king-size beds. Family rooms are an excellent value at usually the same price as doubles. The fantastic in-house spa is a relaxing, revitalizing hideaway, while the outdoor hot tub, overlooking fields and distant mountains, is a calming oasis. Special inclusive spa offers change monthly—massage, facial, and access to the spa facilities for around €80 to €100 is the kind of deal you can expect. The **Brasserie** restaurant serves excellent modern Irish food. Check the website for dinner-bed-and-breakfast offers.

Signposted off N21, Leebrook, approx. 3.3km (2 miles) W of central Tralee. www. ballygarryhouse.com. ✆ **066/712-3322.** 46 units. €195–€250 double, €260–€325 suite. Free parking. Breakfast not included in lower rates. **Amenities:** Restaurant; bar; spa; Wi-Fi (free).

Denny Lane ★ BISTRO   A good option for a quick lunch in Tralee, Denny Lane serves tasty soups, salads, sandwiches, and light lunch specials. The food is good and the atmosphere congenial. They also do breakfast until a very civilized noon (or brunch until 2pm). Dinner on weekends includes a menu of steaks, seafood, burgers, and other favorites all mixed up with a popular tapas menu. Early-bird dinner menus offer three courses, with tea or coffee, for just €23.

11 Denny St., Tralee. www.dennylane.ie. © **066/712-9831.** Lunch entrees €6–€11, dinner entrees €15–€26. Mon–Wed 10am–6pm, Thurs–Sat 10am–11pm (last orders 9pm), Sun 11am–9pm.

Sports & Outdoor Pursuits in Tralee

GOLF   The Arnold Palmer–designed **Tralee Golf Club,** Fenit/Churchill Road, West Barrow, Ardfert (www.traleegolfclub.com; © **066/713-6379**), overlooking the Atlantic 13km (8 miles) northwest of town, is one of the most spectacularly situated courses in Ireland. Greens fees are a pricey €210, although this also allows you to play a second round within a week of the first for €150.

About 40km (25 miles) north of Tralee in the northwest corner of County Kerry is former U.S. President Bill Clinton's favorite Irish course, the **Ballybunion Golf Club,** Ballybunion (www.ballybuniongolfclub.ie; © **068/27146**). This facility has two challenging 18-hole seaside links, both on cliffs overlooking the Shannon River estuary and the Atlantic. Tom Watson has rated Ballybunion's Old Course one of the finest in the world, while the Cashen Course was designed by Robert Trent Jones, Sr. Greens fees are €65 to €210, depending on the time of year.

THE DINGLE PENINSULA

North of the Iveragh Peninsula, the less visited Dingle Peninsula also has much to offer. To call it "undiscovered" would be a stretch—in the summer, little Dingle Town is busy with travelers—but, unlike the Ring of Kerry, it's rarely overrun. Out of the high season, this is a sleepy little place, filled with color and wonderful to explore.

West of Dingle Town, a stunning coastal drive known as the **Slea Head Drive** is lined with archeological sites. (It's also a memorable route for cycling.) Some of Ireland's finest beaches line both sides of the peninsula (see p. 329), and the views are spectacular. Walkers can tackle the challenges of the **Dingle Way** (see p. 330).

Dingle Town

A charming, brightly colored little town at the foot of steep hills, **Dingle** (*An Daingean*) has plenty of hotels and restaurants and makes a good base for exploring the region. The town's most famous resident is an apparently eternal dolphin that adopted the place decades ago and has been bringing in dolphin-loving tourists ever since. The town's busiest time is in August, when the **Dingle Races** draw crowds to watch the horses run every other weekend. (The racetrack is just outside of town on the N86.) In the last week of August, the **Dingle Regatta** fills the harbor with traditional Irish currach boats in a vivid display of color and history.

EXPLORING DINGLE TOWN

Dingle Dolphin Boat Tours ★★ BOAT TOURS   The story of Fungie the Dingle Dolphin is curious and heartwarming (and a bit suspect). According to lore, the bottlenose dolphin was first spotted by Dingle's lighthouse keeper in 1983, as it escorted fishing boats out to sea and then back again at the end of their voyages day after day. The sailors named him, and he became a fixture of harbor life. Fishermen took their children out to swim with him, and he seemed to love human contact. Now people come from miles around to have a few minutes' time with Fungie, and the fishermen ferry them out to meet him. Trips last about 60 minutes and depart roughly every 2 hours in low season and as often as every half-hour in high season. Fungie swims right up to the boats, which stay out long enough to afford views of the picturesque bay. You can also take an early morning trip (8–10am) in a smaller rigid inflatable boat that holds only 10 people. On the morning trips only, you have the option of hiring a wetsuit and getting in the water with Fungie—but you'll need to book (and tell them in advance that you want a wetsuit, which costs extra). The skippers take great lengths to stress that the trips are on Fungie's terms—they don't chase him, and they have no control over whether he puts in an appearance (although he usually does). On the standard trips you don't pay if he doesn't show. Although the little fella was still packing in the crowds at the time of writing, nobody quite knows how old Fungie is. Or if it's still the same dolphin that adopted the town all those years ago. Either way, it's a lovely outing with the kids.

The Pier, Dingle Town. www.dingledolphin.com. ✆ **066/915-2626.** Tour starts at €16 adults; €8 children under 12. Daily, around 11:30am–4pm, weather permitting.

Dingle Oceanworld Aquarium ★ AQUARIUM   This is a nicely designed aquarium, although it's quite small, given the ticket price. As is the norm at such places, it's home to lots of sea critters in creatively designed tanks. You can walk through an aquarium tunnel with fish swimming above and around you, and members of the young staff carry around live lobsters, crabs, starfish, and other "inner space" creatures for kids to touch and pet. The aquarium also has some super-cute Antarctic Gentoo penguins. This compact, hands-on, interactive place makes a good reward for your kids for being so patient while you took pictures of a pile of rocks back up the road. You get a 10% discount if you buy tickets online.

Dingle Harbour, Dingle Town. www.dingle-oceanworld.ie. ✆ **066/915-2111.** Admission €14 adults; €10 seniors and students; €9.50 children; €40–€46.50 family. Daily 10am–5pm. Last admission 1 hr. before closing.

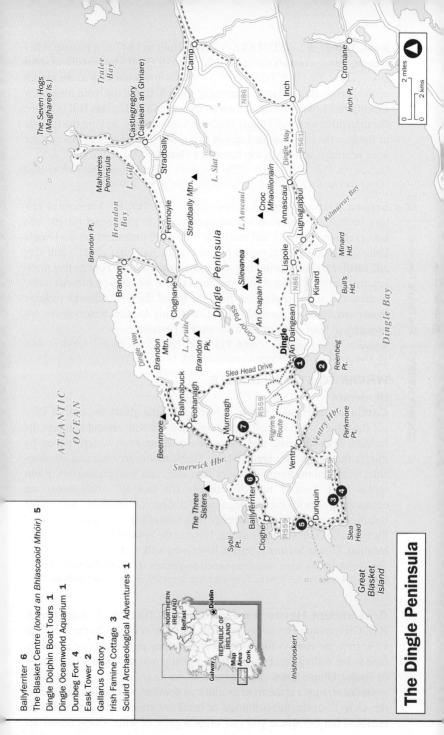

The Dingle Peninsula

Ballyferriter **6**

The Blasket Centre (Ionad an Bhlascaoid Mhóir) **5**

Dingle Dolphin Boat Tours **1**

Dingle Oceanworld Aquarium **1**

Dunbeg Fort **4**

Eask Tower **2**

Gallarus Oratory **7**

Irish Famine Cottage **3**

Sciuird Archaeological Adventures **1**

Eask Tower ★ LANDMARK/VIEW   Built in 1847 as a Famine relief project, this is a remarkable edifice, a 12m-tall (39-ft.) tower built of solid stone nearly 5m (16 ft.) thick with a wooden arrow pointing to the mouth of the harbor. It is certainly interesting to look at, but the main reason for making the 1.6km (1-mile) climb to the summit of Carhoo Hill is to see the incredible views of Dingle Harbour, Connor Pass, and, on the far side of the bay, the peaks of the Iveragh Peninsula. This is a great place to get your bearings, but save a trip here for a clear day.

Carhoo Hill. From Dingle, follow Slea Head Rd. 3.2km (2 miles), turn left at road signposted for Coláiste Ide, and continue another 3.2km (2 miles).

Sciuird Archaeological Adventures ★★ TOUR   For serious history buffs, these tours are a great opportunity to get deeper insight into how prehistoric settlers and early Christians left their mark on the Dingle Peninsula. Led by local expert historians, the tours last about a half-day and involve a short bus journey and some easy walking. Four or five monuments, from the Stone Age to medieval times, are on the route. All tours, limited to 8 to 10 people, start from the top of the pier, although pickups from your hotel are possible if you're staying locally. Reservations are required, at least a day or so in advance if possible.

Holy Ground, Dingle Town. ✆ **066/915-1606.** Tour €20 per person. Apr–Sept daily 10:30am and 2pm; rest of year by appointment.

WHERE TO STAY IN DINGLE

Moderate

Castlewood House ★★★   Overlooking the glassy expanse of Dingle Bay, this lovely whitewashed house is filled with art and antiques. Its location is exceptional, and views of the shimmering water, framed by distant mountains, are breathtaking. Guest rooms are chic and comfortable, with neutral tones, designer furniture, and well-chosen art. Bathrooms have Jacuzzi tubs. Breakfasts (in fact all meals here) are outstanding—including porridge with a dash of whiskey, homemade breads, oranges in caramel, kippers with scrambled eggs, and a light and fluffy omelet with smoked salmon. Despite the beautifully rural feel to the location, Dingle Marina is only a 10-minute walk away.

The Wood, Dingle Town. www.castlewooddingle.com. ✆ **066/915-2788.** 14 units. €148–€164 double, €195 suite. Free parking. Breakfast included. **Amenities:** Wi-Fi (free).

Greenmount House ★★★   A luxurious B&B overlooking Dingle Bay, Greenmount House is one of the best places to stay in the area. The view from the front is like a cliché of what you might imagine all of Ireland to be: rolling green slopes falling gently into the sea with the streets of quaint Dingle town curving around the coastline below. The public areas are arranged at the front as much as possible, so that you can admire the view from the guest lounge or breakfast room. The garden has an enclosed hot tub where you can savor a glass of wine. Guest rooms are bright and spacious; some have polished wood floors and others have skylights, letting the daylight pour in. Breakfasts are delicious and plentiful—try the tasty smoked salmon and scrambled eggs. Hosts Mary and John Curran are incredibly friendly and will even arrange personal tours of the area for you, escorted by a member of their own family.

Upper John St., Dingle Town. www.greenmounthouse.ie. $©$ **066/915-1414.** 14 units. €101 double, €161 suite. 2-night minimum on summer weekends. Free parking. Breakfast included. **Amenities:** Wi-Fi (free).

WHERE TO EAT IN DINGLE

Expensive

The Chart House ★★ IRISH   This friendly restaurant on the outskirts of Dingle is one of the most popular places to indulge in the local produce. The menu is short, but dishes are expertly prepared, filled with regional flavor and a hint of global influences. Expect a Thai curry made with local beef and butternut squash, or Atlantic scallops served with pureé of celeriac and apple. Almost everything on the menu is sourced from providers within the Dingle Peninsula. The three-course early-bird special (6–7pm) has almost as much choice as the evening service for €33.

The Mall, Dingle Town. www.thecharthousedingle.com. $©$ **066/915-2255.** Entrees €20–€29. Mon–Sat 7–10pm, Sun 9am–9pm. Times may vary in winter. Closed Jan to mid-Feb.

Doyle's Seafood Bar ★★★ SEAFOOD   Doyle's is simply one of the best places in the region for topnotch seafood. As you'd expect from a place like this, what you find on the menu depends on the catch of the day; most likely this will include oysters on the half-shell, fresh and delicious. Specialties include fish stew made with white wine and saffron; turbot with red pepper and chive sauce; and black sole with a lemon and parsley butter. Carnivores are taken care of with grilled steak or lamb. The wine list is extensive, and the early-bird menu (€30 for three courses) is served until 7:30pm.

4 John St., Dingle Town. www.doylesofdingle.ie. $©$ **066/915-2674.** Entrees €20–€33. Mon–Sat (and public holidays) 5–9:30pm, Sun 5–7:30pm. Closed Jan.

INEXPENSIVE

Bean in Dingle ★★ CAFE   A little slice of metropolitan cool right in the middle of Dingle, Bean serves one of the finest cups of Joe we've had in Ireland. Bean's beans are all supplied by Badger and Dodo, delightful Irish artisan coffee roasters from Cork. Have it to go or sit at the long, communal wooden table and linger over a slice of tasty homemade cake, provided by a local baker.

Green St., Dingle Town. www.beanindingle.com. $©$ **087/299-2831.** All items €3–€6. Mon–Sat 8:30am–5pm. Closed Sun.

Reel Dingle Fish ★★ FISH & CHIPS   Dingle is not short of an authentic "chipper" or two, and this is one of the best in town. Everything's cooked the traditional way—fish in batter, with piping-hot chips, and no messing around—but the menu has a greater-than-average choice of fresh fish to choose from, including hake, monkfish, pollock, and locally smoked haddock, in addition to the more usual cod and plaice. It also sells homemade burgers crafted from local beef.

Bridge St., Dingle Town. ℗ **066/915-1713.** Fish and chips €5–€12. Mon–Sat 1–10pm, Sun 5–10pm.

DINGLE TOWN SHOPPING

Brian de Staic Jewellery Workshop ★ Brian is a respected jewelry designer who has built up quite a following since he first appeared on the scene more than 30 years ago. He specializes in modern interpretations of ancient Celtic motifs, and you'll find everything from pendants and brooches to earrings, bracelets, and crosses. Some of his work is based on instantly recognizable designs; others are more subtle and abstract. Green St., Dingle Town. www.briandestaic.com. ℗ **066/915-1298.**

Greenlane Gallery ★★ A great selection of new, contemporary art is on sale at this interesting gallery. Styles vary from abstract watercolors and oils to challenging sculpture. Prices vary, inevitably, but several pieces are really quite affordable. Green St., Dingle Town. www.greenlane gallery.com. ℗ **066/915-2018.**

Lisbeth Mulcahy: The Weavers' Shop ★★ Lisbeth Mulcahy is a talented weaver and fashion designer who creates lovely, colorful items of knitwear, hats, throws, and wall hangings. It's all exquisite quality, and the designs are true originals—elegant and distinctive. She also sells a selection of pottery from her husband's workshop (see below). The shop is closed on Sundays from October to May. Green St., Dingle Town. www. lisbethmulcahy.com. ℗ **066/915-1688.**

Louis Mulcahy Workshop ★★ Husband of weaver Lisbeth Mulcahy (see above), Louis Mulcahy is a big name in designer Irish pottery. It's all beautifully made, from Deco-influenced vases to kitchenware, tea sets, and ornaments. Considering what a name he is, Louis's prices are pretty reasonable. Everything can be shipped worldwide, and we say with experience that the shopworkers are experts in packing breakable things so they arrive without a scratch! The workshop, which sprawls over a two-story building with gorgeous views down to the coast, also has a handy cafe. The shop is open daily year-round—until 8pm in the midsummer months. Clogher is 16.5km (10⅓ miles) northwest of Dingle. On R559, Clogher, Ballyferriter. www.louismulcahy.com. ℗ **066/915-6229.**

The Slea Head Drive & Other Dingle Diversions

Looping around the western tip of the Dingle Peninsula, the magnificent **Slea Head Drive** ★★★ offers rugged coastal vistas, unspoiled islands, and mossy archaeological sites—picture-postcard Ireland at its best. At any tourist information center, you can get a guide to the various ruined abbeys and old forts along the way. Sights below are listed in the order

Coumeenoole Beach and Bay on Slea Head.

you'll pass them if you drive the loop clockwise. You can, of course, do the journey in reverse just as well, but we like this way best because it frontloads the "wow factor" of sweeping coastal views as soon as you leave Dingle. *Note:* This is serious Gaeltacht territory, so by law, all signs—even road-hazard signs—are in Gaelic only.

Leaving Dingle by car, head southwest along R559 through the town of Ventry, following the **Slea Head Drive** road markers. **Slea Head,** at the southwestern edge of the peninsula, has pristine beaches, great walks, and extensive archaeological remains such as **Dunbeg Fort (*Dún Beag*)** ★, p. 326. After rounding the Head, go north to the village of **Dunquin (*Dún Chaion*)**, stunningly situated between Slea Head and Clogher Head, where you can catch ferries to the abandoned **Blasket Islands (*Na Blascaodaí;* see p. 326)**, inhabited these days only by seals and seabirds.

After this, the scenery opens up to take in some stark moorland on your right, in contrast to the ever-spectacular coastal views on the left. There are plenty of spots to safely pull over for pictures on this stretch. If the sun is out, this section is jaw-dropping. The weather is also dramatic; incoming squalls can hit you suddenly, like an icy, wet wall. Pause for coffee and a browse of the excellent pottery and crafts at **Louis Mulcahy** ★★ (p. 324), which looks out toward **Clogher Strand,** a pretty coastal inlet (at the 2 o'clock position if you're standing outside the pottery).

A few miles north and east along the coast, the sleepy village of **Ballyferriter (*Baile an Fheirtearaigh*)** ★ has an Iron Age fort with a particularly grim backstory (see box p. 328). Continue along R559 and you'll soon see signs for the **Gallarus Oratory ★,** a beautifully preserved early Christian church. From here, continue on the loop back to Dingle, 8km (5 miles) farther along R559, and you've completed the Slea Head Drive.

Irish Famine Cottage ★ HERITAGE SITE   This cottage isn't a replica; it's a real dwelling, maintained as it would have been at the time it was abandoned during the Great Famine years of the mid–19th century. The humble stone building, scattered with pieces of furniture, is a stark and haunting sight, perched on a windswept cliff overlooking the coast. Sheep and horses graze nearby, adding to the feeling of wildness and isolation. You can't go inside, but looking in through the windows gives a powerful enough impression of what life was really like for the rural poor. Kids get a little bowl of feed to give to the animals in the field. *Note:* The cottage is a short walk uphill from the parking lot, so it may not be suitable for those with mobility problems.

Signposted from R559, Ventry. www.famine-cottage.com. ✆ **066/915-6241** or 087/762-2617. Admission €4 adults; €3 children. Apr–Oct daily 10am–6pm.

Dunbeg Fort (*Dún Beag*) ★ RUINS   Sitting atop a sheer cliff just east of Slea Head, outside the village of Ventry, this 5th-century fort's stony walls rise from the cliff edge as if they were always part of it. The round Iron Age structure's stone walls are still mostly sturdy, although part of the fort tragically fell into the sea during the floods of 2014. Walk around the fort to see where other fortifications and "beehive" huts were built inside the walls thousands of years ago. There's also a mysterious underground passage. (At the time this book was being written, the fort was viewable only from the outside due to storm damage. Call ahead for a repair schedule.)

Dunbeg Fort, Slea Head Dr. www.dunbegfort.com. ✆ **066/915-9755.** Admission €3 adults; €2 children. Daily 9:30am–6pm.

The Blasket Islands ★★ HERITAGE/NATURE SITE   Overshadowed by the more famous Skelligs (see p. 310), the Blaskets are another group of mysterious, abandoned islands off the Kerry coast, but with more recent stories to tell. For hundreds of years these were home to an isolated community with a rich tradition of storytelling and folklore—all in traditional Gaelic, of course—that was well documented in the late 1800s. In 1953, however, the islands were considered too dangerous for habitation and the Irish government ordered a mandatory evacuation. The individual islands have wonderfully evocative names like the **Sleeping Giant** and **Cathedral Rocks,** but the only island you can actually visit is the largest, **Great Blasket,** where a few crumbling buildings and skeletal edifices remain—an eerie ghost town in an outstandingly beautiful setting. See it all in a stunning 13km (8-mile) walking route that stretches to the west end of the island, passing sea cliffs and beaches of ivory sand. You can pick up maps and other information from the **Blasket Centre** on the

Abandoned dwellings dot the Blasket Islands off of Dunquin Bay.

mainland in Dunquin. Trips aboard the *Peig Sayers* (www.greatblasket
island.net/boat-trips; ✆ **066/057-2626**), a rigid inflatable vessel, include a
3-hour stop on Great Blasket *and* a detour to look for Fungie the Dingle
Dolphin (p. 320); it leaves from Dingle Marina (below the tourism office)
at 11am daily from March to October. The cost is €55 per person (no
reduction for kids or seniors). Alternatively, **Marine Tours** (www.marine
tours.ie; ✆ **086/335-3805**) runs full- and half-day tours leaving Ventry at
10am or 1pm daily April to October. Their tour includes 3 hours on Great
Blasket; the rest of the time is spent cruising around the other islands
without making landfall. Tickets are €35 for a morning tour, €60 for a full
day. It also runs a 4-hour **Eco Marine Tour** for €50, but this one is
designed for spotting seals, sharks, and whales and doesn't make
landfall.

The Blasket Centre (*Ionad an Bhlascaoid*): Dunquin (*Dún Chaoin*). www.blasket.ie.
✆ **066/915-6444.** Admission €5 adults; €4 seniors; €3 students and children;
children 7 and under free; €13 families. Apr–Oct daily 10am–6pm. Last admission 45
min. before closing.

Gallarus Oratory ★ RELIGIOUS SITE   This tiny, beehive-shaped
chapel is one of the best-preserved pieces of early Christian architecture
in Ireland. Built sometime between the 7th and 9th centuries A.D., its walls
and roof are made entirely of dry stones without mortar—yet the interior
stays remarkably dry. (Not quite dry enough, sadly, to avoid damage during the heavy floods that hit Ireland in 2014, though the repairs are seam-
less.) The small visitor center features displays on the history of the

A gruesome **TALE IN BALLYFERRITER**

The unassuming village of **Ballyferriter** (*Baile an Fheirtearaigh*), part of the Slea Head Drive, is named after a local rebel named Piaras Ferriter, a poet and soldier who fought in the 1641 rebellion and ultimately became the last area commander to surrender to Oliver Cromwell's English troops.

Just north of the village, however, lie relics of an even darker chapter of the village's history. Follow signs to the moody ruins of the **Dún an Oir Fort,** a defensive citadel dating from the Iron Age. A small memorial is dedicated to 600 Spanish and Irish troops who were massacred here by the English in 1580. Most were beheaded—a fact commemorated by the highly gruesome local names for two adjacent fields nearby. The first, where the executions were carried out, is called "the Field of the Cutting." The second, where their partial remains were buried, is "the Field of the Heads."

Oratory, plus the obligatory information film. If the visitor center is closed, you can just walk around back and straight up the little path to the next field, where the Oratory is located. (Those with mobility problems should note that you can't get any closer than this by car, and the uphill walk takes a minute or two from the parking lot.) Nearby is the single surviving tower of 15th-century **Gallarus Castle.** Tours of the castle can be prebooked at the visitor center—not that there's much to see inside.

Gallarus. www.heritageireland.ie. *©* **066/915-5333.** Free admission. Visitor center Apr–Oct daily 10am–6pm. Signposted down small farm road off R559, 11.8km (7.3 miles) NE of Dingle, 4.8km (3 miles) E of Ballyferriter.

OTHER SCENIC DRIVES

If you're heading back toward Killarney and the Ring of Kerry from here, there are two routes—the main N86 (known locally as the "Low Road"), which is pretty enough, or the smaller but more memorable "High Road," which goes over the mountains via the **Conor Pass.** The road is narrow, and lacks passing places at a few points you really wish it didn't, but the views are nothing short of incredible. The best viewpoint is a small parking area next to a waterfall, just after you begin descending through the pass. To go this way, take R559 (Spa Road) east out of Dingle; on the outskirts of town, when you hit a fork in the road, follow signs for Conor Pass and Tralee, to the right.

The High Road eventually meets up with the main N86, just after the nothing-much village of **Camp**—where there's another scenic alternative for the adventurous. Instead of going the way your GPS will probably steer you, around dull and trafficky Tralee, veer off down the tiny, unnamed road signposted for **Aughils,** on the right as you pass through Camp. This lovely route takes you first by a stretch of modern but idyllic houses (you'll probably dream briefly about moving here), before crossing beautiful moorland, then through another picturesque—and mercifully low—mountain pass. It then joins up with the R561 coast road, just 10 minutes or so from Castlemaine on the Ring of Kerry. But beware—although this way can definitely be a shortcut, especially in rush hours, we mean it when say the road is tiny! The last time we took this route the receptionist at our hotel raised an eyebrow and exclaimed "in a *rental car?*" (And we do not recommend either this or the Conor Pass in heavy rain or icy weather.) But remember, fortune favors the brave. Especially those with good tires.

Sports & Outdoor Pursuits in the Dingle Peninsula

SPECTATOR SPORTS

HORSE RACING   The **Dingle Races** are a major event in the Irish horse-racing calendar, with 20 or so events taking place over a long weekend in mid-August. The incredibly picturesque Ballingtaggart Racecourse is just outside Dingle, on the road to Tralee. For more information, visit **www.dingleraces.ie**.

SAILING   Held over a couple of days in mid-August, the **Dingle Regatta** is one of the highlights of the Irish sailing calendar. The Regatta has no website or central contact number, but information is generally posted a couple of months in advance on its official Facebook page—search for "Dingle Regatta."

OUTDOOR PURSUITS

BEACHES   The Dingle Peninsula is home to several spectacular beaches. The most famous is **Inch Strand**—a 5km-long (3-mile) creamy stretch of sand dunes in the town of Inch (*Inse*). It makes for a beautiful stop on the coast road into Dingle, with a beach cafe (open summer only) and a colony of semi-wild ginger cats that live among the slopes of its parking lot, ever hopeful for scraps. On Kilmurray Bay, **Minard Beach,** in the shadow of Minard Castle, giant sandstone boulders form a beach unlike anything you've ever seen. It's definitely *not* safe for swimming, but ideal for a stroll or a picnic.

The calmest beaches for swimming in this area are east of Castlegregory, on the more protected west side of Tralee Bay. The beach

Horseback riding in Dingle.

walk this way: THE DINGLE WAY

The **Dingle Way** begins in Tralee and circles the peninsula, covering 153km (95 miles) of gorgeous mountain and coastal landscape. The most rugged section is along Brandon Head, on the peninsula's north coast, where the trail passes between Mount Brandon and the ocean. Farther west, the section between Dunquin and Ballyferriter (24km/15 miles) follows an especially lovely stretch of Atlantic coast. For more information, pick up maps from local tourist offices.

The Dingle Way is just one of many itineraries offered by **Hidden Ireland Tours,** Dingle (www.hiddenirelandtours. com; ✆ **251/478-7519** in the U.S., or 087/221-4002), which offers weeklong guided hiking tours through some of Ireland's most beautiful scenery. It also offers hikes around the Kerry Way (see p. 316), Killarney National Park (p. 285), and Skellig Michael (p. 310). Prices include luggage transfers and accommodations. Hikes are available April to September.

at **Maherabeg** has a coveted European Blue Flag (meaning it is exceptionally unpolluted and environmentally safe), and the beaches of **Brandon Bay** are particularly scenic—great for walking and swimming.

CYCLING   Bikes can be rented at **Foxy John Moriarty,** Main Street, Dingle (✆ **066/915-1316**) or the **Mountain Man Outdoor Shop,** Strand Street, Dingle (www.themountainmanshop.com; ✆ **066/915-2400**). The cost is around €15 to €25 per day, or €55 to €80 per week. Employees at both shops can suggest a number of day trips or overnight touring options. Mountain Man offers guided cycle tours, including a gastro tour and an archeological tour of Slea Head. Not to be outdone, Foxy John's has the advantage of also being a pub, although you might want to save your pints until *after* your ride.

DIVING & WATER SPORTS   On the north coast of the Dingle Peninsula, Castlegregory on protected Tralee Bay is the region's go-to place for water sports. **Waterworld,** Harbour House, Scraggane Pier, Castlegregory (www.waterworld.ie; ✆ **066/713-9292**) is a diving center that offers packages including diving, room, and board at good rates. Classes for beginners are available. The house is a short boat ride from most of the diving sites. Windsurfing equipment can be hired from **Jamie Knox Watersports,** Brandon Bay, Castlegregory (www.jamieknox.com; ✆ **066/713-9411**) on the road between Castlegregory and Fahamore. The cost runs from €15 to €30 for 1 hour to €60 to €80 for the whole day. It also offers lessons for surfers of all skill levels; a 2-hour beginner's taster costs €35 (€25 for minors).

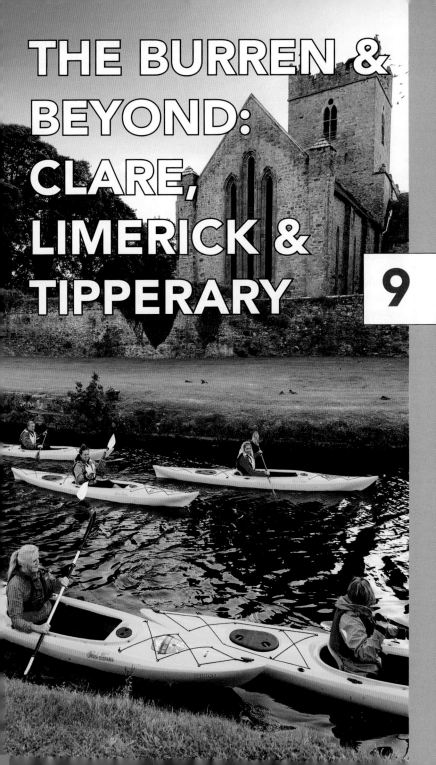

THE BURREN & BEYOND: CLARE, LIMERICK & TIPPERARY

9

N orth of County Kerry, the west coast of Ireland has long drawn visitors entranced by its stunning landscape. From the lush, emerald-green farmland of the Shannon River Valley, head north to the towering Cliffs of Moher, wander through the ancient fortress known as the Rock of Cashel, and finally wind your way up steep roads to the extraordinary lunar landscape of the Burren National Park. However far you go, there's always something wonderful to catch your eye. This is where Ireland begins to get wild.

Bordering Kerry to the north, but entirely separated by the broad Shannon Estuary, **County Clare** is a rugged and beguiling county. Its principal draw is the region known as the Burren, a stark and desolate landscape filled with mysterious, ancient stone dolmens—it's quite unlike anywhere else in the country. As if that wasn't enough to impress, Clare also has the famous Cliffs of Moher, a place of high drama and majestic beauty. The contrast with its neighbor, and rural **County Limerick,** could hardly be more pronounced. Limerick is distinguished by the swirls and eddies of the Shannon River and its valley. To the east, **Tipperary** is filled with pleasant, emerald-green farmland. In truth, Tipperary doesn't contain much else that's worth going out of the way for, with one major exception: the Rock of Cashel, one of Ireland's most spectacular medieval ruins. It's worth a trip across the county all on its own.

ESSENTIALS

Arriving

BY PLANE   Several of the big airlines operate regular scheduled flights into **Shannon Airport,** off the Limerick-Ennis road (N18), County Clare (www.shannonairport.com; ☏ **061/712000**), 24km (15 miles) west of Limerick. If you need a taxi, you can catch one at the airport or prebook with **Shannon Airport Cabs** (www.shannonairportcabs.com; ☏ **061/333-366**). Alternatively, **Bus Éireann** (www.buseireann.ie; ☏ **061/313-333**) provides regular Shannonlink bus service from Shannon Airport to **Colbert Station** in Limerick.

BY BUS   Bus Éireann (www.buseireann.ie; ☏ **061/313-333**) provides regular bus service from all parts of Ireland to most towns listed in this

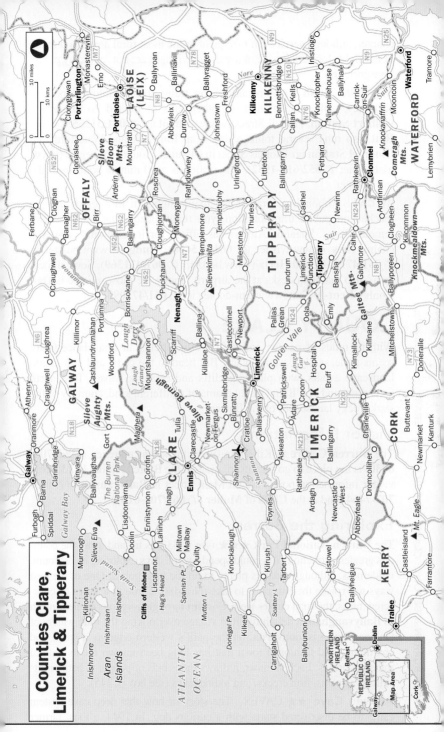

Counties Clare, Limerick & Tipperary

333

chapter, although service isn't frequent in the most rural areas, and many of the sights located outside of towns and villages are not served by public transportation.

BY TRAIN **Irish Rail** operates direct trains from Dublin, Cork, and Killarney, with connections from other parts of Ireland, to Limerick's **Colbert Station,** Parnell Street (www.irishrail.ie; ☏ 061/315555). **Irish Rail** also runs several trains a day from Limerick and Waterford into **Clonmel Station** on Thomas Street in Clonmel, County Tipperary (www.irishrail.ie; ☏ 052/612-1982). The station is a 10-minute walk from the town center.

BY CAR Although several of the major sights in this region can be reached on public transportation, you really need a car for the more remote places. Shannon Airport has offices for international car-rental chains **Avis** (www.avis.ie; ☏ 061/715600), **Budget** (www.budget.ie; ☏ 061/471361), and **Hertz** (www.hertz.ie; ☏ 061/471369). Several local firms also maintain desks at the airport; among the most reliable is **Dan Dooley Rent-A-Car** (www.dan-dooley.ie; ☏ 061/471098).

COUNTY CLARE

With its miles of pasture and softly rolling fields, at first glance Clare seems a pleasantly pastoral place. But head to the coast and a dramatic landscape awaits, with plunging cliffs and crashing waves. Turn north from there and you'll find visual drama of a different kind, courtesy of the stark, rocky landscapes of the Burren.

Visitor Information

The **Burren Centre** in Kilfenora (www.theburrencentre.ie; ☏ 065/708-8030) is the place to go for information on the Burren region. In addition, visitor information points are on Main Street in **Ballyvaughan** (☏ 065/707-7464) and at the **Cliffs of Moher** (☏ 065/708-6141).

Exploring the Burren

The **Burren National Park ★★★** (see p. 337) is far and away the county's greatest attraction. You could spend several days exploring its profound wilderness, although a day is plenty to hit the high points. One of the best ways to explore the Burren is to take the R480. Through a series of corkscrew turns, the road curves from **Corofin** through gorgeous scenery north to **Ballyvaughan,** a delightful little village overlooking the blue waters of Galway Bay. **Lisdoonvarna,** on the park's western edge, is a small and charmingly old-fashioned town that has long been known for its natural mineral springs. Each summer, it draws thousands of people to bathe in its sulfuric streams, iron creeks, and iodine lakes (see box p. 345).

Aillwee Cave ★★ CAVES The story of how this deep cave system came to be discovered starts with a curious dog. In 1944, a local farmer

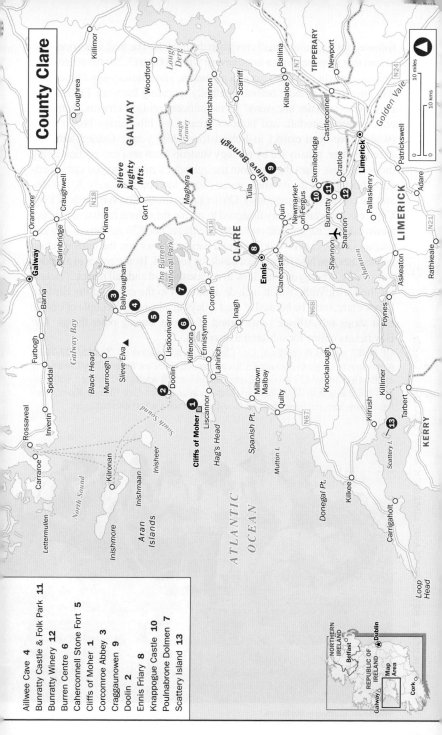

County Clare

Aillwee Cave 4
Bunratty Castle & Folk Park 11
Bunratty Winery 12
Burren Centre 6
Caherconnell Stone Fort 5
Cliffs of Moher 1
Corcomroe Abbey 3
Craggaunowen 9
Doolin 2
Ennis Friary 8
Knappogue Castle 10
Poulnabrone Dolmen 7
Scattery Island 13

followed his dog into a small crevice in the hillside. The man was astonished to find that it opened into a huge cavern with 1,000m (3,280 ft.) of passages running straight into the heart of a mountain. The publicity-shy farmer kept it to himself for decades before eventually spreading the word. Professional cave explorers later uncovered its magnificent bridged chasms, deep caverns, frozen waterfall, and hollows created by hibernating brown bears (which have been extinct in Ireland for 10,000 years). Guided tours are excellent here, usually led by geology students from area universities. Enjoy the spookiness when they turn out the lights for a minute so you can experience the depth of the darkness inside. Tours last approximately 30 minutes and are conducted continuously. On the same site, the **Burren Birds of Prey Centre** is a working aviary designed to mimic the natural habitat of the buzzards, falcons, eagles, and owls that live there. For €70 per person you can take a private "Hawk Walk," where a handler shows you the birds up close and teaches you how to handle a hawk for yourself. It culminates in a guided forest walk, where you learn how to release the bird and call it back. (Tickets for the Hawk Walk, which include admission to the cave and the Birds of Prey Centre, must be booked at least 2 days in advance.) A couple of on-site craft shops sell Aillwee's own brand of cheese, among other things. *Tip:* Buy tickets online for substantial discounts.

Off R480, near Ballyvaughan, Co. Clare. www.aillweecave.ie. (©) **065/707-7036.** Admission to caves: €12 adults; €5.50 children; €35 families. Birds of Prey Centre: €12 adults; €8 children; €29 families. Combined ticket: €18 adults; €10 children; €50 families. Daily July–Aug 10am–6:30pm; Mar–June and Sept–Oct 10am–5:30pm; Nov–Feb 10am–5pm (no flying displays Nov–Dec). Times are first and last tours.

Wildflower spotting in the Burren.

THE burren NATIONAL PARK

The otherworldly landscape of the **Burren National Park** spreads across 1,653 hectares (4,083 acres) carved by nature from bare carboniferous limestone, both desolate and beautiful. Sheets of rock jut and undulate in a kind of moonscape as far as you can see. Amid the rocks, delicate wildflowers somehow find enough dirt to thrive; ferns curl gently around boulders, moss softens hard edges, orchids flower exotically, and violets brighten the landscape. With the flowers come butterflies that thrive on the rare flora. Even the Burren's animals are unusual: The pine marten (small weasels), stoat (ermine), and badger, all rare in the rest of Ireland, are common here.

The Burren began to develop 300 million years ago when layers of shells and sediment were deposited under a tropical sea. Many millions of years later, those layers were exposed by erosion and poor prehistoric farming methods. Since then, it's all been battered by the Irish rain and winds, producing the haunting landscape you see today.

Humans first began to leave their mark here about 7,000 years ago. The park is particularly rich in archaeological remains from the Neolithic through the medieval periods—dolmens and wedge tombs (approximately 120 of them), ring forts (500 of those), round towers, ancient churches, high crosses, monasteries, and holy wells.

Though there's no official entrance, the park is centered at Mullaghmore Mountain—and like all national parks in Ireland, it's completely free to enter. The **Burren Centre** (www.theburrencentre.ie; ℂ 065/708-8030), on R476 to Kilfenora, provides an informative overview with films, landscape models, and interpretive displays. Admission to the center is €6 adults, €5 seniors and students, €4 children age 6 to 16, and €20 families (free for children 5 and under). It's open daily June to August from 9:30am to 5:30pm; mid-March to May and September to October 10am to 5pm. A craft shop and tearoom are also on-site. In June, July, and August, local guide **Tony Kirby** (www.heartofburrenwalks.com; ℂ 065/682-7707) leads 2½-hour guided walks from outside the center at 2:15pm Tuesday and Wednesday, and 10:30am Thursday to Sunday. The cost is €20, including entry to the exhibition. The center is next to the ruins of **Kilfenora Cathedral,** which has some interesting wall carvings—look for the heads above what's left of the doors and windows.

Caherconnell Stone Fort ★ ANCIENT SITE Built sometime around the year A.D. 950, this rugged early medieval ring fort was used as a defensive structure for at least 200 years. It's one of the best-preserved ruins of its kind in Ireland; the dry stone walls are around 3m (9¾ ft.) tall in places, and equally as thick. Today it's partly under the care of an archaeology school, so you'll often see students at work. A visitor center has a cafe and an exhibition focusing on the Burren's forts, dolmens, and other ancient monuments. More entertainingly, you can also see sheepdog demonstrations at the fort from March to October; visit the website to find out when.

On R480, 1km (¾ mile) N of the Poulnabrone Dolmen (see p. 338), near Carran, Co. Clare. www.caherconnell.com. ℂ 065/708-9999. Admission to fort €7 adults; €6

With its unique terrain and meandering walking paths, the Burren lends itself beautifully to walking. The **Burren Way** is a 42km (26-mile) signposted route stretching from Ballyvaughan to Liscannor, incorporating old "green roads"—unpaved former highways that crisscross the Burren landscape in inaccessible areas. (Most were created during the Great Famine as work projects for starving locals.) An information sheet outlining the route is available from any tourist office. You can also contact **Guided Walks and Hikes** (www.burrenguidedwalks.com; © **065/707-6100**) for guided walks and hikes of varying lengths.

seniors and students; €4 children under 12; €17 families. Sheepdog demos: €5 adults; €3 children under 12; €15 families. Joint ticket fort & demos: €10 adults; €8 seniors and students; €6 children under 12; €24.50 families. July–Aug 10am–6pm; May–June and Sept 10am–5:30pm; Mar–Apr and Oct 10:30am–5pm; closed Nov–Feb. Last tour 45 min. before closing.

Corcomroe Abbey ★★ RELIGIOUS SITE/RUINS   Set jewel-like in a languid green valley bounded by rolling hills, the jagged ruins of this Cistercian abbey are breathtaking. Donal Mór O'Brien founded the abbey in 1194, and his grandson, a former king of Thomond, is entombed in the structure's northern wall. Some interesting medieval and Romanesque carvings are set in the stone, including one of a bishop with a crosier. Corcomroe is a lonely spot, except for Easter morning, when people come from miles around to celebrate Mass. It's said to be quite a sight. Look for a mound, surrounded by trees, beside the road on the way out—it's the remains of an ancient ring fort.

Signposted from L1014, near Oughtmama, Co. Clare. No phone. Free admission (open site).

Poulnabrone Dolmen ★ ANCIENT SITE   This portal tomb is an exquisitely preserved prehistoric site, made all the more arresting by the alien Burren landscape in which it sits. Its dolmen (stone table) is huge and surrounded by a natural pavement of rocks. The tomb has been dated back 5,000 years. When it was excavated in the 1980s, the remains of 16 people were found. And yet, it's still a mystery how the gigantic boulders were moved and lifted—the capstone alone weighs 4½ tonnes (5 tons). In summer, you shouldn't have much trouble finding this sight—just look for all the tour buses; at times they literally block the road.

On R480, 1km (¾ mile) S of Caherconnell Stone Fort (see p. 337), near Carran, Co. Clare. Free admission (open site).

Exploring the Clare Coast

One of Ireland's most photographed places, the **Cliffs of Moher** draw thousands of visitors to Clare's remote reaches every day of the year, rain or shine. Rising to vertiginous heights above the Atlantic Ocean, the cliffs are undeniably impressive. The site is well worth a visit, but be aware that in the high season, the crowds can rather spoil the effect.

Farther along the Clare Coast, **Lahinch** is an old-fashioned Victorian seaside resort, with a wide beach and long promenade curving along the horseshoe bay. Golfers already know all about this town—it's renowned for its outstanding links course (see p. 347).

Traditional Irish music is always on heavy rotation in Clare, which has a vibrant music scene. The secluded fishing village of **Doolin,** near Lahinch, is the unofficial capital of Irish traditional music. The village is also a departure point for the short boat trip to the beautiful and isolated **Aran Islands** (see p. 368).

The Clare Coast is dotted with seaside resorts with varying degrees of crowds and beauty, such as **Kilrush, Kilkee, Miltown Malbay,** and **Ennistymon.** You'll also stumble across places with quirky names, like Puffing Hole, Intrinsic Bay, Chimney Hill, Elephant's Teeth, Mutton Island, and Lover's Leap.

Bunratty Castle & Folk Park ★★ HERITAGE SITE   Built in 1425 and restored in the 1950s, Bunratty is an impressive early-15th-century castle, and home to two major tourist attractions: a "living-history" re-creation of a 19th-century village, and a riotous nighttime medieval banquet. You can tour the interior of the castle, which is surprisingly complete, including a fine collection of medieval furniture and art. The restored walled garden is a beautiful place to wander around. However, the folk

In the evening, a medieval banquet takes over the Great Hall of Bunratty Castle.

park is probably the bigger draw here. Actors in period costume wander around as you walk through the authentic-looking village center, complete with everything from a post office and schoolroom to a doctor's office. You can go inside each and chat with the occupants. Meanwhile, professional craftspeople work their trades, using traditional methods. There's even a Victorian-style pub. It's all great fun, and a brilliant way to imbue kids with a sense of history. In the evenings, the medieval banquet takes over the castle's Great Hall. After a full, sit-down meal, actors and musicians in medieval garb put on a lively show of music, dancing, and folk stories. The banquet has two sittings nightly, at 5:30 and 8:45pm. Booking is essential.

Signposted from N18 (Shannon-Limerick Rd.), Bunratty, Co. Clare. www.shannon heritage.com. © **061/360-788.** Admission €11.55 adults; €10.50 seniors and students; €10 children 6–16; children 5 and under free; €30 families. Medieval banquet: €58 adults; €38 children 10–12; €24 children 6–9; free for children 5 and under. Castle: Daily 9am–5:30pm. Last admission to castle 1½ hr. before closing; last admission to park 45 min. before closing.

Bunratty Winery ★ WINERY/FACTORY TOUR   In a coach house dating from 1816, this winery produces traditional medieval wines, including mead—a drink made from honey, fermented grape juice, water, matured spirits, and herbs, a historical favorite of the upper classes. The winery is also one of only a couple of distilleries officially licensed to brew Irish potcheen, a heady potato whiskey that was so popular and pernicious it was banned in 1661, and only made legal again in 1997. Most of the products are made for Bunratty Castle's medieval-style banquets, but visitors to the working winery are welcome to watch the production in progress and taste the brew.

Next to Bunratty Castle, Bunratty, Co. Clare. www.bunrattymead.net. © **061/362-222.** Free admission. Mon–Fri 9:30am–5:30pm.

Cliffs of Moher ★★ NATURAL SITE   The cries of nesting seabirds are faintly audible amid the roar of the Atlantic crashing against the base of these breathtaking cliffs. Undulating for 8km (5 miles) along the coast, the cliffs tower as high as 214m (702 ft.) over the sea. In bad weather, access is (understandably) limited—the wind can blow very hard here. When the weather is fine, a guardrail offers you a small sense of security as you peek over the edge. (Some foolhardy visitors always insist on climbing over it for a better view of the sheer drop—needless to say, this is against the rules and very dangerous.) On a clear day, you can see the Aran Islands in Galway Bay as misty shapes in the distance. Look the other way, however, and you'll see a constant throng of tour groups, coaches, and cars. The enormous visitor center houses gift shops, a high-tech "Cliffs of Moher Experience," and various other exhibits that feel designed to wring every last euro out of this natural wonder. Furthermore, the visitor center has the only (legal) parking, which you can't use without buying entry tickets to the visitor center—effectively turning it into a steep *per person* parking charge. (You may see places beside the narrow road where you could illegally park and walk straight up to the cliffs without paying a cent, but we can't recommend that.) Because of the overwhelming popularity of the cliffs, in the summer it can be very crowded. In July and August, the cliffs stay open until 9pm, and arriving very late in the day is a good way to see the view more quietly. Head up the path beside the visitor center to **O'Brien's Tower** for the best view

The Cliffs of Moher, a perennial tourist attraction.

of the cliffs. The 19th-century tower is a knockout spot for photos, although—surprise!—you'll have to pay an extra €2 to climb the stairs. The crass commercialization cannot completely detract from the beauty of these cliffs, but it is discouraging to see.

Nr. Liscannor, Co. Clare. www.cliffsofmoher.ie. ℃ **065/708-6141.** Admission €6 adults; €4.50 disabled, seniors and students; free for children 15 and under. Price includes parking and visitor center admission. May–Aug daily 8am–9pm; Mar–Apr and Sept–Oct daily 8am–7pm; Nov–Feb daily 9am–5pm. Tower and cliffs may be inaccessible in bad weather.

Craggaunowen ★★ HERITAGE SITE Following the successful castle-plus-open-air-museum template of **Bunratty Castle** (p. 339), Craggaunowen focuses on what life would have been like for the Bronze Age inhabitants of Ireland. A reconstructed "crannog" shows how Celts lived, worked, and defended themselves from the Iron Age right through to the middle of the first millennium. (Records indicate, in fact, that scattered communities lived like this as late as the 1600s.) Other reconstructions to explore here include a 4th-century ring fort and underground passages known as souterrains, thought to have been used for cool storage. (Incidentally, some archaeologists believe there are real souterrains at **Caherconnell Stone Fort**—see p. 337—that have yet to be excavated.) Costumed historian-guides provide demonstrations of the techniques inhabitants of such settlements would have used to cook, build, weave, and so on. Also on display is the Brendan Boat, a replica vessel of the kind Vikings are believed to have sailed to America; it was built in 1976 by explorer Tim Severin, who used it to do just that—a 4,500-mile journey that took him and his crew just over a year. The

Costumed historians illuminate the life of Bronze Age Celts at Craggaunowen.

16th-century **Craggaunowen Castle** is also on the grounds (included in the price).

Kilmurray, near Quin, Co. Clare. www.heritageisland.com. © **061/360788.** Admission €8.50 adults; €7.55 seniors; €5 children 6–16; free for children under 6; €25–€26 families. Easter to mid-Sept daily 10am–5pm. Last admission 1 hr. before closing. Closed mid-Sept to Easter.

Doolin ★★ VILLAGE   Doolin's old pubs and restaurants ring with the sound of fiddle and accordion all year long, earning this secluded fishing village a reputation as the unofficial capital of Irish traditional music. Most famous among them is **Gus O'Connor's Pub** (Fisher St.; www. gusoconnorsdoolin.com; © 065/707-4168), set among a row of thatched fisherman's cottages, about a 10-minute walk from the seafront. Great though the craic is here, the pub's fame inevitably draws crowds, and it can get packed to the rafters on a busy night. If you're looking for something a little more authentic, head up the road to **McGann's** (Main St.; www.mcgannspubdoolin.com; © 065/707-4133); it's less well-known and not so unrelentingly jammed as Gus O'Connor's. In fact, on many nights, there are no locals in Gus's at all—they're all here, downing pints of Guinness and listening to the fiddles. Feel free to join them. Doolin is on R479, about 7.8km (4¾ miles) west of Lisdoonvarna.

Tourist Information Point: at the Hotel Doolin, Fitz's Cross, Doolin, Co. Clare. © **065/ 707-5649.**

Ennis Friary ★ RELIGIOUS SITE/RUINS When you walk around what's left of Ennis Friary, it can be hard to get a sense of its original scale. Records show, however, that in 1375 it was the home and work-place for no less than 350 friars and 600 students. Founded in 1241, this Franciscan abbey was a famous seat of learning in medieval times, mak-ing Ennis a focal point of Western Europe for many years. It was finally forced to close in 1692, and thereafter fell into ruin, but it's been partly restored, and contains many beautifully sculpted medieval tombs, decora-tive fragments, and carvings, including the famous McMahon tomb, with its striking representations of the Passion. The nave and chancel are the oldest parts of the friary, but other structures, such as the 15th-century tower, transept, and sacristy, are also rich in architectural detail.

Abbey St., Ennis, Co. Clare. www.heritageireland.ie. © **065/682-9100.** Admission €5 adults; €4 seniors; €3 children and students; €13 families. Easter–Sept daily 10am–6pm; Oct daily 10am–5pm. Last admission 45 min. before closing.

Knappogue Castle ★★ CASTLE Midway between Bunratty and Ennis, this regal castle was built in 1467 as the home of the MacNamara clan—who, along with the O'Briens, dominated the area for more than 1,000 years. Oliver Cromwell used the castle as a base in the mid–17th century while pillaging the countryside, which is why, unlike many cas-tles, it was largely left intact. The original Norman structure also has elab-orate late-Georgian and Regency wings, added in the early and mid–19th century. Later, in the 20th century, it fell into disrepair, but was rescued by Texan Mark Edwin Andrews (1903–92), a former U.S. Assistant Secre-tary of the Navy. He and his wife, Lavone, an architect, worked closely with area historical societies and returned the castle to its former glory, even furnishing it with 15th-century furniture. The Andrews family then turned Knappogue over to the Irish people. The peaceful walled gardens have been meticulously restored to their Victorian condition—look for the wonderful statue of Bacchus. The gardens supply herbs for the **medieval banquets,** held nightly at 6:30pm from April to October. Tickets cost €50 adults, €33 children 10 to 12, €22 children 6 to 9 (free for children under 6). Reservations are essential. At present the banquets are the only way to see inside the castle, although it's hoped that daytime tours may resume in the future.

Quin, Co. Clare. www.shannonheritage.com. © **061/360-788.** Admission €7 adults; €4 seniors; children 5–16; free for children 4 and under; €17–€20 families.

Scattery Island ★ ISLAND/RUINS Atmospheric monastic ruins dating from the 6th century perch upon this unspoiled island in the Shan-non Estuary near Kilrush, on Clare's south coast. A high, round tower and several churches are all that remain of an extensive settlement founded by St. Senan. To visit the island, ask at the Kilrush information center, just past the pier, or just speak to one of the boat operators who arrange

20-minute ferry rides from the Kilrush marina. Frequency depends on demand; even in summer there may be only one trip per day.

Information center: Merchants Quay, Kilrush, Co. Clare. ☎ **065/682-9100.** Free admission. Ferry prices vary; usually around €10–€20 round-trip.

Where to Stay in County Clare

County Clare contains the most unique and special places to stay in the region. That said, it's perhaps a little surprising that there aren't more of them. Fortunately, there are some real gems among their number.

Aran View Country House ★★   The clue's in the name at this small and friendly hotel in Doolin: The house has a glorious view across 100 acres of rolling green farmland and icy blue sea, out to the fog-wreathed Aran Islands in the distance. The Georgian country house was built in the mid–18th century and later expanded, and its good-size guest rooms maintain a traditional feel. The lounge wisely takes full advantage of the amazing view out front, making this a lovely spot for an early evening pint as the sun goes down. Breakfasts are good and fresh in the beautiful, vaulted-ceiling dining room. Doolin is about a 10-minute drive up the coast from the Cliffs of Moher.

Coast Rd., Doolin, Co. Clare. www.aranview.com. ☎ **065/707-4061.** 13 units. €105–€130 double. Free parking. Breakfast included. **Amenities:** Restaurant; bar; Wi-Fi (free). Closed Oct–Easter.

Fergus View ★★   More breathtaking views are to be had at this sweet B&B near Corofin, one of the gateways to the Burren. You could sit for ages marveling at the long vista of rolling fields and rambling hills, joined by the wonderful owner, Mary, as she brings you a fortifying tray of tea to sip by the open fire. Mary is also an expert on the Burren and all this area has to offer visitors, and will happily share her encyclopedic knowledge. Guest rooms are small and simple, but the beds are comfortable. On the grounds is a self-catering lodge that sleeps five. Fergus View is closed from November to Easter.

On R476 in Kilnaboy, 3.2km (2 miles) N of Corofin, Co. Clare. www.fergusview.com. ☎ **065/683-7606.** 6 units. €78 double. Discounts for 2 nights or more. Free parking. Breakfast included. **Amenities:** Wi-Fi (free). Closed Nov–Easter.

Gregans Castle Hotel ★★★   An elegant 18th-century house in an extraordinary setting, Gregans is not in fact even remotely castle-like, but don't let that bother you. This unique property is one of the most peaceful hotels in Ireland. Manager Simon Haden is the second generation of hoteliers in his family to run the place, although it's been a hotel for much longer—famous guests of the 20th century included J. R. R. Tolkien, who was apparently so inspired by the otherworldly views of the surrounding Burren that he drew on them to describe Mordor in *The Lord of the Rings*. Guest rooms are design-magazine chic, with modern furnishings and bay

If you've been looking for love in all the wrong places, clearly you've never been to Lisdoonvarna. This County Clare town lives for l'amour.

There's a Matchmaker Pub on the main street (inside the Imperial Hotel); two local residents call themselves professional matchmakers (Willie Daly, a horse dealer, and James White, an hotelier); and every autumn, the town hosts the month-long **Lisdoonvarna Matchmaking Festival** (www.matchmaker ireland.com). Thousands of lovelorn singletons come in search of The One, and locals cheer them on. Up and down each street, every atmospheric corner is used for mixers and minglers. Residents stir the pot by hosting romantic breakfasts, dinners, games, and dances. So good are their intentions and so charming is their belief in true love—in the idea that there really is somebody out there for everybody, and that they might find each other in a far-flung corner of western Ireland—that you too may fall for it.

windows. Televisions are banned in the hotel, to enable guests to get maximum benefit from the tranquil surroundings. Even if you can't stretch to the cost of a night here, consider booking a table in the superb restaurant, **Gregans Castle ★★★** (see p. 346). Chef Robbie McCauley's modern Irish cooking is utterly superlative—though if you don't want to splurge, the excellent bar menu is much cheaper. Check the website for some attractive dinner-bed-and-breakfast packages and midweek deals.

Ballyvaughan, Co. Clare. www.gregans.ie. ℂ **065/707-7005.** 22 units. €235–€255 double, €350–€455 suite. Free parking. Breakfast included. **Amenities:** Restaurant; bar; Wi-Fi (free).

Moy House ★★★ An extraordinary tower house built in the 19th century, overlooking the crashing waves of the Atlantic Ocean, Moy House is a unique place. You can climb the four-story central tower for the best view out to sea, although the vistas from some of the guest rooms are almost as good, with acres of green fields leading across to the deep blue sea. Rooms are designed in a muted, contemporary style, with large beds and modern bathrooms. In what has to be a one-of-a-kind feature, one bathroom even has an original, glass-covered well. You can walk down to the beach for a stroll along the dramatic shoreline, or relax in the drawing room—the house is packed with bookshelves from which you can borrow. The restaurant is excellent, with a very strong emphasis on seasonal produce, but it's definitely not cheap at €75 per person for a five-course fixed-price menu. Check the website for good deals, including dinner-bed-and-breakfast packages.

On N67, 1.6km (1 mile) S of Lahinch, Co. Clare. ℂ **065/708-2800.** www.moyhouse. com. 9 units. €185–€200 double, €320–€395 suite. Free parking. Breakfast included. **Amenities:** Restaurant; Internet in public rooms.

9

THE BURREN & BEYOND: CLARE, LIMERICK & TIPPERARY

County Clare

Where to Eat in County Clare

Barrtra Seafood Restaurant ★ SEAFOOD   A friendly, family-run place with a good lineup of simple, tasty seafood, this restaurant looks out over Liscannor Bay. Just look at a map and you'll quickly see why that makes this such a lovely spot in the late evening—the sun sets over the sea on a virtually direct line to the dining room. You can order à la carte, or opt for the surprise menu. You decide whether you want fish, meat, vegetarian, or a mixture and specify anything you *don't* want (or can't eat), and the chef prepares a five-course dinner for your table. Otherwise, your à la carte choices might include oysters or fisherman's broth, perhaps, followed by a juicy steak or almond-encrusted cod with an orange and ginger sauce. Call ahead to check opening times outside the summer season.

Miltown Malbay Rd., Lahinch, Co. Clare. www.barrtra.com. © **065/708-1280.** Five-course menus €32–€37. Mar–Apr and Oct–Dec Fri–Sat 5:30–9pm, Sun noon–7pm; May–Sept Wed–Sat 5:30–9pm, Sun noon–7pm; July–Aug lunch 12:30–4:30pm. Closed Jan–Feb.

Durty Nelly's ★ IRISH/PUB FOOD   You don't walk into a pub called Durty Nelly's expecting haute cuisine, but some welcome surprises are to be found here. It serves appetizing pub food—fish and chips, steak sandwiches, burgers, and salads. Those who don't mind a bit of cheesy tourist novelty can have their picture taken while pouring their own pint of Guinness. Durty Nelly's actually has three dining rooms—the main pub area, the more refined Oyster Restaurant, and the Loft. The latter two offer an upscale version of the same food (good steaks, Thai curries, fresh seafood, and so on). And if you're wondering about the name, "Durty Nelly" was a somewhat ribald heroine of Irish folklore, said to have invented the magical cure-all (and highly alcoholic) variety of moonshine, potcheen (see p. 398).

Next to Bunratty Castle, Bunratty, Co. Clare. www.durtynellys.ie. © **061/364-861.** Pub: Entrees €12–€26. Daily noon–10pm. Oyster Restaurant: Entrees €14–€29. Daily noon–10pm. The Loft: Entrees €14–€29. Daily 5:30–10pm.

Gregans Castle ★★★ MODERN IRISH   Robbie McCauley is the new head chef at the exceptional in-house restaurant of the Gregans Castle Hotel ★★★ in Ballyvaughan (see p. 344). He continues the restaurant's tradition of creating exquisite menus that are easily the equal of top-level restaurants in major cities. The six-course tasting menu forms the entirety of the dinner service, although a casual (and slightly cheaper) dinner menu is available in the **Corkscrew Bar** until 9pm on Monday and Thursday. A typical meal might start with a few expertly prepared canapés, followed by scallops with grapes and hazelnuts, monkfish with brown butter and sea lettuce, or perhaps a beef filet with artichokes and *bordelaise jus*. Desserts, such as the dark chocolate peanut pavé, are sumptuous. If you love Gregans so much that you don't want to leave (and that would be perfectly understandable), rooms start at around €235 per night during high season.

Ballyvaughan, Co. Clare. www.gregans.ie. ℭ **065/707-7005.** Fixed-price menu €70. Tues–Wed and Fri–Sun 6–9pm. Mon and Thurs bar food only 6–9pm. Closed Dec–Jan. Children under 7 only allowed at 6pm sharp.

Vaughan's Anchor Inn ★★ SEAFOOD   A 10-minute drive from the Cliffs of Moher, this excellent pub specializes in topnotch seafood. If you've really worked up an appetite, or possibly have been locked in a room without food for a month, go straight for the gigantic platter of local seafood. Otherwise, just go for the plate of meltingly fresh crab claws with garlic butter, or the traditional fish and chips. A couple of meaty choices are always on the menu, too. At lunchtime you'll find a few sandwiches and nibbles alongside the heartier options. Vaughan's Anchor Inn is on the main street in Liscannor; look for the long white building with the small parking lot on the right, not long after you round the bend and see the small town center ahead of you.

Main St., Liscannor, Co. Clare. www.vaughans.ie. ℭ **065/708-1548.** Entrees €18–€26. Daily 12:30–9pm.

Sports & Outdoor Pursuits in County Clare

BIRD-WATCHING   The **Bridges of Ross,** on the north side of **Loop Head,** is one of the prime autumn bird-watching sites in Ireland, especially during northwest gales, when several rare species have been seen with some consistency. The **lighthouse** at the tip of the head is also a popular spot for watching seabirds.

DOLPHIN-WATCHING   The **Shannon Estuary** is home to about 70 bottlenose dolphins, one of four such resident groups of dolphins in Europe. **Dolphinwatch** (www.dolphinwatch.ie; ℭ **065/905-8156**) runs 2- to 3-hour cruises costing €35 adults, €20 children 15 and under. Advance booking is essential.

GOLF   One of the region's most famous golf courses is at **Lahinch Golf Club,** Lahinch (www.lahinchgolf.com; ℭ **065/708-1003**). Of its two 18-hole links courses, the "Old Course"—the longer championship links

---

The Mass Hole

To say golf is a religious experience in Ireland wouldn't just be hyperbole. Only in Ireland can you experience the unique hazard of the "Mass hole." When the celebration of Mass was outlawed during penal times, secret Masses were often held in hidden dales, culverts, and gorges, out of sight of the British. A few golf links have incorporated such places into their courses. For example, hole 5 at the **Lahinch Golf Course** (above) has a uniquely hidden spot that could easily have served this purpose. Another example is at **Waterville Golf Course** in County Kerry (see p. 299), where the 12th hole is still universally known as the Mass Hole.

Students wait for a break at the Lahinch Surf School.

course—is the one that has given Lahinch its worldwide repute. This course's elevations, especially at the 9th and 13th holes, make for great views, but it also makes wind an integral part of play. Watch the goats, Lahinch's legendary weather forecasters: If they huddle by the clubhouse, it means a storm is approaching. Visitors are welcome to play, especially on weekdays; greens fees are €110 to €210 for the Old Course and a more affordable €25 to €35 for the newer Castle Course.

SURFING   If you've always wanted to try surfing, here's your chance: **Lahinch Surf School** (www.lahinchsurfschool.com; © **087/960-9667**), set up in a hut on Lahinch promenade, specializes in getting people suited up and out on the waves—whether you surf every weekend or have never hit a board in your life. They're friendly and know their stuff. Wetsuits and surfboards are included with the lessons. Average water temps in late summer are 16° C (60.8° F)—so wetsuits are advised for the length of time you're in the water. Private lessons cost around €90 to €120, depending on the time of year; group lessons are around €40. A family of two adults and two kids pay €120 (€25 per extra child) for one 2-hour lesson.

COUNTY LIMERICK

The majority of County Limerick is peaceful, pleasant farmland. The picture-postcard village of **Adare** is definitely worth a visit (although you'll likely see it amidst a row of tourist buses), and the number of good restaurants and hotels nearby make it a good choice for an overnight base.

Lough Gur is also well worth a visit, with its lovely lakeside scenery and intriguing ancient sites. The same cannot quite be said of **Limerick City** (see box p. 350); despite the valiant efforts of the Tourist Board to shake up its image, the city is a rather gritty, unpleasant place. Things have improved over the last decade, most notably with the successful redevelopment of the visitor center at **King John's Castle,** but unless you're really trying to take in everything this island has to offer, County Limerick has better things to see than its eponymous city.

Visitor Information

The **Limerick Tourist Information Centre** on Arthur's Quay, Limerick (© **061/317522**) is open Monday to Friday 9am to 5pm; in summer it's also often open weekends (call for hours). Another office inside the **Adare Heritage Centre,** Main St., Adare (www.adareheritagecentre.ie; © **061/396-255**) is open daily year-round from 9am to 6pm.

Exploring County Limerick

Adare ★★ VILLAGE   Looking like a village plucked from a book of fairy tales, Adare has thatched cottages, black-and-white timbered houses, lichen-covered churches, and romantic ruins, all strewn along the banks of the River Maigue. Unfortunately, all of this means that Adare has been seriously discovered by the tour-bus crowds—even by May, which is still officially off-season, the roads can get clogged at times—but it's absolutely worth a stop nonetheless. Drop in at the **Adare Heritage Centre** on Main Street, roughly in the middle of the village. Part visitor center, part museum on the history of the town, it also has a small craft store and a shop selling Irish woollens. From June to September the center also runs bus tours to Desmond Castle (see p. 263), costing €9 adults; €7 seniors, students and children; and €20 families.

Adare Heritage Centre, Main St., Adare, Co. Limerick. www.adareheritagecentre. ie. © **061/396-666.** Free admission. Daily 9am–5pm.

Foynes Flying Boat Museum ★★ MUSEUM   When Shannon Airport was just a remote patch of undeveloped farmland, this was the center of international aviation in Europe. The first commercial flight

Thatched cottages in the picture-postcard town of Adare.

LIMERICK CITY: worth a visit?

It is synonymous the world over with a type of lively, often lewd verse, but spend much time in Limerick's eponymous capital and you might find yourself making up a few off-color rhymes of your own. With a population of 100,000, it's the Irish Republic's third-largest city (only Dublin and Cork are bigger), with a gritty, urban feel usually associated with much bigger cities. A low point for Limerick came in the late 2000s, when it suffered the ignominy of being named the murder capital of Europe (while the same report declared Ireland to be Europe's safest country overall). Hardly a slogan to put on the welcome sign! Further notoriety came in the early 2010s, when Limerick became the backdrop for a notorious, ongoing feud between criminal gangs.

That said, there have been genuine efforts to make things better. The tourist board is doing its part to clean the place up, with a certain amount of success. A prime example is **King John's Castle** ★ (Nicholas St.; www.shannonheritage.com; ✆ **061/360788**). This stern riverside fortress, dating from 1210, is the centerpiece of Limerick's historic area. But rarely has a historic building been so poorly treated in the modern age; during the 1950s, in an astonishing act of government vandalism, it even had a public housing project built within its central courtyard. Thankfully that's long gone, but the big, modern visitor center

building that's risen in its place still rather spoils the effect. However, a recent renovation has greatly improved the visitor facilities, including high-tech interactive displays. Admission costs €10.50 adults, €9.50 seniors, students and children 6 to 16 (free for children under 6), €23 to €27 families. It's open April to September from 9:30am to 6pm, and October to March from 9:30am to 5pm (last admission 1 hr. before closing).

Located in an 18th-century Customs building with a fine Palladian front, the **Hunt Museum** ★★ (Rutland St.; www.huntmuseum.com; ✆ **061/312833**) has exhibits on ancient Greece and Rome and paintings by Picasso and Renoir. Admission costs €6 adults, €4 seniors and students, €3 children, and €14 families. It's open Monday to Saturday from 10am to 5pm, Sunday and public holidays from 2 to 5pm. For more modern art, try the **Limerick City Gallery of Art** ★ (People's Park at corner of Perry Square and Mallow St.; www.gallery.limerick.ie; ✆ **061/310633**). Besides regularly changing contemporary art exhibitions, the gallery's permanent collection includes work by Irish painters Jack B. Yeats and Sir John Lavery. It's open Monday to Saturday 10am to 5:30pm (until 8pm on Thurs), Sunday noon to 5:30pm (closed on public holidays). Admission is free.

from the U.S. to Europe touched down at Foynes Airport, one hot July morning in 1937. Five years later, this became one end of the first-ever regular service between the two continents. (In the same year, Foynes was also the birthplace of the Irish coffee: After a particularly violent storm turned back a New York–bound flight, the bartender was asked to serve something that would both warm up and calm down the rattled passengers—so he served hot coffee and threw shots of whiskey in for good measure.) At this engaging museum, you can see a replica of the original Pan Am "flying boat," which may make you swear never to complain about a modern flight again. You can also tour the actual terminal building, kept as it was when the airport closed in 1945.

Foynes, Co. Limerick. www.flyingboatmuseum.com. © **069/65416.** Admission €11 adults; €9 seniors and students; €6 children 5–13; free for children under 5; €28 families. Daily June–Sept 9:30am–6pm; mid-Mar to May 9:30am–5pm; Oct to mid-Nov 9:30am–5pm. Last admission 1 hr. before closing. Closed mid-Nov to mid-Mar.

Lough Gur ★★ LAKE/ANCIENT SITES Occupied continuously from the Neolithic period to late medieval times, this lovely lake's shores hold an unusual preponderance of ancient sites, most of which are well-signposted on the R512, the drive that skirts around the lake's edge. Archaeologists have uncovered foundations of a small farmstead built around the year 900; a lake island dwelling built between 500 and 1000; a wedge-shaped tomb that was a communal grave around 2,500 B.C.; and the extraordinary Grange Stone Circle, a 4,000-year-old site with 113 upright stones forming the largest prehistoric stone circle in Ireland. An interesting Heritage Centre helps put it all into context, with exhibits explaining why Neolithic people chose this area to settle. To find the center, turn east off R512 at Reardons Pub in Holycross, take the first left afterward, and follow Lough Gur Road. The lake itself is a great place to explore and have a picnic.

11km (6¾ miles) SE of Limerick City on R512, Lough Gur, Co. Limerick. www. loughgur.com. © **061/385186.** Free access to Lough Gur itself; Heritage Centre €5 adults; €4 seniors and students; €3 children; €15 families. Heritage Centre Mar–late Oct Mon–Fri 10am–5pm, Sat–Sun and public holidays noon–6pm. Late Oct–late Feb Mon–Fri 10am–4pm, Sat–Sun and public holidays noon–4pm.

Where to Stay in County Limerick

Limerick City's economic growth spurt in the 1990s and early 2000s led to the construction of several large, impersonal chain hotels there. But why would you bother? The real finds are in the rural parts of County Limerick, where you can hide away in a lovely old cottage on a tranquil farm, or splurge on a night in a grand country-house retreat.

Adare Manor ★★★ Surrounded by a whopping 340 hectares (840 acres) of landscaped grounds, on the very edge of charming Adare village, this luxurious resort looks impressively Victorian Gothic from the outside. Indoors, the beautifully restored and converted manor house is mostly 19th century, although check out the elaborately carved 15th-century doors on the ground floor. The place looks even more spruce now after a 2017 renovation, which also added a whole new wing, expertly crafted to match the style of the original building, while nearly doubling the number of guest rooms. For decades Adare Manor has been renowned as a golf destination, and now the fully redesigned course has been elevated to championship standard. Archery, clay pigeon shooting, and horseback riding can all be easily arranged. The hotel has three restaurants, including the fantastic **Oak Room** ★★★—one of the best in the region (see p. 354).

Adare, Co. Limerick. www.adaremanor.com. ℰ **061/605200.** 62 units. €595–€700 double; €600–€800 villa. 2-night minimum stay in villas. Free parking. Breakfast included. **Amenities:** 2 restaurants; bar; gym; golf course; pool; room service; spa; Wi-Fi (free).

Courtyard Cottage ★   A former cowshed may not sound like the height of glamour, but this is a beautifully converted, elegant space, a short drive east of Foynes. You really feel away from the herd (no pun intended), with 202 hectares (500 acres) of farmland between you and civilization. And what could be more civilized than going up to the manor house, where the charming owner and family resides, for dinner—or even having it brought to your door if you prefer? (€25; or fend for yourself in the cottage's own kitchen). You can rent this place as a fully self-catering option, or as a B&B, with tasty Irish breakfasts cooked every morning up at the house.

Askeaton, Co. Limerick. ℰ **061/392112** or 087/213-3698. 2 units. €100–€160 per night B&B; €550–€650 per week self-catering. 2-night minimum stay in summer. Free parking. Breakfast included in B&B rate. **Amenities:** Dinner on request (notice required); kitchen; tennis court; no Wi-Fi.

Echo Lodge ★★   This place was once a convent before being converted into a chic and stylish hotel. Guest rooms are relatively small but elegantly decorated with vintage-print wallpapers, tasteful color schemes, flowing curtains, and pleasantly eccentric objets d'art such as mini-Ionic columns for bedside tables. The **Mustard Seed** ★★★ restaurant is one of

Adare Manor Castle Hotel, Golf & Spa Resort in County Limerick.

THERE ONCE WAS A poet FROM LIMERICK...

So how exactly did a genre of bawdy pub poetry come to be associated with Limerick? The answer seems buried nearly 300 years in the past. Nobody really knows who wrote the first sharply worded, five-line poem, but the format became popular in the 18th century, thanks to a group of poets who lived in the town of Croom in County Limerick. Known as the *Fili na Maighe*, or the "Gaelic poets of the Maigue," the poets wrote sardonic, quick-witted poems in Irish that soon became all the rage. Their style was adopted across the region, and within a century, everybody was doing it. Anthologies on the subject list 42 poets and Irish scholars in the county in the 19th century, whose limerick-style compositions covered a range of topics: romance, drinking, personal squabbles, and politics.

But it's possible that the scathing, satiric limerick style we know today rose from an 18th-century battle of wills between poet and pub owner Sean O'Tuama and his boyhood friend Andrias MacCraith. O'Tuama and MacCraith grew up in County Limerick, but after a spectacular falling-out (nobody quite remembers over what), they vented their wit in a series of castigating verses about each other. These became enormously popular, thus birthing the modern limerick. In retrospect, they're kind of cute, although the meter sometimes feels a little stretched. As MacCraith once wrote:

O'Tuama! You boast yourself handy,
At selling good ale and bright brandy
But the fact is your liquor
Makes everyone sicker,
I tell you this, I, your good friend, Andy.

the best in the region (see p. 354). There's usually a good handful of special offers on the website, including dinner-bed-and-breakfast packages. Ballingarry, Co. Limerick (13km/8 miles south of Adare). www.mustardseed.ie. ✆ **069/68508.** 76 units. €69–€115 double, €160 suite. Free parking. Breakfast included. **Amenities:** Restaurant; bar; room service; Wi-Fi (free in public areas only).

Fitzgerald's Woodlands House Hotel ★★ The rooms at this pleasant, modern hotel aren't particularly fancy, but they're enormous—rare for a place that charges just a little more than €100 a night. The hotel makes a big deal out of how good its beds are, thanks to a full 10cm (4 in.) down mattress topper on each of the beds. The in-house **Revas Spa** offers relaxation treatments and a thermal suite to while away the last hint of travel fatigue; you can book couples' packages that include massages and afternoon tea for two for around €280. Deals are also available that include dinner-bed-and-breakfast packages and senior discounts. Adare, Co. Limerick. www.woodlands-hotel.ie. ✆ **061/605100.** 94 units. €110–€170 double, €280–€400 suite. Free parking. Breakfast included. **Amenities:** Restaurant; bar; room service; spa; Wi-Fi (free).

Where to Eat in County Limerick

Dutifully demolishing the rule that the best restaurants are usually found in cities, the rural byways of County Limerick contain several places to eat that would be serious contenders on any "best of" lists for the whole of Ireland.

Foley's at the Pike ★ PUB FOOD/GRILL   Nearly 16km (9 miles) southwest of Adare, just off the main N21 road, this friendly little bar and grill focuses on hearty, unpretentious comfort food, such as steaks, seafood chowder, or maybe a sizzling filet of rainbow trout with lemon and sea salt. Foley's sometimes hosts live music in the evening, though it's more of the local rock band variety than flutes and fiddles. Heading west from Adare on N21, take the R523 turnoff signposted for Athea.

Reens Pike, Ardagh, Co. Limerick. www.foleyspub.ie. ✆ **069/64416.** Entrees €12–€20. Daily noon–9pm.

Mortells ★★ SEAFOOD/DELI   This great little deli restaurant is an excellent lunch option if you're in Limerick City and in need of sustenance. The seafood (much of it local) is beautifully prepared, and cooked right in front of your eyes. There's always a choice of different catches of the day, although you could also opt for a burger or simply a cup of coffee and a sandwich. The lively, chatty staff keeps everything running smoothly.

49 Roaches St., Limerick, Co. Limerick. www.mortellcatering.com. ✆ **061/415457.** Lunch entrees €5–€14. Mon–Sat 8:30am–4:30pm.

The Mustard Seed ★★★ MODERN EUROPEAN   The in-house restaurant of the excellent **Echo Lodge** ★★ (p. 352) is one of the best-loved, and most widely known, in the region. The restaurant's own kitchen garden supplies many of the ingredients. The four-course menus are imaginative and scintillating; after a starter of crab with lemon verbena, you could go for filet of seabass with mussel broth, or ravioli served with a butternut-squash velouté sauce. An eight-course tasting menu is €75; or come before 7:30pm any night except Saturday for the Twilight Dinner, a slightly pared-down version of the main menu for €48. Dinner-bed-and-breakfast deals are often offered on the website.

Echo Lodge hotel, Ballingarry, Co. Limerick (13km/8 miles S of Adare). www.mustardseed.ie. ✆ **069/68508.** Fixed-price four-course dinner €62. Daily 7–9:30pm.

The Oak Room ★★ MODERN IRISH   Another superb hotel restaurant, the Oak Room is part of **Adare Manor** ★★★ (see p. 351). The high stone windows and silver candelabra of the dining room should leave little doubt that this is a place where you're expected to sit up straight—gentlemen, a tie if you please. The food certainly lives up to the elegant surrounds; the five-course set menu may include Dexter beef and swede, Tipperary quail with salsify, or perhaps scallops delicately flavored with truffles. And if you're enjoying the place too much to leave at the meal's end…well, you probably should anyway, since an overnight stay here can cost about the same as your transatlantic airfare home.

Adare, Co. Limerick. www.adaremanor.com. ✆ **061/605200.** Entrees €18–€33. Daily 6–9:30pm.

IF THE story FITZ...

The Wild Geese ★★★ MODERN IRISH What is it about Adare that breeds superlative restaurants? The Wild Geese, in the center of the village, matches fresh, local ingredients with global accents. Chef David Foley constantly changes his menu, but it might include roast chicken stuffed with soft goat's cheese; or salmon rubbed with lemon and tarragon. There's also a vegetarian menu. *Tip:* Sunday lunch, which often features dishes seen on the evening menu, is significantly cheaper than dinner service, at just €24 for two courses.

Adare, Co. Limerick. www.thewild-geese.com. ℰ **061/396451.** Entrees €18–€30. Fixed-price early-bird menus €27–€30. Tues–Sat 6–9:30pm, Sun 12:30–3pm. Closed most of Jan.

Sports & Outdoor Pursuits in County Limerick

FISHING **Celtic Angling,** in Ballingarry, just south of Adare (www.celticangling.com; ℰ **069/68202**), offers daylong salmon-fishing excursions on the Shannon, including pickup from Limerick City, equipment, and licenses. A day's fishing will cost on average €180 to €300 per person, plus €50 to €100 for each additional person in a group. (Owner Paddy Dunworth also offers guided sightseeing trips and hillwalking excursions; check the website for details.)

HORSEBACK RIDING The county's fields provide good turf for horseback riding. Rates run about €25 to €30 per hour. The **Clonshire Equestrian Centre** in Adare (www.clonshire.com; ℰ **061/396770**) offers riding holidays for adults and children. It's also one of the only riding schools in Ireland to offer riding for disabled visitors.

COUNTY TIPPERARY

"It's a long way to Tipperary" as the song goes, and it can certainly feel true when you have the map spread out before you, trying to plan your itinerary. Tipperary's big attractions are few and far enough between that they don't always work conveniently as day trips. (Though the one truly essential site, the **Rock of Cashel,** can easily be worked into a road trip on the N8 between Dublin and Cork.) The relative quietness of Tipperary, however, is also part of its appeal. Far from the tour buses and the bleeping of digital camera shutters, it just may be the welcoming, unspoiled Ireland everyone is looking for.

Visitor Information

The **Clonmel Tourist Office** at 6 Sarsfield St., Clonmel (✆ **052/612-2960**) is open year-round Monday to Friday 9:30am to 1pm and 2 to 4:30pm. The small **Cashel Tourist Office** at the Heritage Centre, Main St., Cashel (✆ **062/61333**) is open 9:30am to 5:30pm daily from March to October and Monday to Friday November to February. A **seasonal office** at Castle Street, Cahir (✆ **052/714-1453**) is open April to September only, Monday to Saturday from 9:30am to 6pm.

Exploring County Tipperary

Clonmel, the capital of Tipperary, is the unassuming gateway to the region. A working town, largely unspoiled by tourism, Clonmel (whose name in Gaelic, *Cluaín Meala,* means "Meadows of Honey") makes a pleasant strategic touring base. Looking at this sleepy place on the banks of the Suir, it's hard to believe that it once withstood a Cromwellian siege for 3 brutal months.

North of Clonmel and deep in the Tipperary countryside, **Cashel,** with its monastic buildings and dramatic setting, is not to be missed. From Cahir, there's a gorgeous drive north through the Galtee Mountains to the pristine 11km (7-mile) **Glen of Aherlow,** a secluded and scenic pass between the plains of counties Tipperary and Limerick (see p. 363 for hiking and walking suggestions in this area).

Ahenny High Crosses ★ RELIGIOUS SITE   You're likely to have this little-known and rarely visited site to yourself, except for the cows whose pasture you cross to reach it. On a bright day, the setting is idyllic and gorgeous. The well-preserved Ahenny high crosses date from the 8th or 9th century. Tradition associates them with seven saintly bishops, all brothers said to have been waylaid and murdered. Their unusual stone "caps," thought by some to represent bishops' miters, more likely suggest the transition from wood crosses, which would have had small roofs to shelter them from the rain. Also note their intricate spiral and cable ornamentation in remarkably high relief, which may have been inspired by earlier Celtic metalwork.

Kil Crispeen Churchyard, Ahenny, Co. Tipperary. 8km (5 miles) N of Carrick-on-Suir, signposted off R697. Free admission (box for donations).

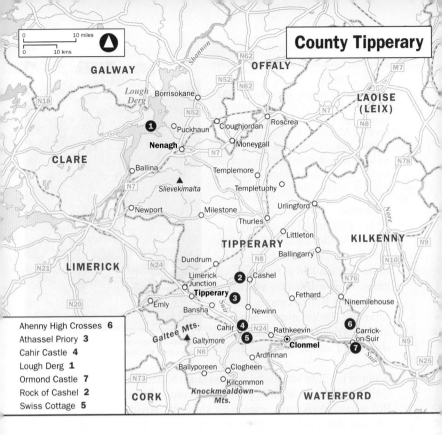

Map legend:

- GALWAY
- OFFALY
- LAOISE (LEIX)
- CLARE
- Lough Derg
- Borrisokane
- Puckhaun
- Cloughjordan
- Roscrea
- Nenagh
- Moneygall
- Ballina
- Templemore
- Slievekimalta
- Templetuohy
- Newport
- Milestone
- Urlingford
- Thurles
- KILKENNY
- Littleton
- TIPPERARY
- Ballingarry
- Dundrum
- Cashel
- LIMERICK
- Limerick Junction
- Tipperary
- Fethard
- Ninemilehouse
- Emly
- Bansha
- Newinn
- Galtee Mts.
- Cahir
- Rathkeevin
- Carrick-on-Suir
- Galtymore
- Clonmel
- Ardfinnan
- Ballyporeen
- Clogheen
- Kilcommon
- CORK
- Knockmealdown Mts.
- WATERFORD

Athassel Priory ★ RELIGIOUS SITE/RUINS   Many delightful details still remain from the original medieval priory that once stood here. An Augustinian priory, founded in the late 12th century, it was once elaborately decorated. The main approach is over a low stone bridge and through a gatehouse. The church entrance is a beautifully carved doorway at the west end, while to the south of the church you can see the graceful arches of the cloister, eroded by time. Look for a carved face protruding from the southwest corner of the chapel tower, about 9m (30 ft.) above ground level.

3km (2 miles) S of Golden, Co. Tipperary. Take signposted road from Golden, on the N74; the priory is in a field just east of the road.

Cahir Castle ★★ CASTLE   On a rock in the middle of the River Suir, this remarkably complete medieval fortress can trace its history from the 3rd century, when a fort was first built on the rock—hence the town's Gaelic name, "City of the Fishing Fort." The present structure, which belonged to the Butler family for 600 years (1375–1961), is Norman. It has a massive keep, high walls, spacious courtyards, original gateways with a portcullis still intact, and a fully restored great hall. The interpretive center offers an engaging 20-minute video introduction to the

357

region's major historic sites, and you can take a guided tour of the castle grounds.

Castle St., Cahir, Co. Tipperary. © **052/744-1011.** Admission €5 adults; €4 seniors; €3 students and children; €13 families. Mid-June to Aug daily 9am–6:30pm; Mar to mid-June and Sept to mid-Oct daily 9:30am–5:30pm; mid-Oct to Feb daily 9:30am–4:30pm. Last admission 1 hr. before closing.

Ormond Castle ★★ CASTLE

This mid-15th-century castle built by Sir Edward MacRichard Butler on a strategic bend of the River Suir has laid in ruins for centuries. What still stands, attached to the ancient battlements, is the last surviving Tudor manor house in Ireland. Trusting that "if he built it, she would come," Thomas Butler constructed an extensive manor in

The massive Norman keep of Cahir Castle towers over the River Suir.

honor of his most successful relation (and childhood friend), Queen Elizabeth I. He was to be disappointed, however—Elizabeth never did visit. But many others have, especially since the Heritage Service partially restored this impressive piece of Irish history. The manor's plasterwork, carvings, period furniture, and collection of original 17th- and 18th-century royal charters will make you glad you came, and leave you wondering why Queen Bess never did.

Signposted from the center of Carrick-on-Suir, Co. Tipperary. © **051/640787.** Admission €5 adults; €4 seniors; €3 students and children; €13 families. Late June to late Oct 10am–6pm. Closed Nov to Feb. Last admission 45 min. before closing.

The Rock of Cashel ★★★ RELIGIOUS SITE/RUINS

One of Ireland's most iconic medieval ruins, this dramatically craggy abbey atop a hill in the center of Cashel dominates views for miles around. The so-called "Rock"—an outcrop of limestone reaching some 60m (197 ft.) into the sky—tells the tales of 16 centuries. It was the seat of the kings of Munster at least as far back as 360, and it remained a royal fortress until 1101, when King Murtagh O'Brien granted it to the church. Among Cashel's many great moments was the legendary baptism of King Aengus by St. Patrick in 448. Remaining on the rock are the ruins of a two-towered chapel, a cruciform cathedral, a 28m (92-ft.) round tower, and a cluster of other medieval monuments. Inside the cathedral, extraordinary and detailed ancient carvings survive in excellent condition. The views of and from the Rock are spectacular. Guided tours are available most days;

check with the visitor center for times. Cashel is just off the N8 motorway. *Note:* The buildings here were being renovated while this book was being written. There may be limited access to the structure throughout 2018, but it is expected to remain open.

Cashel, Co. Tipperary. www.heritageireland.ie. *℗* **062/61437.** Admission €8 adults; €6 seniors; €4 children and students; €20 families. Early June to mid-Sept daily 9am–7pm; mid-Mar to early June and mid-Sept to mid-Oct daily 9am–5:30pm; mid-Oct to mid-Mar daily 9am–4:30pm; last admission 45 min. before closing.

Swiss Cottage ★ HISTORIC HOUSE   A hunting and fishing lodge for the earls of Glengall from around 1812, the Swiss Cottage is a superb example of *cottage orné:* a rustic house embodying the ideal of simplicity that so appealed to the Romantics of the early 19th century. The thatched-roof cottage has extensive timberwork, usually not seen in Ireland, and is believed to have been designed by royal architect John Nash. The interior has some of the first wallpaper commercially produced in Paris. A guided tour (the only way to see the building) lasts approximately 40 minutes.

Off Dublin-Cork Rd. (N8), Kilcommon, Cahir, Co. Tipperary. www.heritageireland.ie. *℗* **052/744-1144.** Guided tour €5 adults; €4 seniors; €3 students and children; €13 families. Early Apr–Oct daily 10am–6pm; last tour 45 min. before closing.

Where to Stay in County Tipperary

Ashley Park House ★★   The enchanting quality of this 18th-century manor-house hotel overlooking Lough Ourna is amplified by the fact that you can row out to an island on the lake and explore an overgrown ruined

The Rock of Cashel, County Tipperary's most iconic heritage site.

petticoat loose & OTHER SCENIC DIVERSIONS

Driving up from County Waterford, you might want to travel via the **Vee Gap,** an 18km-long (11-mile) road winding through the Knockmealdown Mountains from Lismore and Cappoquin in County Waterford to Clogheen in County Tipperary. It's a dramatic drive, which peaks at the Tipperary-Waterford border, where the two slopes of the pass converge to frame the patchwork fields of the Galtee Valley far below.

At this point, numerous walking trails lead to the nearby peaks and down to the mountain lake of **Petticoat Loose**—named after a, shall we say, lady of flexible morals. A more edifying local character was Samuel Grubb, who so loved these slopes that he left instructions to be buried upright overlooking them. Look for the rounded stone cairn off the road between Clogheen and the Vee Gap, where Samuel does indeed stand entombed, facing the Golden Vale of Tipperary.

The Vee Gap also has some terrific walking paths. About 2km (1¼ miles) north of R669 and R668, you reach the highest point in the gap; a parking lot is here, as well as a dirt road continuing down to a lake—**Bay Lough**—nestled into the slope below. This dirt road, once the main thoroughfare over the gap, now offers a fine walk to the shores of the lake, with outstanding views of the valley to the north. For a panoramic perspective of the region, start walking due east from the gap parking lot to the summit of **Sugarloaf Hill;** the hike is extremely steep, but well worth the effort—the views from the ridge are superb.

castle. The house is decorated with heavy references to its historic origins, with Regency-era color schemes and quality antique furniture. Fishing can be arranged on the Lough, as can horseback riding; or you could just stroll around the beautiful gardens, with their vast swathes of peaceful woodland. Four-course dinners, served in the elegant red dining room, can be arranged for around €50 per head.

Off N52, 8km (5 miles) N of Nenagh, Co. Tipperary. www.ashleypark.com. ⓒ **067/ 38223.** 5 units. €150–€160 double. Free parking. Breakfast included. **Amenities:** Dinners on request (notice required); Wi-Fi (free).

Bansha House ★ This Georgian manor house in tiny Bansha, in the shadow of the Galtee Mountains, is 18km (11 miles) southwest of Cashel. Guest rooms are simple and a bit old-fashioned—not all have private bathrooms, for instance, so make sure you ask for one if that's important—but it's cheerful, cozy, and well-run. Guests are free to wander the enormous grounds, and the owners also run a horse-breeding stable next door—ask and they'll take you to meet the occupants. A self-catering cottage on the grounds, overlooking where the horses run, sleeps up to five.

Bansha, Co. Tipperary. www.banshahouse.com. ⓒ **062/54194.** 7 units. €90 double. Free parking. Breakfast included. **Amenities:** Wi-Fi (free).

Hotel Minella ★★   The River Suir babbles along in front of this modern hotel in Clonmel, overlooked by a distant mountain range. Guest rooms are properly spacious, with large, comfortable beds and modern (if rather uninspiring) decor. Some even have their own hot tubs. The hotel has a small spa with a swimming pool, though you'll need to book ahead for treatments. If you want slightly more space, the hotel also has 10 well-equipped apartments on the grounds that can be rented on a self-catering basis. The only real downside to this place is that it's a popular venue for weddings, reunions, and parties, especially in summer.

Coleville Rd., Clonmel, Co. Tipperary. www.hotelminella.com. ✆ **052/612-2388.** 90 units. €140–€150 double. Free parking. Breakfast included. **Amenities:** Restaurant; bar; gym; pool; Wi-Fi (free).

Where to Eat in County Tipperary

The pickings are a little thin in Tipperary—it's more of a lunch-on-the-go kind of place—but it's not without interesting and unique dining options of its own.

Befani's ★ MEDITERRANEAN/TAPAS   This cheerful little restaurant in Clonmel is a pleasant surprise in a region where Irish cooking is king. The tapas lunch menu is short but satisfying, with a couple of nods to exotic flavors (Thai prawns with lemongrass and chili tempura, for instance). In the evening, entrees combine Irish and Mediterranean flavors, such as hake filet with pasta *al Nero di Seppia* (a sauce made with squid ink), and seared scallops with black pudding and fig jam. Befani's also has simple guest rooms available for €75 per night, including breakfast.

6 Sarsfield St., Clonmel, Co. Tipperary. www.befani.com. ✆ **061/617-7893.** Tapas €6–€8; entrees €15–€29. Mon–Sat 9–11am, 12:30–2:30pm, 5:30–9:30pm; Sun 9–11am, 12:30–3:30pm, 5:30–9:30pm. Tapas served Mon–Sun 5:30–9:30pm.

Chez Hans ★★ EUROPEAN   Located in a converted church building—which, rather wonderfully, was bought in the 1860s with a thousand-year lease on terms of 1 shilling per year—Chez Hans is one of the most reliably good restaurants in Cashel. Menus change several times a week, based on what's freshest and best. Seafood features heavily (Dingle king scallops with carpaccio of beef, or maybe a delicious bowl of steamed mussels with garlic breadcrumbs), or you could opt for a sweet fig and walnut tart served with goat cheese. The dining room is a beautiful space with a vaulted ceiling, redolent of the building's past life. Reservations are recommended. The restaurant is a 2-minute walk from the Rock of Cashel.

Rockside, Cashel, Co. Tipperary. www.chezhans.net. ✆ **062/61177.** Entrees €26–€39. Tues–Sat 6–10pm.

The Lazy Bean Café ★ CAFE   This is a place that takes coffee and tea seriously. In addition to an exceptionally fine cup of coffee, you can order tea that comes in a traditional Japanese *suki* teapot. The cafe serves

THE lough derg DRIVE

At the meeting point of counties Clare, Limerick, and Tipperary, the Shannon River's largest lake, Lough Derg—virtually an inland sea—creates a stunning waterscape 40km (25 miles) long and almost 16km (10 miles) wide. The road that circles the lake for 153km (95 miles), the **Lough Derg Drive,** is one of Ireland's great scenic drives, a continuous photo op with panoramas of glistening waters, gentle mountains, and hilly farmlands unspoiled by commercialization.

The drive is also a collage of colorful shoreline towns, starting at the lake's south end with **Killaloe,** County Clare, and **Ballina,** County Tipperary. They're so close that they are essentially one community—only a splendid 13-arch bridge over the Shannon separates them. In the summer, its pubs and bars fill with weekend sailors. **Killaloe** is a picturesque town with lakeside views at almost every turn and restaurants and pubs perched on the shore. **Kincora,** on the highest ground at Killaloe, was traditionally said to be the royal settlement of Brian Boru

and the other O'Brien kings, although no trace of any buildings survives.

Memorable little towns and harborside villages, like **Mountshannon** and **Dromineer,** dot the rest of the Lough Derg Drive. Some towns, like **Terryglass** and **Woodford,** are known for atmospheric old pubs where spontaneous sessions of traditional Irish music are likely to break out. Others, like **Puckane** and **Ballinderry,** offer unique crafts. On the north shore of the lake in County Galway, **Portumna** is worth a visit for its forest park and castle.

The best way to get to Lough Derg is by car or boat. Because the area has limited public transportation, you will need a car to get around the lake. Major roads that lead to Lough Derg are the main Limerick-Dublin road (N7) from points east and south; N6 and N65 from Galway and the west; and N52 from the north. The Lough Derg Drive, which is well signposted, is a combination of R352 on the west bank of the lake and R493, R494, and R495 on the east bank.

very good wraps, bagels, and focaccia sandwiches at lunchtime and has a varied all-day breakfast menu. The cafe also has free Wi-Fi.

The Square, Cahir, Co. Tipperary. www.thelazybeancafe.com. ℂ **052/744-2038.** Lunch €4–€7. Daily 9am–6pm.

Quimby's ★ CAFE/DELI   This cute little cornerside cafe serves tasty snacks and brasserie-style lunches. The menu has plenty of traditional favorites—potato and leek soup, Irish stew, deliciously fluffy potato pancakes—or you could opt for a simple chicken salad or toasted sandwich. It also does a great breakfast if you're tired of hotel fare.

97 Irishtown, Clonmel, Co. Tipperary. ℂ **052/618-0255.** Entrees €8–€14. Mon–Sat 8:30am–5:30pm.

Sports & Outdoor Pursuits in Tipperary

BIRD-WATCHING   As many as 15 species of Irish water birds—including mute swans, coots, gadwalls, and gray herons—can be seen at the **Marlfield Lake Wildfowl Refuge,** several miles west of Clonmel in

Marlfield. On your way, you'll pass signposts for **St. Patrick's Well,** less than 1.6km (1 mile) away, a tranquil spot with an effervescent pool of reputedly healing crystalline water and an ancient Celtic cross rising from the middle of the pool. Legend has it that St. Patrick himself visited here.

CYCLING Centered around the town of Nenagh, the **North Tipperary Cycle Network** consists of three scenic cycling routes around the north Tipperary countryside. Signposted routes pass Lough Derg, small riverside villages, and farmland, before looping back to Nenagh. They vary in length from 30km (18½ miles) to 67km (41½ miles). Maps and other information can be found at **www.alltrails.com**. To hire a bike, contact **Moynana,** 4 Cecil Walk, Nenagh (www.moynans.com; ✆ **067/31293**).

WALKING In the Clonmel area, you'll find some excellent river and hill walks, some more challenging than others. The most spectacular is the ascent of famed **Slievenamon,** a mountain rich in myth. Inexpensive, detailed trail maps for at least a half-dozen walks are available at the Clonmel Tourist Office on Sarsfield Street, Clonmel.

The **Galtee Mountains,** northwest of the Knockmealdowns, offer some great long and short walks. For trail maps and other assistance, contact the **Glen of Aherlow Fáilte Society,** Coach Road, Newtown (www.aherlow.com; ✆ **062/56331**). It's open daily June to October from 9am to 6pm (hours vary the rest of the year). One particularly beautiful trail—a 3-hour round-trip—loops around the sparkling waters of **Lake Muskry,** on the north side of the range. (Ask for directions in Rossadrehid, west of Bansha on the R663.)

COUNTY GALWAY & CONNEMARA

10

F or many travelers to Ireland, Galway is the farthest edge of their journey. Part of the reason they draw the line here is because the depths of the county can look so forbidding—with its bleak bogs, heather-clad moors, and extraordinary light—that it must be the end of all that's worth seeing in Ireland. It isn't, of course, but Galway is just far enough west to escape much of the touristy bustle of Kerry or Cork. And that's a compelling part of its attraction. Here you can climb hills, catch fish, explore history, and get away from it all in the Irish countryside. With its misty mountain-fringed lakes, rugged coastline, and extensive wilderness, County Galway is a wild and wooly area. And yet, nestled just outside its most dramatic and unkempt part—the windswept boggy expanse of Connemara—is one of Ireland's most sophisticated towns. Though small, Galway City has long been a thriving center for the arts, and the winding medieval streets of its oldest quarter have a cultured air.

ESSENTIALS
Arriving

BY BUS Buses from all parts of Ireland arrive daily at **Bus Éireann Travel Centre,** Ceannt Station, off Eyre Square in Galway City (www.buseireann.ie; ✆ **091/562-000**). It also provides daily service to Clifden. Buses to rural areas sometimes run only a handful of times per day, and remote sites may be completely inaccessible without a car.

BY TRAIN Trains from Dublin and Limerick arrive daily at Ceannt Station in Galway City, off Eyre Square. That's pretty much the end of the line, however; to explore the Galway countryside, you'll need to travel by bus or car.

BY CAR Galway City is on the main N18, N17, N63, N67, and M6 roads. Journey time from Dublin is about 2 hours; from Killarney it's about 3 hours; and from Cork it's about 2½ hours. Outside of Galway City, your options in this region get pretty limited if you don't have a car. To hire one in Galway, try **Budget,** 12 Eyre Square (www.budget.ie;

FACING PAGE: Tigh Neachtain, one of many classic pubs in Galway City's Latin Quarter.

⟨ **091/564-570**), or **Europcar** at Motorpark, Headford Road (www. irishcarrentals.com; ⟨ **091/ 396-555**). For car-rental options in Dublin, see p. 91; for Shannon airport, see p. 334.

BY PLANE   Galway has an airport, but as of this writing it has not been used for regular scheduled flights since 2011. Check **www.galway airport.com** for the latest updates.

GALWAY CITY

A small but thriving and cultured city, Galway still has its winding medieval lanes, but it also has a cosmopolitan core. The city's hub is busy **Eyre Square** (pronounced *Air* Square), a few minutes' walk from pretty well all the main sights. The **River Corrib** runs through the town, with the city's artsy historic district on its east bank between **St. Nicholas' Church** and the harbor. (Look for the riverside **Spanish Arch** and the **Spanish Parade,** bearing witness to the city's 16th-century heyday as an international port.) Overlapping the medieval district, the **Latin Quarter** is a small but vibrant section, filled with lively (read: noisy) bars, nightclubs, and restaurants.

To see the highlights, follow the signposted **Tourist Trail of Old Galway** (a handy booklet outlining the trail is available at the tourist office and at most bookshops). The historic core is tiny but tangled, so getting lost is half the fun of going there. You certainly won't want your car in Galway City's center—if you've driven here, you'll want to park and walk. From June to September, the Galway Civic Trust offers free walking tours of medieval Galway. Tours depart from the Hall of the Red Earl (p. 370) at 2pm on Tuesdays and Thursdays. Alternatively, **Histry** (www. histry.ie) is an excellent new smartphone app that provides an interactive, self-guided tour of the historic district. It's available for both Apple and Android phones and costs $1.99; download direct from their respective app stores.

Visitor Information

The **Galway Tourist Office** is on Forster Street, Galway City (www. galway.ie; ⟨ **091/537-700**). The city also has a smaller tourist information point on Eyre Square.

Exploring Galway City

***Corrib Princess* Cruise** ★ TOUR   Sit back and take in the view from this 157-passenger, two-deck boat, as it cruises along the River Corrib out of Galway City. The journey along the river takes in castles, historical sites, and assorted wildlife, while an enthusiastic hostess shows passengers how to fix the perfect Irish coffee and will often try to liven things up with a bit of traditional dancing. It's not for those averse to the full tourist

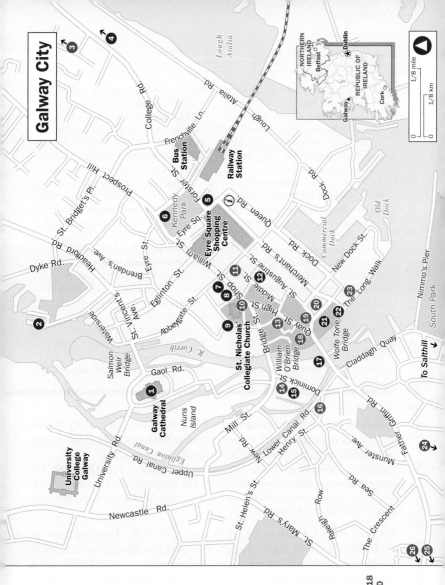

Galway City

Lough Atalia

Bus Station

Railway Station

St. Nicholas' Collegiate Church

Galway Cathedral

University College Galway

Old Dock

Commercial Dock

South Park

Nimmo's Pier

To Salthill

NORTHERN IRELAND
Belfast

REPUBLIC OF IRELAND

Dublin

Cork

0   1/8 mile
0   1/8 km

ATTRACTIONS

Aran Islands Ferries
  ticket office **5**
Corrib Princess **2**
Eyre Square **6**
Galway Arts Centre **15**
Galway Cathedral **1**
Galway City Museum **21**
Galway Fisheries Watchtower
  Museum **17**
Galway Irish Crystal
  Heritage Centre **4**
Hall of the Red Earl **12**
Lynch's Castle **7**
Lynch Memorial Window **8**
St. Nicholas'
  Collegiate Church **9**
Spanish Arch **22**

WHERE TO STAY

The G Hotel **3**
The House Hotel **20**
Marless House **24**
Sea Breeze Lodge **26**

WHERE TO EAT

Aniar **14**
Ard Bia at Nimmo's **23**
The Dough Bros **11**
Gourmet Tart Company **25**
Martine's Quay Street **19**
Oscars Seafood Bistro **16**
The Pie Maker **13**
The Seafood Bar @ Kirwan's **18**
Sheridans Cheesemongers **10**

ⓘ   Information

   Medieval Quarter

When you see the ghostly shapes of the Aran Islands floating 48km (30 miles) out at sea like misty Brigadoon, you instantly understand why these sea-battered and wind-whipped isles have been the subject of fable, song, and film for thousands of years.

All three islands—**Inishmore** (*Inis Mor*), **Inishmaan** (*Inis Meain*), and **Inisheer** (*Inis Oirr*)—are rather strange looking, with a ring of rocks around their outer edges and, inside, small farms surrounded by soft green grass and wildflowers. Life on the islands is deeply isolated. To this day, many of the 1,500 inhabitants maintain a traditional lifestyle, fishing from *currachs* (small crafts made of tarred canvas stretched over timber frames), living in stone cottages, relying on pony-drawn wagons to get around, and speaking Gaelic. They still wear the classic, creamy, handmade *bainin*

sweaters that originated here, as there's nothing better for keeping out the chill.

Inishmore is the largest island and the easiest to reach from Galway. Most visitors disembark from the ferries at **Kilronan** (*Cill Rónáin*), the island's main town (though it's only the size of a village). From there, it's easy to arrange transportation around the island: Horse-drawn buggies can be hailed like taxis as you step off the boat, minivans stand at the ready, and bicycle-rental shops are within sight. Drop in at **Oifig Fáilte** (**Aran Island Tourist Information**) in Kilronan (☏ **099/61263**) to pick up walking maps, ask questions, and generally get yourself going. It's open daily year-round from 10:30am to 5pm.

The islands have some excellent geological sights, including the magnificent **Dún Aengus** ★★ on Inishmore. A ruined 2,000-year-old stone fortress, on

treatment, but the 90-minute trip is very picturesque. You can buy tickets at the dock or at the *Corrib Princess* desk in the tourist office. Be sure to call ahead or check the website for up-to-date sailing times.

Departs from Woodquay, Galway City. www.corribprincess.ie. ☏ **091/563-846.** €17 adults; €15 seniors and students; €8 children; €40 families (2 adults, 3 children; additional children €7). Sailings May–June and Sept daily 12:30 and 2:30pm; July–Aug daily 12:30, 2:30, and 4:30pm.

Galway Arts Centre ★★ CULTURAL CENTER   Once the home of W. B. Yeats's patron, Lady Gregory, this attractive town house held local governmental offices for many years. Today it offers an excellent program of concerts, readings, and exhibitions by Irish and international artists—returning the house to a purpose that Lady Gregory would have appreciated. Usually two or three exhibitions run at any one time.

47 Dominick St., Galway City. www.galwayartscentre.ie. ☏ **091/565-886.** Free admission. Mon–Thurs 10am–5:30pm, Fri 10am–5pm, Sat noon–5pm.

Galway Cathedral ★ CATHEDRAL   Officially the "Cathedral of Our Lady Assumed into Heaven and St. Nicholas," Galway's cathedral has an impressive domed exterior that looks suitably Romanesque in style, although it was actually built in the 1960s. The striking interior has rows of symmetrical stone archways and dramatic lighting.

Contemporary Irish artisans designed the statues, colorful mosaics, and stained-glass windows. The limestone for the walls was cut from local quarries, while the polished floor is made from Connemara marble.

University and Gaol rds., Galway City (by west end of Salmon Weir Bridge). www.galwaycathedral.ie. © **091/563-577** (select option 4). Free admission, donations welcome. Daily 8:30am–6:30pm.

Galway City Museum ★ MUSEUM Overlooking the **Spanish Arch,** built in 1594 by the docks where Spanish galleons used to unload their cargo, this rather endearing modern museum is a good place to acquaint yourself with the city's history. Permanent galleries downstairs relate to Galway's prehistoric and medieval periods, while the upper levels deal with the city's more recent past, including its relationship with the arts. Highlights include a large collection of intricate embroidered textiles, made by a local order of nuns between the 17th and 20th centuries, and some engaging exhibits relating to the history of cinema in the city. A lively program of special events includes talks, touring exhibitions, and hands-on arts workshops.

Spanish Parade, Galway City. www.galwaycitymuseum.ie. © **091/532-460.** Free admission. Easter–Sept Tues–Sat 10am–5pm, Sun noon–5pm. Oct–Easter Tues–Sat 10am–5pm. Closed Sun Oct–Easter.

Galway Fisheries Watchtower Museum ★ MUSEUM   This tiny, free museum is worth visiting for the views of the River Corrib alone. The symmetrical yellow tower was built in 1852 as a lookout from which fishing boats on the river could be monitored; it was in use until commercial net fishing died out in the 1970s. Exhibits tell the story of Galway's fishing heritage and the vital role it played in the city's industry.

Wolfe Tone Bridge, off Father Griffin Rd., Galway City. No phone. Free admission. Mon and Sat 11am–3pm; Tues–Fri 10am–4pm. Closed Sun.

Galway Irish Crystal Heritage Centre ★ FACTORY TOUR   Not as well-known as its feted Waterford rival, Galway Crystal is just as distinctive and beautiful. At this modern visitor center, you can observe master craftspeople at work, from blowing the molten glass to cutting the finished product (weekdays only, although the center is open daily). However, most people just come to browse the huge factory shop, with its glittering array of crystal and other craft items, such as Belleek pottery.

East of the city on main Dublin Rd. (N6), Merlin Park, Co. Galway. www.galwaycrystal. ie. © **091/757-311.** Free admission. Mon–Fri 9am–5:30pm, Sat 10am–5pm, Sun and public holidays noon–5pm.

Hall of the Red Earl ★★ ANCIENT SITE   This fascinating site is what's left of a baronial hall from the Middle Ages, built by the powerful de Burgh family, Anglo-Norman earls who essentially ruled this region in the 13th century. In the late 1200s, they erected what must have been a lavish hall in which to hold court, receive subjects, settle disputes, and generally live it up in true medieval style. The earls were eventually overthrown by local tribes and the building abandoned. Time slowly covered any trace of the building, until the foundations were found during building work in 1997. You can tour the site on glass gangways and view some of the thousands of artifacts that were also unearthed during the excavation.

Custom House, Druid Lane, Galway City. © **091/564-946.** Free admission. May–Sept Mon–Fri 9:30am–4:45pm, Sat 10am–1pm; Oct–Apr Mon–Fri 9am–5pm. Closed Sat Oct–Apr and Sun year-round.

Lynch's Castle ★ HISTORIC HOUSE   Dating from 1490 and renovated in the 19th century, this impressive structure was once home to the Lynch family, who ruled the city for many years. One of the oldest medieval town houses in Ireland, it's now a branch of the Allied Irish Bank.

The Tribes of Galway

By the 15th century, 14 wealthy merchant families ruled Galway Town, giving it a nickname it still bears today—"City of Tribes." These families, mostly of Welsh and Norman origin, ruled as an oligarchy.

As you walk around Galway City, look for these names on storefronts and businesses: Athy, Blake, Bodkin, Browne, Darcy, Deane, Font, French, Joyce, Kirwan, Lynch, Martin, Morris, and Skerret.

Gargoyles preside over the exterior, while inside is a small display describing the building's history.

Abbeygate St. and Shop St., Galway City. ℭ **091/567-041** Free admission. Mon–Wed and Fri 10am–4pm, Thurs 10am–5pm.

St. Nicholas' Collegiate Church ★★ CHURCH   Galway's oldest church, St. Nicholas' was established about 1320. It's claimed that Christopher Columbus prayed here in 1477 before one of his early attempts to reach the New World, although there's no real evidence to suggest it's true. Over the centuries, it has changed from Roman Catholic to Church of Ireland and back again at least four times. In 2002 it became celebrated (and, for some, vilified) for holding the first-ever blessing of a same-sex partnership in an Irish church. Currently, it's under the aegis of the Church of Ireland. Inside are a 12th-century crusader's tomb with a Norman inscription, a carved font from the 16th or 17th century, and a stone lectern with barley-sugar twist columns from the 15th century. You can arrange guided tours conducted by a knowledgeable and enthusiastic church representative. Call or ask at the church for details.

Mainguard and Lombard sts. Galway City. www.stnicholas.ie. ℭ **086/389-8777.** Free admission (donations requested). Daily 9am–7pm; opening times may vary in winter. No tours Sun morning.

Where to Stay In & Around Galway City

The G ★★   Chic designer flourishes and contemporary art grace this modern, luxurious hotel overlooking the glassy waters of Lough Atalia and Galway Bay, about a 5-minute drive northeast of the city

Lively Shop Street in Galway City.

center. Many bedrooms have floor-to-ceiling windows to take full advantage of those views, flooding the place with natural light. Service is outstanding, with charming and attentive staff. Treatments in the beautifully designed spa aren't cheap, but check for special offers—you can sometimes find deals that include a massage, use of the thermal suite, and dinner. (*Tip:* Occasionally these deals work out cheaper than the room-only rate.) Speaking of food, **Gigi's** restaurant serves excellent modern Irish cuisine, with plenty of local meats and seafood; or you can have a more casual meal in one of the hotel's three **Signature Lounges.** The "Dinner and a Movie" package is a good way to fill an evening—a two- or three-course meal in the Signature Lounge (€31–€37 Sun–Thurs, €34–€39 Fri–Sat), plus a ticket to see a movie of your choice at a nearby cinema after dinner.

Wellpark, Galway City. www.theghotel.ie. ✆ **091/865-200.** 101 units. €170–€240 double; €310–€360 suite. Free parking. Breakfast included. **Amenities:** Restaurant; bar; gym; room service; spa; Wi-Fi (free).

The House Hotel ★★   This upbeat, funky hotel is right in the heart of the historic district. Public areas are filled with playful design statements, from polka-dot chairs to hot-pink sofas. Guest rooms, however, are far more muted and restful, with oatmeal, white, or green color schemes and the slightest hint of a retro theme. The restaurant is good and surprisingly reasonable for a hotel of this size in the center of the city, and the in-house cocktail bar is a lively nightspot. That said, you're spoiled for choice when it comes to nightlife in this neighborhood—Galway's buzzing center is literally on your doorstep.

Spanish Parade, Galway City. www.thehousehotel.ie. ✆ **091/538-900.** 134 units. €155–€275 double. Discounted parking at nearby lot (€8 for 24 hr.). Breakfast not included in lower rates. **Amenities:** Restaurant; bar; room service; Wi-Fi (free).

Marless House ★★   This pleasant, friendly B&B in Salthill, a small seaside commuter town immediately west of Galway, is an exceptionally good value for the money. Guest rooms are spacious and spotlessly clean, though some have slightly overwhelming floral color schemes. The thoughtful hosts, Mary and Tom, have arrangements with several local tour companies, so if you want to book an organized trip to one of the major sights in the region—including the Aran Islands or the Cliffs of Moher—the tour bus will pick you up directly from here and drop you back at the end of the day. Mary is a fount of sightseeing information, and will cheerfully help you draw up an itinerary. Breakfasts are delicious and filling.

8 Threadneedle Rd., Salthill, Co. Galway. www.marlesshouse.com. ✆ **091/523-931.** 6 units. €80–€90 double. Free parking. Breakfast included. **Amenities:** Wi-Fi (free).

Sea Breeze Lodge ★★   Another great option in Salthill, just outside Galway City, this stylish little B&B overlooks Galway Bay. The modern gray exterior gives way to smart contemporary spaces inside. Guest rooms are spacious, with polished wood floors and big windows looking out over the bay or garden. Beds are enormous—the larger ones are super king-size, and all have luxurious memory-foam mattresses. Delicious breakfasts are served in a pleasant conservatory overlooking the garden. The B&B can arrange tours of major sights in the area, including an all-day trip to the Aran Islands for €25 per person. There's no restaurant, but the center of Galway is only 5km (3 miles) by car or taxi.

9 Cashelmara, Salthill, Co. Galway. www.seabreezelodge.org. ✆ **091/529-581.** 6 units. €162–€308 double, €292–€342 suite. Free parking. Breakfast included. **Amenities:** Wi-Fi (free).

Where to Stay & Eat on the Aran Islands

Inis Meáin ★★★ Designed to resemble a whale, the low stone structure of this restaurant and B&B is a beautiful sight against the stark horizon—though not as good as the sea views you get from inside. Hosts Ruairi and Marie-Thérèse have created something truly special on the least-visited of the Aran Islands, Inis Meáin, after which the place is named (Ruairi grew up here—get him talking about what life on the island was like during his childhood.) Indeed, for many who spend time here, a stay at this B&B is one of the main reasons to visit the island. The *Financial Times* declared the restaurant one of the best 12 in the world a few years ago, and dining here certainly is a memorable experience. Ruairi creates simple, fresh, delicious meals from produce as local as it comes—including the garden outside and the sea around you. It all depends on what's best that day, but the five-course set menu (€70) might include a starter of fresh sea urchins, followed by John Dory in *grenobloise* sauce. Five enormous, modern guest suites make the most of the stunning views of Galway Bay and the edge of the Burren, with huge windows. The only drawback is the 2-night minimum stay, but that won't feel like a problem once you get here, breathe in the air, and feel the peace wash over you. *Note:* Due to limited space and high demand, you should make reservations as far in advance as possible.

Inis Meáin, Aran Islands, Co. Galway. www.inismeain.com. ✆ **086/826-6026.** 5 units. €730–€1,120 suite. Free parking. Breakfast and HotPot lunch included. **Amenities:** Wi-Fi (free). Closed Oct–Mar.

Inis Meáin, a sought-after restaurant and B&B on the remote Aran Island of the same name.

Kilmurvey House ★★ This pleasant B&B, overlooking Dún Aengus Fort, may look austere outside, but inside it's all cheerful, bright rooms and polished wood floors. Owner Teresa Joyce is extremely welcoming, and her family really does their best to make you feel at home. Guest rooms are surprisingly large, with views across the island countryside. Teresa's home-cooked breakfasts are delicious. (Try the creamy porridge made with whiskey or Bailey's Irish Cream—come on, you're on vacation!) You'll need to fend for yourselves at dinner, but Teresa can recommend a couple of places in the nearby village—and one of the family will even give you a lift there and back. How's that for hospitality?

Kilronan, Inis Mor, Aran Islands, Co. Galway. www.kilmurveyhouse.com. **©** **099/ 61218.** 12 units. €85–€90 double. Free parking. Breakfast included. **Amenities:** Wi-Fi (free). Closed Oct–Mar.

Where to Eat in Galway City

Aniar ★★★ MODERN IRISH This Michelin-starred restaurant in the center of Galway City is one of the best, and most fashionable, places to eat in the region. Head chef Ultan Cooke has won as many fans for his passionate slow-food ethos as for his delicious food. Well, almost as many…okay, it's mainly the food. The menu is tiny but always built around what's in season and best that day. Oysters might be served with cucumber and arrowgrass (a kind of native wild plant that grows in bogs and by the sea), or monkfish with sea buckthorn and mussels. The only downside: the cost. This is not a cheap night out, but how often are you going to be here? *Tip:* Tasting menus are less expensive than you might

September's Galway International Oyster and Seafood Festival draws foodies from far and near.

expect from a place this trendy, at €55 (€85 with paired wines). Needless to say, reservations are essential.

53 Lower Dominick St., Galway City. www.aniarrestaurant.ie. ✆ **091/535-947.** Tasting menus €65–€100. Tues–Thurs 6–9:30pm, Fri–Sat 5:30–9:30pm. Closed Sun–Mon.

Ard Bia at Nimmo's ★★ SEAFOOD/BISTRO/CAFE   The pleasantly rustic dining room at this fashionable restaurant in Galway City doubles as a popular cafe during the day. At any time, the emphasis is the same: delicious, homey flavors, using local and seasonal produce. Stop in for tasty, creative salads and sandwiches at lunch. In the evening, expect local fish (perhaps with a side of roast garlic gnocchi), a plate of fresh boxty, or maybe a tender rib-eye served with lemon-crushed potatoes. The wine list is excellent and reasonably priced—you can drop in for a glass or two without eating, if you don't mind perching on a barstool. The restaurant also has a popular brunch on weekends.

Spanish Arch, Long Walk, Galway City. www.ardbia.com. ✆ **091/561-114.** Lunch entrees €8–€12. Dinner entrees €21–€29. Mon–Fri 10am–3:30pm (lunch served from noon), 6–9pm; Sat–Sun 10am–3pm (lunch served from noon), 6–9pm.

The Dough Bros ★★ PIZZA   The young, the trendy, and just the plain old hungry stand in line for a table at this popular pizza joint in the middle of Galway City. It's a heartwarming tale: Three local boys, in love with Italian cooking since a family trip to Naples as kids, start a food truck after one of them loses his job. Fast-forward a few years and that truck has become a fully fledged restaurant, serving delicious, fresh, wood-baked pizza to hordes of hungry locals. You might go for a classic Neapolitan, with tomato, fresh basil, and buffalo mozzarella, but if you're feeling a bit adventurous, how about the "Hail Caesar," with lemon chicken, smoked pancetta, and arugula? Or the spicy, Indian-influenced Tandoori, with tikka-style chicken pieces, chili, and *raita* (mint and cucumber yogurt)? The dining room is small and informal, and they don't take reservations, so you will probably have to stand in line on Friday and Saturday nights— or do the other traditional thing and get it to go!

Cathedral Building, Middle St., Galway City. www.thedoughbros.ie. ✆ **087/176- 1662.** Entrees €7–€12. No reservations. Tues–Sat noon–10pm, Sun–Mon noon–9pm.

10

COUNTY GALWAY & CONNEMARA

Galway City

Gourmet Tart Company ★ BAKERY/INTERNATIONAL A French-style bakery and patisserie with a restaurant attached, the Gourmet Tart Company is a great place to stop for snacks, light meals, and sweet treats. The home-baked cakes, tarts, and pastries make for a tempting midafternoon snack or a breakfast on the go. (The cafe also does a very good sit-down breakfast if you want to linger.) At lunch it sells sandwiches and assorted deli items to take out. At night, however, a full menu of delicious international fare at very reasonable prices suddenly appears—fish of the day with sautéed potatoes, say, Thai curry with lychees, a goat cheese salad. Brunch is popular on Sundays. The Gourmet Tart Company also has smaller (deli/bakery only) branches on Headford Road, Newcastle Road, Abbeygate Street, and on Raven Terrace in the suburb of Claddagh.

Jameson Court, Salthill, Co. Galway. www.gourmettartco.com. ℂ **091/861-667.** Breakfast €2–€10. Lunch entrees €7.50–€11.50. Dinner entrees €8.50–€12.50. Mon–Sat 7:30am–9pm (last food orders 7:30pm), Sun 7:30am–8pm (last food orders 6pm).

Martine's Quay Street ★★ BISTRO A friendly, cozy restaurant and bar in the center of Galway City, Martine's serves good, Irish-influenced bistro-style cooking, with just a hint of an international accent. The menu is short but well-judged: dishes like hake tempura or chicken liver pâté, followed by the catch of the day, or a juicy rib-eye steak or burger cooked in a charcoal oven. They take their meat seriously here: The specials board includes a "cut of the day," according to what's best. The "Not so Early Bird" menu has limited options, but is a deal at €23 for two courses, or €28 for three (the "not so" because it's available all night, every night). Martine's is also a good choice for a simple, tasty lunch of salads, sandwiches, and a few larger plates, all for around €10 or less.

21 Quay St., Galway City. www.martines.ie. ℂ **091/565-662.** Entrees €14–€30. Daily 12:30–3pm, 5–10:30pm.

Oscar's Seafood Bistro ★★★ SEAFOOD One of the standout seafood restaurants in this part of Ireland, Oscar's is a cheerful, relaxed kind of place. The dining room is filled with modern art, and fabric drapes across the ceiling add a bohemian touch. The menu depends entirely on what's fresh and in season, but you could start with some prawns cooked simply in garlic and butter, followed by filet of monkfish with a chipotle and chorizo sauce; seared Clew Bay scallops with lime drizzle; or a plate of grilled whiting, served with almond and basil pesto. Ingredients are sourced from local producers and farmers' markets. The wine list is good, with plenty of very affordable choices. If you only choose one place to have seafood while you're in Galway, this is the one.

Dominick St., Galway City. www.oscarsbistro.ie. ℂ **091/852-180.** Entrees €14.50–€25.50. Open in the evening Mon–Sat.

The Pie Maker ★★ PIES You can't beat this for an authentic Irish food experience. With its deliciously old-fashioned red-and-gold frontage (just try to pass without taking a picture) and dimly lit, quirky little dining room, it's a cozy and atmospheric place. The menu consists of pies, pies, and more pies, in light, fresh pastry crusts. There are a couple of sweet options, but most are savory with hot, fresh fillings of meat and vegetables, such as roast beef, curried chicken, chicken and mushroom, or sausage and mozzarella. Super-traditional sides come in the form of creamy mashed potatoes and garden peas. And if by some miracle you have room for dessert, try the amazing banoffee pie, a heavenly combination of whipped cream, banana, and toffee, with a crumbly base. Pies can also be ordered to go.

10 Cross St. Upper, Galway City. ℂ **091/513-151.** Entrees €6–€13. Sun–Thurs noon–10pm; Fri–Sat noon–10:30pm.

The Seafood Bar @ Kirwan's ★ SEAFOOD   The exposed stone walls of this elegant downstairs dining room speak to the building's medieval origins. Open the menu, however, and everything suddenly seems bang up to date—this is one of the most popular and reliable restaurants in Galway City for good seafood, dishes like shrimp and clams with chili, fish and chips, or a generous cold seafood platter. Despite the name, the menu has plenty of meat dishes too, so carnivores won't leave disappointed—try the beef with blue-cheese fondant.

Kirwan's Lane, Galway City. www.kirwanslane.com. ℂ **091/568-266.** Entrees €18–€27. Mon–Sat 12:30–2:30pm, 6–10pm; Sun 6–10pm.

Sheridans Cheesemongers ★★ DELI/WINE BAR   This is a delightfully novel idea: an artisan cheese shop and deli, doubling as a bar where you can order a glass of wine and some nibbles. Food comes in the form of delicious cheeseboards and charcuterie, much of it locally produced. So simple, so delicious, and hugely popular too—you might struggle to get one of the few tables during busy times. This is a really good alternative to heavy restaurant food when all you really want is a chat and a sophisticated snack. Oh, and did we mention that the selection of cheese is sensational?

Church Yard St., Galway City. www.sheridanscheesemongers.com. ℂ **091/564-832** or 091/564-829 (shop). Entrees €5–€12. Wine bar: Tues–Fri 1pm–midnight, Sat noon–midnight, closed Sun–Mon. Shop: Mon–Fri 10am–6pm, Sat 9am–6pm, closed Sun.

Shopping in Galway City

Given its status as both a tourist hub and a vibrant arts community, it's no surprise that Galway has fairly good shopping. Some of the best is in tiny clusters of shops in historic buildings, such as the **Cornstore** on Middle Street or the **Grainstore** on Lower Abbeygate Street. **Eyre Square Centre,** the downtown area's largest shopping mall, rather incongruously incorporates a section of Galway's medieval town wall into its complex of 50 shops.

10

COUNTY GALWAY & CONNEMARA

Galway City

Most shops are open Monday to Saturday 9 or 10am to 5:30 or 6pm. In July and August, many stay open late, usually until 9pm on weekdays, and some also open on Sunday from noon to 5pm.

ANTIQUES & VINTAGE CURIOS

The Gaiety Antique & Vintage Store ★ The owners of this friendly store are third-generation antiques dealers and furniture restorers. They specialize in antique furniture, ornaments, and other curios, from Ireland and farther afield. 3 St. Frances St. www.thegaiety.ie. ✆ **091/985-6799.**

BOOKS

Charlie Byrne's Bookshop ★★ Packed floor-to-ceiling with books—secondhand, antiquarian, and new—this wonderfully chaotic bookshop has a huge stock, covering just about anything. It's so beloved that the *Irish Times* named this the best bookshop in Ireland in 2013. It also sells very fetching little cotton tote bags. Cornstore Mall, Middle St. www.charliebyrne.com. ✆ **091/561-766.**

Kenny's Book Shop and Galleries Ltd ★ Another long-standing favorite of Galway bibliophiles, Kenny's has a great selection of new books on all topics, plus secondhand and hard-to-find antiquarian titles. (*Tip:* It delivers free, anywhere in the world, if you prefer to order online.) The bookstore also an interesting little art gallery. Lisobun Retail Park, Tuam Rd. www.kennys.ie. ✆ **091/709-350.**

CRYSTAL, CHINA & SOUVENIRS

Galway Irish Crystal ★★ This local brand of fine crystal rivals Waterford Crystal. At the factory on the edge of town, you can watch the craftspeople at work and purchase armfuls of the stuff yourself. See p. 370 for more details. Dublin Rd., Merlin Park. www.galwaycrystalfactoryshop.com. ✆ **091/757-311.**

Treasure Chest ★ This large craft store and gift emporium in the town center sells china (including Belleek and Royal Doulton), plus Aran sweaters, Irish linens, handicrafts, and a host of other souvenirs. 31–33 William St. www.treasurechest.ie. ✆ **091/563-862.**

JEWELRY

Blacoe ★★ This popular jeweler in the Eyre Square Centre sells Claddagh rings, engagement rings, and a large range of jewelry featuring traditional Irish motifs. Plenty of pieces sell for well under €100. 212 Eyre Square Centre. www.blacoe.ie. ✆ **091/561-003.**

Cobwebs ★★ Located opposite the Spanish Arch, this great little store sells antique and modern jewelry, plus curios, antiques, and objets d'art. 7 Quay Lane. www.cobwebs.ie. ✆ **091/564-388.**

Fallers of Galway ★ Fallers makes and sells the Claddagh ring, a traditional Galway souvenir that symbolizes love and friendship (see box

ESSENTIAL SOUVENIR: THE claddagh RING

Known worldwide as a symbol of love and friendship, the delicate **Claddagh** (pronounced *Clod*-uh) ring is probably a design you'll recognize—two hands holding a heart topped with a crown—even if the name is new to you. Over the years this iconic design has also become a symbol for Ireland and its diaspora.

Claddagh rings first appeared sometime in the 17th century, although the design was based on a much older European tradition, dating back to Roman times. The hands are said to represent friendship, the crown loyalty, and the heart love—the three ingredients of a perfect marriage.

Originally, the ring was a wedding band worn facing out for engagement and facing in for marriage. Though no longer widely worn as a symbol of marriage, it is still frequently worn as a friendship ring and makes a lovely memento. The first rings were made in Galway—or more precisely, just over the Father Griffin Bridge, on the west bank of the River Corrib, in the town of Claddagh. It's now a residential satellite to Galway, but in ancient times it was a kingdom with its own laws, fleet, and customs.

Thomas Dillon's jewelry store on Quay Street (see below) claims to be the original creator of the Claddagh ring—it has been doing a roaring trade in the traditional souvenirs since 1750.

above). It also has a large stock of other jewelry with Celtic motifs. Williamsgate St. www.fallers.com. ℂ **091/561-226.**

Hartmann & Son Ltd. ★ Another maker of Claddagh rings, Hartmann's also specializes in watches and diamonds. This is one of Galway's real high-end jewelry stores. 27–29 William St. www.hartmanns.ie. ℂ **091/562-063.**

Thomas Dillon's Claddagh Gold ★ This chirpily colored little store makes two bold claims: to be the original maker of Claddagh rings (they're the only ones allowed to stamp the rings with "original"), and to be the oldest jewelry store in all of Ireland. If the date it was established—1750—is anything to go by, it's probably true. The shop has a tiny little museum displaying Claddagh rings from the 1700s. 1 Quay St. www.claddaghring.ie. ℂ **091/566-365.**

MUSIC & MUSICAL INSTRUMENTS

P. Powell and Sons ★ Usually just called Powell's, this is an excellent source for instruments—including pennywhistles, bodhráns, and the like—as well as a good range of traditional music CDs. 53 William St. ℂ **091/562-295.**

TWEEDS, WOOLENS & CLOTHING

Irish Tweeds ★ Although not the oldest tweed maker in town by any means, Irish Tweeds has a great selection of traditionally made garments, including snazzy hats, jackets, and nightwear. They also ship worldwide, free of charge. 51 William St. www.irishtweeds.com. ℂ **091/539-745.**

Galway Woollen Market ★   This colorful store is one of the best for traditional, hand-loomed Aran knits, plus lace and other traditional textiles. Visitors who live outside the European Union don't have to pay sales tax on items bought from here. 21 High St. www.aranislandsknitwear.com. ⓒ **091/562-491.**

O'Máille (O'Malley) ★   Another excellent place to buy Aran knitwear and other Irish knits, this store has a claim to fame of its own—when *The Quiet Man* was filmed near here in 1951 (see p. 424), it provided costumes for all the actors, including John Wayne. 16 High St. www.omaille.com. ⓒ **091/562-696.**

Galway City After Dark

THEATER

Druid Theatre ★★ THEATER   Highly respected across Ireland and beyond for its original, cutting-edge productions, the Druid has been one of the region's foremost arts institutions since the 1970s. It's particularly known for premiering new work from up-and-coming writers, so expect to find challenging, intelligent material staged here. The theater also produces new versions of classic plays by Irish, British, and European dramatists. Shows can sell out some time in advance, and are often out on the road (the Druid is a touring company), so it's advisable to check what's on

Kirwan's Lane in the historic Latin Quarter of Galway City.

and make bookings as far ahead as possible. Ticket prices range from around €15 to €45.

Flood St. www.druid.ie. ℰ **091/568-660.** Performance times vary by show.

PUBS & BARS

Crane Bar ★★ Considered one of the best pubs in the city for traditional music, the Crane Bar has live bands every night from 9:30, and on some weekend afternoons too. Admission is usually free, but some sessions in the upstairs bar cost anything from a couple euro to €20. 2 Sea Rd. www.thecranebar.com. ℰ **091/587-419.**

Front Door ★ This cheerful pub, which sprawls over two floors, is a wonderfully social place where you can saunter in at lunchtime for a tasty sandwich and a pint, and find yourself staying for hours. It sometimes shows Irish sports on big TV screens. Cross and High sts. www.frontdoorpub.com. ℰ **091/563-757.**

Halo ★★ Playful decadence is the vibe at this popular nightclub, which pitches itself at a young-but-not-too-young demographic (under 23s are not admitted). It has five bars and a good, slightly retro cocktail menu. 36 Upper Abbeygate St. www.halonightclub.com. ℰ **091/565-976.**

Murty Rabbitt's ★★ This charming and unspoiled late-19th-century pub has a delightfully old-school feel. (It's still run by the same family who owned it all the way back then, too. How's that for tradition?) Rabbitt's sometimes has live music in the evening. 23 Forster St. ℰ **091/566-490.**

Quays Bar ★★ Another good place to hear live music, the Quays has the unusual distinction of having interior decor that was reclaimed from a medieval French church. The what's-on list is a real mixed bag—you could find anything from trad to 80s rock, hip hop to indie. Expect the fun to kick off around 9pm. 11 Quay St. ℰ **091/568-347.**

10

COUNTY GALWAY & CONNEMARA

Galway City

The Galway Races at Ballybrit are a high point of the summer sporting season.

Roisin Dubh ★★   As much a concert venue as it is a bar, this place gets great acts—expect to see a few famous names crop up among the packed program of live music and standup comedy. 9 Dominick St. www.roisindubh. net. ℗ **091/586-540.**

Sports & Outdoor Pursuits Around Galway City

HORSEBACK RIDING   Riding enthusiasts head to **Aille Cross Equestrian Centre,** Aille Cross, Loughrea, County Galway (www.connemaratrails.com; ℗ **091/843-968**), about 32km (20 miles) east of Galway. Run by personable Willy Leahy (who has appeared often on American television), this facility is one of the largest in Ireland, with 50 horses and 20 Connemara ponies. For about €25 to €50 an hour, you can ride through nearby farmlands, woodlands, forest trails, and—a particularly charming experience—along beaches.

Side Trips from Galway City

On the main road inland from Galway City, heading south and east, are a number of attractions perfectly geared for families: the well-preserved medieval town of **Athenry** (see box below), the giant fish tanks of the **Galway Atlantaquaria** (p. 384), and ye-olde-tyme-funne feasting at **Dunguaire Castle** (p. 384). Meanwhile, more literary types may be interested in a string of sites related to one of Ireland's greatest poets, W. B. Yeats (see "A Poetic Soul," p. 440).

ATHENRY: FADED medieval SPLENDOR

Remarkably intact after more than 6 centuries, the medieval town walls of **Athenry**—about 25 minutes' drive east from Galway—surround a charming small town that feels like a time-warp experience. Those walls are some of the best-preserved in Ireland, constructed in the 1300s, with well over half of the original 2km (1⅓ miles) circuit still surviving—up to 5m (16½ ft.) tall in places.

Start with a visit to the **Athenry Heritage Centre** on The Square, in the town center (www.athenryheritagecentre.com; ✆ **091/844-661**). As well as providing all the usual orientation—including maps for walking routes—it has a lively **Medieval Experience.** Aimed mostly at kids, it has plenty of interactive exhibits, dress-up areas, and re-creations of a torture dungeon and medieval street. Admission costs €8 adults, €6.50 children, and €26 families. You can also play Robin Hood by trying your hand at archery; hour-long lessons cost €25. The center is open June to August daily 10:30am to 5pm, and April to May weekdays 10:30am to 5pm (closed Sept–March).

Just a 10-minute walk away, on Court Lane, is the medieval **Athenry Castle.**

Inside its modest tower keep—the only substantial part that survives—are interesting carvings on the main doorway and window arches. Admission costs €5 adults, €4 seniors, €3 students and children, and €13 families. From April to September it's open daily 9:30am to 6pm; last admission 5:15pm. In October, it's open Monday to Thursday 9:30am to 5pm; last admission 4:15pm (closed Nov– March).

Just around the corner from the castle on Bridge Street, check out the ruins of a **Dominican Priory,** built in the mid–13th century and comprehensively destroyed by Cromwell's forces 400 years later. Today it's just a picturesque ruin, incongruously surrounded by modern houses; to medievalists, however, it's of particular interest because of its elaborately carved gravestones.

To reach Athenry from Galway, take the M5 motorway east about 25km (15½ miles) to junction 17, signposted for Athenry and Craughwell. There's also train service hourly from Galway City; the trip takes between 15 and 30 minutes and costs around €6 round-trip.

Heading west out of Galway City, the R336 coast road makes for a lovely scenic drive, snaking along the edge of Galway Bay. The first major stop on the headland is the beach resort of **Salthill** *(Bóthar na Trá),* a summer magnet for Irish families (think the Jersey shore in the U.S., or Blackpool in England). It has a boardwalk and a fine beach, plus lots of bars, fast food, amusement rides, and game arcades, a good respite if you've got kids (as long as you don't mind the crowds). Farther along the R336 are some charming historic towns including Gaelic-speaking **Spiddal** *(An Spidéal).* The road continues as far as **Inverin** *(Indreabhán),* then turns northward, with signposts for **Rossaveal** *(Ros an Mhíl),* ferry port to the **Aran Islands** (see p. 368). Continuing north on R336, you can branch off on R340 to visit **Ros Muc,** site of the **Padraig Pearse Cottage ★** (see p. 386).

Galway Atlantaquaria ★ AQUARIUM   Also known as the National Aquarium of Ireland (the largest in the country), this is a fantastic change of pace for kids who are tired of trudging around historic ruins. One's imagination is captured right from the first exhibit—a dramatic "splash room," where a large, 1-tonne (just under a ton) capacity tank goes off every minute or so with a giant splash, designed to imitate the natural movement of waves on the Galway coast. Highlights of the thoughtful exhibits include an enormous two-story **ocean tank** housing a couple hundred sea creatures (including small sharks); a **wreck tank** that's home to dangerous conger eels; and **touch pools** where kids can handle tame starfish and hermit crabs, under the supervision of the aquarium staff. There's also the opportunity to tickle some inquisitive rays, but make sure your hands are wet first or your touch can burn their sensitive skin. Free talks accompany daily feeding times at 1, 3, and 4pm daily (hourly 11am–5pm in winter)—the schedule for what gets fed when is displayed at the entrance.

The Promenade, Salthill, Co. Galway. www.nationalaquarium.ie. ✆ **091/585-100.** Admission €12 adults; €8.50 seniors; €9 students; €7.50 children 3–16; €22–€33 families. Wed–Fri 10am–5pm, Sat–Sun 10am–6pm. Last admission 45 min. before closing.

Medieval Banquet at Dunguaire Castle ★ CASTLE/ENTER-TAINMENT   One of the better *ye olde worlde* style entertainments in this part of Ireland, the medieval banquet at Dungaire Castle is actually pretty good fun. It's best not to worry about anything silly like historical

Jumping off the Blackrock diving board at the Salthill Promenade.

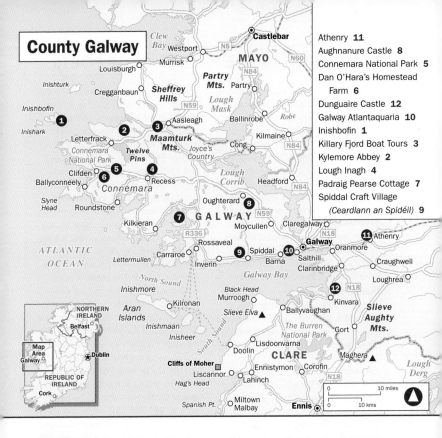

County Galway

accuracy, because that's hardly the point, now, is it? After being welcomed with a goblet of mead, you're seated in a satisfyingly atmospheric candlelit hall, with long communal tables. A (mostly) traditional Irish-style dinner is served—smoked salmon, leek and potato soup, that kind of thing—with jugs of wine left on the table to lubricate the proceedings. A live show follows, featuring song and poetry from some of the great Irish writers (none of them medieval, but remember what we told you about not worrying?). There are two sittings nightly, at 5:30 and 8:45pm, and reservations are essential as far in advance as possible—midsummer dates can get booked up. Dunguaire Castle itself is worth a look around; a tower-house-style late medieval castle built in 1520, it overlooks Galway Bay and was once home to Irish poet and wit Oliver St. John Gogarty (see box p. 386). Outside of the banquet, it's open 10am to 5pm. Dunguaire is near Kinvara, approx. 26km (16 miles) southeast of Galway.

On N67 (Ballyvaughan Rd.), Dunguaire, Co. Galway. www.shannonheritage.com.
📞 **061/360-788.** Banquet €53 adults; €35 children 10–12; €23 children 6–9. Reservations essential. Castle €6 adults; €3.50 seniors and students; €3 children 5–16; children 4 and under free; €17.50 families. Banquets Apr–Oct daily 5:30 and 8:45pm. Castle Apr–Oct daily 10am–5pm; last admission 30 min. before closing.

In the early 1900s, every summer the area southeast of Galway City became a sort of Bloomsbury Society West, as Dublin's greatest literary minds decamped to a cluster of nearby manor homes. About 36km (22⅓ miles) southeast of Galway City, near the northern border of the Burren (see chapter 9), you'll see signs to the beautiful **Coole Park National Forest** (www.coolepark.ie; ✆ **091/631-804**). This was once the country home of the dramatist and arts patron Lady Augusta Gregory (1852–1932), who, along with W. B. Yeats and Edward Martyn, founded the **Abbey Theatre** ★ in Dublin (see p. 169). Sadly, her house no longer stands, but her influence is memorialized in a tree on the grounds on which the following people carved their initials while visiting with her: George Bernard Shaw, Sean O'Casey, John Masefield, Oliver St. John Gogarty, W. B. Yeats, and Douglas Hyde, the first president of Ireland. Clearly, she was an exceptional woman, and this is an exceptional place. The visitor center shows a number of films on Lady Gregory and Coole Park, and has a tearoom, picnic tables, and some lovely nature trails. The visitor center is open daily 10am to 6pm from June to August and 10am to 5pm in April, May, and September (closed last weekend in Sept). Admission is free.

Not too far from the home of his friend, the great poet W. B. Yeats (1865–1939) had his own summer home in Gort at **Thoor Ballylee** (www.yeatsthoor ballylee.org; ✆ **091/631-436**). The restored 16th-century Norman tower house served as the inspiration for his poems "The Winding Stair" and "The Tower." In the interpretive center, an audiovisual presentation examines the poet's life. Also on the grounds are the original Ballylee Mill, partially restored, and a bookshop specializing in Anglo-Irish literature. The tower suffered serious flood damage in 2014, but has since been fully restored by a local community group, the Yeats Thoor Ballylee Society, which runs it as a cultural center. It hosts exhibitions and regular events, such as poetry readings—see the website for a current schedule. The center is open weekdays in May 10am to 2pm and weekends 11am to 5pm; and June to August daily 10am to 6pm. Admission is €7. The rest of the year, the grounds are still open but the tower itself is closed. The site is on the N18 at Gort.

Not too far away from Yeats' and Lady Gregory's summer homes, **Dunguaire Castle** (www.shannonheritage. com; ✆ **061/360-788**) sits on the south shore of Galway Bay, between Gort and Kilcolgan in Kinvara. Once the royal seat of the 7th-century King Guaire of Connaught, the castle was taken over by Oliver St. John Gogarty (1878–1957), Irish surgeon, author, poet, and wit; his great friends Yeats and Lady Gregory were frequent guests. Today, you can enjoy exquisite views of the nearby Burren and Galway Bay from its battlements, and stay for a **medieval banquet** on a summer evening. For more information on the castle, see p. 384.

Pearse Cultural Centre and Padraig Pearse Cottage ★
MUSEUM/HISTORIC HOUSE This small but engaging center is devoted to Padraig Pearse (1879–1916), one of the leaders of Ireland's 1916 Easter Rising. Dublin-based Pearse, who read the Declaration of Independence from the steps of the G.P.O. in Dublin (p. 111), made Connemara his countryside home. The center uses that as a springboard

from which to celebrate the region's culture, and of course there's plenty to say about Pearse's all-too-short life, which ended tragically when he was executed for his part in the rebellion. After visiting the center you can walk over to his humble thatched-roof cottage and look around.

Inbhear, near Ros Muc, Co. Galway. www.heritageireland.ie. ⓒ **091/574292.** Admission €5 adults; €4 seniors; €3 children/students; €13 families. Mid-Mar to Sept daily 9:30am–6pm; Oct to mid-Mar daily 9:30–4pm; last admission 45 min. before closing.

Spiddal Craft Village (*Ceardlann an Spidéil*) ★★ CULTURAL CENTER

On the main road as you enter Spiddal from Galway, this is a fantastic collection of cottage-style crafts stores and workshops. The artists-in-residence here change regularly, but selection is always diverse. At this writing, they include a basket maker, a ceramicist, a jeweler specializing in pieces made from pre-euro Irish coins (you can pick them out by your birth year), a traditional weaver, and a stained-glass artist. Plenty of the work is affordable without stretching the budget too far. Even if you're not buying, it's an inspiring place to browse. The **Builín Blasta Café** sells delicious bakery goods, snacks, and light meals in addition to takeaway deli items. You can contact the individual artists via the main website.

About 15km (9 miles) W of Galway on R336, Spiddal, Co. Galway. www.spiddalcrafts.com. No phone. Mon–Sat 10am–6pm, Sun noon–5pm.

CONNEMARA

If you look for Connemara on road signs, you may be looking forever, because it's not a city or county, but rather a region—and one with a particularly distinct identity. Like the Burren in County Clare, the boundaries are a bit hazy. Most agree that Connemara is west of Galway City, starting at Oughterard and continuing toward the Atlantic. Anyway, you know it when you see it: It's an area of heartbreaking barrenness and unique beauty, with dark bogs and tall jagged mountains punctuated by curving glassy lakes dotted with green islands. The desolate landscape is caused, in part, by an absence of trees: Most native stands were felled and dragged off long ago for building ships, houses, and furniture. As Oscar Wilde wrote, "Connemara is a savage beauty."

It's a varied place—in fact, you could say that there are two Connemaras. South of the Galway-Clifden road (N59) is a vast bog-mantled moorland dotted with lakes, with a low, indented, rocky coastline. North of the Galway-Clifden road, tall quartzite domes and cones form the Maumturks and the Twelve Bens (also called the Twelve Pins), rising toward the breathtaking Killary fjord—the only fjord in this part of Europe.

Note that Connemara is part of the **Gaeltacht,** or Irish-speaking area; many signs are in Gaelic only.

Visitor Information

The **Clifden Tourist Office** is on Galway Road, Clifden (© **095/21163**). Its opening hours are a little unpredictable—generally daily 9am to 5pm in summer, but you might find it closed on spring and fall weekends, and it's closed altogether from mid-October to mid-March.

Getting Around

The main road through Connemara—the N59 highway up from Galway City to **Clifden** and **Leenane** (*Leenaun*)—is hardly a crowded super-highway, but you'll still want to branch off from it to explore the region's wild and rugged coast. Loops such as the R341 from Ballyhinch to Roundstone, the Sky Road from Clifden, or the Connemara Loop from Letterfrack reward travelers who have time to get off the beaten track. Regular **buses** run from Galway to Clifden; the route takes around half an hour longer than by car. Make sure you check the time of the last return journey—they tend to stop quite early in the evening.

Exploring Connemara

As the region's biggest town (though that's not saying much), the seaside town of **Clifden** (*An Clochán*) has an enviable location at the edge of the blue waters of Clifden Bay, where miles of curving, sandy beaches skirt

Overlooking Clifden in Connemara.

the rugged coastline. It's an attractive Victorian town with colorful shop fronts and church steeples thrusting skyward, well provided with restaurants, shops, hotels, and pubs, which makes it a handy base for exploring the area. Still, it's also quite touristy. If you prefer a quieter location, seek out one of the many smaller towns and villages in the area, such as the little fishing port of **Roundstone (*Cloch na Rón*)** ★ on the south coast about 24km (15 miles) away, which also has all the essentials: pristine beaches, comfortable guesthouses, good restaurants, shops, and more than its share of natural charm. North of Clifden, the little community of **Letterfrack (*Leitir Fraic*)** sits at the edge of **Connemara National Park** (see below), close to the extraordinary Gothic **Kylemore Abbey** (p. 392). The tiny village, founded by Quakers, has a handful of pubs and B&Bs in a glorious natural setting. It's near the bright white sands of **Glassillaun Beach** and **Lettergesh,** where horses raced across the sand in the film *The Quiet Man* (see p. 424). North and east of Letterfrack, on the shore of Killary Fjord, **Leenane (*Leenaun*)** is the starting point for a number of excellent scenic hikes.

Aughnanure Castle ★ CASTLE   Standing on an outcrop of rock surrounded by forest and pasture, this sturdy fortress is a well-preserved Irish tower castle with an unusual double *bawn* (fortified enclosure) and a still-complete watchtower that you can climb. It was built around A.D. 1500 as a stronghold of the "Ferocious" O'Flaherty clan, who dominated the region and terrified their neighbors. The castle's fireplaces are so big that you could fit a double bed in them. Aside from the tower the site is mostly a ruin, although you can wander through what remains of the banqueting hall. The grounds also contain the remnants of a dry harbor.

Oughterard, Co. Galway. www.heritageireland.ie. ✆ **091/552-214.** Admission €5 adults; €4 seniors; €3 children; €13 families. Mar–Oct daily 9:30am–6pm. Last admission 45 min. before closing. Closed Nov–Feb.

Connemara National Park ★★★ NATURE SITE   This gorgeous national park encompasses more than 2,000 hectares (4,940 acres) of mountains, bogs, grasslands, and hiking trails. Some of the best trails lead through the peaceful *Gleann Mór* (which means "Big Glen"), through which flows the **River Polladirk,** or up to the **Twelve Bens** (also called the "Twelve Pins"), a small, quartzite mountain range north of the

Galway-Clifden road. None of the Twelve Bens rises above 730m (2,392 ft.), which makes their summits quite accessible to those who don't mind walking at a steep incline. Nearby are the lesser-known, equally lovely **Maumturk** range and the breathtaking **Killary Fjord**—the only fjord in Ireland, indeed this entire region of Europe. Frequent rainfall produces dozens of tiny streams and waterfalls, and the views are spectacular. The excellent visitor center south of the crossroads in **Letterfrack** dispenses general information on the park, as well as providing sustenance in the form of tea, sandwiches, and fresh baked goods.

Visitor center signposted from N59, Letterfrack, Co. Galway. www.connemara nationalpark.ie. © **076/100-2528.** Free admission. Visitor center: Mar–Oct daily 9am–5:30pm (closed Nov–Feb). Park: Daily year-round.

Dan O'Hara's Homestead Farm ★★ HERITAGE SITE This excellent open-air museum tells the story of Connemara, its people, and how they worked this rocky and inhospitable land. Dan O'Hara was a real person who farmed 3 hectares (8 acres) of land for himself and his family, until the potato famine destroyed their livelihood and they were evicted. His tragic tale—recounted at the museum—ends with Dan's children being taken into welfare and him dying broke in New York, where he had eked out a living as a match seller. The reconstructed farmstead is set up exactly as it would have been in the years before the Famine, complete with farm dwellings. The heritage center has exhibits and an informative

Dan O'Hara's Homestead Farm, a reconstructed Famine-era farmstead.

historical film. Also on the grounds of the museum is a dolmen and pre-historic tomb.

About 6.5km (4 miles) E of Clifden off N59 in Lettershea, Co. Galway. www.connemara heritage.com. ℭ **095/21808.** Admission €8 adults; €7 seniors and students; €4 children; €20 families. Apr–Oct daily 10am–6pm; last admission 1 hr. before closing.

Inishbofin ★ ISLAND   A place of seclusion and spectacular beauty, this small emerald-green gem lies 11km (6¾ miles) off the northwest coast of Connemara. Try to come here on a day when the skies are clear enough to deliver the unforgettable views of and from its shores. Once the domain of monks, then the lair of pirate queen Grace O'Malley (see p. 426), later Cromwell's infamous priest prison—you can still see his original, star-shaped barracks—Inishbofin is currently home to just 180 year-round human residents, a seal colony, and a seabird sanctuary. Numerous ferries to the island operate from the port of Cleggan (13km/8 miles northwest of Clifden off N59) daily April through October. **Inishbofin Island Discovery** (www.inishbofinislanddiscovery.com; ℭ **095/ 45819** or 086/171-8829) sails twice a day, or three times a day from late March to mid-October. Round-trip fares are €20 adults, €13 students, €10 children 5 to 18, and €5 children under 5. Seniors go free. *Note:* Reservations are essential, and evening sail times are liable to be brought forward in bad weather—so make sure you keep an eye on the hour.

Inishbofin, Co. Galway.

Killary Fjord Boat Tours ★★ CRUISE   There are roughly 6,000 islands in the North Atlantic archipelago known as the British Isles. Great Britain is the largest, Ireland the second largest, and there's enough variety in the rest to fill an encyclopedia. But this is the only fjord anywhere among them. This pleasant 90-minute cruise gives you ample time to enjoy the gorgeous views, across glassy waters to the oh-so-green hills that seem to cascade down to the shoreline. Weather permitting, you should be able to see three major mountain ranges: the Maumturk and Twelve Bens to the south, and the Mweelreas in County Mayo to the north. If you're lucky, as the cruise approaches the mouth of the Atlantic, you might also get to see dolphins. The boat—designed, they claim, to avoid seasickness, or your money back—has viewing decks inside and out, so the tour can be taken in all weathers. A bar and kitchen on board serves sandwiches and light meals, including fresh Connemara oysters. The boats depart from Nancy's Point, about 2.7km (1½ miles) west of Leenane (Leenaun). Book online for a slight discount on ticket prices.

Signposted on N59, Leenane, Co. Galway. http://killaryfjord.com. ℭ **091/566-736.** Tickets €22.50 adults; €18.50 seniors and students; €11.50 children 11–17; free for children 10 and under; €45–€55 families. Departures daily June–Aug 10:30am, 12:30, 2:30, and 4pm; May and Sept 10:30am, 12:30, and 2:30pm; Apr and Oct 12:30 and 2:30pm.

Cruising on Killary Fjord, the only true fjord in the British Isles.

Kylemore Abbey ★★ RELIGIOUS SITE   As you round yet another bend on the particularly barren stretch of country road around Kylemore, this extraordinary neo-Gothic abbey looms into view, at the base of a wooded hill across mirror-like Kylemore Lake. The facade of the main building—a vast, crenelated 19th-century house—is a splendid example of neo-Gothic architecture. In 1920, its owners donated it to the Benedictine nuns, and the sisters have run a convent boarding school here ever since. You can see a little of the interior, but it's disappointingly plain; the exterior and the grounds are the real reason to visit, especially that breathtaking view across the lake. The highlight is the restored Gothic chapel, an exquisite cathedral in miniature with a plain, somber cemetery to one side; and don't miss the lavish Victorian walled garden. Free, short history talks take place inside the abbey at 11:30am, 1pm, and 3pm daily. From June to August a free guided tour of the walled gardens is given daily at noon. The complex includes a decent restaurant that serves produce grown on the nuns' farm, as well as tea and good scones, a shop with a working pottery studio, and a visitor center. The abbey is most atmospheric when the bells are rung for midday office or for vespers at 6pm.

Kylemore, Co. Galway (follow signs from N59). www.kylemoreabbeytourism.ie. ℭ **095/52011.** Admission €13 adults; €10 seniors; €9 students and children 11–17; children 10 and under free; €26–€35 families. July–Aug daily 9am–7pm; Apr–June daily 9am–6pm; Sept–Oct daily 9:30am–5:30pm; Nov–Mar daily 10am–4:30pm.

Where to Stay in Connemara
EXPENSIVE

Abbeyglen Castle ★★   This is how a stay in a castle should be. The graystone fortress perched on a low hill might look stern and unforgiving from a distance, but inside it's all welcoming charm. It has an overall ambience of slightly faded nobility, with roomy lounges where chairs are grouped around warming fireplaces and huge windows overlook the grounds. At night, guests gather in the piano bar to chat over brandies. Guest rooms are spacious, with four-poster beds and floral fabrics. The friendly staff is happy to arrange fishing trips and packed lunches, and to give you tips on local sights. Dinners are convivial and chatty, and the food is delicious—all sourced locally.

Sky Rd., Clifden, Co. Galway. www.abbeyglen.ie. ✆ **095/21201.** 45 units. €254–€289 double. Breakfast included. Closed early Jan–early Feb. Free parking (if booked online). **Amenities:** Restaurant; bar; Jacuzzi; outdoor pool; sauna; spa; tennis court; Wi-Fi (free).

Ballynahinch Castle ★★   At the side of glass-like Owenmore River, near the foot of Ben Lettery, this gabled manor house looks too good to be true. It's a postcard setting, perfect in almost every way. The 16th-century building, once the seat of the O'Flaherty chieftains, is now a casually elegant hotel. Lounges have towering ceilings and warming fireplaces. Guest rooms are just modern enough, in muted shades of cream and toast; many have fireplaces—and all have orthopedic mattresses. The river is known for its trout and salmon, and your catch can be weighed up each evening in the wood-paneled **Fishermen's Bar.** Dinner in the beautiful **Owenmore Restaurant** is a highlight of any stay.

Recess, Co. Galway. www.ballynahinch-castle.com. ✆ **095/31006.** 40 units. €270–€370 double, €420–€450 suite. Breakfast included. **Amenities:** Restaurant; bar; babysitting; limited room service; tennis courts; Wi-Fi (free).

The neo-Gothic Kylemore Abbey perches on its lakeside site.

WALK THIS WAY: the western way

Nestled between the Maumturk and the Twelve Bens mountains in the heart of Connemara, the waters of **Lough Inagh** lie cupped in a spectacularly beautiful valley, where mountain slopes rise precipitously from the valley floor and small streams cascade into the lake in a series of sparkling waterfalls. The **Western Way,** a walking route that traverses the high country of Galway and Mayo, follows a quiet country road above the R344 through the Lough Inagh Valley.

To reach the beginning of the walk, drive north on the R344, turning right on a side road—look for the sign for Maum Ean—about 200m (656 ft.) before the Lough Inagh Lodge Hotel. Continue on this side road for about 6km (3¾ miles) to a large gravel parking lot on the left. Park here, and follow the well-worn trail 2km (1¼ miles) to the top of the pass, through glorious mountain scenery.

At the top of the pass, which has long been associated with St. Patrick, a small oratory has been built. There's a hollow in the rock known as **Patrick's Bed,** a life-size statue of the saint, and a series of cairns marking the Stations of the Cross. Together, these monuments make a striking ensemble, strangely eerie when the mists descend and conceal the far slopes in their shifting haze. A clear day offers great views, with the Atlantic Ocean and Bertraghboy Bay to the southwest and more mountains to the northeast. The round-trip walking time is about 1 hour.

Delphi Lodge ★★ This Irish country hideaway looks almost too good to be real—a vine-covered 18th-century country house dwarfed by mountains on a 1,000-acre lakefront estate. Calling this place a "lodge" isn't just cute nomenclature; this is very much an actual hunting lodge, and a veritable paradise for fishermen. Everything is arranged to make fishing easy—boats, *ghillies* (guides, though of course you fisherfolk knew that), and licenses are all taken care of. If you don't fish, you can just enjoy the utterly splendid countryside, spending the day hiking the enormous grounds, where filling your lungs with the fresh, loamy air is like a balm for the soul. Afterward, relax by the fire in the cozy library with a sherry from the honor bar, or try your hand at a game in the snooker bar. Guest rooms are comfortable and generously proportioned (though note that the doors don't have locks). The pricier rooms have views of the lake. The excellent dinners here are an event, eaten at a long dining table to encourage conversation. Pride of place on the menu, of course, goes to fish.

The Delphi Estate and Fishery, Leenane, Co. Galway. www.delphilodge.ie. © **095/ 42222.** 12 units. €250–€320 double. Breakfast included. Closed Christmas and New Year's holidays. **Amenities:** Restaurant (guests only); honor bar; Wi-Fi (free).

MODERATE

Currarevagh House ★ This elegant Italianate manor house, built in 1842, sits just outside tiny Oughterard, in the middle of a huge private park, at the edge of the clear blue waters of Lough Corrib. The house is a perfect retreat—its spacious lounges have fires crackling at the hearth, ideal for relaxing on a rainy day. Rooms are large, with floral curtains, and beds are comfortable. The guesthouse can help you plan a host of activities, from pony trekking and hiking to fishing on the Lough (you can even borrow one of the house's own traditionally made boats). Meals in the pink-hued dining room are excellent and often feature the day's catch. There's a 2-night minimum stay on summer weekends.

Oughterard, Co. Galway. www.currarevagh.com. ℰ **091/552-312.** 12 units. €160 double. Breakfast included. **Amenities:** Restaurant; bar; Wi-Fi (free).

Dolphin Beach House ★★★ A beautifully restored early-20th-century homestead, terracotta-hued Dolphin Beach House has awe-inspiring views of the bay at Clifden. The guest rooms are huge and light-filled, with handmade wood beds and high ceilings. The dining room looks out across acres of green fields, giving way to the azure sea beyond. Delicious evening meals are served here, such as local lamb or a catch of the day. (*Note:* Dinner must be booked before you arrive.) The vegetables for the table are grown in the house's own organic garden. Fearghus Foyle is an easy, charming host and also a passionate environmentalist; the house is almost entirely powered by renewable energy sources. Check the website for midweek discounts or special offers that can bring the price down by nearly half.

Lower Sky Rd., Clifden, Co. Galway. www.dolphinbeachhouse.com. ℰ **095/21204.** 4 units. €130–€180. No children under 12. Free parking. Breakfast included. Three-course dinner €40. **Amenities:** Restaurant; Wi-Fi (free).

Renvyle House Hotel ★★ This grand old house on the rocky edge of the Atlantic Ocean seems truly in the middle of nowhere, although it is near Connemara National Park. Still, it's worth the journey, and not just for these breathtaking windswept views. You'll have miles of pristine Irish wilderness to explore; there's also a golf course and a pool—rare amenities in these parts. The poet W. B. Yeats honeymooned here when it was a family home; Winston Churchill was also a regular guest. Lounges are sprawling and wood-floored, warmed by open fires. Guest rooms vary in size and decor—some are grand and spacious, others small and cozy. Most have tasteful, masculine decor. The in-house restaurant offers divine, European-inspired Irish cooking.

Renvyle, Co. Galway. www.renvyle.com. ℰ **095/46100.** 68 units. €148–€207 double. Breakfast included. Closed Jan–Feb. **Amenities:** Restaurant; bar; 7-hole golf course; outdoor pool; 2 tennis courts; Wi-Fi (free).

INEXPENSIVE

The Anglers Return ★ Surrounded by beautiful gardens, this lovely, artsy retreat was built as a hunting lodge in the 19th century; today it's run with great charm by Lynn Hill, a talented artist. Bedrooms are simple and

THE BEST smell IN ALL OF IRELAND?

"There is no fireside like your own fireside."

—Irish Proverb

You don't have to stay for long in Ireland to get used to the strong, smoky, slightly sweet smell of burning turf—dried bricks of peat taken from bogs. There are plenty who don't care for this quintessentially Irish smell, and for sure it can be quite overpowering. But for the rest of us, there's nothing else like it. In fact, if there's another smell so instantly redolent of this land—of cozy evenings by smoky hearths, of tales told and faraway friends—well, we've yet to find it.

Fully a third of the Connemara countryside is classified as bog, and these stark and beautiful boglands—formed over 2,500 years ago—have long been an important source of fuel. (During the Iron Age the Celts also found other use for the bogs, using them to store perishable foods such as butter.) Although no longer the lifeline it once was, cutting and drying turf is still an integral part of the rhythm of the seasons in Connemara.

Cutting requires a special tool, a spade called a *slane*, which slices the turf into bricks about 46cm (18 in.) long. The bricks are first spread out flat to dry, and then stacked in pyramids for further drying.

You can always tell when turf is burning in a home's fireplace—the smoke coming out of the chimney is blue and heavily scented. Regrettably, the bricks are a little too bulky to make good souvenirs, but you might find turf-scented incense and candles in craft stores.

modestly sized, furnished with antiques. The views over the grounds and nearby river are gorgeous. Two of the rooms are en suite; the others have the use of one of two bathrooms located down the corridor—and robes are thoughtfully provided. You can cook your own dinner in the newly outfitted kitchen or on the grills outside. Guests are free to wander the gardens, which are practically an attraction by themselves. Those wanting more seclusion, and a touch of adventure, may want to rent the yurt on the grounds. *Note:* The Anglers Return doesn't accept credit cards; it's cash or check only around here.

Toombeola, Roundstone, Co. Galway. www.anglersreturn.com. © **095/31091.** 5 units. €110–€120 double. 2-night minimum stay B&B. Free parking. Breakfast included. No credit cards. Closed Dec–Jan. **Amenities:** Restaurant; guest lounge; Wi-Fi (free).

Doonmore Hotel ★   This waterfront hotel on Inishbofin island might not be fancy, but the views are extraordinary—from every window you see stunning vistas of the sea and High Island. Guest rooms are quite basic, but families will be pleased to find the spacious units with children's bunk beds. Rooms in the modern extension are furnished with pine furniture and flooded with light. Older rooms in the main house are a little worn but still pleasant. Staff are cheerful, and the restaurant offers good, unpretentious cooking.

Inishbofin Island, Co. Galway. www.doonmorehotel.com. ✆ **095/45804.** 25 units. €95–€110 double. Breakfast included. Closed Nov–Mar. **Amenities:** Restaurant; bar; Wi-Fi (free).

Errisbeg Lodge ★ This mountainside lodge near the little town of Roundstone feels more isolated than it is. Tucked away between the wild countryside and the ocean, its setting is glorious and makes for wonderful, windy walks down to the sandy beach. Guest rooms are simply decorated with pine furniture and floral bedding. All have exquisite mountain or ocean views. This is not a five-star hotel by any means, but the hosts are very friendly and the scenery is breathtaking. *Note:* The lodge doesn't take credit cards.

Just over 1.6km (1 mile) outside of Roundstone on Clifden Rd., Roundstone, Co. Galway. www.errisbeglodge.com. ✆ **095/35807.** 5 units. €80–€110 double. Breakfast included. No credit cards. Closed Dec–Jan. **Amenities:** Wi-Fi (free).

Where to Eat in Connemara

The Carriage Restaurant ★ MODERN CONTINENTAL Locals flock to this restaurant, hidden away in the courtyard at the rear of the Clifden Station House Hotel. The draw is imaginative cooking that manages to infuse even the simplest dish with zest and originality. The chef loves to chargrill and smoke; look for dishes like blackened turbot served with smoked oysters and grilled mushrooms. More casual dining is available in the adjacent bar.

At the rear of the Station House Hotel, on the N59, Clifden, Co. Galway. www. clifdenstationhouse.com. ✆ **095/21699.** Reservations essential. Entrees €15–€25. Daily 6:30–9:30pm. Closed Oct–Apr.

O'Dowd's of Roundstone ★★ SEAFOOD There's not much room in this tiny pub in Roundstone, which means you'll be fighting for space with dozens of hungry locals. But trust them, for they know exactly what they're here for: extremely good, fresh seafood, simple and beautifully prepared. There's nothing complicated about the menu, and that's part of the appeal—Connemara salmon or seafood medley, served in a white wine and cream sauce, or a steaming bowl of beef and Guinness stew to keep carnivores happy. Try the delicious chowder if it's on offer. Needless to say, booking is advisable.

Roundstone, Co. Galway. www.odowdsseafoodbar.com. ✆ **095/35809.** Entrees €13–€29. Daily noon–9pm (food served until 9:30–10pm summer).

Paddy Coyne's Pub ★★ IRISH It can be hard to find this lovely pub in tiny, blink-and-you'll-miss-it Renvyle—just outside blink-just-a-little-bit-longer-and-you'll-miss-it-too Tully—but it's worth the trek. Aside from the postcard-worthy frontage, dating from 1811, this doesn't *look* like the kind of place that's likely to wow you with its cooking. But the numbers of people making their way here for dinner should provide a

TAKING A (moon) SHINE TO POTCHEEN

"Keep your eyes well peeled today, the excise men are on their way, searching for the mountain tay, in the hills of Connemara…"

Potcheen is a potent form of Irish moonshine, traditionally brewed from grain or potatoes. It was banned by the English crown in 1661, in an act that effectively criminalized thousands of distillers overnight. That didn't stop people from making the stuff, however, and after 336 years on the wrong side of the law, potcheen was finally made legal again in 1997.

One 17th-century writer said of potcheen that "it enlighteneth ye heart, casts off melancholy, keeps back old age and breaketh ye wind." Its usefulness didn't stop there, evidently, as history records the drink being used as everything from a bath tonic to a substitute for dynamite.

Potcheen has long been used in fiction as a symbol of Irish nationalism, its contraband status rich with rebellious overtones. The traditional folk song "The Hills of Connemara" describes potcheen being secretly distributed under the noses of excise men.

In 2008, the European Union awarded the drink "Geographical Indicative" protection. This means that only the genuine Irish product is allowed to carry the name (the same status enjoyed by Champagne and Parma ham).

You'll find potcheen for sale in a few souvenir stores. Like most liquors it can be drunk straight, on the rocks, or with a mixer, but at anything from 80 to a massive 180 proof, potcheen packs a mean punch, so enjoy…cautiously.

clue. There's nothing pretentious about the cooking—it's just wonderful, classic Irish fare, done extremely well. Seafood is a specialty—the daily specials are chalked up outside, but expect hake, salmon, mussels, or maybe some Clew Bay oysters, served as they come or with a tasty cheese crumble topping. Burgers are juicy and tender, and the steaks are big enough for three people. Wash it all down with a pint of expertly poured Guinness. Desserts are avowedly traditional (try the homemade trifle). *Note:* It's cash only here, and they don't take reservations either, so arrive early or be prepared to wait.

Tully Cross, Renvyle, Co. Galway. www.paddycoynespub.com. ℂ **095/43499.** Reservations not accepted. Entrees €12–€25. No credit cards. Daily 6–9:30pm (but times vary—call to check).

The Steam Coffee House ★ CAFE   This cute and simple little cafe is one of the best places in Clifden for lunch. The menu isn't fancy, but it's all good: wraps, sandwiches, light meals, and daily specials, everything made with quality ingredients. The soups are particularly tasty, with ever-changing daily specials–you may find minestrone, sweet potato and coconut, or even carrot and orange. The tasty cakes and desserts are great to wash down with the excellent coffee.

Station House Courtyard, off N59 (Galway Rd.), Clifden, Co. Galway. ℂ **095/30600.** Entrees €4–€12. Tues–Sat 9:30am–5:30pm. Closed Sun–Mon.

Veldon's Seafarer ★★ SEAFOOD   The fishermen's nets, captain's wheels, and assorting sailing paraphernalia plastered across the polished wooden walls of this friendly bar and restaurant leaves no doubt as to what the specialty of the house is. You can eat from a fairly simple bar menu—traditional fish and chips, hamburgers, Irish stew—or retreat to the pleasant restaurant area, where you might start with some tasty crab claws with garlic and herb butter, followed up with a plate of sea bream served with lemon and fennel mirepoix (diced vegetables cooked slowly in butter), or chicken stuffed with sweet pimento pepper and smoked cheese.

On the N59, Letterfrack, Co. Galway. www.veldons.ie. ✆ **095/41046.** Bar food €7–€22. Entrees €14.50– €16. Bar daily noon–9pm; restaurant daily 6–9pm (Fri–Sat only in off-season).

Sports & Outdoor Pursuits in Connemara

FISHING   **Lough Corrib** is renowned for brown trout and salmon fishing. Brown trout fishing is usually good from the middle of February, and salmon is best from the end of May. For salmon and sea trout, the **Ballynahinch Castle Hotel** at Ballynahinch, Recess (www.ballynahinch-castle.com; ✆ **095/31006**) is an angler's paradise (see p. 393). Fishing licenses, tackle, maps, and advice are available at the hotel. At **Portarra Lodge,** Tullykyne, Moycullen (www.portarralodge.com; ✆ **091/555-051**), fishing packages include B&B accommodations in a modern guesthouse on the shores of Lough Corrib, dinners, and boats and tackle. Owner Michael Canney is an avid angler and a great guide to this part of Galway. Weekly packages that include half-board, boat, and *ghillie* (guide) are available.

WALKING   **Connemara National Park** ★★★ (see p. 389) has excellent walking trails, some of which lead up the sides of the Twelve Bens. You can get maps at the park's visitor center. From the town of **Leenane** (*Leenaun*), there's an exhilarating 4km (2.4 miles) walk to the picturesque Aasleagh Waterfall (*Eas Liath*) northeast of the Killary Fjord harbor. A 2- to 3-hour walk around the fjord follows the Green Road, a sheep track that was once the primary route from the Renvyle Peninsula to Leenane; along the way you'll even pass a ghost town (a village abandoned after the Famine), where the fields rise at a devilishly steep slope from ruined cottages clustered at the water's edge.

WATERSPORTS & ADVENTURE SPORTS   One-stop shopping for outdoorsy activities—kayaking, waterskiing, hill and coastal walking, rock climbing, archery, you name it—can be found at the **Killary Adventure Company** in Leenane (www.killary.com; ✆ **095/43411**). Rates start at around €30 per session. The **Delphi Adventure Resort** in Leenane (www.delphiadventureresort.com; ✆ **095/42208**) offers courses in kayaking,

CONNEMARA pony TREKKING

The sturdy yet elegant Connemara pony is the only horse breed native to Ireland, though it has received an infusion of Spanish blood over the centuries. Often raised in tiny fields with limestone pastures, the ponies are known for their stamina and gentleness, which make them ideal for amateur riders and young people. Born and bred to traverse the region's rugged terrain, they are adept at scaling short, steep hills and delicately picking their way along rocky shores.

Because much of the countryside is well off the beaten track, pony trekking is actually a fantastic way to cover ground.

It gets you off the busy roads and out into the countryside, even onto the white-sand beaches near Roundstone and elsewhere along the coast. The **Cleggan Beach Riding Centre,** Cleggan (www.clegganridingcentre.com; ✆ **083/388-8135**) offers beach and mountain treks, the most popular being a 3-hour ride to Omey Island at low tide. And near Loughrea, the **Aille Cross Equestrian Centre** (www.connemara-trails.com; ✆ **091/843-968;** see p. 382) can set you up with guided treks for all levels of ability.

windsurfing, and raft building, as well as mountaineering, abseiling, hiking, and archery. Everything is reasonably priced, and the atmosphere is laid-back and friendly.

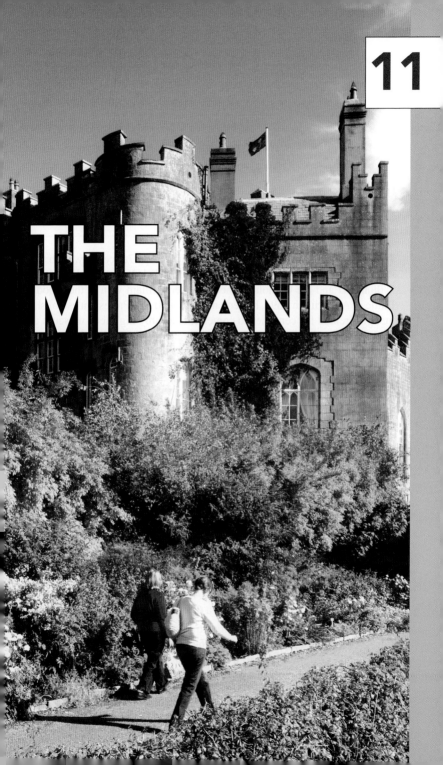

THE MIDLANDS

The Irish Midlands are the country's flatlands—horse country, all soft green grass and sprawling fields, veined with long, winding rivers and picturesque, slow-moving streams. While it doesn't have the glamour of Cork, Kerry, or Galway, there is more to this region than first meets the eye. You can find real gems—like the romantic medieval castles at Charleville and Birr, the atmospheric ancient monastic site at Clonmacnoise, or the surprisingly little-known (and really *very* old indeed) Corlea Trackway.

The most significant history here dates to the late 17th century, with the fateful battle for supremacy between two English kings: the Protestant William III and the Catholic James II. After William won at the bloody Battle of Aughrim in 1691, he cemented the hold of a Protestant establishment in Ireland for centuries to come. The lavishly high-tech museum at Athlone Castle is the best of several in the region that tell this important story.

ESSENTIALS
Arriving

BY CAR By far the best way to get to and around the Midlands is by car. Although Athlone is easy to reach by public transportation from Galway or Dublin, you'll need a car to see the smaller towns and remote sites. Major roads that lead to this area are the main Galway-Dublin road (N6) from points east and west, N62 from the south, and N55 and N61 from the north. For car rentals in Dublin, see p. 91; for rentals from Shannon airport, see p. 334.

BY BUS **Bus Éireann** (www.buseireann.ie; ✆ **061/313333**) runs buses every half hour to 90 minutes, from the main bus station in Galway City to Athlone (journey time 80–100 min.). There are also several buses a day to Birr (around 4 hr.), changing in Athlone or Limerick. From the main bus station in Dublin, buses also go to Athlone about every hour (journey time 2–3 hr.) and a handful of times a day to Birr (3–4 hr.).

BY TRAIN **Irish Rail** operates direct trains from Galway to Athlone Station, Southern Station Road (✆ **090/647-3300**) every 1 to 2 hours; the journey takes 90 minutes. From Dublin trains go to Athlone about every hour; most journeys take just over an hour.

PREVIOUS PAGE: **Lush gardens surround Birr Castle, in County Offaly.**

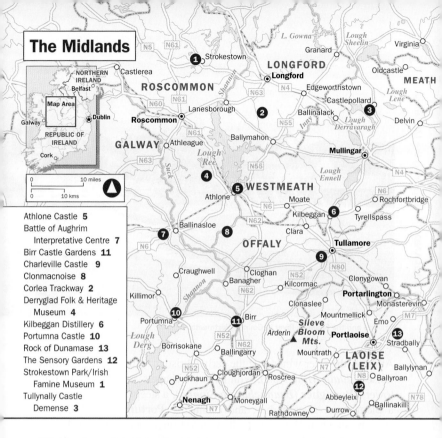

The Midlands

L. Gowna
Lough Sheelin
Virginia

N5 N61 Strokestown Granard Oldcastle

Castlerea LONGFORD MEATH
NORTHERN IRELAND Longford Edgeworthstown
Belfast ROSCOMMON N63 N4 Castlepollard Lough Lene
Map Area N60 N61 Lanesborough Ballinalack Delvin
Galway Dublin Roscommon N55 Lough Derravaragh
REPUBLIC OF IRELAND N61 Ballymahon Mullingar
Cork GALWAY Athleague Lough Ree Lough Ennell N4
N63 N55 N6
Athlone Moate Rochfortbridge
0   10 miles WESTMEATH Kilbeggan Tyrellspass
0   10 kms Ballinasloe N62 Clara
OFFALY Tullamore
N6 N80
Craughwell Cloghan N52 Clonygowan
Banagher Kilcormac Portarlington
Killimor N62 Clonaslee Monasterevin
Portumna Birr Mountmellick Emo M7
Lough Derg Borrisokane Arderin Slieve Bloom Mts. Portlaoise Stradbally
N52 N62 Ballingarry Mountrath LAOISE (LEIX) Ballylynan
Puckhaun Cloughjordan Roscrea N7 N8 Ballyroan
Nenagh Moneygall Abbeyleix Ballinakill
N7 Rathdowney Durrow N78

Athlone Castle **5**
Battle of Aughrim
   Interpretative Centre **7**
Birr Castle Gardens **11**
Charleville Castle **9**
Clonmacnoise **8**
Corlea Trackway **2**
Derryglad Folk & Heritage
   Museum **4**
Kilbeggan Distillery **6**
Portumna Castle **10**
Rock of Dunamase **13**
The Sensory Gardens **12**
Strokestown Park/Irish
   Famine Museum **1**
Tullynally Castle
   Demense **3**

A Note on Listings

Officially the Midlands region covers the counties of Laois, Longford, Offaly, and Westmeath; we've also included a couple of sights in the far eastern part of County Galway, because of their close proximity. Attractions in this region are widely spread out—hiring a car is the only practical way to see the Midlands' best sights without spending excessive amounts of time on public transport (where there's even any at all). Therefore we present them as one list, not split up by county, allowing travelers to pick and choose according to their interests.

EXPLORING THE MIDLANDS

Unsurprisingly, the great Shannon River has for centuries tied this region together. The area's most appealing town of any size—although it's hardly a teeming metropolis, with a population of just over 20,000—is **Athlone (Baile Átha Luain),** on the River Shannon. It's a vibrant place where brightly painted buildings house interesting craft stores and boutiques. It's also a perfect spot to base yourself for exploring the area, with excellent small hotels, charming restaurants, and nightlife. Heading south from

Athlone and the Shannon River in County Westmeath.

Athlone, the river winds past the early Christian settlement of **Clonmac-noise** *(Cluain Mhic Nóis),* with its stone chapels and mysterious round towers; **Banagher** *(Beannchar na Sionna),* a sleepy working town with a picturesque river harbor; and eventually **Portumna Castle,** picturesquely set where the Shannon flows into Lough Derg (see p. 411).

East of the Shannon, the town of **Birr** *(Biorra),* known for its magnificent historic gardens, is south of Banagher, with the Slieve Bloom Mountains rising to its east; the N52 angles northeast from Birr, passing through the county towns of **Tullamore** (County Offaly) and **Mullingar** (Westmeath).

Athlone Castle ★★ CASTLE   Built in 1210 for King John of England, this mighty stone fortress sits on the edge of the Shannon, atop the ruins of an earlier fort built in 1129 as the seat of the chiefs of Connaught. Besieged for almost 6 months in 1641, the castle was attacked again in 1690 and finally fell in 1691 after an intense bombardment by forces sent by William of Orange. The fall of Athlone was a key event in the war that would cement the Protestant establishment in Ireland and ensure British rule, all the way up to the War of Independence in the 1920s. (The Dutch military commander who took the town, Godard van Glinkel, was rewarded for his efforts with the earldom of Athlone.) Three centuries later, in 2012, the castle underwent a multimillion-euro renovation; it now houses eight separate galleries on the history of Athlone, particularly the 1690-91 siege, using plenty of high-tech wizardry. The castle's original medieval walls have been preserved, as have two large cannons dating from the reign of George II, and a pair of 25cm (10-inch) mortars cast in 1856.

Athlone, Co. Westmeath. www.athlonecastle.ie. ✆ **090/644-2130.** Admission €8 adults; €6 seniors and students; €4 children 5–15; free for children 4 and under; €20–€25 families. June–Aug Mon–Sat 10am–6pm, Sun 11am–6pm; Mar–May and Sept–Oct Tues–Sat 10:30am–5:30pm, Sun 11:30am–5:30pm; Nov–Feb Wed–Sat 11am–5pm, Sun noon–5pm. Last admission 1 hr. before closing.

Battle of Aughrim Interpretative Centre ★ BATTLEFIELD

About midway between Galway City and Athlone, just off the M6 motorway, lies this interesting little museum, dedicated to a battle between two kings that took place here in 1691. When James II became king of England in 1685, his days on the throne were already numbered. He had a "flaw" that the Protestant establishment simply couldn't live with: He was a convert to Catholicism. In 1688, James was deposed by Parliament in favor of his own son-in-law—the Protestant William III. Retreating to Ireland, James led a rebellion that was to have far-reaching consequences for Irish history. Aughrim wasn't the most famous nor arguably the most important battle of that war, but it was the last. With the defeat of the so-called Jacobite forces loyal to James, the prospect of a Catholic Ireland was crushed for almost 2½ centuries. The center does a competent job of telling the story through displays and exhibits, plus the obligatory visitor-center film.

R446, Aughrim, near Ballinasloe, Co. Galway. ✆ **090/967-3939.** Admission €5 adults; €4 seniors and students; €3 children 11 and under; €12 families. May–Aug Tues–Sat 10:30am–5pm, Sun 1–5pm. Closed early Sept–Apr.

An open-air market stall in the lively town of Athlone.

THE GREAT telescope

At noble **Birr Castle** ★★ (below), one of the key attractions is not the historic castle itself, nor the beautiful grounds, but a fascinating exhibition on 19th-century science. William Parsons, the 3rd Earl of Birr, was a scientist and astronomer, obsessed with discovering all he could about the night sky. Under his leadership, Birr Castle became an unlikely hub of research into astronomy, photography, and botany. One of his inventions—now known as the Great Telescope—was built in 1845 and soon nicknamed (somewhat sarcastically) the "Leviathan of Parsonstown." Until the 20th century, it was the largest telescope in the world.

The huge astronomical machine may resemble a medieval siege engine, but the key thing about it was that it worked. Using it, Parsons discovered and documented numerous nebulae, some of which were later determined to be hitherto unknown galaxies. He found and named the Crab Nebula, among others. He also discovered that certain galaxies were shaped like spirals. Birr Castle was the only place in the world where the phenomenon could be observed until 1914, when new, more advanced telescopes were developed.

To this day, the Great Telescope is kept in full working order, and demonstrations of its power are held regularly in summer. If you want to witness one of these displays for yourself, call ahead to check times.

Birr Castle Gardens ★★ GARDENS This magnificent 90-room, 17th-century castle stands amid gorgeous sprawling gardens, beautifully crafted as a kind of wonderland. The great house is still lived in by the same family that has owned it for centuries. It is only open to the public from May to August, 6 days a week—and even then for just a handful of pricey guided tours, limited to 15 adults, so advance booking is essential. But the real reason to come to Birr is to see the extraordinary grounds, which are open year-round. The *demesne* (estate) of the Parsons family, now the earls of Rosse, wraps around a peaceful lake and stretches over miles of pastures and wild woodland. There's much to discover—beautiful topiaries, huge box hedges, a lovely wrought-iron bridge, a newly renovated science exhibition, and even a steampunk-esque, 19th-century telescope (see above). There's also a charming tea shop and a play area for kids.

Birr, Co. Offaly. www.birrcastle.com. ✆ **057/912-0336.** Admission to grounds €9 adults; €7.50 seniors, students and children 13–17; €5 children 5–12; free for children 4 and under; €25 families. Castle tours €18 per person; no children under 12 on tours. Grounds: Mid-Mar to Oct daily 9am–6pm; Nov to mid-Mar daily 10am–4pm. Castle tours: May–Aug Mon–Sat 10am, 11:30am, 1pm.

Charleville Castle ★★ CASTLE Now, *this* is a castle. Designed in 1798 by Francis Johnston, the spooky, crenellated Gothic Revival masterpiece took 12 years to build. Today it's considered one of the best of Ireland's early-19th-century castles, with fine limestone walls and plenty of towers, turrets, and battlements—and those who believe in such things say it is haunted. (It has been featured on the TV shows *Ghost Hunters* and *Most Haunted*.) Inside you'll find spectacular plasterwork and hand-carved stairways, as well as secret passageways and dungeons. The castle is open year-round, and scheduled tours run daily from May to August. For the rest of the year, try and book tours a couple of days in advance. Charleville is run by volunteers, so opening times can be a little unpredictable. The volunteers are as accommodating as possible, but do bear in mind that they're running it out of love rather than for profit. ("Tourists who drop in generally find one of the volunteers and get a tour in any case," they explained to us recently.) Prices are a little on the high side, but the money is obviously needed for ongoing restoration work. The fact that the staff, so dedicated and enthusiastic, is all unpaid, makes it easier to justify paying that little bit extra.

Off Birr Rd. (N52), Tullamore, Co. Offaly. www.charlevillecastle.ie. Ⓒ **087/766-4110** or 057/932-3040. Guided tour €20 adults; €12 students age 17–18; €6 children 6–16; free for children under 6. Castle open year-round; June–Aug tours daily 1–5:30pm; Sept–May tours by appointment.

Clonmacnoise ★★★ RELIGIOUS SITE/RUINS   Resting somberly on the east bank of the Shannon, this is one of Ireland's most profound ancient sites. St. Ciaran founded the monastic community of

Performers at Charleville Castle's annual Castlepalooza festival.

Clonmacnoise in 548 at the crucial intersection of the Shannon and the Dublin-Galway land route, and it soon became one of Europe's great centers of learning and culture. For nearly 1,000 years, Clonmacnoise flourished under the patronage of Irish chiefs; the last high king, Rory O'Connor, was buried here in 1198. Clonmacnoise was raided repeatedly by native chiefs, Danes, and Anglo-Normans, until it was finally destroyed by English troops in 1552. Previously the monks always had something to rebuild, but this time the English looted everything. In a report written by a monk from that time, "There was not left a bell, small or large, an image or an altar, or a book, or a gem, or even glass in a window, from the wall of the church out, which was not carried off." Today you can see what was left of the cathedral, a castle, eight churches, two round towers, three sculpted high crosses, and more than 200 monumental slabs. On some stones, the old carvings can still be seen with thoughtful messages in ancient Celtic, such as "A prayer for Daniel."

On R357, 6.5km (4 miles) north of Shannonbridge, Co. Offaly. © **090/967-4195.** Admission €8 adults; €6 seniors; €4 students and children; €20 families. June–Aug daily 9am–6:30pm; mid-Mar to May and Sept–Oct daily 10am–6pm; Nov to mid-Mar daily 10am–5:30pm. Last admission 45 min. before closing.

Corlea Trackway ★★ ANCIENT SITE   This is one of those places that makes you stand back, scratch your head, and marvel at just how *old* Ireland is. The fairly unassuming, modern interpretive center, situated in a bog, contains what at first glance looks like an elevated platform of planks nailed onto rails, like a boardwalk through a marsh or swamp. It is, in fact, an excavated wooden trackway that has been carbon dated to the year 148 B.C. Roughly 18m (59 feet) of original track has been uncovered so far and can be seen on a (free) guided tour. The center also contains an exhibition and a film to put the whole thing into context. A replica version crosses a starkly beautiful section of bog, roughly where the rest of the track is believed to be buried. The weird thing is that the modern version really doesn't look all that different. Was the track built merely as a bridge over the bog, or did it have some religious significance—perhaps

---

Castlepalooza Music & Arts Festival

Haunted it may or may not be, but Charleville Castle (see p. 406) certainly comes to life in early August, when the delightfully laidback and bohemian **Castlepalooza** takes over the grounds. The 3-day festival—which won the award for "Best Small Festival in Europe" in 2009, 2010, and 2011—attracts indie and alternative bands from Ireland and beyond. There are also arts workshops, film screenings, spoken-word performances, and the like. Camping is available on-site during the festival. For more information, and to book tickets, visit **www.castle palooza.com**.

walk this way: **THE SLIEVE BLOOM WAY**

Linking counties Laois and Offaly, the lush and gentle Slieve Bloom mountain range is great hillwalking territory—its tallest peak is just 527m (1,729 ft.), which clocks in at about the same as the 44th tallest in the Wicklow Mountains (see p. 198). The Slieve Blooms also have the great advantage of being decidedly undervisited, so peace and solitude are easy to come by.

The Slieve Bloom Mountains Nature Reserve—Ireland's largest state-owned nature reserve—has several looped hiking trails, including several around **Lough** (lake) **Boora;** one of them has its own sculpture trail. Another takes you through the tiny but charming village of **Clonaslee,** and up to the **Rickets Rock waterfall.** For a touch of scenic wilderness, walk a portion of the **Slieve Bloom Way,** a circular 34km (21-mile) signposted trail that begins and ends in Glenbarrow, County Laois; see **www.slievebloom.ie** for details. Several trained guides live locally and will offer their services if you'd prefer to be taken around by an expert; a full list with contact details is available at **www.slievebloom.ie** (click "Walking," then "Walking Guides").

The terrain also lends itself particularly well to horseback riding; the **Birr Equestrian Centre,** Kingsborough House, Birr, County Offaly (www. birrequestrian.ie; © **087/244-5545**) organizes regular treks and special trips.

Several castles lie within the boundaries of the Slieves, including **Charleville ★★** (see p. 406) and **Portumna ★★** (see p. 411).

For more information, visit **www. slievebloom.ie**.

---

enabling people to reach a part of the bog considered sacred for some long-forgotten reason? Archaeologists disagree, but it's fascinating to contemplate the possibility.

Kenagh, Co. Longford. www.heritageireland.ie. © **043/332-2386.** Free admission. Early Apr to early Oct daily 10am–6pm. Last tour 1 hr. before closing; last admission 45 min. before closing.

Derryglad Folk & Heritage Museum ★ MUSEUM   For a highly concentrated dose of mid-20th-century nostalgia, visit this rather sweet little museum just outside Athlone. You walk through a series of re-created businesses, each little building jam-packed with memorabilia and antiques—a "medical hall" (drugstore), grocery store, hardware store—and a few farmer's crofts. The intriguing **McCormack Photography Room** preserves the collection of a real photography studio that operated in Athlone from 1948 until 2002. As well as antique cameras and developing equipment, it displays photographs from the decades the shop was in operation. Museum guides could hardly be keener to impart their encyclopedic knowledge.

Curraghboy, Co. Roscommon (13.8km/8½ miles NW of Athlone on R362). www. derrygladfolkmuseum.com. © **090/648-8192.** Admission €5 adults; €4.50 seniors and students; €3.50 children. May–Sept Mon–Sat 10am–6pm. Closed Oct–Apr.

The Kilbeggan Distillery ★ FACTORY TOUR   The oldest *licensed* distillery in Ireland, Kilbeggan has been producing whiskey here since 1757. Well, almost—it closed in 1957 and was virtually derelict for 25 years, until locals revived it as a small-time distillery and museum. Full production resumed in the late 2000s, in part using traditional methods and equipment, including oak mash tuns (vats) and a 2-century-old copper still—thought to be the oldest still in day-to-day use anywhere in the world. (They also have a working waterwheel and a steam-powered engine, although these are mostly for show.) Unlike most distilleries, you can wander around yourself, or choose one of the guided tours. The daily Apprentice Tour (€14 per person; hourly 10am–4pm and 4:30pm Apr–Oct, hourly 11am–2pm and 2:30pm Nov–March) includes a master-class tasting of three whiskeys, or, if you prefer, samples to take home. The daily Distillers Tour (€26 per person; 1:30pm Apr–Oct, noon Nov–March) allows you to meet the distillers themselves and take part in a four-whiskey master-class tasting. True enthusiasts can opt for the Connoisseur Experience (€85 per person), a 3½-hour extravaganza that includes lunch and the chance to bottle your own whiskey. It's only available on certain dates; call or go online for schedule.

On N6, E of Athlone, Kilbeggan, Co. Westmeath. www.kilbeggandistillery.com. ℂ **057/933-2134.** No children on tours. Apr–Oct daily 9am–6pm; Nov–Mar daily 10am–4pm.

Sampling whiskeys at the Kilbeggan Distillery.

Portumna Castle and Forest Park ★★ CASTLE/PARK Built in 1609 by Earl Richard Burke, this massive, noble structure on the northern shores of Lough Derg is a particularly fine manor house. Had it not been gutted by fire in 1826, who knows what billionaire might own it now? The fire spared much of the impressive exterior, including its decorative Dutch-style gables and rows of stone mullioned windows; the ground floor is open to the public and contains exhibits on the history of the castle, particularly the so-called "Flight of the Wild Geese" when James II's Jacobite supporters fled Ireland in defeat. The grounds contain a restored walled kitchen garden and a willow maze. Surrounding the castle, the beautiful 560-hectare (1,383-acre) expanse of **Portumna Forest Park** offers trails and signposted walks, plus viewing points, picnic areas, and the remains of a 13th-century Cistercian abbey.

Off N65, Portumna, Co. Galway. ✆ **090/974-1658.** Castle €5 adults; €4 seniors; €3 children and students; €13 families. Free admission to gardens and Forest Park. Castle: Early Apr to mid-Oct daily 9:30am–6pm; late Oct Sat–Sun 9:30am–5pm. Last admission 45 min. before closing. Castle closed Nov–Mar.

The Rock of Dunamase ★ RUINS There isn't much left of the castle that once stood atop this rocky outcrop overlooking a valley near the town of Portlaoise; what remains, however, is a fetching and quite impressive sight. The ruins were once **Dunamase Castle** (though nobody calls it that anymore), built sometime during the 12th century. It clearly didn't last long; records indicate that it was a total ruin by as early as 1350. A much earlier fort is believed to have stood on the same site. A few arched gateways survive intact, and the scattered remains of walls and turrets give a good idea of how large it must have once been. The stunning view from among the ruins, over rolling green fields toward the Slieve Mountains in the distance, is worth the visit alone. The Rock is signposted from the main road, but it's very easy to get lost! So to get there, follow these directions: Leave Portlaoise on N80, heading southeast toward Carlow. Shortly after crossing over the M7 motorway, just outside the town limits, you'll pass some large green industrial sheds. Approximately 1.8km (just over 1 mile) after this you will come to some scattered houses, with a turning on the left, next to a triangular patch of lawn and a telegraph pole. Take this turning; you will start to see the Rock on the hill to your left in about 0.5km (550 yards).

Off of N80 (Portlaoise-Carlow Rd.), about 9km (5½ miles) E of Portlaoise, Co. Laois. Free admission. Daily dawn–dusk.

The Sensory Gardens ★ GARDENS On the grounds of a convent in the town of Abbeyleix, not far from the border between counties Laois and Kilkenny, these gardens were designed by people with learning difficulties. They are intended to be not only accessible but also stimulating to disabled visitors. Plants are chosen for their particularly strong effect on the senses, whether it be their vibrant colors, powerful scent, or tactile

A somber **SORT OF GRANDEUR: STROKESTOWN & ITS FAMINE MUSEUM**

For nearly 4 centuries, from 1600 to 1979, **Strokestown Park House** (www. strokestownpark.ie; ☏ **071/963-3013**) was the seat of the Pakenham-Mahon family. After the Restoration, King Charles II granted the vast estate, which stretches for miles in every direction, to Nicholas Mahon in appreciation for supporting the House of Stewart during the bloody English Civil War. (Quite a reward indeed!) Nicholas's grandson, Thomas, considered the original house, completed in 1697, too small and unimposing, so he upped the ante by hiring Richard Cassels—aka "Richard Castle," the architect behind Russborough House (see p. 196) and Powerscourt House (p. 195)—to build him something more impressive. The result? This stunning 45-room Palladian mansion, a monument to upper-class privilege. In the north wing, note Ireland's last existing galleried kitchen (where the lady of the house could observe the culinary activity without being part of it), and in the south wing, a vaulted stable so magnificent it has been described as an "equine cathedral."

These days Strokestown is also the permanent home of the **Irish National Famine Museum,** one of the country's very best museums devoted to that deadly period in Irish history. It dramatically sets forth not only the natural disaster, but also the shocking cruelty of the British establishment's response. Exhibits include letters penned by some of the tenants of Strokestown during the Famine years.

The pairing of these two historic attractions may seem incongruous, until you learn a little more of Strokestown Park's history—particularly the behavior of Major Denis Mahon, the landlord at Strokestown during the 1840s. When the potato blight struck and famine started to spread, Mahon and his land agents could have done many things to help the hundreds of starving people who lived and worked on the property. Instead they evicted them as soon as it became clear they couldn't pay their rent; callously, Mahon even chartered ships to send his own tenants away from Ireland. In 1847, Major Mahon was shot to death near Strokestown. Two men were hastily (and dubiously) convicted of the crime, but it seems clear that many hungry people had motives.

Strokestown Park is on the main Dublin-Castlebar Road (N5). Admission costs €14 adults, €12 seniors and students, €6 children, and €29 families. It's open daily from mid-March to October 10:30am to 5:30pm (from Nov to mid-March 10:30am–4pm). The house can only be seen on a 45-minute guided tour, at noon, 2:30, and 4pm (2pm only in winter).

The elegant Strokestown Park House in County Roscommon has a dark tale to tell.

appeal. Touches like wind chimes here and there, and even an innovative "humming stone," make this an ingenious and pleasant place to wander.

At Dove House, Main St., Abbeyleix, Co. Laois. ℂ **057/873-1325.** Free admission (donations requested). June–Sept Mon–Fri 9am–4pm, Sat–Sun and public holidays 2–6pm; Oct–May Mon–Fri 9am–4pm.

Tullynally Castle Gardens ★ CASTLE/GARDENS   A turreted and towered Gothic Revival manor, this creamy white castle is dazzling. It has been the home of the Pakenham family, the earls of Longford, since 1655. Frustratingly, the building itself is only open to prebooked groups of 20 or more. But the 12-hectare (30-acre) grounds are an attraction in themselves. Highlights include a large kitchen garden, where the grass is kept short by grazing llamas; forest trails and a riverside walk; and an idyllic path leading to a Victorian grotto. Tullynally is near Lough Derravaragh, a tranquil spot featured in the legendary Irish tale *The Children of Lir.* Check the website for events listings, including classical concerts—the only way you're likely to get inside the castle without being part of a large group.

About 32km (20 miles) E of Longford and 21km (13 miles) N of Mullingar, off the main Dublin-Sligo Rd. (N4), Castlepollard, Co. Westmeath. www.tullynallycastle.ie. ℂ **044/966-1856.** Gardens €6 adults; €3 children; €16 families. Castle open for pre-booked group tours—call for information. Garden open Apr–Sept Thurs–Sun and public holidays 11am–5pm. Open daily during Heritage Week in Aug.

WHERE TO STAY IN THE MIDLANDS

Athlone, on the southern tip of Lough Rea and almost halfway between Galway and Dublin, makes a natural base from which to explore the Midlands region. It has a couple of modern chain hotels, although it seems a shame to come all this way and stay in one when you could be waking up to a home-cooked breakfast in a sweet little Irish farmhouse instead.

Athlone

Bastion ★★   This delightful B&B is run by the lovely Anthony and Vinny McCay, who have converted an old Athlone town house into a chic, rather bohemian getaway. The decor fills the place with light and cheer, from the whitewashed walls and polished wood floors in the bedrooms to the sophisticated furniture and slightly Moroccan-style accent pieces strewn here and there. Breakfasts are served across the street at the wonderful **Bastion Kitchen** (see p. 416). Two minor downsides: Two of the bedrooms have shared bathrooms, and those with mobility problems should be sure to ask for a room on the lower floors—there are quite a few stairs to climb.

2 Bastion St., Athlone, Co. Westmeath. www.thebastion.net. ℂ **090/649-4954.** 7 units. €65–€75 double. No parking (street parking nearby). Breakfast not included in lower rates. **Amenities:** Wi-Fi (free).

Hodson Bay Hotel ★★ The deep blue waters of Hodson Bay stretch out before this modern spa hotel just outside Athlone. Views of the bay are stunning, which somewhat makes up for what the guest rooms lack in character, with their rather bland, corporate look. (Needless to say, you should ask for a room on the bay side.) Rooms in the "Retreat" wing are better designed, but also more expensive. The spa is excellent, with a huge list of treatments—starting with a simple half-hour facial for €55, rising to, on the more indulgent end of the scale, a 105-minute "Double Decadence," starting with champagne, chocolate, and strawberries in a private outdoor hot tub, followed by a massage for two in the couple's treatment suite (€135 per person). The hotel has two good restaurants and a pub, and the center of Athlone is only a 10-minute drive away. Check the website for package deals and special offers.

Signposted off N61, 7km (4½ miles) NW of Athlone, Co. Westmeath. www. hodsonbayhotel.com. © **090/644-2000.** 176 units. €110–€215. Free parking. Breakfast included. **Amenities:** 2 restaurants; bar; pool; room service; spa; Wi-Fi (free).

Wineport Lodge ★★ This romantic, modern hotel overlooking Lough Rea is a truly relaxing getaway. The contemporary bedrooms have plenty of space, and balconies offer views of the Lough—great for watching the glassy waters turn orange as the sun goes down. The hotel spa is surprisingly good value for a place like this; choices range from a simple aromatherapy bath for €45 to a deeply relaxing full-body hot-stone massage for €110. The restaurant is equally excellent. Good-value dinner-bed-and-breakfast packages are available.

Glasson, Athlone, Co. Westmeath. www.wineport.ie. © **090/643-9010.** 30 units. €180–€290 double, €260–€360 suite. Free parking. **Amenities:** Restaurant; bar; room service; spa; Wi-Fi (free).

Birr

Emmett House ★ A corner terrace house with a cozy, authentic interior, Emmett House is a satisfyingly traditional B&B. Guest rooms are a bit of a mixture; some nicely reference the 18th-century origins of the house, with antique-style furniture (including a beautiful four-poster in one room), but others are plainer and more modern. They're a decent enough size, though (given their age), and everything is spotlessly clean. Breakfasts are tasty and filling, and the welcome from host Maureen is genuine and friendly.

Emmett Square, Birr, Co. Offaly. www.emmethouse.com. © **057/916-9885.** 4 units. €100–€120 double. 2-night minimum stay in summer. No parking (street parking nearby). Breakfast included. **Amenities:** Wi-Fi (free).

Longford

Viewmount House ★★ Tranquil, elegant gardens await at this lovely country-house B&B just outside Longford. Guest rooms are done

leprechauns: **YOU'RE DOING IT ALL WRONG**

For better or worse, leprechauns have long been known around the world as a symbol of Ireland. Usually portrayed as little green creatures, grinning broadly, they are absurd, cartoonish figures, with which we've all grown up.

Originally, though, they were something much different. The word "leprechaun" comes from the Irish *leath bhrógan*, meaning "shoemaker." And in early folklore, leprechauns were often depicted as cobblers by trade. Though they were elven, mischievous creatures, they weren't evil exactly—just prone to the occasional malicious practical joke.

In those days, different regions of Ireland had their own versions of the Leprechaun folklore, although with a few elements of common ground. One of those was the leprechaun's clothing. Originally, all leprechauns were portrayed

as wearing *red* coats, not the green you see today. The green coats came much later in the 20th century, probably invented by foreigners to denote their Irishness.

Where that pot of gold came from, though, is anybody's guess.

Today, leprechauns also have some less whimsical connotations in Irish society. The description is used by the Irish to describe the crass side of the tourism industry. And on an even more unpleasant note, it's used by some of the worst elements among Northern Irish Unionists as a term of abuse for the Gaelic language.

So bear all this in mind when you consider buying that figurine of a leprechaun ironing an Irish flag. There's more to the myth than yellow hearts and green clovers.

in a pleasingly old-fashioned style, with antique wood furniture and plenty of space. Some have little sitting areas and rolltop tubs in the bathrooms. Viewmount also has a deserved reputation as one of the best places to eat in the area; the **VM Restaurant** serves superb modern Irish cuisine, worth the splurge at €60 for four courses. Check the website for special offers, including good midweek dinner-bed-and-breakfast deals.

Dublin Rd., Longford, Co. Longford. www.viewmounthouse.com. © **043/334-1919.** 12 units. €160–€180 double. Free parking. Breakfast included. **Amenities:** Restaurant; Wi-Fi (free).

WHERE TO EAT IN THE MIDLANDS

Most small towns in this area have little in the way of restaurant life. In some villages, the only place in town serving food at all is the pub. But **Athlone** has some good restaurants, plus a couple of sophisticated coffee shops. Along with the choices below, most of the hotels listed above have excellent restaurants.

Abbeyleix

The Gallic Kitchen @ Bramley ★ BREAKFAST/BISTRO   If you've come this way from Dublin, there's a good chance you've already sampled Gallic Kitchen's tasty pies, quiches, and desserts—these folks started out running a stall at Dublin's **Temple Bar Food Market** (see p. 158), which is still very popular. This is the main HQ, however, and it's a great spot for breakfast or a light lunch. Everything's fresh and homemade, and don't even think about leaving without trying a slice of cake or delicious tart for dessert.

Main St., Abbeyleix, Co. Laois. www.gallickitchen.com. ℭ **086/605-8208.** All items €3–€6. Wed–Sat 9:30am–5pm, Sun 10am–5pm.

Athlone

Al Mezza ★★ MIDDLE EASTERN/MEDITERRANEAN   Athlone is an unlikely location in which to find a topnotch Lebanese restaurant, but Al Mezza has fast become one of the best places to eat in the area. After seating you at one of the nicely shabby-chic tables (ours was an old sewing table), the staff helpfully takes you through the options—especially useful if you're not familiar with Middle Eastern food. Order off the menu for healthy, delicious meat and fish dishes (try the chicken shawarma, or the sea bream, simply served with cilantro and garlic), or go for the *mezza* plate, filled with tasty small servings of traditional Lebanese dishes (the hummus is a must, of course). These are designed to be shared, and vegetarian options are available. Round the meal off with some sweet baklava and ice cream. There's a good wine list, too.

Bastion St., Athlone, Co. Westmeath. https://almezza.ie. ℭ **090/649-8765.** Mezza plates (for 2 people) €52–€64. Entrees €13–€22. Wed–Thurs 5–9:30pm; Fri–Sat 5–10pm; Sun–Mon 5–9pm. Closed Tues.

Bastion Kitchen ★★ CAFE   Delicious, healthy meals are served at this charming little cafe and deli. Organic pitta sandwiches; salads served with fresh falafel or quinoa cakes; and excellent daily soups—try the pea, kale, and coconut broth served with spelt bread, if it's on offer. Most items can be ordered to go. Not all the food here invites you to polish your halo—the fresh scones are more than enough to tempt you straight out of diet mode.

1 Bastion St., Athlone, Co. Westmeath. www.bastionkitchen.com. ℭ **090/649-8369.** All items €5–€11. Mon–Fri 8:30am–5pm, Sat 9am–5pm, Sun noon–5pm.

Beans & Leaves ★ CAFE   This cheerful cafe/deli is another great place for a quick, healthy lunch in Athlone. In addition to excellent sandwiches, it offers tasty light meals: fishcakes, seafood chowder, and specials such as a steaming-hot plate of tasty chicken curry. Desserts are well worth checking out.

Lloyds Lane, Athlone, Co. Westmeath. ℭ **090/643-3534.** Lunch entrees €5–€12. Mon–Sat 9:15am–5pm, Sun 10am–5pm.

THE OLDEST pub IN IRELAND

Who can lay claim to the title of Ireland's oldest pub? It's a vexing question, with several contenders battling it out. **The Brazen Head ★★★** in Dublin (see p.166) has been serving customers since 1198, making it an oft-cited candidate for the honor—although detractors would scoff that most of the building was replaced in the 17th century, thus disqualifying it. The other big contender is **Sean's Bar ★★**, Main Street in Athlone (www.seansbar.ie; © **090/649-2358**). Records show that a drinking establishment of some kind or another has been on this site since the astonishingly far-away date of A.D. 900. The fact that a section of wall is believed to be original further strengthens the claim—but again, the extent to which it can be considered *the same pub* is debatable.

The dispute was finally settled when the *Guinness Book of Records* ruled in favor of Sean's. Presumably this means that it's now acceptable to call it officially Ireland's oldest pub. And, although some of the decor is modern, the fact that you still have to duck low to get in the door gives it an *olde* feel. All the same, to look at the place you'd certainly never guess that it's been serving customers since half a millennium before Columbus sailed to America.

Hatters' Lane Bistro ★★ BISTRO   Black-and-white portraits of movie stars adorn the walls of this friendly little bistro in the center of Athlone. The menu doesn't present too many surprises, but it's all done very well—roast pork glazed with honey and mustard, lamb shank with garlic and herb mashed potato, or perhaps roast duck with plum sauce. For dessert, try the Toblerone cheesecake and warm chocolate sauce—it's made with a Swiss chocolate-bar brand that's been popular here since the '70s. The set menu is a pretty good deal at €24 for two courses, €29 for three (served all night Mon–Fri, or until 6pm Fri–Sat).

Strand St., Athlone, Co. Westmeath. www.hatterslane.ie. © **090/647-3077.** Entrees €16.50–€28. Mon–Sat 5:30–9:45pm. Closed Sun.

Thyme ★★★ MODERN IRISH   Offering fine dining without being overly fussy or formal, this excellent bistro is one of the best places to eat in Athlone—or anywhere in the Midlands, come to that. Local ingredients feature heavily on the imaginative menu; to start, you may be offered young buck cheese mousse with candied walnuts, then maybe a loin of County Cork Wagyu beef with smoked potatoes, or cod with wild garlic aioli. The "value menu," served until 6:30pm on Friday, till 6pm Saturday, and all night the rest of the week, offers similar dishes at a very reasonable €25 for two courses, €30 for three. Be sure to make reservations, especially on weekends.

Costume Place, Athlone, Co. Westmeath. www.thymerestaurant.ie. © **090/647-8850.** Entrees €18–€30. Mon–Sat 5–10pm, Sun 1–8pm.

Tullamore

The Blue Apron ★★★ IRISH   This great little bistro is in Tullamore, about 3.4km (2 miles) northeast of **Charleville Castle** (see p. 406). Start with a plate of tender king scallops with prawn toast, or a spiced pear and Cashel blue cheese salad, before choosing from honey-and-thyme-glazed duck breast or slow-roasted lamb with garlic potatoes and rosemary jus. A full vegetarian menu is always available (try the sweet roast vegetable and honey log with goat cheese). The fixed-price Sunday lunch menu (€24 for two courses, €28 for three) is a great, and very filling, choice—don't expect to get much done afterward.

Harbour St., Tullamore, Co. Offaly. www.theblueapronrestaurant.ie. ℭ **057/936-0106.** Entrees €18–€28. Thurs–Sat 5:30–10pm, Wed 5:30–9pm, Sun 12:30–9pm.

The Coffee Club ★ CAFE   A popular lunch place with Tullamore locals, this busy, friendly cafe serves a huge range of sandwiches from the deli counter, plus delicious, healthy stir-fries (you choose the ingredients), salads, and other snacks. The upstairs dining room, lined with shelves full of secondhand books, is a quieter, more relaxed space. Appropriately enough, given the name, the cafe also serves an extremely fine cup of joe. Everything on the menu can be ordered to go.

Harbour St., Tullamore, Co. Offaly. ℭ **057/933-0015.** Entrees €5–€12. Wed–Mon 8am–6pm, Tues 9am–6pm.

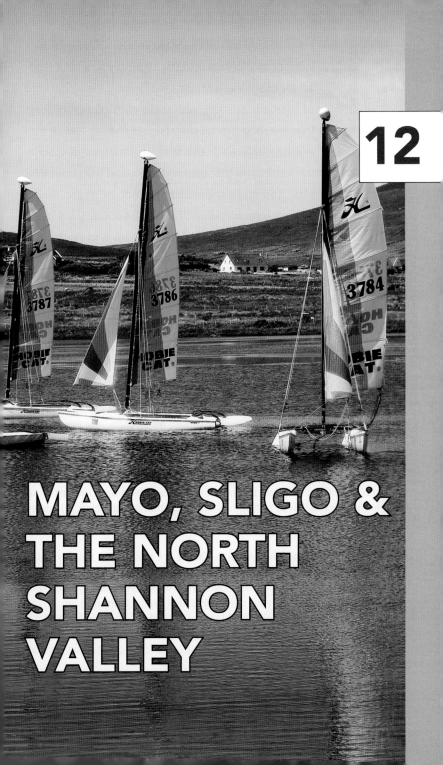

MAYO, SLIGO & THE NORTH SHANNON VALLEY

T he strikingly beautiful landscape of Galway segues without any fanfare into the strikingly beautiful landscape of southern Mayo. Like Galway, Mayo is a land of dramatic scenery, with rocky cliffs plunging down into the opaque blue waters of the icy sea. If you head farther north, you'll reach the smooth pastures of County Sligo, the classic landscape that inspired the great Irish poet William Butler Yeats. The main appeal here is not its towns, which tend to be functional farm communities, but the countryside itself. Though the region is dotted with fairy-tale castles and mysterious prehistoric sites, its biggest gift to the visitor is tranquility.

ESSENTIALS

Arriving

BY BUS   **Bus Éireann** runs daily bus service to Sligo Town from Dublin, Galway, and other points including Derry in Northern Ireland. It provides daily service to major towns in Mayo. The bus station in Sligo is on Lord Edward Street.

BY TRAIN   Trains from Dublin and other major points arrive daily at **Westport** in Mayo, and **Sligo Town** in Sligo. The train station in Westport is on Altamont Street, about a 10-minute walk from the town center; in Sligo it's on Lord Edward Street, next to the bus station.

BY CAR   Mayo can be reached by four major highways: N84 from the south; N59 from the south and north; and N5 and N60 from the east. Four other major roads lead to Sligo: N4 from Dublin and the east, N17 from Galway and the south, N15 from Donegal to the north, and N16 from Northern Ireland.

BY PLANE   **Ireland West Airport Knock** in Charlestown, County Mayo (www.knockairport.com; ✆ **094/936-8100**) is becoming quite a popular hub for budget airlines from the U.K. **Flybe** (www.flybe.com; ✆ **037/1700-2000** in the U.K. only) runs daily scheduled flights from London, Liverpool, Edinburgh, Birmingham, Manchester, and Bristol. There are also a handful of scheduled flights from airports in France, Spain, Italy, Portugal, Bosnia, Finland, and Croatia—but none from other points within Ireland.

PREVIOUS PAGE: **Sailboats on Keem Bay on Achill Island, off the coast of County Mayo.**

COUNTY MAYO

For experienced Ireland travelers, Mayo is the place they escape to after visiting Galway—its rugged coastal scenery is similar, but it has less of the traffic and tourist overload from which Galway suffers in the summer. It's a delightfully unpredictable place, where the terrain changes at the turn of a steering wheel, from lush and green to stark, desert-like, and mountainous. This region was hit so hard by the Great Famine that, in certain ways, it has never quite recovered. Starvation and emigration emptied it then, and that emptiness is still palpable.

In 1951, the tiny village of **Cong** became the setting for the John Ford film *The Quiet Man,* starring John Wayne and Maureen O'Hara (see box p. 424). Surprisingly, the county still vigorously celebrates this 65-year-old connection to cinematic stardust—the townsfolk of Cong even paid for a bronze statue of the film's stars in 2013. Younger readers may be more familiar with the area thanks to the CW series *Reign,* which is filmed at Ashford Castle.

Among Mayo's other attractions are the mysterious 5,000-year-old settlement at **Céide Fields,** the religious shrine at **Knock,** and some of Europe's best fishing waters at **Lough Conn, Lough Mask,** and the **River Moy** (see p. 436). It's such a storied angler's destination that **Ballina** (*Béal an Átha*), Mayo's largest town, calls itself the home of the Irish salmon.

Among the relics of the movie *The Quiet Man,* set in the Mayo village of Cong, is this re-created crofter's cottage.

Visitor Information

The main tourist information center for County Mayo is the **Westport Tourist Office,** Bridge Street, Westport (www.mayo.ie; ✆ **098/25711**). Other offices are on Pearse Street, **Ballina** (✆ **096/72800**) and in the Old Courthouse on Abbey Street in **Cong** (✆ **094/954-6542**).

Exploring County Mayo

Because it's a rural county with no major cities or many large towns, County Mayo feels a bit like a place without a center. Towns such as Castlebar, Claremorris, and Ballinrobe in the southern part of the county, and Ballina in the northern reaches, make good places to stop, refill the tank, and have lunch, but they offer little to make you linger. The county's attractions lie in the countryside, and in smaller communities like Foxford, Ballycastle, and Louisburgh.

County Mayo's loveliest town, **Westport (*Cathair na Mairt*)** ★, nestles on the shore of Clew Bay and makes an excellent touring base. Once a major port, it was designed by the famed architect Richard Cassels (he of Leinster House [p. 112] and Powerscourt House [p. 195]) with a tree-lined mall, rows of Georgian buildings, and an octagonal central mall. From here, you can take a scenic drive west to **Achill Island (*An Caol*)** (see p. 430) or catch a ferry to the bay's **Clare Island,** once the home of Mayo's legendary "Pirate Queen," Grace O'Malley (see p. 423). Southeast of Westport, **Croagh Patrick,** a 750m (2,460-ft.) mountain, dominates the views of western Mayo for miles. St. Patrick is said to have spent the 40 days of Lent praying here in the year 441. To commemorate that, on the last Sunday of July, thousands of Irish people make a pilgrimage to the site, which has become known as St. Patrick's Holy Mountain.

A short drive inland from Westport, in **Castlebar,** you can pick up the R310 road, which swings north past the clear, mountain-ringed waters of **Lough Cullin** and **Lough Conn** and eventually to **Ballina (*Béal an Átha*).** A dramatic coastal drive runs along the R314 from Ballina to Downpatrick Head, passing through the secluded harbor village of **Killala (*Cill Alaidh* or *Cill Ála*).** Outside Killala on the road R314, several ruined friaries are worth a stop, particularly **Moyne Abbey** ★ (see p. 430) and **Rosserk Abbey** ★ (see p. 431).

IN & AROUND WESTPORT

Ballintubber Abbey ★★ CHURCH   This abbey is a real survivor—one of only a few Irish churches in continuous use for almost 800 years. Founded in 1216 by Cathal O'Connor, king of Connaught, it has endured fires, numerous attacks, pestilences, and anti-Catholic pogroms. Although Oliver Cromwell's forces thoroughly dismantled the abbey—they even carried off its roof in 1653 in an effort to finally suppress it—clerics continued discreetly conducting religious rites. Today it's an impressively

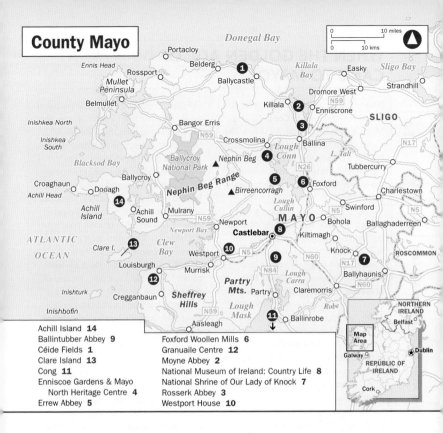

County Mayo

Donegal Bay
Portacloy
Ennis Head
Rossport
Mullet
Peninsula
Belmullet
Belderg ❶
Ballycastle
Killala
Bay
Easky   Sligo Bay
Strandhill
Dromore West
Killala ❷
Enniscrone
SLIGO
Inishkea North
Inishkea
South
Bangor Erris
N59
Crossmolina
Lough
Conn
Ballina
N17
Blacksod Bay
Ballycroy
National Park
Nephin Beg ▲
❹
L. Talt
Tubbercurry
N26
Croaghaun
Achill Head
Dooagh
Ballycroy
Nephin Beg Range
❺
▲ Birreencorragh
❻ Foxford
Charlestown
Achill
Island
❶❹ Achill
Sound
Mulrany
N59
Lough
Cullin
N5
Swinford
N5
Ballaghaderreen
Newport
Newport Bay
Castlebar
M A Y O Bohola
ATLANTIC
OCEAN
Clare I.
❶❸
Clew
Bay
Westport
Murrisk
N5
❿
❾
Kiltimagh
Knock ❼
N60
N17
ROSCOMMON
Louisburgh
Ballyhaunis
N60
Inishturk
Cregganbaun
❶❷
Sheffrey
Hills
Partry
Mts.
N59
Lough
Mask
Partry
Lough
Carra
Claremorris
Robe
NORTHERN
IRELAND
Belfast
Inishbofin
Aasleagh
❶❶
Ballinrobe

Achill Island **14**
Ballintubber Abbey **9**
Céide Fields **1**
Clare Island **13**
Cong **11**
Enniscoe Gardens & Mayo
   North Heritage Centre **4**
Errew Abbey **5**

Foxford Woollen Mills **6**
Granuaile Centre **12**
Moyne Abbey **2**
National Museum of Ireland: Country Life **8**
National Shrine of Our Lady of Knock **7**
Rosserk Abbey **3**
Westport House **10**

Map
Area
Galway
Dublin
REPUBLIC OF
IRELAND
Cork

restored church, with 13th-century windows on the right side of the nave and a doorway dating to the 15th century. Guided tours are available weekdays (and on weekends by prior arrangement) from 9:30am to 5pm; there's no charge, but donations of €4 per person are requested. The **Celtic Furrow** visitor center illuminates the abbey's troubled and fascinating history as part of a wider examination of spiritual life in Ireland dating back 5,000 years.

Ballintubber, Co. Mayo, off the Galway-Castlebar Rd. (N84), about 21.5km (13½ miles) E of Westport. www.ballintubberabbey.ie. ☏ **094/903-0934.** Free admission; donations requested. Abbey: Daily 9am–midnight. Celtic Furrow: July–Aug daily 10am–5pm.

Clare Island ★★ ISLAND   Floating about 5km (3 miles) off the Mayo coast, just beyond Clew Bay, Clare Island is a place of unspoiled splendor. Inhabited for 5,000 years and once quite populous—1,700 people lived there in the early 19th century—Clare is now home to only about 150 year-round islanders, plus perhaps as many sheep. But the island is best known as the haunt of Grace O'Malley, the "Pirate Queen," who controlled the coastal waters 400 years ago (see p. 426). O'Malley's modest

WHEN THE GOLDEN AGE OF hollywood CAME TO MAYO

When director John Ford descended on the sweet little town of **Cong,** County Mayo, to make his classic 1951 film *The Quiet Man,* starring John Wayne and Maureen O'Hara, the town's profile sky-rocketed. Tourists were soon visiting in the tens of thousands, and Cong was transformed.

But what's really surprising is that visitors still flock here on Quiet Man pilgrimages, even though the film is well over half a century old, and Cong merrily continues to hang its hat on its brief brush with stardust. The **Quiet Man Museum,** Circular Road (www.quietman-cong.com/cong-museum; ✆ **094/954-6089**), is a charming little thatched cottage that has been transformed into an exact replica of John Wayne's house in the movie, right down to the furniture. From April to October, it's open daily from 10am to 4pm. Admission costs €5 adults; €4 seniors, students, and children; and €15 families. The museum usually run tours of the village every day at 11am, and other times if demand is high.

Just around the corner on Abbey Street are the ruins of **Cong Abbey.** Founded in 623, it was rebuilt in the 12th century, then comprehensively destroyed by Henry VIII in the 1540s. The ruins are an open site, which you can wander at leisure—but even here there's a reminder of this town's love affair with an old Hollywood movie. The **Quiet Man Statue,** a full-size bronze of Maureen O'Hara being whisked off her feet by John Wayne, was unveiled just outside the abbey in 2013. Since then it's become an almost obligatory focal point for souvenir selfies.

Unfortunately, the countless movie fans Cong has attracted haven't always treated the town with respect. The actual cottage used as John Wayne's house is little more than a pile of rocks now, having been gradually torn apart over the years by souvenir hunters. The museum will tell you where it is if you really want to see for yourself. Just don't be one of *those* people.

Aside from the Quiet Man, Cong is most famous as the location of **Ashford Castle ★★★**. Built in the 13th century, it is one of Ireland's biggest and most complete medieval castles. Unfortunately, you can't tour the inside unless palatial luxury is within your price range, as it is now a super-exclusive hotel and resort (see p. 432). However, there's nothing to stop you driving up and having a wander around the grounds. And if you want to spend a little more time here, consider the more modest splurge of dinner at **Wilde's ★★★** (p. 435), an outstanding restaurant in the former estate keeper's house.

Cong is roughly halfway between Galway and Westport, on R344, R345, and R346.

castle and the partially restored Cistercian abbey where she is buried are among the island's few attractions—the main draw is the island's remote natural beauty. Two ferry services operate out of Roonagh Harbour, 29km (18 miles) south of Westport: **O'Malley's Ferry Service** (www.omalley ferries.com; ✆ **098/25045**) and **Clare Island Ferries** (www.clareisland ferry.com; ✆ **098/23737** or 086/851-5003). The round-trip fare for the 15-minute journey is around €15.

Co. Mayo. www.clareisland.info.

Granuaile Centre ★ MUSEUM   This small but rather charming museum is devoted to a particularly cool local hero: Grace O'Malley, also known as "the Pirate Queen" (see p. 426). Today she is feted as a defender of the rights of the people of Mayo as much as for being a ruthless pirate—but the pirate stuff is more fun. The center, set in a former church building, offers a historical film, some engaging exhibits that tell the story of O'Malley's life, and displays on the wider history of the area, particularly during the Great Famine. A short drive from the Roonagh Harbour ferry to Clare Island (see p. 423), it makes a worthwhile introduction to O'Malley's life and times, but call ahead first if getting here involves more than a minor detour—opening times can be a little unpredictable, especially in winter.

Church St., Louisburgh, Co. Mayo, 21km (13 miles) W of Westport on R334. www.granuaile.org. ℂ **098/66341.** Admission €5 adults; €2.50 seniors and students; children free. Mon–Fri 10am–5pm. Call ahead to check times, particularly in winter.

The National Museum of Ireland: Country Life ★★ MUSEUM   The countryside outpost of Ireland's multi-site national museum (the others are all in Dublin—see chapter 4), this one specializes in Irish life, trade, culture, and tradition since the mid–19th century. Absorbing exhibits deal with folklore; the natural environment and how local communities have relied on it for survival; political and social upheaval, particularly in the years preceding the Great Famine; traditional trades and crafts; and the changing life of the Irish people at home and at work. You could easily spend 3 hours wandering around here. The museum also has a thoughtful program of changing exhibitions. As at all the National Museum sites, entry is completely free. On the grounds opposite the museum is **Turlough Park House,** a moderately sized country house built for the wealthy Fitzgerald family in the 1860s. You can wander the rooms, which have been kept much as they would have been in the house's Victorian heyday, complete with original furniture.

Signposted from N5, Turlough Park, about 8km (5 miles) E of Castlebar, Co. Mayo. www.museum.ie/Country-Life. ℂ **094/903-1755.** Free admission. Tues–Sat 10am–5pm, Sun 2–5pm. Closed Mon.

Westport House ★★ HISTORIC HOUSE/THEME PARK   This is the sort of family-friendly attraction that requires a deep breath before listing everything there is to do here. It's all centered around an elegant late-18th-century residence—the home of Lord Altamont, the Marquess of Sligo and a descendant, it is said, of Pirate Queen Grace O'Malley (hence the bronze statue of her on the grounds). The work of Richard Cassels and James Wyatt, the house has a graceful staircase of ornate white Sicilian marble, unusual Art Nouveau glass and carvings, family heirlooms, and silver. The grandeur of the residence is undeniable, but during the summer months a large proportion of visitors come here without even setting foot in the building—just follow the whoops and cheers

local hero: **GRACE O'MALLEY, THE PIRATE QUEEN**

By all accounts, Grace O'Malley—a.k.a. the "Pirate Queen"—was a woman ahead of her time. Born in 1530 on **Clare Island** (see p. 423), she grew up to be an adventurer, pirate, gambler, mercenary, traitor, chieftain, noblewoman, and general badass. And while she is remembered now with affection, at the time she was feared and despised in equal measure.

Even as a child, Grace was fiercely independent. When her mother refused to let her sail with her father, she cut off her hair and dressed in boys' clothing. Her father called her *"Grainne Mhaol,"* or "Bald Grace," later shortened to Granuaile (pronounced Graw-nya-*wayl*), a nickname she'd carry all her life.

At 16, Grace married Donal O'Flaherty, second in line to the O'Flaherty clan chieftain, who ruled all of Connacht. Her career as a pirate began a few years later when the city of Galway, one of the largest trading posts in northern Europe, refused to do business with the O'Flahertys. Grace used her fleet of fast galleys to waylay slower vessels on their way into Galway Harbour. She then offered safe passage for a fee in lieu of pillaging the ships.

She is most fondly remembered for refusing to trade her lands in return for an English title, a common practice of the day.

When the English captured her sons in 1593, she went to London to try to win their release. In an extraordinary turn of events, she actually secured a meeting with Queen Elizabeth herself. History records that the two women got on quite well (although legend has it that Grace initially tried to smuggle a knife in with her, in case things went differently). A deal was struck; Elizabeth agreed to release Grace's sons and to return some captured lands, if Grace would agree to renounce piracy. This she did and returned to Ireland triumphantly.

The truce did not last, however. Grace got her sons back, but not her property—so she took up piracy again and continued her legendary seafaring career until her death from natural causes in 1600.

---

of a couple thousand excited children and you'll find the sprawling **Pirate Adventure Park.** Here kids can burn off energy on the swinging pirate ship, log ride, go-karts, swan-shaped pedal boats, and giant bouncy castle. When that's over you can all tour the gardens together in a Toytown-sized express train. Very young children can enjoy some slightly gentler fun at the **Pirate's Den** play area (an extra €5–€7 per child, depending on age). Upping the ante even further, the **Adventure Activity Centre** is the latest addition, piling on bungee jumping, zip wires, tree climbing, archery, and a host of other high-adrenaline amusements. All activities at the Adventure Activity Centre must be paid for separately; prices start at €9 for a child's zip-wire ride and rise to €28 for a couple's water "zorbing," which involves traversing a body of water while entirely trapped inside a giant bubble. You know, for fun! *Note:* As of this writing, Westport House planned to close for a new country music

Sedate Westport House has a popular Pirate Adventure Park in its backyard.

festival, **Harvest Festival,** over the last week in August. The jury's out as to whether this will be a yearly event—so call or go online to check if you're planning to visit around that time.

The Westport Demense, Westport, Co. Mayo. www.westporthouse.ie. © **098/27766.** House, Gardens, and Pirate Park: €21 adults; €19 seniors and students; €16.50 children; €60–€75 families. House and Gardens only: €13 adults; €10 seniors and students; €6.50 children. House and Gardens: June–Aug daily 10am–6pm; Sept–Oct and Mar–May daily 10am–4pm; Nov–Dec and Feb weekends 10am–4pm (daily 10am–4pm the week before Christmas). Pirate Adventure Park: June Wed–Fri 10am–3pm, Sat–Sun 11am–6pm; July–Aug daily 11am–6pm. Adventure Activity Centre: June weekends 11am–6pm; July–late Aug daily 11am–6pm. Check online for off-season and school-breaks opening times.

IN & AROUND BALLINA

Céide Fields ★★ ANCIENT SITE   In a breathtaking setting above huge chalk cliffs that plunge hundreds of feet down into a deep blue sea, an ancient people once lived, worked, and buried their dead. But nobody knew this until the 1930s, when a local farmer noticed the stones in his fields were piled in strange patterns. More than 40 years later, his archaeologist son explored the discovery further. Under the turf, he found Stone Age fields, megalithic tombs, and the foundations of a village. Standing

Céide Fields Visitor Centre interprets the amazing megalithic relics found on this remote clifftop site.

amid it now, you can see a pattern of farm fields as they were laid out 5,000 years ago (predating the Egyptian pyramids). Preserved for millennia beneath the bog, the site is both fascinating and inscrutable. To a casual observer, it's little more than piles of stones, but the visitor center makes it meaningful in a series of displays, films, and tours. The pyramid-shaped center itself is designed to fit in with the dramatic surroundings—you can see the building from miles away. It also contains a cafeteria, which comes as a relief since this hilly, rocky site is miles of winding roads from anywhere.

On R314, 8km (5 miles) W of Ballycastle, Co. Mayo. www.heritageireland.ie. © **096/ 43325.** Admission €5 adults; €4 seniors; €3 students and children; €13 families. June–Sept daily 10am–6pm; Apr–May and Oct daily 10am–5pm; last tour 1 hr. before closing. Closed Nov–Mar.

Enniscoe Gardens & Mayo North Heritage Centre ★ GENE-ALOGY CENTER   Part of the huge Enniscoe estate—where you can stay in the charming manor house (**Enniscoe House** ★★, see p. 432)—these beautiful gardens comprise woods, parkland, and part of Lough Conn. One of the highlights is an 18th-century walled garden that has been restored to the layout it had in the estate's Victorian heyday. The on-site **Mayo North Heritage Centre** (www.northmayogenealogy.com) is the ideal place to start if you're checking out your roots. It offers extensive records such as church registers (Catholic, Presbyterian, Methodist, and others); registers of births, marriages, and deaths; estate and probate records; property leases and rent rolls; school registers; emigrant rolls; and census records. Research fees, which give you access to expert genealogists, range from €30 for a basic search to €150 and up for a full history report, which may take several weeks to finish (results are sent to you on completion). A little museum displays a somewhat random collection of historic farm equipment and household items from the early to mid–20th century.

On Lough Conn, about 3.2km (2 miles) S of Crossmolina, off R315, Enniscoe, Castlehill, Ballina, Co. Mayo. www.enniscoe.com/gardens. © **096/31809.** Gardens and musem: €10 adults, €3 students and children. Gardens and Heritage Centre: Apr–Oct Mon–Fri 11am–5pm, Sat–Sun and public holidays 1:30–5:30pm. For genealogical inquiries only, year-round Mon–Fri 10am–4pm.

Errew Abbey ★ RELIGIOUS SITE This atmospheric ruined 13th-century Augustinian church sits on a tiny peninsula in Lough Conn. The cloister is well-preserved, as is the chancel with altar and *piscina,* a stone basin used for disposing of the water used during Mass. An oratory of massive stone walls in fields adjacent to the abbey stands on the site of a church founded in the 6th century. It's known locally by the marvelous tongue-twisting name *Templenagalliaghdoo,* which means "Church of the Black Nun."

Near Crossmolina, Co. Mayo. No phone. Free admission (open site). Signposted about 3.2km (2 miles) S of Crossmolina on the Castlebar Rd., then 5km (3 miles) down a side road.

Foxford Woollen Mills Visitor Centre ★ FACTORY TOUR This popular Irish brand of knitwear and tweed was founded by a nun, Mother Agnes Morragh Bernard, in the late 19th century. Mother Agnes's idea was to build a new local industry to try to ameliorate the effects of the Great Famine. Ever since then the mill has thrived, producing rugs, clothing, and the like. Not only did her scheme help to stave off poverty for the local workforce, but the brand became hugely successful in Ireland and beyond. You can tour the mills and visit the on-site museum, which tells the story in detail. A guided tour, available April to November, leaves every 20 minutes and takes 45 minutes or so; alternatively you can borrow a self-guided multimedia version that takes around an hour to complete. (Be aware that the mills stop work for the weekend at noon on Friday; although you can still take a tour, the machinery won't be working.) Also on-site are two art galleries, a jewelry workshop, a restaurant, and of course a gift shop, where you can stock up on the stylish products themselves.

St. Joseph's Place, Foxford, Co. Mayo. www.foxfordwoollenmills.com. © **094/925-6104.** Free admission. Tour €10 adults; €8 seniors and students; free for children 15 and under. Centre: Mon–Sat 10am–6pm, Sun noon–6pm. Tours: Apr–Nov Mon–Sat 10am–4:30pm, Sun noon–4:30pm.

A TRIP TO achill island

The rugged, bog-filled, sparsely populated coast of counties Mayo and Sligo makes for scenic drives to secluded outposts. Leading the list is **Achill Island,** a heather-filled slip of land with sandy beaches and spectacular views of waves crashing against rocky cliffs.

Once you've crossed the bridge from the mainland, follow a winding road across the island to the little town of **Keel,** a trip that requires patience but rewards you with a camera full of photos. About 5.7km (3½ miles) west of Keel, you'll find the secluded Blue Flag beach of **Keem Bay** (it was once a major fishing ground—basking shark were caught here commercially up until the 1950s—but no more). You can reach the bay along a small cliff-top road, which passes by cliff faces containing rich seams of glittering amethyst. Apparently it's not uncommon to find chunks of the stuff lying loose after a heavy rainfall.

Speaking of remarkable finds: Hidden on the slopes of **Mount Slievemore,** Achill's tallest mountain, are the remains of an **abandoned village.** The hundred or so crumbling stone cottages of the nameless ghost town date back to sometime around the 12th century. It was deserted during the Great Famine,

although some cottages are known to have been in occasional use until the very early years of the 20th century, a traditional practice known as "booleying"—seasonal occupation by farming communities, which continued here long after it had died out in the rest of Ireland. Mount Slievemore is between Keel and Doogort, in the central northeastern part of Achill Island.

At Kildavnet, between Derreen and Coughmore, in the southeastern corner of the island, you'll find **Granuaile's Tower.** This impressive 15th-century tower house was owned by Grace O'Malley, the "Pirate Queen," who caused all manner of havoc for the English around these parts in the 16th century (see box p. 426). There's not a great deal to see, but it's a stunning spot to admire. Nearby **Kildavnet Church** is thought by some archaeologists to date from the 8th century.

To get to the Achill Island bridge, take N59 heading northwest out of Westport, then join R319, signposted to Achill. The drive from Westport to the crossing is about 42km (26 miles) and should take around 40 minutes. Once you're on Achill Island, Keel is about another 14km (8⅔ miles) down the same road.

Moyne Abbey ★ RELIGIOUS SITE/RUINS   Established in the mid-1400s and destroyed in the 16th century by Sir Richard Bingham, the English governor appointed to suppress rebellion in Connaught, Moyne Abbey is a picturesque ruin between Killala and Ballina. Parts of the exterior are relatively complete, although the roof is completely gone. The closer you get, the more of a ruin you realize it is. The tower looks quite well-preserved from a distance—until you look to the upper level, that is, where the whole structure appears as if it's been snapped off by a giant hand. Moyne Abbey is a peaceful place, and gazing through its moldering old windows or over a misty carpet of green fields, you can fully understand why the monks chose this spot.

On R314 btw. Killala and Ballina. No phone. Free admission (open site).

National Shrine of Our Lady of Knock and the Church of the Apparition ★ SHRINE Ireland's version of Lourdes, Our Lady of Knock draws pilgrims, mostly Irish Catholic, in droves. It all stems from a day in August 1879 when two young local girls said they saw Joseph, Mary, and St. John standing in bright light in front of the southern tower of the parish church. Soon, 13 other witnesses claimed to have seen the same thing. Before long, miracles were occurring fast and furious, as sick and lame visitors to the church were pronouncing themselves healed. Knock came to the world's attention in 1979, when Pope John Paul II visited the shrine. More than 10,000 pilgrims still visit every year, and during Novena week in August (marking the anniversary of the miracle), the shrine holds special twice-daily ceremonies and other commemorative events. There's not much to the town of Knock on the whole—it sits unspectacularly at the intersection of the N17 and R323 roads—but it's filled with increasingly large, modern religious structures, including a huge circular basilica that seats 7,000 and contains artifacts or furnishings from every county in Ireland. The grounds also hold a folk museum (with a few letters relating to the original testimonies) and a religious bookshop.

On the N17 Galway Rd., Knock, Co. Mayo. www.knock-shrine.ie. ✆ **094/938-8100.** Free admission to shrine. Museum €4 adults and students; €3 seniors and children; free for children under 5. Shrine and grounds: Late May–Aug daily 9am–7:30pm (9am–8:30pm and 9:30–11pm during Novena week); Sept–Dec daily 10am–5pm; Jan–late May 9am–6pm. Museum: Daily 10am–6pm.

Rosserk Abbey ★ RELIGIOUS SITE/RUINS About 3km (2 miles) from Moyne Abbey (p. 430), Rosserk Abbey, sitting at the edge of the River Rosserk, is in many ways its twin. Both are evocative ruins, built at the same time, and destroyed at the same time by Bingham's troops. Rosserk Abbey, however, is today in much better shape than Moyne. Its chapel windows are well-preserved, and the church's *piscina* (once used for washing altar vessels) is still here, carved with angels. On its lower-left-hand column is a delightful detail: a tiny, elegant carving of a round tower that recalls its 23m-tall (75-foot) counterpart in nearby Killala. Climb the winding stone stair for a lovely vista out across the bay.

On R314 btw. Killala and Ballina. Signposted. No phone. Free admission (open site).

Where to Stay in County Mayo

This region of Ireland is not the most abundant ground for topnotch places to stay. Even the major towns have only a smattering of decent B&Bs and small hotels. However, some gems are to be found in the deepest reaches of the countryside. It takes effort to get to these places, but the journey will be worth it.

EXPENSIVE

Ashford Castle ★★★ This extraordinary, fairy-tale-like castle has entertained plenty of famous guests over the years—Grace Kelly, Ronald Reagan, Brad Pitt, Pierce Brosnan, and Tony Blair, to name just a few. It also has a list of awards and commendations as long as your arm, including best hotel in Ireland, and third best in Europe overall, from *Condé Nast Traveler* in 2012. Ashford Castle was built in the 13th century and still looks every inch the palatial abode, thanks to the suits of armor and priceless antiques lining the walls and the huge four-poster beds filling the sumptuous guest rooms. The grounds are stunning—the castle overlooks Lough Corrib, with acres of forest and landscaped gardens. A luxurious range of spa treatments is on hand

Inside the palatial Ashford Castle, now a swank hotel.

to soothe and pamper guests. The restaurant is as excellent as you'd expect (don't even think about dressing down), although a less formal eatery is on the grounds, too (see p. 435). Of course, you'll virtually need a chest full of solid gold treasure to afford a night here—although, if it makes any difference at all, the dinner-bed-and-breakfast packages are pretty good. Check the website for special deals, especially in the off-season.

On R346, on the eastern approach to Cong, Co. Mayo. www.ashford.ie. ⓒ **094/ 954-6003.** 83 units. €410–€865 double; €1,550–€2,250 stateroom; €2,500–€4,500 suite. Free parking. Breakfast included. **Amenities:** 2 restaurants; bar; gym; massage treatments; estate sports including golf, fishing, and clay pigeon shooting; Wi-Fi (free).

Enniscoe House ★★ Flanked by Mount Nephin on one side and the shimmering waters of Lough Conn on the other, Enniscoe is a stunningly restored mid-18th-century mansion. Very little has been significantly altered from the original structure, so the place is overflowing with wonderful period details (one room even has its original silk wallpaper). Bedrooms are spacious with big windows and antique half-tester beds. Bathrooms are modern and elegantly designed. Susan Kellett and her son, DJ, run the place with a natural flair for hospitality. Susan is a great cook, too; make sure you book one of her excellent dinners. The grounds are big and offer enough to do that you could spend a day here without ever stepping back into the outside world (see **Enniscoe Gardens,** p. 428). The

Enniscoe estate also has a couple of self-catering cottages available if you want more privacy.

Castlehill, Ballina, Co. Mayo. www.enniscoe.com. © **096/31112.** 6 units. €180–€260 double. Dinner €50. Free parking. Breakfast included. **Amenities:** Guest lounge; Wi-Fi (free) in public areas.

MODERATE

The Bervie ★★★ Overlooking the Atlantic Ocean on **Achill Island** (see p. 430), the Bervie is an inspiring place to stay. Husband-and-wife hosts John and Elizabeth Barrett spent years lovingly restoring the building. Elizabeth actually grew up in this house; it's been a B&B since the 1930s, although today it's a far more sophisticated place than she remembers from her childhood. Guest rooms are large and spacious, with well-chosen furniture (most of it made locally) and tasteful art. Some rooms directly overlook the sea—and what a view! You can see some of the other islands dotted around the bay from certain rooms, while others have a dramatic view of cliffs. Light pours in from huge windows, and the whispering of the waves soothes you off to a restful sleep. Elizabeth's home-cooked breakfasts are to die for, and after years of being advance-notice-only, the outstanding dinners are now a permanent fixture. Menus might offer black sole, Clare Island salmon, or chicken flavored with lemon and thyme. There's a good (and reasonably priced) wine list, too. The Bervie has a 2-night minimum on weekends, but the higher rate also includes dinner.

The Strand, Keel, Achill, Co. Mayo. www.bervie-guesthouse-achill.com. © **098/43114.** 14 units. €110–€140 double. Weekend dinner-bed-and-breakfast €320–€350 (2 nights inclusive). Free parking. Breakfast included. Dinner €45. **Amenities:** Restaurant; Wi-Fi (free).

Westport Coast Hotel ★ This pleasant, modern hotel on the Quay in Westport overlooks the smooth, dreamy waters of Clew Bay and the mountains behind. It's worth paying a little extra for a room with a view or a spacious suite if your budget will stretch to it. The **Veda** spa has plenty of affordable treatments, from an invigorating 15-minute Indian head massage (€20) to relaxing full-body treatments (€70–€90). The top-floor restaurant, which looks out over the bay, serves tasty, crowd-pleasing fare (leg of lamb, roast chicken, steaks—you get the picture). Check the website for dinner-bed-and-breakfast deals.

The Quay, Westport, Co. Mayo. www.westportcoasthotel.ie. © **098/29000.** 85 units. €160–€240 double, €220–€400 suite. Breakfast included. Free parking. **Amenities:** Restaurant; bar; pool; spa; Wi-Fi (free).

Where to Eat in County Mayo

An Port Mor ★★ SEAFOOD/MODERN IRISH At this multi-award-winning seafood restaurant in Westport, local catches dominate the menu—you can easily find Clew Bay scallops, or blue trout (yes, *blue*) from Curran served with tarragon and canola. The seafood is excellent, but it's not all that's on the menu; expect juicy steaks served with something fresh and tasty like red onion marmalade, as well as local chicken or lamb. Everything is impeccably presented, and the atmosphere in the cheerful dining room is relaxed. Service is excellent, too.

Bridge St., Westport, Co. Mayo. www.anportmor.com. (C) **098/26730.** Entrees €15–€28. Daily 5pm–midnight.

The Beehive ★ CAFE   There aren't many places to eat on Achill Island, and this homey craft-store-cum-cafe is one of the best. (Technically, they say, this is a "Craft Coffee Shop.") Stop and refuel on excellent sandwiches and cakes, or a bowl of homemade soup (the chowder is particularly good). The craft store isn't bad, either. The Beehive overlooks the beach at Keel, and you can sit outside with your food on a warm day.

Keel, Achill Island, Co. Mayo. (C) **086/854-2009.** €5–€11. Daily 9:30am–6pm. Closed Nov–Easter.

Dillons ★★ INTERNATIONAL   A cobblestone courtyard leads into this friendly, cozy bar and restaurant, buzzing with atmosphere. Tasty, unfussy, quality pub food is the mainstay: thick broths served with soda bread, gourmet burgers, seafood pies and creamy mashed potato, or maybe a steaming-hot plate of fish and chips washed down with a refreshing pint of ale. The menu contains plenty of vegetarian and gluten-free options. Desserts are of the stick-to-the-ribs comfort-food variety: Think warm chocolate pudding, say, or a fruit crumble with thick custard. An unexpected bit of trivia about this place: The stone floor was originally part of the notorious **Kilmainham Gaol** in Dublin (see p. 99).

Dillon Terrace, Ballina, Co. Mayo. www. dillonsbarandrestaurant.com. (C) **096/72230.** Entrees €14–€23. Fixed-price three-course menu €25. Mon–Sat 5–9pm, Sun 1–9pm.

The Helm ★ SEAFOOD/BISTRO   The hungriest diners are welcomed with open arms at this relaxed Westport bar-restaurant, which specializes in local seafood—tackle the delicious fisherman's platter, if it's on offer, only if you're wearing elasticated pants. Rich seafood chowder is a particular specialty. In addition to the fishy options, main dishes include steaks, rack of lamb, and pork chops. Lunch service is more traditional, with Irish stew alongside fish and chips. The comfort-food desserts include pies, crumbles, and even jelly and ice cream. The Helm is also a B&B with a few self-catering apartments.

The Harbour, Westport, Co. Mayo. www.thehelm.ie. (C) **098/26398.** Entrees €15–€23. Mon–Fri 7am–11:30pm, Sat–Sun 6:30am–12:30am. Food served until about 9:30pm.

The Hungry Monk Café ★ CAFE   "We don't do fast food," says the blackboard on the wall at this friendly cafe in Cong. "We do fresh wholesome Irish food as quick as we can!" That sums it up, really. The Hungry

Monk is just the kind of cozy place to break up a long day's sightseeing: simple cooking, light lunches and snacks, served in a warm cottage atmosphere. The lunch menu consists mostly of tasty sandwiches and salads, creatively prepared with local ingredients. Or you could just linger over a cup of coffee and a sweet, such as the delicious cheesecake. The Hungry Monk doesn't serve dinner, but snacks and light meals are offered until late afternoon.

Abbey St., Cong, Co. Mayo. www.hungrymonkcong.com. © **094/954-5842.** Entrees €3–€10. Mon–Sat 10am–5pm (also Sun on Bank Holiday weekends only).

Wilde's at the Lodge at Ashford ★★★ MODERN IRISH   If, like the other 99% of us, you can't quite swing a night at **Ashford Castle** ★★★ (see p. 432), then you might find this a viable alternative for a slice of upper-crust Irish glamour. Lisloughrey Lodge was once home to the estate managers of Ashford, but now it's run as a boutique hotel with a fantastic restaurant. Wilde's is overseen by Jonathan Keane, an up-and-coming star of the Irish culinary world. His modern Irish cooking is deliciously inventive; just a glance at the menu is enough to give you an idea of his celebratory approach to food. From the tasting menu (or "Menu of Discovery"), you might be offered mackerel with horseradish and nasturtium, duck with orange and pine, or wild turbot with monk's beard (we presume the Tuscan vegetable), and, to finish, a deliciously smooth and sweet concoction of white chocolate, mango, and passion fruit. The somewhat more straightforward children's menu should please the junior palate (entrees €8). The dining room has a

walk this way: **PORTACLOY**

The region to the east of the Mullet Peninsula has a spectacular array of sheer sea cliffs and rugged, craggy islands. The small, secluded beach at **Portacloy,** 14km (8⅔ miles) north of Glenamoy on the R314, is a good starting point for a dramatic walk. On a sunny day, its aquamarine waters and fine-grained white sand recall the Mediterranean more than the North Atlantic.

From the concrete quay at the beach's western edge, head north up the steep green slopes of the nearest hill. The sea views from here are breathtaking. Don't be too distracted by the fantastic vista or adorable little sheep—the boggy slopes on which you are walking end precipitously at an unmarked cliff edge. The walk is therefore **not** recommended for children, and should not be undertaken in bad weather. Resist the urge to get a better view of the mysterious sea caves, or to reach the outermost edges of the coast's promontories. Instead, using the farmer's fence as a guide, head west toward the striking profile of **Benwee Head,** about 2.4km (1½ miles) away. This will give you gorgeous views of blue sea and rocky countryside. Return the same way to finish with a swim in the chilly, tranquil waters of Portacloy.

fantastic view of Lough Corrib. If you want to spend the night, doubles start at around €410.

On the grounds of Ashford Castle, Cong, Co. Mayo. www.thelodgeac.com. ℂ **094/954-5400.** Tasting menus €50–€60. Mar–Oct Mon–Sat 6:30–9pm, Sun 1–3:30pm and 6:30–9pm; Nov–Feb Thurs–Sat 6:30–9pm, Sun 1–3:30pm and 6:30–9pm.

Sports & Outdoor Pursuits in County Mayo

FISHING   The waters of the River Moy and loughs Carrowmore, Conn, and Cullin are renowned fishing destinations, particularly for salmon and trout. To arrange a day's fishing, contact **Cloonamoyne Fishery,** Castle-hill, near Crossmolina, Ballina (www.cloonamoynefishery.com; ℂ **096/963-1928).** The fishery rents fully equipped boats and tackle, teaches fly-casting, and provides transport to and from all fishing: for brown trout on loughs Conn and Cullin; for salmon on loughs Beltra, Furnace, and Fee-agh; and for salmon and seatrout on the rivers Moy and Deel. Daily rates are around €30 for a rowboat, €60 for a boat with engine, and €120 for a boat with engine and *ghillie* (guide).

Obtain a permit and state fishing license at the **Mayo Angling Advice Centre,** at the Tiernan Bros. fishing tackle shop, Upper Main Street, Fox-ford (www.themoy.com; ℂ **094/925-6731).** It also offers a range of services, including boat hire and ghillies.

For fishing tackle, try **Kingfisher Bates,** Pier Road, Enniscrone (ℂ **096/36733)** or the **Ballina Angling Centre,** Unit 55, Ridge Pool Road, Ballina (ℂ **096/21850).** On Achill Island, get fishing tackle at **Supervalu Supermarket,** Achill Sound (ℂ **098/45211).** Also a good place to stock up on supplies, it's the smallish white-and-red building on the right, immediately after the bridge crossing from the mainland.

HORSEBACK RIDING   One of the best riding centers in the West is **Drummindoo Stud & Equestrian Centre,** Knockranny, Westport (www.drummindoo.com; ℂ **098/25616).**

KAYAKING   Courses for adults and children are at the **Atlantic Adventure Centre,** in Lecanvey, just outside of Westport (www.atlanticadventurecentre.com; ℂ **098/64806).** Most of the kayaking is done at the Blue Flag beaches at Old Head, Bertra, and Carramore. Very reasonable accommodations rates are available for campers. The adventure center has all you need for a wide range of activities, from canoeing to rock climbing.

WINDSURFING & OTHER WATERSPORTS   With constant wind off the Atlantic Ocean, Achill Island is ideal for windsurfing, hang gliding, or any activities that involve a breeze. If you want to try it out, get in touch with the **Achill Outdoor Education Centre** on R319, between Cashel and Bunacurry (www.achilloutdoor.com; ℂ **098/47253).** It does plenty of other outdoor activities, including powerboating, raft building, and body boarding. For other options, you can also try the Atlantic Adventure Centre (above).

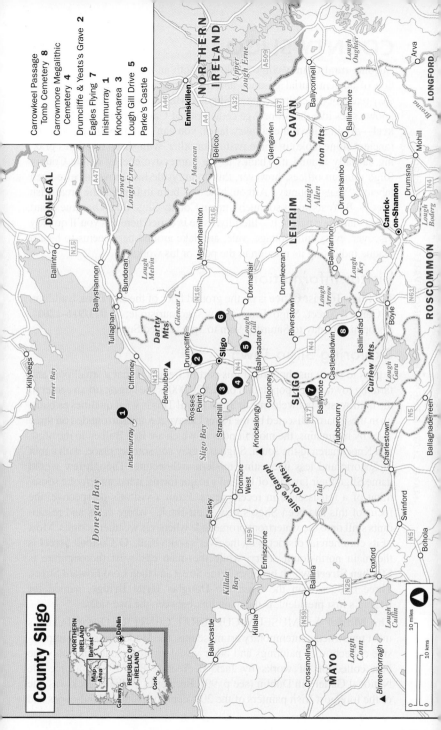

County Sligo

Carrowkeel Passage Tomb Cemetery	**8**
Carrowmore Megalithic Cemetery	**4**
Drumcliffe & Yeats's Grave	**2**
Eagles Flying	**7**
Inishmurray	**1**
Knocknarea	**3**
Lough Gill Drive	**5**
Parke's Castle	**6**

COUNTY SLIGO

Bucolic, rural County Sligo is blessed with an extraordinary concentration of ancient burial grounds and pre-Christian sites, most of them in easy reach of the county capital, **Sligo Town.** It's more than just the well-known sites like the Stone Age cemeteries at **Carrowmore** and **Carrowkeel**—driving down the country lanes, you can't help spotting a *dolmen* (ancient stone table) in some pasture or other, with sheep or ponies grazing casually around it. Thanks to the impressive energy of the County Sligo tourism offices, however, this countryside has above all else been labeled "Yeats Country." Although he was born in Dublin, the great Irish poet W. B. Yeats spent so much time in County Sligo that it became a part of him, and he a part of it—literally, as he is buried here. As you'll quickly discover, every hill, cottage, vale, and lake around here seems to bear a plaque indicating its relation to the poet or his works.

Visitor Information

The **Sligo Tourist Office** is on the ground floor of the Old Bank Building, O'Connell Street, Sligo Town (www.sligotourism.ie; ✆ **071/916-1201**). It's open Monday to Saturday 9am to 5pm (closed Sun).

Exploring Sligo Town

It goes to show just how rural this part of Ireland is that a small port and farming town with a population of just 20,000 is the largest urban center in the northwest—but welcome to Sligo Town! This is what qualifies as built-up in these parts. Bisected by the River Garavogue and surrounded on three sides by mountains, the most famous of which are Ben Bulben to the north and Knocknarea to the south, Sligo is a gray and somber place, with a mix of historic and less interesting modern architecture. Though few would name Sligo their favorite of Ireland's major towns, it has undergone something of a renaissance in recent years. From a visitor's perspective, the focus of this has been Sligo's new "Left Bank," where cafes and restaurants spill onto the waterfront promenade whenever weather permits. Most of its commercial district is on the river's south bank. **O'Connell Street** is the main north-south artery, while the main east-west thoroughfare is **Stephen Street,** which becomes Wine Street and then Lord Edward Street. Three bridges span the river; the **Douglas Hyde Bridge,** named for Ireland's first president, is the main link between the two sides.

The Model ★★ MUSEUM/CULTURAL CENTER   One of Ireland's most renowned contemporary art museums, the Model houses an impressive collection of paintings and other visual art. It includes probably the best collection of works by Jack B. Yeats (1871–1957) outside the National Gallery in Dublin (see p. 99). Brother of William, Jack was one of the foremost Irish painters of the 20th century, painting landscapes and

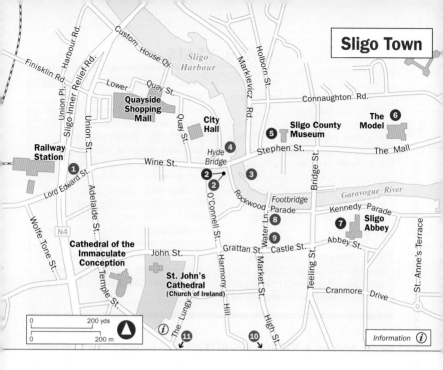

Sligo Town

Sligo Harbour

Finisklin Rd. · Harbour Rd. · Custom House Qy. · Lower Quay St. · Quay St. · Markievicz Rd. · Holborn St. · Connaughton Rd.

Union Pl. · Sligo Inner Relief Rd. · Union St. · **Quayside Shopping Mall** · **City Hall** · **Sligo County Museum** ⑤ · **The Model** ⑥

Railway Station ① · Lord Edward St. · Adelaide St. · Wine St. · Hyde Bridge · Stephen St. · The Mall

Wolfe Tone St. · N4 · **Cathedral of the Immaculate Conception** · John St. · **St. John's Cathedral (Church of Ireland)** · O'Connell St. · Rockwood Parade · Garavogue River · Footbridge Parade · Kennedy Parade · **Sligo Abbey** ⑦ · St. Anne's Terrace

② ② ③ ④ ⑧ ⑨ · Water Ln. · Harmony Hill · Grattan St. · Castle St. · Abbey St. · Teeling St. · Cranmore Drive · Market St. · High St. · The Lungy

0 — 200 yds / 0 — 200 m

⑪ ⑩ · Information ⓘ

NORTHERN IRELAND · Belfast · Sligo Town · Galway · Dublin · REPUBLIC OF IRELAND · Cork

ATTRACTIONS
The Model 6
Sligo Abbey 7
Sligo County Museum 5
Yeats Memorial Building 2

WHERE TO STAY
The Glasshouse 4
Ross Farmhouse 10
Sligo Park Hotel 10
Temple House 11

WHERE TO EAT
Coach Lane at Donaghy's Bar 1
Eala Bhan 8
Kate's Kitchen 9
Lilly's & Lolly's Cafe 2
Osta Café & Wine Bar 3

---

figures in a bold Expressionist style. Other luminaries of the Irish art world represented here include Louis le Brocquy (1916–2012), an extraordinary figurative painter; and the portraitist Estella Solomons (1882–1968). The museum's program of temporary and special exhibitions is varied and imaginative. The Model is also a venue for live music and film screenings. Check the website for up-to-date listings.

The Mall, Sligo Town. www.themodel.ie. ℂ **071/914-1405.** Free admission to exhibitions; tickets to other events free to around €25. Tues–Sat 10am–5pm, Sun 10:30am–3:30pm. Closed Mon.

a poetic soul: **W. B. YEATS**

One of Ireland's greatest and most beloved writers, **William Butler Yeats** (1865–1939) had Sligo in his soul.

The first of Ireland's four Nobel laureates, Yeats (pronounced "Yates") was a poet, playwright, and politician. He was at the forefront of the Celtic Revival, which celebrated and championed native Irish culture and heritage. Drawing heavily upon the traditional folklore of Ireland, his work was steeped in myth and imagination.

Yeats grew up amid Sligo's verdant hills and dales, now known (by the tourist board at least) as "Yeats Country." In fact, parts of the county's tourism industry seem to focus on little else. You can cruise Lough Gill while listening to a live recital of Yeats's poetry; follow Yeats trails and buy a hundred items of Yeats memorabilia; and visit dozens of his purported haunts—some reputedly still spooked by his ghost, and some of which have only tenuous connections with the man.

Yeats died in Menton, on the French Riviera, in 1939. Knowing he was ill, he stated, "If I die here, bury me up there on the mountain, and then after a year or so, dig me up and bring me privately to Sligo." True to his wishes, in 1948 his body was moved to Sligo and reinterred at **Drumcliffe Church** (see p. 442).

Sligo Abbey ★ RELIGIOUS SITE/RUIN   Founded as a Dominican house in 1252 by Maurice Fitzgerald, Earl of Kildare, Sligo Abbey was the center of early Sligo Town. It thrived for centuries and flourished in medieval times when it was the burial place of the chiefs and earls of Sligo. But, as with other affluent religious settlements, the abbey was under constant attack, and it was finally destroyed in 1641. Much restoration work has been done in recent years; the fine cloisters contain outstanding examples of stone carving, and the 15th-century altar is one of the few intact medieval altars in Ireland.

Abbey St., Sligo Town. www.heritageireland.ie. © **071/914-6406.** Admission €5 adults; €4 seniors; €3 students and children; €13 families. Apr to mid-Oct daily 10am–6pm; last admission 45 min. before closing.

Sligo County Museum ★ MUSEUM   This museum in the center of Sligo Town presents a good overview of the county's history from ancient times to the present day. The most interesting sections cover the region's extraordinary prehistoric heritage, including a couple of ancient artifacts. (Sligo is, after all, where you'll find one of the world's oldest buildings by some measures, the Carrowmore Megalithic Cemetery—see p. 441.) The other standout sections are devoted to two of Sligo's most famous residents: the poet W. B. Yeats (see box above), whose mother was from Sligo and whose affinity with the county drastically influenced his work; and Constance Markievicz (see box p. 443), an aristocrat who grew up in Sligo and went on to become a prominent Irish revolutionary.

Stephen St., Sligo Town. © **071/911-1679.** Free admission. May–Sept Tues–Sat 9:30am–12:30pm, 2–4:50pm; Oct–Apr Tues–Sat 9:30am–12:30pm. Closed Sun and Mon.

Yeats Memorial Building ★ MUSEUM   Located in a distinctive red-and-white town house building on the Douglas Hyde Bridge, this engaging little museum, art gallery, and heritage center acts as a kind of focal point for the W. B. Yeats–related attractions in County Sligo. Exhibitions focus on the life and work of the great poet, and the 19th- and 20th-century literary canon of which he was a major part. The center also has an art gallery, featuring work by contemporary artists, many of them Sligo-based, and presents courses, workshops, and lectures during the summer months. It's also a good place to stop for a bite to eat, at **Lily's & Lolly's Café** ★ (see p. 448). For more on Yeats, see "A Poetic Soul" on p. 440.

Douglas Hyde Bridge, Sligo Town. www.yeatssociety.com. ⓒ **071/914-2693.** Free admission. Tues–Sat 10am–5pm. Closed Sun and Mon.

Farther Afield in County Sligo

The area around Sligo Town is known for its ancient burial grounds and pagan sites, some dating from the Stone Age. These include the vast Neolithic cemetery **Carrowmore,** the atmospheric hilltop cairn grave of **Knocknarea,** and the haunting Neolithic mountaintop cemetery of **Carrowkeel.** Some lesser sites are also open to the public, but most are not. The Irish are passionate about property rights, so don't go clambering over a fence for a better photo without getting permission first.

At the foot of Knocknarea is the delightful resort area of **Strandhill,** 8km (5 miles) from Sligo Town. Stretching into Sligo Bay, Strandhill has a sand dune beach and a patch of land nearby called Coney Island, which is usually credited as the namesake of New York's amusement park. Across the bay is another resort, **Rosses Point.**

Carrowkeel Passage Tomb Cemetery ★★ ANCIENT SITE   Atop a hill overlooking Lough Arrow, this ancient passage-tomb cemetery is impressive, isolated, and frequently empty. Its 14 cairns, dolmens, and stone circles date from the Stone Age (ca. 5000 B.C.), and it's easy to feel a mystical connection to that history, standing among the cold, ageless rocks. The tombs face **Carrowmore** ★★★ (below) in the far distance below and are aligned with the summer solstice. The walk uphill from the parking lot takes about 20 minutes, but the exercise is worth the effort. This is a simple site—no visitor center, no tea shop, no admission fee—nothing but ancient mystery.

Signposted on N4 btw. Sligo Town and Boyle, Co. Sligo. No phone. Free admission (open site).

Carrowmore Megalithic Cemetery ★★★ ANCIENT SITE   This is one of the great sacred landscapes of the ancient world. At the center of the Coolera Peninsula sits a massive passage grave that once had a Stonehenge-like stone circle of its own. Around that were as many as 200 additional stone circles and passage graves arranged in an intricate and mysterious design. Over the years, some of the stones have been moved;

An ancient stone circle at Carrowmore Megalithic Cemetery.

more than 60 circles and passage graves still exist, although the site spreads out so far that many of them lie in adjacent farmland. Look for your first dolmen in a paddock next to the road about a mile before you reach the site. The dolmens were the actual graves, once covered in stones and earth. Some of these sites are open to visitors, and you can get a map to them from the visitor center. (Not all are, however; be careful not to trespass on private land.) On the main site, the oldest tomb is thought to date from around 3,700 B.C.—making it one of the oldest pieces of free-standing stone architecture in the world. From Carrowmore, you can see the hilltop cairn grave of **Knocknarea ★** (see p. 445), which is about 4km (2½ miles) away. The visitor center has good exhibits and guided tours. Follow signs from Woodville Road heading west out of Sligo Town, or from R292 at Ransboro.

Carrowmore, Co. Sligo. www.heritageireland.ie. *(?)* **071/916-1534.** Admission €5 adults; €4 seniors; €3 students and children; €13 families. Apr–Oct daily 10am–6pm; last admission 1 hr. before closing. Closed mid-Oct to Mar.

Drumcliffe Church ★ CHURCH/GRAVESITE   An essential stop for Yeats fans, this square-towered village church, where Yeats' great-grandfather was once rector, was the poet's chosen burial site. (See "A Poetic Soul," p. 440.) His grave is marked with a dark, modest stone just left of the church, alongside his young wife, Georgie Hyde-Lee (when they married in 1917, he was 52 and she was 23). His epitaph, "CAST A COLD EYE ON LIFE, ON DEATH…." comes from his poem "Under Ben Bulben." While you're here,

local hero: **CONSTANCE MARKIEVICZ**

Aristocrat, suffragette, revolutionary, and politician, Constance Markievicz (1868–1927) was one of the most influential Irish women of the 20th century and a key figure in the country's struggle for independence from Britain.

Born in London to Anglo-Irish gentry, Constance became aware of the realities of life for the poor in Ireland at an early age. Her father, Sir Henry Gore-Booth, owned Lissadell House, a great estate in County Sligo. Unlike many landowners of the time, he was widely loved by his tenants; during an outbreak of famine when Constance was eleven, he provided them with life-saving food relief.

In 1900 Constance married a Polish count, Casimir Markievicz (1874–1932), and the two settled in Dublin. By this time she was actively involved in the fight for women's suffrage. It wasn't long before she began to move in revolutionary circles too. (One story has it that she was finally persuaded to join Sinn Fein, the political party set up in 1905 to fight for independence, after discovering a collection of rousing pamphlets left behind at a remote country cottage.)

In 1914 her revolutionary career began in earnest when she joined the Irish Citizens Army. She became known for her leading role in gun-running missions, alongside Douglas Hyde (1860–1949), who would later become the first President of Ireland. During the Easter Rising of 1916 she manned barricades in St. Stephen's Green, Dublin, engaging in gunfights with British soldiers.

After the Rising was put down, Markievicz, along with many of her fellow revolutionaries, was sentenced to death. But the court commuted her sentence to life in prison because she was a woman. In a

Countess Constance Markievicz.

withering comeback, she shot back from the dock, "I wish you had the decency to shoot me."

In the end Markievicz served only a year in prison, including solitary confinement at the notorious **Kilmainham Gaol ★★★** (see p. 99), although she would later be jailed again for sedition. It was while serving a sentence in 1918 that she learned she had become the first woman elected to the British Parliament. She refused to take her seat and was later elected to the Irish Dáil.

Following the War of Independence, Markievicz was to achieve another political first for women, when she was appointed Minister for Labor in the new Irish government—the first woman in Europe to serve at cabinet level.

also check out the 11th-century high cross in the churchyard—its faded eastern side shows Christ, Daniel in the lions' den, Adam and Eve, and Cain murdering Abel. The site also has a little visitor center and cafe.

Drumcliffe. 10km (6½ miles) N of Sligo Town, on the N15 road.

Eagles Flying ★★ AVIARY   Some of the biggest birds of prey in the world are displayed at this aviary and educational center near Ballymote. Eagles, vultures, owls, and falcons take part in an hour-long flying show daily at 11am and 3pm—outside or in a purpose-built arena. Most of the awe-inspiring birds who live at the center can be handled by visitors (under close supervision, of course). For young children who prefer their animals a little less intimidating, the center has a petting zoo, home to lambs, chinchillas, donkeys, rabbits, and even raccoons (which are not native to Ireland but have slowly been spreading here as an invasive species since the early 2010s).

Ballymote, Co. Sligo. www.eaglesflying.com. ✆ **071/918-9310.** Admission €12 adults; €11 students; €7 children 3–16; free for children 2 and under; €36 families. Late Mar to early Nov daily 10:30am–12:30pm, 2:30–4:30pm. Bird shows 11am and 3pm.

Inishmurray ★★ ISLAND/ RUINS   Northwest of Sligo Bay, this tiny, uninhabited island shelters an ancient past. The haunting ruins of St. Molaise, a 6th-century monastic settlement that was destroyed by the Vikings in 807, stands within its circular walls. You can still see the remains of several churches, beehive cells, altars, and an assemblage of "cursing stones" once used to bring ruin on those who presumably deserved it. In the 19th and early 20th centuries, however, Inishmurray harbored a different identity: a thriving illicit trade in the distilling of moonshine whiskey. The last permanent residents left the island in 1948; their ruined houses can still be seen, battered by the elements. Boat trips to the island are operated by **Inishmurray Island Trips** (www.inishmurray islandtrips.com; ✆ **087/254-0190**) and **Ewing's Sea Angling and Boat Charters** (www.sligoboatcharters. com; ✆ **086/891-3618**). Expect to

An abandoned cottage on the island of Inishmurray.

pay around €45 adults, €40 children, and you may need a minimum group size of four. Call or visit the websites for details and sailing times.

NW of Sligo Bay, 6km (3¾ miles) offshore. Ferries leave from Mullaghmore or Rosses Point.

Knocknarea ★ ANCIENT SITE From the low vantage point of **Carrowmore ★★★** (see p. 441), if you study the mountain ranges that ring the surrounding valley, you'll notice a stone cairn in the center of each one. (As any local schoolchild will tell you, from certain angles this has the effect of making them look decidedly, well, boob-shaped.) One of these is the unexcavated **Knocknarea.** Local legend has it that this is the grave of the "fairy queen" Queen Maeve—better known to most people these days as Queen Mab, the subject of one of the most famous speeches written by William Shakespeare in *Romeo and Juliet.* If you have the energy to make the relatively gentle 30-minute climb to the top, the views are extraordinary.

Knocknarea, about 6.4km (4 miles) W of Sligo, Co. Sligo. No phone. Free admission (open site). Signposted from small farm road btw. Cullenduff and Knocknarea, and from R292 heading south from Strandhill. Follow signs for mescan meadhbha chambered cairn.

Parke's Castle ★ CASTLE On the north side of the Lough Gill Drive (see p. 446), just over the County Leitrim border, Parke's Castle stands out as a lone outpost amid the natural tableau of lake view and woodland scenery. Named after an English family that gained possession of it during the 1620 plantation of Leitrim (when land was confiscated from the Irish and given to favored English families), this castle was originally the stronghold of the O'Rourke clan, rulers of the Kingdom of Bréifne. Beautifully restored using Irish oak and traditional craftsmanship, it exemplifies the 17th-century fortified manor house. At this writing, access to the upper levels was restricted because of restoration work; this should be finished by early 2019. In the visitor center, informative exhibits and a splendid audiovisual show illustrate the history of the castle and the surrounding area.

On R286, 11.2km (7 miles) east of Sligo Town, Co. Leitrim. www.heritageireland.ie. © **071/916-4149.** Admission €5 adults; €4 seniors; €3 students and children; €13 families. Early Apr to Sept daily 10am–6pm; last admission 45 min. before closing.

Where to Stay in County Sligo

As with County Mayo, most of the best places to stay in County Sligo are hidden in the countryside.

MODERATE

Sligo Park Hotel ★ A pleasant little park surrounds this convenient, cheap-ish hotel in Sligo Town. Guest rooms are simply furnished in a contemporary style, with muted color schemes of gray and brown, and

THE lough gill DRIVE

An essential stop on Yeats Country pilgrimages is this beautiful lake, which figured prominently in the writings of W. B. Yeats. A well-signposted drive-yourself tour around the lake's perimeter covers 42km (26 miles) and takes less than an hour.

To start, head 1.6km (1 mile) south of Sligo Town and follow the signs for Lough Gill. Within 3.2km (2 miles) you'll be on the lower edge of the shoreline. Among the sites are **Parke's Castle** (see p. 445); **Dooney Rock,** with its own nature trail and lakeside walk (inspiration for the poem "Fiddler of Dooney"); the **Lake Isle of Innisfree,** made famous in poetry and song; and the **Hazelwood Sculpture Trail,** a unique forest walk along the shores of Lough Gill, with 13 wood sculptures. At the lake's east end, branch off to visit **Dromahair,** a delightful village on the River Bonet.

The road along Lough Gill's upper shore brings you back to the northern end of Sligo Town. Continue north on the main road (N15), and you'll see the graceful profile of **Ben Bulben** (519m/1,702 ft.), one of the Dartry Mountains, rising off to your right. One of Yeats' last poems, "Under Ben Bulben," alludes to this majestic rock formation as a silent sentinel looming over Irish history.

If you prefer to see all this beautiful scenery from the water itself, **Lough Gill Cruises** take you around Lough Gill and the Garavogue River aboard the 72-passenger *Wild Rose* waterbus as you listen to the poetry of Yeats. The boat departs from Parke's Castle daily at 12:30pm; tours last around an hour. During summer only there are also 3-hour trips daily from Doorly Park in Sligo at 2:30pm. Tickets for the hour-long tour are €15 adults, €13 seniors and students, €7.50 children; for the 3-hour version it's €18 adults, €15 seniors and students, €9 children. Trips to Innisfree, sunset cruises, and dinner cruises are also scheduled. Visit www.roseofinnisfree.com or call ☏ **071/916-4266** for details and booking.

good-size bathrooms. One or two rooms could do with some TLC around the edges, though the public areas are sleek and well-designed. Family rooms only cost a little more than doubles. This hotel won't win any awards for heart-of-Ireland atmosphere, but as a clean, modern base, it's a good option in a region that's short on choice. *One word of caution:* The hotel is also a popular venue for weddings and other events, so noise can sometimes be a problem on weekends. You might want to ask for a room as far away from the bar as possible.

Pearse Rd., Sligo Town. www.sligoparkhotel.com. ☏ **071/919-0400.** 136 units. €119–€184 double, €169–€219 suite. Free parking. Breakfast not included in lower rates. **Amenities:** Restaurant; bar; pool; room service; sauna; Wi-Fi (free).

Temple House ★★★ This is quite simply *the* place to stay in the northwest if you're after a unique and historic B&B experience. Make no mistake: Temple House is not a hotel, and it's not full of five-star extras—but for historical authenticity, beautiful surroundings, and sheer, unforgettable charm, we think it's unbeatable. The delightful young custodians of the estate, Roderick and Helena Perceval, are now more than a decade into their painstaking restoration of the 1665 manor house. Once a thriving country estate, it had fallen slowly into near-ruin during the turbulent years of the 20th century. (When we first stayed, the 18th-century silk curtains in one room, now fully restored, would literally crumble to the touch). Now the huge guest rooms are packed with interesting antiques, but have completely modern, recently renovated bathrooms. Nightly dinners are more akin to parties, with all guests seated around an enormous old table enjoying outstanding food. Breakfasts hit the spot, too, with plenty of homemade treats. The beautiful grounds include a boating lake, a walled garden, and even a ruined Knights Templar castle—hence the name. Supposedly there are a couple of resident ghosts roaming around, although they must be of a very Bacchanalian kind, with such a welcoming and convivial atmosphere as this. There is also a self-catering cottage on the grounds.

Ballymote, Ballinacarrow, Co. Sligo. www.templehouse.ie. ✆ **071/918-3329.** 6 units. €100–€210 double. Dinner €45 (no dinner Sun). Free parking. Breakfast included. **Amenities:** Wi-Fi (free). Closed Dec–Mar.

INEXPENSIVE

The Glasshouse ★   A solid, modern option in Sligo Town, the Glasshouse overlooks the River Garavogue and resembles a gleaming, modern ship from the outside. The public areas inside either look bold and funky or like an explosion in a kitsch factory, depending on your point of view: multicolored circles on the carpet, misshapen blue sofas, and a bright orange signature color in the towering atrium. Bedrooms are a little more refined, with muted tones and modern art on the walls. There is an in-house restaurant, although you could eat more cheaply in town. The appropriately named **View Bar** looks out over Sligo Town and has live music (if you are sensitive to noise, ask for a room away from the bar when you book). A few years ago, places like this were all but unheard-of in Sligo, and the Glasshouse offers a good alternative for those who want a decently priced, convenient, and contemporary place to stay.

Swan Point, Sligo Town. www.theglasshouse.ie. ✆ **071/919-4300.** 116 units. €119–€179 double, €149–€209 suite. 2-night minimum some weekends. Free parking. Breakfast not included in lower rates. **Amenities:** Restaurant; 2 bars; room service; Internet (broadband/via TV).

Ross Farmhouse ★★   Not far from Carrowkeel (see p. 441), Ross Farmhouse is a restored 1880s cottage, surrounded by acres and acres of rolling farmland. The cheerful owners, Nicholas and Oriel Hill-Wilkinson, see this place as their pride and joy, and it shows in the gregarious welcome they give guests. Bedrooms are reasonably sized, with simple, unfussy furnishings. One is a family room, and another is fully accessible to wheelchairs. Downstairs are two lovely guest lounges, filled with antiques. An open peat fire warms the hearth in winter. Breakfasts are good, and they'll cook for you in the evenings if you book in advance (very reasonable at €35 per person; there's a good wine list, too, or you can bring your own). In addition to all the countryside walks, ancient ruins, and sweet little towns you could wish for, the area has some of the best horseback riding in Ireland—ask if you'd like recommendations for local riding centers. *Note:* Not all bedrooms have a private bathroom, so specify when you book if you want one.

Riverstown, Co. Sligo. Follow signs from Drumfin on N4 or Coola on R284. www.rossfarmhousesligo.com. ℂ **071/916-5140.** 6 units. €90 double. Free parking. Breakfast included. **Amenities:** Wi-Fi (free).

Where to Eat in Sligo Town

Coach Lane at Donaghy's ★★ IRISH/INTERNATIONAL   A very popular spot with Sligo residents, Coach Lane has two dining rooms: a bar, serving easy crowd-pleasers such as burgers, fish and chips, and shepherd's pie; and a more upmarket, gastropub-style restaurant. Most ingredients are regionally sourced, and the seafood is particularly good. Try the rich French onion soup, then dive into a hearty plate of steak and chips, or filet of cod served with samphire (a salty green vegetable that grows only by the sea) and white wine butter.

1–2 Lord Edward St., Sligo Town. www.coachlane.ie. ℂ **071/916-2417.** Entrees €19–€25. Bar food: daily 3–9:30pm. Restaurant: daily 5:30–10pm.

Eala Bhan ★★★ INTERNATIONAL   Local meats and seafood are featured at this popular brasserie in Sligo Town. The menu takes traditional brasserie classics and adds a light touch of creative flair—tender rack of local lamb comes with *courgette* (zucchini) puree and pesto mash while the seabass is balanced by a piquant pea-and-lemon risotto and a rich champagne cream sauce. Three-course set menus are good value and feature many dishes from the main menus. The early-bird menu (served until 6:20pm daily) is just €25 for three courses. The lunch menu is almost as extensive as dinner, with a few lighter options such as poached chicken salad or seafood chowder.

Rockwood Parade, Sligo Town. www.ealabhan.ie. ℂ **071/914-5823.** Entrees €18–€28. Mon–Sat noon–3pm, 5–9:30pm; Sun 12:30–3pm, 5–9:30pm.

Kate's Kitchen ★★ DELI   This great delicatessen has a large stock of gourmet foods, Irish cheese, fresh bread, salads, chutneys, and other tasty items that just beg to be put together to make an elegant picnic or lunch on the go. It also has a small shop selling bath products and a particularly nice range of handmade chocolates—perfect for gifts, if you can keep yourself from raiding them before the journey home.

3 Castle St., Sligo Town. www.kateskitchen.ie. ℂ **071/914-3022.** Most items €4–€8. Mon–Sat 8:30am–5:30pm.

Lily's & Lolly's Café ★ CAFE   Handy for a quick and tasty lunch, this cheery cafe inside the **Yeats Memorial Building** ★ (see p. 441) serves reasonably priced wraps, panini, and light meals, in addition to homemade cakes and pies. The cafe is next to the Garavogue River; you can sit outside on a sunny little terrace when the weather's fine.

At the Yeats Memorial Building, Douglas Hyde Bridge, Sligo Town. ☏ **071/914-4727.** All items €3–€8. Tues–Sat 10am–5pm. Closed Sun and Mon.

Osta Café and Wine Bar ★★ CAFE   The owners of this sweet cafe overlooking the river in Sligo are big believers in the slow-food and organic movements, and their delicious, healthful food makes superb use of ingredients from small, local producers. There are usually only a few dishes on offer every day, but you're virtually guaranteed to find something properly, authentically Irish—hot pot (a kind of meat and vegetable stew), perhaps, or omelets made from smoked Gubbeen cheese and potato. Soups are a specialty, too. Even the sandwiches qualify as local—they're made with deliciously fresh bread from a nearby bakery. In the early evening on Thursday to Saturday, the food switches to a simple but tasty tapas menu. *Tip:* A Gaelic-speaking group meets here every Friday evening, which makes it a good time to drop by if you fancy eavesdropping on some of the language used.

Garavogue Weir, off Stephen St., Sligo Town. www.osta.ie. ☏ **071/914-4639.** Entrees €5–€8. Mon–Wed and Sat 8am–6pm, Thurs–Fri 8am–7pm, Fri 8am–8pm, Sun 9am–5pm.

Shopping in Sligo Town

Sligo Town has some great little boutiques and independent local businesses. Most shops are open Monday to Saturday 9am to 6pm; some may have extended hours in July and August.

The Cat & the Moon ★★   Named after a Yeats poem, this is a great place to shop for Irish crafts and jewelry. They design their own silver rings and pendants with Celtic motifs. In addition, the shop stocks an interesting range of art, ceramics, candles, and other handicrafts, and always seems to offer something in the way of unique finds and souvenirs. 4 Castle St., Sligo Town. www.thecatandthemoon.com. ☏ **071/914-3686.**

Michael Quirke ★★   Michael Quirke is a real Sligo character. He used to be a butcher, but got bored with it and decided to follow his real passion: woodcarving. Out went the meat and in came the artisan tools, and his shop became a studio. Now he spends his time carving and selling exquisite statues, ornaments, and objets d'art out of Irish wood, with a particular focus on figures from Irish mythology. His carvings are quite affordable for the quality. Wine St., Sligo Town. ☏ **071/914-2624.**

Wehrly Bros. Ltd ★★   The granddaddy of Sligo jewelry stores, this firm has been trading from behind its elegant black-and-gold storefront since 1875. It specializes in diamond rings, watches, and pearls, with a wide range of designer jewelry. It also sells Waterford crystal. 3 O'Connell St., Sligo Town. www.wehrlybros.ie. ☏ **071/914-2252.**

Sports & Outdoor Pursuits in County Sligo

CYCLING With its lakes and woodlands, Yeats Country is particularly good biking territory. To rent a bike, contact **Chain Driven Cycles,** 23 High St., Sligo Town (www.chaindrivencycles.com; ℭ **071/912-9008**). Prices start at around €9 per day.

HORSEBACK RIDING Arrange an hour or a day of horseback riding on the beach, in the countryside, or over mountain trails through **Sligo Riding Centre,** Carrowmore (www.sligoridingcentre.com; ℭ **087/230-4828**) or at **Woodlands Equestrian**

Horseback riding in the Sligo countryside.

Centre, Loughill, near Ballymote (www.woodlandsequestrian.ie; ℭ **071/918-4207**). Rates average around €25 to €45 per hour.

DONEGAL &
THE ATLANTIC
HIGHLANDS

13

W hen the signs change into Gaelic, the landscape opens up into great sweeping views of rocky hills and barren shores, and a freezing mist blows off the sea, you know you've reached Donegal. The austere beauty of this county can be almost too bleak, but it is also unforgettable. On a clear day, you can stand at the edge of the sea at Malin Head, and, despite the sun, the sea spray will blow a chill right through you. It feels as if you're standing at the edge of the world.

County Donegal's natural wonders include the magnificent Slieve League cliffs and remote beaches tucked into the bays and inlets of its sharply indented coast. Few tourists make it this far, however. The towns of Donegal are perhaps the least developed for tourism in Ireland; the county has some truly fantastic places to stay, but they tend to be hidden away amid mountainous roads and tiny seaside towns. Buildings are made of cold stone, and villages perch on the slopes of precipitous hillsides; road signs vary from cryptic to nonexistent. When you stop to take a wander, you can't help but worry whether the car's brakes will hold. But take the chance. You will spend half your time lost, but wherever you're headed, you'll get there eventually, most likely with a few adventures along the way. And the people in Donegal are as nice as can be—meeting them is worth the trip in itself.

ESSENTIALS

Arriving

BY BUS   **Bus Éireann** (www.buseireann.ie; ✆ **074/912-1309**) operates daily bus service to Donegal Town from Dublin, Derry, Sligo, Galway, and other points. Buy tickets in advance online for the best price.

BY TRAIN   Trains in this part of the country are extremely scarce. Donegal Town no longer even has a train station. You can catch a train as far as Sligo and then switch to bus, but it's easiest to take a bus all the way.

BY CAR   The only practical way to get around the remote attractions of County Donegal is by car. If you're driving from the south, Donegal is reached on N15 from Sligo or A46 from Northern Ireland; N56 is the main road from Donegal Town circling around the rest of the county.

PREVIOUS PAGE: **Hiking in Ards Forest Park.**

BY PLANE **Donegal Airport,** Carrickfinn, near Letterkenny (www. donegalairport.ie; ✆ **074/954-8284**), also known as Carrickfinn Airport, is very slowly growing as a budget airline hub. Currently a couple of scheduled flights connect per day with Dublin and about three flights per week with Glasgow in the U.K., all operated by **Aer Lingus** (www.aerlingus. com; ✆ **1890/800-600**).

DONEGAL TOWN & DONEGAL BAY

Overseen by a low, gloomy castle at the edge of the picturesque estuary of the River Eske on Donegal Bay, Donegal Town is a tiny burg, with just 2,500 residents. As recently as the 1940s, the town's triangular central mall (called "the Diamond"), set at the meeting point of roads from Killybegs, Ballyshannon, and Ballybofey, was used as a market for trading livestock and goods. Today the marketing takes the form of tweeds and tourist goods, as the Diamond is surrounded by little crafts shops and small hotels of variable quality. In the center stands an obelisk erected in memory of four 17th-century Irish clerics from the local abbey (see p. 455) who wrote *The Annals of the Four Masters,* the first recorded history of Gaelic Ireland.

Visitor Information

The **Donegal Discover Ireland Centre** is on Quay Street, Donegal Town (✆ **074/972-1148**). The seasonal **Ardara Heritage Centre** (✆ **074/954-1704**) is on the main road through Ardara; it's closed from November to Easter. Admission costs €2.54, €1.27 seniors and students, and €0.63 children 13 and under.

Exploring Donegal Town

Donegal Bay Waterbus ★ BOAT TOUR These guided 75-minute tours of Donegal Bay take place daily on a modern, two-deck boat. Points of interest along the way include the **Old Abbey** ★ (see p. 455); the aptly

---

Summer Fests in Donegal Town

If you're heading this way in early July, check out **www.donegaltown.ie** for details of the town's laidback annual **Summer Festival.** The program is an enthusiastic mixture of free concerts (from local bands that, in all probability, you've never heard of) and family-friendly fun and games. The festival lasts 4 days, with the biggest events scheduled over a weekend. And if you're heading this way later in the summer, you might be able to catch the **Donegal Food Festival.** Held over a weekend in late August, the festival brings together chefs, restaurateurs, and artisan food providers from all over Ireland. Visit www.atasteofdonegal.com for more details.

IRISH only!

Although English is the day-to-day language spoken by the overwhelming majority of Irish people, there are places where you will hear a more ancient tongue being spoken: Gaelic, the Celtic language indigenous to these shores. While only about 3% of Irish people speak Gaelic as their main language, many more understand or can speak a little.

In the interest of promoting and preserving the language, there are certain regions, known as **Gaeltacht,** where English is forbidden on official signage. These areas are spread all over the country, but some of the biggest are in Donegal, Mayo, and Kerry. When you're driving around Gaeltract districts, all the road signs will be in Gaelic—even emergency signs and place names. This can get confusing pretty fast, so in this book we've included the Gaelic names as well

as the English names for the places where you're likely to encounter it. (Donegal has an unusually high proportion of native speakers—more than a third of residents of the Rosguill Peninsula [see p. 466], for example, speak Gaelic as their main language.)

The Gaeltacht laws aren't without controversy. A few years ago, the government caused outrage when it forced Dingle to change its much-loved name to the entirely made-up Gaelic *An Daingean* (see p. 319). But one thing you won't have any problem with is communicating with locals. Nobody in Ireland speaks *only* Gaelic. In fact, despite the efforts to save the ancient tongue, there is a general feeling of pessimism about its chances for long-term survival—so if you do manage to hear Gaelic being used by native speakers, it's an experience you may want to savor.

named **Seal Island,** home to a colony of about 200 noisy seals; and **The Hassans,** a port from which many emigrants from the northern part of the country left for the New World. The guides are enthusiastic and knowledgeable; unfortunately, their commentary is nonstop (guides have even been known to play the keyboard to fill in moments of silence). The views, however, are wonderful. There's a bar on board, plus seniors get free tea, coffee, and bottled water (ask for a voucher when picking up your tickets). Sailing times are usually morning and afternoon or evening but are dependent upon tides and weather, so call ahead. Buy tickets from the office on Quay Street—it's the white-and-blue building next to Dom's Pier 1 Bar.
The Pier, Donegal Town. www.donegalbaywaterbus.com. (C) **074/972-3666.** Tour €20 adults; €12 students 17–23 (must have student ID); €7 children 5–16; free for children 4 and under. No credit cards. Closed Nov–Feb.

Donegal Castle ★ CASTLE Built in the 15th century on the banks of the River Eske, this solid graystone castle was once the chief stronghold for the O'Donnells, a powerful Donegal clan. In the 17th century, during the Plantation period, it was taken over by Sir Basil Brook, who added an extension with 10 gables, a large bay window, and smaller mullioned windows in Jacobean style. Much of the building has survived the centuries, and both the interior and exterior of the castle were beautifully restored in

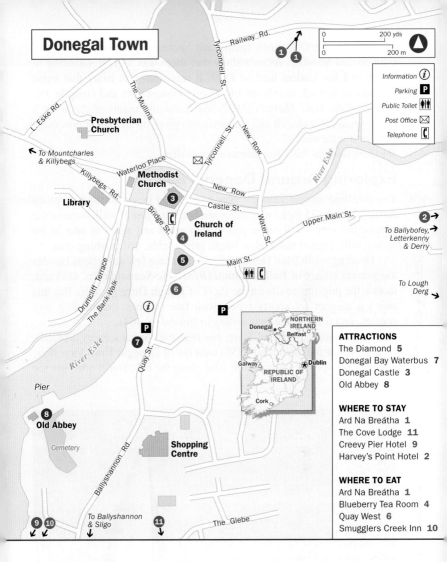

Donegal Town

To Mountcharles & Killybegs

Presbyterian Church

Methodist Church

Library

Church of Ireland

Pier

Old Abbey

Cemetery

Shopping Centre

To Ballyshannon & Sligo

The Glebe

To Ballybofey, Letterkenny & Derry

To Lough Derg

Railway Rd.

Tyrconnell St.

New Row

River Eske

L. Eske Rd.

The Mullins

Waterloo Place

New Row

Castle St.

Upper Main St.

Water St.

Main St.

Bridge St.

Drumcliff Terrace

The Bank Walk

River Eske

Quay St.

Ballyshannon Rd.

Killybegs Rd.

| 0 | 200 yds |
| 0 | 200 m |

Information ⓘ
Parking P
Public Toilet 🚻
Post Office ✉
Telephone C

NORTHERN IRELAND

Donegal • Belfast ○

Galway ○ ★ Dublin

REPUBLIC OF IRELAND

Cork ○

ATTRACTIONS
The Diamond **5**
Donegal Bay Waterbus **7**
Donegal Castle **3**
Old Abbey **8**

WHERE TO STAY
Ard Na Breátha **1**
The Cove Lodge **11**
Creevy Pier Hotel **9**
Harvey's Point Hotel **2**

WHERE TO EAT
Ard Na Breátha **1**
Blueberry Tea Room **4**
Quay West **6**
Smugglers Creek Inn **10**

the 1990s. Guided tours run hourly and are included in the admission price.

Castle St., Donegal Town. www.heritageireland.ie. ⓒ **074/972-2405.** Admission €5 adults; €4 seniors; €3 students and children; €13 families. Easter to mid-Sept daily 10am–6pm; mid-Sept to Easter Thurs–Mon 9:30am–4:30pm; last admission 45 min. before closing.

Old Abbey ★ RELIGIOUS SITE/RUINS   Sitting in a peaceful spot on the quay in Donegal Town, where the River Eske meets Donegal Bay, this ruined Franciscan monastery was founded in 1474 by the first Red Hugh O'Donnell and his wife, Nuala O'Brien of Munster. It was generously endowed by the O'Donnell family and became an important center of religion and learning; records show that there was a great gathering of clergy and lay leaders here in 1539. It was from this friary that some scholars undertook to salvage old Gaelic manuscripts and compile *The Annals of the Four Masters* (1632–36). Enough remains of the abbey's glory—ruins of a church and a cloister—to give you an idea of how magnificent it once was.

The Quay, Donegal Town. Free admission (open site).

Exploring Around Donegal Bay

The coastline around Donegal Bay is wild and beautiful. Speeds much above 55kmph (35 mph) are dangerous, but that's just as well, because the spectacular views will cause you to stop again and again to take in the rolling hills, jagged mountains, bright green fields, and crashing seas.

Heading south from Donegal Town, there are few attractions besides the historic village of **Ballyshannon** (***Béal Átha Seanaidh***) (p. 458) and, inland, the pilgrimage site on the shore of **Lough Derg** (p. 459). But this area's a magnet for sporty types, with fine beaches, outstanding golf courses, and some of the best surfing in Ireland (p. 464).

To the north of Donegal Town, however, the coastal scenery is breathtaking. Follow the main road (N56) west out of Donegal Town for a slow, winding, but spectacularly scenic drive along the bay. You'll often see the

Huge Donegal Bay offers many options for sailing and other water sports.

County Donegal

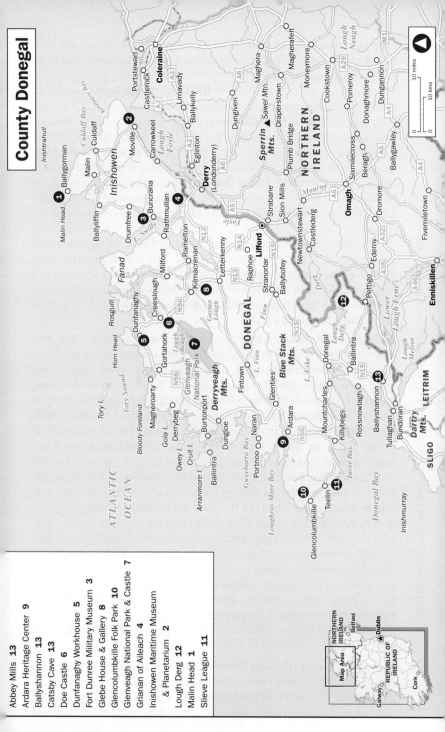

Abbey Mills **13**
Ardara Heritage Center **9**
Ballyshannon **13**
Catsby Cave **13**
Doe Castle **6**
Dunfanaghy Workhouse **5**
Fort Dunree Military Museum **3**
Glebe House & Gallery **8**
Glencolumbkille Folk Park **10**
Glenveagh National Park & Castle **7**
Grianan of Aileach **4**
Inishowen Maritime Museum
 & Planetarium **2**
Lough Derg **12**
Malin Head **1**
Slieve League **11**

457

distinctive thatched-roof cottages typical of this area, with rounded roofs held down by ropes (called *sugans*) fastened beneath the eaves to help the thatch resist the strong sea winds.

Just before the fishing village of **Killybegs *(Ceala Beaga),*** where the main N56 road swings inland, continue on the coastal road R263 through Killybegs to **Kilcar *(Cill Chártha),*** where you can pick up Donegal tweeds at a bargain at **Studio Donegal** (the Glebe Mill; http://studiodonegal.ie). Truly spectacular photo ops await at **Slieve League *(Sliabh Liag)*** (p. 460), with its perilously high sea cliffs crashing down into the waters below. (Take the turnoff for the Bunglass viewing point at Carrick.) The traditional end of the west coast drive is the heritage site of **Glencolumbkille *(Gleann Cholm Cille),*** 48km (30 miles) from Donegal Town (below).

To continue touring from Glencolumbkille, follow the signs directing you on the R230 to Ardara *(Árd an Rátha).* This is a breathtaking drive through **Glengesh Pass,** a narrow, sinuous, scenic roadway that rises to a height of 270m (886 ft.) before plunging in hairpin curves into the valley below to reach the village of **Ardara *(Árd an Rátha)*—**ready to take on **the Atlantic Highlands,** p. 465.

Ballyshannon (*Béal Átha Seanaidh*) ★★ VILLAGE   The first proper town you'll come to on a drive south of Donegal Town is this busy, pretty little place, built on a hill, with a 15th-century town center. Some claim (rather dubiously) that Ballyshannon is the oldest town in Ireland, in part because traces have been found of permanent settlements dating as far back as 4000 b.c. Ballyshannon is also the location of **Abbey Mills** (© **071/985-1260**), a heritage center and craft store. Part of a ruined Cistercian abbey, the mill still has a working waterwheel. (Opening hours vary—generally Monday to Saturday 10am to 5pm, summer months only; entry is free, but leave a few coins in the collection box by the waterwheel to help pay for its upkeep.) While you're here, check out tiny **Catsby Cave,** about 50m (164 ft.) along the riverbank. During the years of British occupation, when Catholicism was outlawed (from the 16th– until the mid–19th century), priests would give Mass here in secret. You can still see the remains of an altar, chiseled from the rock. Admission is free. Ballyshannon is known for its lively pubs, many of which have reliably good traditional music—never more so than during a weekend in late July or early August, when the streets come alive for the **Ballyshannon Folk Festival** (www.ballyshannonfolkfestival.com).

Tourism Office: The Bridge, Ballyshannon, Co. Donegal. © **071/982-2856.** About 22km (13½ miles) S of Donegal Town on N15.

Glencolumbkille (*Gleann Cholm Cille*) ★★ HERITAGE SITE   An extraordinarily beautiful outpost overlooking the Atlantic Ocean, Glencolumbkille is sited in a lush green valley, west of the dark boglands. It is said that St. Columba established a monastery here in the 6th century and

Ballyshannon lays claim to being the oldest town in Ireland.

gave his name to the glen (its Gaelic name—*Gleann Cholm Cille*—means "Glen of Columba's Church"). Today it's home to the **Glencolumbkille Folk Village,** a wonderful "living history" park and craft center, set up and maintained entirely by local people. In a series of small traditional cottages, the park tells the story of this remote community in an engaging way. Guided tours are available, or you can take it at your own pace. Don't leave without browsing the *sheebeen*—a little store selling traditional local products (seaweed wine, anyone?). There are miniature playhouses to entertain the children, while a tearoom serves traditional Irish stews and *brútin* (a stew of hot milk and potatoes). Guinness cake is a house specialty.

On R263, about 26km (16 miles) NW of Killybegs, Glencolumbkille, Co. Donegal. www.gleanncholmcille.ie/folkvillage.htm. Ⓒ **074/973-0017.** Admission €4.50 adults; €4 seniors and students; €2.50 children 7–16; free for children under 7; €12 families. Easter–Sept Mon–Sat 10am–6pm, Sun noon–6pm.

Lough Derg ★★ NATURE SITE This beautiful island-dotted lake lies about 16km (10 miles) east of Donegal Town. Legend has it that St. Patrick spent 40 days and 40 nights fasting in a cavern at this secluded spot, and since then it has been revered as a place of penance and pilgrimage. From June 1 to August 15, thousands of Irish Catholics take turns

walk this way: **CLIMBING SLIEVE LEAGUE**

There are two ways to see Slieve League—and rarely has the phrase "the easy way or the hard way" been more appropriate.

The walking path is a truly spectacular hike across stunning countryside, about 10km (6¼ miles) in length, which takes between 4 and 5 hours. The summits of Slieve League, rising almost 600m (1,968 ft.) above the sea, are often capped in clouds, and you shouldn't undertake the walk if there are high winds or any danger at all of losing visibility along the way. In any case, this is only for the fearless and fit. And we *really* mean fearless; the high point (literally) is the frankly terrifying **One Man's Pass,** a footpath so narrow that it can only take one person at a time—and it's *on top of* the cliff, with a 450m (1,500-ft.) drop on

one side and a perilously steep incline on the other. Your starting point will be the Bunglass lookout point; you'll end up at Trabane Strand in Malin Beg, a few miles southwest of Glencolumbkille. Be sure to arrange a pickup at the end.

So where does "the easy way" come into all this? The less intrepid (or possibly just "sane") can take a shuttle bus from the visitor center up to the best viewing point. You won't be able to see the vista from the cliffs, but you'll get a great view *of* them.

Sliabh Liag Tours (www.sliabhliag tours.ie; ☏ 087/671-1944) runs a tour from Carrick and can arrange to drop you off at the best (and more manageable) walking points on the way back. Tours are all customized; call for information.

coming to Lough Derg to do penance for 3 days at a time, remaining awake and eating nothing but tea and toast. It's considered one of the most rigorous pilgrimages in all of Christendom.

Co. Donegal. Take R232 to Pettigo, then R233 for 8km (5 miles).

Slieve League ★★ NATURE SITE   It's surprising that these towering sea cliffs aren't better known, because they're almost three times the height of their far more feted southern cousins, the **Cliffs of Moher** (see p. 340), and arguably even more spectacular. Needless to say, given the remote location, they also get a tiny fraction of the visitors that the Cliffs of Moher attract. The **Slieve League Cliffs Centre** (www.slieveleague cliffs.ie; ☏ 074/973-9077) in Teelin, about 3km (1⅔ miles) southwest of Carrick, is a friendly little visitor center, run by an archaeologist and an artist, with a very good cafe and a crafts store. At the main lookout point in Bunglass, there's no snazzy visitor center, no handy parking, no guide ropes, and no admission fees—just the wild, ominous beauty of this rugged, far-flung outpost. If you really want to test yourself against the terrain, try the hike to the top of the cliff (see box above).

Slieve League Centre: Teelin, Carrick, Co. Donegal (signposted from R263). www.slieveleaguecliffs.ie. ☏ *074/973-9077.* Free admission. Mar–Nov daily 10:30am–5:30pm.

Where to Stay in Donegal Town & Donegal Bay

Ard Na Breátha ★★   Beautifully converted into a comfortable, modern guesthouse, Ard Na Breátha sits on a working farm. Bedrooms are summery and spacious, with bright colors, polished wood floors, and antique-style iron frame beds in some rooms. Family rooms are only €20 to €40 more than standard doubles. The pleasant guest lounge has a fireplace and a little bar, too. In the restaurant, evening meals are sophisticated if unashamedly traditional in style, with plenty of local and seasonal ingredients (many supplied from the guesthouse's own farm, of course). Prebooking for dinner is essential. The B&B is located right on the edge of Donegal Town, although the farm makes it feel quite rural, enhanced by views of the mountains in the distance.

Railway Park, Middle Drumrooske, Co. Donegal. www.ardnabreatha.com. ✆ **074/972-2288.** 6 units. €94–€113 double. Free parking. Breakfast included. **Amenities:** Restaurant; bar; Wi-Fi (free). Closed mid-Jan to mid-Feb.

The Cove Lodge ★   This sweet, modern B&B just outside Donegal Town is set between soothing green hills on one side and lovely views of Donegal Bay on the other. Hosts Joan and Liam create a genuine and warm atmosphere. Rooms are comfortable, spacious, and spotless. The homemade breakfasts are excellent—try the delicious porridge with honey and cinnamon. Cove Lodge is about 3.5km (2½ miles) from the town center; if you don't have a car, a taxi out here costs around €6.

Drumgowan, Donegal Town, Co. Donegal. www.thecovelodgebandb.com. ✆ **074/972-2288.** 6 units. €70–€85 double. Free parking. Breakfast included. **Amenities:** Wi-Fi (free).

Creevy Pier Hotel ★   The coastline in this part of Ireland isn't short of hotels and restaurants with magnificent views, but this one is up there with the best. The dining room looks straight out over Donegal Bay, framed by distant mountains—it's a magnificent spot from which to watch the sun go down. The **Pier Restaurant** is good, with plenty of local seafood options; the bar has live music most weekends in summer. Bedrooms are fairly basic, but pleasant and well-equipped. Special offers are often available, especially out of season. The only negative is the hotel's popularity with wedding and pre-wedding parties; you might want to check whether any are planned over the dates of your stay.

About 7km (4½ miles) from Ballyshannon, signposted from R231, in Kildoney Glebe, Co. Donegal. www.creevypierhotel.com. ✆ **071/985-8355.** 10 units. €100 double. Free parking. Breakfast included. **Amenities:** Restaurant; bar; room service; Wi-Fi (free).

Harvey's Point Hotel ★★★   This lakeside hotel on Lough Eske, a 15-minute drive from Donegal Town, is much loved by regulars, and it's easy to see why. The views of the lake from the hotel are pristine. Rooms

On the shore of Lough Eske, Harvey's Point Hotel is a popular country getaway.

and bathrooms are spacious, modern, and very comfortable. The decor is traditional throughout, with marble bathrooms, striped wallpaper, and antique reproduction beds. All guest rooms are suites, with seating areas and plenty of space to relax. Downstairs, the restaurant serves rich meals with exquisite views of the lake—afternoon tea here is absolutely decadent, with fresh-baked scones, cakes, and homemade jam. The wood-paneled bar has the feel of a private club, and a good selection of wine and whiskey to go with it. The place has the ambience of an exclusive getaway, as if you're hiding from the world. No wonder it's won so many awards.

At Lough Eske, about 7km (4½ miles) from Donegal Town, off N15, Co. Donegal. www.harveyspoint.com. © **074/972-2208.** 10 units. €200–€260 double. Free parking. Breakfast included. **Amenities:** Restaurant; bar; room service; Wi-Fi (free).

Where to Eat in Donegal Town & Donegal Bay

Blueberry Tea Room ★ CAFE   A buttermilk-colored shopfront, adorned with little baskets of azaleas; twinkling fairy lights and walls filled with knick-knacks; and the friendliest owner in Donegal—what more could you want from a small-town cafe? If the answer's "tasty, simple lunches in huge portions," guess what, you're in luck there, too! This simple, no-nonsense cafe serves tea, cake, and traditional Irish lunches. The homemade soups are a specialty (served with or without a toasted sandwich), or you could fill up on a hearty plate of steak fajitas, or breaded chicken with pasta and house special sauce. The cafe also has a little deli selling Irish cheese, breads, muffins, and other tasty treats to go. The only discernable snag is that it doesn't take credit cards.

Castle St., Donegal Town. ✆ **074/972-2933**. Entrees €3–€10. Mon–Sat 9am–7pm. Closed Sun.

Quay West ★★ IRISH   Romantic, contemporary food is served up in this delightful place overlooking Donegal Bay. The food is modern without a hint of pretension. Start with a plate of local shellfish with fresh sourdough toast, then for your main course try a char-grilled steak (a house specialty), or stick with the local seafood and opt for a plate of fresh smoked haddock from Killbegs. A small selection of more international dishes (especially South Asian) includes a delicious panko-crumbed chicken with basil pesto. Desserts are mostly of the indulgent, comfort-food variety. Resist if you dare the profiteroles with dark chocolate ganache sauce and you are a better person than us.

Quay St., Donegal Town. ✆ **074/972-1590**. Entrees €15–€24. Wed–Thurs 5–9pm, Fri–Sat 5–10pm, Sun 5–9pm. Closed Mon–Tues.

Smugglers Creek Inn ★ SEAFOOD   With a breathtakingly beautiful clifftop view of Donegal Bay, this mid-19th-century inn is a fantastic place to come and watch the sun setting over the Atlantic Ocean. See if you can get a table outside or in the conservatory. Order from the bar snack menu, or a full meal a la carte in the restaurant. The steaks are good, but the seafood is really what's best here: chowder, smoked mackerel, scampi, crab claws, or the "symphony of seafood" platter. Vegetarians are better catered for than you might expect at a little restaurant in the back of beyond; try the delicious brie and sweet pepper tartlet. Wash it all down with a pint of local ale. The menu is decidedly more limited during the day, but the sandwich menu is a welcome alternative to a huge lunch. Note that service can be a little slow, however, especially when it's busy.

Cliff Rd., Rossnowlagh, Co. Donegal. www.smugglerscreekinn.com. ✆ **071/985-2367**. Bar food €7.50–€14. Entrees €13–€25. Apr–Oct noon–5pm, 6–9:30pm; Nov–Mar Fri–Sun noon–5pm, 6–9:30pm.

Sports & Outdoor Pursuits Around Donegal Bay

BEACHES   Donegal Bay's beaches are wide, sandy, clean, and flat—ideal for walking. **Ballyshannon** has a good beach, but it gets crowded; **Rossnowlagh** and **Bundoran** are both better options. On the North Donegal Bay drive, **Glencolumbkille** has two fine beaches: one a flat, sandy beach at the end of Glencolumbkille village, where the R263 swings left; the other a tiny gem of a beach surrounded by a horseshoe of cliffs, accessible from the small road signposted to Malin More (off the R263) about 1.6km (1 mile) southwest of town.

CYCLING If you're very fit, the north side of Donegal Bay has great cycling roads—tremendously scenic but with some demanding climbs. One good but arduous route from Donegal Town follows the coast roads west to Glencolumbkille (day 1), continues north to Ardara and Dawros Head via Glengesh Pass (day 2), and then returns to Donegal (day 3). It takes in some of the most spectacular coastal scenery in Ireland along the way, but follows small winding roads that must be shared with cars. Rental bikes are available in Donegal Town from **Ted's Bike Shop** (✆ **074/974-0774**) on Killybegs Road for around €15 per day.

FISHING Surrounded by waters that hold shark, skate, pollock, conger, cod, and mackerel, **Killybegs** is one of the most active centers on the northwest coast for commercial and sport sea fishing. **Brian McGilloway** (www.killybegsangling.com; ✆ **087/220-0982** or ✆ 074/973-1181) operates full-day fishing expeditions on the 12m (39-foot) MV *Meridian* from Blackrock Pier in Killybegs. Prices are €500 per day, or €300 per half-day for up to 12 people, plus €10 per person for rod, reel, and tackle. McGilloway also runs evening mackerel fishing trips (€40 per person, groups of 5 or more). Daily departure times vary according to demand; reservations are required.

GOLF The Donegal Bay coast is home to two outstanding 18-hole championship seaside golf courses. **Donegal Golf Club,** Murvagh, Ballintra (www.donegalgolfclub.ie; ✆ **074/973-4054**) is 5km (3 miles) north of Rossnowlagh and 11km (6¾ miles) south of Donegal Town. It's a par-73 course with greens fees of €120 May to September, €90 April to October, €50 November to March. The **Bundoran Golf Club,** off the Sligo-Ballyshannon road (N15) in Bundoran (www.bundorangolfclub. com; ✆ **071/984-1302**), is a par-69 course designed by Harry Vardon. Greens fees are around €35 weekdays, €45 weekends.

SURFING **Bundoran** is popular with surfers for its steady waves; it has hosted the European Surfing Championships. Rossnowlagh also has excellent surf and attracts lots of surfers. When the surf is up, you can rent boards and wetsuits locally from around €5 to €10 per hour per item.

WALKING The peninsula to the west of Killybegs offers some of the most spectacular coastal scenery in Ireland, much of it accessible only from the sea or on foot. Besides the **Slieve League** hike (see p. 460), there's a spectacular coastal walk between Glencolumbkille and the town of **Maghera** (not so much a town as a small cluster of houses). Begin by hiking up to the Martello tower on Glen Head, which overlooks Glencolumbkille to the north, then continue along the cliff face for 24km (15 miles), passing only one remote outpost of human habitation along the way, the tiny town of **Port.** For isolated sea splendor, this is one of the finest walks in Ireland, but only experienced walkers with adequate provisions should undertake it, and only in fine weather.

THE ATLANTIC HIGHLANDS

This is the most isolated part of Donegal, which is the most isolated county in Ireland, so it doesn't get much more rugged, exhilarating, and, well…*isolated* than this. At a certain point when you're driving through the highlands, the signs drop all pretense at bilingualism and switch entirely to Gaelic. It's disorienting—one minute you know exactly where you are and the next you haven't a clue. And at that moment—which almost always occurs on a mountainside by a rushing stream amid rocky terrain—you're in the true Donegal.

The best place to start a tour of Donegal's Atlantic Highlands is at **Ardara** *(Árd an Rátha),* an adorable village about 40km (25 miles) northwest of Donegal Town. From there, weave your way up the coast. This drive can take 4 hours or 4 days, depending on your schedule and interests. Our advice is to take your time. You may never come this way again, and you will want to remember every moment.

Exploring the Atlantic Highlands

Looking as if it were carved from stone, charming little **Ardara** is known for its exceptional tweed and wool creations. Astride a narrow river in a steep gulch, it is a pleasant place to stop, chat with the locals, and do a bit of shopping or maybe have a cup of tea in its small but useful **Heritage Centre** on the N56 main road through the village (open Easter–Sept). If you happen to arrive in June, you may catch the **Ardara Weavers Fair,** which has been going on since the 18th century and features spectacular works in wool.

Heading north from Ardara, the N26 passes through the neat-as-a-pin little town of **Glenties** *(Na Gleanta),* where playwright Brian Friel set his play *Dancing at Lughnasa,* and eventually curves inland to gorgeous **Glenveagh National Park** ★★★ (see p. 468) and **Mount Errigal,** Donegal's highest mountain. Just east of the park, the surprisingly good **Glebe House and Gallery** ★★ (see p. 467) sits on lovely Lough Gartan.

The Wild Atlantic Way

Intended to be Ireland's answer to the Pacific Coast Highway in the U.S., the Wild Atlantic way is a new, 2,500km (1,550-mile) marked road trail, stretching the entire length of the west coast. The trail, which runs from Malin Head in the north (see p. 474) all the way to Cork in the south, can be a handy way of navigating to some of the main sights, especially in more rural and isolated areas. Look for brown road signs with a thick white squiggle in a blue box (like two W's linked together). More information, including a full list of the points of interest covered, can be found at **www.wildatlanticway.com**.

Road sign for the Wild Atlantic Way.

It would be a shame, however, not to sample some scenic coastal detours along the way. The southernmost is on R261, taking in two pleasant resort towns—**Naran *(An Fhearthainn)*** and **Portnoo**—both favorites with Irish families in the summer. Your next option is at Dungloe, where you can split off on coastal R259 to visit **the Rosses,** a rock-strewn land punctuated by mountains, rivers, and glassy lakes. On this loop you'll pass **Burtonport *(Ailt an Chorrain),*** where, it's said, more salmon and lobster are landed than at any other port in the country. The next coastal loop heading north is on R257, swinging through Derrybeg and Gortahork. This is known as the **Bloody Foreland,** from the fact that its rocks take on a ruddy color when lit by the setting sun. If you can arrange to be driving through here at sunset on a clear day, you are in for a treat.

If you follow N56 to the top rim of Donegal, you'll find a series of small peninsulas like fingers jabbing out into the sea. West to east, they are **Horn Head *(Corrán Binne),*** with spectacular cliffs towering 180m (590 feet) above the ocean; **Rosguill *(Ros Goill);*** and the **Fanad,** jutting out between Mulroy Bay and the glassy waters of Lough Swilly. Each peninsula has its own driving circuit. Horn Head's clifftop drive is the most spectacular but also rather perilous; you may want to opt instead for Rosguill's scenic 16km (10-mile) Atlantic Drive, or, if you have more time, the Fanad's 73km (45-mile) circuit. At the base of the Horn Head peninsula, pretty **Dunfanaghy *(Dún Fionnachaidh)*** can be a good option for an overnight stay, with a fine beach and an intriguing heritage center, the **Dunfanaghy Workhouse** (see p. 467). Between Horn Head and Ros-guill, **Doe Castle** (see p. 467) is also well worth a stop. At the base of the Fanad, the tiny village of **Rathmelton** *(Ráth Mealtain)* is eminently pho-tographic, with its gray Georgian warehouses reflected in the mirrorlike water of the lake.

About 10 minutes' drive north of Rathmelton, on the coast of Lough Swilly, the village of **Rathmullan** *(Ráth Maoláin)* is an excellent stop-ping point, with an evocative ruined abbey, a beautiful stretch of flat, sandy beach, and a couple of good hotels (splurge on the **Rathmullan House ★★★** if you can swing it—see p. 469).

Doe Castle *(Caisleán na dTuath)* ★ CASTLE   This little 600-year-old castle at the edge of a mirrorlike lake is so perfect it's hard to believe it's real. A battlement wall with round towers at the corners encloses the central tower house, which was once the stronghold of Clan Sweeney. Built in the early 16th century, the castle was extensively restored in the 18th century and was a used as a home until 1843. Uninhabited since then, it's now maintained by Historic Ireland. It's a lovely little place, surrounded on three sides by the waters of Sheep Haven Bay, and on the fourth by a moat carved into the bedrock that forms its foundation. The view from the battlements across the bay is superb. If the entrance is locked, you can usu-ally get the key from the caretaker in the house nearest the castle.

5.6km (3½ miles) off N56; turnoff signposted just S of Creeslough, Co. Donegal. Free admission. Daily dawn–dusk.

Dunfanaghy Workhouse ★ MUSEUM   This rather unassuming graystone building was the scene of great hardship and fear in the 19th century, when it was one of around 100,000 workhouses set up to feed and house the poor during the Great Famine. Their approach was hardly altru-istic, however; fearing that merely feeding people would engender a "something-for-nothing" culture in the poor, the authorities decreed that they should perform backbreaking labor in return for their bread. It's esti-mated that workhouses killed around a million people in Ireland. This particular one housed about 300 inmates. The museum does a good job of describing their daily lives, as well as providing a history of the Famine in this area. One exhibit focuses particularly on a local girl, "Wee Hannah" Herrity, who lived here and survived to tell the tale—which she did, in extensive conversation with a local biographer.

Just W of Dunfanaghy on N56, Co. Donegal. www.dunfanaghyworkhouse.ie. *C* **074/913-6540.** Admission €4.50 adults; €3.50 seniors, students, and children; €12.50 families. July–Aug daily 9:30am–5:30pm; May–June and Sept–Oct daily 9:30am–5pm; Apr Mon–Sat 9:30am–5pm; Nov–Mar Mon–Wed 9:30am–4:30pm.

Glebe House & Gallery ★★★ ART MUSEUM   What a pleasant surprise, in such a remote location, to find an art gallery as good as this. This early-19th-century house on the shores of Lake Gartan was once home to noted English painter Derek Hill (1916–2000), who donated the house, along with his personal art collection, to the Irish state in the 1980s. And what a collection—highlights include paintings by Picasso, Renoir, Jack Yeats, and Oskar Kokoschka, along with rare Islamic and Far Eastern art and original William Morris prints. About 300 works are on display from the permanent collection, plus temporary and special exhibitions. The house itself is worth seeing too—a handsome Regency building, surrounded by pretty woods and gardens, stretching down to the Lough. The house can only be visited on a guided tour, and space is limited to 15 people at a time.

Signposted from R251, 17km (10½ miles) NE of Letterkenny, Church Hill, Co. Donegal. http://glebegallery.ie. *©* **074/913-7071.** Admission €5 adults; €4 seniors; €3 students and children; €13 families. Gallery: July–Aug daily 11am–6:30pm; late May–June, Sept and Easter week Sat–Thurs 11am–6:30pm. Last tour 1 hr. before closing. Grounds open year-round.

Glenveagh National Park and Castle ★★★ NATURE SITE/CASTLE

This thickly wooded valley is peaceful now, but its history is dark. Nestling at its heart, **Glenveagh Castle** was originally the home of the infamously cruel landlord John George Adair, who evicted scores of struggling tenant farmers in the freezing winter of 1861, leaving many to die, ostensibly because their presence on his estate was ruining his view. If the tale is true, it's divine justice that this estate now belongs to all of the people of Ireland. Today the fairy-tale setting includes woodlands, herds of red deer, alpine gardens, a crystal-clear lake, and the highest mountain in Donegal, Mount Errigal. There's a visitor center with a little shop, and a charming tearoom in the castle. You can also go on ranger-led walks of the park for €10. Cars must be parked at the visitor center, but a shuttle bus can take you up to the castle for €3 round-trip (€2 seniors, students, and children).

Visitor Centre and Castle: Church Hill, Co. Donegal (signposted from R251, 24.4km/15 miles NE of Letterkenny). www.glenveaghnationalpark.ie. *©* **076/100-2537.** Free park admission. Castle: €7 adults; €5 seniors, students and children; €15 families. Visitor center and castle: Mar–Oct daily 9:15am–5:30pm; Nov–Mar daily 9:15am–4:45pm; last admission 1 hr. before closing.

Once the home of a brutal English landlord, Glenveagh Castle and its luxe gardens now belong to the Irish people.

Where to Stay in the Atlantic Highlands

Arnold's Hotel ★   Near the harbor in Dunfanaghy, this simple but pleasant hotel overlooks Sheep Haven Bay. The overly bright interior decor won't win any design awards, but guest rooms have all the basics and comfortable beds. Ask for a room with a view of the bay. Family rooms cost about €30 more than doubles. The owners also run horseback-riding stables; weeklong holiday packages, including accommodations and guided trail rides, are available. Check the website for details.

On N56, Dunfanaghy, Co. Donegal. www.arnoldshotel.com. ℭ **074/913-6208.** 32 units. €140–€154 double. Free parking. Breakfast not included in lower rates. **Amenities:** Restaurant; bar; Wi-Fi (free).

Castle Grove Hotel ★★   Lancelot "Capability" Brown, the famous English landscaper who virtually invented landscape gardening in the 18th century, laid out the elegant grounds at this inviting white manor house. Inside the decor is avowedly traditional in style, with plenty of period detail and heritage hues. Rooms have antique furnishings (including a four-poster bed in one). All have views of the grounds. Breakfasts are outstanding, and the **Castle Grove restaurant** (p. 470) is one of the best in the region. Check the website for dinner-bed-and-breakfast packages.

Ballymaleel, off Ramelton Rd., Letterkenny, Co. Donegal. www.castlegrove.com. ℭ **074/915-1118.** 16 units. €130–€160 double, €220 suite. 2-night minimum on weekends. Breakfast included. **Amenities:** Restaurant; bar; room service; access to nearby golf courses; tennis courts; Wi-Fi (free).

Rathmullan House ★★★   Right on the edge of Lough Swilly, this delightful mid-18th-century mansion is one of our favorite places to stay in the northwest. The guest lounges are warm and hospitable, with sumptuous period decor and fires crackling in the hearth on cold days. Bedrooms are spacious and extremely comfortable; rooms in the modern extension lose nothing in terms of style and charm to the rooms in the older section of the house. Some have fireplaces and deep roll-top bathtubs. Superior rooms have even more space. Family rooms can work out to be only slightly more expensive than standard doubles. The house has a swimming pool, but you can also take a short stroll down to the beach of the beautiful Lough. The **Cook & Gardener** ★★★ (p. 470) restaurant is outstanding, deserving its reputation as one of the top places to eat in Donegal; alternatively, the **Tap Room** bar serves stone-baked pizza and craft beers. Check the website for discounts and special rates—particularly outside the busiest times of year, when you can often find deals like dinner-bed-and-breakfast packages for around €115 per person—very good value for a place like this.

On R247 (Chapel Rd.), Rathmullan, Co. Donegal. ℭ **074/915-8188.** www.rathmullan house.com. 32 units. €210–€260 double. Free parking. Breakfast included. **Amenities:** Restaurant; pool; Wi-Fi (free).

Where to Eat in the Atlantic Highlands

Castle Grove ★★ IRISH   This place has won plenty of awards over the years, and it's easy to see why—the food is superb and a top recommendation if you're staying here or nearby. Seasonal menus present classic Irish flavors with a modern edge: asparagus with blood-orange hollandaise, followed by beef filet with onion jam, or Barbary duck prepared with honey and clove. **Castle Grove ★★** is also a very good hotel—see p. 469 for review.

Ballymaleel, off Ramelton Rd., Letterkenny, Co. Donegal. www.castlegrove.com. ✆ **074/915-1118.** Entrees €22–€30. Daily 6:30–9:30pm. No children under 10 allowed after 7pm.

The Cook & Gardener ★★★ IRISH   It's entirely befitting that, as one of the very best hotels in Donegal, **Rathmullan House ★★★** (p. 469) would also have one of its best restaurants. Many of the ingredients have come no greater distance than the house's own gardens, and most of the rest haven't traveled all that much farther. The menu changes daily, but expect dishes such as Mulroy Bay scallops with cauliflower puree, or free-range Glin Valley roast chicken with parsnip puree and chard. If you're not in the mood for a formal dinner, head to the hotel bar for a more casual menu of sandwiches, burgers, and stone-baked pizza.

Rathmullan House hotel, R247 (Chapel Rd.), Rathmullan, Co. Donegal. www.rathmullan house.com. ✆ **074/915-8188.** Entrees €18–€30. Daily 1–2:30pm and 6:30–8:30pm.

The Rusty Oven ★ PIZZA   Locals love this place, hidden in a courtyard behind Patsy Dan's Pub, and they throng here night after night for the gorgeous handmade pizzas, baked traditionally in a wood-fired oven. The atmosphere is very casual—it's a bit like eating in someone's living room, in a good way. In the summer, dining happens outside, on the bohemian courtyard, beneath the trees. It's best to not be in a hurry, for the pizzas are made at a leisurely pace. But sometimes someone's playing guitar, and everyone sings, and the mood is chill. Every pizza is good: The margarita is made with slow-roasted tomatoes and Irish mozzarella; the Sundance pairs spicy chorizo with caramelized onions. The pizza base is light as a feather, and there's homemade ice cream for dessert.

Off Market Square, behind Patsy Dan's Pub, Dunfanaghy, Co. Donegal. No phone. Entrees €8–€12. Daily 5–10pm.

Sheila's Coffee & Cream ★ CAFE   This cozy cafe at the Ardara Heritage Centre (see p. 453) is a welcome find. Drop in for a fine cup of coffee and a restorative slice of cake, or a light lunch—soups, Irish stew, salads, and filling sandwiches. The bread is home-baked, and the ever-present Sheila herself is quite delightful. The cafe stays open until 9pm on Friday and Saturday in summer.

Ardara Heritage Centre, Ardara, Co. Donegal. ℰ **074/953-7905.** Entrees €4.50– €10.50. Mon–Sat 9am–6pm. Closed Sun.

Sports & Outdoor Pursuits in the Atlantic Highlands

BEACHES There are Blue Flag beaches in **Portnoo** and **Navan. Magheroarty,** near Falcarragh on the northern coast, has a breathtaking beach, unspoiled by crowds or development. The same goes for **Tramore** beach on the western side of Horn Head near Dunfanaghy; you have to hike a short distance, but the rewards are seclusion and miles of creamy sand.

GOLF On the Rosguill peninsula, one of Ireland's most challenging golf courses is the **Rosapenna Golf Club,** on Atlantic Drive in Downings (www.rosapenna.ie; ℰ **074/915-5000**), an 18-hole championship seaside par-70 links course laid out in 1983 by Tom Morris of St. Andrews. It also has the newer Sandy Hills links, which was named the top course in the whole of Ireland and Britain by *Golf World* magazine in 2008. Greens fees are €110, but you'll get a €25 discount if you book your tee time online. The twilight rate is €55. It's closed from October to March.

HORSEBACK RIDING **Dunfanaghy Stables,** Arnold's Hotel, Dunfanaghy, Co. Donegal (www.dunfanaghystables.com; ℰ **074/910-0980**) specializes in trail riding on the surrounding beaches, dunes, and mountain trails. An hour's ride is €32 adults, €27 children. Between May and September the stables also offers guided trail-riding holidays, including meals and accommodations.

WALKING The **Ards Forest Park,** on a peninsula jutting into Sheep Haven Bay about 5.6km (3½ miles) south of Dunfanaghy on N56, has lots of signposted forest trails as well as an area of dunes along the water. You can buy a guidebook as you enter the park.

For a bit more of a challenge, try some scenic hiking on **Horn Head,** signposted off N56 just west of Dunfanaghy. From the concrete lookout point, a trail leads out to a ruined castle on the headland and continues south along a line of impressive quartzite sea cliffs that glitter in the sun.

THE INISHOWEN PENINSULA

Driving around the northernmost point of Ireland is worth doing just so you can say you did. You stood on Malin Head and felt the icy mist come in on a wind that hit you like a fist. You have felt the satisfaction that comes from knowing there is no farther to go.

There is, however, more to this land than that. Around the edges are ancient sites, beautiful beaches, and charming villages. At its center are gorgeous views, mountains, and quiet, vivid green pastures. If you are looking to get lost, this is a great place to do it—although (perhaps paradoxically, given its decided dearth of traffic) the Inishowen Peninsula circuit is very well signposted, with all directions clearly printed in English and Irish, miles and kilometers.

Exploring the Inishowen Peninsula

The Inishowen *(Inis Eoghain)* Peninsula reaches out from Lough Foyle to the east and Lough Swilly to the west toward **Malin Head ★★** (see p. 474), its farthest point.

From Donegal Town, take N15 through the scenic Barnesmore Gap—a vast open stretch through the Blue Stack Mountains—to N13 and on to Letterkenny *(Leitir Ceanainn),* the largest town in County Donegal, set on a hillside overlooking the River Swilly. From there, head north on N13, then east on R238, to Buncrana, an excellent place to rest and have a meal. Near Buncrana are a couple of worthwhile stops—Fort Dunree Military Museum ★★ (p. 473) to the north, and the much more ancient hilltop fort known as Grianan of Aileach ★ (see p. 473), a short drive south of Buncrana.

Ascend a corkscrew road (R238) from Buncrana through the Gap of Mamore, a mountain pass that rises 240m (787 ft.). Head east to the beach town of Ballylifflin and on to Malin *(Málainn),* with its picturesque stone bridge and village green. From there, it's another 20-minute drive north on R242 to Malin Head *(Cionn Mhélanna),* a satisfyingly remote place at the end of the road (see p. 474).

From Malin Head, head back on R242/238 to **Culdaff** *(Cúil Dabhcha),* a sleepy waterfront village with a pretty beach. On its main street, the Clonca Church is a solid 17th-century structure with a fine carved high cross. The coastal road leads from here to picturesque **Inishowen Head** (follow signs off the R241 onto a side road, follow

The Northern Lights silhouette Linsfort Church on Malin Head.

that to its end, and walk the rest of the way to the headland). It's eerily isolated, but the views are stupendous—on clear days, you can see all the way to the Antrim Coast.

Continuing around the peninsula, follow coastal road R241 southwest to **Greencastle** *(An Cáisleá Nua),* site of the quirky **Inishowen Maritime Museum and Planetarium ★** (see p. 473).

Fort Dunree Military Museum ★★ MUSEUM Rising precipitously from the cliffs beside Lough Swilly, this impressive-looking fort was constructed as a defensive lookout in the event of a French invasion during the Napoleonic Wars. It later became part of Irish sea defenses against German invasion during the First World War. Neither came, and today Dunree serves as an informative museum. Spread partly through subsurface bunkers, the exhibitions tell the history of the fort, and of the local area as a whole. It also serves as the starting point for scenic walks around Dunree Point along three recommended walking paths. The museum has a handy coffee shop overlooking the Lough.

Signposted on the coast road, about 11 km (7 miles) N of Buncrana, Co. Donegal. www.dunree.pro.ie. © **074/936-1817.** Admission €7 adults; €5 seniors and children. Mon–Fri 10:30am–4:30pm. Closed weekends.

Grianan of Aileach ★★ ANCIENT SITE Built high atop a hill outside the village of Burt, this beautifully preserved ring fort can be seen from miles away, a crown made of stone. Experts think the existing structure was built in the 6th or 7th century A.D., although the site had already been used for many centuries by then. There's evidence it may have originally been a temple of the sun as long ago as 1700 B.C. From the mid–5th century A.D. to the early 12th century A.D., this was the seat of the kingdom of Aileach, home to the O'Neills, the chieftains of this area. The view from the top is spectacular. The waters of the two lakes—Lough Swilly and Lough Foyle—sparkle in the distance, and you can make out the shape of the entire peninsula. The round fort is made of stone without mortar; the walls are terraced, giving access to the top.

Signposted on N13, behind the town of Burt, about 16km (10 miles) S of Buncrana, Co. Donegal. Parking by the church at the base of the hill. Free admission. Mid-June to Sept daily 9am–9pm; Oct to mid-June daily 9am–7:30pm. Gate not locked out of hours mid-June to Sept Fri–Sun.

Inishowen Maritime Museum & Planetarium ★ MUSEUM/ PLANETARIUM Overlooking Loch Foyle, this small but engaging museum packs all it can into the Old Coast Guard building for the harbor town of Greencastle. It follows the town's maritime history from the armadas of the 16th century, through emigration to the modern-day lifeboat crews and their selflessly heroic work. There's also a planetarium, complete with a full-dome digital theater presenting more or less hourly shows such as "Sea Monsters—A Prehistoric Adventure" and "Dynamic Earth."

The Harbour, Greencastle, Co. Donegal. www.inishowenmaritime.com. ☏ **074/938-1363.** Museum only: €5 adults; €4 seniors and students; €3 children. Museum plus planetarium: €10 adults; €8 seniors and students; €6 children. Easter–Sept Mon–Sat 9:30am–5:30pm, Sun noon–5:30pm; Oct–Easter Mon–Fri 9:15am–5:30pm. Last admission 30 min. before closing.

Malin Head (Cionn Mhélanna) ★★ NATURE SITE   On this stunning promontory, the road goes no farther—the next stop west is New York. Even on a sunny day, the wind often howls and temperatures can be 10 degrees colder than it is just a few miles south. To reach Malin Head, take R242 north until it turns into a small, unnamed road. Following the few signs, meander past a small cluster of houses until you reach rocky **Banba's Crown (Fíorcheann Éireann),** the farthest point of the headland. Winds permitting, you can even wander down to the edge of the land and catch a glimpse of some old concrete huts built in World War II as lookout points. To the west of them is the dramatically named **Hell's Hole,** a natural land formation where waves crash deafeningly against the craggy shore. To the east, a path leads to a hermit's cave known as the **Wee House of Malin.** There's a little information board that explains all this—but you may be too busy gazing at the incredible view to notice.
Ballyhillin, Co. Donegal.

Where to Stay on the Inishowen Peninsula

Ballyliffin Lodge ★★   With impressive views of **Malin Head** ★★★ (above), this hotel is a relaxing place to stay. Bedrooms, which take full advantage of the gorgeous views, are nice and spacious, with muted, autumnal decor. The hotel can help organize plenty of activities, from horseback riding to surfing and golf. The in-house spa, **Rock Crystal,** provides a welcome respite at the end of a long day's travel, with prices that are a lot more reasonable than they would be in an equivalent place in a more visited part of the country. The in-house restaurant is good but pricey—a bowl of pasta with tomatoes and basil will set you back €16.

Shore Rd., Ballyliffin, Co. Donegal. www.ballyliffinlodge.com. ☏ **074/937-8200.** 40 units. €124–€222 double. Breakfast not included in lower rates. **Amenities:** Restaurant; bar; gym; pool; room service; spa; Wi-Fi (free).

Inishowen Gateway ★   This large, modern hotel is a particularly appealing choice for families. It overlooks Lough Swilly—a dramatic view that's either glorious in sunshine or stark and moody in the rain. Guest rooms are basic and quite small, but they tick enough boxes so long as you're not craving anything too fancy. Meanwhile, the spa and pool are welcome places to unwind. This place has excellent facilities for kids—a supervised play area, Planet Active, has plenty to keep the little ones busy,

The Inishowen Gateway Hotel in Buncrana overlooks Lough Swilly.

including game tables, video games, and soft play for younger kids. If you book a family room package then you even get one free craft workshop per child (and can book others for just €10 each).

Railway Rd., Buncrana, Co. Donegal. www.inishowengateway.com. © **074/936-1144.** 80 units. €85–€185 double. Free parking. Breakfast included. **Amenities:** Restaurant; bar; gym; pool; spa; Wi-Fi (free).

The Strand ★   Another place with views of Malin Head, this modest but friendly hotel also has views of Pollan Strand, a 2-mile stretch of beach outside Ballyliffin. Accommodations aren't overly fancy, but they're modern and comfortable, with deep tubs in the bathrooms. Family rooms sleep up to four; one room is fully accessible for wheelchair users.

Shore Rd., Ballyliffin, Co. Donegal. www.ballyliffinstrandhotel.com. © **074/937-6107.** 21 units. €120 double. Free parking. Breakfast included. **Amenities:** Restaurant; bar; Wi-Fi (free).

Where to Eat on the Inishowen Peninsula

The Drift Inn ★★ BISTRO/PUB FOOD   This cheerful pub in Buncrana with the pun-tastic name is loved by locals for its top-quality food, almost all of it locally sourced. There are plenty of names on the menu that you probably will have seen on signs while driving here. You could opt for roast guinea fowl served with bacon and leek mashed potato, or a risotto of butternut squash and Parmesan cheese. Be aware—food is only served Thursday to Sunday, although the pub is open daily.

Railway Rd., Buncrana, Co. Donegal. www.thedriftinn.ie. ℗ **074/936-1999.** Main courses €15–€26. Thurs 2–9:30pm, Fri–Sat 1–9:15pm, Sun 1–8:45pm.

Nancy's Barn ★ CAFE   With its red shutters and gray stone walls, this place looks so pretty from the outside on a sunny day, you may stop to take a picture and end up going inside for lunch out of curiosity. Fortunately, chances of disappointment are low—Nancy's serves fine sandwiches, toasties, salads, soups, and other light meals. They also bake their own cakes and scones.

On the main road through Ballyliffin, Co. Donegal. ℗ **074/937-6556.** Entrees €4–€10. Daily 9:30am–5:30pm.

Ubiquitous ★★ INTERNATIONAL   Don't spend too much time puzzling over whether the name is relevant to anything—we suspect it just sounded good, although it does allow for the rather catchy local nickname of "the Ubiq." This fun and relaxed bar-restaurant offers modern, unpretentious comfort food with global flavors. The steaks are excellent, or you could opt for a Thai curry, Cajun fish, or a plate of rich buttermilk-fried chicken. Desserts are serious comfort-food territory; don't even pretend you can't find room for a custard tart or chocolate fudge cake. It serves

Surfing Pollan Bay.

food until 10pm most evenings, which is practically all night in this neck of the woods.

47 Upper Main St., Buncrana, Co. Donegal. www.ubiquitousrestaurant.com. © **074/932-2320.** Entrees €15–€23. Set menus €21–€25. Mon–Sat 4–10pm, Sun 3–9pm.

Sports & Outdoor Pursuits in the Inishowen Peninsula

GOLF   A definite center for golf in Ireland, the Inishowen has four 18-hole golf courses. Two are at the **Ballyliffin Golf Club,** Ballyliffin (www.ballyliffingolfclub.com; © **074/937-6119**). Greens fees are €140 to €160. The **North West Golf Club,** Fahan, Buncrana (www.northwest golfclub.com; © **074/936-1715**), founded in 1890, is a par-69 seaside course with greens fees of around €50 weekdays, €60 weekends. After 4pm the twilight rate is €30. **Greencastle Golf Course** in Greencastle (www.greencastlegolfclub.com; © **074/938-1013**) is a par-69 parkland course with greens fees of around €25 to €30.

SURFING   The Inishowen Peninsula's northwest coast presents some of the most challenging surfing conditions in Europe. For information and classes, contact the **Inishowen Surf School,** Hill Road, Buncrana (www. inishowensurfschool.com; © **087/7773323**).

BELFAST

14

The vibrant and beautiful six counties of Ireland still under British rule are all the more fascinating for their troubled history. At their epicenter is Belfast, the capital of Northern Ireland—a curious combination of faded grandeur and forward-looking optimism. Belfast boomed in the 19th century as prosperity flowed from its vast textile and shipbuilding industries. The 20th century was not so kind to the city, which spent decades in decline, riven with political divisions and terrorism. But an entire generation has grown up since those troubled years ended in the 1990s, and with them, Belfast has forged a new identity, complete with an artsy, edgy underground.

The old Belfast is still here—both in its grand old Victorian buildings in the center and some old-school, never-the-twain-shall-meet Protestant and Catholic neighborhoods in the suburbs. But new developments signal change and renewal, such as the Titanic Quarter, with its sleek new museums and modern visitor attractions. This is a lively, funky, youthful, and complicated city. Come and let it surprise you.

ESSENTIALS
Arriving

BY PLANE Belfast has two airports: **Belfast International** (www.belfast airport.com; ℂ **028/9448-4848**) and **Belfast City Airport** (www.belfastcity airport.com; ℂ **028/9093-9093**). **Aer Lingus** (www.aerlingus.com; ℂ **01/ 814-1111**), **British Airways** (www.ba.com; ℂ **189/0626-747** in Ireland, or 084/4493-0787 in the U.K.), and **Easyjet** (www.easyjet.com; ℂ **084/3104-1000**) operate regular scheduled flights from Britain to Belfast. In the summer, **Thomas Cook** (www.thomascookairlines.com; ℂ **0800/107-3409** from the U.K. only) offers a limited number of direct flights from Salt Lake City to Belfast. Other intercontinental routes require a change in London or Manchester. You can also fly direct to Belfast from several European cities.

BY BUS **Ulsterbus** (www.translink.co.uk; ℂ **028/9066-6630**) runs buses from Dublin to Belfast and towns across Northern Ireland. From Dublin Airport, **AirCoach** (www.aircoach.ie; ℂ **01/844-7118**) also runs a regular

FACING PAGE: **Artsy Belfast is forging a new post-Troubles identity.**

nonstop service to Belfast. Round-trip tickets are between €20 and €25 (£16 and £22) and the trip takes just under 2 hours. (Book online for discounts.) In Belfast, the main bus station is **Europa Bus Centre** on Glengall Street.

BY TRAIN   Belfast has two train stations: Great Victoria Street Station and Belfast Central Station on East Bridge Street. Contact **Northern Ireland Railways** (www.translink.co.uk; © **028/9066-6630**) for tickets. The journey from Dublin takes about 2½ hours.

BY CAR   Driving from Dublin to Belfast is easy; just go north up the M1 motorway. From Dublin airport, the journey takes about 90 minutes in good traffic. From Sligo Town, take N16 and A4 west; from there it's 200km (124 miles), about 2½ hours.

[Fast FACTS] BELFAST

ATMs/Banks   ATMs are easy to find in central Belfast. Several banks around Donegall Square include **Ulster Bank** (© **028/9024-4112**) and **Bank of Ireland** (© **028/9043-3420**).

Currency   As part of the United Kingdom, Northern Ireland uses the **pound sterling,** not the euro. The cheapest way to get local currency is to use an ATM. The pound/euro exchange rate fluctuates, but it currently hovers between parity and around €1.15.

Dentists   For dental emergencies, your hotel can contact a dentist for you. Otherwise, you could try **Dublin Road Dental Practice,** 23 Dublin Rd. (© **028/9032-5345**), or **Lisburn Road Dental Clinic,** 424 Lisburn Rd. (© **028/9038-2262**).

Doctors   For medical emergencies, dial © **999.** For non-emergencies, your hotel can call you a doctor. Otherwise there's **Ormeau Health Centre,** 120 Ormeau Rd. (© **028/9032-6030**), or the **Crumlin Road Health Centre,** 94–100 Crumlin Rd. (© **028/9074-1188**).

Emergencies   For police, fire, or other emergencies, dial © **999.**

Pharmacies   Belfast has branches of **Boots the Chemist** at 35–47 Donegall Place (© **028/9024-2332**) and 17–21 Great Northern Mall (© **028/9031-0530**).

Post Offices   Main branches in Belfast include 16–22 Bedford St. and 12–14 Bridge St.

Taxis   You can catch a taxi at the stand in front of City Hall. Alternatively, try phoning **Value Cabs** (© **028/9080-9080**), **Courtesy Cabs** (© **028/9032-9988**), or **Gransha Taxis** (© **028/9060-2092**).

Visitor Information

The main tourist information center for the city is the **Belfast Welcome Centre** at 9 Donegall Square, BT1 5GJ (www.visitbelfast.com; © **028/9024-6609**). From June to September it's open Monday to Saturday 9am to 7pm and Sunday 11am to 4pm; and October to May Monday to Saturday from 9am to 5:30pm and Sunday 11am to 4pm. The staff at the center can help book accommodations in the city, and they also have a

VISITING NORTHERN IRELAND: f.a.q.

What is Northern Ireland? It's still part of Ireland, right?

Yes—and no. It's a part of the island of Ireland, but not the Republic of Ireland.

I'm confused. Is it a different country or not?

Bear with us—this is complicated. Northern Ireland is part of the United Kingdom. It has been a separate entity from the rest of Ireland since 1921. If "entity" sounds a little vague, that's because— get this—there isn't even an official term to describe what Northern Ireland is. (Trust us, we checked.) It is referred to, variously, as a country, a nation, a region, and a province. Note, however, that your mobile phone company will treat Northern Ireland as the U.K., so inform them in advance if you plan to cross the border, to avoid international roaming charges. Also, check that your travel insurance and any car-rental agreements are equally valid in Northern Ireland.

Will I need to show my passport at the border crossing?

No, because there really isn't a border crossing. In fact, it can be hard to tell when you've entered Northern Ireland— except that the road signs change from miles to kilometers. Signs around the border usually show both.

What are those letters and numbers at the end of Northern Irish addresses?

They're British-style postal codes. Postcodes are still in the process of being introduced to the Republic, but almost every address in Northern Ireland has one. This is actually a big advantage if you're driving, as it makes GPS navigation much easier.

Does Northern Ireland use the euro?

No. The currency in Northern Ireland is the **British pound (sterling).** In practice, euros are accepted in some border areas, at tourist attractions and hotels; however, you may be given change in pounds. (And just try using those pounds in the rest of Ireland!) And if you're traveling onward to Britain, be aware that Northern Irish pounds look completely different from standard ones, and many businesses won't accept them. (They're legally obliged to, but...well, *you* try arguing.)

What about the Brexit vote? Has that changed anything?

The whole thing is a hot mess. In fact, we literally don't know what to tell you. At this writing, less than a year until the supposed date of Britain's exit from the European Union in March 2019, nobody has any clue how the border will look afterward. The sad fact is that the British government's handling of the situation has been inept and shockingly irresponsible. The Good Friday Agreement, which bought peace and stability to Northern Ireland in 1998, may collapse; or the U.K. could hold a new referendum and decide to stay in the E.U., in which case nothing will happen. It's generally believed that a return to violence in the region is unlikely, but the possibility of a hard border, with customs checks and a military presence, must be taken seriously. Any predictions made now could be completely out of date in a month, though, so our only advice is this: Keep up with the latest developments.

bureau de change and left-luggage facility. Smaller visitor information points are at **Belfast International Airport** (© 028/9448-4677) and **George Best Belfast City Airport** (© 028/9093-5372).

City Layout

Small and easily traversed, central Belfast is best explored by walking. The main tourist districts are as follows.

CITY CENTER   Dominated by the impressive domed City Hall (see p. 486), the bustling **Donegall Square** area is the best place for shopping, particularly along **Donegall Place,** which extends north from the square, onto **Royal Avenue. Bedford Street,** which travels south from Donegall Square, becomes **Dublin Road,** which leads to:

UNIVERSITY QUARTER   The leafy area around Queen's University (see p. 492) contains the Botanic Gardens (see p. 483), art galleries, and museums, as well as a buzzing nightlife scene.

GOLDEN MILE   Southwest of Donegall Square, the stretch of **Great Victoria Street** leading to Bradbury Place is the city's best address for restaurants and pubs, although it's a bit hyperbolically named. As one local said to us, "It's not a mile and it's not golden. But it's nice enough."

CATHEDRAL QUARTER   North of Donegall Square, surrounding Donegall Street, **Belfast Cathedral** (see p. 491) presides over this area with many vast Victorian warehouses. The district has quite a buzzing feel, with plenty of interesting shops.

TITANIC QUARTER   Northeast of the city center, a series of big commercial developments have recently gone up around Belfast Harbour. Here you'll find several big purpose-built attractions.

Getting Around

BY BUS   **Metro** (www.translink.co.uk; ✆ **028/9066-6630**) city buses depart from Donegall Square East, West, and North, plus Upper Queen Street, Wellington Place, Chichester Street, and Castle Street, and from bus stops throughout the city. The cheapest way to use the buses is to buy a Metro Day ticket, which allows unlimited travel all day for £3.90 (£3.40 after 9:30am).

BY CAR   If you've brought a **car** into Belfast, it's best to leave it parked and take public transport or walk around the city. If you must drive and want to park downtown, look for a blue p sign that shows a parking lot. No parking is allowed in "control zones," marked by pink-and-yellow signs.

BY TAXI   **Taxis** are available at all main rail stations, ports, and airports, and in front of City Hall. Most metered taxis are London-type black cabs with a yellow disk on the window. Other taxis may not have meters, so ask in advance what the fare to your destination will be. You can hail a taxi on the street, although it rarely takes long for a cab to arrive if you call.

BY BIKE   Belfast has recently adopted a public bike-sharing system. "Belfast Bikes"—formally "Coca-Cola Zero Belfast Bikes," though absolutely nobody calls them that—are available at more than 30 unmanned rental stations around the city. You can set up an account at the station's terminal, or by downloading the *Nextbike* app for your smartphone. When you're done, simply return the bike to any station. Prices start at £0.5 per hour. See **www.belfastbikes.co.uk** for details.

EXPLORING BELFAST

Belfast's wealthy past has left the city with some handsome industrial remnants. However, it's the more troubled, 20th-century Belfast that many visitors find most intriguing, and a **Black Taxi Tour ★★★** (see p. 484) is a unique way to explore that history. Meanwhile, there's a whole mini-industry of attractions related to the most famous shipwreck in history. Because the SS *Titanic* was built in Belfast—a curious symbol of pride for natives of this city—shipwreck aficionados (aka "Titanoraks") are drawn to the bold **Titanic Belfast** museum (p. 488) and the **Titanic's Dock & Pump-House** (p. 489) in the newly regenerated harbor district.

Top Attractions

Belfast Botanic Gardens & Palm House ★★ GARDENS   Dating from 1828, these gardens were first laid out by the Belfast Botanic and Horticultural Society, but their most important feature came along 10 years later, when noted Belfast architect Charles Lanyon designed the

The Victorian-era Palm House, centerpiece of the Belfast Botanic Gardens.

beautiful glass-and-cast-iron conservatory. Now known as the Palm House, this curvilinear Victorian glasshouse contains an excellent variety of tropical plants, including sugarcane, coffee, cinnamon, banana, aloe, ivory nut, rubber, bamboo, guava, and spindly birds of paradise. If the weather's fine, stroll in the outdoor rose gardens, which date back to 1927. The **Ulster Museum** (p. 490) is also on the grounds.

College Park, Botanic Avenue, Belfast, BT7 1LP. © **028/9049-1813.** Free admission. Palm House Apr–Sept daily 10am–4:45pm; Oct–Mar daily 10am–3:45pm. Gardens mid-Apr to Aug daily 10am–9pm; Sept to mid-Apr daily 10am–sunset (hours can vary in winter; call ahead).

Black Taxi Tour ★★★ TOUR For many years, Belfast was best known for its most conflicted neighborhoods, where in the 1970s and '80s protest and violence occurred daily. Peace has held on the Catholic Falls Road and its nearby parallel, the Protestant Shankill Road, for 20 years. A growing industry supports this enterprising tourism initiative, with the Black Taxi Tour company's **Belfast Political & Mural** tour by far the best option. Tours are conducted in London-style cabs that take you through the neighborhoods, past the barbed wire, towering dividing walls, and partisan murals, as guides explain their significance. Drivers, who are all locals, are relaxed, patient, and unbiased, with a talent for explaining this complicated history to outsiders in an easy and engaging way. Tours aren't just limited to politics; the guides will also take you to see the *Titanic* shipyard or on a day-long tour to see the locations where *Game of Thrones* is filmed (one of many such tours that have sprung up; see box, p. 522).

Belfast street murals can be viewed via open-top bus tour or Black Taxi tours.

Belfast Attractions

485

The standard tour lasts about 90 minutes, and guides will pick you up and drop you off anywhere in the city.

www.belfasttours.com. ℂ **028/9064-2264.** £35 for up to 3 passengers, then £15 for each additional passenger, up to 6 people.

City Hall ★ ARCHITECTURAL SITE   A testament to the city's grand industrial past, this domed building of granite, marble, and stained glass dominates central Belfast. Built in classical Renaissance style in 1906, it has white Portland stone walls and a soft green copper dome. Several statues dot the grounds, including a grim-faced Queen Victoria, who stands out front looking as if she wished she were anywhere else. Bronze figures around her represent the textile and shipbuilding industries that powered Belfast's success. There's also a memorial to the victims of the *Titanic* disaster. Inside the building, the elaborate entry hall is heavy with marble but lightened by stained glass and a rotunda with a painted ceiling. Somehow it all manages not to be tacky. A new 16-room exhibition center opened in 2018. Free hour-long guided tours offer a surprisingly absorbing insight into the building's history.

Donegall Sq. North, Belfast, BT1 5GS. ℂ **028/9032-0202.** Free admission. Mon–Fri 10am–5pm, Sat–Sun 10am–4pm. Guided tours June–Sept Mon–Fri 10, 11am, 2, and 4pm; Sat–Sun noon, 2, 3, and 4pm; Oct–May Mon–Fri 11am, 2, and 3pm; Sat–Sun noon, 2, and 3pm.

Spring Market outside Belfast's City Hall, on Donegall Square.

the art of conflict: BELFAST'S STREET MURALS

Painted by amateur artists—albeit very talented ones—the huge street murals in West Belfast tell tales of history, strife, anger, or peace. The densest concentration is around the **Falls and Shankill roads**—the epicenter of the conflict during the Troubles, from the late 1960s to the mid-1990s. The Falls Road is staunchly Catholic and Republican (largely those who want Ireland united as a single country). Shankill, just half a mile away, is resolutely Protestant and Loyalist (those who want Northern Ireland to remain part of the United Kingdom).

While all are deeply political, there is a noticeable difference in the tone of these murals. Those on the Falls Road tend to be about solidarity with the downtrodden (and not just in Ireland—you'll see murals about war and oppression in other parts of the world, too). By contrast, the Shankill murals are more strident, featuring more violent and threatening imagery, although some of the most offensive examples were removed a few years ago by the government.

Perhaps the most famous political mural in Ireland is on the corner of Falls Road and Sevastopol Street, at one end of the surprisingly small Sinn Fein headquarters: a mural of the late hunger striker **Bobby Sands** (1954–81). Locals in all districts are very proud of their murals and are fine with visitors taking photos. Still, you should exercise the usual caution you would in any rough city neighborhood. It's best to avoid these parts of town on **parade days**—ostensibly celebratory events, they tend toward displays of nationalism, erupting into street violence. The biggest, and most controversial, is the Protestant "Orange Order" parade on July 12th. Any parades likely to cause trouble are well covered by the local media, so it's easy to know when one is coming up.

The best, safest, and certainly the most informative way to see the murals is to take a **Black Taxi Tour ★★★** (p. 484). The tours are a real Belfast highlight, and could hardly be more convenient—the drivers will pick you up at your hotel and drop you off anywhere you like in the city.

Crown Liquor Saloon ★★★ ARCHITECTURAL SITE/PUB   Easily the most impressive Victorian pub in the city, and possibly the best building in Belfast, the Crown Liquor Saloon piles on the atmosphere. The old "gin palace" owes its ornate appearance to Italian workers who came to Ireland in the late 19th century to work on churches but ended up building this, in 1873. Some of the finer features definitely have something ecclesiastical about them, from the stained glass in the windows to the pew-like "snugs," their elaborately carved doors designed to shield the more refined class of Victorians from their fellow drinkers. The floors are intricately tiled, and the ceiling is gorgeous hammered copper. This place was considered so important to the iconography of Belfast that it was actually bought for the nation by the National Trust in the 1970s, ensuring its impeccable upkeep while it continues to run as a working pub.

46 Great Victoria St., Belfast, BT2 7BA. www.nicholsonspubs.co.uk/thecrownliquor saloonbelfast. © **028/9024-3187.** Mon–Sat 11:30am–midnight, Sun 12:30–11pm.

Crumlin Road Gaol ★★ HISTORIC SITE   From 1846 until its closure 150 years later, Crumlin Road Gaol (known as "The Crum") was one of the most notorious prisons in Northern Ireland. Improbable though it sounds, the Crum is now used as a conference center and wedding venue (festive!), although the original structure has been excellently preserved. The building brings to mind the popular image of a Victorian-era prison, with its forbidding, fortress-like exterior and row upon row of cells. An informative 75-minute tour takes you around the building, filling in some fascinating details of what prison life was like. It would take a hard person indeed not to shudder as you walk down the claustrophobic underground tunnel connecting to the old courthouse across the street, or stand inside the condemned cell from which prisoners made their final journeys until 1961. Book online for ticket discounts.

53–55 Crumlin Rd., Belfast, BT4 6ST. www.crumlinroadgaol.com. ✆ **028/9074-1500.** Admission £12 adults; £10 seniors and students; £6.50 children 5–15; free for children 4 and under; £30 families. Daily 10am–4:30pm (last tour).

SS Nomadic ★★ SHIP   The last working ship in the White Star Line fleet, the *Nomadic* was built in Belfast as a tender to the most famous ocean liner in history—the ill-fated SS *Titanic.* (Tenders were small steamships that ferried passengers and supplies to and from the oceangoing behemoths.) After seeing action in both World Wars—first press-ganged into service by the French Navy, then used by the British to evacuate Cherbourg, where she came under fire from the Nazis—*Nomadic* returned to work as a tender until 1968. She spent the next 35 years in France as a *bateau mouche* floating restaurant, before bailiffs seized the poor ship in 2003. *Nomadic* looked destined for the scrap heap, until the people of Belfast raised enough money to rescue her. After a decade-long restoration, *Nomadic* has been returned to her original 1911 glory. You can tour the whole vessel, from the cramped and claustrophobic crew quarters to the bridge and upper deck. Exhibitions along the way tell the full story behind *Nomadic,* along with profiles of passengers who sailed on her throughout the years. Daily ticket numbers are limited due to space—book in advance if possible.

Hamilton Dock, Queens Rd., Belfast, BT3 9DT. www.nomadicbelfast.com. ✆ **028/9076-6386.** Admission £7 adults; £5 seniors, students, and children 5–16; free for children under 5; £20 families. Combined ticket with Titanic Belfast (including Discovery Tour) £18 adults; £14.50 seniors and students; £8 children 5–16; free for children 4 and under; £44 families. June–July daily 10am–7pm; Aug daily 10am–8pm; Apr–May and Sept daily 10am–6pm; Oct–Mar daily 11am–5pm.

Titanic Belfast ★★★ MUSEUM   This ambitious and impressive museum, which opened to huge fanfare in 2012, tells the story of the *Titanic* in revelatory detail. Located next to the site where the doomed vessel was built, the angular aluminum-clad frontage juts out in four directions at the height of the ship's actual bow. You can explore the

Titanic Belfast discovery tour.

museum yourself or take an hour-long "Discovery Tour" of its innovative galleries. Exhibitions cover everything from the *Titanic*'s construction to her triumphant launch, disastrous sinking, and the lasting cultural phenomenon that rose in her wake. A special ride takes you on a virtual tour of the shipyard to see how *Titanic* and her sister ship, *Olympic*, were built. In a split-level gallery you can even "visit" the wreck, via huge high-definition screens and other interactive gizmos. Finally, the **Ocean Exploration Centre** offers high-tech exhibits on the science of sea exploration, including a live link to an undersea probe. Needless to say, an extremely well-stocked gift shop is at the end. Crowds can swell at busy times, so it's advisable to book ahead in summer.

1 Olympic Way, Belfast, BT3 9DP. www.titanicbelfast.com. ✆ **028/9076-6386.** Admission (includes entry to SS *Nomadic*) £18 adults; £14.50 seniors and students; £8 children 5–16; free for children 4 and under; £44 families. Discovery Tour £8.50 adults, £7.50 children. Combined ticket with Discovery Tour and SS *Nomadic* £30 adults, £20 children. Parking £1.50 per hr. for 1st hr., £1 per hr. afterward. June–July daily 9am–7pm; Aug daily 9am–8pm; Apr–May and Sept daily 9am–6pm; Oct–Mar daily 10am–5pm. Last admission 1 hr. 45 min. before closing.

Titanic Boat Tour ★★ TOUR

Many of Belfast's historic shipyard buildings were demolished in the early 2000s to make way for new development, opening up long-obscured views of the harbor from the river. While there really aren't that many *Titanic*-related sights left, this jaunty and informative hour-long boat trip offers a pleasant introduction to Belfast's maritime past. With typically dry Belfast wit, the crew T-shirts read, "She was alright when she left here." In summer, the tour goes as far as Musgrave Channel, home to a large breeding colony of seals. The departure point is on Donegall Quay, to the left of the big fish sculpture.

The Obel, 66 Donegall Quay, Belfast, BT3 3NG. www.laganboatcompany.com. ✆ **028/9024-0124.** Admission £10 adults; free for children 5 and under; £35 families. Times vary, but generally June–Aug daily 12:30, 2, and 3:30pm; Mar–Apr and Sept–Oct daily 12:30 and 2pm (always call to check daily times).

Titanic's Dock & Pump-House ★★ MUSEUM

Another of Belfast's ship-related attractions, this fascinating self-guided tour takes you around the dry docks at the old Harland and Wolff shipyard, where *Titanic* and *Olympic* were constructed from 1909–11. Designed to appeal to a general audience, not just enthusiasts, it's a great way to learn what it was really like to work here at the turn of the last century, when Belfast was one of the world's greatest industrial cities. The enormous Edwardian pump house, which could drain a staggering 21 million gallons of water in just over 90 minutes, is worth the price of admission alone. An audio-visual room includes rare film footage of the *Titanic in situ* at the dock. The large visitor center has interesting exhibits, a gift shop, and a cafe.

Queen's Rd., Queen's Island, Belfast, BT3 9DT. www.titanicsdock.com. © **028/9073-7813.** Admission £5 adults; £3.50 children 5–16; free for children under 5; £12 families. Parking £1.50 per hr. Apr–Oct daily 10am–5pm; Nov–Dec daily 10am–4pm; Jan–Mar daily 10:30am–5pm.

Ulster Museum ★★★ MUSEUM   One of Ireland's best museums, the Ulster Museum has a comprehensive collection of everything from dinosaur bones and prehistoric artifacts to art and other treasures from Ireland and around the world. Highlights include 16th- to 18th-century Dutch and Italian paintings; a hoard of priceless 16th-century Spanish jewelry, recovered off the coast near Belfast in the 1960s; clothes, textiles, and ceramics from Asia and Africa; and items relating to the Ascendancy, the period of Protestant rule in Ireland that finally came to a head with the rebellion of 1798. The Life and Death in Ancient Egypt exhibit has about 2,000 artifacts from Pharaonic times (including a mummy), as well as items from ancient Mesopotamia, Rome, and Greece. The museum's calendar often has special exhibitions, talks, and even the occasional concert; check the website to see what's on.

At the Botanic Gardens, Belfast, BT9 5AB. www.nmni.com/um. © **028/9044-0000.** Free admission. Tues–Sun 10am–5pm. Closed Mon (except public holidays).

The Wee Tram Tour ★★ TOUR   A fun way to see the Titanic Quarter, this lively tram tour takes you around the docks in about half an hour—including a few areas you can't see any other way. The guides are adept at telling the history as a story, rather than a dry recitation of facts, while on-board multimedia screens give you extra info to put it all into context. The circular route includes all the highlights of the docks, including the museums and dry dock; **HMS *Caroline,*** the last surviving ship of the Battle of Jutland (1916), permanently moored here; and the towering landmarks **Samson and Goliath**—two 140m (459-ft.) cranes that have come to symbolize the docks and Belfast's industrial heritage (even though they only date from the 1960s and '70s, when shipbuilding was already in decline). Trams run every half-hour from either **Titanic Belfast** (p. 488) or **SS *Nomadic*** (p. 488). You buy tickets on board; possible upgrades include entry to the **Titanic's Dock & Pump-House** (p. 489) or HMS *Caroline*.

Departs from Titanic Belfast, 1 Olympic Way, Belfast, BT3 9DP; or SS *Nomadic*, Hamilton Dock, Queens Rd., Belfast, BT3 9DT. www.theweetram.com. No phone. Admission £5 adults; £4 seniors, students, and children 5–16; free for children under 5; £15 families. Combined ticket with Titanic's Dock & Pump-House £7 adults; £6 seniors, students, and children 5–16; free for children under 5; £21 families. Combined ticket with HMS *Caroline* £12 adults; £10 seniors and students; £7 children 5–16; free for children under 5; £24–£31 families. Tours every 30 min from Titanic Belfast and SS *Nomadic* noon–5pm, Sun 2–5pm.

Other Attractions

Belfast Castle ★ CASTLE   Northwest of downtown and 120m (394 ft.) above sea level stands Belfast Castle, its 80-hectare (198-acre) estate spreading down the slopes of what is now **Cave Hill Country Park** ★ (see below). Dating from 1870, this was the family residence of the third marquis of Donegall, and it was built in the style of Balmoral Castle, the Scottish residence of the British monarch. The outside is more interesting than the inside, which has been sadly modernized over the years and is now a popular wedding venue. The estate, though, is a lovely place to visit, offering sweeping views of Belfast and the lough. Its cellars contain a Victorian arcade, a restaurant (open daily 11am–5pm, and Tues until 9pm), and a shop selling antiques and crafts. According to legend, a white cat brought the castle residents luck, so look around for carvings featuring this much-loved feline.

Signposted off Antrim Rd., 4km (2½ miles) N of city center, Belfast, BT15 5GR. www.belfastcastle.co.uk. © **028/9077-6925.** Free admission and parking. Tues–Sat 9am–10pm, Sun 9am–5:30pm, Mon 9am–6pm.

Belfast Cathedral (St. Anne's) ★ CATHEDRAL   Although the foundation stone on this monumental cathedral, also known as **St. Anne's,** was laid in 1899, it remained incomplete for more than a century; even now it still awaits a steeple. Blending architectural genres from Romanesque to Victorian to modern, the huge structure is more attractive inside than out. In the nave, the ceiling soars above black-and-white marble walls and stone floors, and elaborate stained-glass windows flood it with color on a sunny day. Carvings that represent life in Belfast top the 10 pillars. The cathedral's most impressive features are the delicate mosaic ceilings of the tympanum, and a baptistery constructed of thousands of pieces of glass.

Donegall St., Belfast, BT1 2HB. www.belfastcathedral.org. © **028/9032-8332.** £5 adults; £4 seniors and students; £3 children 5–12; free for children 4 and under; £12 families. Mon–Sat 9am–5:15pm, Sun 1–3pm.

Cave Hill Country Park ★★ PARK   Atop a 360m (1,181-foot) basalt cliff, this park offers panoramic views, walking trails, and archaeological and historical sights (including **Belfast Castle** ★, above). Its name derives from five small caves thought to have been Neolithic iron mines; several other ancient sites are scattered about the place, often unmarked. These include stone cairns, dolmens, and **McArt's Fort**—the remains of an ancient defensive hill fort in which Wolfe Tone and his fellow United Irishmen planned the 1798 rebellion. It's mostly gone now, but you can explore the ruins, which sit atop the park's most famous viewpoint. The

Cave Hill Visitor Centre, on the second floor of Belfast Castle, contains a diverting exhibition on the history of the park and the castle. You can also pick up maps of the park here. For a great walk around the entire park, check out **www.walkni.com**, a site promoting hiking in Northern Ireland. To explore the park's mountain-bike trails, rent a **Belfast Bikes** (see p. 482) or hire a proper mountain bike at **Full Cycle,** 326 Crumlin Rd. (www.fullcyclebikeshop.co.uk; ✆ **028/9074-1569**); make reservations at least 24 hours in advance, preferably a full week ahead.

Visitor Centre: Belfast Castle, off Antrim Rd., 6.5km (4 miles) N of city center, Belfast, BT15 5GR. www.belfastcity.gov.uk/parksandopenspaces. ✆ **028/9077-6925.** Free admission. Park: 7:30am–dusk. Visitor Centre: Tues–Sat 9am–10pm, Sun–Mon 9am–5:30pm.

Cultúrlann Macadam Ó Flaich ★ CULTURAL CENTER Located in a former church building on the notorious Falls Road (a Republican stronghold during the Troubles), this cultural and arts center is a friendly, inclusive place. It has a handy cafe, a tourist information point, and a well-stocked shop full of Irish interest books, traditional crafts, and music CDs. The **Dillon Gallery,** West Belfast's only public art gallery, showcases work by Irish artists and those from farther afield. The center's theater has a varied program of traditional music, plays, spoken word events, and films. Check website for listings.

216 Falls Rd., Belfast, BT12 6AH. www.culturlann.ie. ✆ **028/9096-4180.** Free admission. Mon–Thurs 9am–6pm, Fri–Sat 9am–9pm, Sun 10am–4pm.

Queen's University ★ UNIVERSITY Founded in 1845 during the reign of Queen Victoria to provide nondenominational higher education, this is Northern Ireland's most prestigious university. The turreted main building, an imposing example of 19th-century Tudor Revival, may remind you of England's Oxford; its design was based on the Founder's Tower at Magdalen College. But there's much more to this university, which sprawls through 250 buildings and where 17,500 students are studying at any given time. The surrounding neighborhood is a quiet, attractive place to wander, and University Square on the north side of campus is simply beautiful. At one end of the square, Union Theological College,

Queen's University, founded in 1845.

dating from 1853, housed Northern Ireland's Parliament after the partition of Ireland in 1921 until its abolition in 1972. Tours of the campus can be arranged on request; contact the university's welcome center for details. Access to parts of the campus may be restricted during exam times.

Queen's Welcome Centre, Queen's University, University Rd., Belfast, BT7 1NN. www.qub.ac.uk/home/welcome-centre. © **028/9097-5252.** Free admission; tour £3.50. Mon–Fri 8am–5pm; also Sat–Sun 11am–4pm during summer vacation.

Especially for Kids

Belfast Zoo ★ ZOO   On the northern slopes of Cave Hill, near **Cave Hill Country Park** ★★ (p. 491), this zoo emphasizes conservation and education. Many rare species are bred here, including Hawaiian geese, lowland gorillas, red lechwe (a kind of antelope), sea bears, Barbary lions, and golden lion tamarins. The **Rainforest House** is a tropical environment filled with birds and jungle creatures. Most activity days are quite kid-oriented, although there are some more grown-up events too, such as all-day photography competitions. Special tours and events run all year. Check the website for up-to-date listings.

Antrim Rd., Belfast, BT36 7PN. www.belfastzoo.co.uk. © **028/9077-6277.** Admission £13 adults; £6.50 seniors, students, and children 4–16; free for children 3 and under; £33.50 families. Apr–Sept daily 10am–7pm (last admission 5pm; animal houses close 6pm). Oct–Mar daily 10am–4pm (last admission 2:30pm; animal houses close 3:30pm).

W5 ★ SCIENCE CENTER   This great science play center for kids is part of the Odyssey Complex, a huge modern entertainment center in the Titanic District. Properly known as "Whowhatwhenwherewhy"—you can see why they abbreviate it to W5—this high-tech, interactive learning environment lets kids try out over 250 individual activities, all in the spirit of science-based fun. They can create animated cartoons, try to beat a lie detector test, even present the weather on TV; plus, the center hosts lots of special events and temporary exhibitions. The Odyssey also contains a cinema, bowling alley, shops, restaurants, and a sports arena.

2 Queen's Quay, BT3 9QQ. www.w5online.co.uk. © **028/9046-7700.** Admission £10 adults; £8 seniors and students; £7.50 children; £28–£49 families. Mon–Fri 10am–5pm, Sat 10am–6pm, Sun noon–6pm. Last admission 1 hr. before closing.

Outlying Attractions: Belfast Lough

Belfast built up around the mouth of this coastal inlet; today the city's outer suburbs stretch along its north and south shores. There are a few worthwhile sights here, all doable on an easy short trip out of the city proper. A dozen miles or so to the northeast, just off the M3 motorway, the castle town of **Carrickfergus** offers a nice break from the hustle and bustle of the city, along with some fresh sea air. Locals like to say that Carrickfergus was thriving when Belfast was a sandbank, and looking around its winding medieval streets and traces of city walls, it's easy to believe.

On the other side of the Lough, **Cultra** is a relatively nondescript residential suburb with one big attraction—the excellent **Ulster Folk & Transport Museum** ★★★ (see p. 495).

Andrew Jackson Cottage and U.S. Rangers Centre ★ HISTORIC HOUSE   This re-created 18th-century dwelling is built in the style of cottages once lived in by Scotch-Irish settlers—including the ancestors of Andrew Jackson (1767–1845), the seventh President of the United States and the first president of Irish extraction. The cottage is decorated as it would have looked in the 1750s; also here is an exhibition devoted to the life of Jackson. Although it's a faithful reproduction, the house isn't the actual home of the Jacksons—that was demolished in the 19th century. Next door is a very small museum devoted to the U.S. Rangers, who were stationed in Carrickfergus during World War II.

2 Boneybefore, Carrickfergus, BT38 7EQ. ⓒ **028/9335-8241.** Free admission. Wed–Sun 11am–3pm.

Carrickfergus Castle ★ CASTLE   Built in 1180 by John de Courcy, this massive Norman keep was Ireland's first real castle, designed to loom darkly over the entrance to Belfast Lough. Centuries later, its defensive location would prove prophetic, as William of Orange landed here on June 14, 1690, en route to the Battle of the Boyne. The central part dates to the 12th century, the thick outer walls were completed 100 years later, and the gun ports are a comparatively new addition (only 400 years old). The outside is more impressive than the inside, which has been largely outfitted to trigger kids' interests, with waxwork figures riding horses, threatening to shoot people over the walls, et cetera. Sometimes actors in medieval costume add a touch of hammy fun. The castle has a visitor center and a small museum. In the summer, medieval banquets, a medieval fair, and a crafts market all add a touch of play and pageantry.

Marine Highway, Carrickfergus, BT38 7BG. ⓒ **028/9335-1273.** Admission £5 adults; £3 seniors, students, and children; £13 families. Apr–Sept Mon–Thurs 8:30am–5pm, Fri–Sat 8:30am–8pm, Sun 9:30am–8pm; Oct–Mar daily 10am–4pm. Last admission 30 min. before closing.

Carrickfergus Castle guards the entrance to Belfast Lough.

Ulster Folk & Transport Museum ★★★ MUSEUM/ HERITAGE SITE One of Northern Ireland's best living-history museums, the Ulster Folk & Transport Museum is made up of buildings rescued from demolition and reconstructed, piece by piece. Mostly dating from the 19th century, they include houses, schools, a chemist's shop, a pub, and even a working farm. The level of detail is impressive—the shops are fully decked out as they would have been in Victorian times, complete with shelves overflowing with authentic bottles, jars, and items of clothing. Costumed guides add to the fun. As you wander about, you may encounter a Victorian housewife engaged in day-to-day domestic drudgery, or watch a village blacksmith working away in a forge using authentic period methods. Frequent special events include craft demonstrations, classes, or horse-drawn vehicle days. The connected **Transport Museum** contains a wealth of historic vehicles, from old cars and small planes to buses and trams.

Viewing ship models at the Ulster Folk & Transport Museum.

Signposted off A2 (Bangor Rd.), Cultra, Hollywood, BT18 0EU. www.nmni.com/uftm. ⓒ **028/9042-8428.** Folk or Transport Museum: £9 adults; £7 seniors and students; £5.50 children 5–17; free for children 4 and under; £19–£25 families. Combined ticket: £11 adults; £8.50 seniors and students; £6 children 5–17; free for children 4 and under; £22–£29 families. Tues–Fri 10am–4pm, Sat–Sun 11am–4pm. Closed Mon except public holidays.

WHERE TO STAY IN BELFAST

Belfast's hotel scene has grown in leaps and bounds during the last few years. A decade ago, expecting to find a top-quality boutique hotel or B&B for under £100 per room was a tough task; today, however, you have much more to choose from. Best of all, because Belfast is still developing as a major tourist destination, prices remain relatively low—although depending on where you're from, that advantage can be quickly wiped out by the exchange rate, which is often worse for pounds than for euros.

EXPENSIVE

Europa Hotel ★★ For some time this has been the lodging of choice for big-name politicians, diplomats, and celebrities visiting Belfast. The decor is subtly masculine; the lobby has marble floors with a modern gas fireplace to take the edge off the chill. The large guest rooms are contemporary in style, with comfortable beds and sizeable bathrooms. A little rubber ducky in a top hat awaits you as you enter the bathroom (you can take it home if you want). Downstairs is a piano bar and the laidback **Causerie** restaurant. Check the website for deals such as dinner-bed-and-breakfast discounts or a package that includes entry to the Titanic Belfast.

Great Victoria St. Belfast, BT2 7AP. www.hastingshotels.com/europa-belfast. © **028/ 9027-1066.** 272 units. £153–£288 double, £405 suite. Parking £18 per day. Breakfast not included in lower rates. **Amenities:** Restaurant; 2 bars; gym; room service; Wi-Fi (free).

The Merchant Hotel ★★★   One of Ireland's most luxurious hotels, the Merchant is a real treat. The Victorian building was once a bank, and the conversion is stunning, from the grand dining room (lacquered and gilded Corinthian columns, marble floors, ceiling friezes) to an elegant cocktail lounge (chandeliers and a gently curved, dark wood bar). Guest rooms are thoroughly modern, but ask for one with Art Deco–style decor as opposed to traditional—they're larger and better designed. The excellent **spa** comes complete with hydrotherapy pool and treatment rooms, and a rooftop gym has an eight-person hot tub with lovely city views. The **Great Room Restaurant** serves topnotch modern Irish cuisine. Afternoon tea is a bit of an event here, and popular, so book ahead if you want to indulge. Service is impeccable, and the staff could hardly be friendlier or more helpful.

The Merchant Hotel, converted from a Victorian-era bank.

16 Skipper St., Belfast, BT1 2DZ. www.themerchanthotel.com. © **028/9023-4888.** 62 units. £160–£319 double, £280–£560 suite. Valet parking. Breakfast not included in lower rates. Dinner-bed-and-breakfast packages available. **Amenities:** Restaurant; bar; gym; spa; Wi-Fi (free).

MODERATE

Malmaison Belfast ★   This is the only Irish outpost of Malmaison, a British mini-chain that specializes in turning unusual historic buildings into hip boutique hotels. This one used to be a seed warehouse, of all things. It's a gorgeous four-story building, with weathered stone walls and tall arched windows. Inside, they've done beautiful things with the soaring space, using a chic, playful design that

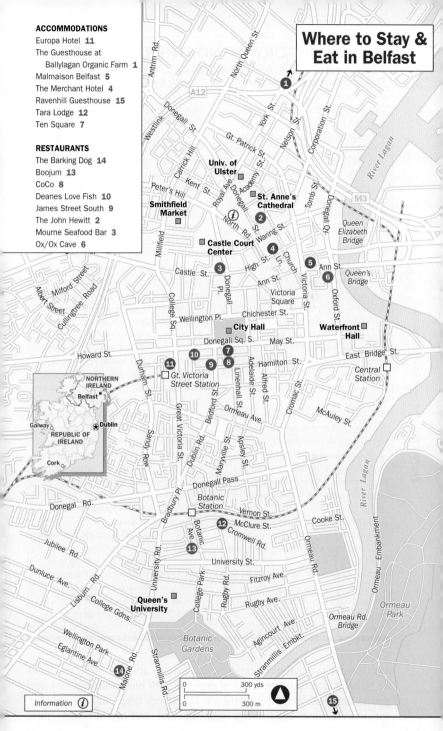

ACCOMMODATIONS

Europa Hotel **11**
The Guesthouse at
 Ballylagan Organic Farm **1**
Malmaison Belfast **5**
The Merchant Hotel **4**
Ravenhill Guesthouse **15**
Tara Lodge **12**
Ten Square **7**

RESTAURANTS

The Barking Dog **14**
Boojum **13**
CoCo **8**
Deanes Love Fish **10**
James Street South **9**
The John Hewitt **2**
Mourne Seafood Bar **3**
Ox/Ox Cave **6**

NORTHERN
IRELAND
Belfast

Galway
REPUBLIC OF
IRELAND
Dublin

Cork

Information ⓘ

0   300 yds
0   300 m

A brief HISTORY OF NORTHERN IRELAND

Shelves upon shelves of books have been written in an attempt to unravel the complicated history and politics of Northern Ireland. Only a fool would expect to be able to do it clearly and concisely, in just a few short paragraphs. So here goes.

In 1921, after nearly a thousand years of occupation and more rebellions and civil wars than you could count, Ireland won its independence from the United Kingdom. At least, *most* of it did. The U.K. didn't want to give it all up, nor did the Protestant, pro-British majority of the north. So a compromise was reached: The northern counties of Antrim, Armagh, Down, Fermanagh, Londonderry, and Tyrone (known collectively as "Ulster") were split off to form a new country called Northern Ireland. This, in turn, would stay part of the United Kingdom—a U.K. state, effectively. It was a messy deal, but at least they would stop killing each other. What could possibly go wrong?

Well…a lot. For a start, the Catholic minority in Northern Ireland was treated appallingly, discriminated against in almost every aspect of life, from work and housing to elections and policing. Not unreasonably, they wondered if they would be better off in the Republic of Ireland too. Things came to a head in the late 1960s, when the Catholic population began an intense civil rights campaign. Their marches and demonstrations were crushed by the authorities, sometimes with brute violence—which spurred the reemergence of the Irish Republican Army (IRA), a paramilitary group that had first appeared early in the 20th century.

After the "Bloody Sunday" massacre in 1971, when the British army opened fire on a peaceful protest in Derry (see p. 539), the IRA launched a terror campaign aimed at civilians, both in Northern Ireland and the British mainland. Bombs were planted in bus stops, cafes, schools, pubs, and shopping malls, killing many innocent people. Politicians were assassinated. (In 1985, Prime Minister Margaret Thatcher was inches away from being killed by a bomb.) The British army, meanwhile, patrolled Northern Irish streets and colluded with pro-U.K. terrorist groups. People were thrown in jail for crimes they didn't commit. There were shootings and bombings almost weekly. Over 3,000 died, and tens of thousands were injured—mostly just ordinary folk who were in the wrong place at the wrong time.

The struggle continued for decades, until the so-called "Good Friday Agreement" was negotiated, with the help of U.S. President Bill Clinton, in 1997. While it didn't end all political and religious violence, it did change the atmosphere considerably. A massive constitutional overhaul, the agreement ended institutional discrimination against the Catholic minority, installed power sharing, and devolved government. Paramilitary groups such as the IRA agreed to disarm. Mortal enemies agreed to share power together, peacefully.

Skip forward 20 years, and the region is still at peace. Sporadic flare-ups of violence do happen, but nothing even remotely approaching what it was. Meanwhile, a new generation has grown up who weren't even alive when the so-called "Troubles" came to an end.

retains some original industrial touches. Carpets are dark-hued, and walls are painted in deep matte colors of gray and dark blue, with exposed steel girders here and there. Bedrooms are large, very quiet, and comfortable, with neutral colors, low lighting, huge beds, and modern bathrooms—most have separate baths and showers. Breakfasts are large and varied. **Chez Mal** is the good in-house brasserie restaurant (dinner-bed-and-breakfast packages are available), and the bar is lively.

34-38 Victoria St., Belfast, BT1 3GH. www.malmaison.com/locations/belfast. © **028/9600-1405.** 62 units. £95–£195 double, £280–£420 suite. Discounted parking at nearby lot (£10 per day). Breakfast not included in lower rates. **Amenities:** Restaurant; bar; gym; room service; Wi-Fi (free).

Ten Square ★★ Set in a recently renovated historic Belfast building, minutes from all the sights, this boutique hotel aims to emulate five-star luxury hotels at a fraction of the cost. Its decor deliberately contrasts styles—exposed stone and tall arched windows in public areas; bedrooms treading the line between chic and kitsch, with polka-dotted carpet and blue velvet fabrics. The king-size beds, draped in pure white linens, are very firm. The overall effect works pretty stylishly. **Jospers** restaurant specializes in Irish meats, particularly steak, and also serves afternoon tea with all the extras. Check the website for deals, including a *Titanic*-themed package.

Yorkshire House, 10 Donegall Sq., Belfast, BT1 5JD. www.tensquare.co.uk. © **028/9024-1001.** 23 units. £115–£160 double. Breakfast included. Street parking only. **Amenities:** Restaurant; bar; Wi-Fi (free).

INEXPENSIVE

The Guesthouse at Ballylagan Organic Farm ★★ Ballylagan is a fully certified working organic farm (the first in Northern Ireland, no less) and at the center of it all is this welcoming little 1840s farmhouse. Covered by lush vines, the two-story graystone building looks as if it, too, has grown out of the landscape. Patricia and Tom Gilbert are passionate about what they do, and that ethos shines through, especially in the food. All breakfast ingredients are completely organic (of course), from the fresh-baked bread to the bacon and sausages at breakfast; home-cooked dinners can be provided, too, if booked in advance. (Due to licensing restrictions, they can't serve wine, but you're welcome to bring your own.) The guest rooms are in a separate building from the owners' home, giving everyone a bit of privacy. Painted in soothing colors, the bedrooms are large enough to easily fit a sofa and a couple of chairs in addition to the extremely comfortable beds. Tea and homemade cakes await your arrival in the guest lounge. For an extra charge of £10 you can have the use of a wood-burning stove in your room. A quiet night's sleep is guaranteed—Ballyclare is about 21km (13 miles) north of Belfast.

12 Ballylagan Rd., Straid, Ballyclare, Belfast, BT39 9NF. www.ballylagan.com. © **028/9332-2129.** 4 units. £70–£95 double. 2-night minimum stay. Free parking. Breakfast included in guesthouse lodging. **Amenities:** Wi-Fi (free).

Ravenhill Guesthouse ★ A friendly welcome awaits from hosts Roger and Olive, whose handsome Victorian corner house has been converted into one of the best B&Bs in Belfast. They're the sort of hosts for whom nothing seems too much trouble in order to make guests feel right at home. The recently renovated bedrooms are simple but neat as a pin, with print fabrics and views of the street. You're in a residential area here but not far from the action; the city center is about a 10-minute cab or bus ride away. Roger cooks delicious breakfasts, and guests can expect the full Ulster fry, in addition to options such as kippers with parsley butter and scrambled eggs. They also bake their own traditional Irish wheaten bread from scratch, even down to milling their own flour.

690 Ravenhill Rd., Belfast, BT6 0BZ. www.ravenhillhouse.com. © **028/9020-7444.** 5 units. £95–£115 double. 2-night minimum stay in summer. Free parking. Breakfast included. **Amenities:** Wi-Fi (free).

Tara Lodge ★★ When Tara Lodge opened in the mid-2000s, it was part of a fresh new wave of modern, inexpensive, boutique-style hotels in Belfast, a city where good budget accommodations were scarce. It has more competition these days, but Tara Lodge still manages to get everything just about right. The simple, contemporary guest rooms are perhaps a little small, but the beds are large and comfortable. Breakfasts are very good and offer plenty of choice. The **Botanic Gardens ★** (see p. 483) and **Ulster Museum ★★★** (see p. 490) are 10 minutes away on foot; it's a short cab ride to the city center. The hotel doesn't have a full restaurant, but plenty of good eateries are within easy reach. Tara Lodge sometimes offers excellent package deals, including bed, breakfast, and a *Game of Thrones* locations tour for just £72 per person.

36 Cromwell Rd., Belfast, BT7 1JW. www.taralodge.com. © **028/9059-0900.** 34 units. £95–£135 double. Free parking. Breakfast included. **Amenities:** Wi-Fi (free).

WHERE TO EAT IN BELFAST

A prominent British journalist tells the story of ordering a fried breakfast in Belfast, sometime in the 1970s. "No sausage," he asked the waitress. When his food arrived, there were sausages on the plate. He sent it back, asking again for no sausage. But back it came, with sausages still there. "But I said no sausages," he complained. "Chef says sausage is compulsory," came the taciturn reply. These days the Belfast dining scene is, happily, much more cosmopolitan. The number of top restaurants in the city seems to grow every year, from funky gastropubs to chic fine dining.

EXPENSIVE

CoCo ★★ MODERN EUROPEAN/INTERNATIONAL Coco's stylishly whimsical dining room is plastered in modern art along with posters and photo-collages that set the tone. The contemporary menu is full of welcome surprises that innovate without overcrowding the more traditional ingredients; an appetizer of goat's cheese ravioli is served with candied walnuts, for example, while a spiced chicken salad comes with ginger, mint, and glass noodles. For dessert, try the blood-orange carpaccio with yogurt sorbet. Prices are a little high for the evening service, but the three-course pre-theater menu is just £19. It also has a popular Sunday lunch.

7-11 Linenhall St., Belfast, BT2 8AA. www.cocobelfast.com. ℭ **028/9031-1150.** Entrees £16–£23. Mon–Fri noon–3pm, 5:30–9:30pm; Sat 5:30–9:30pm; Sun 1–9pm.

James Street South ★★★ MODERN IRISH One of Belfast's leading restaurants, James Street South has built a great reputation on creative, modern Irish cuisine. With exposed brick walls and an industrial-chic vibe, the place may look unpretentious, but the food is outstanding—dishes such Dundrum crab with a bisque reduction, Guinness-cured salmon, local beef sirloin with a cheddar cheese crust, or cod with pickled rhubarb and smoked buttered leeks. Splurge on the "Taste of Ulster" tasting menu (£50 for four courses; £70 with paired wines).

21 James St. South, Belfast, BT2 7GA. www.jamesstreetsouth.co.uk. ℭ **028/9043-4310.** Entrees £16–£28. Mon–Tues 5:30–10:30pm; Wed–Sat 12:30–2:30pm, 5:30–10:30pm.

Ox ★★★ MODERN EUROPEAN Contemporary, seasonal, well-balanced flavors form the small but sumptuous menus at this Michelin-starred restaurant. The tasting menus change constantly, with local and seasonal availability a constant priority, but expect dishes such as a piquant tomato, onion, and black-garlic galette; creamy bisque made with salsify and ink; or perhaps salted halibut with buttermilk and dill. A full vegetarian menu is always available. Paired wines are just £30 extra. The service strikes precisely the right balance between professionalism and friendliness—the waitstaff really know their stuff, without ever making you feel like you need to sit up straighter—and the modern dining room provides a sophisticated backdrop. Be sure to make reservations. If, however, you can't quite stretch to dinner here, you can sample the restaurant's excellent wine list in the entirely informal **Ox Cave** (the French, wine-filled kind), the adjacent wine bar, while enjoying cheese, nibbles, and light bites.

1 Oxford St., Belfast, BT1 3LA. www.oxbelfast.com. ℭ **028/9031-4121.** Tasting menus £50–£55. Tues–Fri 12:15–2:30pm and 6–9:30pm; Sat 1–2:30pm and 6–9:30pm. Closed Sun–Mon.

MODERATE

The Barking Dog ★★ IRISH/INTERNATIONAL There's something quintessentially Belfast about this place—quirky, artsy, lively, but ultimately no-nonsense. The dining room has a funky pub feel, with exposed brick walls and old candelabras balanced on battered wood tables. If you sit in the front garden, you're separated from the street by a fence with paw prints all over it. The menu is balanced and straightforward—a juicy cheeseburger with fat French fries, for example, or a simple fish pie. Vegetarian choices are more than the usual "mushroom pie" variety—herb gnocchi, perhaps, or sweet potato ravioli. The selection of "nibbles" (good value for the money at five for £12) puts a nicely

Irish-style twist on tapas. The Barking Dog has a good lunch menu, and the Sunday brunch is popular.

33-35 Malone Rd., Belfast, BT9 6RU. www.barkingdogbelfast.com. © **028/9066-1885.** Entrees £11–£30. Mon–Thurs noon–3pm and 5–10pm; Fri–Sat noon–3pm and 5:30–11pm; Sun 12–9pm. No children after 9pm.

Deanes Love Fish (Etc.) ★★ SEAFOOD   Deep breath here, because this review is six rolled into one. The mini-empire run by local celebrity chef Michael Deane has so far expanded to half a dozen restaurants; while each has its charms, **Deanes Love Fish** is probably our favorite. Adjacent to **Eipic** (© **028/9033-1134),** Deane's flagship formal restaurant on Howard Street (known for very good Irish-French cuisine), the more casual Love Fish is just as good, but less expensive. Here you'll find plates such as roast local salmon, cooked in olive oil and lemon with anchovy butter sauce; crab and chile linguine; beer-battered fish and chips; or maybe a buttery plaice *meunière*. Late in the evening a menu of nibbles and snacks includes prawns on toast, smoked salmon with Guinness wheat bread, or a seafood platter if you're hungry. And the lunch at Love Fish is one of the city's best food bargains, where all main dishes cost just £6.50. Also here is the excellent **Meat Locker** (© **028/9033-1134),** a laid-back grill where you can enjoy a pre-theater menu with main courses priced at around £10.

Michael Deane's other culinary outposts, scattered around the city, each cater to a slightly different crowd. The **Deli-Bistro** (© **028/9024-8800**) and **Deli/Vin Café** (© **028/9024-8830**), a tapas bar, share premises at 44 Bedford Street; while in the University Quarter, next to the Ulster Museum, is the informal bistro **Deanes at Queens** (1 College Gardens; © **028/9038-2111**). The newest addition is Chef Deane's foray into Italian cooking, **Deane & Decano** (© **028/9066-3108**), on Lisburn Road. Take your pick!

36–40 Howard St., Belfast, BT1 6PF. www.michaeldeane.co.uk. © **028/9033-1134.** Entrees £10–£24. Mon–Sat noon–10pm.

Mourne Seafood Bar ★★ SEAFOOD   This is one of the best places in Belfast for top-quality seafood. The dining room has a casual air—this is a seafood *bar* after all—but the food speaks for itself. Oysters are a specialty, served traditionally with Tabasco and lemon or in more elaborate ways, such as with pickled ginger and soy dressing. Alternatively, you could go for some spicy piri-piri prawns with fresh focaccia bread to start, followed by one of the fresh daily specials like seared scallops with pea risotto. The atmosphere is relaxed and convivial, and the prices are thoroughly reasonable for food this good. The restaurant doesn't take reservations at lunchtime, but evening booking is essential. A second branch is located on Main Street in Dundrum, just outside Newcastle, County Down (© **028/4375-1377**).

34–36 Bank St., Belfast, BT1 1HL. www.mourneseafood.com. © **028/9024-8544.** Entrees £9–£23. Mon–Thurs noon–9:30pm; Fri–Sat noon–4pm, 5–10pm; Sun 1–9pm.

INEXPENSIVE

Boojum ★★ MEXICAN   Lines have been known to stretch way down the street at busy times for this jaunty, no-frills emporium, where the food is excellent and fresh as can be. The menu is pretty simple—just choose from burritos, tacos, fajitas, or salad, then your main meat or veg ingredients, and one of several kinds of salsa. (Brave souls will want to try the fiery *naga*; the less masochistic may prefer the tasty *salsa verde*.) Wash it all down with a soda or a nice cold bottle of Mexican beer. Boojum has a few tables, but most people get theirs to go. Other branches are on Chichester Street (ⓒ **028/9023-0600**) and Great Victoria Street (ⓒ **028/9023-3200**)—or, if you're lucky, you might spot the Boojum food truck somewhere around town.

Botanic Ave., Belfast, BT1 1JL. www.boojummex.com. ⓒ **028/9031-5334.** All items £5–£7.50. Daily 11:30am–10pm.

The John Hewitt ★ IRISH/INTERNATIONAL   Near the Belfast Cathedral, this atmospheric bar is a popular hangout with locals. The gastropub-style lunch menu is a real crowd-pleaser: soup of the day with crusty bread, haddock and chips, steak and ale pie, and so on. After lunch service, the menu shifts to nibbles and sharing bowls. It doesn't serve food in the evenings or any time on Sunday, but you may still want to drop by—the John Hewitt is one of the best spots in the city for live music, with bands every night from 9:30pm or 4pm on Saturday. (Check the website for full listings—Tuesday is traditional Irish night.) Admission to gigs is usually free.

51 Donegall St., Belfast, BT1 2FH. www.thejohnhewitt.com. ⓒ **028/9023-3768.** Entrees £4–£10. Mon–Fri 11:30am–1am, Sat noon–1am, Sun 7pm–midnight. Food served Mon–Sat noon–3pm.

SHOPPING

Belfast is a surprisingly good place to shop. Start at Donegall Place, where the streets are lined with shops and the Victorian arcades are filled with gift and jewelry stores. Good buys are to be had on Belleek china, linen, and crystal from County Tyrone. Shops are typically open weekdays from 9 or 9:30am to 5 or 5:30pm, and open later on weekends.

The main shopping street is **Royal Avenue,** home of several well-known chain stores, while the **Westfield Castlecourt Shopping Centre** on Royal Avenue and the glass-domed **Victoria Square** shopping center are Belfast's main downtown multi-story shopping malls.

Built in 1896, the iron-and-glass **St. George's Market** (May and Oxford sts.; ⓒ **028/9043-5704**) has a number of different street markets. On Friday, the **Variety Market** (6am–3pm) is packed with 250 stalls of fresh produce, antiques, clothing, and bric-a-brac. On Saturdays, the **City Food and Craft Market** (9am–3pm) specializes in artisan foods, with plenty of tempting fresh snacks on offer, plus an assortment of local crafts.

The **Sunday Market** (10am–4pm) is a happy combination of the two, although the balance tends to be in favor of crafts.

ANTIQUES

Archive's Antiques Centre ★ Several dealers sell their wares at this sprawling center, with specialists in everything from silverware to pub memorabilia and militaria. 88 Donegall Pass, Belfast, BT7 1BX. www.archivesantiques-centre.co.uk. ✆ **028/9023-2383.**

Oakland Antiques ★★ This enormous antiques emporium specializes in furniture, glassware, and other household items from the 18th to early 20th centuries. 137 Donegall Pass, Belfast, BT7 1DS. www.oaklandantiques.co.uk. ✆ **028/9023-0176.**

BOOKS & STATIONERY

No Alibis ★★ Here's a mystery to solve. You walk into this independent bookstore empty-handed and come out carrying a bag filled with books and a lighter wallet. What happened in there? *J'accuse* No Alibis, with its excellent stock devoted to crime fiction from all over the world. 83 Botanic Ave., Belfast, BT7 1JL. www.noalibis.com. ✆ **028/9031-9601.**

CRAFTS, DESIGN & HOMEWARE

The Wicker Man ★★ Don't be put off by how humdrum this place looks from the outside; within lies an inventive selection of crafts, art, and other souvenirs, from clocks and jewelry to bath products and musical instruments. This is one of the best places in Belfast to shop for gifts. 44–46 High St., Belfast, BT1 2BE. www.thewickerman.co.uk. ✆ **028/9024-3550.**

FASHION & CLOTHING

The Bureau ★★ When this place opened in the late 1980s, it was something of a harbinger of the modern, cultured city Belfast would slowly become in the 1990s and 2000s. Today it remains one of the city's major men's fashion boutiques, selling a fantastic range of clothes and footwear from its airy, stylish shop on Newtownards Road, east of the Titanic Quarter. Portview, 310 Newtownards Rd., Belfast BT4 1HE. www.thebureaubelfast.com. ✆ **028/9046-0190.**

Rojo ★★ An absolute must for the well-heeled woman, Rojo specializes in women's shoes and boots, from a wide selection of top designers. It also sells beautiful handbags and other accessories. Rojo isn't cheap, but the range is second to none in the city. 613 Lisburn Way, Belfast, BT9 7GT. www.rojoshoes.co.uk. ✆ **028/9066-6998.**

JEWELRY

Steensons ★★★ Behind Belfast City Hall, this long-established showroom sells an outstanding collection of gold and silver jewelry. Most of what's on sale are from Steensons' own designs, although it sells work by other top Irish designers, too. It's known for its beautiful pieces made for *Game of Thrones* (see box p. 522); other popular lines include elegant limited-edition pieces launched to commemorate the *Titanic* (the owner's grandfather was a crewmember). There's also a branch on Toberwine Street in Glenarm, County Antrim (✆ **028/2884-1445**). Bedford St., Belfast, BT2 7FD. www.thesteensons.com. ✆ **028/9024-8269.**

BELFAST AFTER DARK

Belfast has a plethora of historic pubs serving friendly local crowds, along with a fast-growing scene of late-night bars for the young and trendy, mostly clustered in the University Quarter. If you're looking for a traditional pub, several of the best are tucked away in the pedestrian lanes off Donegall Place.

The **licensing laws** in Northern Ireland aren't as notoriously strict as they used to be. Pub hours are generally Monday to Saturday from 11:30am to 11pm and Sunday from 12:30 to 2:30pm and 7 to 10pm, but some stay open until 1am, especially on Friday and Saturday nights; bars stay open later. Nightclubs tend not to get busy until after the pubs close; admission ranges from a few pounds to about £15.

BARS & CLUBS

Apartment ★★★ This glamorous cocktail bar with a fantastic view of Belfast City Hall is popular with a young and sophisticated crowd, drawn by top DJs (from about 9:30pm on weekend nights) and an excellent cocktail list. It also serves good food. 2 Donegal Sq. West, Belfast, BT1 6JA. www.apartmentbelfast.com. ✆ **028/9099-4120.**

THE PERFORMING ARTS

Belfast Empire ★ This former music hall is now one of the city's busiest live venues, with acts a few times a week (some big names, mostly of an indie/alternative variety) and standup comedy every Tuesday. It's also a busy bar and nightclub, open until 1am every night except Sunday. 42 Botanic Ave., Belfast, BT1 1JQ. www.thebelfastempire.com. ✆ **028/9024-9276.**

Black Box ★★ This eclectic venue has a great program of theater, spoken word, cabaret, film, and other live events, as well as exhibition spaces featuring whatever's interesting in the worlds of photography and visual art. From Wednesday to Sunday nights, the Green Room bar offers pizza, beer, and free live music. The slightly bohemian crowd is a great mix of ages, the music a similarly mixed bag of styles. 18–22 Hill St., Belfast, BT1 2LA. www.blackboxbelfast.com. ✆ **028/9024-4400.**

Grand Opera House ★★ One of the main landmarks of Belfast's Golden Mile, the Grand Opera House opened in 1895. The interior is full of late-Victorian detail, including a grand auditorium with an elaborately painted frieze on the high ceiling. Severely damaged twice by IRA bombs, it underwent a full restoration in the early 2000s. A cornerstone of the Belfast live arts scene, it hosts a tremendous variety of shows, from touring plays, ballet, and opera to big-ticket musicals and concerts. Ticket prices vary, but expect to pay between £15 and £30 for most shows. Check the website for the current schedule. 2–4 Great Victoria St., Belfast, BT2 7HR. www.goh.co.uk. ⓒ **028/9024-1919.**

Lyric Theatre ★★　The Lyric is a highly respected repertory theater (the only one in Northern Ireland), producing original work and hosting a varied program of touring plays all year. Ticket prices vary but are generally between £10 and £25. In 2011, the Lyric played a walk-on part in history, when it was the venue for a meeting between the Queen and Martin McGuinness (the former IRA commander, who was Deputy First Minister of Northern Ireland from 2007–2017). 55 Ridgeway St., Belfast, BT9 5FP. www.lyrictheatre.co.uk. ⓒ **028/9038-1081.**

PUBS

Crown Liquor Saloon ★★★　There's a very real possibility that this impeccably restored Victorian gin palace is the handsomest pub in the world. See full review p. 487. 46 Great Victoria St., Belfast, BT2 7BA. www. nicholsonspubs.co.uk/thecrownliquorsaloonbelfast. ⓒ **028/9024-3187.**

Kelly's Cellars ★★　One of a couple pubs claiming to be Belfast's oldest, Kelly's Cellars certainly looks the part, with low doorways and a selection of vintage fishing nets, lanterns, and other bric-a-brac hanging

The Crown Liquor Saloon, a Belfast landmark.

from the high-beamed ceiling. It's also considered one of the best pubs in town for live traditional music; sessions are usually held on Tuesdays, Wednesdays, and Thursdays from 8:30pm on, and Saturdays from 4:30pm. 30–32 Bank St., Belfast, BT1 1HL. www.kellyscellars.com. © **028/ 9024-6058.**

The Morning Star ★ Another lovely traditional pub, the Morning Star has been in business since at least 1810. Originally it was next to a stagecoach terminus, providing sunrise pick-me-ups for overnight passengers—hence the name. The pub is famously hard to find: Pottinger's Entry is a small, pedestrian-only alleyway off High Street, across from the post office; look for the iron arch over the entrance. 17–19 Pottinger's Entry, Belfast, BT1 4DT. www.themorningstarbar.com. © **028/9023-5986.**

White's Tavern ★★ White's Tavern has been serving liquor since 1630, which makes it an even older establishment than all of the above (though technically not the oldest pub; it began life as a wine shop). It was renovated in 2014 to keep it looking…well, decidedly *not* new, and that's exactly why people love the place. The decor is all old whiskey bottles and vintage photos, with the quintessentially Irish smell of burning peat wafting from the fireplace. The upstairs bar turns into a nightclub on weekends (admission £5). Every other Monday in summer it turns the courtyard into a makeshift cinema, showing retro movies—for free (free popcorn, too). See the website for listings. The entrance to Winecellar Entry is between High and Rosemary streets. 2–4 Winecellar Entry, Belfast, BT1 1QN. www.whitesbelfast.com. © **028/9031-2582.**

14

BELFAST

Belfast After Dark

DAY TRIPS FROM BELFAST

15

M edieval castles, mountain ranges, coastal drives, and one of the most spectacular (and certainly unique) landscapes you'll find anywhere—all are within easy reach of Belfast. That is, if you don't mind driving down tiny, winding roads that take at least twice as long as they should to get anywhere. Though the destinations covered in this chapter are no more than 60 miles in any direction from Northern Ireland's capital, it could take you up to 90 minutes to drive there—more if you take the scenic way. And frankly, why wouldn't you?

As if that wasn't enough, the countryside these winding roads lead to is simply breathtaking—the verdant greens of the **Glens of Antrim,** the rugged **Mourne Mountains,** and the famously craggy coastline to the **Giant's Causeway,** surely one of the world's great natural wonders. Take the time to get out of your car and explore what this region has to offer. You may even leave thinking this was the highlight of your trip.

ESSENTIALS
Arriving

BY CAR Most of the attractions listed in this chapter are easily accessible by car, with a journey time of between 1 and 2 hours (at most) from Belfast. Roads are good in the regions around the city, although traffic can be a problem, particularly during rush hour. In reasonable traffic, Comber is about a half-hour drive from the city; Strangford and Armagh, about an hour; Newcastle, 1¼ hours; Bushmills and the Giant's Causeway, 1½ hours.

BY BUS Ulsterbus (www.translink.co.uk; © **028/9066-6630**) runs buses from Belfast to Downpatrick, Carrickfergus, and Ballymena. While several other towns are reachable by bus, routes are long and circuitous—you're better off driving, or joining an organized tour.

BY TRAIN Translink (www.translink.co.uk; © **028/9066-6630**) has train connections with several towns in the region, including Lisburn, Armagh, Bangor, and Portrush, although journey times can be long. The Translink/Ulsterbus website has a great journey planner.

FACING PAGE: **Near Ballycastle, on the Antrim Coast, a herd of sheep claims right of way.**

THE ANTRIM COAST

The most extraordinary stretch of countryside in Northern Ireland, the glorious Antrim Coast Highway stretches north and west from Belfast, curving around toward Donegal. This beautiful rocky shoreline includes the North's most striking sights: the awe-inspiring **Giant's Causeway** (p. 515) and the picturesque **Carrick-a-Rede Rope Bridge** (p. 512). Along the way, the coastal drive meanders under bridges and stone arches, passing crescent bays, sandy beaches, harbors, and huge rock formations. The ocean gleams beside you as you curve along its craggy shores, and the light creates intense colors. In the spring and autumn, you often have the road all to yourself.

The drive is more or less equidistant from Belfast and Derry. It's possible to see all the sights in 1 day, staying in either city, although most travelers prefer to get a room on the coast and take their time.

Visitor Information

The principal tourist information centers in North Antrim are at Narrow Gauge Road, Larne (☎ **028/2826-2450**); Sheskburn House, 14 Bayview Rd., Ballycastle (☎ **028/2076-2024**); and the **Giant's Causeway Information Centre,** Main St., Bushmills (☎ **028/2073-0390**). All offices are open daily year-round, though the Larne and Ballycastle offices are closed Sundays outside the midsummer season. The Giant's Causeway office stays open until 6pm in July and August.

Exploring the Antrim Coast

Carnlough ★ VILLAGE   The first major stop along the Antrim Coast Drive is this quiet village, known for its glassy harbor bobbing with sailboats. It's a lovely place to wander around, sampling interesting little shops and restaurants. Just outside Carnlough is a peaceful yet little-known waterfall called **Cranny Falls.** To get there, look for a marked 1-mile walking trail beginning on the waterfront. After crossing the white-stone bridge, the route goes through idyllic countryside, following an abandoned railway bed, past a disused quarry, until it reaches the falls. Along the way, occasional markers tell you more about the history of the area.

Fishermen sell their daily catch in Carnlough's scenic harbor.

Carnlough, Co. Antrim.

Day Trips from Belfast

Inishowen

Rathlin I.

Giant's Causeway

Fair Head

Torr Head

Moville

Portrush

Portstewart

Ballintoy

Bushmills

Ballycastle

Castlerock

Coleraine

Armoy

Cushendun

Lough Foyle

Limavady

Ballymoney

Cushendall

Red Bay

Ballykelly

Garvagh

Trostan

Carnlough Bay

LONDONDERRY (DERRY)

Kilrea

Bunn

Antrim Mts.

Carnlough

Glenarm

Dungiven

Broughshane

ANTRIM

Sperrin Mts.

Maghera

Ballymena

Larne

Sawel Mtn.

Draperstown

Magherafelt

Island Magee

Cranagh

Ballyclare

Whitehead

Moneymore

Randalstown

Carrickfergus

To Douglas, Heysham, Liverpool

TYRONE

Cookstown

Antrim

Greenisland

Belfast Lough

Pomeroy

Coal Island

Belfast Int'l

Newtownabbey

Bangor

Donaghadee

Sixmilecross

Lough Neagh

Glengormley

Crumlin

BELFAST

Newtownards

Ards Peninsula

Dungannon

Peatlands Park

Lisburn

Comber

Ballygawley

Craigavon

Lurgan

Saintfield

Killinchy

Portavogie

Augher

Portadown

Dromore

Aughnacloy

Tandragee

Ballynahinch

DOWN

Killyleagh

Portaferry

Armagh

Scarva

Banbridge

Downpatrick

Strangford

Middletown

Markethill

Castlewellan

Dundrum

Ardglass

Monaghan

ARMAGH

Rathfriland

Newcastle

IRISH

MONAGHAN

Keady

Newry

Mourne Mts.

Dundrum Bay

SEA

Ballybay

Slieve Gullion

Warrenpoint

Annalong

Castleblayney

Forkhill

Omeath

Silent Valley

Cootehill

Carlingford

Kilkeel

Dundalk

Greenore

Carlingford Lough

0   10 miles
0   10 kms

Northern Ireland counties shown are the historic counties. UK counties were reorganized after 1973.

North Channel

To Troon
To Cairnryan
To Stranraer

Sheep herder along the avenue of ancient beech trees known as Dark Hedges.

Carrick-a-Rede Rope Bridge ★★★ BRIDGE   Each spring, local fishermen put up this rope bridge across a chasm 18m (59 ft.) wide and 24m (79 ft.) deep, swinging over the sea between the mainland and a small island. The bridge has a practical purpose—allowing access to the island's salmon fishery, which it's been doing since 1755 (don't worry, they do regular maintenance). Visitors can use it for a thrilling walk and the chance to call out to each other, "Don't look down!" (By the way, that is *excellent* advice.) If you are acrophobic, stay clear; and if you don't know whether you are, this is not the place to find out. *Note:* A 19km (12-mile) coastal cliff path leads between the Giant's Causeway (p. 515) and the rope bridge. It is always open and is worth the exhaustion.

8km (5 miles) W of Ballycastle off the A2 road. 119A Whitepark Rd., Ballintoy, Co. Antrim, BT54 6LS. www.nationaltrust.org.uk/carrick-a-rede. ℂ **028/2076-9839.** Admission £7 adults; £3.50 children; £17.50 families. July–Aug daily 9:30am–7pm; Mar–June and Sept–Oct daily 9:30am–6pm; Nov–Feb daily 9:30am–3:30pm.

Cushendun ★ VILLAGE   Back in the 1950s, the National Trust bought most of this charming seaside village to preserve it from over-development. Today, the seafront is lined with an elegant sweep of perfect white Cornish-style cottages, and the quaint teashops do a bustling trade. The Glendun River winds through the village, crossed by a lovely old stone bridge, while down on the beach are some atmospheric sea caves. Just north of the village, in a field overlooking the coast, stand the scant remains of **Curra Castle.** Cushendun is a good place to stop and take

THE antrim coast DRIVE

One of the most memorable routes in Ireland, the 96km (60-mile) drive along the Antrim coast offers sweeping views of midnight-blue seas against gray unforgiving cliffs and deep green hillsides. Starting from Carrickfergus, just north of Belfast, it runs to **Portrush,** a few miles past the spectacular **Giant's Causeway.** You could do the whole journey in a couple of hours, but allow much longer if you can—it's the sort of drive you want to savor.

Once you join the coast road (A2), about 26km (16 miles) north of Carrickfergus, the first town is **Glenarm,** decked out with castle walls and a barbican gate. In the picturesque seaside village of **Carnlough ★** (p. 510), you can take a pleasant hike to a waterfall. On up the coast, you'll find the National Trust village of **Cushendun ★** (p. 512), known for its tea shops and whitewashed cottages.

For the most spectacular views, detour off the main A2 road at Cushendun onto the **Torr Head Scenic Road ★★** (p. 517). Just note that this narrow, rugged, cliffside road can induce vertigo as it climbs in seemingly perilous fashion to the tops of hills that are bigger than you might think. On a clear day, you can see all the way to Scotland.

In the late spring and summer, you can take a ferry from the bustling beach town of **Ballycastle** to **Rathlin Island** (see p. 514), where seals and nesting birds make their homes at the **Kebble National Reserve.** Or take a 15-minute detour south on the A22 from Ballycastle to see the picturesque **Dark Hedges,** a beautiful avenue of 200-year-old beech trees that intertwine overhead. (It's just past the Gracehill Golf Club on Bregah Road.)

Farther west, the heart-stopping **Carrick-a-Rede Rope Bridge ★★★** (p. 512) allows the brave to cross on foot over to a small island just off the coast. Others may prefer to press straight on to the postcard-perfect little town of **Ballintoy,** filled with charming stone cottages and flowery gardens. Ballintoy is stretched out at the edge of **Whitepark Bay,** a wide, crystalline curve of sandy beach at the foot of rocky hills surrounded by green farms. On a sunny day, you might find it hard to go farther.

The last major stop is the eerily lunar **Giant's Causeway ★★★** (p. 515), one of the world's true natural wonders. And after all that adventure, don't you think you've earned yourself a tipple—to enjoy later, if you're the one driving—at the **Old Bushmills Distillery ★★** (p. 516)?

pictures before heading on down the main A2 road—or, if you want the most amazing views, the **Torr Head Scenic Road ★★** (see p. 517). Cushendun, Co. Antrim.

Dunluce Castle ★★ CASTLE   Between the Giant's Causeway and the busy harbor town of Portrush, the coastline is dominated by the hulking skeletal outline of what must have once been a glorious castle. This was the main fort of the Irish MacDonnells, chiefs of Antrim. From the 14th to the 17th century, it was the largest and most sophisticated castle in the North, with a series of fortifications built on rocky outcrops extending into the sea. In 1639, part of the castle fell into the sea, taking some of the

GOING TO THE birds: A TRIP TO RATHLIN ISLAND

Want to get close to nature? Plan a trip to **Rathlin Island,** 10km (6 miles) off the coast north of Ballycastle. The tiny island is 6km (3¾ miles) long, less than 1.5km (1 mile) wide, and almost completely treeless, with rugged coastal cliffs, a small beach, and crowds of seals and seabirds in spring and summer. Once you get there, you'll realize that it's not quite as isolated as it seems—there's a resident population of about 100 people, plus a pub, a fish-and-chip shop, and a couple of guesthouses, should you miss the last boat to shore.

Start with a visit to the **Boat House Museum and Visitor Centre,** near the ferry landing at Church Bay (✆ **028/ 2076-2024**). The center contains an exhibit on the history of the islands, as well as plenty of handy visitor information. It's open from April to September, daily 10am to 5pm (call to check if you're visiting in April or September—opening and closing dates vary). Admission is free.

Rathlin is a favorite bird-watching spot, especially in spring and early summer when the birds are nesting. Given that there's little else to do here, it's no surprise that the island's biggest draw is bird-watching at the **Kebble National Nature Reserve** (✆ **028/7035-9963**) on the western side of the island, and the **RSPB**

Rathlin Seabird Centre (✆ **028/2076-0062**), located in an old lighthouse. There's no charge for entry, but you have to be let in by the warden; call in advance to arrange a time. From here you can watch colorful puffins, guillemots, kittiwakes, fulmars, razorbills, and other birds. It's open April and the first half of September, daily from 11am to 4pm, and from May to August, daily from 10am to 5pm.

Boat trips operate daily from Ballycastle pier; the crossing takes 50 minutes. Boat schedules vary and are always subject to weather conditions, but there are usually several crossings a day. (Do check for cancellations in bad weather, though.) To check times and book tickets, call **Rathlin Island Ferry** (www.rathlinbally castleferry.com; ✆ **028/2076-9299**). Round-trip tickets cost £12 adults, £6 children, and £32 families; it's advisable to book in advance.

If you find yourself wanting to stay a little longer, **Coolnagrock B&B** (www. rathlin-island.co.uk; ✆ **028/2076-3983**), which has distant views of the Mull of Kintyre in Scotland, costs from £70 for a double. It's open April to October.

For more information about Rathlin, visit **www.rathlin-island.co.uk**.

An abandoned house at Ushet Point on south Rathlin Island.

Photo ops abound on the weird and wonderful Giant's Causeway.

servants with it; soon after that, it was allowed to fall into a beautiful ruin. The 17th-century courtyard survives, including a few buildings. The site incorporates two of the original Norman towers dating from 1305. *One enticing footnote:* A recent archaeological dig here uncovered the remains of a town thought to have been destroyed during a rebellion in 1641. Only a tiny fraction of what is now believed to exist has so far been excavated. 87 Dunluce Rd., Bushmills, Co. Antrim, BT57 8UY. ⓒ **028/2073-1938.** Admission £5 adults; £3 seniors, students, and children 4–16; free for children 3 and under; £13 families. Daily 10am–5pm (4pm in Dec and Jan); last admission 30 min. before closing. Call to confirm times in winter.

Giant's Causeway ★★★ NATURE SITE   A UNESCO World Heritage Site, this is an extraordinary sight indeed. Sitting at the foot of steep cliffs and stretching out into the sea, it is a natural formation of thousands of tightly packed basalt columns. The tops of the columns form flat stepping stones, all of which are perfectly hexagonal. They measure about 30cm (12 in.) in diameter; some are very short, others are as tall as 12m (39 ft.). Scientists believe they were formed 60 or 70 million years ago by volcanic eruptions and cooling lava. The ancients, on the other hand, believed the rock formation to be the work of giants. To reach the causeway, you walk from the parking area down a steep path for nearly 1.6km (1 mile), past amphitheaters of stone columns and formations with fanciful names like Honeycomb, Wishing Well, Giant's Granny, King and his Nobles, and Lover's Leap. If you wish, you can then climb up a wooden

THE GIANT'S CAUSEWAY: A poet's-eye VIEW

With what tremendous force, aerial powers,
Once did ye rage in subterraneous bowers.
When roused by torturing fires from all your cayes.
Ye swept the glowing lava's sulphurous wayes;
Ye then beheld the thundering waters pass
Through wide rent gulfs, and changed to instant gas;
Struggling for vent again they upward roll.
And burst their narrow bounds from pole to pole.
'Twas nature's throe, and from the labouring frame
The solid strata, midst encircling flame
Severed and torn, their serried peaks upreared
And o'er the foamy surge the new-formed land appeared.

—From "The Giant's Causeway"
by William Hamilton Drummond (1778–1865)

staircase to Benbane Head to take in the views, and then walk back along the cliff top. Regular shuttle service from the visitor center is available for those who can't face the hike. *Note:* The high-tech, underground visitor center has a cafe, shop, interpretive center, and hugely expensive parking, justifying the fairly steep admission price. However, the Causeway itself is a free, open site, so if you can find safe and legal parking, there's nothing to stop you from walking down on your own.

44 Causeway Rd., Bushmills, Co. Antrim, BT57 8SU. www.nationaltrust.org.uk/giants-causeway. *©* **028/2073-1855.** Visitor center and parking: £10.50 adults; £5.25 children; £26.25 families. Visitor center July–Aug daily 9am–7pm; Mar–June and Sept–Oct daily 9am–6pm; Nov–Feb daily 9am–5pm.

The Old Bushmills Distillery ★★ FACTORY TOUR   Licensed to distill spirits in 1608, but with historical references dating from as far back as 1276, this distillery is endlessly popular. Visitors can tour the working sections and watch the whiskey-making process, starting with fresh water from the adjacent River Bush and continuing through distillation, fermentation, and bottling. At the end of the tour, you can sample the wares in the **Potstill Bar,** where you can learn more about the history of the distillery. Tours last about 25 minutes. The Bushmills coffee shop serves tea, coffee, homemade snacks, and lunch. *Tip:* Try to visit during the week for the full experience. Although tours do take place on weekends, the distillery itself is only in operation from Monday to Friday. The same is true for the "silent season," early July through early August—when the distillery shuts down for annual maintenance, but tours continue as normal.

2 Distillery Rd., Co. Antrim, BT57 8XH. www.bushmills.com. *©* **028/2073-3218.** Admission £8 adults; £7 seniors and students; £4.50 children 8–17; £23 families. No

children under 8 on tour. Apr–Oct tours about every 20 min. Mar–Oct Mon–Sat 9:15am–4:45pm, Sun noon–4:45pm (last tours 4pm); Nov–Feb Mon–Sat 10am–4:45pm, Sun noon–4:45pm (last tours 3:30pm).

Torr Head Scenic Road ★★ SCENIC DRIVE   This diversion is spectacular, but it's not for those with a fear of heights or narrow dirt roads; nor is it a good idea to drive in bad weather. But on a sunny, dry day, the brave can follow signs from **Cushendun** ★ (p. 512) up a steep hill at the edge of town onto the Torr Head Scenic Road. After a precipitous climb, the road narrows further and inches its way along the edge of the cliff overlooking the sea. Along the way are places to park and take in the sweeping views. On a clear day, you can see all the way to the Mull of Kintyre in Scotland. Arguably the best views of all are to be had at Murlough Bay (follow the signs).

Torr Rd., heading N out of Cushendun, Co. Antrim.

Where to Stay on the Antrim Coast
MODERATE

Causeway Smithy ★★★   A short hop from the Giant's Causeway (you can just see it in the distance, across rolling green fields), this warm and friendly B&B is a fantastic find. The guest rooms are simple but stylish, with polished wood floors and contemporary print wallpaper. Big bay windows look out over the verdant countryside, flooding the rooms with light during the day. Each of the three rooms is located in a separate annex, and you have your own key, so you'll have more of a feeling of freedom and privacy than is usual in countryside B&Bs. Tasty breakfasts are served in a guest lounge. There's no restaurant, but owner Denise is full of recommendations about where to go in the evenings.

270 Whitepark Rd., Bushmills, Co. Antrim, BT57 8SN. www.causewaysmithybnb. com. ✆ **075/1506-6975.** 3 units. £70 double. Free parking. Rates include breakfast. **Amenities:** Wi-Fi (free).

Whitepark House ★★   This fantastic little place, just a couple of miles from the Carrick-a-Rede Rope Bridge (see p. 512), was built in the mid-1700s and still retains a traditional feel. Beds are wrought iron framed; one is a four-poster, while the others have canopies. Heavy silk fabrics lift the design of the room. Views of the well-tended garden are sweet, but ask for a room overlooking the sea if you want to wake up to a spectacular vista. Bob and Siobhan Isles are genuinely warm people; the fact that they've won awards for their hospitality comes as no surprise whatsoever. Breakfasts are delicious—the full Ulster fry is the specialty, of course, but Bob also takes care of his vegetarian guests (he is one himself). What a lovely, idyllic find along the Antrim coast road.

150 Whitepark Rd., Ballintoy, Co. Antrim, BT54 6NH. www.whiteparkhouse.com. ✆ **028/2073-1482.** 3 units. £90–£130 double. Free parking. Breakfast included. Children must occupy their own room (no discount). **Amenities:** Wi-Fi (free).

INEXPENSIVE

Londonderry Arms Hotel ★   A pleasant Georgian inn in Carnlough, the Londonderry Arms is a well-run, traditional kind of place. The building has its quirks—most of the inn is original, with a well-designed modern extension. Bedrooms are simple but comfortable, and a couple have views of the nearby sea. Triple and quad rooms can offer great savings for families or groups. (Check the website for special offers.) The old place could do with a facelift, in truth, but for this price most of us would accept the odd creak and frayed edge. An unexpected piece of historical trivia about this place: Winston Churchill was once (briefly) the landlord. He inherited it and sold it soon afterward, although he is known to have stayed here at least once.

20 Harbour Rd., Carnlough, Co. Antrim, BT44 0EU. www.glensofantrim.com. ⓒ **028/ 2888-5255.** 35 units. £60–£75 double. Limited free parking (on street). Breakfast not included in lower rates. **Amenities:** Restaurant; bar; room service; Wi-Fi (free).

Lurig View ★   The atmosphere at this sweet little B&B in Glenariff feels akin to a family home. The manager, Rose Ward, and her husband, Chris, are friendly as can be, and happy to help with planning sightseeing trips, making dinner reservations, and so on. Bedrooms are simple but decorated with paintings of flowers chosen to match the accent colors of the room—an inventive touch. Breakfast is served outside if the weather's good. If you really must, the guest lounge has a TV, but a better choice is to get out and explore. Glenariff, a pretty little town a few miles south of Cushendun, is a popular coastal stop; a forest park is within about 10 minutes' drive, and the beach is a short walk from the front door.

38 Glen Rd., Glenariff, Ballymena, Co. Antrim, BT44 0RF. www.lurigview.co.uk. ⓒ **028/2177-1618.** 3 units. £70 double. Free parking. Breakfast included. **Amenities:** Wi-Fi (free).

Where to Eat on the Antrim Coast
MODERATE

Smuggler's Inn ★ IRISH/INTERNATIONAL   A convenient lunch spot right across from the Giant's Causeway, the Smuggler's Inn serves traditional pub lunches. Choose from a few sandwiches and light snack options, or go for the full works with hefty burgers, fish and chips, or chicken *goujons* (strips of meat, breaded and deep-fried). There's also a separate children's menu. In the evening it's much the same kind of thing but pushed up a notch in terms of choice—a couple of steaks join the menu, as does the occasional dish with a bit more ambition, such as roast duck with fruity red cabbage and a sherry reduction. Like several places around here, euros are accepted as well as pounds. The Smuggler's Inn also has rooms available for around £100 per night.

306 Whitepark Rd., Giant's Causeway, Bushmills, Co. Antrim, BT57 8SL. www.smugglers innireland.com. ⓒ **028/2073-1577.** Entrees £10–£18. Food served daily noon–2:30pm and 4:30–9pm.

INEXPENSIVE

Red Door Tea Room ★★ CAFE   This little cottage tearoom is cozy and welcoming inside, with a turf-burning stove and the day's menu chalked onto blackboards behind the counter. But if the weather allows you'll want to sit outside—the view from the garden over lush green fields to Ballintoy Harbour is stunning. The Red Door serves tempting fresh cakes and desserts, like the delicious Victoria sponge cake (two layers, separated by jam and cream). It also serves good light lunches if you want something a little more substantial. Salads, soups, bagels, sandwiches, or plates of tasty fresh fish are quite good. It all adds up to a welcome and idyllic rest stop along the Antrim coast road. Although the Red Door officially closes at 5pm, you may find it open into the evening on busy days in summer.

Ballintoy Harbour, Ballintoy, Co. Antrim, BT54 6NA. ℂ **028/2076-9048.** Entrees £9–£14. Easter week and June–Sept daily 11am–5pm; Easter–May and Sept–Easter daily 11am–4pm.

Thyme & Co. ★ MODERN IRISH   Another great little cafe on the Antrim coast drive, Thyme and Co. serves delicious, healthful lunches. Ingredients are locally sourced, and the short menu is thoughtfully put together. Dine on freshly baked pies, fishcakes made from salmon and smoked haddock (something of a house specialty), or gourmet sandwiches and wraps. The dining room is a pleasant kind of space, and the staff is always friendly and cheerful. The cafe stays open into the evenings on Fridays and Saturdays in summer, when it sometimes serves thin-crust pizzas—a popular choice with locals. It does takeout too, useful if you're staying nearby and your hotel doesn't provide dinner.

5 Quay Rd., Ballycastle, Co. Antrim, BT54 6BJ. www.facebook.com/thymeand cocafe. ℂ **028/2076-9851.** Entrees £5–£12. Tues–Fri 8:30am–4:30pm, Sat 9:30am–4:30pm.

Sports & Outdoor Pursuits

ADVENTURE SPORTS   The **Ardclinis Activity Centre,** 11 High St., Cushendall, BT44 0NB (www.ardclinis.com; ℂ **028/2177-1340**), offers a range of year-round outdoor programs and courses, covering everything

---

The Red Hand of Ulster

Around Belfast and Northern Ireland, you'll frequently come across representations of a red hand. It's carved in door frames, painted on walls and ceilings, and even planted in red flowers in gardens. Known as the Red Hand of Ulster, it is one of the symbols of the region. According to one version of the old tale, the hand can trace its history from a battle between two men competing to be king of Ulster. They held a race (some say by boat; others say it took place on horseback) and agreed that the first man to touch Ulster soil would win. As one man fell behind, he pulled his sword and cut off his right hand, then with his left, flung the bloody hand ahead of his competitor, winning the right to rule.

from rock climbing and mountain biking to windsurfing and rafting, for people age 14 and over.

GOLF North Antrim has several notable courses, including champion pro golfer Darren Clarke's home course, the **Royal Portrush Golf Club,** Dunluce Road, Portrush (www.royalportrushgolfclub.com; ✆ **028/7082-2311**). Royal Portrush has two links courses; its celebrated Dunluce Course has been ranked number 3 in the United Kingdom. Greens fees here range from £205 on summer weekends to a mere £70 November to March.

PONY TREKKING **Watertop Farm Family Activity Centre,** 188 Cushendall Rd., Ballycastle (www.watertopfarm.co.uk; ✆ **028/2076-2576**), offers pony trekking and other outdoor activities. In the Portrush area, contact **Maddybenny Riding Centre,** Loguestown Road, Portrush (www.maddybenny.com; ✆ **028/7082-3394**); Maddybenny also has a good B&B (£80 double) and some self-catering cottages. In Castlerock you'll find **Hill Farm Riding and Trekking Centre,** 47 Altikeeragh Rd. (www.hillfarmridingcentre.co.uk; ✆ **028/7084-8629**). Fees are typically around £15 to £25 per hour-long ride.

WALKING A section of the **Ulster Way,** 904km (560 miles) of marked trail, follows the North Antrim Coast from Glenarm to Portstewart. The **Moyle Way** offers a spectacular inland detour from Ballycastle south for 37km (26 miles) to Glenariff Forest Park. Last, but far from least, the **Causeway Coast Path** stretches for 47km (33 miles) from Ballintoy Harbour in the east to Bushfoot Strand, near Bushmills, in the west. Short of sprouting wings, this is the best way to take in the full splendor of the North Antrim Coast. Comprehensive guides to each route, including downloadable maps of each stage, can be found on the excellent Northern Ireland walker's website **www.walkni.com**.

THE ARDS PENINSULA & MOURNE MOUNTAINS

The Ards Peninsula, beginning about 16km (10 miles) east of Belfast, curls around **Strangford Lough.** A wildlife reserve of great natural beauty, it's also lined with historic buildings and ancient sites, from the austere **Castle Ward** and the elegant **Mount Stewart House** to the mysterious, megalithic **Giant's Ring.** All are an easy drive from Belfast city center—you can reach most sights in half an hour, perfect for a day trip.

More outdoorsy types will want to press on to explore the Mourne Mountains, the highest mountains in Northern Ireland. The rocky landscape here is breathtaking—all gray granite, yellow gorse, purple heather, and white stone cottages. Remote and traversed by few roads, the mountains—complete with barren, windswept moors—are left to hikers and walkers. The ancestral home of the Brontës is here, in ruins. But the region is not desolate: You have forest parks, sandy beaches, lush gardens, and, of course, pubs to explore.

Visitor Information

The **Portaferry Tourist Information Office** at the Stables, Castle St., Portaferry (© **028/4272-9882**) is open daily Easter through September. The **Newcastle Tourist Information Centre** at 10–14 Central Promenade, Newcastle (© **028/4372-2222**) and the **Silent Valley Visitor Centre** on Head Road, Kilkeel, Newry (© **084/5744-0088**) are both open daily year-round.

Exploring the Ards Peninsula

Two roads traverse the **Ards Peninsula:** A20 (the Lough road) and A2 (the coast road). The Lough road is the more scenic. At the southern tip of the peninsula in Portferry; you'll need to take a 15-minute car ferry ride (www.nidirect.gov.uk/articles/strangford-ferry-timetable; © **030/0200-7898**) to get back to the mainland, in Strangford. Ferries run twice an hour more or less from 7:45am to 10:45pm (11:15pm on Sat).

Castle Espie Wetland Centre ★ NATURE SITE   This marvelous wildlife center, named for a castle that has long since ceased to be, is home to a virtual United Nations of rare migratory geese, ducks, and swans. Some birds are so accustomed to visitors that they will eat grain from their hands, so kids can have the disarming experience of meeting Hooper swans eye to eye. Guided trails are designed for children and families, and the center sponsors activities and events year-round. Every summer, the "duckery" becomes home to dozens of adorable, newly hatched goslings, ducklings, and cygnets. The book and gift shop is enticing, the kids' play area is excellent, and the restaurant serves good lunches and home-baked cakes.

78 Ballydrain Rd., Comber, Co. Down, BT23 6EA. www.wwt.org.uk/wetland-centres/castle-espie. © **028/9187-4146.** Admission £8 adults; £7 seniors and students; £4.50 children 4–16; children 3 and under free; £22 families. Daily 10am–5pm (5:30pm on summer weekends). In winter, last admission 3:30pm.

Castle Ward ★★ HISTORIC HOUSE   About 2km (1¼ miles) west of Strangford village, this grand manor house dates from 1760. A hybrid of architectural styles melding Gothic with neoclassical, it sits on a 280-hectare (692-acre) country estate. Inside, kids can dress up in period clothes and play with period toys, while outside they can roam formal gardens, woodlands, lakes, and seashore, and even ride a tractor-trailer out to see the farm animals. A theater in the stable yard hosts operatic performances in summer. Castle Ward has achieved a degree of latter-day fame as

khaleesi **DOES IT**

The most popular TV show in the world is filmed in Northern Ireland, and the publicity that HBO's *Game of Thrones* has brought to the region has been a massive boon for tourism. Major filming locations have included **Castle Ward** ★★ (p. 521); **Cushendun** ★ (p. 512) and **Ballintoy** (p. 513) on the Antrim Coast Drive; and the **Tollymore Forest Park** ★★ in County Down (p. 528). Several companies now offer locations tours, but some of the best, and longest-running, come from **Brit Movie Tours.**

The epic, 9-hour **Northern Locations with Giant's Causeway** tour takes in many of the most scenic places used in the show. It really packs in a lot, in addition to various fan-related fun along the way, such as a quiz (dressing up is not unheard of). It includes a 90-minute visit to the Causeway (p. 515), which hasn't actually appeared in the show (but it would seem silly to pass and not stop). Tours depart daily at 9am from the main tourism office in Donegall Square, Belfast, and return roughly 9 hours later. Tickets cost £35 adults and £20 children. Private tours, in a people carrier, can be booked for £360 to £570, depending on the number of people (maximum six).

The **Game of Thrones Filming Locations** tour, another 9-hour event, takes in some locations to the south of Belfast, including Castle Ward. This option includes even more in the way of Westerosian hijinks, including photo ops with the prop Direwolf pups used in the show (important note: not actual puppies) and the chance to sit on an imitation Iron Throne. Tours depart at 9am from Donegall Square, Belfast; from March to August, there are tours on Friday, Saturday, and Sunday; in February and September–October, tours are on certain Saturdays only. Call or go online to check the schedule and make reservations in advance, as this one runs less often than the Northern Locations tour. Tickets cost £55 adults and £40 children under 12, or £490 to £570 for the private version.

Disabled travelers should also note that, because of the historic and sometimes remote nature of the locations visited, neither tour is wheelchair-accessible.

For details and booking, call ℭ **0844/247-1007** in Northern Ireland and Britain (ℭ **44/207-118-1007** in the rest of the world) or visit **www.brit movietours.com**.

Winterfell, one of the key locations for HBO's *Game of Thrones* (above)—albeit heavily disguised.
Park Rd., Strangford, Co. Down, BT30 7LS. www.nationaltrust.org.uk/castle-ward. ℭ **028/4488-1204.** Admission £8.60 adults, £4.30 children; £21.50 families. Grounds: Apr–Oct daily 10am–6pm; Nov–Mar daily 10am–4pm. House: Mar–Oct daily noon–5pm. House closed Nov–Feb.

Giant's Ring ★★ ANCIENT SITE   Only a few miles from Belfast, this massive and mysterious prehistoric earthwork, 180m (590 ft.) in diameter, has at its center a megalithic chamber with a single capstone. Ancient burial rings like this were thought to be protected by fairies and were left untouched, but this one is quite an exception. In the 19th century, it was used as a racetrack, and the high embankment around it served as grandstands. Today, its dignity has been restored, and it is a place of wonder for the few travelers who make the journey. It's 6km (3¾ miles) southwest of Belfast center, west off A24.

Near Shaw's Bridge, off Ballynahatty Rd., Ballynahatty, Co. Down, BT8 8LE. Free admission (open site).

Grey Abbey ★ RELIGIOUS SITE   On the eastern shore of Strangford Lough, the striking ruins of Grey Abbey sit amid a beautifully landscaped setting, perfect for a picnic. Founded in 1193 by the Cistercians, it contained one of the earliest Gothic churches in Ireland. Many Cistercian ruins were quite elaborate, but this one is surprisingly plain. Amid the ruined choirs is a fragmented stone effigy of a knight in armor, possibly a likeness of John de Courcy, husband of the abbey's founder, Affreca of Cumbria. There's a reconstructed medieval herb garden, and a small visitor center has exhibits on the abbey's history.

Main St., Greyabbey, Co. Down, BT22 2NQ. ℂ **028/9181-1491.** Free admission. Abbey: Daily dawn–dusk. Visitor center: Mon–Thurs 8am–4:30pm, Fri 8am–1pm; closed Sat–Sun.

Legananny Dolmen ★ ANCIENT SITE   This renowned granite *dolmen* (Neolithic tomb) on the southern slope of Slieve Croob looks, in the words of one archaeologist, like "a coffin on stilts." This must be one of the most photographed dolmens in Ireland, but only when you see it up close can you fully appreciate its awesome size, with a massive capstone that seems weightlessly poised on supporting uprights. The dolmen is signposted about halfway between Dromara and Castelwellan on the lower slopes of Slieve Croob Mountain, about 40km (25 miles) south of Belfast.

Signposted off Legananny Rd. Leitrim, Co. Down, BT32 3QR. No phone. Free admission (open site).

Mount Stewart House, Garden, and Temple of the Winds ★★ HISTORIC HOUSE/GARDENS   Once the home of Lord Castlereagh, this 18th-century house sits on the eastern shore of Strangford Lough. Named one of the 10 best in the world by Britain's *Daily Telegraph* newspaper in 2014, its lush gardens are a candidate for UNESCO World Heritage status. An impressive array of unusual plants flourish here, thanks to a rare mild microclimate—the gardens almost never experience bad frosts. Inside the house, the excellent art collection includes the *Hambletonian* by George Stubbs and family portraits by Pompeo Batoni and Anton Raphael Mengs. The Temple of the Winds, a fine 18th-century banqueting house, is also on the estate, but it's only open Sunday afternoons (and not in winter). Admission to the house is by guided tour only.

Portaferry Rd., Newtownards, Co. Down, BT22 2AD. www.nationaltrust.org.uk/mount-stewart. ℂ **028/4278-8387.** House & Lakeside Garden: £9.50 adults; £4.70 children; £23.50 families. House: Mar–Oct daily 11am–5pm; Nov–Dec weekends 11am–3pm. Gardens: Mar–Oct daily 10am–6pm; Nov–Feb daily 10am–4pm. Temple: Mar–Oct Sun 2–5pm; closed Nov–Mar. Last admission 1 hr. before closing.

JOINING THE national trust

Several of Ulster's best historic sites are managed by the **National Trust,** a not-for-profit organization that preserves thousands of buildings and areas of natural beauty across the U.K. (including Northern Ireland), keeping them accessible to the public. Taking out a yearly membership gives you unlimited free admission to all of them, which can work out cheaper if you plan to visit several. If you also happen to be visiting Britain on your trip, or within the same year, it could be a wise investment.

The current membership costs are £67 for individuals, £110 for couples, and £74 to £118 for families. You can sign up for membership at any National Trust property, or join in advance online at **www.nationaltrust.org.uk**.

American visitors can also join the U.S. wing of the National Trust, the **Royal Oak Foundation**. Visit **www.royal-oak. org** or call ℂ **212/480-2889** or for more information. Royal Oak members get the same benefits, plus money off lectures, tours, and other special events held in the United States.

Nendrum Monastic Site ★ RELIGIOUS SITE   Hidden away on an isolated island, this site dates from the 5th century. It's much older than Grey Abbey across the water, and the remains of the ancient community founded by St. Mochaoi (St. Mahee) are fascinating. Foundations show the outline of ancient churches, a round tower, and beehive cells. Other interesting details are concentric stone ramparts and a sundial, reconstructed from long-broken pieces. Its visitor center shows informative videos and has insightful exhibits. The road to Mahee Island crosses a causeway to Reagh Island and a bridge still protected by the 15th-century Mahee Castle.

Mahee Island, Ringneill Rd., Comber, Co. Down, BT23 6EP. ℂ **028/9082-3207.** Free admission (open site). Visitor center: Apr–May Tues–Sun 10am–5pm; June to mid-Sept daily 10am–5pm; Mar and mid-Sept–Oct Tues–Sun noon–4pm; Nov–Feb Sun noon–4pm.

Portaferry Castle ★ CASTLE   Though it's little more than a small 16th-century tower house, at one time Portaferry Castle, together with another tower house in Strangford, controlled all the ship traffic through the Narrows. This piece of history stands right beside the Portaferry visitor center; it's worth popping your head in for a peek.

Castle St., Portaferry, Co. Down. Free admission. Easter–Aug daily 10am–5pm.

Exploring the Mourne Mountains

Below the Ards Peninsula, the A2 continues south to the **Mourne Mountains** area, although if you're going there directly from Belfast, the A24 is a good shortcut. The drive from Belfast directly to Newcastle should take just under an hour. If you're driving up from Dublin, turn east off the Dublin-Belfast Road at Newry and take A2, following the north shore of

Carlingford Lough, between the mountains and the sea. It's a drive you won't soon forget.

This outdoorsy region is dominated by the massive barren peak of **Slieve Donard** (839m/2,752 ft.). From the top, the view takes in the full length of Strangford Lough, Lough Neagh, the Isle of Man, and, on a crystalline day, the west coasts of Wales and Scotland. (The recommended ascent of Slieve Donard is from Donard Park on the south side of Newcastle.) If that's too high for you, head to the heart of the Mournes, to the exquisite **Silent Valley Reservoir** (see p. 527). Recreational opportunities abound (see p. 530), but it also has some intriguing old ruins to explore. **Newcastle,** a lively traditional seaside resort with a golden sand beach and one of the finest golf courses in Ireland, makes a good base for exploring the area; several small coastal towns strung along the A2 road—**Kilkeel, Rostrevor,** and **Warrenpoint**—offer their own low-key charms.

Castlewellan Forest Park ★★ NATURE SITE   Surrounding a fine trout lake and watched over by the stately mid-19th-century Castelwellan Castle (sadly closed to the public), this forest park just begs for picnics and outdoor activities. Woodland walks, a formal walled garden, and an interesting lakeside sculpture trail are among its attractions. Anglers can fish for trout (brown and rainbow) in the lake. The **Peace Maze,** planted in 2000, is an enormous hedge maze designed to represent the path to peace in Northern Ireland. The real draw is the **National Arboretum,** opened in 1740 and now 10 times its original size. The largest of its three greenhouses features aquatic plants and a collection of free-flying tropical birds. The town of Castlewellan, elegantly laid out around two squares, is a short distance away, as is the ancient fort of **Drumena Cashel** (see below).

Forest Office: The Grange, Castlewellan Forest Park, Castlewellan, Co. Down, BT31 9BU. 🕿 **028/4377-8664.** Admission and parking £5. Daily 10am–sunset.

Drumena Cashel ★ ANCIENT SITE   Ireland once had thousands of fortifications like this irregularly shaped stone-ring fort, a farmstead dating from the early Christian period; this is one of the better-preserved examples. During the age of the Viking invasions, it likely provided protection for the local

Canoeing on the lake at Castlewellan Forest Park.

DOWNPATRICK: sainted TOWN

Legend has it that when St. Patrick came to Ireland in A.D. 432 to begin his missionary work, strong winds blew his boat to the ancient fortified town of Downpatrick, at the south end of Strangford Lough. He'd meant to sail up the coast to County Antrim, where as a young slave he had tended flocks on Slemish Mountain. Instead, as fate would have it, he settled here and converted the local chieftain Dichu and his followers to Christianity. Over the next 30 years, Patrick roamed through Ireland carrying out his work, but this is where he died. Some believe he is buried in the graveyard of Downpatrick Cathedral, although there's no proof. Because of all of this, the town tends to be crowded, largely with Catholic pilgrims, around St. Patrick's Day.

Stop in first at the **Down County Museum** (www.downcountymuseum.com; ☏ **028/4461-5218**), the Mall, English St., BT30 6AH. Set in a converted jail, the museum tells the story of Down from the Stone Age to the present day. It also has a handy tearoom. The museum opens weekdays from 10am to 4:30pm and weekends 1:30 to 5pm. Entry is free.

Almost next door to the museum, at the end of the English Street cul-de-sac, is **Down Cathedral** (www.downcathedral.org; ☏ **028/4461-4922**). Excavations show that Downpatrick was a *dún* (fort), perhaps from the Bronze Age, and its earliest structures were built on the site where this church now sits. Ancient fortifications ultimately gave way to a series of churches, each built atop the ruins of the previous incarnation, over 1,800 years. The current cathedral is an 18th- and 19th-century reconstruction of its 13th- and 16th-century predecessors. Just south of the cathedral stands a relatively recent monolith inscribed with the name "Patric." By some accounts, it roughly marks the grave of the saint, who is said to have died at Saul, 3km (2 miles) northeast. The tradition identifying this site as Patrick's grave seems to go back no further than the 12th century, though, when John de Courcy reputedly transferred the bones of saints Columba and Brigid to lie beside those of St. Patrick. The cathedral is open to visitors Monday to Saturday from 9:30am to 4pm (and for services only on Sun). Entry is free.

A 5-minute walk away, the modern glass-and-steel **St. Patrick Centre,** 53A Market St., BT30 6LZ (www.saintpatrickcentre.com; ☏ **028/4461-9000**) tells the story of Ireland's patron saint through high-tech displays and exhibits. It also has an exhibition devoted to the legacy of Irish missionaries who helped spread Christianity in Europe in the latter half of the first millennium. The center is open Monday to Saturday from 9am to 5pm; also Sunday 1 to 5pm in July and August. Unsurprisingly, there's always something going on here on St. Patrick's Day. Entry costs £6 adults; £4 seniors, students, and children; and £14 families.

Downpatrick is about 34km (21 miles) southeast of Belfast. To get there from the city by car, take A24 then A7; the drive takes just under 40 minutes. You can also get there by bus (a 1-hr. trip) from the Europa Bus Station on Great Victoria Street.

population. Its walls, partially rebuilt in the mid-1920s, measure 2.7m (9 ft.) to 3.6m (12 ft.) thick. The *souterrain* (underground stone tunnel) is T-shaped and was likely used in ancient times for cold storage.

Signposted from A25, 3km (2 miles) SW of Castlewellan, Co. Down. Free (open site).

Dundrum Castle ★ CASTLE The oldest visible portions of this castle's striking and extensive ruins date from the 12th century. This was once one of the mightiest of the Norman castles in Northern Ireland (second only to Carrickfergus), and it still commands the imagination, if nothing else. It's on the site of an early Irish fortification (of which nothing is visible now). The enormous keep was built in the 13th century, as was the gatehouse. It was the home of the Maginnis family until the 17th century, when it was captured by Oliver Cromwell's army, who destroyed it in 1652. The hilltop setting is lovely, and the views from the keep's parapet are panoramic.

6.5km (4 miles) E of Newcastle, off A2, Dundrum, Co. Down, BT33 0NF. ℂ **028/9181-1491.** Free admission. Castle: June–Aug daily 10am–5pm; Mar–May and Sept Tues–Sun 10am–5pm; Oct–Mar Sun noon–4pm. Last admission 30 min. before closing. Grounds: Daily year-round.

Greencastle Royal Castle ★ CASTLE The first castle on this site, built in 1261, faced its companion, Carlingford Castle, across the mouth of the lough. It was then a two-story rectangular tower surrounded by a curtain wall with corner towers. Very little of that survives; most of what you see is from the 14th century. It served as a royal garrison until it was destroyed by Cromwell's forces in 1652. Opening times are somewhat unpredictable, so if you want to see inside, call ahead.

6.5km (4 miles) SW of Kilkeel, Greencastle, Cranfield Point, Co. Down, BT34 4LR. ℂ **028/9082-3207.** Free admission. July–Sept daily 10am–5pm. Closed Oct–June.

Silent Valley Mountain Park ★★ NATURE SITE Created by the Mourne Wall (see box p. 529) and dam, the Silent Valley Reservoir is the major source of water for County Down. Easy, well-marked paths wind around the lake, and there's a coffee shop by the Silent Valley Information Centre. A shuttle bus takes visitors from the center to the top of nearby Ben Crom; it runs on weekends in May, June, and September and daily in July and August.

Information Centre: Head Rd., Kilkeel, Newry, Co. Down, BT34 4HU www.niwater.com/silent-valley. ℂ **084/5744-0088.** Free admission. Parking £5 per car. May–Sept daily 10am–6:30pm; Oct–Apr daily 10am–4pm.

Hiking the Mourne Mountains.

Tollymore Forest Park ★★ NATURE SITE All that's left of the once-glorious Tollymore House is this delightful 480-hectare (1,186-acre) wildlife and forest park. The park offers a number of walks up into the north slopes of the Mourne Mountains or along the Shimna River (known for its exceptionally fine salmon). The Shimna walk has several beguiling little landmarks, including caves and grottos. The park is scattered with follies, such as faux-medieval castle gatehouses and other fanciful fakes. The forest is a nature preserve inhabited by a host of local wildlife like badgers, foxes, otters, and pine martens. And don't miss the trees for the forest—some exotic species here include the magnificent Himalayan cedars and a 30m (98-ft.) sequoia in the arboretum.

Off B180, 3.2km (2 miles) NW of Newcastle, Tullybrannigan Rd., Newcastle, County Down. ✆ **028/4372-2428.** Free admission. Parking £5. Daily 10am–dusk.

Where to Stay in the Ards Peninsula & Mourne Mountains

Ards Peninsula sights are close enough to Belfast to allow you to get back to your Belfast hotel for the night, but if you're venturing out to the Mourne Mountains—particularly if you're engaging in the outdoor activities for which the area is justly famed—you'll need a place to lay your head overnight.

The Carriage House ★★ With a view of Dundrum Castle on one side, and a shimmering bay dotted with sailboats on the other, it's little wonder that this lovely little B&B inspires artistic sentiment. Owner Maureen Griffith is a collector of unique art, and her creative eye has furnished almost every corner of her terraced house with something wonderful to look at. She's also a great cook; breakfasts here are special, including produce picked fresh from the garden. She doesn't cook evening meals, but will recommend places to eat within walking distance.

71 Main St., Dundrum, Co. Down, BT33 0LU. www.carriagehousedundrum.com. ✆ **028/4375-1635.** 3 units. £80 double. Free parking (on street). Breakfast included. **Amenities:** Garden; Wi-Fi (free).

Dunnanelly Country House ★★★ Just outside Downpatrick, this delightful country mansion is a truly idyllic retreat, set on beautiful grounds that stretch for miles. The decor inside mixes a feeling of history with a playful edge: traditional, Regency-style color schemes and furnishings offset by pieces of modern art, an interesting sculpture, or (memorably) an antique rocking horse, complete with mouth open in an oh-so-happy-to-see-you grin. The guest rooms are thoughtfully designed with large, modern bathrooms and have lovely views of the estate, tempting you to take a gentle stroll or invigorating hike. And you may need that exercise to help work off the hearty and delicious breakfasts. Guests have the use of a conservatory, a sitting room, and a separate game room.

Between 1904 and 1922, the 36km (22-mile) dry-stone Mourne Wall and dam was built to enclose Silent Valley. The **Mourne Wall Trek** follows the wall in a circuit that climbs over 15 of the Mourne Mountains' main peaks. The steep path is more than most hikers want to take on, and probably shouldn't be attempted in a single day (though some serious hikers have done it in a day). But it is a fine, long walk for experienced ramblers and offers wonderful views. You can join the pathway at several different places, and you can hike either clockwise or counter-clockwise. For more information about the route, including maps and a photo log of every stage, go to **www.mourne wall.co.uk**.

There's no dinner, but the owners can cheerfully point you in the direction of the best local pubs.

26 Rocks Chapel Rd., Downpatrick, Co. Down, BT30 9BA. www.dunnanelly countryhouse.com. ☎ **077/1277-9085.** 6 units. £100 double. Free parking. Breakfast included. No children under 12 unless all 3 rooms booked by same group. **Amenities:** Wi-Fi (free).

The Slieve Donard Spa and Resort ★★ The spindly, neo-Gothic turret of this 1897 hotel stands like a beacon overlooking Dundrum Bay. The surroundings are certainly dramatic, but inside this is a relaxing, luxurious place. Bedrooms are good-sized and modern; many have views of the bay and Mourne Mountains. Executive bedrooms are bigger and have air-conditioning—a bonus if you're visiting during a rare heat wave. The excellent spa has a long list of treatments, from Ayurvedic regimens to hot stone massages and full-body salt scrubs. (Prices aren't cheap, however—expect to pay between £75 and £170 for a 1- to 2-hour signature treatment.) The two restaurants are the formal **Oak Room** and the more relaxed **Percy French.** Dinner-bed-and-breakfast packages offer good savings.

Downs Rd., Newcastle, Co. Down, BT33 0AH. www.hastingshotels.com. ☎ **028/ 4372-1066.** 180 units. £180 double. Free parking. Breakfast included. **Amenities:** 2 restaurants; bar; gym; pool; room service; spa; Wi-Fi (£10 per day).

Where to Eat in the Ards Peninsula & Mourne Mountains

Brunel's ★★★ IRISH Local flavors are prepared with imaginative flair at this excellent restaurant just a mile from the Slieve Donard Spa and Resort (see above). Mussels fresh from Strangford Lough are a simple but choice lead-in to a dish of coley (a fish similar to cod) cooked with chorizo risotto and red pepper caramel, or lamb with hazelnut puree and samphire. This is the kind of place where you'll witness a sea of cellphones taking photos of each course before commencing demolition of the artful

15

DAY TRIPS FROM BELFAST

The Ards Peninsula & Mourne Mountains

arrangements on the plate. The early-evening menu is a bargain—two courses for just £17, or three for £19—served until 7:30pm Wednesday to Friday. Another moneysaving tip: Main dishes at lunch generally cost half, or even a third, of what you pay in the evening.

32 Downs Rd, Newcastle, Co. Down, BT33 0HJ. www.brunelsrestaurant.co.uk. ☏ **028/4372-3951.** Entrees £16–£28. Mon–Tues 10am–2:30pm; Wed–Thurs 10am–2:30pm, 5:30–9pm; Fri–Sat 10am–2:30pm, 5:30–9:30pm; Sun 10am–8pm.

The Daily Grind ★ CAFE   A great place to know about for a quick lunch in Downpatrick, this funky cafe is a favorite of locals. It specializes in creative and tasty sandwiches, which go down nicely with a cup of fresh coffee if you can forgive the atrociously punning names ("Buy One Get One Brie," "Pitta Pocket or Two"—you get the idea). Try the Daily Grind Special, a delicious salad served with toast and chili jam. It also does tempting gateaux. The cafe closes at a disappointing early 3:30pm, however—you may want to have your afternoon treat a little early.

St. Patrick's Ave., Downpatrick, BT30 6DW. ☏ **028/4461-7173.** Entrees £4–£7. Mon–Sat 10am–3:30pm.

Mourne Seafood Bar ★★ SEAFOOD   Situated just a street back from the quay in Dundrum, this seaside outpost of one of Belfast's best restaurants (see p. 502) is worth traveling for if you're staying in the countryside—or worth a detour for a leisurely lunch. The menu is strictly oriented around whatever's good and fresh that day, but you may well be offered crab claws with chili butter, smoked haddock with potato cake and leek, or scallops with linguini and wilted greens. Prices are surprisingly reasonable, too. The only real snag is that it's hardly an undiscovered gem—you'll be lucky to get a table for dinner without a reservation on weekends, especially in summer.

10 Main St., Dundrum, Co. Down, BT33 0LU. www.mourneseafood.com. ☏ **028/4375-1377.** Entrees £12–£15. Thurs–Fri 12:30–3pm, 5–10pm; Sat–Sun 12:30–10pm. Closed Mon–Wed.

Sports & Outdoor Pursuits

ADVENTURE SPORTS   For canoeing, rock climbing, bushcraft, watersports, and a variety of other intrepid activities in the Mourne Mountains, contact **One Great Adventure,** the Grange Yard, Castlewellan Forest Park, Castlewellan (www.onegreatadventure.com; ☏ **028/4377-0714**).

CYCLING   The foothills of the Mournes around Castlewellan are ideal for cycling, with panoramic vistas and very little traffic. In these parts, the perfect year-round outfitter is **Ross Cycles,** 44 Clarkhill Rd. (☏ **028/4377-8029**), signposted from the Clough-Castlewellan Road, .8km (½ mile) out of Castlewellan. The shop carries mountain bikes for the whole family, including children's seats. You can park and ride, or request local delivery. Daily rates start at around £10, with family and weekly rates available.

Biking through the Mourne Mountains.

DIVING   The Ards Peninsula's loughs and offshore waters are a diver's dream—remarkably clear and littered with wrecks. One of Europe's finest training centers, **DV Diving,** 138 Mount Stewart Rd., Newtownards, County Down (www.dvdiving.co.uk; 𝄞 **028/9186-1686**), offers diving courses.

GOLF   **Royal County Down ★**, Newcastle, County Down (www.royal countydown.org; 𝄞 **028/4372-3314**), is nestled in huge sand dunes with the Mourne Mountains in the background. This 18-hole, par-71 championship course was created in 1889 and is still considered to be among the best. Greens fees are £220 to £240, depending on the day and time of year. (In winter and early spring, prices drop to £85–£125.) Not too far away, the **Kilkeel Golf Club,** Mourne Park, Ballyardle, Kilkeel (www.kilkeel golfclub.org; 𝄞 **028/4176-5095**), is a beautiful parkland course on the historic Kilmorey Estate. Greens fees are around £20 to £35, less on Mondays and Wednesdays.

HORSEBACK RIDING   The **Mount Pleasant Trekking & Horse Riding Centre,** Bannonstown Rd., Castlewellan (www.mountpleasantcentre. com; 𝄞 **028/4377-8651**), offers group trekking tours into **Castlewellan Forest Park** (see p. 525). For riding in **Tollymore Forest Park** (see p. 528) or on local trails, contact the **Mourne Trail Riding Centre,** 96 Castlewellan Rd., Newcastle, County Down (www.mournetrailridingcentre.co.uk; 𝄞 **028/4372-4351**). It has quality horses and offers beach rides for skilled riders. Expect to pay around £25 per hour.

COUNTY ARMAGH

A green, rolling stretch of gentle hills and small villages, County Armagh is also one of Northern Ireland's most rebellious Republican regions—you'll notice police watchtowers atop some hills, as well as the occasional barracks (mostly empty these days).

The handsome cathedral town of Armagh City makes a good touring base. A short distance outside the city, the small town of Bessbrook has historic cottages, the forests of Slieve Gullion, and ancient Navan Fort, the most important archaeological site in Ulster. The area's greatest natural attraction is a 40-minute drive north of Armagh City: Lough Neagh, Ireland's largest lake (see box p. 535).

Visitor Information

The **Armagh Visitor Information Centre,** 40 Upper English St., Armagh (© **028/3752-1800**), is the main information point for the surrounding area. It's open all year, daily from 9:30am to 5:30pm.

Exploring County Armagh

Armagh City's name, from the Irish *ard Macha* (Macha's height), refers to the pagan queen Macha, who is said to have built a fortress here. It's no coincidence that St. Patrick chose to base himself here when he was spreading Christianity—it was a bold challenge to the native paganism. The simple stone church that he built in the 5th century is now the stately St. Patrick's Church of Ireland Cathedral (p. 534). (Not to be outdone, Armagh City's Roman Catholic cathedral is also called St. Patrick's—see p. 534.) East of the town center, the city also boasts The Mall, a lush park lined with handsome Georgian town houses built of the colorful local limestone. To get to Armagh City from Belfast, take M1 and A3 southwest for 64km (40 miles); the journey takes a little less than an hour.

Armagh County Museum ★ MUSEUM   Intriguing Armagh-related artifacts going back to the Neolithic Age fill this history museum on the Mall. Highlights include a collection of 19th-century Irish bog oak jewelry; Irish police uniforms from the 1820s up to the mid–20th century; and a collection of elaborate fans from around the world, from as far back as the 1700s. Chillingly, the museum also has a genuine scold's bridle, an iron torture instrument and "correctional" device that was placed over a woman's head, with a spike inside her mouth to prevent her from talking. It's part of the same National Museums Northern Ireland collective that includes the excellent **Ulster Museum ★★★** (see p. 490) and the **Folk & Transport Museum ★★★** (see p. 495).

The Mall East, Armagh City, BT61 9BE. www.armagh.co.uk/armaghcountymuseum. © **028/3752-3070.** Free admission. Mon–Fri 10am–5pm; Sat 10am–1pm, 2–5pm. Closed Sun.

Armagh Observatory and Planetarium ★★ PLANETARIUM

This state-of-the-art planetarium is a fantastic place for kids with an interest in science and astronomy. The digital projection system, which has 3D elements, is impressive. Shows with dramatic, spacey titles such as "Beyond the Blue" or "Edge of Darkness," full of crashes and zooms and loud space facts, run every weekday afternoon (usually at 1 or 2pm); on Saturdays from 11am to 4pm, shows range from the gentle 15-minute "Astronaut George," aimed at very young children, to documentaries on constellations and astronomers. *Note:* All seats must be booked in advance, and you must arrive 30 minutes before

The historic Armagh Observatory, next to the state-of-the-art Armagh Astronomy Centre.

start time to pick up your tickets. During summer (and other school vacation periods) there's usually a full program every day. Outside the planetarium, take a stroll around the **Astropark**, filled with scale models of planets. You'll pass the 200-year-old **Armagh Observatory** (still a working observatory and not open to the public).

College Hill, Armagh City, BT61 9DB. www.armaghplanet.com. *(*) **028/3752-3689.** Admission to show and exhibition area £6 adults; £5 seniors and children under 16; £20 families. Mon–Sat 10am–5pm. Closed Sun.

Benburb Valley Park ★★ NATURE SITE

This rather lovely sylvan park 11km (7 miles) northeast of Armagh on the River Blackwater contains the ruins of **Benburb Castle**, a squat fortress-like ruin dating from the Plantation of Ulster in the early 1600s. It occupies an impressive cliffside spot overlooking a gorge. In 1646, an Irish army defeated an Anglo-Scottish invasion force at Benburb, thus ending the brief Scottish bid to rule Ireland. The castle is on the grounds of a Servite priory; admission is free, but you have to arrange in advance if you want to do more than see it from the outside. Call the priory at *(*) **028/375-8241** for more information, or contact the nearby **Benburb Valley Heritage Centre** (*(*) **028/3754-9885**), which has exhibits on the area's history.

89 Milltown Rd., Benburb (take B128 off A29), Co. Armagh, BT71 7LY. *(*) **028/3754-8170.** Park: Free admission. Heritage Centre: £3. Park daily until dusk. Heritage Centre Apr–Sept Mon–Sat 10am–5pm.

Navan Fort and Centre ★★ ANCIENT SITE Believed to have been the royal and religious capital of Ulster from 1150 B.C. until the spread of Christianity, the Navan Fort is a mysterious place. Its central circular earthwork enclosure holds a smaller circular structure, and it all encloses an Iron Age burial mound. Even today, scientists do not really know what it was used for, although they know that it was all set on fire around 95 B.C., possibly as part of a ritual. The excellent interpretive center puts it all into context, complete with exhibition and reconstructed Iron Age houses. Admission rates are discounted slightly in the winter.

On A28, signposted from Armagh center, 81 Killylea Rd., Co. Armagh, BT60 4LD. www.armagh.co.uk/navan-centre-fort. ✆ **028/3752-9644.** Admission Apr–Sept £6.80 adults; £4.50 children; £5.60 seniors and students; £18.50 families. Admission Oct–Mar £5.60 adults; £4.20 seniors and students; £3.40 children; £16.40 families. Apr–Sept daily 10am–5:30pm (last admission 4pm); Oct–Mar daily 10am–4pm (last admission 3pm).

Peatlands Park ★ NATURE SITE As the name implies, Peatlands Park is a park filled with peat. It's also big—more than 240 hectares (593 acres)—and the peat bogs and small lakes are surprisingly lovely. The whole thing is a nature reserve, so you wander through it on a well-designed system of walking paths, or, slightly more fun on rainy days, you ride through it on a narrow-gauge railway. Nature walks and events are offered through the year. The park is southwest of Lough Neagh, just across the border into County Tyrone.

33 Derryhubbert Rd. 11km (6¾ miles) SE of Dungannon, at exit 13 off M1, Co Tyrone, BT71 6NW. ✆ **028/3839-9195.** Free admission to park. Rail ride £3 adults; £2 seniors and children 5–16; £5 families; free for children 4 and under. Vehicle access to park May to mid-Sept daily 9am–9pm; Apr and mid-Sept to Oct daily 9am–7pm; Nov–Mar daily 9am–4:30pm. Railway July–Aug Sat, Sun, and bank holiday Mon only 1–4pm.

St. Patrick's Church of Ireland Cathedral ★ CATHEDRAL Built on the site of St. Patrick's 5th-century church, Armagh's Anglican cathedral dates from the 13th century, although much of the current square-towered brown stone church was built in the 1830s. Inside the church are the remains of an 11th-century Celtic cross, and a strange granite carved figure known as the Tandragee Idol, which dates from the Iron Age. A stone slab on the exterior wall of the north transept marks the spot where Brian Boru, the high king of Ireland who died in the last great battle with the Vikings in 1014, is buried.

43 Abbey St, Armagh City, BT61 7DY. www.stpatricks-cathedral.org. ✆ **028/3752-3142.** Admission £3 adults; £2 seniors and students; free for children. Apr–Oct daily 9am–5pm; Nov–Mar daily 9am–4pm.

St. Patrick's Roman Catholic Cathedral ★ CATHEDRAL Built in the mid-1800s, this Catholic cathedral is a grand Gothic Revival building on a hill, its slim twin spires dominating its portion of the town. Outside it's monochromatic gray, but inside is another story, as vividly painted

LOUGH neagh

Now here's a great creation story: Irish lore maintains that Lough Neagh—the largest lake in Ireland—was created by the mighty giant Fionn MacCumhail (Finn McCool) when he dug up a chunk of earth to fling into the sea to create the Isle of Man. It must have been a sizeable chunk indeed, to gouge out this 396sq.-km (153 sq.-mile) lake.

The **Lough Neagh Discovery Centre**, Oxford Island, Craigavon, Co. Armagh (www.oxfordisland.com; ☏ **028/ 3832-2205**), is open Monday to Friday 9am to 5pm and Saturday and Sunday 10am to 5pm (6pm Apr–Sept). Admission is free. Part of an enormous, lush nature reserve, the center has an exhibition on the Lough and its history, plus information about the best walking trails. It also hosts occasional guided walks (or "rambles") through the reserve; prices and times of any upcoming tours are advertised on the website. There's also a cafe, craft shop, and tourist information center—where, handily, you can rent a pair of binoculars.

However, before you think about taking a dip in the cool, glassy waters,

consider this: The lake's claim to fame is its massive population of eels. Yep, the waters are positively infested with the slimy creatures. Hundreds of tons of eels are taken from Lough Neagh and exported each year, mainly to Germany and Holland. The ages-old eel-extraction method involves "long lines," baited with up to 100 hooks. As many as 200 boats trailing these lines are on the lake each night (the best time to go fishing for eels). So maybe take a raincheck on that swim.

If you're not entirely creeped out by that, however, you can take a **boat trip** on the lovely lake. Boats depart regularly from the nearby **Kinnego Marina** (☏ **028/ 3832-7573**), signposted from the main road. The trip lasts about 45 minutes and costs about £10 for adults, £7 for children. It's advisable to call in advance to book.

For windsurfing on Lough Neagh, try **Craigavon Watersports Centre,** 1 Lake Rd., Craigavon, County Armagh, BT64 1AS (www.craigavonactivity.org/ watersports-centre; ☏ **028/3834-2669**).

mosaics bathe it in color. Unfortunately, a renovation in the 1980s added some modern touches that stand out starkly against its otherwise perfect 19th-century authenticity.

Cathedral Rd., Armagh City, BT61 7QX. www.armaghparish.net. ☏ **028/3752-2813.** Free admission. Daily 8am–dusk. Opening times can vary; call to check.

Where to Stay & Eat in County Armagh

Cross Square Hotel ★   This humble but pleasant inn sits on the main square in Crossmaglen, a little village about 20 miles south of Armagh town. Guest rooms are modern and fairly spacious; some overlook the square itself. Family rooms are enormous, with space enough for six people. A very good in-house restaurant has won awards locally—handy in a part of the country with limited options when it comes to dining. The restaurant also serves traditional afternoon tea (book ahead). The downstairs bar sometimes has live music sessions on weekends—these can go on late, so light sleepers beware. Service is efficient and friendly.

Crossmaglen is near the border with the Republic; it only takes slightly longer to drive here from Dublin than it does from Belfast (about an hour and 15 min.), so this could be a good stop if you're working your way up through Northern Ireland from the southern end.

O'Fiaich Sq., Crossmaglen, Co. Armagh, BT35 9AA. www.crosssquarehotel.co.uk. ℰ **028/3086-0505.** 15 units. £95 double. Free parking. Breakfast included. **Amenities:** Wi-Fi (free).

Embers ★★ CAFE/GRILL   For a reviving snack or meal in Armagh town, check out this casual spot, a 3-minute walk from St. Patrick's Church of Ireland Cathedral (p. 534). Embers serves great coffee and sandwiches, plus a full menu of crowd-pleasing bar-food favorites. It's very much "something for everyone" territory—fish and chips, fajitas, ribs, steaks, salads, and so on. Chase it all down with a comforting plate of deep-dish apple pie, served with a scoop of ice cream. The early-bird special—available every day except Sunday from 5 to 7pm—is an excellent value at £13 for two courses, £15 for three.

7 Market St., Armagh City, BT61 7BW. www.embersrestaurant.co.uk. ℰ **028/3751-8544.** Entrees £10–£22. Sun–Thurs 9am–9:15pm, Fri–Sat 9am–10:30pm.

Newforge House ★★★   What's not to love? Great food, warm hosts, and a restful night's sleep in a four-poster bed await you in this idyllic country mansion, only a half-hour's drive southwest of Belfast. Host John Mathers, whose family has owned this house since it was built in the early 18th century, is a trained chef, and his gourmet dinners are a real treat. (It's also open to non-guests, so be sure to make dinner reservations by noon on the day.) Seasonal menus, prepared with many ingredients from the house's own garden, feature local meats and seafood. Guest rooms are spacious and light-filled, with floor-to-ceiling windows; one room has a four-poster, while another has a king-size canopy bed. Check the website for special offers, including romantic weekend breaks.

58 Newforge Rd., Magheralin (halfway btw. Lisburn and Craigavon), Co. Armagh, BT67 0QL. www.newforgehouse.com. ℰ **028/9261-1255.** 6 units. £129–£199 double. 2-night minimum on certain dates. Free parking. Breakfast included. Dinner £40. **Amenities:** Wi-Fi (free).

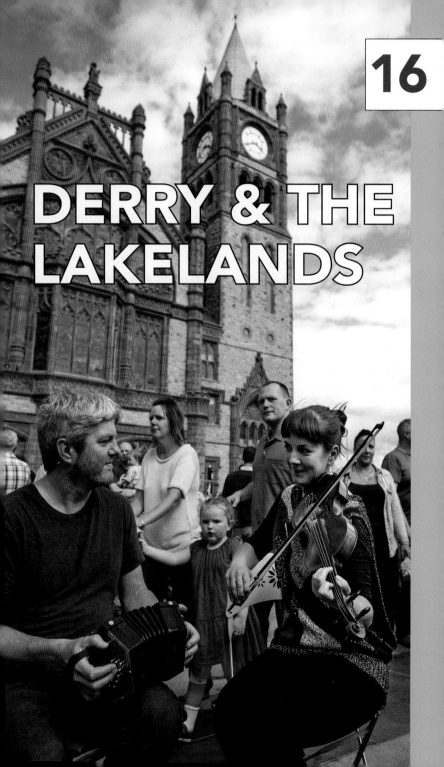

16

DERRY & THE LAKELANDS

You'd expect a city with two names to have some stories to tell. And sure enough, Northern Ireland's second city is full of surprises. Derry—officially, but by no means universally, called Londonderry—is reveling in an identity reboot. The 20th century was unkind to this city, where some of the very worst times of the so-called "Troubles" played out. For years its name—sorry, *names*—may as well have been printed on a traveler's map next to the medieval warning "Here Be Dragons." It was a place to avoid. But things have changed enormously in the past 2 decades, and in the 21st century, an undeniable spirit of optimism and renewal now reigns. While it's still not as handsome or buzzing as Belfast, the energy propelling Derry's cultural shift makes this a fascinating time to visit.

Derry is also strategically located, with the Northwest Passage and the Sperrins (see p. 550) all within an hour's drive. It's conveniently also at the edge of Donegal's picturesque Inishowen Peninsula (see chapter 13), with the Giant's Causeway and the North Antrim Coast (see p. 513) within day-trip distance. This makes Derry an ideal base of operations from which to explore some of Ireland's most unspoiled regions.

ESSENTIALS
Arriving

BY PLANE   Service to **Derry Airport** (www.cityofderryairport.com; ℂ **028/7181-0784**) is provided by the budget airline **Ryanair** (www.ryanair.com; ℂ **0818/303030** in Ireland, 0871/246-0000 in the U.K.) from London Stansted, Liverpool, and Glasgow, plus a limited service to and from Majorca in Spain.

BY TRAIN   **Northern Ireland Railways** (www.translink.co.uk; ℂ **028/9066-6630**) operates frequent trains from Belfast, which arrive at the Londonderry/Derry Station—known by everyone as **Waterside Railway Station** (ℂ **028/7134-2228**), on Duke Street, on the east side of the Foyle River. The journey takes about 2 hours. A free Linkline bus brings passengers from the train station to the city center.

BY BUS   The fastest bus between Belfast and Derry, the no. 212, operated by **Ulsterbus** (www.translink.co.uk; ℂ **028/9066-6630**), takes just under 2 hours. Ulsterbus also has service from Portrush and Portstewart. From the Republic, **Bus Éireann** (www.buseireann.ie; ✆ **091/562000**) offers a few buses a day from Galway (about 5½ hr.), Cork (7–9 hr.), and Dublin (around 6 hr.). Most of the long-distance routes involve changes.

DERRY CITY

Northern Ireland's second city is a vibrant place, surrounded by 17th-century walls that you can climb, walking the ramparts all the way around the town center. Although they were the focus of attacks and sieges for centuries, the 5-foot-thick fortifications are solid and unbroken to this day. Historians believe the city was modeled on the French Renaissance town of Vitry-Le-Francois, which in turn was based on a Roman military camp, with two main streets forming a central cross and ending in four city gates. It's made for walking, combining a medieval center with sprawling Georgian and Victorian neighborhoods.

Within Ireland, though, Derry is not known for its architecture, but for the fact that, in the 1960s and 1970s, the North's civil rights movement was born here, and baptized in blood on the streets. The "Bloody Sunday" massacre in 1972, in which British troops killed 14 peaceful civil rights protesters in Derry, shocked the world and led to years of violent unrest. In the **Bogside,** as the neighborhood at the bottom of the hill west of the walled section is known, the famed mural reading "You Are Now Entering Free Derry" remains as a symbol of those times.

The sculpture *Hands Across the Divide* symbolizes an end to sectarian strife.

DERRY OR LONDONDERRY: what's in a name?

The short answer is: quite a lot.

Depending on which side of the border you're on, Northern Ireland's second city is called two different things. Road signs and maps in the Republic say **Derry;** in Northern Ireland they point to **Londonderry.**

This stubborn dispute dates to the Plantation of Ulster in the 1600s, when English settlers were given land in Ireland as an attempt to entrench Protestant rule. A new city was founded by the City of London trade guilds and named Londonderry in their honor. Nationalists have always objected to the term, preferring Derry, an Anglicization of *Daire Calgaich,* the name of the much older settlement that once stood on the same site.

During the Troubles, the dispute was a cause celebre. Many attempts have been made to find a solution, including several unsuccessful court cases. Loyalists fiercely defend the name. But having a city with two names poses a knotty problem for residents and visitors alike—what to call it?

The best advice is just to be tactful. If you're drinking in a pub with a big Irish tricolor on the side, it's probably best to use Derry; but if they're flying the British flag, opt for Londonderry. Of the two, Derry is probably the more commonly used in town, and certainly throughout the Republic, so we've chosen to call it Derry in this book.

Fed up with having to make a political statement whenever they talk about their own city, residents have long since tried to find an acceptable solution to the Derry/Londonderry dilemma. In the 1990s, local radio DJ Gerry Anderson suggested the wry compromise "Stroke City." (American readers: Stroke is a slash in the U.K.) Quick-witted locals swiftly nicknamed the DJ "Gerry/Londongerry."

To see more evidence of how far back this titular dispute goes, look no further than a United States road atlas. Near Manchester, New Hampshire, is a small old town called Derry. In the early 19th century there was a dispute over its name, so a group of residents set up a new town just to the south called—you guessed it—Londonderry.

Happily, much of that sectarian strife seems to be behind Derry now, and it has begun to reinvent itself as a center of culture and commerce. Symbolic of the changes in Derry is the ***Hands Across the Divide*** sculpture that you pass as you cross the Craigavon Bridge into town. Erected 20 years after Bloody Sunday, it is a bronze sculpture of two men reaching out toward one another.

Visitor Information

The **Derry Tourist Information Centre** is at 44 Foyle St., Derry, B48 6AT (www.visitderry.com/Visitor-Info/Visitor-Information-Centre; ✆ **028/ 7126-7284**). It's open daily year-round; from May to September, hours are Monday to Saturday 9am to 6pm (7pm June–Aug) and Sunday 10am to 5pm; in April and October the hours are Monday to Friday 9am to 5:30pm and Sunday 10am to 5pm; and from November to March the hours are Monday to Friday 9:30am to 5pm and Sunday 10am to 4pm.

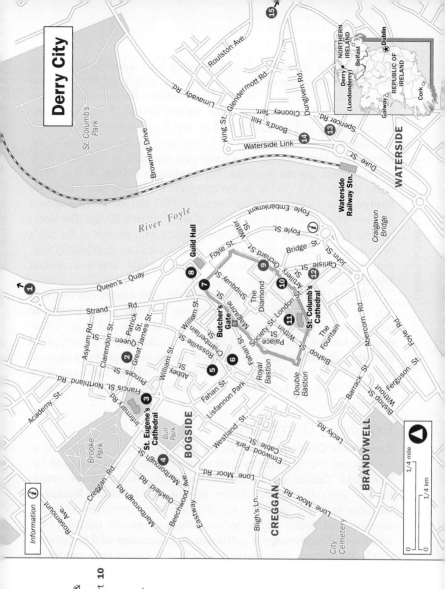

Derry City

ATTRACTIONS

Bloody Sunday Monument & Bogside Murals **6**
Centre for Contemporary Art **10**
Guildhall **8**
Museum of Free Derry **5**
St. Columb's Cathedral **11**
St. Eugene's Cathedral **3**
Tower Museum **7**

WHERE TO STAY

Saddler's House & the Old Rectory **2**
Serendipity House **4**
Troy Hall **1**

WHERE TO EAT

Badgers **9**
The Belfray Country Inn Bistro **15**
Browns **14**
Primrose Café **12**
The Sooty Olive **13**

City Layout

The focal point of Derry is the **Diamond,** a large square holding a war memorial in the center of the city. Four streets radiate out from the Diamond: Bishop, Ferryquay, Shipquay, and Butcher. Each extends for several blocks and ends at a gateway (Bishop's Gate, Ferryquay Gate, Shipquay Gate, and Butcher's Gate) cut into the thick city walls.

Although the original walled city was built on the west bank of the River Foyle, Derry has spread across to the east bank as well, with three bridges connecting the two sides. The **Craigavon Bridge,** built in 1933, is one of only a few double-decker bridges in the British Isles. The **Foyle Bridge,** Ireland's longest bridge, opened in 1984 and provides a dual-lane highway about 3.2km (2 miles) north of the Craigavon Bridge. The sleek, modern **Peace Bridge** links Ebrington Square with the rest of the city's central area. Its name refers to the fact that it joins two traditionally warring districts, the mostly Catholic **Cityside** and the largely Protestant **Waterside.**

West of the river are two major areas: the walled **inner city** and, outside the walls to the west, the area known as the **Bogside. Waterside** refers to streets near the waterfront, where most hotels and many restaurants are located. Also in Waterside is a small grassy viewing point called the **Top of the Hill,** where you can enjoy spectacular eagle's-eye views of the city. You'll never find your own way there, so take a taxi and bring your map. Short of a helicopter tour, this is the best way to get your initial bearings.

Exploring Derry City

Centre for Contemporary Art ★ ART MUSEUM   Drop in here to see new and touring works by contemporary artists from Ireland and farther afield. Themed seasons include visual art, film screenings, performances, and public debates. Recent seasons have included a fascinating but rather gruesome immersive installation centered around the concept of microbes and decay; and a performance-based project linking LGBT issues with climate change. It's all serious and fascinating stuff for grownup minds. With strong international links, the center often hosts residencies for artists from across the globe. Admission to most events is free, but there may be a charge for some; check website for up-to-date listings.

10–12 Artillery St., Derry, BT48 6RG. www.cca-derry-londonderry.org. © **028/7137-3538.** Free admission. Tues–Sat noon–6pm.

Guildhall ★ ARCHITECTURAL SITE   Just outside the city walls, between Shipquay Gate and the River Foyle, this Tudor Gothic–style building looks much like its counterpart in London. The site's original structure was constructed in 1890, but it was rebuilt after a fire in 1908 and again after a series of sectarian bombings in 1972. The hall is

THE bogside: THE PEOPLE'S GALLERY

In many ways, the recent history of Derry is embodied in the district known as the Bogside. In the 1960s and 1970s, the neighborhood bore witness to violent scenes that shocked the world. Today, it's known as much for its powerful street art, chronicling those troubled decades of the late 20th century.

Located just outside the walled city center, the Bogside was developed in the 19th and early 20th centuries as a home for Catholic workers. In the late 1960s, civil rights protests became regular events here, and the residents declared their neighborhood as "Free Derry," independent of local and British government. The situation came to a head on January 30, 1972, later to be known as "Bloody Sunday," when British troops opened fire on a peaceful demonstration, killing 14 civilians. The soldiers said they'd been fired upon first; eventually, in 2010, after an inquiry that lasted 12 years and cost nearly £200 million, the British government finally accepted this was completely untrue and apologized.

Most of the Bogside has been redeveloped, but the Free Derry corner remains, near a house painted with the mural reading "YOU ARE NOW ENTERING FREE DERRY." Since the 1990s, local artists known as the **Bogside Artists** have painted more murals around the district, similar to those on the Falls Road in Belfast (see p. 487). Though some are overtly political in nature, many depict simple yet powerful messages of peace. This has effectively turned parts of the Bogside into a free art museum, and together the murals have become known as the **People's Gallery.**

distinguished by its huge, four-faced clock (designed to resemble Big Ben) and 23 stained-glass windows made by Ulster craftsmen, which illustrate almost every episode of note in the city's history. The hall is used as a civic center for concerts, plays, and exhibitions. A nice bit of historical trivia: The Guildhall clock is designed not to strike between midnight and sunrise. This is because at the time it was finished in 1890, the management of an expensive hotel nearby protested that a clock striking every hour through the night would disturb sleeping guests.

Shipquay Place, Derry, BT48 6DQ. © **028/7137-6510.** Free admission. Daily 10am–5:30pm. Free guided tours July–Aug; inquire at reception.

Museum of Free Derry ★★ MUSEUM Outside this small museum is an extraordinary piece of art, which may at first glance look like a long, rusty iron wall. But look again—it's a model of the actual sound waves from the 21 seconds in which the crowd on Bloody Sunday sang the civil rights anthem "We will overcome," shortly before 26 of them were shot, and 14 killed, by the British Army. Such a thought-provoking statement nicely frames the story told inside the museum, which reopened in a new location after a long refurbishment in 2017. Thousands of documents and artifacts related to the Irish Catholic civil rights movement of the mid- and late 20th century are housed here, while displays tell the story of Bloody

Sunday and other key events in the "Troubles" of the 1960s to '90s. The timeline is clearly laid out and easy to understand; the calm, level tone makes the impact all the more powerful. The **Bogside** (see p. 543) naturally becomes the focus for much of this history—so afterward, why not take one of the excellent **Free Derry Tours** of the district, which leave from the museum?

55 Glenfada Park, Derry, BT48 9DR. www.museumoffreederry.org. ✆ **028/7136-0880.** Admission £4 adults; £3 seniors, students, and children. Mon–Fri 9:30am–4:30pm (all year); Apr–Sept Sat 1–4pm; July–Sept Sun 1–4pm.

St. Columb's Cathedral ★ CATHEDRAL

Within the city walls, near the Bishop's Gate, this Protestant cathedral was built by the Church of Ireland between 1628 and 1633 as a prime example of the so-called "Planters Gothic" style of architecture. It was the first cathedral built in Europe after the Reformation, although several sections were added afterward, including the impressive spire and stained-glass windows depicting scenes from the siege of 1688–1689. The chapter house contains a display of city relics such as four massive original padlocks for the city gates. On the porch, a small stone inscribed "IN TEMPLO VERUS DEUS EST VEREO COLENDUS" ("The true God is in His temple and is to be truly worshipped") is part of the original 1164 church. An old mortar shell on the porch was fired into the churchyard during the great siege of 1689; in its hollow core it held proposed terms of surrender. Flags around the chancel window were captured during the siege, a pivotal moment in William of Orange's war against James II. The war and its aftermath had a far-reaching effect on Ireland, leading to the so-called "Plantation," whereby land was confiscated from Irish Catholics and given to favored Protestant (mostly English) families—thus cementing Protestant hegemony for centuries. The war was ultimately decided at the Battle of the Boyne (see p. 56), which is still commemorated annually in Northern Ireland by controversial parades, led by the Protestant Orange Order, on and around July 12.

London St., Derry, BT48 6RQ. www.stcolumbscathedral.org. ✆ **028/7126-7313.** Requested donation £2 adults; £2 seniors, students, and children. Mon–Sat 9am–5pm; Sun for services only.

St. Eugene's Cathedral ★★ CATHEDRAL

Designed in the Gothic Revival style, Derry's Roman Catholic cathedral is appropriately located in the heart of the Bogside district, just beyond the city walls. The foundation was laid in 1851, but work continued until 1873. The spire was added in 1902. It's built of local sandstone and is known for its stained-glass windows depicting the Crucifixion, designed by famed stained-glass makers Meyer and Company of Munich.

Francis St., Derry, BT48 9AP. www.steugenescathedral.com. ✆ **028/7126-2894.** Free admission. Mon–Sat 7am–9pm, Sun 7am–6:30pm.

CLIMBING THE walls

One of the best ways to explore Derry is via its 17th-century stone walls, about 1.6km (1 mile) in circumference and more than 5m (16 ft.) thick. Climb the stairs to the top and you can circle the entire walled city in about 30 minutes. There are a number of stairways off of the parapets, so you'll never get stuck up there. If you start at the **Diamond,** as the square in the center of the walled section is called, walk down Butcher Street to climb the steps at **Butcher's Gate,** a security checkpoint between the Bogside and the city during the Troubles. Walk to the right across **Castle Gate,** built in 1865, and on to **Magazine Gate,** which was once near a powder magazine. Shortly after, you'll pass **O'Doherty's Tower,** which houses the worthwhile Tower Museum (p. 546). From there you can see the brick walls of the Guildhall (p. 542).

Farther along, you'll pass **Shipquay Gate,** once located very near the port, back when the waters passed closer to the town center. The walls turn uphill from there, past the Millennium Forum concert hall, and up to **Ferryquay Gate.** Here in 1688, local apprentice boys saved the town from attacking Catholic forces by locking the city gates—thus saving the town from attack, but launching the Great Siege of Derry, which lasted for months. (By the time it ended, nearly a quarter of the town's population was dead.)

Next you'll pass **Bishop's Gate,** where a tall brick tower just outside the gate is all that remains of the **Old Gaol.** The rebel Wolfe Tone was imprisoned here after the unsuccessful uprising in 1798. Farther along, the **Double Bastion** holds a military tower with elaborate equipment used to keep an eye on the Bogside—it's usually splashed with paint hurled at it by Republicans. From there you can easily access the serene churchyard of **St. Columb's Cathedral** (p. 544). From the next stretch of wall, you have a good view over the political murals of the Bogside down the hill.

A bit farther along the wall, an empty plinth stands where once there was a statue of Rev. George Walker, a governor of the city during the siege of 1689. It was blown up by the IRA in 1973. The small chapel nearby is the **Chapel of St. Augustine** (1872), and the building across the street from it with metal grates over the windows is the **Apprentice Boys' Memorial Hall,** commemorating the boys from the Great Siege of Derry. Walk but a short way farther, and you're back to Butcher's Gate.

Walk the 17th-century walls of Derry City for views and a history lesson.

The Tower Museum ★★

MUSEUM This engaging museum chronicles the history of Derry from the earliest times to the 21st century. It's located in **O'Doherty Tower,** a reconstructed medieval fortress originally built in the early 17th century (rather wonderfully to pay off a tax debt, rather than for any specific defensive purpose). The **Story of Derry** exhibition presents a chronology of life in the city from the first monastic settlers through the Plantation era, up to the turbulent 20th century, when the city was a focus of the civil rights movement. The main attraction, however, is the large, multifloor exhibition **An Armada Shipwreck,** which tells the story of *La Trinidad Valencera,* part of the massive Spanish Armada that attempted to invade England in

Derry's history is told in the Tower Museum, a 17th-century fortress.

1588. Separated from the main fleet, the ship sank during a storm. Four hundred years later the wreck was salvaged, together with an extraordinary hoard of treasure including clothes, shoes, pottery, cannons, goblets, and other items that reveal tantalizing glimpses of life on board.

Union Hall Place, Derry, BT48 6LU. www.derrystrabane.com/towermuseum. © **028/ 7137-2411.** Admission £4 adults; £2.40 seniors and students; £2 children; £9 families. Daily 10am–5:30pm. Last admission 1 hr. before closing.

Where to Stay in Derry

INEXPENSIVE

Saddler's House & the Old Rectory ★★   Two charming buildings full of character with one pair of owners, these lovely B&Bs are among the best accommodations in Derry. Choose from the elegant **Merchant's House,** which was built in the mid–19th century (one of relatively few town houses from that period left in Derry), or **Saddler's House,** a slightly simpler, late-Victorian building. (Check-in for both is at the Saddler's House.) Each house has been beautifully maintained and renovated with design-magazine interiors and antiques scattered about. Breakfast is served in whichever house you choose. The same owners also have three self-catering places in Derry, including a small terraced cottage opposite the cathedral, an apartment in the old pumphouse, within the walled part of the city, and a 1950s-style apartment. *Tip:* The Merchant's House family room sleeps up to five and has its own kitchen, for just £100 to £135 per night.

36 Great James St., Derry, BT48 7DB. www.thesaddlershouse.com. ✆ **028/7126-9691.** 7 units. £60–£90 double. Limited free parking (on street); otherwise, paid street parking nearby. Breakfast included. **Amenities:** Wi-Fi (free).

Serendipity House ★   This popular B&B at the top of the hill overlooking Derry has few frills but is a handy, well-priced option. Rooms are small but neat, with modern decor; most have lovely town views. Bathrooms are tiny but clean. Most rooms have en suite facilities, but a few have bathrooms a short distance away; if this matters to you, ask when you book. Breakfasts are of the carb-heavy, eggs-and-bacon variety, although fresh scones and pancakes are sometimes on offer. The old city is a pleasant 10-minute walk downhill—which means a pretty steep 10-minute walk uphill when you're coming home later. But taxis are plentiful in Derry if you can't face the climb. The same owners also have a second B&B, **Angel House,** located on Marlborough Street in the city center.

26 Marlborough St, Derry, BT48 9AY. www.serendipityrooms.co.uk/bed-breakfast/serendipity-house. ✆ **028/7126-4229.** 5 units. £70–£100 double. Free parking. Breakfast included. **Amenities:** Wi-Fi (free).

Troy Hall ★★   How delightfully unexpected to find this lavish Victorian mansion so close to the Derry city center. Troy Hall was built in 1897, complete with the Gothic Revival flourishes that were so popular in the period. Turrets give the redbrick exterior an almost fairy-tale look, while the sweeping back lawn is a remnant of what was once a huge estate. The building suffered terribly over the years, until the current owners restored it to its beautiful condition. Spacious guest rooms are individually designed but share a country-house-style chic, furnished with handmade wood or wrought-iron beds and occasional antiques. Family rooms sleep up to five. Excellent breakfasts are served in the well-restored dining room. Central Derry is about 5 minutes by car or cab, and a bus stop is nearby.

9 Troy Park, Culmore Rd., Derry, BT48 7RL. www.troyhall.co.uk. ✆ **078/8436-1669.** 3 units. £85 double. Free parking. Rates include breakfast. **Amenities:** Wi-Fi (free).

Where to Eat in Derry
EXPENSIVE

Browns ★★ BRASSERIE   One of Derry's best restaurants, Browns serves excellent Irish food with international influences. The menu uses plenty of local and regional ingredients, embracing traditional flavors with a touch of well-judged, modern innovation. Menus change frequently, but start with fresh Donegal crab or local wood pigeon, if they're on the menu. Afterward, how about monkfish with samphire and butter-milk, or beef filet with caramelized onion and broccoli? Vegetarians will be delighted to see a full menu of non-meaty options, including some tasty spiced falafel, served with creamed kale. A nine-course tasting menu costs £45 (£75 with wines) and a three-course early-bird special is £25. A more casual sister branch, **Browns in Town** (✆ **028/7136-2889**), is on Strand Road.

1 Bonds Hill, Derry, BT47 6DW. www.brownsrestaurant.com. ✆ **028/7134-5180.** Entrees £19–£25. Tues–Thurs noon–3pm, 5:30–9pm; Fri–Sat noon–3pm, 5–10pm; Sun noon–3pm.

MODERATE

The Belfray Country Inn Bistro ★ BISTRO   The dining room at this big hotel and restaurant, a short drive outside Derry, adds a rococo touch to the feel of a country pub. A lot of things are gilded here. For the food, imagine posh pub fare and you've got it about right. The best dishes come from the grill—thick juicy steaks, lamb cutlets, and chicken esca-lope, with all the trimmings—but there are also several stir-fry and vege-tarian options, as well as an extensive kids' menu. Weekend "carvery" (buffet-style) roasts are hugely popular; they're served Friday to Sunday from midday to 3:30pm. The inn also offers spacious rooms with big beds and neutral decor, but they're a bit pricey (around £115) given the loca-tion. The Belfray is on Glendshane Road (A6), about 5.5km (3[bf1/2] miles) southwest of Derry city center.

171 Glenshane Rd., Derry, BT47 3EN. www.thebelfraycountryinn.co.uk. ✆ **028/7130-1480.** Fixed-price menus £12–£25. Daily noon–3:30pm, 5–9:30pm.

The Sooty Olive ★ IRISH   Named after a kind of fishing lure, this trendy eatery in central Derry specializes in locally sourced food, and serves it with class. The decor in the small dining room makes the most of the exposed brick walls, contrasting it with tasteful leather chairs and sofas. Similarly, the cooking makes the most of local ingredients in dishes like sea bream with black pudding and new potatoes, or duck breast with potato fondant. It also serves steak and skinny fries, as well as plenty of vegetarian options. Desserts are to die for. The wine list is small but well-chosen; try a bottle of the dark and spicy Basilisk Australian Shiraz (£30).

160–164 Spencer Rd., Derry, BT47 6AH. www.thesootyolive.com. ✆ **028/7134-6040.** Fixed-price menus £19–£22. Mon–Thurs noon–2:30pm, 5–9pm; Fri–Sat noon–2:30pm, 5–10pm; Sun 1–9pm.

INEXPENSIVE

Badgers ★ IRISH   A friendly local pub right in the center of Derry, Badgers serves hearty traditional grub—stews, fish and chips, steak and Guinness pie, burgers, and the like—plus a few lighter options such as hot sandwiches and wraps. Plates are generous, and of course, you can wash it all down with a pint of the black stuff. The dining room is satisfyingly unreconstructed with plenty of polished wood and low hanging lamps. No matter what the time of day, there always seem to be a few locals propping up the bar, which helps keep the atmosphere authentic.

16–18 Orchard St., Derry, BT48 6EG. ℓ **028/7136-0763.** Entrees £6–£12. Food served Mon–Thurs noon–7pm, Fri–Sat noon–9pm, Sun noon–4pm. No children after 9pm.

Primrose Café ★★ CAFE   This lovely cafe is nicely old-fashioned without being at all stuffy. Drop in for a bowl of delicious soup, fresh sandwiches, or a tasty pie (served with a side of excellent chips—that's thick-cut fries around here). Or you could just have a plate of homemade scones and some tea, served the proper way in a teapot with fine china. Service is cheery and prices are reasonable—just what you want for a casual lunch on the go. A second branch is at 2 Atlantic Quay (ℓ **028/ 7136-5511**).

53/55 Strand Rd., Derry, BT48 6JJ. https://primrose-ni.com. ℓ **028/7137-3744.** Lunch £4–£10. Mon–Sat 8am–10pm, Sun 10am–6pm.

Derry After Dark

Derry pubs are an important part of the local fabric; hanging out in one is a good way to meet locals. Boozers are tied into the local music scene, so you'll frequently find bands playing. Pubs even host debating contests, in the midst of which you'll hear Irish eloquence at its well-lubricated best. Along **Waterloo Street,** just outside the city walls, a handful of Derry's most traditional and popular pubs are known for their live music. Walk from one end of Waterloo to the other—an act that will take you all of 2 minutes—and you'll likely find the bar for you.

Bennigan's ★★   A fairly new addition to the top-tier of Derry's live music scene, Bennigan's is known for its fantastic live jazz, which attracts performers from all over Ireland (and beyond). Sessions usually start at around 9pm. 13 John St., Derry, BT48 6JY. www.bennigansbar.com. ℓ **028/7126-9127.**

Peadar O'Donnells ★★★   "Peadars" to the locals, this is one of the best places in Derry to hear traditional live music. Sessions are every night except Monday; generally they run from 10:30pm to about 1am weekdays, 7pm to 1am Saturdays, and 5pm to 1am Sundays—although spontaneous sessions have been known to start up pretty much anytime. The craic is lively and the atmosphere is buzzing. 59–63 Waterloo St., Derry, BT48 6HD. www.peadars.com. ℓ **028/7126-7295.**

River Inn ★★   Allegedly Derry's oldest pub (the city walls form part of the building), the River Inn opened its doors in the 17th century. It also serves food, although people come for the atmosphere. 34–38 Shipquay St., Derry, BT48 6DW. www.riverinn1684.com. ℓ **028/7137-1965.**

DAY TRIPS TO THE SPERRIN MOUNTAINS

The beautiful Sperrin Mountains, a short drive southeast of Derry in County Tyrone, are filled with scenic walks, national parks, and extraordinary views, plus one really must-see site: The **Ulster American Folk Park** (see p. 552). This is splendid, wide-open walking country, home to golden plover, red grouse, and thousands upon thousands of fluffy white sheep. There's no shortage of ancient sites, including standing stones (about 1,000 have been counted in these hills), high crosses, dolmens, and hill forts. Whether you're traveling on foot, wheels, or horseback, be sure to traverse the **Glenshane Pass** between Mullaghmore (545m/1,788 ft.) and Carntogher (455m/1,492 ft.), and the **Sawel Mountain Drive** along the east face of the mountain. The vistas along these routes through the Sperrins will remind you why you've gone out of your way to spend time in Tyrone.

Visitor Information

The **An Creagán Visitors' Centre,** on the A505 road just outside Creggan (see below) is a good place to start, with tourist information and an interesting exhibition on the history of the area. Other area sites include the **Cookstown Tourist Information Centre,** Burn Road, Cookstown (✆ 028/8676-9949), the **Dungannon Visitor Information Centre,** 26 Market Square, Dungannon (✆ 028/8772-8600), the **Omagh Tourist Information Centre** at the Strule Arts Centre, Townhall Square, Omagh (✆ 028/8224-7831), and the **Strabane Visitor Information Centre,** at the Alley Arts and Conference Centre, 1A Railway St., Strabane (✆ 028/7138-4444). Generally they are open Monday to Saturday year-round from about 10am to 5pm; the Dungannon and Cookstown centers also open on Sundays in midsummer.

Exploring the Sperrins

An Creagán Visitors' Centre ★ INTERPRETIVE CENTER   Beautifully designed to fit in with the craggy countryside around, this modern center is an excellent place to get your bearings when you first arrive in the Sperrins. A small gallery has an interactive exhibit about the mountains and the area; a few Bronze Age artifacts excavated from nearby sites are also on display. The helpful staff will give you all the information you need on walking and cycling routes, as well as maps and bicycle rentals (bikes can be rented for roughly £10 per day, £7 per half-day, or £35 per week). The center has a restaurant and craft shop, and even owns a few self-catering properties if you're interested in staying longer. (Prices start at about £120 for a one-bedroom cottage in the low season, £180 in the high season.)

A505, Creggan (about 60km/37 miles SE of Derry), Omagh, Co. Tyrone. www.an-creagan.com. ✆ **028/8076-1112.** Free admission. Daily 10am–9pm.

Derry, Tyrone & Fermanagh

An Creagán Visitors' Centre **10**
Beaghmore Stone Circles **11**
Belleek Visitors Centre **1**
Castle Coole **6**
Crom Estate **7**
Devenish Island **5**
Drum Manor Forest Park **12**
Enniskillen Castle **4**
Florence Court **2**
Gortin Glen Forest Park **9**
Marble Arch Caves **3**
Ulster American Folk Park **8**

Northern Ireland counties shown are
the historic counties. UK counties were
reorganized after 1973.

Beaghmore Stone Circles ★ ANCIENT SITE In 1945, seven stone circles and a complex assembly of cairns and alignments were uncovered here, in remote moorland north of Evishbrack Mountain and near Davagh Forest Park on the southern edge of the Sperrins. Arranged inside the largest circle are around 800 small stones, christened the "Dragon's Teeth." No one knows what this intriguing bit of Bronze Age stonework was built for, but it may have involved astronomical observation and calculation. The layout has also led archaeologists to believe that the stones surround unexcavated megalithic tombs.

17km (11 miles) NW of Cookstown, signposted from A505, Co. Tyrone. No phone. Free admission (open site).

Drum Manor Forest Park ★ NATURE SITE   Once a private estate, this extensive park and woodland has numerous trails and three old walled gardens, one of them designed as a butterfly garden. Also on the grounds are a visitor center, a heronry, and a pond that attracts a variety of wildfowl.

4km (2½ miles) W of Cookstown on A505, Co. Tyrone. ℂ **028/8675-9311** (forest ranger). Admission £3.50 per car; pedestrians £1 adults, 50p children. Daily 8am–dusk.

Gortin Glen Forest Park ★★ NATURE SITE   Nearly 400 hectares (988 acres) of conifers make up this serene nature park. The woodlands provide habitat for a variety of wildlife, including a herd of Japanese sika deer. A forest drive offers splendid views of the Sperrins. Here you'll also find a nature center, wildlife enclosures, trails, and a cafe. The park has three separate marked walking trails; details can be found at the visitor center on the B48 road just south of Gortin. The long-distance **Ulster Way** hiking trail also passes through the park; for more information on the Ulster Way, visit **www.walkni.com/ulsterway**.

Visitor Center: On B48 (Glenpark Rd.), about 4km (2½ miles) S of Gortin, Co. Tyrone. ℂ **028/8167-0666.** Free admission; parking £5. Visitor center: Daily 10am–dusk.

Ulster American Folk Park ★★★ HERITAGE SITE   Another of the region's excellent "living history" outdoor museums, this one celebrates and commemorates the links between Ulster and the New World. It chronicles the story of those 18th- and 19th-century emigrants who left their homes in the north of Ireland to seek a new life overseas. The park contains authentic structures from the period— some of them actual dwellings reconstructed from elsewhere—to give an accurate impression of the life they left behind. After looking around the humble thatched cottages, you can explore a small town street, complete with convincingly decked-out shops, manned by costumed actors. Next you'll see a full-size replica emigrant ship, and finally examples of the kinds of frontier, log-cabin-type homes the emigrants lived in when they

The Ulster American Folk Park is a "living history" museum.

settled in the United States. The park has an active schedule of special events, including a respected bluegrass festival around the tail end of August or the beginning of September. Check the website for full listings.

2 Mellon Rd., Castletown, Co. Tyrone BT78 5QU. www.nmni.com. © **028/8224-3292.** Admission £9 adults; £7 seniors and students; £5.50 children 5–17; £19–£25 families. Prices rise by a few pounds on major event days. Tues–Sat 10am–5pm. Closed Mon except for NI Bank Holidays.

THE FERMANAGH LAKELANDS

In the extreme southwest corner of Northern Ireland, County Fermanagh is a resort area dominated by **Lough Erne,** a long, narrow lake with 154 islands and countless coves and inlets. The **Shannon-Erne Waterway** links the lough to the Shannon River system through the Republic of Ireland. Were you to cruise the whole length of the waterway between the village of Leitrim and Lough Erne, you'd travel 65km (40 miles), past 16 lochs, three lakes, and the Woodford River, all ripe for exploration. At the south end of Lough Erne, **Enniskillen** is a good touring base for the region, with many overnight options if you intend to spend much time here—it's a 90-minute to 2-hour drive from Derry City.

In medieval times, a chain of island monasteries stretched across the waters of Lough Erne, establishing it as a haven for those seeking peace and contemplation. Traces of those monasteries can still be found on those unspoiled islands—and the Fermanagh Lakelands remains a peaceful place to get away from it all.

Visitor Information

The **Fermanagh Tourist Information Centre,** Wellington Road, Enniskillen, Co. Fermanagh, BT74 7EF (© **028/6632-3110**), is open year-round Monday to Friday 9:30am to 5pm and Saturday 11am to 5pm; (also Sun 11am–5pm June–Sept). For an introduction to the Fermanagh Lakelands on the web, check out **www.fermanaghlakelands.com**.

Exploring the Lakelands

The hub of this lakeland paradise—wedged between Upper Lough Erne to the south and Lower Lough Erne to the north—is **Enniskillen,** a delightful resort town that was the medieval seat of the Maguire clan and a major crossroads between Ulster and Connaught. Both Oscar Wilde and Samuel Beckett were once students here at the royal school. A handful of lovely historic homes are dotted around the midsection of the lake as well, including **Castle Coole ★** (p. 554), the **Crom Estate ★★** (p. 554), and **Florence Court ★★** (p. 556). At the northern tip of the lake, near the Republic of Ireland border, **Belleek** (p. 557) is known the world over for its trademark delicate bone chinaware.

CRUISING LOUGH ERNE by boat

One of the best ways to explore Lough Erne is by boat. **Erne Tours Ltd.,** Enniskillen (www.ernetoursltd.com; ✆ **028/6632-2882**), operates 2-hour cruises on Lower Lough Erne aboard the *MV Kestrel*, departing daily May through September from the delightfully named Round "O" Jetty, Brook Park, Enniskillen. Tours include a 45-minute stop on **Devenish Island ★★** (see p. 555). Erne Tours also runs dinner cruises; call for schedules. Upper Lough Erne cruises are operated on Sundays and Bank Holidays by **Share Holiday Village,** Smith's Strand, Lisnaskea (www.sharevillage.org; ✆ **028/6772-2122**). Fares for both cruises start at £10 adults, £9 seniors, and £6 for children under 16. Call for reservations and to confirm times.

Independent boatmen offer ferry crossings to some of the many islands in Lough Erne. Besides Devenish Island, **White Island** and **Boa Island** are rich in archaeological and early Christian remains. On White Island, seven stone figures remain from a vanished 10th-century monastery inside a ruined 12th-century church. (The ferry to White Island runs from Castle Archdale Marina in Irvinestown; ✆ **028/6862-1892;** fare £5 round-trip.) Boa Island is connected to the shore by bridges; poke around the cemetery at the island's west end to find two ancient idols of the god Janus (with faces looking both ways), thought to date from the 1st century.

Castle Coole ★ HISTORIC HOUSE   Not really a castle at all, Coole is in fact a lavish stately home on the east bank of Lower Lough Erne. This quintessential neoclassical mansion was designed by James Wyatt for the Earl of Belmore and completed in 1796. Its rooms include a state bedroom hung with crimson silk, said to have been prepared for George IV (1762–1830). Other features include a Chinese-style sitting room, magnificent woodwork, fireplaces, and furniture dating from the 1830s. A nearly 600-hectare (1,482-acre) woodland estate surrounds the house. A classical music series runs from May to October.

2.4km (1½ miles) SE of Enniskillen on A4, Co. Fermanagh, BT74 6JY. www.national trust.org.uk/castle-coole. ✆ **028/6632-2690.** House: £5 adults; £2 children; £12 families. Grounds only (cars): £3 adults, £2 children, £9 families. Grounds only (walkers): £2.50 adults; £1.50 children; £6.50 families. House open June–Aug daily 11am–5pm; May and Sept Wed–Mon 11am–5pm; Mar–Apr weekends 11am–5pm (also daily during Easter week). Grounds open Mar–Oct daily 10am–7pm; Nov–Feb daily 10am–4pm. Last admission 30 min. before closing; last house tour 1 hr. before closing.

Crom Estate ★★ NATURE SITE   On the east bank of Upper Lough Erne, this nearly 800-hectare (1,976-acre) nature reserve is a splendid National Trust–owned estate, with forest, parks, wetlands, fen meadows, and an award-winning lakeshore visitor center. The numerous trails have concealed places for observing birds and wildlife. You can rent a rowboat and row your way out to the islands. A 19th-century castle is also located on the grounds, though it's not open to visitors. The estate is a great place to fish for bream and roach; permits and day tickets are available at the gate lodge. During the summer, weekends frequently feature special programs and guided nature walks. The estate also has several cottages available for rent by the week (about £300–£850). Call or check the National Trust website for more information.

34km (21 miles) S of Enniskillen via A4 and A34, then take signposted right turn. Upper Lough Erne, Newtownbutler, Co. Fermanagh, BT92 8AP. www.nationaltrust. org.uk/crom. ⓒ **028/6773-8118.** Admission £6 adults; £14 families. June–Aug daily 10am–7pm; mid-Mar to May and Sept–Oct daily 10am–6pm. Visitor center mid-Mar to Sept daily 11am–5pm; Oct Sat–Sun 11am–5pm. Closed Nov to mid-Mar. Last admission 1 hr. before closing.

Devenish Island ★★ NATURE SITE The most extensive of the ancient Christian sites in Lough Erne, Devenish Island is a marvelous mélange of remnants and ruins, providing a glimpse into the lake's mystical past. In the 6th century, St. Molaise founded a monastic community here, to which the Augustinian Abbey of St. Mary was added in the 12th century. In other words, this is hallowed ground, even more so for the legend that the Old Testament prophet Jeremiah is buried somewhere nearby—if you can figure that one out. The jewel of Devenish is the perfectly intact 12th-century round tower, which was erected with Vikings in mind. A regular ferry to Devenish Island used to run in July and August from Trory Point, 6.5km (4 miles) from Enniskillen on A32, but at this writing it had stopped operating until further notice. Until it gets back up and running, the only way to get out there is to take the Lough Erne cruise offered by **Erne Tours** (see p. 554). Alternatively, you could check at the jetty for a private ferryman to take you. To reach the jetty, take A32 north from Enniskillen toward nearby Irvinestown; after about 2 miles you will come to a roundabout. Almost immediately turn left (next to the gas station) down a small country road. After about ¾ mile you'll come to a fork in the road; turn left and look for the jetty on your right.

2.4km (1½ miles) downstream from Enniskillen, Co. Fermanagh, BT94 2FE. ⓒ **028/ 9082-3207.** Admission to round tower £3 adults; £2 seniors and children.

Enniskillen Castle ★★ CASTLE/MUSEUM On the banks of Lower Lough Erne in Enniskillen, this impressive castle was built sometime around the first half of the 14th century, but was significantly remodeled in the 17th. It's unusual in that the design owes more to the Scottish Baronial style of castle—note the small round turrets, redolent of Gothic motifs—than the fortress-like English-French style that predominates throughout Ireland. The castle is home to two museums, included in the ticket price, which were recently reopened after a major renovation. **Fermanagh County Museum** tells the story of the region's colorful history, with interesting sections on local crafts and the development of the castle from medieval times onward. The **Inniskillings Museum** houses the castle's large collection of militaria, historic weapons, uniforms, and other artifacts dating back to the 1600s.

Castle Barracks, Enniskillen, Co. Fermanagh, BT74 7HL. www.enniskillencastle. co.uk. ℰ **028/6632-5000.** Admission £5 adults; £3.50 seniors, students, and children; £13.50 families. Mon–Fri 9:30am–5pm, Sat–Sun 11am–5pm (Oct–May closed Sun).

Florence Court ★★ HISTORIC HOUSE Set among dramatic hills, 13km (8 miles) southwest of Lower Lough Erne and Enniskillen, this 18th-century Palladian mansion was originally the seat of the earls of Enniskillen. Its interior is rich in rococo plasterwork and antique Irish furniture, while outside is a fine walled garden, an icehouse, and a water-wheel-driven sawmill. The forest park offers a number of trails, one leading to the top of Mount Cuilcagh (nearly 660m/2,165 ft.). Florence Court is the sister property to Castle Coole (see p. 554).

Eniskillen Castle overlooks Lower Lough Erne.

Florence Court, off A32, Enniskillen, Co. Fermanagh, BT92 1DB. www.nationaltrust. org.uk/florence-court. ℰ **028/6634-8249.** Admission £6 adults; £3 children; £15 families. House tour £4 adults; £2 children; £10 families. House June–Aug daily 11am–5pm; May and Sept Sat–Thurs 11am–5pm; mid-Mar to Apr and Oct Sat–Sun 11am–5pm (also daily Easter week). Gardens and park Mar–Oct daily 10am–7pm; Nov–Feb daily 10am–4pm. Open public holidays. Last admission 1 hr. before closing.

Marble Arch Caves ★★ CAVES   Near the Florence Court estate (see above), these UNESCO-listed caves are among the finest in Europe for exploring underground rivers, winding passages, and hidden chambers. Electrically powered boat tours take visitors underground, and knowledgeable guides explain the origins of the amazing stalactites and stalagmites. Tours last 75 minutes and leave at 15-minute intervals. The caves are occasionally closed after heavy rains, so phone ahead before making the trip if there's been particularly bad weather recently.

Marlbank Rd., off A32, Co. Fermanagh, BT92 1EW. www.marblearchcavesgeopark. com. ℰ **028/6634-8855.** Admission £9.80 adults; £6.95 seniors and students; £6.70 children; £23.70–£26.80 families. Reservations recommended. July–Aug daily 10am–5pm (last tour); Mar–June and Sept daily 10am–4:30pm (last tour); Oct daily 10:30am–3pm.

Perhaps the most famous Irish homeware brand in the world after Waterford Crystal, Belleek Pottery has been making fine china since 1864. The **Belleek Visitor Centre,** Belleek, County Fermanagh (www.belleek.ie; © **028/6865-9300**), is the world headquarters of the brand. You can visit their museum—which displays unique objects of Belleek pottery, such as the extraordinary International Centre Piece vase created for the 1900 Paris Expo—and also take factory tours. But of course, the reason most people come is to visit the enormous gift shop. If you're not a china expert but still want to bring back some Belleek pieces from your trip, here are a few tips to ensure that your purchases become heirlooms:

○ The Belleek Heirloom Centre has the best selection of patterns from which to choose, giving you lots of options and a wide price range.

○ At the center, all the china is displayed around the room. You walk around looking at all the pieces, and then note the item numbers of those pieces you like. Take the numbers to the central counter, and the boxed china pieces are brought to you.

○ Ask to see the pieces in the boxes to ensure they are what you wanted. Take the pieces from the sales assistant and look at them closely. This is delicate

china, and it can have tiny imperfections that you can only see by getting up close and personal. Be particularly conscious of the bottom of the piece—look for tiny hairline cracks. We bought a lovely Belleek vase once that looked perfect, but leaked through a nearly invisible crack.

○ The center will ship internationally if you don't want to risk taking your purchases on a plane.

○ If it looks good to you and you love it—buy it! You may not get the chance again.

The Belleek Centre is open July to September weekdays 9am to 6pm, Saturday 10am to 6pm, and Sunday 2 to 5pm; March to June weekdays 9am to 5:30pm, Saturday 10am to 5:30pm, and Sunday noon to 5:30pm; October to December weekdays 9am to 6pm, Saturday 10am to 5:30pm, Sunday noon to 5pm; and January to February weekdays 9am to 5:30pm, closed weekends.

On weekdays, factory tours run every half-hour from 9:30am to 12:15pm and 1:45 to 4pm (last tour 3pm on Fri). From June to September, there are also Saturday tours from 10:30am to 12:15pm and 2 to 4pm. Tour tickets cost £5 adults, £3 seniors and students, £10 families, and free for children age 11 and under.

Where to Stay in the Fermanagh Lakelands
EXPENSIVE

Castle Leslie ★★★   Actually just across the border in the Republic, this historic estate surrounded by lush grounds is one of the very best places to stay in the North, having welcomed a dazzling list of luminaries over the years (W. B. Yeats was a houseguest, Winston Churchill was a cousin of the Leslie family, and Paul McCartney and Heather Mills were married here in 2002). Strolling around the house you'll wander past Wordsworth's harp, the Bechstein grand piano on which Wagner composed *Tristan and Isolde,* and Winston Churchill's baby clothes, among many other things. Guest rooms are individually designed to varying degrees of grandeur; most are located in the converted hunting lodge, although guests with deeper pockets can stay in the main house for the full "Downton Abbey" effect. The outstanding **Snaffles Restaurant** offers sophisticated dishes prepared with local ingredients, such as filet of seabass with red pepper drops and baby carrots, or roast chicken with garlic and citrus dressing. You can also opt for a more casual meal at **Conor's Bar and Lounge.** On the several hundred acres of grounds, horseback riding, clay pigeon shooting, and other outdoor activities can be arranged; there's also an elegant spa to smooth away the few cares you have left. The price is incredibly reasonable for what you get.

Glaslough, Co. Monaghan (Republic of Ireland). www.castleleslie.com. © **047/ 88100.** 62 units. £118–£245 double. 2-night minimum in summer. Dinner-bed-and-breakfast packages available. Free parking. Breakfast included. **Amenities:** Restaurants (2); bar; room service; spa; Wi-Fi (free).

MODERATE

Belmore Court Motel ★ At this quality budget option on the edge of Enniskillen, basic rooms are laid out like a traditional American motel (virtually unheard of in Europe). They're clean and modern, with compact kitchen areas and free Wi-Fi. Pay just a little more, however, and you get a lot of extra space, plus nice little touches like Nespresso machines, breakfast, and even (in the executive rooms) little balconies. Family rooms, which sleep up to four, cost just a bit more than doubles. The location, although not the most romantic spot in Enniskillen, isn't too far from the town center and nearby sights such as **Enniskillen Castle** ★★ (p. 555) or **Castle Coole** ★ (p. 554).

Tempo Rd., Enniskillen, Co. Fermanagh, BT74 6HX. www.motel.co.uk. © **028/6632-6633.** 60 units. £55–£108 double. Free parking. Breakfast included. **Amenities:** Wi-Fi (free).

The Enniskillen Hotel ★ This stylish boutique hotel in central Enniskillen has a wonderfully *bon vivant* streak. Bedrooms are modern and chic, with subtle lighting and plenty of dark grays and oatmeal hues. The bar, **Wilde's,** specializes in whiskey and sometimes hosts special tasting sessions; you can also take light meals here. Or you can dine in the excellent **Beckett's Grill,** where the relatively small menu focuses on barbecue, with a few fish options, too. Special offers, including dinner-bed-and-breakfast packages and family weekends (with passes for a local play center), are excellent values. The hotel is on the eastern side of the city, about a 20-minute walk from **Enniskillen Castle** ★★ (see p. 555).

72 Forthill St., Enniskillen, Co. Fermanagh, BT74 6AJ. www.enniskillenhotel.com. © **028/6632-1177.** 35 units. £80–£100 double, £120–£183 suite. Free parking. Breakfast included. **Amenities:** Restaurant; bar; room service; Wi-Fi (free).

Finn Lough ★★ This surely qualifies as one of the most unique places to stay in Ireland. The five-star lakeside compound at Finn Lough has a very unique feature: so-called "bubble domes," individual plastic dome cottages from which you can see the wide sky and verdant countryside all around you, all the time. If such an open environment isn't for you (although you're surrounded by foliage for privacy), more traditional cottages are tucked away around the compound, in the woods or at the edge of the lake. Most have three bedrooms, a kitchen, and a living room, as well as good Wi-Fi; some have working fireplaces. You can dine in the on-site restaurant (inclusive packages are available), hire kayaks to paddle out on the pristine lake, or rent a mountain bike and explore the forests. On the other hand, you could just hide yourself away in your own cottage and enjoy the peace. If you're looking for true isolation combined with elegance, this could be the place for you.

Letter Rd., Enniskillen, Co. Fermanagh, BT93 2BB. www.finnlough.com. © **028/6638-0360.** 15 units. £260–£420 bubble dome (nightly), £170–£350 cottages (per 2-night minimum). Free parking. No breakfast. **Amenities:** Wi-Fi (free).

Where to Eat in the Fermanagh Lakelands

The Jolly Sandwich ★ CAFE This bright, light sandwich shop is a cheery place to grab a quick lunch or breakfast or create a picnic to go. As the name suggests, the specialty is freshly made sandwiches of all kinds, but there's more to this place than that. Towering stacks of American-style pancakes are often available, as well as homemade scones, elaborate cakes, gorgeous layered coffees, and steaming pots of tea.

3 Darling St., Enniskillen, Co. Fermanagh, BT74 7DP. www.thejollysandwichbar.co.uk. © **028/6632-2277.** All items £4–£8. Mon–Sat 7:30am–4:15pm. Closed Sun.

The Taphouse ★★ IRISH/INTERNATIONAL Converted into a gastropub, this handsome old stone building is a good-looking place, with exposed stone walls, rugged wood floors, and leather furniture. The front bar is sleek and modern, contrasting beautifully with the aged setting. Dishes are smart reinterpretations of traditional pub food. You might start with smoked salmon and wholegrain mustard–flavored cream cheese, for instance, or on a rainy day try the soup with Guinness and treacle bread. Main courses could include a creamy Thai curry, Moroccan spiced lamb. Desserts are old-school comfort food—try the homemade cheesecake, with a new flavor each week.

46 Old Tempo Rd., Enniskillen, Co. Fermanagh BT74 4RR. www.thetaphouse enniskillen.com. © **028/6634-6800.** Entrees £9–£20. Daily 11am–11pm (food served until about 9pm).

Tully Mill ★★ IRISH Relaxed and sophisticated, this bistro on the edge of the Florence Court estate (p. 556) is located inside an old watermill. Plenty of local flavors find their way onto the three-course set menus, including some from the mill's own walled garden. Start with some goat cheese from Fivemiletown, County Tyrone; then go for a slow-roasted breast of Fermanagh chicken with Bushmills sauce, or perhaps a simple local steak. Sunday lunches are popular here, with plenty of interesting fish and vegetarian options alongside traditional plates of roast meats. The quiet grounds also contain a few self-catering cottages; prices in summer start at around £250 for the weekend, £400 for the full week.

On the Florence Court estate, Co. Fermanagh BT92 1FN. www.tullymill.com. ✆ **028/6634-9879.** Three-course menu £35. Fri–Sat 5–10pm, Sun noon–5pm.

Sports & Outdoor Pursuits in the Lakelands

BIRD-WATCHING   These lakelands are prime bird-watching territory. You'll find hooper swans, great-crested grebes, golden plovers, curlews, corncrakes, kingfishers, herons, merlins, peregrines, kestrels, and sparrow hawks. On Upper Lough Erne, the primary habitats are reed swamps, flooded drumlins, and fens; on the lower lake, the habitats of choice are the less-visited islands and the hay meadows. Two important preserves are at **Crom Estate ★★** (p. 554) and the **Castle Caldwell Forest and Islands** on Lower Lough Erne, near Belleek. The preserve includes a stretch of the lough's shoreline; the picturesque 17th-century ruins of Castle Caldwell itself stand nearby.

Fishing in the Fermanagh Lakelands.

BOATING Lough Erne is an explorer's dream, and you can take that dream all the way to the Atlantic if you want. The price range for fully equipped, four- to eight-berth cruisers is around £650 to £1,250 per week, including tax, depending on the season and the size of the boat. The many local cruiser-hire companies include **Erne Marine,** Bellanaleck (www.erne-marine.com; ℂ **077/0812-7700**), and **Carrickcraft,** Lurgan (www.cruise-ireland.com; ℂ **028/3834-4993** or 01/278-1666 from the Republic). On Lower Lough Erne, you can hire motorboats from **Manor House Marine,** Killadeas (www.manormarine.com; ℂ **028/6862-8100**). Charges average £65 to £90 for a half-day and £90 to £130 for a full day, depending on the size of the boat (maximum 8 people). You'll have to pay a refundable deposit before heading out.

FISHING If you can't catch a fish here, you will really have to question your technique. The best time for salmon is February to mid-June; for trout, mid-March to June or mid-August until late September. As for coarse fishing, about a dozen species await your line in the area's lakes and rivers. For on-the-spot info, tackle, and bait, try **Home, Field and Stream,** 18 Church St., Enniskillen (www.hfs-online.com; ℂ **028/6634-0758**). For locally arranged game fishing, call or drop in on **Melvin Tackle,** Main Street, Garrison, Co. Fermanagh (ℂ **078/7144-3304**). All necessary permits and licenses are available at the **Fermanagh Tourist Information Centre** (see p. 553).

WALKING The southwestern branch of the **Ulster Way** follows the western shores of Lough Erne, between the lake and the border. The area is full of other great walks as well. One excellent 11km (6.75-mile; 3–7 hr.) hike leads from a starting point near Florence Court and the Marble Arch Caves (p. 556) to the summit of **Mount Cuilcagh** (656m/2,152 ft.). For a detailed description of the route and downloadable map, visit **www.walkni.com/walks/585/cuilcagh-mountain**.

17 PLANNING YOUR TRIP TO IRELAND

C hances are you've been looking forward to your trip to Ireland for some time. You've probably set aside a significant amount of hard-earned cash, taken time off from work, school, or other commitments, and now want to make the most of your holiday. To accomplish that, you'll need to plan carefully. The aim of this chapter is to provide you with the information you need and answer any questions you might have, including: When to go? How to get there? Should you book a tour or travel independently? How much will it all cost? Here you'll find plenty of resources to help you make the most of your Irish adventure.

GETTING THERE
By Plane

The Republic of Ireland has three major international airports. They are, in order of size, **Dublin (DUB)** (www.dublinairport.com; ✆ **1/814-1111**), **Cork (ORK)** (www.cork-airport.com; ✆ **021/431-3131**), and **Shannon** (www.shannonairport.com; ✆ **061/712000**). Northern Ireland's main airport is **Belfast International Airport (BFS)** (www.belfastairport.com; ✆ **028/9448-4848**).

The Republic of Ireland has several smaller regional airports. The airports at Donegal and Kerry offer service to Dublin; in addition, the airports at Donegal, Kerry, and Knock receive some (limited) European traffic. In Northern Ireland, the secondary airports are Belfast City Airport and Derry City Airport. Airline service to these smaller airports changes frequently, so be sure to consult your preferred airline or travel agent as soon as you begin to sketch out your itinerary.

Begin thinking about flying plans at least 6 months ahead of time. Consider exchange-rate movements: Fares may be calculated in U.S. dollars, British pounds, or euros, depending on the airline. The key window for finding a **deal** is usually between 5 and 6 months ahead of your departure, according to a study of some 21 million fare transactions by the Airline Reporting Corporation (a middleman between travel agencies and the airlines). They also found that those who booked on a Sunday statistically found the best rates (on average paying 19% less than those who booked midweek).

FACING PAGE: **Northern Ireland's spectacular Antrim Coast Drive.**

563

The glory days of generous **frequent-flyer programs** and bucket loads of free miles are no more, but those who collect miles via credit cards (rather than trying to fly to get them) are having better luck getting free trips nowadays. The key strategy is to get a card that will work with a number of airlines, rather than one branded by a particular airline (the latter usually have less generous rates of return and more draconian fees). The forum **Flyertalk.com** is a handy resource for learning how to get the most out of your miles (both for airlines and hotels); such companies as **AwardMagic.com** and **IFlyWithMiles.com** can help stressed travelers redeem miles for flights for a flat fee that's usually far less than a ticket from the United States to Ireland would have cost.

Run searches through the regular online agents such as Expedia, as well as metasearch engines like **DoHop.com**, **Kayak.com**, and **Skyscanner.net**. For complex journeys, with multiple departures, doing multiple searches (so that affordable intra-European airlines such as Ryanair, Flybe, and EasyJet show up on the search) is a good way to find deals; a specialist flight agent such as **RoundtheWorldFlights.com** or **AirTreks.com** will also likely save you money.

By Ferry

If you're traveling to Ireland from Britain or the Continent, traveling by ferry is a good alternative to flying. Several car and passenger ferries offer reasonably comfortable furnishings, cabin berths (for longer crossings), restaurants, duty-free shopping, and lounges. You may be surprised, however, by how long it takes, even from super-near neighbor Britain; the quickest U.K.-to-Ireland ferry route is Holyhead to Dublin, which is a little over 3 hours; the sailing from Fishguard to Dublin takes well over 7 hours. From Cherbourg in France it's a whopping 18 hours.

Prices fluctuate seasonally and depend on your route, time of travel, and whether you are on foot or in a car. Check with your travel agent for up-to-date details, but the lowest one-way adult fare in high season on the Holyhead to Dublin ferry starts at £30. A car usually costs about £80 including one adult passenger, plus £30 per extra adult, £15 extra child.

Irish Ferries (www.irishferries.ie; ℭ **0818/300-400** in the Republic of Ireland, or ℭ **353/818-300-400** in Northern Ireland/U.K.) operates between Pembroke, Wales, and Rosslare, County Wexford. It also sails from Cherbourg and Rosscoff in France.

Stena Line (www.stenaline.com; ℭ **01/204-7777**) sails from Fishguard, Wales, to Rosslare; and from Cairnryan, Scotland, and Liverpool, England, to Belfast, Northern Ireland.

P&O Irish Sea Ferries (www.poferries.com; ℭ **0871/664-2121** in Britain, ℭ **01/407-3434** in Ireland, or ℭ **352/3420-808-294** in the rest of the world) operates from Liverpool to Dublin and from Cairnryan, Scotland, to Larne, County Antrim, Northern Ireland.

TRIPS & TOURS

Package Tours

Package tours are simply a way to buy the airfare, accommodations, and other elements of your trip (such as car rentals, airport transfers, and even activities) at the same time and often at discounted prices.

One good source for package deals of all kinds is the airlines themselves. Most major airlines offer air/land packages, with surprisingly cheap hotel deals. Several big online travel agencies—such as **Expedia** (www.expedia.com), **Travelocity** (www.travelocity.com), **Orbitz** (www.orbitz.com), and **Lastminute** (www.lastminute.com)—also do a brisk business in packages.

Fully escorted tours mean a travel company takes care of absolutely everything, including airfare, hotels, meals, tours, admission costs, and local transportation. Although we hope this book will help you plan your trip independently and safely, many travelers still prefer the convenience and peace of mind that a fully escorted tour offers. They are particularly good for inexperienced travelers or people with limited mobility. They can also be a great way to make new friends. On the downside, you'll have little opportunity for serendipitous interactions with locals. The tours can be jam-packed with activities, leaving little room for individual sightseeing, whim, or adventure. Plus they often focus on heavily trafficked sites, so you often miss out on many lesser-known gems.

Discover Ireland (www.discoverireland.com) can give advice on escorted tours and publishes up-to-the-minute deals on the front page of its website. **C.I.E. Tours** (www.cietours.com; ✆ 01/703-1888) offers fully escorted tours, self-guided tours, and individual chauffeur-driven tours. **Hidden Ireland Tours** (www.hiddenirelandtours.com; ✆ 087/221-4002 or 125/1478-7519 outside Ireland) specializes in off-the-beaten-path tours of Kerry, Galway, and Donegal. **Authentic Ireland** (www.authenticireland.com; ✆ 01/293-3088 or 188/8443-5259 outside Ireland) organizes escorted, self-guided, and private tours, as well as themed tours such as castle and golfing vacations. Those wanting to combine their trip with learning opportunities might be interested in the **International Summer School** program at the National University of Ireland, Galway (University Rd., Galway, Co. Galway; www.nuigalway.ie/international-summer-school), which includes courses on Irish language and history. Contact the course administrator at ✆ 091/495-442 for more information.

Special Interest Tours

GOLF

A host of U.S. companies offer package golf tours. Among them is **Premier Golf** (www.premiergolf.com; ✆ 866/260-4409).

CYCLING

All-inclusive bicycle trips in Ireland can be booked from the United States with either **Backroads** (www.backroads.com; ✆ 800/462-2848) or **VBT** (www.vbt.com; ✆ 800/245-3868), both well-regarded companies. Tour packages include bikes, gear, luggage transportation via a support van, good food, and rooms in local inns and hotels of character—everything bundled into one price. In Ireland, **Irish Cycling Safaris,** Belfield Bike Shop, Belfield House, University College Dublin (www.cyclingsafaris. com; ✆ 01/260-0749), offers cycling trips to practically every part of Ireland, including B&B stays and some meals.

HIKING

For a full walking holiday package to County Kerry or County Clare and Connemara, the U.S.–based **Backroads** (www.backroads.com; ✆ 800/462-2848) is one highly recommended operator. For guided walks in the southwest of Ireland, contact **Ireland Walk Hike Bike** (www.ireland walkhikebike.com; ✆ 066/718-6181).

HORSEBACK RIDING

Hidden Trails (www.hiddentrails.com; ✆ 888/987-2457 from the U.S. or Canada) offers 7-day guided riding tours in several regions in Ireland, including the Wicklow Mountains, West Cork, and Connemara. Tours are graded easy, moderate, or challenging, and include lodging and meals (breakfast, picnic lunch, and dinner).

GETTING AROUND
By Car

Although Ireland has a reasonably extensive network of public transportation, it will only be useful if you don't mind being confined to the major towns and cities, or depending on organized tours for attractions that are farther afield. Trains tend not to go to charming small towns and villages, and great houses and castles are usually miles from any major town. Bus service to places off the beaten track can be infrequent.

Renting a car is not for everyone—particularly if you're not used to driving on small, winding European country roads (and on the *left* side of the road). But if you're intrepid enough to do it, this is by far the best way to get around. It will give you the most freedom and open up more choices to you than any other way of getting around. Put simply: Rent a car and you'll see more of Ireland.

In the summer, weekly rental rates on a manual-transmission compact vehicle begin at around €160 and ascend steeply. Rates are much cheaper out of season.

Unless your stay in Ireland extends beyond 6 months, your own valid driver's license (provided you've had it for at least 6 months) is all you need to drive in Ireland. Rules and restrictions for car rentals correspond roughly to those in other European nations and the U.S., with two important distinctions: Most rental-car agencies in the Republic won't rent to you (1) if you're under 25 or over age 74 (there's no upper age limit in the North) or (2) if your license has been valid for less than a year.

DRIVING LAWS, TIPS & WARNINGS

Highway safety has become a critical issue in Ireland during the past several years. The number of highway fatalities is high for such a small nation—Ireland regularly comes out near the bottom of European league tables for accident rates. In an effort to rein in Irish drivers, the Republic now uses a penalty "points" system similar to that in the U.K. and the U.S. Although visitors won't have points added to their licenses, they may still be fined if they speed or commit driving infractions.

All distances and speed limits on road signs in the Republic of Ireland are in **kilometers,** while in Northern Ireland they are in **miles.** Take care if you're driving around the borderlands—the border is unmarked, so you can cross over from one side to the other without knowing it. It's easy to get confused and speed accidentally.

Getting used to left-side driving, left-handed stick shift, narrow roads, and a new landscape all present a challenge, especially if you're driving solo—it's helpful if you have somebody along to navigate. Some people even use tricks such as sticking a big arrow to the dashboard reminding you that the left is your default lane.

A GPS navigation device can be invaluable in finding your way around, especially in the remote countryside. Nearly all rental firms offer them.

Roundabouts (what Americans call traffic circles or rotaries) are found on most major roads and take a little getting used to. Remember always to yield to traffic coming from the right as you approach a roundabout and follow the traffic to the left, signaling before you exit the circle.

One signal that could be misleading to U.S. drivers is a flashing amber light at a pedestrian traffic light. This almost always follows a red light, and it means yield to pedestrians but proceed when the crossing is clear.

The Republic has relatively few types of roads. **Motorways (M)** are major highways, the equivalent of interstates in the U.S. **National (N)** roads, which link major cities, are rarely more than two lanes in each direction (and are sometimes as small as one American-size lane). Most pass directly through towns, making cross-country trips longer than you'd

road rules **IN A NUTSHELL**

1. Drive on the left side of the road.

2. Road signs are in kilometers, except in Northern Ireland, where they are in miles.

3. On motorways, the left lane is the traveling lane. The right lane is for passing.

4. Everyone must wear a seat belt by law. Young children must be in age-appropriate child seats.

5. Children 11 and under are not allowed to sit in the front seat.

6. When entering a roundabout (traffic circle), give way to traffic coming from the right.

7. Another roundabout rule: Always go *left* (clockwise) around the circle.

8. Speed limits are 50 kmph (31 mph) in urban areas; 80 kmph (50 mph) on regional and local roads; 100 kmph (62 mph) on national roads, including divided highways (called dual carriageways); and 120 kmph (75 mph) on freeways (called motorways).

expect. **Regional (R)** roads have one lane of traffic traveling in each direction and generally link smaller cities and towns. Last are the rural or unclassified roads, often the most scenic back roads. These can be poorly signposted, very narrow, and a bit rough, but they usually travel through beautiful countryside.

Both the Republic and Northern Ireland have severe laws against **drunk driving.** The legal limit is 35 micrograms of alcohol per 100 milliliters of breath. What that equates to varies by person, but even one pint of beer can be enough to put you over the limit. The general rule is: Do not drink and drive.

RENTING A CAR

Most rental companies offer their best prices to customers who reserve in advance from their home country. Ireland is a small country, and in high season it can virtually run out of rental cars—but long before it does, it runs out of *affordable* rental cars. Note that weekly rentals are almost always less expensive than day rentals, and keep in mind that the vast majority of available rental cars have **manual transmissions** (stick shifts). Automatics are available, but for a premium. *Another word of warning:* Fuel is very expensive in Ireland.

By law, you must be between the ages of 25 and 75 to rent a car in Ireland. The only documentation you should need is your driver's license and photo I.D., such as a passport, plus a printout of your reservation if you have one.

When you reserve a car, be sure to ask if the price includes: all taxes including value-added tax (VAT); breakdown assistance; unlimited mileage; personal accident or liability insurance (PAI); collision-damage waiver (CDW); theft waiver; and any other insurance options. If not, ask what these extras cost, because they can make a big dent in your bottom line. The CDW and other insurance might be covered by your credit card if you use the card to pay for the rental; check with your card issuer to be sure that there are no restrictions on that coverage in Ireland. (Not all cards do offer insurance protection for car rentals in Ireland.) Some travelers like to live dangerously and waive optional insurance. But when no CDW is purchased, many rental agencies will make you pay for any damages on the spot when you return the car—making even the smallest dent or scratch a potentially costly experience. To avoid any issues, take cellphone photos of your car with a time stamp, so that you have any dents and dings recorded and won't be charged for it.

If your credit card doesn't cover the CDW, consider buying Car Rental Collision Coverage from a third party. **Travel Guard** (www.travelguard.com; ✆ **1800/826-4919** in the U.S. and Canada) will insure you for around US$8 to US$10 per day. In the U.K., **Insurance 4 Car Hire** (www.insurance4carhire.com; ✆ **0344/892-1770**) offers similar coverage.

By Train

Train travel is generally the fastest way to get around the country. **Iarnród Éireann (Irish Rail)** (www.irishrail.ie; ✆ **1850/366222** or 01/836-6222) operates the train services in Ireland. Most lines radiate from Dublin to other principal cities and towns. From Dublin, the journey time to Cork is about 2½ hours; to Belfast, just over 2 hours; to Galway, just under 2½ hours; to Killarney, 3¼ hours; to Sligo, 3 hours; and to Waterford, about 2¼ hours.

In addition to Irish Rail service between Dublin and Belfast, **Translink** (www.translink.co.uk; ✆ **028/9066-6630**) operates routes from Belfast that include Coleraine, Derry, and 21 other localities in Northern Ireland.

One useful piece of lingo: When buying any sort of travel tickets—air, ferry, train, or bus—a "single" means one-way, a "return" is round-trip.

RAIL PASSES

The greatest value in European travel has traditionally been the **rail pass,** a single ticket allowing you unlimited travel (or travel on a certain number of days) within a set time period. The granddaddy of passes, the **Eurail Pass** covers some 28 countries, including Ireland (thanks to recent changes, these passes now apply to both the Republic and Northern Ireland). However, if you're a citizen of the European Union (or a long-term resident), you'll need to purchase the equivalent **Interrail Pass** instead. See the box on p. 34 for details.

By Bus

Bus Éireann (www.buseireann.ie; ✆ **01/836-6111**) operates an extensive system of express bus services, as well as local service, to nearly every town in Ireland. The Bus Éireann website provides timetables and fares for bus service throughout the country. Similarly, **Translink** provides detailed information on services within Northern Ireland (www.translink.co.uk; ✆ **028/9066-6630**). Bus travel in both countries is affordable, reliable, and comfortable—but also slow (see map on p. 573).

By Plane

Ireland is such a small country that there is very little point in flying from one end to the other. In any case, the options for internal flights seem to get more limited every year, partly because of improved roads and faster rail journey times. Daily flights on the Dublin–Kerry and Dublin–Donegal routes are operated by **Aer Lingus** (www.aerlingus.com) and **British Airways** (www.britishairways.com).

By Bike

Cycling is an ideal way to explore the Irish landscape. Distances are quite manageable, and many hostels, B&Bs, and hotels offer bike storage and luggage transfers for touring cyclists.

As mentioned earlier, roads in Ireland are categorized as **M** (Motorway), **N** (National), or **R** (Regional). When it comes to bikes, it is illegal to cycle on motorways, but R roads are always suitable for cycling, as are the N roads in outlying areas with little traffic. Be prepared, however, for two inevitable obstacles: wind and hills. Outside the Midlands, hills are just about everywhere, and those on the back roads can have thigh-burning grades. (*Tip:* If you're biking in the west, plan your route from south to north—the same direction as the prevailing winds.) Note that you can bring your bike on all passenger ferries to Ireland's islands, often for no extra charge.

Rental agencies with depots nationwide include **Raleigh** (www.raleigh.ie; ✆ **01/465-9659**) and **Emerald Cycles/Ireland Rent-A-Bike** (www.irelandrentabike.com; ✆ **061/416983**). Mountain and cross-country bike-rental rates average around €20 per day, €80 per week. You can also rent a car bike carrier for €40 per week (good for up to three bikes). On top of the hire price, you'll also have to fork over a refundable deposit, probably of around €50 per bike.

Irish Rail Routes

Area Codes

Area codes in Ireland range from one number (the Dublin area code is "1") to three. Area codes are included in all listings in this guide. Within Ireland, you dial 0 before the area code. Outside of Ireland, however, you do not dial 0 before the area code.

Business Hours

Banks are generally open 10am to 4pm Monday to Wednesday and Friday and 10am to 5pm on Thursday. **Post offices** (also known as An Post) are generally open from 9am to 5:30pm Monday to Friday and 9am to 1:30pm on Saturday. Some take an hour for lunch from 1 to 2pm, and small or rural branches may close on Saturday. **Museums and sights** are generally open 10am to 5pm Tuesday to Saturday and 2 to 5pm on Sunday. **Shops** generally open 9am to 6pm Monday to Saturday with late opening on Thursday until 7 or 8pm. Most shops in larger towns and cities will also open on Sundays (typically from late morning to late afternoon). Major shops, such as department stores, often stay open much later than other businesses.

Cellphones

See "Mobile Phones," later in this section.

Disabled Travelers

For disabled travelers, Ireland is a mixed bag. Its modern buildings and cities are generally accessible, but many of its historic buildings often lack wheelchair access. Trains can be accessed by wheelchairs but only with assistance. If you plan to travel by train in Ireland, check out Iarnród Éireann's website (**www. irishrail.ie**), which includes services for travelers with disabilities.

Finding accessible lodging can be tricky in Ireland. Many buildings here are hundreds of years old, and older hotels, small guesthouses, and landmark buildings still have steps outside and in. The rule of thumb should be: Never assume that a B&B, hotel, or restaurant has accessible facilities—ask about your requirements before booking. To research options prior to your trip, one excellent online resource is **www.disability.ie**. For advice on travel to Northern Ireland, contact **Disability Action** (www. disabilityaction.org; ✆ **028/9029-7880**). The Northern Ireland Tourist Board also publishes a helpful annual "Information Guide to Accessible Accommodation," available from any of its offices worldwide.

Doctors

Healthcare in Ireland is comparable to that in other European nations. In the Irish system, private doctors and hospitals provide care and patients purchase healthcare insurance. See individual listings under "Fast Facts" in chapters 4 and 14.

Drinking Laws

The minimum legal age to buy alcohol in Ireland is 18. Children under 18 are allowed in pubs until 9pm, or 10pm from May to September, so long as they're with their parents or guardians. (In practice, pubs serving food often have separate dining areas, which can accommodate children later.) Pubs are allowed to stay open until 11:30pm during the week, and around 12:30am on weekends, though some have licenses that allow them to stay open later. Many pubs choose to close earlier on Sundays. These times are roughly comparable in Northern Ireland.

A restaurant can serve alcohol to diners if it has a liquor license (restaurants with no liquor license may allow you to bring your own alcoholic beverages—we state in our restaurant listings if this is the case). Alcohol is for sale at dedicated liquor stores (or "Off Licenses"), in addition to supermarkets and convenience stores. **Important note:** Drunk-driving laws in Ireland are very strict. Even a single pint of beer could be enough to put you over the limit. If you're arrested

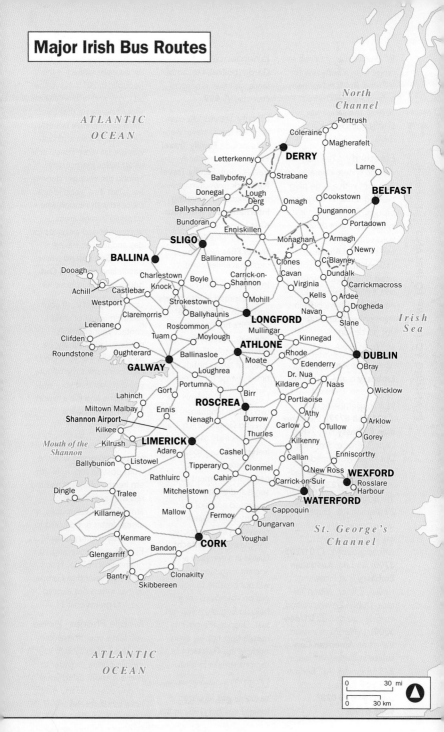

Major Irish Bus Routes

ATLANTIC
OCEAN

North
Channel

Portrush
Coleraine
Magherafelt
DERRY
Larne
Letterkenny
Ballybofey
Strabane
BELFAST
Donegal
Lough
Derg
Cookstown
Omagh
Dungannon
Ballyshannon
Portadown
Bundoran
Enniskillen
Armagh
SLIGO
Monaghan
Newry
Clones
C. Blayney
BALLINA
Ballinamore
Cavan
Dundalk
Carrickmacross
Dooagh
Charlestown
Boyle
Carrick-on-Shannon
Virginia
Kells
Ardee
Drogheda
Achill
Knock
Mohill
Navan
Castlebar
Strokestown
Slane
Westport
Claremorris
Ballyhaunis
LONGFORD
Irish
Sea
Leenane
Roscommon
Mullingar
Clifden
Tuam
Moylough
Kinnegad
Roundstone
Oughterard
Ballinasloe
ATHLONE
Rhode
DUBLIN
GALWAY
Loughrea
Moate
Edenderry
Bray
Portumna
Dr. Nua
Kildare
Naas
Wicklow
Gort
Birr
Portlaoise
Lahinch
Ennis
ROSCREA
Athy
Arklow
Miltown Malbay
Nenagh
Durrow
Carlow
Tullow
Gorey
Shannon Airport
Thurles
Kilkenny
Kilkee
LIMERICK
Cashel
Callan
Enniscorthy
Kilrush
Adare
Tipperary
Clonmel
New Ross
WEXFORD
Ballybunion
Listowel
Cahir
Carrick-on-Suir
Rosslare
Harbour
Dingle
Rathluirc
Mitchelstown
WATERFORD
Killarney
Mallow
Fermoy
Cappoquin
Tralee
Dungarvan
St. George's
Channel
Kenmare
Youghal
Glengarriff
Bandon
CORK
Bantry
Clonakilty
Skibbereen

Mouth of the
Shannon

ATLANTIC
OCEAN

| 0 | 30 mi |
| 0 | 30 km |

573

for drunk driving, penalties range from a hefty fine to jail time. Rules in Northern Ireland are even more severe. The safest way is simply not to drink and drive.

Electricity   The Irish electric system operates on 220 volts with a large plug bearing three rectangular prongs. The Northern Irish system operates on 250 volts with a similar plug. To use standard American 110-volt appliances, you'll need both a transformer and a plug adapter. Most new laptops have built-in transformers, but some do not, so beware.

Embassies & Consulates   The **American Embassy** is at 42 Elgin Rd., Ballsbridge, Dublin 4 (dublin.usembassy.gov; ✆ 01/668-8777); the **Canadian Embassy** is at 7–8 Wilton Terrace, 3rd floor, Dublin 2 (www.canada international.gc.ca/ireland-irlande; ✆ 01/234-4000); the **British Embassy** is at 29 Merrion Rd., Dublin 2 (www.gov.uk/government/world/organisations/british-embassy-dublin; ✆ 01/205-3700); and the **Australian Embassy** is at Fitzwilton House, 7 floor, Wilton Terrace, Dublin 2 (www.ireland.embassy.gov.au; ✆ 01/664-5300). In Northern Ireland, there's an **American Consulate** at Danesfort House, 223 Stranmillis Rd., Belfast BT9 5GR (belfast.usconsulate.gov; ✆ 028/9038-6100).

Emergencies   For the **Garda (police)**, fire, ambulance, or other emergencies, dial ✆ **999.**

Family Travel   Recommended family travel websites include **Family Travel Forum** (www.myfamily travels.com), **Family Travel Network** (www.familytravel network.com), **Traveling Internationally with Your Kids** (www.travelwithyour kids.com), and **Family Travel Files** (www.the familytravelfiles.com).

Internet & Wi-Fi   Wi-Fi is widespread in Irish hotels and B&Bs, even in rural areas. It's not universal, however. Most B&Bs and smaller hotels provide it free, but larger hotels sometimes charge for access.

Language   Ireland has two official languages: English and Gaelic (which is also known as Irish). All native Irish people can speak English. There is a strong national movement to preserve and expand the language, so areas of the country where Gaelic is protected and promoted are known as **Gaeltacht.** Gaelic is a complex and ancient language that you will not be able to figure out on your own; ask for help (in English) if you get lost. Despite the government's best hopes, everybody in the Gaeltacht regions speaks English.

LGBT Travelers   Homosexuality was legalized in Ireland in 1993 (1982 in the North), and same-sex marriages were ratified in the Republic in 2015. Nevertheless, gay and lesbian visitors should be aware that this is still a conservative country. Cities like Dublin and Galway are far more liberal in its attitudes (particularly among the younger generation), but it's a good idea to proceed with caution when traveling in rural areas. Recommended websites for gay and lesbian travelers include **Gay Ireland** (www.gay-ireland.com) and **Outhouse** (www.outhouse.ie).

Lost Property   If your passport is lost or stolen, contact your country's embassy immediately. Be sure to tell all of your credit card companies the minute you discover that your wallet is gone and file a report at the nearest police station.

Mail   In Ireland, mailboxes are painted green with the word post on top. In Northern Ireland, they are painted red with a royal coat of arms. From the Republic, an airmail letter or postcard to any other country outside Europe, not exceeding 100 grams, costs €1.35. From Northern Ireland to Europe, airmail letters not exceeding 100 grams cost £1.00.

Mobile Phones   Before you leave your home country, check directly with your mobile phone provider to find out about using your phone overseas. You may have to ask for the "international roaming" capability to be switched on **before** you're overseas.

Unfortunately, using your own phone in Ireland can prove very expensive. Most mobile phone companies charge very large premiums on call charges made while abroad. If you use a smartphone, such as an iPhone or Android, turn off features such as location services and push notifications, or you could face *enormous* data roaming charges. Always use Wi-Fi if you need to download anything.

Some travelers prefer to **rent** a phone for their trip to Ireland. You can do this from any number of overseas sites; several Irish phone companies have kiosks at the main airports, and car-rental agencies can usually rent you a phone for the duration of your stay.

Another option is to purchase a **disposable** pay-as-you-go phone. Disposable phones aren't quite as big here as in some countries, due to the relatively low cost of phone contracts; however, you can buy them quite cheaply from mobile phone stores (most airports and any town of reasonable size will have one). Disposable smartphones are also available. For a handy rundown of the cheapest deals on pay-as-you-go phones, check out www.moneyguideireland.com/cheapest-mobile-phone-charges.html.

Call charges in Ireland, and across the European Union, are much lower than they are in many other parts of the world, including the U.S.; on pay-as-you-go, expect to pay around €0.35 per minute. You are not charged for incoming calls.

Money   The Republic of Ireland uses the European currency known as the **euro** (€). Euro notes come in denominations of €5, €10, €20, €50, €100, €200, and €500. The euro is divided into 100 cents; coins come in denominations of €2, €1, 50¢, 20¢, 10¢, 5¢, 2¢, and 1¢.

As part of the United Kingdom, Northern Ireland uses the British **pound sterling** (£). Notes come in denominations of £5, £10, £20, £50, and £100. Coins are issued in £2, £1, 50p, 20p, 10p, 5p, 2p, and 1p denominations.

The British pound is not accepted in the Republic, and the euro is not accepted in the North—if you're traveling in both parts of Ireland you'll need some of both currencies, although shops on the border tend to accept both. Note that pounds issued in Northern Ireland, while legal tender in Great Britain, actually *look* different. You may find that cabdrivers and small business owners in the North won't accept bills issued in Great Britain, and vice-versa. In that case, you can change the money into locally issued versions

at any large central bank, free of charge.

Note for international travelers: Exchange rates can fluctuate wildly in the space of just a few weeks; before departing, consult a currency exchange website such as **www.xe.com** to check up-to-the-minute rates.

When it comes to obtaining foreign currency, please, **skip the currency exchange kiosks** in airports, train stations, and elsewhere. These give the poorest rates and charge exorbitant fees. Instead, order a small amount of foreign currency from your bank before leaving home, and then use your **debit card** for the duration of your trip. ATMs (in Ireland also called "cash machines" or "cash points") will give you a favorable rate, and you can withdraw however much cash you need for a day or so. The **Cirrus** and **Plus** ATM networks span the globe; check the back of your bank card to see which network you're on. Before you depart, be sure you know your personal identification number (PIN) and daily withdrawal limit. Confirm with your bank that your PIN will work in Europe, and be sure to let them know the dates and destinations to which you're traveling—you don't want to find your card frozen while you're abroad!

Credit cards are accepted just about

everywhere, save street markets, small independent retailers, street-food vendors, and occasional small or family-owned businesses. However, North American visitors should note that American Express is accepted far less widely than at home, and Diners Club only at the most high-flying establishments. To be sure of your credit line, bring a Visa or MasterCard as well.

Many retailers ask for your 4-digit PIN to be entered into a keypad near the cash register. In restaurants, a server might bring a hand-held device to your table to authorize payment. If you're visiting from a country (such as the U.S.), where Chip and PIN are less prevalent, some retailers may be reluctant to accept swipe cards. Be prepared to argue your case: Swipe cards are still valid and the same machines that read the smartcard chips can also read your magnetic strip. (Still, carry some cash with you, just in case.)

WHAT THINGS COST IN IRELAND

A pint of Guinness in the Temple Bar nightlife district in Dublin	€7
A pint of Guinness in Doolin, County Clare, with live traditional music	€4.50
High tea at the Shelbourne Hotel, Dublin	€49
Coffee and a homemade slice of cake at Lily's and Loly's Cafe in Sligo Town	€5.85
A 10-course chef's tasting menu at Anair, Galway City	€110 per person
Dinner for two at the Black Pig Winebar, Kinsale	€75
Fish and chips at Leo Burdock's, Dublin	€8
An 18-hole round of golf	€30–€150
An afternoon of horseback riding	€25–€50
1-day bicycle rental in the countryside	€20
Train ticket from Dublin to Galway	€33
Train ticket from Dublin to Belfast	€22
Kissing the Blarney Stone (Blarney Castle admission plus tip to attendant holding your legs)	€16
Visiting the Cliffs of Moher (admission plus parking)	€6 per person
A claddagh ring from Thomas Dillon's in Galway	€25–€900
A Waterford crystal goblet	€45
An authentic Aran Island sweater	€60
One night in a top hotel in Dublin	€200 and up
One night in a budget hotel in Dublin	around €70
One night in a country hotel in County Cork	around €120
One night in a B&B on the Ring of Kerry in high season	€100 and up
One night in a B&B on the Ring of Kerry the rest of the year.	around €70

Passports   See "Embassies & Consulates," earlier in this section, for whom to contact if you lose yours while traveling in Ireland. For country-specific information, please contact the following agencies:

For Residents of Australia   Contact the **Australian Passport Information Service** (www.passports.gov.au; ✆ **131-232**).

For Residents of Canada   Contact the central **Passport Office,** Department of Foreign Affairs and International Trade, Ottawa, ON K1A 0G3 (www.ppt.gc.ca; ✆ **800/567-6868**).

For Residents of New Zealand   Contact the **Passports Office,** Department of Internal Affairs (www.passports.govt.nz; ✆ **0800/225-050** in New Zealand or 04/463-9360).

For Residents of the United Kingdom   Visit your nearest passport office, major post office, or travel agency or contact the **United Kingdom Passport Service** (www.gov.uk/government/organisations/hm-passport-office; ✆ **0300/222-0000**).

For Residents of the United States   To find your regional passport office, either check the U.S. State Department website (**www.state.gov**) or call the **National Passport Information Center** toll-free

number (✆ **877/487-2778**) for automated information.

Pharmacies   Drugstores are called "chemists" and are found in every city, town, and most villages of any size. You'll find individual listings under "Fast Facts" in chapters 4 and 14.

Police   In the Republic of Ireland, a law enforcement officer is called a **Garda,** a member of the *Garda Síochána* ("Guardian of the Peace"); in the plural, it's **Gardaí** (pronounced *Gardee*) or simply "the Guards." Dial ✆ **999** to reach the Gardaí in an emergency. Except for special detachments, Irish police are unarmed and wear dark blue uniforms. In Northern Ireland you can also reach the police by dialing ✆ **999.**

Safety   By U.S. standards, Ireland is very safe, but, particularly in the cities, it's not safe enough to warrant carelessness. Be wary of the usual tourists' plagues: pickpockets, purse snatchers, and car thieves. Do not leave cars unlocked or cameras and other expensive equipment unattended. Ask at your hotel which areas are safe and which are not. Take a taxi back to your hotel if you're out very late.

In Northern Ireland, safety has to be a somewhat greater concern. Violence is no longer commonplace, and your visit here should be every bit as safe as in the rest of Ireland.

However, occasional flare-ups do happen, especially during the Orange marching season in the late summer. Visitors rarely have problems with this because they are not the targets of unrest. Still, keep abreast of things by reading or watching the news.

Senior Travel   In Ireland, seniors are referred to as "O.A.P.'s" (short for "Old Age Pensioners"). People over age 60 often qualify for reduced admission to museums and other attractions. Always ask about an O.A.P. discount if special rates aren't posted. **Discover Ireland** (p.565) can offer advice on how to find the best discounts.

Smoking   Ireland and Northern Ireland both have broad antismoking laws that ban smoking in all public places, including bars, restaurants, and hotel lobbies. However, most restaurants and pubs have covered outdoor smoking areas.

Taxes   As in many European countries, sales tax (VAT, or value-added tax) is often already included in the price shown on price tags. In the Republic, VAT rates vary—for hotels, restaurants, and car rentals, it is 13.5%; for souvenirs and gifts, it is 23%. In Northern Ireland, the VAT is 20% across the board. VAT charged on services such as hotel stays, meals, car rentals, and entertainment cannot be refunded to visitors, but the VAT on products such as souvenirs is refundable. Save your receipts and present them at the Global Refund Desk when you get to the airport (they're located airside in the main terminals at Dublin and Shannon; in Dublin the desk is now an automated kiosk, located on the left just after you pass the Starbucks on the way to the departure gates). They can usually issue you a refund there and then. Some larger stores can issue you a Global Refund form and refund your VAT themselves, although you'll need to know your passport number, flight number, and departure time. In practice, this is usually much more fuss than it's worth.

Telephones In the Republic, the telephone system is known as Eircom; in Northern Ireland, it's BT (British Telecom). Every effort has been made to ensure that the numbers and information in this guide were accurate at the time of writing.

Overseas calls from Ireland can be quite costly, whether you use a local phone card or your own calling card.

To call Ireland from home:

1. **Dial the international access code:** 011 from the U.S., 00 from the U.K., 0011 from Australia, or 0170 from New Zealand.

2. **Dial the country code:** 353 for the Republic, 44 for the North.

3. **Dial the local number,** remembering to omit the initial 0, which is for use only within Ireland (for example, to call the County Kerry number 066/12345 from the United States, you'd dial 011-353-66/12345).

To make international calls from Ireland: First dial 00, then the country code (U.S. or Canada 1, U.K. 44, Australia 61, New Zealand 64). Next you dial the area code and local number. For example, to call the U.S. number ☎ 212/000-0000 you'd dial ☎ 00-1-212/000-0000. The toll-free international access code for AT&T is ☎ **1-800-550-000;** for Sprint it's ☎ **1-800-552001;** and for MCI it's ☎ **1-800-551-001.**

To make local calls: To dial a local number within the same area code, drop the initial 0. To dial a number within Ireland but in a different area code, use the initial 0.

As in many parts of the world, phone booths are slowly disappearing. Calls from a phone booth usually require coin payment, but at some you need a **calling card** (in the Republic) or **phone card** (in the North)—prepaid computerized cards that you insert into the phone instead of coins. They can be purchased in post offices, grocery stores,

and shops (such as newsstands).

Time Ireland follows Greenwich Mean Time from November to March, and British Summer Time from April to October. Ireland is 5 hours ahead of the eastern United States. Ireland's latitude makes for longer days and shorter nights in the summer and the reverse in the winter. In June, the sun doesn't fully set until around 11pm, but in December, it is dark by 4pm.

Tipping For taxi drivers, hairdressers, and other providers of service, tip an average of 10 to 15%. For restaurants, the policy is usually printed on the menu—either a gratuity of 10 to 15% is automatically added to your bill, or it's left up to you. As a rule, bartenders do not expect a tip, except when table service is provided.

Toilets Public toilets are usually simply called "toilets" or are marked with international symbols. In the Republic of Ireland, some of the older ones carry the Gaelic words FIR (men) and MNA (women). Free restrooms are usually available to customers at sightseeing attractions, museums, hotels, restaurants, pubs, shops, and theaters. Many gas stations (called "petrol stations" in Ireland) have public toilets, and a few even have baby-changing facilities.

Visas Citizens of the United States, Canada, Australia, and New Zealand entering the Republic of Ireland or Northern Ireland for a stay of up to 3 months do not need a visa, but a valid **passport** is required. For citizens of the United Kingdom, when traveling on flights originating in Britain, the same rules apply as they would for travel to any other member state of the European Union (E.U.).

Water Tap water throughout the island of Ireland is generally safe. However, some areas in the west of Ireland have been battling with out-of-date water-purification systems. Always carry a large bottle of water with you.

Wi-Fi See "Internet & Wi-Fi," earlier in this section.

Women Travelers

Women should expect few problems traveling in Ireland. You may attract a little attention if you eat alone in a restaurant at night—a sight that is still relatively uncommon in Ireland outside of the major cities—but you won't be hassled. If you drink in a pub on your own, though, expect all kinds of attention—a woman drinking alone is still considered to be "on the market," even if she's reading a book, talking on her cellphone to her fiancé, or doing a crossword puzzle. So be prepared to fend them off. (Irish men almost always respond well to polite rejection, though.) Take a cab home at night and follow all the usual caution you use when you travel anywhere. Essentially, don't do anything in Ireland that you wouldn't do at home.

Index

Accommodations

Restaurants

PHOTO CREDITS

p. ii, T. Slack/Shutterstock.com; p. iii, Courtesy of Tourism Ireland/Chris Hill; p. 1, Sandra Mori/ Shutterstock.com; p. 3, Owen J Fitzpatrick/Shutterstock.com; p. 4, Courtesy of Tourism Ireland/Bren Whelan; p. 5, Courtesy of Tourism Ireland/Chris Hill; p. 6, Courtesy of Fáilte Ireland; p. 8, Courtesy of Fáilte Ireland; p. 9, Courtesy of Fáilte Ireland/Neal Houghton; p. 10, Courtesy of Tourism Ireland/ Chris Hill; p. 12, Courtesy of Tourism Ireland/Lorna Lee; p. 15, Courtesy of Fishy Fishy; p. 17, Courtesy of Tourism Ireland/Chris Hill; p. 20, Courtesy of Tourism Ireland; p. 21, ilolab/Shutterstock.com; p. 23, Tourism Ireland/Brian Morrison; p. 26, Courtesy of Fáilte Ireland/Rob Durston; p. 31, Courtesy of Fáilte Ireland/Martin Fleming; p. 35, Courtesy of Tourism Ireland/Chris Hill; p. 38, Sergio; p. 39, Maciek A; p. 45, Courtesy of Tourism Ireland/Stephen Power; p. 48, Stefano_Valeri; p. 50, Courtesy of Fáilte Ireland; p. 53, Courtesy of Tourism Ireland/Caspar Diederik/@storytravelers; p. 54, Courtesy of Fáilte Ireland/Rob Durston; p. 57, Courtesy of Tourism Ireland/Tony Pleavin; p. 58, Courtesy of Tourism Ireland/Chris Hill; p. 62, Courtesy of Fáilte Ireland/Ruth Medjber; p. 65, glynnis2009; p. 66, Courtesy of Tourism Ireland/Brian Morrison; p. 71, Courtesy of Fáilte Ireland; p. 73, Courtesy of Fáilte Ireland/Rob Durston; p. 80, Kelly Neilson/Shutterstock.com; p. 85, Courtesy of Tourism Ireland; p. 87, Courtesy of Tourism Ireland; p. 88, James Horan; p. 96, Courtesy of Fáilte Ireland/Rob Durston; p. 97, Lauren Orr; p. 98, James Horan; p. 103, Courtesy of Tourism Ireland/Brian Morrison; p. 105, Courtesy of The Dub Web Fest Team; p. 110, Courtesy of Tourism Ireland; p. 115, William Murphy; p. 117, Courtesy of Tourism Ireland/James Fennell; p. 118, Courtesy of Fáilte Ireland/Rob Durston; p. 122, Courtesy of Butlers Chocolate; p. 126, Courtesy of the Clarence Hotel; p. 128, Courtesy of the Radisson Blu; p. 140, William Murphy; p. 144, Courtesy of San Lorenzo; p. 146, Courtesy of Tourism Ireland; p. 148, Courtesy of Lemon Crepe; p. 150, Courtesy of Aqua/Paul Sherwood; p. 151, Courtesy of Fáilte Ireland/ Andrew Bradley; p. 154, Courtesy of Tourism Ireland; p. 159, Courtesy of Tourism Ireland/Jason Baxter; p. 163, Courtesy of Tourism Ireland; p. 167, Chad and Steph; p. 171, Courtesy of Tourism Ireland/ Brian Morrison; p. 177, Courtesy of Tourism Ireland/Tony Pleavin; p. 180, Bjoern Alberts; p. 185, Irish National Stud/Fáilte Ireland; p. 188, Courtesy of Barberstown Castle; p. 192, Courtesy of Fáilte Ireland/Neal Houghton; p. 194, Courtesy of Tourism Ireland; p. 195, Courtesy of Tourism Ireland/ Brian Morrison; p. 199, Courtesy of Tourism Ireland/Chris Hill; p. 202, Semmick Photo; p. 203, Courtesy of Fáilte Ireland/Liam Murphy; p. 207, Courtesy of Fáilte Ireland/Leo Byrne; p. 211, Courtesy of Fáilte Ireland/Andrew Bradley; p. 212, Courtesy of Fáilte Ireland/Luke Myers; p. 213, left, Courtesy of Tourism Ireland/George Munday; p. 213, right, Courtesy of Tourism Ireland; p. 214, walshphotos; p. 221, top, Courtesy of Fáilte Ireland; p. 221, bottom, Courtesy of Fáilte Ireland; p. 224, Courtesy of Tourism Ireland/Brian Morrison; p. 226, Courtesy of Aldridge Lodge; p. 230, Courtesy of Fáilte Ireland/ Finn Richards; p. 232, Courtesy of Fáilte Ireland/Finn Richards; p. 236, Courtesy of Kytelers Inn; p. 238, Andrei Nekrassov; p. 242, Courtesy of Fáilte Ireland/Andrew Bradley; p. 244, Courtesy of Tourism Ireland/Chris Hill; p. 245, Courtesy of Tourism Ireland/Siobhan Russell; p. 247, Courtesy of Tourism Ireland/Jed Niezgoda www.venividiphoto.net; p. 254, Courtesy of Fáilte Ireland/Andrew Bradley; p. 259, Courtesy of Fáilte Ireland/Liam Murphy; p. 260, Courtesy of Ballymaloe Cookery School; p. 262, Courtesy of Tourism Ireland/Chris Hill; p. 263, Courtesy of Tourism Ireland/Tony Pleavin; p. 266, Courtesy of Tourism Ireland/Chris Hill; p. 269, Courtesy of the Spaniard; p. 276, Courtesy of Tourism Ireland/Arthur Ward; p. 281, Courtesy of Tourism Ireland/Chris Hill; p. 286, Courtesy of Tourism Ireland/ Stephen Power; p. 288, Courtesy of Tourism Ireland; p. 296, Courtesy of Aghadoe Heights Hotel & Spa; p. 300, mozzercork; p. 301, Courtesy of Tourism Ireland/©Raymond Fogarty/Valerie O'Sullivan; p. 309, Janelle Lugge; p. 325, Courtesy of Tourism Ireland/Chris Hill; p. 327, Courtesy of Tourism Ireland/Chris Hill; p. 329, Greg Fellmann; p. 331, Courtesy of Fáilte Ireland/Fennell Photography; p. 336, Michael Mc Lughlin; p. 339, Courtesy of Tourism Ireland/Stephen Power; p. 341, Meghan Lamb; p. 342, Courtesy of Tourism Ireland; p. 348, Courtesy of Lahinch Surf School; p. 349, Photo Derek Cullen Fáilte Ireland; p. 352, Courtesy of Tourism Ireland/George Munday; p. 358, Courtesy of Fáilte Ireland/ Liam Murphy; p. 359, Richard Melichar; p. 364, Courtesy of Tourism Ireland/Brian Morrison; p. 371, Courtesy of Tourism Ireland; p. 373, Courtesy of Inis Meian; p. 374, Courtesy of Tourism Ireland/ Chris Hill; p. 380, Rihardzz; p. 382, Courtesy of Tourism Ireland; p. 384, Courtesy of Tourism Ireland;

p. 388, Courtesy of Tourism Ireland/Chris Hill; p. 390, Courtesy of Fáilte Ireland; p. 392, Courtesy of Killary Fjord Boat Tours; p. 393, Noradoa; p. 401, Courtesy of Tourism Ireland; p. 404, Gabriela Insuratelu; p. 405, Courtesy of Fáilte Ireland/Fennell Photography; p. 407, Ian Murphy; p. 410, Courtesy of Fáilte Ireland/Simon Crowe; p. 412, Courtesy of Tourism Ireland/Gareth McCormack; p. 419, Courtesy of Tourism Ireland; p. 421, LunaseeStudios/Shutterstock.com; p. 427, Gabriela Insuratelu; p. 428, Courtesy of Tourism Ireland; p. 432, Courtesy of Tourism Ireland/Brian Morrison; p. 442, Courtesy of Tourism Ireland/Alison Crummy; p. 443, Brendan Howard/Shutterstock.com; p. 444, Courtesy of Fáilte Ireland, Tourism Ireland/Peter McCabe; p. 450, Courtesy of Tourism Ireland/Gardiner Mitchell Photography; p. 451, Courtesy of Fáilte Ireland/Martin Fleming; p. 456, Courtesy of Tourism Ireland/Gardiner Mitchell Photography; p. 459, Greg Clarke; p. 462, Courtesy of Harvey's Point Hotel; p. 466, Courtesy of Tourism Ireland/Lukasz Warzecha; p. 468, Courtesy of Tourism Ireland/Gardiner Mitchell Photography; p. 472, Courtesy of Fáilte Ireland/Adam Rory Porter; p. 475, Courtesy of Inishowen Gateway Hotel; p. 476, Courtesy of Fáilte Ireland; p. 478, Courtesy of Tourism Ireland/Tony Pleavin; p. 483, Courtesy of Tourism Ireland/Tony Pleavin; p. 484, Courtesy of Tourism Ireland/Paul Lindsay; p. 486, Courtesy of Tourism Ireland/Paul Lindsay; p. 489, Courtesy of Tourism Ireland/Chris Hill; p. 492, Courtesy of Tourism Ireland/Tony Pleavin; p. 494, SurangaSL; p. 495, Courtesy of Tourism Ireland; p. 496, Courtesy of Tourism Ireland/Brian Morrison; p. 506, Courtesy of Tourism Ireland/Brian Morrison; p. 508, Courtesy of Tourism Ireland/Brian Morrison; p. 510, Courtesy of Tourism Ireland/Brian Morrison; p. 512, Courtesy of Tourism Ireland; p. 514, Courtesy of Tourism Ireland/Bernie Brown; p. 515, Courtesy of Tourism Ireland/Chris Hill; p. 525, Courtesy of Tourism Ireland/George Munday; p. 527, Courtesy of Tourism Ireland/Gareth McCormack Photography; p. 531, Courtesy of Tourism Ireland/Chris Hill; p. 533, Courtesy of Tourism Ireland/Steffan Hill; p. 537, Courtesy of Tourism Ireland/Gardiner Mitchell Photography; p. 539, Courtesy of Tourism Ireland/Chris Hill; p. 545, Courtesy of Tourism Ireland/Chris Hill; p. 546, Courtesy of Tourism Ireland/Gardiner Mitchell Photography; p. 552, Courtesy of Tourism Ireland/Brian Morrison; p. 556, Courtesy of Tourism Ireland/Gardiner Mitchell Photography; p. 560, Courtesy of Tourism Ireland/Gardiner Mitchell Photography; p. 562, Courtesy of Tourism Ireland/Arthur Ward.

Before, During, or After your use of a Frommer's guidebook... you'll want to consult

FROMMERS.COM

FROMMERS.COM IS KEPT UP-TO-DATE, WITH:

NEWS
The latest events (and deals) to affect your next vacation

BLOGS
Opinionated comments by our outspoken staff

FORUMS
Post your travel questions, get answers from other readers

SLIDESHOWS
On weekly-changing, practical but inspiring topics of travel

CONTESTS
Enabling you to win free trips

PODCASTS
Of our weekly, nationwide radio show

DESTINATIONS
Hundreds of cities, their hotels, restaurants and sights

TRIP IDEAS
Valuable, offbeat suggestions for your next vacation

AND MUCH MORE!

Frommers.com